ABRAHAM LINCOLN'S
PHILOSOPHY
OF COMMON SENSE

An Analytical Biography of a Great Mind

PART I

EDWARD J. KEMPF

NOTE ABOUT THE COVERS

The *blue-green, rough-grained* cloth used on the covers of this three-part publication was selected by the author, since it "expresses the dominant traits of Lincoln's personality. Ever melancholic, he found cheer in friendship and humorous stories of frustrated vanity, and in working for freedom with truth and justice under equitable legal rights for all mankind."

SPECIAL PUBLICATIONS

OF

THE NEW YORK ACADEMY OF SCIENCES

VOLUME VI

NEW YORK

PUBLISHED BY THE ACADEMY

March, 1965

PLATE 1. President Lincoln, November 1863. Photograph by Alexander Gardner.

To Dorothy

My wife and associate through fifty years in research
studies of the dynamics of life

Special Publications of The New York Academy of Sciences

VOLUME VI

HAROLD E. WHIPPLE, *Editor*
MARVIN I. SPITZER, *Managing Editor*

CONTENTS: PARTS I, II, AND III

PART II

PART III

LIST OF ILLUSTRATIONS

PREFACE

I have written *Abraham Lincoln's Philosophy of Common Sense* as a scientifically oriented analytical biography. The relative estimations of the depth of formative impressions of his conditioning experiences on the development of his mind and personality are based on my experiences as a physician, specialized for fifty years in the allied disciplines of psychiatry, psychobiology, psychopathology and psychoanalysis. My books *Psychopathology* and *The Autonomic Functions and the Personality* and numerous papers and monographs on physiology of attitude and ego-organization, psychology of the family, holistic laws of life, laws of attitude, phylogeny and ontogeny of bisexual differentiation, comparative conditioned neuroses, basic biodynamics, and psychotherapeutics of neuroses and psychoses attest to my biodynamic understanding of human behavior.

Edward J. Kempf

Wading River, N.Y.

INTRODUCTION

Abraham Lincoln's self-analytical comments, in autobiographical sketches and numerous letters and lectures, provide the humanitarian sciences with invaluable evidence on *why* and *how* he reasoned out and applied his philosophical common-sense understanding of the social motivations of human nature and the universal need of maintaining constitutional government by free people to advance their welfare in common with that of the nation.

Common sense is cultivated primarily by thinking consistently, analytically, and logically, to reduce pain and frustration and secondarily to increase success and pleasure in work to live.

Common-sense understanding of sensory experience is recognized in science as the basis of development of realistic, practical, scientific, and philosophical thinking. Informed common sense is the means of evolution of higher levels of intelligence, civilization, and social organization, from primitive self-authorized "gangster" systems of government and tyrannical subjugation and exploitation of defenceless, unorganized people, toward more sympathetic cooperative culture of equality of legal rights and privileges of self-determination. The most understanding humanitarian philosophies of history have been thought out by men with deep sympathetic natures who have experienced bitter suffering with their people under the yoke of legalized privilege and injustice.

Sir William Osler, master physician, has commented in an essay on *A Way of Life:* "Everyone has a philosophy of life in thought, in word, or in deed, worked out for himself unconsciously . . . as it grows with growth."

Abraham Lincoln's philosophy of human nature and human relations developed consciously, purposefully, as well as unconsciously, in a sequence of steps of increasing moral comprehensions and practical realizations. By studiously thinking out self-righting understandings, analytically, ethically, and humorously, of his personal experiences to overcome provocations, by social injustice, of daily repetitive nervous tendencies to diplopia and "melancholy," leading to headache, indigestion, mental distraction, and anxiety, he developed profound understanding of egoistic motivations of himself and other people and extraordinary inspirational moral drive to improve social justice. These personality characterizing compensations followed, as I have shown in a previous publication in the *Archives of Neurology and Psychiatry* (1952), an accidental injury of his brain in childhood that left him with certain residual disabilities of nervous functioning.

This book presents an analytical study of the decisive experiences and steps in the development of Lincoln's understanding of human nature and his common-sense philosophy of ethical personal relations in love, law, and political organization, as shown by authentic records of what he did, said, and wrote, up to becoming president and as president of the United States.

When Abraham Lincoln was persuaded by his law partner, W. H. Herndon, to read a new book on the life of Edmund Burke, he glanced through some of its pages for several minutes and then commented: "No sir. I've read enough of it. It is like all the others. Biographies, as generally written, are not only misleading but false. . . . In most instances they commemorate a lie and cheat posterity of the truth."

We have taken Lincoln at his word and given only thoroughly checked and verified information on the noble and beautiful and crude and vulgar thoughts and acts of his life in their provocative environmental situations for their natural psychobiodynamic worth, regardless of popular prejudices and idealizing legends of martyred hero worship now being cultivated. The following analytical biography is frank, factual, and humanly realistic. Its presentation is not intentionally sentimental and romantic. Its material is naturally so, for Lincoln was a person of deep sentiments, attachments, and convictions, and his life was involved in an unusual series of romantic and tragic experiences that led eventually to gloomy triumphs and fateful death.

Biographies differentiate into three types: popular, historical, and analytical. The popular type is written by skillful romancers to satisfy the preferences and prejudices of an easy reading public. It usually includes a series of glowing accounts of the more important situations in the life of the subject with selected excerpts of such of his productions as will excite popular admiration. The result is entertaining superficial reading about the life of an unusual person as the writer would have him known. Popular eulogizing of the tragic hero in America is producing, as it has myths and legends of the heroes of other nations, portraits in monuments, books, movies, and plays of Lincoln which cultivate many false ideas about him as a man. By reading selected epigrammatic passages from his expressions, most American people have no realistic understanding of how Lincoln's mind developed and how carefully, thoroughly and consistently he labored to master personal, physical, educational, legal, and political deficiencies and to think out basic principles of human behavior as a boy, young man, legislator, lawyer, and leader of freedom-loving people.

Historical biography gives more reliable and extensive accounts from existing records of the economic, political, and other social conditions in which the subject lived and his reactions to them and influence upon them, with the purpose largely of establishing his place in history. Such biography is not primarily interested in the psychodynamics of experience-conditioning development of the subject's personality, ideas, convictions, and unconscious determinants of conscious volitional reasoning. All preceding biographies of Lincoln, other than the psychoanalytical study by Pierce Clark, are either popular or historical in type.

Analytical biography is a recent scientific development evolving from the combined discoveries of psychology, psychiatry, psychoanalysis, philosophy, sociology, physiology, genetics, biology, and medical practice, on the natural determinations of human behavior. No man's mind is the product of free-will selections of experience-detached knowledge and abstract reasoning, as long erroneously assumed by academic, religious, and popular psychology. Mental development is the product of hereditary endowment and bodily growth, reacting in a natural sequence of stages and pyramiding levels of self-righting, self-expressive, self-understanding egocentric organization, to the conditioning influences of climate and nutrition, and cultures of interactions of needs, desires, attitudes, habits, speech, work, demands, approvals, condemnations, and beliefs in the family, school, community, and nation.

Unlike the popular and historical biographer, the analytical biographer must have sufficient psychiatric and psychoanalytic, as well as general medical, psychological, and sociological experience, to recognize and correlate the major social characteristics of his subject's personality. These must include basic inborn aptitudes and repetitive autonomic pressures of emotional cravings and energy of drives for developing more effective and pleasurable self-expression in creative work toward achieving greater self-realization of being a desired, respected, and influential person by his social group. Thereby he most enjoys self-respect with social respectability and peace of mind.

Analytical biography correlates the natural sequences of particular stages and levels of concomitant development of personality with body, under particular experience-conditioning environmental excitations and inhibitions of particular forms of acquisitive and avoidance behavior. It must show the steps in sequence of formation of the subject's characteristic egoistic-social attitudes, in interaction with such attitudes of particular persons—cooperatively to acquire and give particular pleasurable exchanges of sympathetic work-easing appeals, approvals, praises and rewards, and competitively to avoid and to give antipathic work-increasing demands, disapprovals, condemnations, and punishments.

It must show how such social experiences have conditioned particular allied and conflicting acquisitive and avoidance compulsions and convictions of what to think and do and what not to think and do, in order to be justified as morally right and good and not be condemned as wrong and evil. It must show how these socially conditioned egoistic biases continue to act unconsciously, involitionally, and influence conscious volitional thinking throughout childhood, adolescence, and maturity in a pyramiding series of levels of mental organization. It must show how such fixed conditioned reactions, when too much alike and excited in conflicting ways in unavoidable situations, under decreasing limitations of time and increasing danger of failure and punishment, produce indecision with tendency to progressive split mindedness, illogical thinking, and anxiety with depression or rage. Thereby analytical biography is able to take any egoistic reaction   pattern of a person and reversely trace its conditioning steps in development back to its earliest formative experiences. Thus we can learn to understand the sequences of development and compulsive consistencies and contradictions of a person's behavior and foreknow what he will probably do in equivalent situations in the future.

Analytical biography is written for the serious student of human nature and human relations, the psychologist, sociologist, and anthropologist, the physician, lawyer, judge, editor, commentator, teacher, minister, politician, and dramatist, and the general reader who wants to be realistically and not sentimentally informed about a particular person and human nature in general. The analytical understanding of the endless pressures of equilibrating against disequilibrating interactions of egotistic attitudes between persons in their daily cooperative and competitive interests is now emerging as a dynamic science of human behavior. It will eventually become man's most enlightening contribution to understanding the greater development of his mind, his interpersonal interactions, and social organizations.

An analytical biography of a man like Lincoln, which would cover the development of his understanding of human nature and political organization, as he worked out his principles and policies in interaction with the social conditions of his time, must have a universal cultural frame of reference. His political philosophy has aroused international as well as national interest. He is now recognized by historians as our greatest, most influential president. He has become, within less than 100 years, the subject of more biographical volumes and papers and more editorial and oratorical commentaries and quotations in more languages than any statesman in history. This interest is profoundly revolutionary. It reveals irrepressible human needs and desires to understand Lincoln's philosophy of human nature, human relations, and national social organization.

Lincoln's propositions and applications of the principle of divine right to self-government with equalitarian legal rights to justice for all persons, regardless of race, creed, political office, social class, wealth, or education, continue to be discussed and advocated by religious and political organizations in every civilized land. They assert the fundamental needs and aspirations of the individual person to live respectably in freedom of ethical self-expression and self-determination, to be the divinely intended natural moral foundation of the integrity of the human mind and of democratic government. They deny the ancient unilateral assumption of divine right of kings and hereditary or self-established ruling classes to govern without the free consent of the governed.

Lincoln's humanitarian statements include less well known basic psychological and sociological as well as better known political principles. They are consistent with the moral cultures of Mosaic law, Buddhism, Confucianism, and Christianity. He often referred to his principles as his "philosophy," and in this application of the term he was correct. It is indeed applied wisdom in consistent psychological, moral, and political arguments expressed in numerous speeches, lectures, notes, stories, and letters. It is a philosophy built on the common-sense *realizations* of natural truths of human behavior rather than interpretations of so-called divine *revelations*. Such truths have accumulated through the ages by analytical observations of many minds to reduce suffering and improve the practical culture of more equitable social relations, toward the greater cooperative development of the individual and the people with greater organization of the state. They are now being analyzed and applied by the sciences of living behavior.

The political philosophy of Abraham Lincoln has contributed effectively practical, equitable applications of analytically informed, sympathetic common sense to the natural political organization of human interactions in everyday life under guarantees of equalitarian rights of freedom of constitutional government. Before Lincoln's presidency the meaning of the Constitution of the United States on federal versus state sovereign rights, and the powers conferred by it on the president, on Congress, on the Supreme Court, and the people, were confused by two opposed cultural interpretations of human needs and rights, completely equalitarian and racially unilateral. The indissoluble solidarity of federal government based on inviolable contracts between states, majority rule with consideration and not suppression of dissenting minorities, the emancipation of mankind as morally and legally possessing personal rights above property rights, and the need for legal restriction of power and privilege inherent in monopoly, have become under his leadership and teaching, essential to the democratic way of life in America.

Most biographers seem to have regarded Lincoln's unusual personal characteristics and unique expressions of political philosophy as the free-willed product of enigmatic genius. Important studies have been published with selected excerpts of his productions and accounts of stimulating situations by Herndon, Lamon, Davis, Raymond, Barton, Tarbell, Charnwood, Stephenson, Masters, Clark, Sandburg, Angle, Randall, Thomas, and many others. No biography of Lincoln, however, has presented a basically realistic understanding of the psychobiodynamics of the man's mental development, for no one suspected, until I found the evidence, that Lincoln's brain had been injured in childhood, leaving residual impairments of certain highly necessary nervous functions that had been counterbalanced by developing special volitional compensations, repeated constantly to maintain normal mental integrity. Conditioning formative effects of the utmost importance on his personality and philosophical view of life by certain experiences in his childhood, adolescence, and manhood are not even mentioned in the most important biographies, although he described them self-analytically and told them to friends to indicate their influence on his mind.

Abraham Lincoln's personality and facial expression were often said to have had certain enigmatical qualities of unfathomable mystery, by such important observers and students of his life as his close political and business friends and neighbors who knew him personally. At times his inner personal, visual, emotional, and mental experiences were as deeply puzzling to himself. The great sculptors and painters of Lincoln's face have not understood the profoundly significant meaning of its endlessly sad, divergent eyes and gloomy expression, covered by earnest and humorous but diffident tensions of volitional self-control. Of these artists only Gutzon Borglum seems to have intuitively sensed that the left side of Lincoln's face was for some reason, unknown to him, mentally less active and developed than the right.

This personal dualism interested me greatly and, while modeling, about 12 years ago, a portrait of Lincoln from the 1860 life mask by Volk and numerous photographs, my professional training as a psychiatrist led me, from the differences in measurements of his eyes and the right and left sides of his face, and the growth of the facial bones on each side, to the conclusion that he had been functionally embarrassed and disconcerted throughout life, by the nervous after-effects of a serious injury of his brain in childhood. Investigation produced evidence from Lincoln's own statement, given fully later, that accounts for the injury. When nine years old he had been kicked in the forehead by a horse and "thought dead for awhile."

The nature of the cerebral damage and how it influenced the development of his personality and mind, hence public career, became then a question of absorbing interest. Extensive reading of the more important biographies showed that, although the accident was generally known, it was ignored, and injury of the brain had never been suspected. When I found that practically all of the evidence on the life of Lincoln, when properly correlated and evaluated, revealed the endlessly gloomy effect of nervous and emotional instability on his mind, and how he analyzed and disciplined himself to overcome it, thereby developing the most salutary understanding in history of human nature, human relations, and social organization, I felt obliged to present an account of this profoundly important achievement in an analytical biography.

That Lincoln's cerebral condition was never recognized by his personal physicians is understandable, since he received no medical aid after the injury in the wilderness of southern Indiana, and little was known in his time of the physiology of the brain. Some recent medical observers have suggested that Lincoln's facial asymmetry developed possibly through habitually making voluntary efforts to correct a congenital strabismus. The marked differences in the muscular tonus of the two sides of his face seem to have been regarded superficially by most of his friends and biographers as an oddity of habitual expression. Although his keenly observing law partner and biographer, W. H. Herndon, has said from repeated observation that Lincoln's gloomy sadness seemed to have "organic and functional" causes, the cerebral basis of his neurosis was never recognized by any of his medical biographers, including such eminent physicians as Holt (1910), Hornell (1914), Clark (1933), Shutes (1933), and Wold (1948).

Collection of physical evidence on the cerebral injury has been a relatively simple task, but the correlation of personal and social evidence, showing how it affected, with other conditioning experiences, the development of his personality, self-understanding, and philosophy of human relations, has been far more complex, requiring a complete study, in order of development, of all of his extant publications with the most reliable collateral evidence as provided by numerous biographers.

It will be confirmed by recorded evidence in the following chapters that Lincoln, as a man from his late twenties until his death, hence no doubt since the cerebral injury in childhood, had a hypersensitive, involitionally unstable nervous system that was aggravated by increasing strain of diplopia under emotional stress and fatigue, to augment a daily tendency to gloomy visual consciousness. These nervous reactions tended to become incapacitating when excited by certain kinds of unjust accusations and frustrations that discredited his self-respect and moral integrity. His melancholic disposition was also conditioned by regressive, nostalgic fixations of love for the memories of a certain childhood pet and for certain persons who had tragic deaths under similar conditions of fateful determination.

This organic and emotionally conditioned vicious circle was always potentially disposed to become active, and when aroused it tended to last for a day to several weeks. It will be shown how, three times, under fateful conditions involving hopeless frustration of love, Lincoln developed extreme anxiety and dangerous depression. It will be shown how, consistently with these reactions, he interpreted a certain experience of double vision of his face and some of his dreams, as the occult presentiment of fateful destiny. It will also become evident why he sensed intuitively that he would carry on the work he most loved, promotion of equalitarian legal rights and justice for all mankind, and that his life would end in tragedy as had the lives of those he most loved.

The evidence will show that Lincoln was born with a superior hereditary intellectual and constitutional endowment from unusual grandparents, for developing self-reliantly an intelligent mind. It will show how he learned as a child to make the most of his natural propensity to question causes of events in everyday life that interested him, so that he could not only understand them but describe them logically and convincingly to other people. We will see how his natural method of self-education, under the encouragement of maternal interest, though opposed by paternal prejudice, but free of the intense dogmas of badly informed teachers, led to the development of a mind that gave as full consideration as possible to the pros and cons of issues and propositions, to learn truth and reality. It will be seen how Lincoln learned never entirely to close his mind to the possibility of changes occurring in the relative values of causes and effects nor to develop a conviction beyond peradventure of doubt, except in certain supreme situations, lest some unknown condition or unforeseen contingency might arise and make his beliefs and decisions erroneous and unjustifiable and increase gloomy feelings of moral frustration. The common-sense method of equilibrating logically and mathematically reasoning from experience and evidence to tentative conclusions, as consistently developed by young Lincoln, is the method effectively adopted by the modern scientific mind as so profoundly applied by Darwin in biology and Newton and Einstein in physics.

Lincoln worked all his life to overcome the effects of his neuro-psychopathological vicious circle without ever freeing himself from them. His own statements will show how he needed to feel that he was being right and kind in order to avoid being "melancholy," and how he cultivated intentionally, to maintain better self-control, a calm, cautious, good humored, patient, and thoroughly just and conscientious attitude to overcome emotions aroused by the trials and stresses of everyday life. They also show how he developed practical analytic insight into the ways of the self- and socially interested ego leading to cultivation constantly of a common-sense philosophy of human relations. It will be seen how he compensated against his endlessly regressive tendency to become distracted and how he improved his memory and powers of self-expression by reading aloud each day in order to better mentally visualize and auditize the meanings of what he read. It will be shown in his words why, daily, he needed to seek sympathetic communications with friends who enjoyed trading humorous stories about the frustrations of egotism, so that he could enjoy laughing with them and overcome his melancholic disposition.

Since few people know that, besides his legal and political speeches, he wrote and lectured on such important psychological subjects as the egocentric interests of the personality and its political ambitions, on friendship, wit, the treatment of alcoholism, and on the economic and political implications of inventions, railroads, canals, agriculture, and slave labor, and capital and labor, we present them fully. Since few people know that Lincoln was a deeply nostalgic poet, we present his more characteristic works and show how his emotional attachments developed and influenced him in his immortal expressions of sentiment on human relations. He was an exceptionally well informed student of the *Bible* and of Shakespeare, of Aesop, Bunyan, Washington, Jefferson, Clay, Webster, and other great humanitarian moralists, and it will be shown how these sources of wisdom influenced his philosophy of human nature, law, and social organization.

Lincoln's realization of the importance of free egoistic self-determination for the healthy organization of mind under equalitarian rights of sympathetic social cooperation and competition preceded modern realizations of these functions by many years. His practical advice on the psychotherapy of alcoholism and other psychopathological frustrations, as suggested in his lectures presented later in full, preceded by 100 years similar methods being applied today in the best psychiatric institutions. In the knowledge of modern psychology, Lincoln's philosophy of human nature and human relations is far more fundamental than Freud's theory of mental development and social organization through repression of forbidden sexual desires.

The most significant letters, notes, poems, speeches, papers, and authentic stories, inclusive of his life through childhood, youth, and maturity up to and through his presidency, are presented in categorical orders to give in appropriate sequences his hard earned improvements in humanitarian wisdom. His speeches often express similar ideas and feelings in different ways to different audiences. They show, better than any other evidence, Lincoln's genius for understanding people and expressing himself so that they would understand him. He did this naturally, as he would tell the same story in different ways to different people so that they would react with enjoyment of its wit.

Only by reading Lincoln's commentaries fully, in correlation with established evidence on the interpersonal, political and, other social situations that stimulated them, can we obtain an intimate feeling and realistic understanding and appreciation of the development of the personality, mind, and philosophy of the man as he lived.

In Chapter I the best established evidence on Lincoln's physical constitution as a matured man is presented to show in detail the compensatory after-effects of the injury of his brain in childhood. This is the man as known by his contemporaries before and during his presidency. The following chapters portray the development of his mind. In Chapter II is given his family history with a view to accounting for his unusual hereditary mental endowment. In Chapters III to VI are presented the personalities of Lincoln's parents and their influences on the development of his personality in childhood and youth. Lincoln's statements revealing belief in the honesty of his mother and his moral sensitivity about the promiscuity of her relatives, and his conviction that he was the legitimate son of Thomas Lincoln, and why he respected his father's honesty and hated his tyranny are adequately accounted for with additional evidence so correlated for the first time in any biography. How he educated himself as a boy and worked out a method of cross checking the pros and cons of his information and reasoning for truth and reality, that later established him as a superior lawyer, statesman, and president, is given with impressive experiences as he related them.

Chapter VII portrays his life as a young man in New Salem, Ill., and Chapter VIII presents the best evidence known on his tragic romance with Ann Rutledge. It indicates how the encouraging admiration of this lovely, intelligent, virtuously idealistic granddaughter of a signer of the Declaration of Independence and grandniece of a founder of the Constitution of the United States, for Lincoln's ability as a debater, inspired him to decide not to become a blacksmith, as he had contemplated, but to study law and politics and uphold to the best of his ability the intent of the founders of the Constitution of the United States. Chapters IX and X give his important experiences as a crude but apt young lawyer, legislator, and politician and his neurotic courtship of Mary Owens.

In Chapter XI he meets for the first time Stephen A. Douglas, the man who will have more critical influence on his life, political career, and philosophy of democracy, up to the presidency, than any other person. In Chapter XII are presented Lincoln's ideas on the importance of friendship and his neurotic rivalry with Douglas in the courtship of Mary Todd. Chapters XIII and XIV give, in Lincoln's words, accounts of the sympathetic but neurotic dependence of two bachelors on each other and how he talked Joshua Speed into marrying Fanny Henning and then eventually talked Speed into talking himself into marrying Mary Todd.

Chapter XV gives Lincoln's nostalgic poetry and shows how this deeply fixed mood influenced his philosophy of living. Chapters XVI, XVII, and XVIII follow him through Congress and his discouraging failures as a politician. In Chapters XIX and XX Lincoln's philosophy as an eminent lawyer is presented with his most famous cases and what his more intimate contemporaries thought of him. Chapter XXI portrays him as a family man and analyzes his expressions of loyalty to his aging stepmother and management of a moody old father and undependable stepbrother, and his sympathetic interest in maternal as well as paternal relatives.

Chapters XXII to XLII give accounts, largely in Lincoln's own words, of his revival of interest in politics and his uncompromising opposition to the policies of Senator Douglas that would extend states' rights to slavery in the western territories. They show how he envied Douglas more than any other man and how the Lincoln-Douglas rivalries and debates in law and politics, which began in Speed's store in Springfield some 20 years before their political race in 1858 for election to the United States Senate, were resumed. They show how Douglas generally dominated him in winning public approvals in debates and state and national politics, and how Lincoln's envious inferiority influenced him in opposing the national political ambitions of Douglas until he finally defeated him for the presidency of the United States in 1860.

The personal and political conflicts between Lincoln and Douglas constitute the most dramatic romance of obsessive jealousy of human nature and its fateful political consequences in American history, if not world history. Although the major part of the record is largely presented in the chronological order of its development in Lincoln's words, many of Douglas' critical replies to Lincoln are given in his words.

Chapters XLIII and XLIV give Lincoln's reasoning on the selection of his cabinet to solve the intricate political problem that confronted him as president-elect when the southern states seceded and organized the Confederacy. Chapter XLV gives his astute efforts to convince the divided, confused people of the northern and southern states that they must preserve the Union as an indissoluble constitutional contract between states. Chapter XLVI presents his appeal for peace in his inaugural address. Here it will be seen how the jealous rivalry in love and politics between Lincoln and Douglas reached its dramatic climax during the the inaugural address and the amazing sequel of the grand march of the inaugural ball.

Chapter XLVII presents the grounds for Lincoln's philosophy of administration of democratic government. Chapter XLVIII shows how he met crises, and XLIX presents his justifications of suppression of rebellion. Chapter L treats his administration of unprecedented civil involvements of military suspension of the writ of habeas corpus. Chapters LI and LII cover Lincoln's military strategy in 1861-62, and Chapter LIII gives the dilemmas of emancipation. Chapters LIV and LV give his letters and addresses as statesman and emancipator in 1863. Chapter LVI presents his military strategy in 1863, LVII the trials of reconstruction in 1864, LVIII his military strategy of 1864, and LIX covers his final political and military triumphs and tragic death. Chapter LX describes his private life as President and LXI that of Mrs. Lincoln after his death. Chapter LXII discusses his philosophy of morals and religion.

He who has learned to read Lincoln studiously comes to enjoy the growth of his wisdom and literary style as one does the development of the music of great masters. As one reads his productions again and again, appreciation grows for his severe cultivation of clarity, simplicity, economy, beauty, and depth of expression of humanitarian sympathies with meticulous choice of words. He who would like to understand the processes involved in the development of Lincoln's personality, mind, and philosophy will obtain the best understanding by reading his letters, papers, notes, and speeches in the chronological order as presented.

Besides the members of Lincoln's boyhood family, five persons, Ann Rutledge, Joshua Speed, Mary Todd, Stephen A. Douglas, and William H. Herndon, had unusually impressive influences on his life up to the presidency. Of these, Stephen A. Douglas was by far the most critically important and determinative. Brief biographical sketches of these people are inserted in the chapters where they enter the scene in order that the reader will better grasp the nature of their personal influences on Lincoln's mind.

Collections of Lincoln's written or otherwise recorded productions as known at the time of publication have been presented by Raymond (1865), Nicolay and Hay (1890), Hertz (1931), Basler (1949), and The Abraham Lincoln Association (1953). The last has become, through the meticulous research of collateral recorded material, and the correction of former misinformation and erroneous statements and the elimination of false documents, by an organization of highly competent scholars, editors and librarians, under the supervision of Roy P. Basler, editor of Rutgers University Press, the most authoritative and complete presentation of Lincoln's productions. This *Collected Works of Abraham Lincoln* is accepted here as authentic and his letters, notes, and speeches and spelling are quoted from it.

Abstracts from editorial comments and notes in the *Collected Works,* made with reference to particular situations relative to particular letters or speeches of Lincoln, have been added at the time of quotation where they provided interesting information, and I am most indebted to the *Collected Works* for such collateral information. Other material on Lincoln is credited to the source as used. Extensive correlation of material from many contemporary and later biographies and historical records has been made, in order to present as accurate and complete an account as possible of the most important conditioning physical and social factors in the development of Lincoln's personality and philosophy.

I am particularly indebted to the late Dr. John F. Fulton, former Sterling Professor of Physiology at Yale University Medical School, and Dr. Henry A. Riley, Professor of Clinical Neurology at Columbia University College of Physicians and Surgeons, for their kindly assistance in interpreting the facial evidence of Lincoln's cerebral injury and its possible pathology. I am, however, responsible for the diagnosis as presented.

The photographs of Lincoln have been selected to show the facial evidence of the organic neurosis and the changes in his face and character with age and work. A photograph of Volk's life mask of Lincoln (1860) in my possession is presented to show the depression in his forehead produced by the old injury. The life mask of President Lincoln by Mills (1864) has been added for comparison.

I have taken the liberty of including, at the request of friends who are interested in this study, a photograph of myself with my sculpture of president-elect Lincoln, in which I tried to portray the inspired, resolutely moral, but diffident, kindly humored prophet of fraternalism who would fight to establish equal legal rights for all mankind and to preserve the Constitution and the Union.

Because of the specialized method of presenting the study of Lincoln's personal development I have relied mostly on the assistance of Dorothy Clarke Kempf, my wife, who is also a physician and specialist in psychiatry. For a thousand and one invaluable discriminating literary criticisms and editorial suggestions in preparing the manuscript I am immeasurably indebted to her. Without her help I could not have written this book.

I wish to extend my thanks in particular to the following publishers and authors for my abstractions and quotations of material from special publications bearing on the life of Lincoln which have been essential sources of information for this biographical analysis: to the World Publishing Co., from *Herndon's Life of Lincoln;* to The Viking Press, Inc., from *The Hidden Lincoln* by Emanuel Hertz; to Horace Liveright & Co, from *Abraham Lincoln, A New Portrait* by Emanuel Hertz; to Rutgers University Press, from *The Lincoln Reader* by Paul M. Angle; to Alfred A. Knopf, from *Abraham Lincoln* by Benjamin P. Thomas; to McClure Co., from *The Reminiscences of Carl Schurz;* to Houghton Mifflin Co., from *The Real Lincoln* by Jesse W. Weik, and *The Diary of Gideon Welles;* to Harcourt, Brace & World, Inc., from *Mary Lincoln* by Carl Sandburg and Paul M. Angle; to Dodd, Mead & Co., from

Lincoln the President by J. G. Randall; to Little, Brown & Co., from *Mary Lincoln* by Ruth Painter Randall; and to Frederick A. Praeger, Inc., from *The West Point Atlas of the Civil War* by V. T. Esposito.

I am also particularly indebted to the Department of Lincolniana, Lincoln Memorial University, to the McClellan Lincoln Collection in Brown University Library, to Louis A. Warren, Director of the Lincoln National Life Foundation, and to the Library of Congress and the Illinois State Historical Library for special points of information and for photographs of Lincoln, Mrs. Lincoln, Douglas, and their contemporaries, and to The American Museum of Natural History and H. C. Shapiro and Clarence L. Hay for anthropological notes and reproductions of Mills' life mask of Lincoln from *Natural History*.

To Mrs. Eunice Thomas Miner, Executive Director of The New York Academy of Sciences I feel particularly grateful for her interest and encouragement in publishing this book as a contribution to the new social science of analytical biography, and to Editors Harold E. Whipple, Marvin I. Spitzer and Mary Louise Byrd for numerous suggestions in improving the manuscript.

Chapter I

LINCOLN'S PHYSICAL CONSTITUTION

The biographical analysis of the development of the personality and political philosophy of Abraham Lincoln is simplified and best facilitated by first considering his physical make-up and constitutional energic type as an adult, for evidence of genetic, endocrine, neural and other bodily determining factors. We can then advantageously follow his family origin and cultural development, with the decisive experiences of his life in correlation with his physical constitution.

Hereditary Determination

Lincoln's unusual bodily and personal characteristics, particularly his long legs and arms relative to a torso of average length, his large hands, long fingers and flat feet, narrow stooped shoulders and misshapen chest, the longish dimensions of his face and upward deviation (hyperphoria) of left eye, melancholy disposition and relaxed social attitude, have long been taken, in the medical sciences, as associated characters indicating an unusual hereditary (genic) and congenital and later environmental determination.

As in the growth of any unicellular or multicellular organism, the biological question is, what bodily characters are hereditary and what characters are acquired from environmental nutritional and stressing energic effects on growth. Each gene in an hereditary chromosomal complement produces highly specific enzymatic action on the cytoplasmic differentiation of cells and on the growth of tissues and organs, and the effects of these specific actions are qualified by allied and antagonistic actions of many other genes. Moreover, as cells must work to maintain equilibrating cytoplasmic interactions with other cells of their bodily environmental and with external environmental energies, the specific cytoplasmic qualitative genic effects become differentiated by environmental action in quantities, ratios, timing and positions, throughout embryonic and postnatal development. As the specific effects of any form of hereditary determination vary more or less in each organism at different ages in interaction with other genic determinants and with its environmental energies, inferences of hereditary effects in Lincoln's case must include environmental modifications of these effects.

Upon finding "a classic example of the Marfan syndrome" in a male (7 to 11 years of age) in Lincoln's lineage, Schwartz (1964) compared measurements of his subject's hands and head with Lincoln's as taken from casts and photographs and descriptions of his bodily and personal characteristics by contemporaries, particularly Herndon, and assumed

1

that Lincoln likewise had a similar syndrome "derived from an ancestor common to both individuals." The last ancestor in common was Mordecai Lincoln II, born in Massachusetts in 1686. He was the fourth antecedent (great-great-grandfather) of Abraham Lincoln by his first wife, and the eighth antecedent of the Marfan boy by a male line of descendents from a second wife. The transmission of a special autosomal genic mutation has been assumed to have been repeated through four generations of four male and four female antecedents of Lincoln in one line, and eight generations of eight male and eight female antecedents of a distant relative in another line. As genic mutations may arise in reproduction of the germ plasm sperm and ova of one generation, and be transmitted, modified, or eliminated by chance in crossing in the next, the assumption of a genic determination common to both individuals, as the basic factor producing assumed similarities of body growth is questionable.

The Marfan syndrome was first described by A. B. Marfan in 1896, as a set of bodily and personal characteristics, defined now *(American Medical Dictionary)* as "a congenital and hereditary condition characterized by arachnodactyly with bilateral ectopia lentis," meaning long, thin, spiderlike fingers and toes and tendency to pathological displacement of the lens of both eyes, leading to reduction of vision and eventual blindness. As the effects attributed to a Marfan mutation vary greatly in individuals of the same pedigree and immediate family, the formerly limited syndrome has been enlarged to include other abnormal bodily and personal characteristics. The mutation seems to produce the growth of distrophic, inelastic connective tissue which is attended by long thin growth of arms, legs and ribs, with tendency to deformation of the sternum making a bulging "pigeon" breast or a concave breast with malposition of lungs and heart, flabby skin with little subcutaneous fat, loose joints, hernia, arterial aneurism, and, generally, an apathetic, listless, doleful personality with weak mental integrity and social indifference. Gothic palate and myopia, hyperopia, strabismus, and tendency to glaucoma have recently been included in the syndrome by some observers. Death follows frequently in youth from respiratory or cardiac disease or, later, from rupture of an aneurism. As an intellectually superior mind and socially active disposition with normal eyes have been observed in otherwise typical cases of long, thin body growth; and low energy, myopia and other anomalies appear in short thick persons of the same family; such opposite characters have been assumed by some medical geneticists to be variations of the effects of the same mutation.

A. M. Gordon (1962) described a case of Marfan's syndrome in a young male, and compared such bodily characteristics with Lincoln's. He chose to attribute the latter to an hereditary genic determination transmitted by his mother, Nancy Hanks, as she had a long thin body seemingly more like the Marfan type although she was socially energetic and intelligent, whereas his father, Tom, who had a average short, thick, powerful physique, was lazy, ill-tempered and unintelligent.

Schwartz and Gordon have both freely interpreted Herndon's description of Lincoln's bones, particularly of his arms, legs and hands and head and face, as being long and thin and characteristic of Marfan genic determination, whereas Herndon described him as being "thin, wirey, sinewy, raw and heavy boned." Neither Schwartz or Gordon has given due consideration to comparative anthropological measurements and environmental modifications of Lincoln's physique.

H. L. Shapiro (1953), Chairman of the Department of Anthropology, American Museum of Natural History, has pointed out that "the tall, gaunt figure [of Abraham Lincoln], with its cadaverous face" was of "the type" now recognized in anthropology as "the Southern Mountaineer." Lincoln, he said, was perhaps "more the product of the Kentucky Hills where he was born and of the people that first settled there than we realize."

Shapiro made a series of significant measurements from a bronze cast of a life mask of Lincoln taken in 1865, on his 56th birthday, by Clark Mills. Comparison of these measurements with a composite of measurements of 272 skulls of "Old Americans" of comparable native origin led Shapiro to a number of significant inferences. He found that Lincoln's height was seven and one-half inches above this average and his face was "exceedingly wide at the cheekbones" and his jaw was "rarely matched in width," his forehead was high, wide and sloping and the face above the mouth was long and the nose long but wide, and the mouth wide. The unusual width of the jaw so overbalanced that of the forehead that the latter seemed to be narrow. Shapiro said that "some of Herndon's observations were sound" but he "was wrong" in describing Lincoln's forehead as "narrow." "Among the racial strains to be found in Lincoln's geography," he said, "one could match these dimensions easily only among Indians." The American ancestry of Lincoln includes English, Scotch and probably Dutch, and they have undergone a marked increase in height in successive generations in the Appalachian country, Shapiro said. Particularly in Kentucky where Lincoln was born, and in Tennessee, unusually tall, lanky, powerful men like Lincoln and the Enloes and Brownfields were so common that the type has become established in anthropology and in the public mind as typical of the mountains of the limestone country.

Schwartz has presented an interesting chart of an "inferential pedigree" of the male line of antecedents and descendents of Lincoln and of his Marfan relative. It includes a number of males and a female who seem to have had some anomalous physical condition that might be assumed, regardless of long-thin or short-thick physiques, as possibly to have been a more or less vigorous or submerged effect of a Marfan mutation.

In Lincoln's case, Schwartz has included the unusual length of his arms and legs relative to the torso, unusual length of the fingers relative to the breadth of the hands, with anomaly of the fingers of the left hand being longer than the right whereas the right thumb was longer than the left. He also emphasized the leathery skin with little subcutaneous fat, protruding ears, asymmetrical differences in growth of the bones of the right and left sides of his face, hyperopia, and strabismus of the left eye, as possible Marfan characters.

Asymmetrical differences in growth of bilateral organs are not infrequent in the Marfan syndrome but this does not permit the geneticist to attribute them entirely to genic determination. Possible effects of special environmental stresses must be included. Lincoln, from early youth throughout his physical development, chopped wood with a heavy axe daily for many hours, and in such occupation the left hand in a right handed person carries more stress and does more work than the right hand. Whereas Marfans are usually long thin-boned and muscularly weak and mentally dull, socially withdrawn and apathetic, Lincoln, as a boy and man, had unusually heavy, long bones, powerful arms, legs, hands and back, large head and face, and an intelligently active mind with endless drive at self-education and improvement toward giving social service.

An environmental cause of the asymmetrical development of the right and left bones of Lincoln's face and the subnormal neuromuscular tonus of the left side, and hyperphoria of the left eye, his melancholy disposition and euphoric compensation will be shown later in this and other chapters to have followed after the accidental fracture of his skull and probable injury of his brain in childhood.

Lincoln's face gave evidence of unusual hereditary genetic predispositions in its embryonic development, hence in the later development of his brain and personality. The creases in the skin of the human face are produced principally by the activities of the facial muscles with attachments to the skin. In most faces, the creases that run on each side from the nose continue around the upper lip and back of the corners of the mouth, and then pass more or less distinctly around the lower lip and under the chin. In Lincoln's face, as shown by two life masks and photographs, the creases on each side of the nose run halfway around the upper lip and then turn sharply backward, above the corners of the mouth. Here they join deep creases that run downward in front of the cheekbones, between the muscles of the cheek and the muscles of the mouth, and then curve forward to pass under the chin where they meet, giving the mouth and chin strong expression. The expressive effect of this unusual, though not rare, type of facial creasing was enhanced by the unusual length and breadth of his face.

A second cousin, David Lincoln, had facial creases similar to those of Abraham. Also a third cousin, Jonas Basham, whose grandmother, Mimi Hanks, was a first cousin of Lincoln's mother, Nancy Hanks, inherited facial creases remarkably similar to those of Abraham Lincoln, indicating maternal as well as paternal hereditary factors for this unusual characteristic.

Three genetic moles, one on the right side and two on the left side of the face, gave, in relation to these creases, a distinguishing quality to Lincoln's face which, once seen, was not likely to be forgotten, and was, therefore, socially and politically invaluable. The largest and most prominent mole was located on the right side, just above the crease as it turns backward from the upper lip to join the crease lying between the muscles of mastication and the mouth. The mole actually divided the crease, producing a perpetually dimpled, smiling effect on that side of the face. On the left side of the face, one of the other two moles lies on the cheek above the crease where it turns backward from the upper lip, and the other lies lower down on the side of the face, in back of the crease, after it joins the mouth muscle-cheek muscle crease. Their positions in relation to the right mole indicate that early in embryonic development, when the head was very small and the face was beginning to form, the right and left moles appeared in symmetrically opposite positions. If so, the left one later became divided and the two parts separated progressively as the muscles and bones of the face enlarged.

Although the psychological effect of these facial characteristics is now unknowable, they gave his face a ready-to-smile set and an unusually comical quality that surely must have reinforced the development of his great sense of humor and propensity for laughing. They probably also combined with other unusual, inherited and acquired facial and bodily qualities, in reinforcing the formation, in his boyhood, of the conviction that he was an unusual person, predestined to perform some great mission to be revealed to him, that developed later into his unique, fixed lifelong, humanitarian inspiration and compulsion.

When an adult, his hair was coarse and black, and his eyes were small, grey and deeply set. His ears were large, thick-lobed, and extended out at almost right angles to his head. His usually long and generally disheveled hair hid this grotesque, comical inferiority. His nose was not relatively oversized, but it looked large because of his thin face. The nostrils did not extend as far into the tip of the nose as in most people, which made the end look heavy. Lincoln was said, when young, to have been somewhat sensitive about his nose, but not about his ears.

Hypersensitive Hypokinetic Constitution

Lincoln's body growth and energic constitution show evidence of some endocrine imbalance. He was a long, thin baby at birth, with unusually long arms and legs. Lincoln grew to six feet four inches in height and generally weighed less than 180 lbs. His legs and arms were disproportionately long for his body, which when seated was about the length of an average six footer. His chest was narrow and described as flat.

The skin of his face was weather-beaten, coarse, deeply grained, dark and generally had a sallow or muddy color. Many years of close exposure in youth before an open wood fire, where he read, possibly left a permanently dystrophic effect. Deep creases over the forehead and at the outside corners of the eyes and around the mouth indicate an unusual amount of facial work in using the eyes, and in talking and laughing.

The neuromuscular tonus of his body was more relaxed than in the average man. This was shown in the slow, drawling, staccato monotone of his speech, and the deliberate, contemplative, meditative manner and slow mental reaction time, and flat feet. He seems also to have had lower blood pressure than normal, which probably, when too low, contributed to the production of nervous depression. Self-conscious of his height, he tended to slouch in posture, with stooping at the shoulders and bending slightly at the knees, but he characteristically held his chin up; indicating an ego-attitude of humility counterbalanced with well-determined self-reliance and self-respect.

Dr. K. C. Wold has also reviewed the evidence on Lincoln's physical constitution in relation to his health. He concluded that any endocrino-pathy was limited to indications of some thyroid disfunction and possibly a slight postpubertal overactivity of the pituitary which might account for his disproportionately long legs and arms. Attempts to explain Lincoln's melancholic disposition on an endocrinological basis would be, he says rightly, "merely a venture in the realm of fancy."

However, even though not fully known, it would be more erroneous to disregard the indications of some degree of pituitary, thyroid and gonadal endocrinopathy, than not to consider these factors as having possibly contributed to his hypokinetic constitution. Many years of hard farm work and wood chopping from childhood to manhood, out of dire necessity for living, gave him an unusually large and powerful muscular development of hands and arms, back and shoulders. His neck, though strong, was long and scrawny looking in relation to his head and sloping shoulders. His lower jaw was long and heavy and inclined to the acro-megalic form.

His constitutional morphology was predominantly Kretschmerian (1936) asthenic, or Sheldonian (1940) ectomorphic and cerebrotonic, and his energic constitution was Kempfian (1941) hypokinetic. These qualities indicate that Lincoln was probably somewhat hyperpituitary and hypo-gonadal in endocrine ratio. His constitution disposed toward some reduction of autonomic pressure of energy in sexual directions and tended to produce shyness with women and a preference for the company of men, factors endlessly contributory and determinative in influence on the social conditioning and development of his personality.

His slow, drawling speech, slow reaction time and mental deliberate-ness, and pedestrian rhythm in style of speaking and writing were so con-sistent with his energic constitution and morphology that the latter, obviously, largely determined the former. In Lincoln the physiopsycholog-ical order of reactions dominated the psychophysiological. In other words, he must be and was always guided by his feelings in what he said and did,

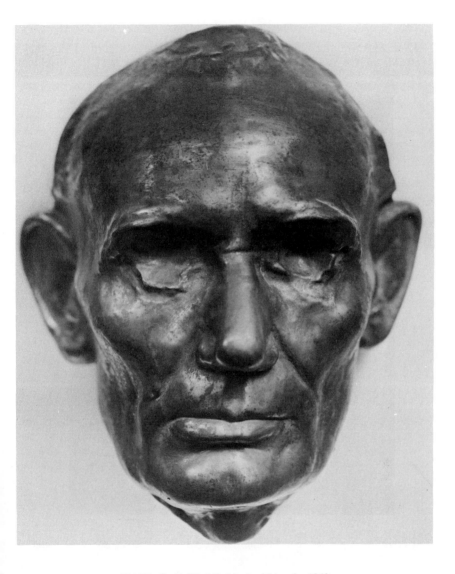

PLATE 2. Volk's Life Mask of Lincoln, 1860.

for if they did not support him in the work of fulfilling certain self-commitments he would become miserable, if not melancholic.

Meaning of Facial Asymmetries

If we examine the full face photographs* of Lincoln, and of the Volk (1860) life mask,† and the Mills (1865) mask,‡ we see that the forehead

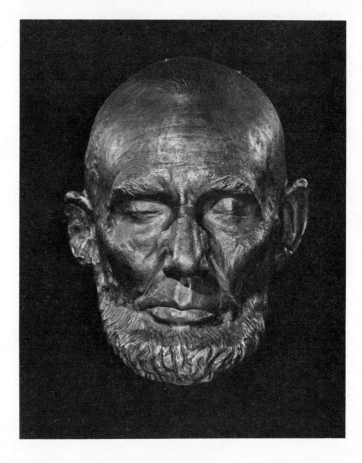

PLATE 3. Mills' Life Mask of Lincoln, 1865. Courtesy of Mr. Clarence L. Hay and the American Museum of Natural History.

is wide, high and bulges slightly in the middle. There is an unusual depression in the Volk mask with a palpable edge near the midline above

*See Frontispiece. Lincoln's full face photograph, age 54.
†Illustration No. 2. Life Mask by Volk, 1860.
‡Illustration No. 3. Life Mask by Mills, 1865.

the left eye. I have examined the Mills mask and found a similar depression in its forehead.

In Lincoln's photographs and both masks the left eye sets higher than the right. His left eyebrow is usually elevated more than the right to keep the upper lid retracted and the pupil of the left eye exposed. The tendency of the left eye to turn upward uncovered more of the white surface of the sclera below the iris, giving a slightly dull, weak, staring effect on that side, in strong disharmony with the more active right eye and face. The left eye in the best frontal photographs is shown definitely to be out of focus and turned reflexly slightly upward and outward. This effect is due to the inferior oblique muscle of the eye being stronger than the weakened superior oblique which turns the eye inward and downward. Lincoln's right eye functioned normally and dominantly for general vision and reading.

Further examination of the face shows that the left half of the upper lip is somewhat thicker than the right and less expressive, that is, less involitionally and volitionally active. The right half of the lower lip protrudes markedly and is pulled toward the right by the mouth and cheek muscles. This action also characteristically pulls the nose definitely toward the right. The right side of the chin is larger than the left, indicating stronger muscle tonus and development from more active use. Although his larynx was large, he had a rasping, high pitched voice that grew shrill and squeaky upon emotional excitement, indicating some imbalance of vocal cord or pharyngeal muscle tension.

Further examination of the Volk mask, especially when measured for similar right and left points from the midline, also shows marked differences in the growth of the bones. Although such differences may be genetic, or developmental in relation to loss of teeth and use, and cannot be taken as definitely indicative of the effects of an injury of the brain in youth like the differences in tonic contraction of the ocular and facial muscles, they should be considered and functionally correlated. His cheekbones were unusually high and prominent. The right was larger than the left, and the right orbital ridge and lower jaw were more heavily developed than the left, giving the whole face a decided morphological curve toward the right.

This deformation becomes distinctly visible when the fullface photographs are turned upside down. When the Volk mask is turned upside down, or viewed from below upward, the larger size of the face and the greater prominence of its lip, chin and lower jaw, and the greater depression of the face under the cheekbone, on the right side, is impressive.

Fracture of Skull and Injury of Brain in Boyhood

All of these differences in facial muscle and bone development, like the weakened functioning of the left ocular and facial muscles in particular, indicated to me that Lincoln had suffered a serious injury of his brain in childhood. The sharp depression in the forehead above the left eye with a definitely palpable edge, in the life masks, shows where his skull had been fractured, and the permanent differences in the nervous tone of the ocular and facial muscles of the two sides indicate that his brain was then permanently injured.

Evidence that such an accident occurred was given by Lincoln in his letter to Scripps (1860), where he told that "in his tenth year he was kicked by a horse and apparently killed for a while." More extensive descriptions of the accident by Lincoln to Herndon, and by Dennis Hanks who was living with the Lincolns at the time, provide details of what happened. Although descriptions in Herndon's several accounts (Herndon, 1889; Hertz, 1938) are slightly different, their essentials coincide as combined here.

"Mr. Lincoln told me," Herndon said, "that he had to shell corn with his hands and take it to mill in a sack on horseback, corn in one side and rocks in the other [to balance]. He went to the mill on his father's old [unshod] mare [and] had to wait his turn to grind. It was getting late in the evening and he was some two miles from home . . . ; he hitched in his old mare to the sweep-pole or lever that turned the wheel and, being in a hurry to get through with his grist, he urged her to full speed, round and round, . . . faster and faster, . . . [and as] he struck her with a stick . . . [he started] to say: 'Get up—you old hussy.' . . . Just as he uttered: 'Get up,' [he] was kicked in the forehead." "Miller Gorden picked up the bleeding, senseless boy, whom he took for dead and at once sent for his father . . . ." "Abe lay unconscious all night." As he regained consciousness he blurted out 'You old hussy.' "He finished the sentence just as he intended to speak it, commencing where he left off. Lincoln told me this and he and I used to speculate on it."

Young Abe was said, many years later by a cousin, Dennis Hanks, who lived with the Lincolns at the time and was 10 years older, not to have regained consciousness until the next day. He seemed to have recovered without serious mental or physical after-effects since he received no medical attention for the head injury (see Chapter V).

Fractures of the skull and cerebral after-effects were never suspected, or at least never reported by any of Lincoln's physicians although, after 30, he consulted several for treatment of "hypochondria" and other nervous symptoms. This is not surprising for it was not until after 1890, upon application of X-ray photography and neurophysiology that we learned how to explain some of the cerebral effects and nervous consequences of fracture of the skull.

Lincoln was also struck on the head with a club in a fight with Negro marauders while taking a flatboat down the Mississippi, when either 19 or 22. This blow, he said, left a permanent scar. However, it probably did no further damage, for he routed the hoodlums, saved his cargo and continued the journey.

Congenital injury of the nervous system has also been suggested to account for the ocular and facial symptoms but this is discredited by the definite history of a blow on the head in childhood that knocked him unconscious for many hours.*

Diagnosis of Cerebral Lesion

Although modern neurology requires a far more complete examination of the living subject for positive and negative evidence of nervous impairment to make a diagnosis, consideration of several places of brain injury that might have produced the unusual complex of symptoms, as far as known in Mr. Lincoln's case, is highly desirable.

The kick on the forehead over the left eye evidently fractured the skull at the point of impact and must have violently snapped the head and neck backward. The size and depth of the depression is evidence of its severity. It is most likely that a subdural hemorrhage of considerable size developed here, besides points of hemorrhage elsewhere. The left frontal lobe was certainly damaged, which, in a right-handed, right-eyed person, would have modifying after-effects on his personality, which will be considered later.

The evident, permanent weakness of conjugate movements of the left eye, with tendency to turn slightly upward and outward, and weakness in tonus of the left facial muscles, constitutes a symptom complex that cannot be satisfactorily explained by a single area of permanent brain injury. The lifelong discordance of functioning of the laryngeal muscles is also indicative of additional involvement of involitional nervous action, as is also his daily mental distractibility and moody frustration, as will be seen in many later chapters.

Hydrostatic repercussion within the skull on the opposite side might have damaged by shock, if not by another subdural hemorrhage, the right cerebral cortex in the middle area of the precentral gyrus, supplying motor impulses to the left eye, eyelid, face and pharynx. Penfield and Rasmussen (1950) state that elimination of the precentral gyrus below the arm area produces temporary paralysis of the opposite side of the face, which recovers leaving a residual minor weakness of the lower part only. It sometimes also interferes with mastication and pharyngeal movement and speaking, but functional recovery to normal generally follows here also. Since the facial muscles on both sides have bilateral cortical innervation, the effects of such an injury in a boy would probably have been largely compensated for within a few months, hence more permanent damage probably occurred in some other area.

---

*Mock (1950) reports that about seven per cent of untreated fractures of the skull in children end fatally. Most such fractures were caused, before the automobile, by being kicked in the head. Electronic recording has now shown that an appalling amount of damage to the brain, heretofore unsuspected, follows from blows on the head, at the point of impact and from hydrostatic repercussion (contra-coup), and through the production of numerous, small (petechial) internal hemorrhages as well as subdural blood clots, without external evidence of fracture.

Several small hemorrhages in the brainstem would have produced the particular permanent ocular and facial effects. If one partly damaged the nucleus of the left fourth nerve to the superior oblique muscle, so as to weaken it, the left eye would then tend continuously to turn more or less upward and outward, as shown in many of Lincoln's photographs, while leaving some degree of volitional coordination. If another point of hemorrhage damaged the nucleus of the left seventh nerve, the left facial muscles would be permanently weakened, likewise with some retention of volitional control. Persistent laryngeal tensions, producing a rasping, high pitched voice, might have also followed from another petechial hemorrhage that impaired vagus innervation.

The weakening of the left facial muscles would probably have only minor, secondary effects on the personality. The production of a high pitched, rasping voice was more important, but Lincoln largely overcame this professional deficiency by speaking thoughtfully, slowly and deliberately, always with the intention of expressing himself simply and directly so as to be clearly understood. However, he spoke in a slow staccato monotone, indicating deficiency in sense of inflection,—a serious impairment in a public speaker.

Frontal lobe impairment on the left side (of a right-eyed and right-handed person) of the corticothalamic system of integration of nervous interactions would have reduced the egoistic volitional production of conscious visual imagery of self-in-its-environment, requiring compensatory development of the right corticothalamic connections to serve this indispensable function. More stimulation than in normal people would then be necessary in order to remain mentally acutely active. A person with such a cerebral lesion would have, in order to keep his mind working at a highly attentive sensory discriminating level, to keep himself involved in emotionally stimulating situations by cultivating exciting social interests and objectives. As will be seen in later chapters, Lincoln did just this, constantly, through his passion for realistic accuracy and simplicity of reasoning, truth, directness, honesty, kindness and friendliness of self-expression, and upholding the equalitarian moral and legal rights of all people, cultivating a moralizing sense of humor, and challenging illegally exercised political and judicial authority.

The most significant of his symptoms was the repetitive tendency, when not being stimulated by environmental activities to lapse automatically into a lower conscious state of mental detachment, tending to sadness and gloominess, with characteristic facial expression. This was described by some of his friends as "ugly and stupid looking" and others as "dull," "sad and abstract," "detached" and "withdrawn." When a man in his forties, he told his friends that he was never without "melancholy." Upon being stimulated in a way that aroused emotivating interest, such as some incident or some interpersonal talk, his facial expression was observed to change quickly from dull indifference to animated interest, with a tendency to smile and laugh.

As a humorist telling moral stories of frustrated vanities and a humanist seeking freedom and peace of mind for all people as well as himself, he carried on endlessly to overcome his subconscious tendency to lapse into a rut of sad, gloomy, visual, mental preoccupation over the fateful futility of life. He also intentionally cultivated special forms of self-stimulation in habits of reading aloud to himself and other people, memorizing, and writing out his reasonings. By reading aloud, he told Herndon, he gained the benefit of hearing as well as seeing what he read, enabling him thereby to remember more easily. By writing out his reasons for and against making decisions he formed stable convictions.

Records of descriptions of Lincoln's physical and personal disabilities as a boy and man, by himself and neighbors and friends, are numerous, many of which are presented in later chapters. The earliest is that of Josiah Crawford in Gentryville, Ind. He employed the boy Lincoln, loaned him books for study and liked to jest him about the way he "stuck out" his lower lip, apparently regarding it as a boy's eccentric habit. When Lincoln returned to southern Indiana in 1844, age 35, to make a speech, his lower lip still protruded abnormally. When Crawford asked him about his books for making the speech, Lincoln, remembering his joking, replied humorously, "I haven't any. Sticking out my lip is all I need." Tarbell (1924) who has retold the story, saw in it evidence that "this habit, fallen into in youth, resulted in that protruberance of the lower lip which is a distinguishing characteristic of his face," an interpretation held generally by his medical and lay biographers.

Diplopia and Eyestrain

Decoordination of the left eye with dominant right eye was more serious in Lincoln's case than usual in that his persistence in reading tended to produce severe eyestrain that increased upon fatigue, moral frustration or emotional excitement, with the sequelae of headache, nausea, indigestion, chills, mental distraction and gloominess. In youth and maturity Lincoln was unable to focus both eyes for any length of time without volitional strain. Herein existed a definite unconscious involitional determinant of a special form of self-righting compensation on conscious learning. He must not only use right eye vision against out-of-focus left eye vision, but he must consciously and conscientiously see in his mind's eye the morally right and better side of himself in sympathetic interaction with other people, in order to reduce the stress of visualizing himself as being wrong, unkind or unjust in ways that caused gloomy frustration of his egoistic self-respect and will to live.

The continuous tendency of visual decoordination was sufficient to increase nervous fatigue and depression of mood or "spirit" upon prolonged use of the eyes, particularly for reading. Such conditions tend in most youths to induce discouragement of reading, and lethargy with laziness. Despite this impairment, young Lincoln was an eager student and liked to lie on the floor and read aloud by the light of the open wood fire. Later, as a man, he often read in a reclining position on a couch or the floor. His work as a lawyer and politician required him to read excessively, and he adapted to this by learning to scan pages rapidly for essentials and by developing a highly retentive memory. When it was unnecessary to use his eyes or mind he would lapse into a characteristic, disinterested mental state.

The earliest definite evidence of observation of Lincoln's visual de-coordination has been recorded by Dr. T. H. Shastid (1929), an oculist who practised in Pittsfield, Ill. It was described to him by his father who, when a boy, lived in New Salem and knew Abe Lincoln, storekeeper and postmaster of the village. Shastid described him as a melancholy but kindly spoken person who liked to amuse children as well as grown-ups. "Abe" would sit on a box in front of the store when not waiting on a customer, generally with a dejected and abstracted expression. He liked in summer to lie on the ground near the store, with his bare feet elevated against the trunk of a tree and read.

Shastid noticed that Lincoln's left eye looked queer at times and would suddenly turn upward. Some 20 years later he saw Lincoln in several debates with Douglas and in several trials as a lawyer. He then recognized the eye condition as being produced by a weakness of the left eye muscles that turned the eyeball upward. Upon excitement this condition would suddenly increase and produce a severe divergent squint.

Dr. Shastid diagnosed Lincoln's eye condition, from his father's description, as hyperphoria. The continuous eyestrain, he pointed out, was at least partly the cause of moodiness or "chronic inexpressible blues." He thought that Lincoln was possibly also color blind, for he said to Dr. Shastid's grandmother that he did not enjoy beauty in flowers and sunsets like other people. However, Lincoln's description, in this period, of colors in the scene of an Indian massacre (see later chapter) indicate that his perception of colors was not entirely deficient.

In 1857, at 48, he bought, upon the recommendation of a friend while shopping in a jewelry store, his first pair of "spectacles" for reading. He tried on several pairs and paid 37-1/2 cents for the glasses that he liked best. Until a few years before he probably had effective accommodation of the right eye, although it was always attended by more or less strain from decoordination of the left.

The following reports on Lincoln's eyes and glasses are taken from several later authoritative investigations. The glasses were reported by Almer Coe of Chicago to have in each lens the strength of plus 6.75 diopters. This indicated that Lincoln probably had four or four and a half diopters of hyperopia or far sightedness at 48. This severe disability had no doubt been developing for a number of years and required constant effort to produce sufficient accommodation for reading.

Dr. W. H. Crisp (1932), opthalmologist, recorded the following observations. Fullface photographs show an upward deviation of the left eye, great enough to produce a lack of fusion of its images with the right eye. The two eyes did not work together, possibly as a result of a vertical strabismus of the left.

Dr. S. Mitchell (1914) found evidence of left hyperphoria and sugtested that the corrugations of his brow and crow's feet at each corner of the eyes showed that he habitually used auxiliary facial muscles to support the external muscles of the eyes in the work for visual coordination.

Dr. K. C. Wold (1948) has suggested that the diplopia was caused by a decoordination of the external muscles of the left eye which was inherently connected in some way with the other facial asymmetries.

No physician of record, in so far as I know, has offered an explanation of the nervous origin and nature of the asymmetrical functioning of the left facial and ocular muscles, although some of the nervous effects of eyestrain have been discussed.

Most people with diplopia learn how to disregard the dimmer visual image by concentrating mentally on the image of the dominant eye. When both eyes are used in focal coordination, volitional effort is necessary, and this eventually produces mental visual fatigue and organic eyestrain tending to cause headache. Under mental or physical fatigue or emotional excitement, visual decoordination increases (as noticed at times in Lincoln by his contemporaries) and the stronger image is underlapped by more or less of a shadowy, weaker image, increasing mental confusion and uneasiness. Lincoln learned in boyhood to cultivate a calm, humorous, patient, kindly attitude and friendly interpersonal assurances, and a common-sense philosophy of life that generally protected him from emotional provocation and increase of this distress. However, he had a singularly impressive mystifying experience with more persistent diplopia after a fatiguing day upon the evening of his election as President. His description and interpretation of this experience to Ward Lamon and Noah Brooks is given in Chapter XLII. The strange mystery of his double vision and its superstitious meaning for him has been cited by many biographers as an indication that Lincoln had clairvoyant sensitivity. It seems evident now that it was the simple result of an old injury of his brain in childhood.

Through his adult years Lincoln had many nervous attacks, characterized by eyestrain and headache with nausea and indigestion, so severe that often he became unable to work and had to lie down with a cold compress over his eyes. He had couches in his law office, at home, and in the White House, for this purpose.

Borglum's Interpretation of Lincoln's Face

Gutzon Borglum, sculptor of the great marble head of Lincoln in the Capitol rotunda at Washington, made extensive comparative measurements of the photographs and masks of Lincoln, and studies of his notes, letters, speeches and life history before attempting the portrait.

In an essay on Lincoln, Borglum gave interpretations of the relative meanings of the right and left sides of his face as indicated by its lines and measurements. He saw the greater strength of functioning of the right side relative to the left. The lines around the right eye and its direct convergence showed that it was more active, that is, dominant, and that he naturally thought and planned with the visualized imagery of this eye. He was "naturally a merry soul changed by sadness." The lines around Lincoln's mouth and its displacement towards the right indicated that "he smiled very, very often when his nature took no part in it."

Borglum noticed that the tip of the nose was also turned toward the right but he did not give any particular significance to this. However, he saw that the left eye was "wide open" and out of focus, "indecisive," "noncommittal and dreamy." The left side of the face seemed "primitive," "immature" and "unfinished." Its weak expression was "sad and undetermined" in contrast to the determined strength of the right side. The left brow was "anxious, ever slightly elevated and concerned." Written on his face was "humor, pathos, half-smile, half-sadness; half-anger, half-forgiveness, half-determination, half-pause; . . . a dual Nature struggling with a dual problem delivering a single result."

Borglum's description of Lincoln's face is the most careful and thorough given heretofore by any artist or biographer, but he made no attempt to find why the left side was characterless, weak and undeveloped and the right side expressed the real personality and state of mind of Lincoln.

Enigmatical Character of Facial Expression

The right side of Lincoln's face was animated and normally emotionally expressive, whereas the left side functioned more weakly, looked duller and strangely out of harmony. The meaning of the duality and uncoordinated changes in his facial expression baffled everyone. Strangers who estimated the man by his dull, perplexed face and sad, tired eyes were always astonished by the quick change of his expression to alertness when he became interested in their conversation and wanted to make some contribution to it. Many officials, including lawyers, generals and members of his cabinet, upon first acquaintance, thought themselves superior to this ugly, dull, sad, weak man, only to find themselves amazed and mastered by his ready wit, common sense, logical intelligence and strength of character upon being required to look out for himself.

Herndon was no doubt the most frequent, intimate and interested daily observer of Lincoln's personality and physical constitution, as his law partner, through the years of 1843 to 1861. He has stated (1889) that Lincoln's most marked and persistent characteristic was a predisposition to become melancholy or sad and abstracted. This attitude showed in his facial expression when sitting alone or in a group and not taking an active interest in the conversation. Many other intimate friends of Lincoln were similarly impressed, as recorded in various biographies. Some of his friends thought, because of the muddy, leathery condition of his skin, this facial lapse was due to chronic indigestion and "insufficient secretion of bile." The morbidity was caused, Herndon said, by some "occult condition" that could not be explained by observation or reasoning. It was "ingrained, . . . necessarily hereditary . . . a part of his nature." "Lincoln was a sad looking man whose melancholy dripped from him as he walked." "The look of sadness was more or less accentuated by a peculiarity of one eye [left], the pupil of which had a tendency to turn or roll slightly toward the upper lid, whereas the other one maintained its normal position equidistant between the upper and lower lids." He also noticed that the tip of his nose and mouth turned toward the right. "Mr. Lincoln was a peculiar, mysterious man . . . had a double consciousness, a double life." He "quickly passed from one state of consciousness to another and different state." (Letter to J. Weik, February 21, 1891; Hertz, 1938.)

Actually, as Lincoln's life mask and photographs show, the right half of the lower lip always protruded more than the left half and was pulled with the other muscles of the mouth slightly to the right side. When reading intently or thinking actively the degree of dominance in neuromuscular activity of the right side of his face tended generally to increase over that of the relatively hypotonic left, which gave his expression a perplexed quality that was misunderstood as a sign of mental confusion by those who would read his face. (See additional information by Herndon in Chapter XIX.)

Preference for Photographs of Right Side of Face

The collected photographs of Lincoln published by Frederick Hill Meserve and Carl Sandburg (1944), and by Stefan Lorant (1952), show that in many of them he has a similar, serious, solemn, dignified, unsmiling but kindly, reposeful, mentally inactive facial expression. In a few, the face is so moody and depressed and unusually perplexed, and the eyestrain so marked, that many people doubt if they are authentic reproductions. Not until one examines the lines of the eyes, mouth and skin closely in such photographs is the identity fully established.

The differences in expression of the two sides of his face seem to have influenced Lincoln, or his photographers, to prefer the right side since most photographs were taken from the right quarter or profile. Only a few were taken from the left side or in front. Although a laugher, he tended to keep his mouth closed firmly, with more protrusion of the right side of the lower lip than the left. Even though Mrs. Lincoln often chided him for persisting in looking too solemn, he could not be persuaded to smile freely before the camera. Herndon (Hertz, 1938) said that from the moment Lincoln faced the camera his face would grow serious and sad.

Lincoln's face was completely shaven until, in his campaign for the presidency in 1860, he was persuaded by a young girl's suggestion to grow a beard. The numerous changes in the style of cutting his beard and hair indicate that he and his barbers or Mrs. Lincoln indulged in no little experimenting for satisfactory effects. His photographs show how they tried a number of different trimmings with one constant feature, namely, shaving of the upper lip and lower lip and upper half of the chin, while letting a beard grow on the lower half of the chin and throat and sides of his face. The coarse, black hair of his head was generally cut so as to remain unusually long, probably for reducing the prominence of his ears. He was self-conscious about his hair, and parted it on either side as he fancied, but it was soon disheveled by the nervous habit of running his fingers through it.

Chapter II

LINCOLN'S FAMILY ORIGIN

The psychobiological analysis of the development of the mind and personality of Abraham Lincoln and his philosophy of moral, legal and political relations of free people under a constitutional government must include the influence on the social estimations of himself, from childhood on, of what he knew and believed about his forbears. The evidence of his genealogy on which he was uninformed, worked out since his death, is also important for our purpose to indicate the possible strength of his hereditary endowment from paternal and maternal sources and the influence of their vigorous culture of freedom and independence on their descendants. Biographers have disagreed on the origin and character of Lincoln's mother, Nancy Hanks, hence we present a thorough research of all the known positive evidence to establish her identity and show why he was ashamed of her family.

Lincoln wrote a short autobiographical letter in December 1859, upon the insistence of his friend, Jesse W. Fell of Bloomington, Ill., for a brief history of his life for publication, so that people who were considering him as a presidential candidate might know something about him. After his nomination by the Republican party in 1860, he wrote another, somewhat more detailed account, upon the request of John Locke Scripps of the *Chicago Tribune*. This was expressed in the third person for use as campaign material. The two letters have become biographically and historically Lincoln's most important personal documents in that they reveal how far back he was able to trace his ancestry and how simply, directly, frankly and humbly he thought of himself and his family. Upon giving the letter to Fell he said: "There is not much of it, for the reason, I suppose, that there is not much of me. If anything be made of it, I wish it to be modest, and not to go beyond the material."

Autobiographical Letters

The Fell letter:

"I was born, Feb. 12, 1809, in Hardin County, Kentucky. My parents were both born in Virginia, of undistinguished families—second families, perhaps I should say. My mother, who died in my tenth year, was of a family of the name of Hanks, some of whom now reside in Adams and others in Macon County, Illinois. My paternal grandfather, Abraham Lincoln, emigrated from Rockingham County, Virginia, to Kentucky, about 1781 or or 2, where, a year or two later, he was killed by indians,* not in battle, but

*He was killed in 1786, according to a statement by his son Mordecai Lincoln, in a legal document to establish the title of his father's land. Lincoln gave the year as 1784 in his statement to Scripps made a year later.

by stealth, when he was laboring to open a farm in the forest. His ancestors, who were Quakers, went to Virginia from Berks County, Pennsylvania. An effort to identify them with the New England family of the same name ended in nothing more definite, than a similarity of Christian names in both families, such as Enoch, Levi, Mordecai, Solomon, Abraham, and the like.

"My father, at the death of his father, was but six years of age; and he grew up, litterally [sic] without education. He removed from Kentucky to what is now Spencer county, Indiana, in my eighth year. We reached our new home about the time the state came into the union [1816]. It was a wild region, with many bears and other wild animals still in the woods. There I grew up. There were some schools, so called; but no qualification was ever required of a teacher beyond *'readin, writin and cipherin,'* [sic] to the Rule of Three. If a straggler supposed to understand latin, happened to sojourn in the neighborhood, he was looked upon as a wizzard [sic]. There was absolutely nothing to excite ambition for education. Of course when I came of age I did not know much. Still somehow, I could read, write and cipher to the Rule of Three; but that was all. I have not been to school since. The little advance I now have upon this store of education, I have picked up from time to time under the pressure of necessity.

"I was raised to farm work, which I continued until I was twenty-two. At twenty-one I came to Illinois, and passed the first year in Illinois— Macon County. Then I got to New-Salem, (at that time in Sangamon, now in Menard County, where I remained a year as a sort of Clerk in a store. Then came the Black-Hawk war; and I was elected a Captain of Volunteers— a success which gave me more pleasure than any I have had since. I went through the campaign, was elated, ran for the Legislature the same year (1832) and was beaten— the only time I have been beaten by the people. The next, and three succeeding biennial elections, I was elected to the Legislature. I was not a candidate afterwards. During this Legislative period I had studied law, and removed to Springfield to practice it. In 1846 I was once elected to the lower House of Congress. Was not a candidate for re-election. From 1849 to 1854, both inclusive, practiced law more assiduously than ever before. Always a whig in politics, and generally on the whig electoral tickets, making active canvasses. I was losing interest in politics, when the repeal of the Missouri Compromise aroused me again. What I have done since then is pretty well known.

"If any personal description of me is thought desirable, it may be said, I am, in height, six feet, four inches, nearly; lean in flesh, weighing, on an average, one hundred and eighty pounds; dark complexion, with coarse black hair, and grey eyes— no other marks or brands recollected."

When John Locke Scripps asked Lincoln for material to be used in a campaign biography he replied: "Why Scripps, it is a great piece of folly to attempt to make anything out of me or my early life. It can all be condensed into a single sentence, and that sentence you will find in Gray's Elegy, 'the short and simple annals of the Poor.' That's my life, and that's all you or anyone else can make out of it." (Herndon, 1889.)

The Scripps letter (June, 1860) begins with the time and place of his birth and then continues, with significant amplifications, the history of his family. It is presented in this book in chronological sections to correspond with events that he seemed to think constituted turns of the cycle of destiny in his life.

"Abraham Lincoln was born Feb. 12, 1809, then in Hardin, now in the more recently formed county of Larue, Kentucky. His father, Thomas, & grand-father, Abraham, were born in Rockingham county Virginia, whither their ancestors had come from Berks county Pennsylvania. His lineage has been traced no farther back than this. The family were originally quakers, though in later times they have fallen away from the peculiar habits of that people. The grand-father Abraham, had four brothers—Isaac, Jacob, John & Thomas. So far as known, the descendants of Jacob and John are still in Virginia. Isaac went to a place near where Virginia, North Carolina, and Tennesse, join; and his descendants are in that region. Thomas came to Kentucky, and after many years, died there, whence his descendants went to Missouri. Abraham, grandfather of the subject of this sketch, came to Kentucky, and was killed by indians about the year 1784. He left a widow, three sons and two daughters. The eldest son, Mordecai, remained in Kentucky till late in life, when he removed to Hancock county, Illinois, where soon after he died, and where several of his descendants still reside. The second son, Josiah, removed at an early day to a place on Blue River, now within Harrison [Hancock] county, Indiana; but no recent information of him, or his family, has been obtained. The eldest sister, Mary, married Ralph Crume and some of her descendants are now known to be in Breckenridge county Kentucky. The second sister, Nancy, married William Brumfield, and her family are not known to have left Kentucky, but there is no recent information from them. Thomas, the youngest son, and father of the present subject, by the early death of his father, and very narrow circumstances of his mother, even in childhood was a wandering laboring boy, and grew up litterally (sic) without education. He never did more in the way of writing than to bunglingly sign his own name. Before he was grown, he passed one year as a hired hand with his uncle Isaac on Wata[u]ga, a branch of the Holsteen [Holston] River. Getting back into Kentucky, and having reached his 28th year, he married Nancy Hanks—mother of the present subject—in the year 1806. She also was born in Virginia; and relatives of hers of the name of Hanks, and of other names, now reside in Coles, in Macon, and in Adams counties, Illinois, and also in Iowa."

In both autobiographical letters Lincoln wrote proudly of his father's family but made the least possible reference to his mother's relatives. The reasons for this attitude will become obvious in the history of the Hanks family and will indicate as well the severity of his moral self-discipline.

Lincoln Forebears

Genealogists have traced the Lincoln ancestry back to the Englishman, Samuel Lincoln, who settled in Massachusetts in 1637. The city, borough and county of Lincoln and the Lincoln Cathedral in England are evidence of the social virility of this very old family. Abraham Lincoln said that his first American ancestor settled in Hingham, Mass., "or was it

Hanghim." The general hereditary soundness of this family in America is shown by the number of its sons who have been successful in business, military and public affairs. Lincoln's direct ancestors migrated from Massachusetts to Pennsylvania, then to Virginia and Kentucky. Tarbell (1900; 1924) and Barton (1925; 1927) have given authentic historical accounts of the family in successive generations from Samuel Lincoln, great-great-great-great-grandfather, to the birth of Abraham.

Abraham Lincoln's information about his family probably extended vaguely back to his great grandfather, John Lincoln, who with his wife, Rebecca, and children migrated from Pennsylvania into the Shenandoah Valley of Virginia in 1768. He was a Quaker, farmer and iron worker like his father and established himself successfully in Rockingham County. He had four sons and four daughters, owned 600 acres and was, as his will indicated, a religious man. Abraham, his oldest son, the President's grandfather, was born in 1744 in a prosperous community in Pennsylvania with good schools. He was educated in the fundamentals, like his father, brothers and sisters, as shown by their signatures on documents. He accompanied his parents to Virginia and, like his father, became a good farmer, blacksmith and general craftsman.

Abraham was a young man of exceptional ability. Within two years, by 1770, he had established himself socially and accumulated sufficient means to marry. The origin of his wife, Bersheba, the paternal grandmother of President Lincoln, is still not conclusively known. Some biographers have stated from unproven traditions in families who claim identification with President Lincoln, that Abraham married twice, first Mary Shipley and then Bersheba. This has been discredited by Barton (1927). Documentary evidence shows that the Lincoln children were born after he married Bersheba. Her later history indicates that she was a young woman of strong moral character, excellent mind and, for then, good education. Family tradition says that she was one of the aristocratic Herring family and married against her father's disapproval of her husband as "too poor and plain." Abraham was given 210 acres by his father, and six years later enlarged his farm to 260 acres. He served in the Revolution as a captain, and in 1778 as a judge advocate of a military court.

Although well established in a prosperous community, with a family of four children, Abraham became enchanted by the tales of his cousin, Daniel Boone, about the vast wilderness of cheap, fertile land that lay west of the mountains. He sold his farm in 1780 and went to Kentucky, the land of promise, where he bought title to several large tracts amounting to over 2,000 acres. He moved his family there in 1782 in a wagon train that included a cousin and several neighbors and their families.

By 1786 he had surveyed his lands and increased them to 3,000 acres, and with the building of a well-provisioned cabin, almost completed, he and Bersheba were on the way to great prosperity. They now had three sons and two daughters, Mordecai, 14, Josiah, 12, Mary, 10, Thomas, 8, and little Ann (Tarbell, 1924). Then he was killed by a marauding Indian as described by Lincoln. Abraham Lincoln thought that his father was about six years old at the time, but according to the best evidence Thomas Lincoln was born January 5th, 1778. Evidently the hearsay record as passed by word of mouth among members of the Lincoln family, varied considerably in time but was more accurate for place. For a vivid account of this family legend, as young Abraham probably often heard it told, see the statement of Dennis Hanks (Hertz, 1938).

The estate inventory that Bersheba Lincoln filed in Bardstown, then county seat of Washington County, Ky., shows that she was well supplied with horses, cows, farm implements, guns and house furnishings to maintain a comfortable home for her children. She moved into the more secure vicinity of her husband's cousin, Captain Hannaiah Lincoln, near Springfield in Washington County. He was succeeding in business and regarded as a "gentleman." Mordecai devoted himself to the care of his mother, brothers and sisters and proved himself an able young man. The tax lists show that Bersheba was able to retain ownership of most of her lands up to 1793—further evidence that she was a woman of superior intelligence. Her written request, dated 1801, that a license be granted to William Brumfield to marry her daughter Ann (called Nancy by President Lincoln and by Barton, 1927) proves that her education was better than the slurred, phonetical English generally spoken in the wilderness. She probably taught her children to read and write for they were more or less literate and religious people, devout readers of the Bible.

Mordecai who, according to his nephew, Abraham Lincoln, had the "best brains of the family," married, bought 300 acres near Springfield in Washington County and became a successful farmer and an important member of the Washington County community. His great obsession was killing Indians, good or bad, whenever he could. Bersheba's second son, Josiah, also married when a young man and became a successful farmer on land bought adjacent to Mordecai. Mordecai and Josiah were good neighbors with Joseph Hanks and Richard Berry who had married Shipley sisters in Virginia and migrated to Kentucky with their families. No doubt all were intimate friends and helped each other in clearing fields, building cabins and doing other heavy farm work.

Tom Lincoln before Marriage

All of Bersheba's children married much younger than Thomas. He did not seem to follow the rate of development that characterized his brothers and sisters. Traditions and documents dated before his marriage indicate that either he was more troubled and restless than his brothers and sisters or matured more slowly and was not as bright. He hired out at doing farm work for neighbors while growing up, and spent a year or so with his Uncle Isaac Lincoln's family in Tennessee before 1797. When he returned to Washington County he enlisted, from 18 to 20, in the local militia and lived with his brothers and sisters at least part of the time, working at any job as needed. Sometime around 1801 he learned the carpenter's trade from Joseph Hanks in Elizabethtown, a son of Mordecai's neighbor, Joseph Hanks, Sr. He became a good craftsman and the owner of a fine set of tools. In 1803, age 26, he bought, for 118 pounds—money probably inherited through his mother—238 acres on Mill Creek in Hardin County, near his sister Nancy Brumfield's home, 12 miles from Elizabethtown. Documentary evidence cited by Tarbell (1924), Warren (1926), and Barton (1927) showed that he served on a jury in 1803, as a road supervisor in 1804, and as a sheriff's deputy in 1806. His signatures at this time are legible and correctly spelled. He proposed marriage to Sarah Bush, an intelligent, better educated young woman but was turned down. In 1806, age 28 or 29, he took a flatboat of produce for a local merchant down the Ohio and Mississippi rivers to New Orleans and earned enough money to marry Nancy Hanks.

Hanks Forebears

The origin and identity of Nancy Hanks Lincoln, Abraham Lincoln's mother, has been held by most biographers, including Thomas (1952), as not having been conclusively established. Such important investigators as Herndon (1889), Hitchcock (1899) and Tarbell (1900; 1924), Warren (1926; 1945), Barton (1925; 1927) and Hertz (1938) have disagreed on the meaning of the indicative evidence. According to the best record, the birth date of Lincoln's mother, as now supposed to have been written by him in 1851, in his father's bible, was February 5, 1784.

She was reported by Lamon (1872) and Herndon (1889), as stated by her first cousin, Dennis Hanks, who knew her well, to have been the illegitimate daughter of the Lucy Hanks who married Henry Sparrow in 1791. This, Abraham Lincoln seems to have been told and believed to be true, as shown by his autobiographical letters and what he is reported by Herndon to have said to him about it (See Chapter V).

After the death of Lincoln, Herndon devoted much of his time to collecting evidence on the President's boyhood family and his mother's origin. He questioned old relatives and neighbors of Indiana and Kentucky. His best sources were the cousins of Lincoln's mother, John Hanks, regarded by the President as a respectable, reliable and truthful man, and Dennis Hanks, who was a more willing but less trustworthy and more inaccurate informer, and the statements of Lincoln himself. The versions of Dennis and John Hanks, although somewhat contradictory, it is now established, agreed sufficiently to fit in with other traditions and indicative documentary evidence. Both tried to conceal the illegitimate origin of President Lincoln's mother under the name of Nancy Sparrow, as the daughter of Henry Sparrow, although she was seven years old when he married her mother. Their misleading first statements contradicted Lincoln's statement in the Scripps letter that his mother's name was Nancy Hanks, but were later corrected by Dennis (Hertz, 1938). The suppositions of Herndon (1889) and Weik (1922) have been verified by Warren (1926) and Barton (1927) who made far more accurate and extensive investigations of the Kentucky records.

Mrs. Caroline Hanks Hitchcock, dissatisfied with the Hanks-Herndon identification of Lincoln's mother, made an extensive personal investigation of the Hanks family in Kentucky. She also traced the Hanks genealogy to England, showing it was an artisan family as far back as King Alfred the Great. Benjamin Hanks settled in Plymouth, Mass., in 1699. He had 11 children and some of his early descendants went to Pennsylvania and later to Virginia, the Carolinas, Kentucky, and Tennessee.

Records of wills, deeds, taxes, lawsuits and tombstones are generally reliable, but may be confusing when relatives living at the same time in the same locality have the same names. Family traditions, though more intimate, are often erroneous unless given with names and accurate dates and places of the generation in question.

Tarbell (1924) argued that Lincoln's mother was the Nancy Hanks who was a daughter of Joseph Hanks, a well-to-do farmer who lived in Nelson County, Ky., as indicated by his will drawn in 1793 and filed in Bardstown. It recognized his wife, Nanny (née Nancy Shipley), and five sons, Thomas, William, Charles and Joseph, and three daughters, Elizabeth, Polly and Nancy. He bequeathed to each boy a horse and to each girl a heifer, and to his wife his whole estate to be divided equally upon her death "among all my children."

The will made no mention of a daughter Lucy, and this was taken by Tarbell as proof that Lucy Hanks (Sparrow) of Mercer County, came from another Hanks family and was not the mother of Nancy Hanks Lincoln. Joseph Hanks died in 1893 and his wife Nancy followed soon after, and Tarbell and Hitchcock further assumed, although they admitted the evidence was inconclusive, that their youngest daughter, Nancy, thereafter lived with her neighboring relatives, the Berry family, until she married Tom Lincoln in 1806.

It was the purpose of Hitchcock and Tarbell to discredit the claims of Dennis Hanks that he was born (in 1799) the illegitimate son of an unmarried Nancy Hanks who was a daughter of Joseph Hanks and later became Mrs. Levi Hall. They tried also to discredit Dennis' claim that he was a cousin of Abraham Lincoln's mother, as the incredible fabrication of a weak-minded man acting under the suggestive questioning of Herndon, who had grown vindictive after Lincoln's death. Tarbell also discredited John Hanks' statement that he was a cousin of Lincoln's mother and, moreover, she either overlooked or ignored Lincoln's own identification of John Hanks as a "first cousin of Abraham's mother." Since John was a son of William Hanks, Abraham's mother could not have been William's sister Nancy, for that would have made her John's aunt. The evidence says that Lincoln's mother Nancy was the illegitimate daughter of Lucy Hanks, and Lucy was William's sister and not the wife of one of his brothers before she married Henry Sparrow.

The unexpurgated history of Dennis Hanks on the identity of Nancy Hanks Lincoln, as supported by the documentary evidence recorded by Warren (1926) and Barton (1925, 1927), gives us some account of what Lincoln was often told and probably believed about his mother's family and why he was ashamed of it. Dennis stated several times: "My mother and Abe's grandmother were sisters. My mother was Nancy Hanks. Abe's grandmother was Lucy Hanks which was my mother's sister. The woman that raised me was Elizabeth Sparrow the sister of Lucy and Nancy and the other sister her name was Polly Friend. So you see there were four sisters that were Hankses." [From a letter to Herndon in 1866, cited by Warren (1926).]

Who Was Lucy Hanks?

Warren (1926) and Barton (1925; 1927) have disagreed on her identity. Barton showed from an enumeration of the population taken in 1782 by the state of Virginia, and included in the United States Census of 1790, that Joseph Hanks lived then in northwestern Virginia on a tributary of the Potomac River (Patterson Creek), and had a family of 11 persons "all white." He deduced from this and Joseph Hanks' will and other documentary evidence that the 11 consisted of Joseph and wife and five sons and four daughters. He concluded that Lucy was the oldest daughter, born about 1765, 10 years before the Revolution. Warren (1926) claims from the same evidence, plus the Shipley tradition, that Lucy was Joseph Hanks' daughter-in-law, born Shipley. Barton's account, however, seems more consistent with the statement of Dennis Hanks and with Lincoln's reticence about his mother, to be shown in Chapter V.

The family of Joseph Hanks, in Lucy's youth, was poor but reputable and of average "second class" Virginia standing, with many relatives serving honorably in the Revolution. When Washington and Lafayette forced Cornwallis to surrender at Yorktown in 1781, only a day's ride from Lucy's home in tidal Virginia, she was 16 and already a remarkable young woman. Even though Governor Berkley had, with popular approval, publicly and officially thanked God that Virginia had no free schools and printing presses, she had the initiative and imagination to learn to read and write as well as most business men and public officials in her community. (The sons and daughters of the aristocratic families were tutored or sent to private schools and finished their education in England.) Lucy Hanks had the energy, pride and mental integrity to disregard Virginia's cold, hard, class prejudice and educate herself—then a remarkable ambition. She was no doubt regarded with envy and amazement by her own family, since her father and brothers signed their names with a mark. That she was unusually intelligent, vivacious, vigorously sexed and probably beautiful, is indicated by her remarkable career later and the vigorous flourish of her writing and self-expression.

In 1782, Joseph Hanks sold his home in tidal Virginia and moved his family up the Potomac River to Patterson Creek, near its confluence with the Shenandoah. Here Lucy, unmarried, at the age of 18, gave birth to a daughter on February 4, 1784. It seems that her lover betrayed her confidence but she refused to prosecute him for marriage, since his identity was never recorded. She named her baby Nancy, and the family tradition, as seems to have been believed by her illustrious grandson, alleged that its father was "a young Virginia aristocrat."

Abraham Lincoln liked to think, according to Herndon's report of his confidential talk with him (see Chapter V), that he inherited his unusual mental abilities through his mother from this grandfather, even though he had betrayed his grandmother. Why, in his sympathy for his mother, did he not appreciate the remarkably superior mental qualities of her mother—qualities of which he had inherited so much? The answer lies perhaps in her premarital history.

Bastardy was then a serious offense in Virginia, and Lucy Hanks was no doubt subjected to intolerant ridicule, derision and threats of prosecution. Her father is said to have become alarmed for her safety and hastily mortgaged his farm for the pitiful sum of 21 pounds, nine shillings, Virginia money, and moved his family that spring, as the records show, west of the mountains into the wilderness of Nelson County, Ky. The mortgage was foreclosed November 9, 1784, upon failure of redemption.

It is not known how long Lucy stayed with her family but it is thought that she was soon obliged to leave home and look out for herself and child, because bastardy was also an offense in Kentucky. We surmise that some of her family had probably grown deeply resentful of her wilful attitude, for her father disregarded her in his will.

She seems to have gone to Mercer County some 50 miles away to live, probably working as a servant. The first positive record of her exists in an indictment filed against her by a grand jury of that county in November, 1789, "for fornication." The first summons was not served and a second was issued on March 23, 1790. Before the court convened, Henry Sparrow (a friend Barton thinks she probably had known in Virginia when he served in Lafayette's army) offered to marry her. The following request for a license was written out and signed by herself and attested by two friends. It stated: "I do certify that I am of age and give my approbation freely for henry Sparrow to git out Lisons this or enny other day given under my hand this day of April 26th, 1790 [wi] doy Lucey Hanks. Test Robert michel, John bery."

Lucy's handwriting is done with a vigorous, defiant flourish. The word "approbation" was first misspelled, then crossed out and spelled correctly. Such bungling was not uncommon for well-educated people of that time, as shown by the letters of eminent men, including George Washington. Warren (1926) found that the mysterious letters "doy" are preceded in the original document by two very faint letters "wi," showing that Lucy Hanks signed herself as a "widow." From this clue and the fact that

Mrs. Joseph Hanks was a Shipley, he inferred that Lucy was not the daughter of Joseph Hanks but a Shipley relative of his wife who had married one of Joseph's sons.

This guess seems unnecessary and only confuses the Hanks history, for no record indicating such a marriage has been found. Mrs. Joseph Hanks (née Shipley) was one of Abraham Lincoln's great grandmothers in either case.

It seems more likely that Lucy Hanks protected herself and her child by living among strange people in a sparsely settled community as a widow, a method mothers of bastard children not infrequently use effectively. Common law marriages and illegitimate children were not uncommon among pioneer women although they lost respectability under the social proprieties and were subject to persecution by religiously obsessed officials. Lucy Hanks is thought, from the record of her progeny, to have had a second illegitimate daughter, Polly, in Mercer County before she married Henry Sparrow. Polly Hanks, who was said to have been a sister of Lincoln's mother, never married though she had six children, all of whom bore her name and lived to maturity. Later, one of Polly's daughters (Sophie), a month younger than Abraham, lived with Tom Lincoln's family in Indiana (Morgan, 1920).

Lucy Hanks married Henry Sparrow on April 26, 1790. She was a good, faithful wife and bore him eight children, two of whom became prominent ministers and contributed to the development of civilization in that part of Kentucky. Her children and grandchildren and great grandchildren have been honest, God-fearing citizens. Some became members of the state legislature, others were successful in business and the professions, and some fought for the North and others for the South in the Civil War (Barton, 1927).

An explanation now seems well enough established of why Lincoln always felt sadly about his mother's family and was reticent and cautious about making its history public during his campaign for election as President. (See Chapter V for the letter he wrote to John Hanks in 1860.)

Nancy Hanks' Girlhood

Dennis stated (Herndon 1889; Hertz, 1938) that Henry Sparrow objected to raising Lucy's illegitimate daughter Nancy as one of his family and she was taken into the home of her aunt Elizabeth Hanks Sparrow some time after her marriage to Thomas Sparrow. Nancy was then about 12 years old and had no doubt been taught to read and write by her mother before they became separated. The history of "Nancy Hanks" thereafter became confused in the careless gossip of neighbors about two people, aunt and niece, having the same name and living at the same time in closely related families.

In 1799, Lincoln's mother's Aunt Nancy, the youngest daughter of Joseph Hanks and sister of Lucy Hanks, his grandmother, gave birth to an illegitimate son, Dennis Hanks. His father was Charles Friend. Later she married Levi Hall, her brother's wife's brother, and he too refused to raise a "base born" child, so Dennis was also taken in by Thomas and Elizabeth Hanks Sparrow who were raising Nancy and were childless. According to Dennis, his cousin Nancy, who was 14 years older, lived with the Sparrows until she was about 16 when she began to work out as a servant. She had become known by the neighbors as Nancy Sparrow (leading to no little confusion among biographers). Since her foster parents sent Dennis to school they probably did as much for Nancy when possible.

Nancy like other pioneer girls learned, through hard work, farming with homemaking, and had become by 16 particularly adept at sewing. It seems established that she lived mostly thereafter with her cousin Richard Berry Jr.'s family until she reached womanhood. Here also lived Sarah Mitchell, several years older, who had been held captive by Indians since childhood. Upon being returned to her people she had to learn their ways of speaking, working and living, and Nancy became her devoted friend and teacher. Sarah married in 1800 and named her daughter Nancy, and six years later Nancy married and named her daughter Sarah.

Marriage of Tom Lincoln and Nancy Hanks

The Berrys were prosperous farmers and close neighbors of Mordecai and Josiah Lincoln. Tom Lincoln often visited his brother's home and probably knew both Nancys well. He bought a farm on Mill Creek but gave it up to work for carpenter Joseph Hanks in Elizabethtown. Here he learned the craft and began in 1805 to court Joseph's niece Nancy, after Sarah Bush had refused to marry him.

Herndon stated in many letters (Hertz, 1938) that Tom Lincoln and Nancy Hanks had not been legally married since no record of it could be found in Hardin County, where Lincoln was born. Later, evidence was found that finally proved the legality, time and place of marriage, much to the chagrin of Herndon and Weik. The request for a bond, as required by Kentucky law, granting Thomas Lincoln the right to marry Nancy Hanks, was found in the Washington County records, signed on June 10, 1806, by Thomas Lincoln and "Richard Berry, garden" (guardian). Another record shows that two days later, on June 12, 1806, Thomas Lincoln and Nancy Hanks were married by Rev. Jesse Head, deacon of the Methodist Episcopal Church. This was stated by him in a written list of marriages that he performed in 1806 and 1807. This date of the marriage has been confirmed in Thomas Lincoln's Bible.

Further evidence that Nancy grew to womanhood while living with her mother's relatives and that she made herself useful and much beloved is shown by the big wedding given by the Berrys in their house, as described many years later by a guest, Dr. C. C. Graham.

The development of every child's personality and social attitude is based largely on his hereditary and acquired physical constitution and the conditioning formative pressures in childhood of the sympathetic encouraging and antipathic critical attitudes of its parents, siblings and other impressive people toward itself and one another. The most insidiously conditioning influences, upon the child's egoistic integration of self-confidence in its social worth and respectability, are not the physical qualities of the home and parents as much as the consistency or inconsistency of their principles, mores, and sexual attitudes. The loves and hates of the parents for each other and the child determine the constructive and destructive processes of its early integrative organization, hence wherein it will grow strong and wherein weak in character as an adult.

Abraham Lincoln's personal development was, in its early conditioning and training by familial and community cultural influences, unusual, and the extraordinary hereditary qualities of his physical and mental constitution combined to produce in manhood a social attitude of unique proportions, out of qualities common in American people. The principles of his philosophy were rooted in the characters and beliefs of his father and mother. It is necessary, therefore, to consider every important angle of the record, good and bad, moral and immoral, in order to see the family situations of his youth as realistically as possible.

Lincoln's Father

Tom Lincoln was a man about five feet, eight inches tall and weighed about 180 pounds when his children were born. He was muscular and powerful, but of restless disposition, and for some time the "best man" in his community. He lost one eye by accident and saw weakly with the other. His eyes were dark grey, hair black, and shoulders a little stooped. His character seems to have changed greatly from a restless, dissatisfied, though industrious young man, to moody impulsiveness in middle age, to deteriorating dependence on his son later. He was easy-going, congenial and, like his brother Mordecai, was a natural master at telling humorous stories. He liked hunting, fishing and loafing, but was a man of good morals, had no vices, was honest and a good farmer, carpenter and craftsman. [From Herndon (1889), Weik (1922), Tarbell (1924), Warren (1926), Barton (1925), and statements to Herndon by John Hanks, Dennis Hanks, Nat Grigsby, Elizabeth Crawford and others who knew him for many years in Kentucky and Indiana (Hertz, 1938).]

Before his marriage Tom Lincoln began the migratory restlessness characteristic of his ancestors and pioneer neighbors, ever seeking wealth in more and better land. As we follow his quest for fortune we find that he made a number of unsuccessful, poorly thought out, moody attempts at establishing a farm home in the wilderness of Kentucky, Indiana, and Illinois.

Titles to land in central Kentucky had become hopelessly entangled through prior, unsurveyed, overlapping grants and claims, resulting in many lawsuits and feuds. The 238 acres that Tom Lincoln bought in 1803 on Mill Creek for 118 pounds produced a lawsuit which he won. Although it was near his sister's home he gave up farming after his marriage, bought lots and built a cabin in Elizabethtown near Joseph Hanks with whom he had learned carpentering. Here his first child, Sarah, was born in 1807.

He soon grew discontented and moved to a cabin on the farm of George Brownfield for whom he worked as a carpenter and farm hand. Late in 1808 he acquired 348 acres of wilderness on Nolin Creek for $200, also in Hardin County, about two and a half miles from Hodgenville. Here he built another dirt-floor log cabin, and here Abraham was born in 1809. In the spring of 1811 he sold the place with its mortgaged title for $78, after spending three crop seasons and two winters on it (Barton, 1925). The ground had proven unsuitable for farming and he moved to a more fertile tract of some 30 acres on Knob Creek which he bought despite its mortgaged and legally doubtful title.

In 1814 he sold his Mill Creek tract for 100 pounds and he later sold his rights to the Knob Creek land for less than he paid after cultivating it four years. In 1816 he moved from the slave state of Kentucky, across the Ohio River to that part of the Northwest Territory that was being made into the free state of Indiana. In Spencer County he lived near an old friend as a "squatter" until he bought clear title to 80 acres from the Federal government.

In 1830 Tom Lincoln suddenly sold this land, after having cleared and cultivated it for 13 years, for less than he paid for it, even though he had just built an attractive new cabin of hewn timbers on it. The population of the community was increasing and his skill as a carpenter was well known; but, highly suggestible, he had become imbued with the yearning to follow the Hanks family to the Illinois prairies. Here he made two more attempts at settling, and finished as an old man—though poor and dependent on his son—wanting to move to Missouri. We will see (Chapter XXI) how Lincoln managed to keep father and step-brother from going to Missouri. Herndon (1889) argued that Tom Lincoln was driven to move from Kentucky to Indiana to escape from gossip alleging his sterility and illegitimacy of his wife's children. The absurdity of this suspicion is proven by the number of times Tom moved after his second marriage.

Tom Lincoln's character must be measured by the cultural standards of poor, lonely, restless, wilderness people. He was a useful citizen as a carpenter, independent of mind, venturesome, and an enthusiastic beginner but weak finisher. He was too illiterate, easy-going and affable to search through the legal tangles of doubtful titles and keep defending his claims, in litigation, although he did win a suit for payment of cut timber that he had sold. He seems to have been ambitious, like most pioneers, to own large tracts of wild land but eventually sold or lost them. Although not lacking in courage to make one venture after another, he was insufficiently thrifty, consistent and industrious ever to be economically successful in any. He is said to have paid all his debts, and to have worked conscientiously for other people but leisurely and indifferently for his own family. He served his community at times as road supervisor and juryman, and probably was not weak-minded and given to terrifying epileptic attacks with visual hallucinations, as attributed by Stephenson (1922), for he lived until his 74th year. Mention is made in some letters of his family about his ill condition in his last years but nothing indicates nervous disease.

Lincoln's Mother

When Nancy married, in 1806, she was about 22 years old and Tom about 29. Both were unusually old for pioneer marriage. The best descriptions of Lincoln's mother were obtained by Herndon after the death of her illustrious son, from her cousins John and Dennis Hanks, and her neighbors in Indiana, Mrs. Elizabeth Crawford, William Wood, and Nat Grigsby (Hertz, 1938).

John described Nancy in Kentucky: "I knew Mrs. Nancy Lincoln, or Nancy Hanks before her marriage. She was a tall, slender woman, dark skinned, black hair and eyes, her face was sharp and angular, forehead big. She was beyond all doubts an intellectual woman, rather extraordinary if anything . . . her nature was kindness, mildness, tenderness, obedience to her husband. Abraham was like his mother very much. She was a Baptist by profession."*

The portrayals by other neighbors in Indiana (1816-1817), describe Nancy when she was 32 to 34 years old. They make her about five feet eight inches tall and about 130 pounds in weight. According to Dennis Hanks, who lived with the Lincolns during her last two years in Indiana and knew her probably better than any neighbor, she was "spare made, tall and slender, had dark hair and blueish green eyes." She was "immovably calm; keen, shrewd, smart, had a strong memory, quick perception and good judgment." "She was spiritually and ideally inclined, not dull, not material, not heavy in thought, feeling, or action." "She was most affectionate, keen and loving, and never out of temper."

Nat Grigsby described Mrs. Lincoln as having dark hair, light hazel eyes, sharp features, high forehead, "complexion light and exceedingly fair. . . . a woman known for the extraordinary strength of her mind among the family and all who knew her; she was superior to her husband in every way. She was a brilliant woman, a woman of great good sense and

*This description was written by Herndon during an interview with John Hanks and it is not valid to assume, as Warren has (Lincoln Lore, 995, 1948) on the basis of Lincoln's letter to John in August 1860 (see Chapter 5), that John Hanks never saw Nancy after her marriage when he was four years old. He was 14 when she moved to Indiana and he never saw her after that; but he had lived only a day's horseback ride from the Lincolns on Knob Creek, and pioneers thought little of walking or riding for several days just to visit each other and talk, to get over loneliness. William Hanks with John and other members of his family almost certainly exchanged visits many times with the Lincolns and the Sparrows who lived nearby. Hence John's description of Nancy Lincoln may be considered as a reliable though meager sketch of her appearance when living in Kentucky after her marriage.

morality. . . . Thomas Lincoln and his wife were really happy in each other's presence, loved one another."

William Wood said: "Abe got his mind and fixed morals from his good mother. Mrs. Lincoln was a very smart, intelligent, and intellectual woman; she was naturally strong-minded; was a gentle, kind, and tender woman, a Christian of the Baptist persuasion, she was a remarkable woman truly and indeed."

The above descriptions by those who knew Nancy Lincoln agree on her physique, character and intelligence but disagree on the color of her eyes. No description of his mother is known to have been given by Abraham, but we are inclined to infer from his nostalgia and poem to her memory (see Chapter XV) that she tried bravely to make the most of a hard life that grew sadly disappointing in Indiana.

The literacy of Nancy has been questioned, since a deed to a piece of land in Hardin County was found signed by "Tom Leincoln" and "Nancy, her X mark, Lincoln." The "bungled" first signature was no doubt Tom Lincoln's but Nancy's name was signed with her mark although she was present in the clerk's office as recorded by Samuel Haycraft, Deputy Clerk of Hardin County. Her mark, however, is not certain evidence of illiteracy, as some biographers have insisted, for an answer to a bill of chancery of September 7, 1813 was signed "Thomas his X mark Lincoln." An exhibit in a lawsuit was signed the same way on September 5, 1814.

In Collected Works (1, 263) is the record, dated 10, 25, 1841, of an indenture to Abraham Lincoln by his father and stepmother. It is signed:

Thomas Lincoln (SEAL)

her
Sarah   X   Lincoln (SEAL)
mark

It is well known that Sarah Bush Lincoln had a literate education. The document is in Abraham's hand except for Thomas Lincoln's signature. The signature on a pioneer document by an X mark is obviously insufficient and unreliable evidence of illiteracy.

Abraham Lincoln said that his mother read the Bible and taught him to write. His statements were always made with such thoughtful care and accuracy that we accept them as true.

Nancy Lincoln's Children

Sarah, the first child of Tom and Nancy Lincoln, was born on February 10, 1807, as recorded in the Lincoln family bible in Abraham Lincoln's handwriting. This date is 243 days after June 12, 1806, when her parents were married. If Sarah was conceived after the wedding it means that she lacked at least 37 days of being a full-term baby. Under primitive conditions it would probably not have survived, even if nursed. We therefore assume that Nancy Hanks conceived before marriage. The latter possibility most impressed Herndon and he gave it as "proof" that Lincoln's mother "fell before her marriage." (See Chapter V.)

Nancy was 25 when her son Abraham was born, on February 12, 1809, in the log cabin on Nolin Creek, two miles from Hodgenville in Hardin County, Ky. According to Tarbell's (1924) reconstructed account, while she was in labor Tom Lincoln hurried down the road to fetch a neighboring midwife and is said to have met young Abe Enloe, then a boy of 15. When Abe was told of Nancy's labor, he offered to go after the midwife so that Tom could immediately return home. This incident perhaps gave material for gossip, for Abe Enloe is said to have jokingly boasted that he was the father of Abraham Lincoln and the baby was named after him in gratitude. (See Enloe's statement later.)

Dennis Hanks, a boy of 10 when Abraham was born, upon being told of the new son, ran two miles from his home to Nancy's to be the first boy to touch the baby for good luck. As he held it in his arms it cried so vigorously that he gave it up, saying, "Aunt [Mrs. Sparrow], take him, he'll never come to much."

Three years after the birth of Abraham, another son was born to Nancy and she named him Tom in honor of her husband. He died in infancy. Since Abraham had been named after his paternal grandfather we may take Nancy's names for her sons as indicative evidence that she was devoted to her husband and that he was the father of her children. The name of her daughter, Sarah, after her friend, Sarah Mitchell Thompson, spoke volumes for a warm, affectionate personality that thought in the magnitude of lifetime loyalties.

Chapter III

CHILDHOOD

The science of egoistic attitude analysis has shown that the social attitudes of the members of a family, as a binding, unavoidable social group, have, by repetitive pressures of sympathetic appeal and approval of cooperations and critical resentment of oppositions, formative influences on the instinctive development of the egoistic social attitudes of each person, through infancy, adolescence, and maturity. The influences of the persons in Lincoln's family were insidiously persuasive, living in the interdependent intimacy of a one room cabin, nearly isolated in a primeval wilderness. The use of crude, handmade tools, furniture and clothing, hard living, low literacy, slurred speech, few books, no newspapers, numerous pet superstitions, and meager religious, commercial, and other outside social affiliations, limited the development of their minds, knowledge, thinking, and habits. Such family groups must not be judged by modern standards of living if we would understand them.

Out of thousands of such families grew many vigorous builders of the nation, and among these now stands one above all in influence of force of personality and moral political principles. He had not only extraordinary inheritance of genius for self-education and self-righting sociability, but extraordinary combinations of conditioning social experiences in childhood that so molded fundamentally the development of his egoistic social attitude that it continued consistently in almost the same form with little change as a man. Biographical analysis searches for evidence of such inborn aptitudes and conditioning experiences, estimates their molding forces on the development of egoistic attitude and correlates them with the eventual course and results of adult behavior.

The Spirit of 1776 and Union Forever

Both of Lincoln's parents were born in Virginia, the home state of of George Washington and Thomas Jefferson, when the colonial states were winning the struggle for independence and organizing themselves into the United States. They were impressionable children during the exciting talk about establishing the nation as a union of states under a constitution. Abraham was born during the presidency of Jefferson, and his alert, imaginative, young mind soon reflected the influence on his parents of that illustrious statesman's philosophy of constitutional democracy as being founded on the will of free people and not on the divine right of kings. The ultimate elimination of slavery was the belief of his Baptist elders. Nowhere in the culture of civilization were the lawful rights of the common people to equalitarian justice with dignity and

freedom of expression held more fundamental to the solidarity of constitutional government, than by the Founding Fathers and their near
descendants.

Practical Parents

Tom Lincoln was in his prime and a good woodsman, farmer, carpenter
and cabinet maker. He was strong and brave, and loved the carefree,
easy-going, independent, day-by-day living by hunting, trapping, fishing
and farming in the wilderness. Proud of being honest, he built, for pay,
snug, warm, nicely hewn log cabins and made useful furniture and farm
tools. He was disposed, however, to do no more for his family than was
emotivated by necessity, and the cabins he built for it, until his second
marriage, were of rough logs with clay floors. He probably read very
little, if at all, but liked to sit around with a group and make big talk,
mostly about things and events of daily life, superstitious beliefs, laws,
politics, the eradication of slavery, and the westward migration. At home
he required, with firmness and sometimes temper, respectful attention to
visitors from his children.

Abraham's mother was said by relatives and neighbors, and we know
from the social attitudes of her children, to have been thoughtful, affectionate, cheerful, sweet, kindly, self-sacrificing, and devoted to her
family. She was skillful with her hands and could make yarn, weave it
into cloth and make clothing, tan skins, and do any necessary house and
farm work. She believed, with her husband, in living by the moral precepts
of the Bible, and must have been tactful, wise and patient in early cultivating in her children profound respect for its Christian teaching and an
attitude of willing obedience to their parents, for both Sarah and Abe were
unusually considerate, respectful, kind and pleasing youngsters. Abraham
Lincoln said that his mother read the Bible when he was a child and
'guided his hand' to show him how to write. However, some biographers
have persisted in inferring, from the failure to find any signature of
Nancy, other than her mark on one deed, that this "mother" teacher was
Sarah Bush Johnston, the second Mrs. Lincoln, who came into the family
when Abe was 10 years old. We have shown in the previous chapter, from
signatures of Thomas Lincoln and Sarah Bush Johnston, why this inference is probably wrong.

Old Kentucky Home

The earliest memories of Abraham Lincoln went back to the little log
cabin with one room, a door and one window, a big fireplace and clay
floor, on Knob Creek in Hardin County, Ky., where he lived from his
third to his eighth year. It was situated near the main road from Louisville to Nashville and, whatever conditions had influenced Tom Lincoln to
move within two years from a nice new cabin in Elizabethtown to an
isolated farm on Nolan Creek and then move again within three years to

Knob Creek, we find that the last place had grassy, fertile ground and provided a better livelihood with less exertion. Here an enchanting, clear stream teeming with fish rushed through a fertile little valley, and forest-covered hills abounded in game. Here we are able to begin, from Lincoln's own stories of his childhood, the reconstruction of decisive events in his early mental integration and their profound effects later in his thinking.

The First Six Years

Ralph Walso Emerson, Lincoln's contemporary, might well have had the children of the pioneers in mind when he wrote:

> "Cast the bantling on the rocks,
> Suckle him with the she wolf's teat,
> Wintered with the hawk and fox,
> Power and Speed be hands and feet."

Unusual men and women develop from children able to show, by six years of age, unusual emotional and intellectual potentialities and capacities in the free expressions of everyday life. Retrospective analyses of adults and the free play of children have proven that the personality, in order to integrate itself and develop normally, must pass through a sequence of pleasurable levels of egoistic attitudinal transformation and holistic organization. The natural completion of each level in time with its physical development is basic for the next higher integration of the ego-organization and the social maturation of its expressions of love, fear and hate. We therefore follow the early development of Abraham Lincoln's personality, as the basis of his adult personality and philosophy, by reconstructing formative experiences in these periods, from his history.

The baby was delivered by a granny midwife in the second labor of a tall, slender woman, probably without unusual cranial stress at birth. Its genetic endowment proved an unusually strong combination from a weak-minded father, a strong-minded mother and three or possibly four exceptionally strong-minded grandparents. The first, naturally inherent, emotional and mental trials for an infant generally come with weaning it prematurely from pleasurable nursing dependence on its mother's breast for food and her kindly attentions for its excretory and other physical comforts. Integrative steps toward developing a vocally communicative egoistic attitude start with the first cry of birth, and the child needs thereafter repeated, spontaneous, gentle, considerate, affectionate responses to its efforts, and reassurances that it is loved and wanted, in order to continue the development of a really sound, speaking integrity. Wilderness babies were breast fed, and soon given occasional bits of cooked vegetables to bite on, until they weaned themselves with teething. Thereby they had time to develop and organize fundamental, socially possessive, self-determinative reflexes naturally, in coordination with the free play of learning to vocalize their desires while trying to get satisfaction for them. We can be reasonably sure that this was little Abe's good fortune, for he had the trustful, affectionate, self-confident attitude of a happy, talkative child who trusted his mother completely. Pioneer infants in the wilderness that had to be weaned prematurely and fed artificially usually died.

After oral weaning, young children become more self-reliantly integrated as they continue consistent, positive emotional and mental activities, with encouragement in learning from the mother and father how to say and do things in ways that win their happy instinctive approval as right. Too much lying and critical negation by parents in "don't" disapprovals of wrong doing, tends to produce a neurotically conditioned, self-doubtful, confused, contrary compelled child mind. We know, from Abe's later, irrepressible, good humored propensity in boyhood for talking and asking questions, even against his father's vigorous disapprovals, that a self-confident, expressive egoistic attitude was freely cultivated from the very beginning of voicing his needs. This most important start came probably not so much by virtue of his mother's psychological foresight as, better, out of her love and enjoyment of her child's pleasure in freely talking to her about any of his natural needs, curiosities, interests, and successes.

Also, his childhood egoistic self-reliance seems to have developed consistently, in due time, control of excretory functioning without having to make repressions of natural infantile pleasures and curiosities because of fear of punishment or ridicule about being unclean or losing self-control. Freudian egoistic attitude analysis has shown that the conditioning influence of this childhood phase of development continues throughout life. As a boy and man Lincoln was careless about his personal appearance and money, but very conscientious about other people's money, his fees, debts, opinions, and judgments. He was unusually inquisitive and talkative and loved to tell vulgar, witty, humorous stories, and cultivated, eagerly, proper spelling and grammatical use of words. However, as a lawyer, he developed chronic constipation naturally consequent upon being overly conscientious about having to be right, morally clean, truthful, honest, and just.

Doubtless the natural curiosity in early childhood of experimenting with the pleasurable feelings and functions of the genitals, fundamental for later psychosexual maturation, evolved in due order about the third year. It is quite likely that he had learned by six, by observation of himself and the mating behavior of animals and the talk of his elders, that these organs were used for pleasures other than urinating, and genital union of males with females had some relation to the production of young. He seems not to have been fooled about the mystery of birth nor impressively threatened with punishment for such interest. There may have been some casual disapproval of too eager curiosity but it seems not to have disturbed the natural course of sexual development of his personality.

He seems, however, to have been perplexed as a child over the family gossip about his mother's birth and her father, and the unmarried mothers of his illegitimate cousins. He became shy with girls in adolescence, and remained shy with women as a man, but an honorable need, as will be seen later, for self-repression in his adolescent years amply accounts for this bias of social attitude.

Self-Reliance

For clothing, the Lincoln children were dressed, like their mother, through summer and winter, in ankle length, sack-like, homespun, linsey-woolsey tow shirts with sleeves and a buttonless hole for the neck, which she made. They probably had no underwear in winter and certainly none in summer. Tanned animal skins served as blankets and coats. Little Sarah and Abe, happy, vigorous and healthy, learned early to care for themselves as best they could, and display their achievements with modest joy and assimilate their failures with laughter. The vital urge to learn and grow up and become self-reliant naturally developed with irrepressible curiosity under the intimate, revealing conditions of living with carefree adults in a little one room cabin. The plain talk at home, store, mill and meeting house about practical daily interests, and discussion of the Biblical philosophy of living helpfully and justly, encouraged pride in knowing how to be useful, honest, truthful, and fair. They developed an eager, free curiosity, with mutual exchange of sympathies and information that continually revealed to each other the natural emotional interests of their lives.

They learned keenly from babyhood to read face-to-face and eye-to-eye the loves, hates, jealousies, hungers, fears, ambitions and prejudices of each other and their elders, with an instant understanding, not equalled under more civilized, sophisticated and shallow, egotistical affectations and pretensions. In primitive living, where each person's welfare often depends on immediate decisions, and companionship includes only a few people, mutual trust and confidence is indispensable, and everyone must be natural, truthful, and honest. To cheat or lie, or to become arrogant, superior and affected ends in being distrusted and shunned by neighbors, and living made almost unbearable.

The Primal Triangle

The first naturally inherent inhibition of steps in development of possessive, aggressive egotism begins for children, more or less intensely, with the first period of shedding the deciduous teeth. The teeth are the child's most aggressive organs and the loss of the first tooth shocks the child's happy, self-loving, self-reliant perfectionism and it tends to regress temporarily into more or less of a defensive phase of awkward shyness and diffidence. A modified compensatory self-reliance resumes vigorous expression again instinctively with the emergence of permanent teeth.

This impressionable period usually begins in the sixth year and magnifies the effects of other concomitant emotional crises.

The normal sequence of mental and emotional transformations in the development of the child's personality must include a final self-compensatory, cardiorespiratory attitudinal-emotional conversion to produce vigor of self-expression. It must give up the last traces of residual inclinations to infantile, mother-dependent, appealing, too easily frustrated, regressive self-helplessness, in order to develop hardy, compensatory, extroverting, independent, courageous pride in self-helpfulness. Therewith it loves increasing adventure in tests of self-reliance and ability, and its cardiorespiratory emotivation and range of compensatory functioning grows stronger as each task is mastered.

Young Abe's attitude by six, we find, was resolutely turned in the manly direction and away from too intimate dependence on his mother. He identified himself with his father as a carpenter, woodsman and humorist, imitated some of his better ways with increasing skill, and seems to have lost jealousy of his father's right to possession of his mother. Wherein he had a kindly, patient, tolerant, good-humored father, his attitudinal conversion was made easily, by resignation and not through fear that compelled repression of competitive sexual impulses. A jealous, tyrannical father generally interferes with his young son's rival interests inconsiderately, and prematurely forces it to quit its mother dependence in ways that offend and injure the development of its self-respect and self-reliance. Wherein the father unjustly punishes and suppresses the child's wilful challenges of his authority, it tends to accumulate hurt feelings and develop moody resentments against unjust interference with its natural need of personal rights. If his father completely defeats him he tends to develop habitual repression of hate, leading to introversion of affection and an effeminate submissive attitude. If the child's mother supports him in ignoring and frustrating his father's authority his self-reliance increases in vain, egotistical show-offish aggressiveness.

If the parents are considerate in their desires and conflicts with each other and with the child, and let be right who is really so, they all develop a sound sense of the social balance of cooperating and opposing personal interests and learn to live sensibly by the equalitarian social rule, *do unto others as you wish to be done by*. In triangular variations of conflicting adjustments between parents and child, any one's approval of another as right implies a relative degree of superiority. Young Lincoln's mother must have been very natural, frank, truthful, and honest for he believed her implicitly and obeyed her word willingly. "What my mother said was always the truth and law to me." She probably never lied to him so he never doubted her word. She was conscientiously dutiful to her husband's wishes, although more intelligent, for Abe always felt himself to be duty bound to respect his father's authority until he came of age. Later, as a lawyer and president, he held religiously that the law, whatever it is, should be obeyed and executed until anulled. However, he was set in attitude to challenge the legal validity of the judgment of his father and even that of the Supreme Court of the United States. We ask: how did such an unusually vigorous, self-reliant, judicial egoistic attitude in a man get set in childhood?

We know that Lincoln's father, although usually a good humored, quiet, easy-going, kindly man, was inclined at times to arrive impulsively at decisions of great importance and impose them upon his family. Young Abe learned confidently, but cautiously, how to adjust himself to his temperamental will and wherein he could master his weakness. The Lincoln family's interpersonal relations seem to have been unusually frank and free of conflicting emotivations such as generally produce in children a confused discrimination of right from wrong, for young Abe early developed a remarkable sense of proportions in retributive justice as the incidents of his childhood presented in this book show. Interests, experiences, and episodes have been selected for authenticity and psychological importance in revealing crucial formative influences on the development of his personality. Few of Lincoln's biographers have given them due consideration, although psychoanalysis has long shown that childhood trials that seem trivial to older people often have specific constructive or deformative effects on development of the mind that continue throughout life. Experiences like the well known story of his rescue from drowning by a playmate, or dropping a soft pawpaw in a cap which he thought was his playmate's only to find that it was his own, are interesting but of little psychological importance beyond showing that Abe was a natural boy.

First Psychic Trauma

Lincoln told the following tragic story about his childhood pet pig to Frederick C. Iglehart who retold it in "The Speaking Oak" with fair reproduction of his style of speech (Hertz, 1939). The story reveals the unusual force and persistence of Lincoln's early love-possessive characteristics and the great persistence of their special conditioning through his life. (Italics inserted by me for characterization.)

One moonlight night when they were walking on a country road they noticed just ahead of them six little pigs with their noses together. Lincoln said: "Those little pigs are lost; let us help them find their mother." When at last they found the hole in the fence and their mother, Lincoln began:

> "I never see a pig that I do not think of my first pet. When a boy six years old I went over to a neighboring farm. A litter of striped pigs had recently been born, and I was so crazy about them that they could not get me away from them. The man filled me with supreme delight by saying: 'Abe, you may have one of those pigs, if you can git him home.'
>
> " 'I will attend to that,' I said. I had on a tow shirt reaching to my feet, which my mother made, and I made a fold in the garment, and in it, as a sack, I carried my pig home. I had an old bee-gum, a hollow log, put corn

shucks and stable litter and leaves in it for a bed and tucked him in for the night.

"He squealed for his mother nearly all night. In the morning I brought him corn meal, bran, bread, milk, everything I could think of, but he would not touch any of them; he did not seem to have time or energy for anything but to squeal. At last my mother said to me: 'Abe, take that pig home; it will die if you keep it here.'

"What my mother said was always the truth and the law to me, and though it about broke my heart I took the pet back. The mother was so glad to see him and he so glad to see her. After she had given him his dinner, he looked so pretty I could not stand it, and I begged the man to let me take him back, and I put him in the tow sack as I had done before and carried him to our house.

"Mother protested and I cried, and she broke down and relented, and said I might try him one more day. He would not eat a thing I brought him, and mother sent me back with him again, and I carried him back and forth to his meals for two weeks, when we taught him to eat, and he was mine for good.

"That pig was my companion. I played with him, I taught him many tricks. We used to play hide and go seek. *I can see his little face now peeping around the corner of the house to see whether I was coming after him.* After a while he got too heavy for me to carry him around, and then he followed me everywhere—to the barn, to plowed ground, the woods. Many a day I have spent in the woods brushing the leaves away and helping him to find the acorns and nuts. *Sometimes he would take a lazy spell and rub against my legs, and stop in front of me, and lie down before me, and say in a language which I understood; 'Abe, why don't you carry me like you used to?'*

"When he grew larger, I turned the tables on him and made him carry me, and he did just as happily as I ever did the same service for him. Father fed him corn, piles of it, and how he did eat! And he grew large, too large for his happiness and mine. There was talk about the house of the hog being fat enough to kill. At the table I heard father say he was going to kill the hog the next day. My heart got as heavy as lead.

"The next morning father had a barrel of water ready and was heating the stones that were to be thrown into it to make hot water for the scalding, and I slipped out and took my pet with me to the forest. When father found out what had happened, he yelled as loud as he could: 'You, Abe, fetch back that hog! You Abe, You, Abe, fetch back that hog!! The louder he called the farther and faster I went, till we were out of hearing of the voice. We stayed in the woods till night.

"On returning, I was severely scolded. After a restless night, I went to get my pig for another days's hiding, but found that father had arisen before me and fastened my pet in the pen. I knew then all hope was gone. I did not eat any breakfast, but started for the woods. I had not gone far when *I heard the pig squeal, and, knowing what it meant, I ran as fast as I could to get away from the sound.*

"Being quite hungry, at noon I started for home. Reaching the edge of the clearing, I saw the hog, dressed, hanging from a pole near the house, and I began to blubber. I could not stand it and went back into the woods again, where I found some nuts that stayed my appetite till night, when I returned home. They never could get me to eat a bit of the meat, neither tenderloin, nor rib, nor sausage, nor souse. And months after, when the cured ham came on the table, it made me sad and sick even to look at it.

"The next morning I went out into the yard, and saw the red place on the ground where the throat had been cut with the knife, and taking a chip, *I scraped the blood and hair that had been scattered, into a pile and burned it up. Then I found some soft dirt, which I carried in the folds of my tow shirt, and scattered it over the ground to cover up every trace of the killing of my pet.*

"*The dirt did not do its work very well, for to this day, whenever I see a pig like the little fellows we have just met in the road, my heart goes back to that pet pig, and to the old home, and the dear ones there."*

Conditioned Consequences of Tragedy

Lincoln, as a man, retained many of the socially conditioned personal traits of his childhood, particularly an unusually strong, kindly, affectionate, natural, unaffected, unpretentious attitude that persisted against great obstacles in working to get what he loved. Besides exchanges of affection with his mother, sister, and father, Abe's pet pig provided the natural enjoyment of such relations with another living thing of great importance to him. At the age of six, during the critical period of final conversion of egoistic attitude from possessive dependence on his mother to more self-reliant independence, he had successfully mothered and fed a baby pig as his own property, and raised and trained it as a pet. Daily they had played and talked together in their own ways and it developed for him the psychological values and affections of a deeply-loved person. This boy and his young pig responded to each other more intimately than pets do with adults. Each belonged to the other. Such deeply pleasurable emotional attachments in this period of development of a child's egoistic social attitude have formative effects that endure throughout life as an adult. The strength of young Abe's emotivation that became so tragically conditioned, is evident in the *persistence* with which he carried his pet to its mother for nursing, alone, over a little used road in a wilderness still inhabited by wildcat, panther, and bear. Obviously he was, even as a child, remarkably self-reliant and self-respectful.

When his father inconsiderately announced, in his habitual authoritative, blunt manner, that he would kill the pig the next morning, the boy, greatly shocked and distressed, resolutely planned to save its life. Had his father shown more patient understanding and sympathetic consideration of his feelings by saying that he realized how it hurt him to have his pig killed and that he felt badly about having to do it before winter came, and given the boy ample time to adjust himself and accept it as necessary, his distress would not have been so sharp, deep, and bitter. But his father ignored his protests, rights, and feelings when he relentlessly cut its throat. As Abe ran from the scene and heard its death squeal, his once beloved father became changed into a ruthless tyrant who had violently offended his personal rights and self-respect and had on his hands the life blood of his pet which, in his intensely affectionate attachment to it, was a part of himself. His mother, no doubt, sensed the serious nature of her young son's bitter anguish and tried to comfort him by saying something about how sorry she felt about it all but he should accept that his father had to do it out of necessity. Abe evidently obediently accepted the death of his pet as its inevitable fate as he cleaned up and burned its hair and blood and covered the spot with fresh earth, in unforgettable bitter loneliness of soul.

Since Lincoln freely told this story to a friend when a man, upon being reminded of it by the young pigs on the road, and the whole episode was, no doubt, talked over freely by the family in his presence more than once, he had not repressed its painful memories to forget them. Rather, he had often reflected over them with rudimentary philosophical understanding. However, he was as a boy unforgettably impressed, for the first time, by the fateful destiny of life, and the indifference to his rights and affections which his father had assumed as necessary. His egoistic attitude toward life was thereafter conditioned to resent, more intensely than normal, unnecessary violations of human and animal rights, to hate tyrannical injustice, and to be deeply inclined to see life as a tragic fatalist.

Such potentially gloomy implications of the fate of his love attachments followed thereafter, as naturally as the conditioning of nausea and indigestion that he experienced whenever the family ate some of the flesh of this pig. Later, as a man, his appetite was limited by feelings of revulsion.

As late as 1855, when traveling on a country road with Herndon, who told the story, Lincoln recognized the squeal of a young pig that was being killed. He instantly leaped out of the buggy, grabbed a club and beat off an old sow. When she ran he said, "By jingo, the unnatural old brute shall not devour her own progeny" (Hertz, 1838).

When a boy Lincoln developed a repugnance for hunting, and bloodshed became nervously sickening to him. When President, the cruelty and killing of the Civil War harassed him endlessly. However, the details with which he told his story show that he liked to meditate on the tragic scenes of how he tried to save the life of his pet and his father killed it and he cleaned up its blood. Many years later the fatalism of Shakespeare's tragedies, Macbeth and Hamlet, so deeply fascinated him that he memorized impressive parts of them.

Abe's relations with his pet has another important lifelong effect on the basic pattern of development of his egoistic attitude and self-expression. They had, he said, talked a language that they could understand. This experience prepared him to have an unusually intense fascination for Aesop's fables when he learned to read. Here human ambitions, passions, follies and virtues are presented under the guise of animals that speak with wisdom. Through the Aesopian fable, with its terse moral or philosophical ending, young Abe learned the art of telling entertaining stories with practical humorous or witty ending that had a useful moral connotation. This art he used so effectively as a boy, and later as a lawyer, politician, and President that it contributed in a major way to his success in influencing people to adopt his reasoning.

The destined fate of young Abe's pet by his father's will, in the critical year of his psychological conversion of egoistic attitude, had another deeply impressive conditioning influence on the development of self-reliance and consistency of sense of justice. Instead of his will being broken down in hateful moody resentment by the experience, it made him even more resolute. Young Abe was proud of his mother's heroic character and loved the name she gave him and the rules of personal rights that she taught him. He knew that his name *Abraham* honored the name of his father's father and the patriarch Abraham. She had probably read to him from the Bible about the life of Abraham and how he was chosen by the Lord God to command his children to live with justice and judgment and produce a mighty nation. His name now assumed for him a supremely transcendent meaning that served as a fixed, profoundly inspiring conviction. He could endure his bitter experience and submit to his father's authority but he would transcend him through self-identification with the first great lawgiver and judge in Biblical history. He believed with definite conviction that he was also 'chosen' by destiny to make laws that would give people a more equitable sense of justice and maintain a greater nation. The faith in his star remained a guiding inspiration for the rest of his life. We will see, later, that he never made a final decision that involved the disposition of conflicting claims and rights, without heeding this inner voice, no matter how great or small the issue.

His heart became set upon fighting against dominating injustice wherever he met it, set ready to oppose, when he became a man, tyranny of slavery. When he became a father his attitude went to the opposite extreme of his father's intolerance, in being endlessly patient and tolerant of the wilful impositions on himself of his own wife and children.

We know from the psychoanalysis of obsessive compulsions and beliefs how they often begin unconsciously in the unavoidable fates of the child when it must sacrifice its great love for its mother in honor of its father's rights and authority. When this sorrowful conversion happens to be combined with the death of its substitute love-object, the apprehension of a similar tragic fate tends to repeat itself with cumulative force upon each similar experience. Such fateful inclination of mind conditions the entire course of attitudinal development throughout adolescence and maturity. The destined fate of his pet suggested to young Abraham the unforgettable presentiment that his own future was destined still to be involved in more tragedy. Three times more Lincoln had to endure the untimely death of the one he most loved, and twice with serious depressive effects.

Chapter IV

BOYHOOD

Boyhood and girlhood differentiates naturally from childhood with the emergence of permanent teeth and physiopsychological conversion of egoistic attitude from parasitic mother dependence to proud love of being self-reliant in characteristic ways. Boys and girls now become more eager to learn from other people besides their parents, whose knowledge of the meanings of life has long been thoroughly explored, if not exhausted.

The Lincoln cabin was situated on the main road from Louisville, Ky. to Nashville, Tenn., beside clear, dashing Knob Creek near its confluence with Rolling Fork River. Nearby was a tavern and a grist mill. Travelers on horse back and in wagons passed by the cabin daily and sometimes stopped to get a refreshing drink of water and trade talk with Tom and Nancy Lincoln, much to the delight of inquisitive young Sarah and Abe.

The potential power of the brain for mental development is shown early by the questions children impulsively ask and the ease with which they learn and remember answers. Abe's curiosity, by six, was inexhaustible. He would ask strangers more questions than they could readily answer. Here Abe learned the art of being sociable with strangers in a crude but most effective way. Grinning with anticipation he "fetched" fresh water or whatever was desired, knowing that it always won the gratitude of people and opened their minds to inquisitive approach. Lincoln as a man developed unusual ability for mixing with strangers and readily establishing friendly relations through exchanging ideas for the pleasure of it. We can with certainty trace the beginning of this invaluable self-cultivation back to Knob Creek. Here pleasure in the art of service, so essential later in politics, gushed from his irrepressible nature with each encouraging success so that a lonely young boy, who otherwise might have passed shyly into manhood, was ready to be awakened suddenly to the value of book learning.

First Girl

Young Abe's eager love was relieved in the usual way with children, through diversion of interest in playmates, particularly one of the opposite sex about his age. Knob Creek was probably the scene of Lincoln's story of his first love [as told to Wayne Whipple (Hertz, 1939)], since it mentions travelers on a wagon road that passed near his home. It contains important clues to young Abe's self-reliance under dutiful submission to the authoritative rights of ownership by his father, and on the awakening of interest in learning to read and romance imaginatively. (Italics are inserted for indications of character formation).

"One day, when I was a little codger, a wagon with a lady and two girls and a man broke down near us, and while they were fixing up, they cooked in our kitchen. *The woman had books and read us stories, and they were the first I ever heard. I took a great fancy to one of the girls;* and when they were gone I thought of her a great deal, and one day when I was sitting out in the sun by the house I wrote out a story in my mind. I thought I took my father's horse and followed the wagon, and I finally found it, and they were surprised to see me. I talked with the girl and persuaded her to elope with me; and that night I put her on my horse, and we started off across the prairie. After several hours we came to a camp, and when we rode up we found it was the one we left a few hours before, and went in. The next night we tried it again, and the same thing happened— the horse came back to the same place; and then *we concluded that we ought not to elope. I stayed until I had persuaded her father to give her to me.* I always meant to write that story and publish it, and I began once; but I concluded it was not much of a story. But I think that was the beginning of love with me."

The ease with which the woman won young Abe's admiration shows that he expressed himself freely to his own mother without fear of rejection. His confidence in the imagination of being able to persuade the little girl to elope with him indicates that he had long learned how to understand and persuade his sister to cooperate with him. The manner in which the love fantasy circulated around need of approval from the girl's father, and in twice getting lost after eloping and being brought home by his father's horse, indicates that little Abe's mother had taught him well, through working on his love and devotion to her, to believe that he should obey his father dutifully and willingly. His confidence in being able to persuade the girl's father to consent to his love shows that he was often able to persuade his own father to give consent to his desires and that with all their hardships the Lincolns were a happy, peaceful family.

As the strange, attractive lady read the enchanting stories she awakened in the boy the desire to learn to read for the pleasure of entertaining others. This became one of Lincoln's greatest pleasures and it started very likely with the lady's intuition, from his intelligent questioning, that by example she might show him the way to knowledge in books.

Search for Fundamentals

When Abraham Lincoln was asked by Reverend J. P. Gulliver, in an interview in 1860, how he happened to cultivate such unusual power of "putting things," he replied as retold by Carpenter (1866) (italics inserted):

"I can say this, that among my earliest recollections I remember how, when a mere child, I used to get irritated when anybody talked to me in a way I could not understand. *I don't think I ever got angry at anything else in my life. But that always disturbed my temper, and has ever since.* I can remember going to my little bedroom after hearing the neighbors talk of an evening with my father, and spending no small part of the night walking up and down, and trying to make out what was *the exact meaning of some of their, to me, dark sayings.* I could not sleep, though I often tried to, when I got on such a hunt for an idea, until I had caught it; and when I thought I had got it, I was not satisfied until I had repeated it over and over, until I put it in language plain enough, as I thought, for any boy I knew to comprehend. *This was a kind of passion with me, and it stuck by me; for I am never easy now, when I am handling a thought, till I have bounded it north, and bounded it south, and bounded it east, and bounded it west.* Perhaps that accounts for the characteristic you observe in my speeches, though I never put the two things together before."

Herndon also wrote of this ability but he criticized Gulliver's story as being fanciful about Abe's little room and pacing the floor while others slept. He pointed out that Lincoln's childhood home consisted of a one room cabin and when young he probably slept as was customary in a cradle and later in the loft. His parents would probably not have permitted much wandering about at night. Nevertheless the essential part of the story is probably Lincoln's and indicates how early in childhood he felt he must understand the meaning of what people said and be able to express himself so that he would be clearly understood.

The dark, mysterious sayings of adults before intelligent children obsess them to learn their meanings and pass them on to playmates. The strength of this boy's compulsion to understand the double talk of his elders indicates that he had become perplexed about the moral question of the paternity of their children, several of whom were illegitimate.

First School

Lincoln wrote for Scripps: "Before leaving Kentucky he and his sister were sent for short periods to A.B.C. schools, the first kept by Zachariah Riney, and the second by Caleb Hazel. . . . At this time his father resided on Knob Creek." Abe was six to seven and his sister eight to nine years of age. Barton (1925) says it was not a free school. Anyone who could read, write, and do arithmetic could take pupils for a small fee. Zachariah Riney taught a little group of children for a few weeks in winter. They had no books, but education was started by learning to spell out loud and recite more or less as a group in sing-song unison with the teacher. Sarah is said to have been more diligent than her brother and liked to learn her lessons whereas Abe liked playing better.

Religion and Mores

Tom and Nancy Lincoln held Baptist affiliations and attended "prayer meeting" in the little log church a few miles from home when the itinerant minister made his monthly visit. Like most Protestants they also attended other denominational meetings. Sometimes a minister stayed with the Lincolns and young Abe was much impressed by their application of biblical law on what was right and wrong in the world. Baptists were more numerous in Kentucky in this period than other denominations and were the most active opponents of slavery. They had, with the separation of the state from Virginia, fought unsuccessfully to abolish the institution as un-Christian. It was their argument that slavery was tolerated under the federal constitution by agreement between the northern and southern states and therefore all of the states were responsible for its existence; that as the people realized its immoral impositions on personal rights, its degradation of womanhood, and its opposition to Christian religious principles, its encouragement of idleness and vice on slave holders and its uneconomical labor, it would naturally be abandoned by the southern states. Tom Lincoln was strongly opposed to slavery and no doubt young Abe heard the question discussed in the way of Thomas Jefferson, Henry Clay, and Baptist teaching many times in his home. Hardin County had then over 1,200 slaves on its tax lists and Washington County had nearly as many. The slavery that young Abe knew was probably kindly and without the brutal chain gangs that he saw later (Barton, 1925).

In the Kentucky backwoods everyone was more or less superstitious and believed in signs and the supernatural magic of spirits. Ghost and witch tales mystified the night, and vague clairvoyant prophesies were accepted retrospectively with conviction. It seems that young Abe took particular delight in challenging beliefs that violated natural processes with too big skips of realistic probability, but he retained all his life belief that portents, signs, and dreams gave hints of the predestination of future events just as they did in the days of the prophets. Baptists were strong believers in predestination and revelation and herein was probably an influential source of his childhood conviction of destiny.

The Lincolns had relatives and friends in three counties near Hardin. The roads were rough and hilly and horseback was generally the easiest way to travel. Walking or riding 10, 20, or even 100 miles to attend to some business or just to visit for a day or two was not out of the ordinary. Abe went with his parents to the village of Elizabethtown, capital of Hardin County, and probably also to Bardstown in Nelson, Springfield in Washington, and possibly even to more distant Harrodsburg in Mercer County, where his grandmother, Lucy Hanks Sparrow lived. Elizabethtown was only nine miles away but the road was very hilly, so Tom Lincoln generally "traded" in Bardstown unless he had business in court.

Horse racing; whiskey distilling and drinking; wrestling matches; wolf, deer, bear, and turkey hunting; camp meetings; barn dances; house and barn raisings; political meetings; elections; murder trials; weddings; and funerals provided most of the excitement.

Unusual Intelligence

Perhaps the best indication that Lincoln possessed unusual intelligence and self-reliance early in boyhood is found in the story told to Herndon by Mentor Graham, who helped Lincoln later in his studies in New Salem,

Ill. Graham knew Tom Lincoln and his young son in Kentucky and met them on one occasion in a gathering of people where a man had killed his wife. As they stood about making comments, one of them turned to young Abe, who had been silently taking in every opinion, and asked him what he thought of it. The group expected the boy to mutter something and shuffle away in embarrassment but instead he answered, after serious deliberation, in a clear voice with such maturity of judgment as to astonish everyone. Unfortunately, what he said was not recorded but we may guess that it was a practical application of Mosaic law.

Vivid Memory

Lincoln's memory, when an eminent lawyer and president, was extraordinary for the vividness and accuracy of details and number of childhood events that he could recall. Instances of this will appear in the order of their occurrence but we give here some illustrations as evidence that he did not have a repressed unconscious, such as is usually developed by children to forget social guilt as charged by playmates.

When president, he was asked if he could remember anything of the War of 1812. He replied that he could and told of the time he caught a fish and was taking it home when he met a soldier on the road, and having been taught to be "good" to soldiers he gave it to him. He was probably then under six years of age. He remembered well how his playmate Austin Gollaher had saved him from drowning in Knob Creek, and the chores he did for his parents in this period. When presented with a cane by a committee of old Kentucky friends of his boyhood, President Lincoln is reported to have said:

> "I remember the old home very well. Our farm was composed of three fields, which lay in the valley surrounded by high hills and deep gorges. Sometimes when there came a big rain in the hills the water would come down the gorges and spread over the farm. The last thing I remember of doing there was one Saturday afternoon; the other boys planted corn in what we called the 'big field'—it contained seven acres—and I dropped the pumpkin seed. I dropped two seeds for every other hill and every other row. The next Sunday morning there came a big rain in the hills; it did not rain a drop in the valley, but the water, coming down through the gorges, washed ground, corn, pumpkin seeds and all clear off the field."

The most remarkable evidence of Lincoln's keen discriminatory observations in childhood and clarity of memory retention for life exists in his letter (5, 28, 1860) to Sam Haycraft, former clerk of the court in Elizabethtown, Ky.

> ". . . I do not think I ever saw you, though I very well know who you are—so well that I recognized your handwriting, on opening your letter, before I saw the signature. My recollection is that Ben Helm was first clerk, that you succeeded him, that Jack Thomas and William Farleigh graduated in the same office, and that your handwritings were all very similar. Am I right?"

Helm was clerk of Hardin County from 1800-1817; Haycraft served from 1817-1851. Thomas and Farleigh were deputy clerks and practiced law in Hardin County.

In 1814, Thomas and Nancy Lincoln probably took their little son, age five to six, to the clerk's office in Elizabethtown when they sold the Mill Creek property. It is quite probable that he was also taken to Elizabethtown during the litigation over the title to the Knob Creek farm. Abe was then age six to seven and interested in learning to write. It seems that he saw the handwriting of Ben Helm at this time and his memory of it was so retentive that he recognized, 40 years later, the similarities in the handwriting of Haycraft and other clerks with it. The letter gives some indication of the extraordinary development of his mental powers of discriminatory observation at an early age, and his pride in it throughout his life.

Loss of Knob Creek Farm

We give in some detail the circumstances of the loss of the Knob Creek farm, for it no doubt greatly impressed young Abe in his seventh year. His father had bought, with payment of 200 dollars, 30 acres on Knob Creek from George Lindsey, even though he was unable to obtain a clear title to the land since it was part of a 10,000-acre tract held under a patent in 1786 by a Philadelphia family. Tom paid some of the taxes on his claim and planned to complete payment upon receipt of title. He won a suit brought against him and Lindsey as trespassers and obtained thereby strong assurance that his title was valid. However, when a second suit was instituted (1, 1, 1815) against him and other "squatters," he decided to abdicate and finally sold his rights for 75 dollars. He had cleared and cultivated the land through four years but had grown discouraged after the flood that eroded much of the soil. Doubtless there was much discussion in the Lincoln household about the injustice of the litigation and the complex land laws and titles and the cost of fighting in court against a wealthy claimant with prior title. The squatters who remained and contested the suit won title to their lands in 1818, about a year after Tom Lincoln moved to Indiana. Young Abe was much impressed by his father's reasons for yielding his rights to the farm, for he said in his Scripps letter (1860) that difficulty in establishing land titles in Kentucky and dislike of slavery there and the assurance of a federal title to cheap land in the free territory of Indiana influenced his father to move. The litigation and his father's inability to protect his mother's home seems to have greatly impressed young Lincoln, for later, reading books on law and government became his chief interest.

New Start in Indiana

In 1816 Tom Lincoln built a flatboat near his home on Rolling Fork of Salt River and loaded it with his tools and two large casks of whiskey for bartering. The federal government was giving assured titles to good land in Indiana for two dollars an acre and he was determined to visit his old friend Tom Carter on Pigeon Creek in Spencer County and find out for himself. He drifted the 40 miles down Salt River without incident, but when he entered the Ohio the current swamped his overloaded craft despite his skill as a riverman. He had taken a loaded flatboat down the Ohio and Mississippi to New Orleans about 10 years before without incident. After recovering his tools and some of the whiskey he reached Thompson's Ferry in Perry County and then traveled overland to Gentry-ville, then a village of a few straggling cabins and a store and mill. He staked out a quarter section claim about two miles from the village on a ridge overlooking Pigeon Creek bottoms. The upland was safe from floods but covered with large trees and devoid of water. The nearest spring was a long quarter of a mile down in the valley. He seems not to have thought much of Abe having to carry water that distance up hill each day nor of what a drought might do to his corn. He then walked 70 miles over the wilderness road to Vincennes and filed his claim. Later he paid 160 dollars for 80 acres of it and relinquished title to the remainder.

Tom Lincoln then returned to Kentucky to get his wife and two children who, in the meantime, had been visiting with Hanks and Lincoln relatives. In December of 1816 the family moved to Indiana. Tom and Nancy each rode a horse, with a child and a bundle of bedding and utensils. Sarah was about ten and Abe nearly eight years of age, and probably all took turns at walking to rest the horses. They also drove a cow and several hogs along with them.*

The living conditions provided by Tom Lincoln for his family have often been described as "mean," but they were no better or worse than the first homes of many pioneers. It was generally the practice on moving into new wilderness to first build a three-sided shed of poles for a temporary shelter and then build a log cabin as the land was cleared of trees. Two stout, forked trees, standing not too far apart on fairly level ground, were topped and a strong pole laid across the forks. The whole was finished off with smaller poles and covered with sod and grass. Skins and cloth lined it and formed the rear wall, and a fireplace was built in front of it. Its southern exposure made it fairly comfortable except in high wind with snow or rain. Keeping the fire going was the most important problem, especially in winter, and an ample supply of dry, dead wood was indispensable. This became Abe's chore which he performed efficiently. Through a year, the family lived in this primitive shelter while they cut down trees to clear a corn patch and build a "house." It was made of unhewn logs and had only one room about 14 feet square with an entrance and an open stone fireplace with an outside chimney made of sticks plastered with mud. It had no door, window, or floor and they moved in before completing it.

*For a more detailed account see Barton (1925) who lived in this section of Kentucky.

As in most pioneer homes, the furniture consisted of a few hand-made, three-legged stools, beds made of poles stuck between the logs and covered with a mattress of sacks filled with feathers, corn husks, or dry leaves and grass. Deer, bear, and cattle skins were used for blankets. A split log table, a big kettle, pot and skillet for cooking over the open fireplace, a few knives, forks and spoons, and tin and pewter dishes for serving food completed the equipment.

The immediate problem of the Lincoln family was getting feed for the horses, cow, pigs, and chickens, and enough land cleared in time to raise corn and vegetables. Deer, bear, turkey, pigeons, panther, wildcat and small game were abundant, and with salt pork, ground corn meal, sorghum molasses and wild nuts, fruits, and berries, they fared well enough. Either Nancy or Tom seems to have sent word back to Kentucky with a happy account of the family's prosperity, for by 1818 Tom and Elizabeth Sparrow with Dennis and Sophie Hanks and Levi and Nancy Hall had joined them on Pigeon Creek. "Granny" Betsy Sparrow and her husband lived in the old pole shed, and the rest of the flock crowded into the cabin.

Abe's First Wild Turkey

When a boy, Abe liked to fish and play games more than going to school. He was far more persistent than his friends in working out his objectives. In his Scripps letter, he gave the following description, in the third person, of himself as a boy hunter in Indiana, although forbidden by his father to use his gun.

> "At this place A. took an early start as a hunter, which was never much improved afterwards. (A few days before the completion of his eigth [sic] year, in the absence of his father, a flock of wild turkeys approached the new log-cabin, and A. with a rifle gun, standing inside, shot through a crack, and killed one of them. He has never since pulled a trigger on any larger game.)"

Tom and Dennis hunted at every opportunity. Bear hunting with dogs was the great sport of the community, for bruin liked to raid the cattle and hog pens. With all the opportunity for hunting Abe had lost this interest by the time he reached adolescence and preferred to spend his free time in reading and athletic sports.

"Puttin' In Too Much"

The extremely sympathetic warmth, freedom, intimacy of give and take of democratic life among parents, children, and relatives, all living together in a pole shed and one-room cabin, isolated for miles in the great forest, developed an affectionate attachment of each for the other that distance and time and death could not break. For this Indiana home Abraham Lincoln later had an endlessly recurrent nostalgic attachment. He enjoyed talking and asking questions, and when conversation was going on he was generally around listening for a chance to contribute his share.

Sometimes his father would get provoked and take him aside to "tend to him for puttin' in too much." It was his father's rule not to whip his children before "company" as a matter of pride in "being polite." He had great respect for himself and his family, and seems not to have punished Abe severely enough to break his willful spirit or even to make him submissive in fear of his anger.

Herein was one of the repetitive reaction patterns that influenced the development of young Abe's unusual self-confidence and self-respect, with a remarkable sense of proportion in retributive justice. Rules of politeness embarrassed him and he confided in Dennis that he was afraid he could never learn to apply them, for his father said it was not polite to ask strangers questions, and he "just couldn't stop asking questions."

His father did not always control himself and postpone the disciplining. We get an intimate sketch of this from Dennis through Herndon (Hertz, 1938). Although it was written 40 years later, it gives us an idea of father and son attitudes in the presence of strangers.

> "Abe was a good boy, an affectionate one, a boy who loved his father and mother dearly and well, always minding well. Sometimes Abe was a little rude. When strangers would ride along and up to his father's fence, Abe always, through pride and to tease his father, would be sure to ask the stranger the first question, for which his father sould sometimes knock him a rod. Abe was then rude and a forward boy. Abe, when whipped by his father, never balled, but dropped a kind of silent unwelcome tear, as evidence of his sensations or other feelings."

On the whole, Tom respected and trusted his son and encouraged his initiative. One day he sent him to buy a certain horse from a neighbor with the following instructions: "You may offer him fifty dollars for the horse; but if you can't get it for that, you may give him as much as sixty dollars for it." Young Abe went to the neighbor and said: "Father told me I might offer fifty dollars for that horse you have for sale; but if I couldn't get it for fifty dollars I might give you as much as sixty for it. I have made up my mind that I won't give you but fifty dollars for the horse." He remained firm and got the horse for his price.

Hoosier School Days

In his Scripps letter, Lincoln has given us a glimpse of his Indiana schooling. "While here A. went to A.B.C. schools by littles, kept successively by Andrew Crawford, —— Sweeney, and Azel W. Dorsey. He does not remember any other. . . . A. now thinks that the agregate [sic] of all of his schooling did not amount to one year."

In his early school days Abe had a self-respectful attitude that resented belittling attentions from anyone. He was eagerly ambitious for winning superiorities through competition in any kind of work or play. His long, skinny arms and legs, big nose, coarse, black, long, unshorn, unkempt hair, ever-ready grin, freckled face, and wide spreading ears made him a delightful target for good natured teasing. He met it with the ready give and take of wit of a mischievous, playful, vigorous, uninhibited boy.

The attitude of Abe's blunt-spoken, illiterate father toward education has been described by some biographers as discouraging and by others as encouraging. It seems that he appreciated the incompetence of illiteracy for making a living, and wanted his son to learn sufficient "readin', writin' and 'rithmetic" to carry on, but otherwise thought that he wasted time in getting more education, when there was so much work to be done in clearing and farming and building houses, barns, fences, and furniture. We can be quite certain that Abe's reading at home was often opposed by his father but openly encouraged by his mother and later by his stepmother.

Abe was an exceptionally good natured, happy, laughing, sweet, kindly, intelligent boy. He was skillful with his hands, and learned from his father how to use the axe for cutting logs and splitting rails, and to use other wood-working tools for making farm implements and household utensils and furniture. He continued this mechanical interest throughout life, and, when lawyer and president, contributed to the development of several mechanical inventions. This interest certainly had an enormous influence, from boyhood to manhood, on self-education with a common-sense, factual, logical, mechanistic interpretation and understanding of everything in life.

Dennis, who had considerable schooling for that time, has given (Hertz, 1938) a vivid description of the first steps:

> "About Abe's early education and his sister's education, let me say this; their mother first learned them the ABCs. . . . She learned them out of Webster's old spelling book; it belonged to me and cost in those days 75¢, it being covered with calf skin or such like covering. I taught Abe to write with a buzzard's quill which I killed with a rifle, and having made a pen, put Abe's hand in mine and moving his fingers by my hand to give him the idea how to write. We had no geese then, for the country was a forest. I tried to kill an eagle but he was too smart; wanted to learn Abe to write with that. Lincoln's mother learned him to read the Bible, study it and the stories in it and all that was moral and affectionate in it, repeating to Abe and his sister when very young. Lincoln was often much moved by the stories."

This account of Lincoln's early education probably includes the last years in Kentucky as well as the first years in Indiana, since the Sparrows and Lincolns were close neighbors in both places.

For ink, Abe used berry juices, and, for something to write on when paper was not to be had, he shaved smooth a piece of clapboard and used it over and over until it was worn out.

His total schooling was less than one year, including the "blab" school in Kentucky before he was eight and the school with books in Indiana at nine, ten, and seventeen. Sarah continued to be a better pupil than her brother who was "tollerable lazy" and liked to play pranks in school, but when they graduated from the speller to the reader he became interested in learning. School was held in the Indiana wilderness in winter, as in Kentucky, when someone moved into the neighborhood who had sufficient literacy to teach children.

The first lessons were confined to reading and writing by copying the words of *Dillworth's Speller* until they were memorized, although often without definition and meaning. The children learned by all spelling out loud and reciting at the same time under the critical administrations of the teacher who believed in keeping them busy and forcing education on their wild, playful spirits by "lickin and larnin." This method, incidentally, trained children to control attention in a noisy crowd. Abe Lincoln, as a man, had unusual powers of concentration and control of attention for reading quietly to himself where other people were talking, or, as a lawyer, in pleading a case before an indifferent jury. As an orator before a noisy, hostile or heckling crowd, his self-control and ready wit were masterful.

It was probably in his mother's time that Lincoln began the study of *Murray's English Reader.* Years later he said that it was the best textbook ever given to an American boy.

Chapter V

LINCOLN'S ATTITUDES TOWARD HIS PARENTS

Abraham was in his tenth year when his mother died, on October 5, 1818, after an illness of seven days from "milk sickness." This disease is characterized by extreme diarrhea, trembling, chills, emaciation, and delirium. It is acquired from the milk or butter of a cow that has been poisoned through eating snakeroot, a native plant, and is often fatal to cattle as well as man. A number of people were then desperately ill, and Nancy Lincoln, ever a helpful neighbor, went among them nursing and giving aid and comfort however she could. The malady was fatal to her foster mother, "Grannie" Betsy Hanks Sparrow and her husband, who lived in the pole shed, and to Aunt Nancy Hanks Hall (Dennis Hanks' mother) and her husband.

When she realized that she was dying, Nancy Lincoln called her children, Sarah and Abraham, to her bedside. Her cousin, Dennis Hanks, who was present, described the scene to Herndon (Hertz, 1938). "She told them to be good and kind to their father, to one another, and to the world, expressing a hope that they might live as they had been taught by her to love men, love, reverence and worship God. Here in this rude house, of the milk sickness, died one of the very best women of the whole race, known for kindness, tenderness, charity and love to the world."

Gloomy Fate

Tom Lincoln, with the help of Dennis and Abraham, split a log into boards and made a rough coffin in which they tenderly laid Nancy's body. They buried her near the aunt who raised her, on a knoll in the forest on their land, about half a mile from home.

The lonely gloom that fate so swiftly cast upon the boy's mind left unforgettable memories of his mother. A path has since been cut along the trail he made from the cabin to her grave, where often he went to commune with her in spirit. There were no funeral rites to relieve the bitter sadness, since no minister was to be had, and no stone was placed to mark her grave for public view.

When we search through accounts by neighbors of Lincoln's mother's last years and illness for a cause that might have imbued her son with saddened memories of her, and hate of his father for unkindness, nothing of particular significance is apparent except that the house had never been completed and made as comfortable as possible for living. No doubt Nancy had asked her husband to put in a door and window for protection against the weather. His indifference, as a carpenter who could easily have done this in a few days, might have made a boy of nine feel resentful if he thought that it made his mother's life harder than she could bear. But the death of five people in the family within a short time from the same disease indicates that such blame was unlikely, since two of them lived under worse housing conditions. Tom Lincoln's careless attitude, later, toward the memory of his wife, however, probably contributed to the deep, silent aversion against him that was already started in the mind of his son.

Judging from the statements made many years later by Lincoln about his mother, he thought she contracted her fatal illness through trying to save the lives of other sick people. It reaffirmed his fatalistic belief, generally held by Baptist pioneers, that the time and way of death is pre-destined, and nothing can change its course. His mother, he believed, died by the will of her Maker, the Father of all life, and he submitted, in his great love and devotion to her, with unforgettable oppressive sadness but without feelings of antireligious resentment.

Belief in fatalistic predestination, generally found in wilderness peoples almost wholly dependent on the uncontrollable forces of nature, leans to the culture of submissive resignation and profound fixation of gloomy sympathetic affection among the living for memories of the dead. In modern urban peoples, having greater protection and mastery over the forces of nature, and more diverse mental activity, the dead, after burial rites, are more easily forgotten.

Depressing Effect of Injury of
Young Lincoln's Brain

A nine-year-old boy might have "outgrown" much of his nostalgic love-regressive mother attachment in time, as longings for her faded and the vigorous surge of adolescence forced him on to prepare for the conquests of manhood, if it had not been for an accident a few weeks after her death that damaged parts of his brain.

In the first chapter we have described the accident and discussed the organic pathology of the injury of Lincoln's brain. We have now come to the time of the accident and need to reconsider briefly its physiological and psychological effects on the development of his mind and personality. "In his tenth year," in the words of Lincoln in his Scripps letter, "he was kicked by a horse and apparently killed for a time." He was taken home and recovered without medical treatment. No physician lived nearer than 20 miles and little was known then in medical science about treating injuries of the brain.

Although Lincoln, and those who knew him, thought that he had recovered completely from the injury, there is definite evidence that he suffered a frontal fracture of the skull and serious, permanent damage to certain parts of his brain. We know from Shastid's observations later, that in his twenties, hence no doubt since the accident, Lincoln's left eye was more or less turned upward and decoordinated from the right, and when he got excited the condition grew worse. We have Crawford's observation that the boy's lower lip "stuck out" in an unusual way (see Chapter I), and we have statements of neighbors that he seemed depressed and less active in this period.

Most children and adults with double vision resulting from accidents become poor readers, and poor competitors where success depends on continuous use of the eyes and pleasurably visualizing foresight. A boy with an ordinary brain capacity for developing intelligence, and with ordinary suggestive inspiration from his elders to educate himself, would have been greatly discouraged after such an injury, for he would soon have become conditioned by experience to know that such efforts lead to eye strain and headaches. As a boy Lincoln discovered that he could read more easily while lying on his back on the floor or a couch or tilting back in a chair. It was a posture taken reflexly to relieve his eye strain.

Retributive Justice to his Mother and Father

Lincoln's father soon grew indifferent to his unfinished obligation to the memory of his wife, and young Abraham became increasingly unhappy over thoughts of his mother lying without Christian funeral rites in a grave in the forest. She had been in her way a true Christian, and taught her children to cherish and practice in everyday life its fundamental rule, *do unto others as you would have them do unto you.* He knew that she wanted a Christian burial, and his conscience could not rest until she was properly committed to her Maker. He was said by neighbors to have saved money earned through doing chores and three years later (1821) wrote to Reverend David Elkins, an old friend of his mother whom he had known in Kentucky, that he would pay the expense if he would come and perform the funeral service.

Lincoln's comments to friends and in poems and letters at different times many years later, reveal that he always remembered his mother with reverential love and respect and regarded his father with dutiful loyalty but cool aversion. For young Abe the feeling of unexpressed resentment, at six years of age against his father for the inconsiderate, tyrannical manner of killing his pet pig, without respect for his tender feelings and natural rights, was in beginning adolescence associatively superimposed by more aversive feeling against him for being indifferent to his religious obligation to his mother. In order to simplify the analytical study of Lincoln's attitudes as a boy and man toward his mother and father for their melancholy effects on the course of development of his attitude toward life in general, we will consider here his most intimate expressions of feeling about them.

Many of Lincoln's biographers, like Tarbell, have assumed that his mother probably did not tell her children much about her early life and family relations, and whatever she told them soon became a faint, unimportant memory for a rapidly growing, healthy, venturesome boy.

The unreality of such notions of personal psychology has long been demonstrated by the evidence of experimental physiological psychology and, independently, by psychoanalysis. It shows that in every person's mind its orderly conditioning sensory experiences in childhood, youth, and adulthood with the family and other persons produce connected sensory impressions in the brain that continue unconsciously, involitionally active, and determine with present environmental excitements the conscious volitional associative processes of thinking. The products of Lincoln's mind as a boy and man, as a lawyer and president, show that his memories and feelings about his parents continued to have unusually active influences on his attitude toward love and life, largely through his method of mental culture. The death of a person who has had a formative influence on the development of another person's egoistic attitude does not extinguish this effect. While it is naturally reduced by lack of repetitive stimulation, it tends to continue active, particularly if it is cultivated by fondness for nostalgic memories.

Melancholy Presentiment of Regressive Love

Lincoln was a home-loving boy and he continued to love his childhood memories of home and his "dear ones" with such unusual intensity of devotion that it constituted a distinguishing characteristic of his personality that never waned. His nostalgia colored his sentiment as a lawyer and as president.

Melancholy preoccupation of adolescence in meditation over the feeling of destination of love and life ending in death, in connection with memories of his mother's fate, is evident in the numerous passages on such trials of human nature that he memorized from the Bible. How this mood continued in his love for nostalgic poetry and more mature philosophical contemplations on the meaning and destiny of life will be presented in later chapters as they appear in later years.

After his return to his boyhood home in 1845 he yielded to meditative moods and wrote a series of poems expressing the revival of boyhood memories. The following little poem, which he is said to have written at that time, expresses tenderly his sentiment of frustration of love.

My Angel Mother

All that I am, All that I hope to be,
  I owe to my Angel mother.
My hand she guided as I learned to write,
My feet she guided in the ways of right,
My hopes she nourished, as a flame of light,—
But now I wander like a child at night,—
God bless her soul, God bless her memory,
  Nancy, my Angel mother.

The philosophy of these lines is characteristic of Lincoln's mood, although their authenticity has not been established. Many biographers have interpreted Lincoln's use of the phrase "my angel mother" as having been in reference to his stepmother. Speed (1896) has told us definitely that he often spoke of his real mother as his "angel mother," hence, obviously, it could not have referred to his living stepmother whom he called his "saintly mother."

Attitude Toward his Dying Father

Lincoln's most intimate expressions of feelings about his parents were made in 1851 in a message to his dying father, and a few months later to his law partner, William Herndon, about his regard for his mother.

In the collection of papers given by Robert T. Lincoln to the Library of Congress was a letter to Abraham Lincoln by Dennis Hanks written in May 1849 about his father's (Tom Lincoln's) ill health (Sandburg, 1950). He is "anxious to see you before He dies & I am told that His Cries for you the last few days are truely Heart-Rendering. . . . He craves to See you all the time . . . his only Child that is his own flush [sic] & blood."

When his old father declined in health, so that the end appeared near, Lincoln naturally felt, upon being told, that he should go to see him before he died. A long day's journey away, he did not go, but gave reasons in the following letter to John Johnston that were intended both to justify himself and to soothe his father's mind. It marked the sad closing of the most unpleasant personal relationship of his life. His memories of the childhood tragedies caused by his father must naturally have been deeply stirred.

Springfield, Jany, 12, 1851-

Dear Brother:

On the day before yesterday I received a letter from Harriet, written at Greenup. She says she has just returned from your house; and that Father [is very] low, and will hardly recover. She also s[ays] you have written me two letters; and that [although] you do not expect me to come now, yo[u wonder] that I did not write. I received both your [letters, and] although I have not answered them, it is no [t because] I have forgotten them, or been uninterested about them—but because it appeared to me I could write nothing which could do any good. You already know I desire that neither Father or Mother shall be in want of any comfort either in health or sickness while they live; and I feel sure you have not failed to use my name, if necessary, to procure a doctor, or any thing else for Father in his present sickness. My business is such that I could hardly leave home now, if it were not, as it is, that my own wife is sick-abed. (It is a case of baby-sickness, and I suppose is not dangerous.) I sincerely hope Father may yet recover his health; but at all events tell him to remember to call upon, and confide in, our great, and good, and merciful Maker; who will not turn away from him in any extremity. He notes the fall of a sparrow, and numbers the hairs of our heads; and He will not forget the dying man, who puts his trust in Him. Say to him that if we could meet now, it is doubtful whether it would not be more painful than pleasant; but that if it be his lot to go now, he will soon have a joyous [meeting] with the many loved ones gone before; and where [the rest] of us, through the help of God, hope ere-long [to join] them."

This letter was found somewhat damaged and the bracketed words were added for completion by Nicolay and Hay, probably under Robert Lincoln's direction. Thomas Lincoln died five days later, January 17, 1851, "age 73 years and 11 days."

The record of his family in his father's Bible was completed in Lincoln's hand, so that it seems he may have attended his father's funeral but proof of this is lacking. Thomas (1953) and other biographers state that he did not attend. The births and marriages and deaths have been recorded, but the order is not entirely chronological. It begins with the dates of birth of Thomas Lincoln and Nancy Hanks and their marriage. Then follows: "Sarah Lincoln Daughter of Thos. and Nancy Lincoln, was born Feb. 10th 1807. Abraham Lincoln, Son of Thos. & Nancy Lincoln, was born Feb. 12th 1809." It then states that Sarah Bush was first married to Daniel Johnston, and afterward to Thomas Lincoln, and gives the date of her birth. Then follows the date of birth and marriage of Sarah's son John D. Johnston, and the births of his seven children. Next are recorded in the following order the marriage of Thomas Lincoln to Sarah Johnston, the marriage of Lincoln's sister, and his own marriage, and then John D. Johnston's second marriage. After this list the following entry was made: "Nancy Lincoln wife of Thos. Lincoln, died October 5th, 1818." Next Lincoln recorded the deaths of his sister and his father as if he thought they all belonged together without regard to the differences in time.

Meaning of "the Fall of a Sparrow"

The allegorical reference to the fall of a sparrow in his letter to his dying father is not original with Lincoln. It is an adaptation from Matthew, Chapter 10, verses 29, 30, 31. "Are not two sparrows sold for a farthing? And one of them shall not fall on the ground without your Father. But the very hairs of your head are all numbered. Fear not therefore, ye are of more value than many sparrows."

An attitude analysis of Lincoln's personality must give his philosophical advice to his dying father studied consideration of its meaning at the time it was written. The anticipation of his father's death must have awakened many emotionally impressive memories of his own childhood, particularly about the life and death of his mother and the development of himself as a person under dutiful submission to the authoritative, possessive rights over him of his parents.

Nancy Hanks, the illegitimate daughter of Lucy Hanks, was known, after her adoption by her "Aunt Betsy" (Mrs. Elizabeth Hanks Sparrow), as Nancy Sparrow, until her marriage. Her first child, Sarah, was born eight months later, probably following premarital conception. Thereby Lincoln's consoling reference to the biblical teaching that death is noticed by our Maker, even as "the fall of a sparrow," is deeply indicative of his memories and moral feelings about his mother's fall before marriage, in the imminence of the death of his father who was responsible for it. It was the choice of a number of suitable biblical metaphors familiar to him. Hence it was the choice of his unconscious emotivations, decisively conditioned long past by the great problem of his childhood. The metaphor expresses the moral cast of his memories and feelings about the unmoral side of his mother's life, her illegitimate birth by a promiscuous mother, and her own premarital conception.

"He notes the fall of a sparrow" is given additional meaning by association in his troubled mind with the next part of the sentence, "and numbers the hairs of our heads; and He will not forget the dying man, who puts his trust in Him." Here Lincoln expresses belief in the fateful predestination of each person by his Maker. He was inspired by such belief in his own destiny to become a law maker for his people, like the prophet Abraham. His preoccupations about the hairs of his head and habitual nervous combing with his fingers, his adoption of a child's suggestion to grow a beard, and his variations of having his hair and beard cut signify the depth of his self-conscious superstitions on predestination. In his habitual nostalgia Lincoln often meditated, as he confided to Herndon, on the destiny of life and death for himself in relation to the illegitimacy of birth of his mother leading to his own mental endowments.

The last part of the letter expresses Lincoln's old feelings of resentment and aversion for his father's authoritative injustice many years past. "Say to him that if we could meet now it is doubtful whether it would not be more painful than pleasant." This unhappy refusal to see his father is tempered by the rest of the sentence, "but that if it be his lot to go now, he will soon have a joyous meeting with many loved ones gone before and where the rest of us through the help of God, hope ere long to join them."

Lincoln's sentiment, suggesting to his father that he look forward in death to meeting his mother again and ere long he would join them in a new way of life could hardly have been written without belief that he was his real son.

Myths of the Illegitimate Birth of Lincoln

A few months after the death of his father, while he and his law partner, William Herndon, were riding together in a buggy to attend a trial that involved a question of heredity, Lincoln felt moved to talk about his mother more freely than any other time of which we have a record. Herndon has given the story repeatedly and consistently as follows, in several letters to Lamon and Weik (Hertz, 1938), with inclusion of his unwarranted suspicion that Lincoln believed himself also to have been an illegitimately conceived child.

"On the subject of his ancestry and origin I only remember one time when Mr. Lincoln ever referred to it. It was about 1850 [he also said 1851], when he and I were driving in his one-horse buggy to the court in Menard

County, Illinois. The suit we were going to try was one in which we were likely, either directly or collaterally to touch upon the subject of hereditary traits. During the ride, he spoke for the first time in my hearing, of his mother, dwelling on her characteristics, and mentioning and enumerating what qualities he inherited from her. He said, among other things, that she was the illegitimate daughter of Lucy Hanks and a well-bred Virginia farmer or planter; and he argued that from this last source came his power of analysis, his logic, his mental activity, his ambition, and all the qualities that distinguished him from the other members and descendants of the Hanks family. His theory in discussing the matter of hereditary traits had been, that, for certain reasons, illegitimate children are oftentimes sturdier and brighter than those born in lawful wedlock; and in his case, he believed that his better nature and fine qualities came from this broad-minded, unknown Virginian. The revelation—painful as it was—called up the recollection of his mother, and, as the buggy jolted over the road, he added ruefully 'God bless my mother; all that I am or ever hope to be I owe to her' and immediately lapsed into silence.

"This is a substantial statement," Herndon wrote to Lamon, "made to me by Lincoln . . . about which there is, nor can be any material mistake and in these last expressions *I have sometimes thought that Lincoln intended to include himself. I do not assert this to be so; it only SEEMS SO; by a loose intendment made by me, a loose impression made by me.* The manner of Lincoln I shall never forget—nor what was said, nor the place, whatever may become of time." (Hertz, 1938.) (Italics inserted.)

Lincoln seemed, according to Herndon, to disregard his father as a source of any of his better characteristics, but we know that he was proud of his Lincoln ancestry. The death of Lincoln's father, a short time before this event, probably as much as the nature of the law suit, induced a nostalgic, confiding, reminiscent mood.

Science has since dispelled Lincoln's fancy, by proving that a weak father may produce sperm having certain strong genetic determinants that may combine with strong genetic determinants inherited from the mother so as to produce a child endowed with unusually strong physical and mental abilities.

Herndon has pretended to quote Lincoln although the idiom is his own. The sincerity and truthfulness of recording his own facts and memories of Lincoln have generally proven reliable and keenly discerning, although his interpretations and conclusions have often been found erroneous. He did not make notes of this conversation at the time, but no doubt often thought of it, and only recorded it retrospectively 15 years later, after President Lincoln's death. It is not likely that a lawyer who had Lincoln's confidence would forget a statement so surprising and revealing by a man so important to him. Herndon repeated his statement a number of times, with more or less dramatic wording and sometimes with the addition that Lincoln had asked him to keep it confidential while he lived. He published his memories and inferences before he had established some reasonable evidence of their truth. Feeling guilty under the bitter public criticism heaped upon him for being unjust to his great friend's memory, he searched the gossip of Lincoln's neighbors in Indiana and Kentucky, and of the Hanks relatives of Nancy. The material he gathered on this question he believed should be given to the American people but he did not do this without biased judgment.

Herndon became convinced, as he said, that "Nancy Hanks fell before her marriage" and that Tom Lincoln was sterile and not the father of Sarah and Abraham, but he never attempted to answer the logical question, that if Nancy was sexually promiscuous before and after her marriage in Kentucky, as he believed, why did she not continue such inclinations in Indiana. Her reputation with the Gentryville neighbors— that of being a loving, obedient, devoted wife and mother and most helpful neighbor who made heroic self-sacrifices to minister to the sick— denied his belief.

Unfortunately, Weik, in writing *Herndon's Lincoln* (1889), gave Herndon's information and inferences about Lincoln inadequately and his letters were suppressed and hidden from the public by Lincoln's son Robert's insistence, until released in 1938 to Hertz for publication. They show that after 1867 Herndon confidentially discussed his material with Ward Lamon who bought his entire collection for a biography of Abraham Lincoln and repeated Herndon's story. Other biographers, including Arnold, Carpenter, Hart, Weik, and Nicolay and Hay, have also repeated parts of it. Herndon continued to think, with admitted reservation of doubt, however, until his death in 1890, that Lincoln was an extramarital son, even though he had found himself badly mistaken about the marriage of Lincoln's parents, which he once published as probably not having been legally consummated.

Since Herndon's death, Tarbell and many other biographers have rejected his entire statement of Lincoln's account as a malicious falsification. Barton and others have accepted it as being essentially true about his mother's illegitimate birth and consistent with many established facts that would otherwise be inexplicable. Herndon was charged with having been disappointed and resentful over not receiving an appointment to office in Lincoln's administration and of being an habitual drunkard whose words were unreliable. As will become evident later, such personal damnations have proven untrue.

In reply to the charges of his enemies Herndon said: "Mr. Lincoln was my good friend. While this is true I was under an obligation to the world of readers—living and to live during all coming time—as long as Lincoln's memory lives in the world. Lincoln rose over so many disadvantages that he seems to me a hero, having lived a grand good life. . . . I know so much of Lincoln's trials and troubles and difficulties that I see and feel them all as my own—so closely do they touch me and my good dead friend."

Herndon's interpretation that Lincoln believed himself to be an illegitimate son is not given credence now by any reliable biographer.

The reason for Lincoln's reticence about his mother and her family in his autobiographical letters is fairly evident. In the one to Fell he did not even give her Christian name. In the Scripps letter he only said that his father "married Nancy Hanks—mother of the present subject—in the year 1806. She was also born in Virginia."

Contributary Ground for Herndon's Myth

Previous to Herndon's publications, assertions of the illegitimate birth of Lincoln's mother and of Lincoln himself were first made in Kentucky, as a political defamation during the presidential campaign of 1860. They were based on neighborhood gossip 40 years old. Herndon properly judged its refutation or verification to be important for history.

Lincoln's enemies in Kentucky (then a slave state and Democratic stronghold) had spread the story that Abraham Enloe was his illegitimate father. Herndon was greatly impressed by this old gossip for it coincided with a statement by Dennis Hanks after Lincoln's death that Tom Lincoln was unable to have children because "accident and nature cut things short." Since Nancy had three children in Kentucky and none in Indiana, and Sarah Bush Johnston, Tom's second wife, had three children by her first husband and none by her second, he became persuaded that Dennis meant Tom's "accident" occurred before his marriage. Herndon knew Dennis to be an impressionable, plausible prevaricator but he accepted his statement since it coincided with the hearsay of Tom's neighbors in Kentucky and Indiana that he had small testicles.

A number of publications, besides Herndon's, were made to establish the extramarital origin of Abraham Lincoln. Of these, Weik (1922) listed "The Sad Story Of Nancy Hanks," by Lucinda Boyd of Virginia; "Truth Stranger Than Fiction," by W. M. Coleman of Texas; "The True Genesis of a Wonderful Man," by James Cathey of North Carolina; and "The Parentage of Lincoln," by D. J. Knotts of South Carolina. The most preposterous of all the published legends was that by Knotts. He said baldly that John C. Calhoun paid Tom Lincoln five hundred dollars to marry Nancy Hanks and take her out of Virginia, and the child born to her was none other than Abraham Lincoln. Although the story utterly disregarded the fact that Abraham was born as the second child three years after the marriage of his parents, it was republished many times and is still believed by some people. Other gossip was based merely on the similarities of Lincoln to tall, slender, long armed, long legged men who lived in the neighborhood of his birth.

Herndon was inclined for many years to believe the legend that Abe Enloe was Abraham Lincoln's real father, until it was finally discredited by a letter he received from Charles Friend of Hardin County, Ky., written in 1889 in answer to his inquiries. Charles was the grandson of Charles Friend, the reputed father of Dennis Hanks. It said:

"While living in Hodgenville there came a man from Illinois who said that it was reported in that state that Abe Enloe was Abe Lincoln's father. I heard the question put to old Uncle Abe Enloe, by my brother-in-law, Mr. A. H. Redman. There was another gentleman present, Dr. W. H. Holt. Redman asked if it was true that he, Abe Enloe, was Abe's father. The old man . . . remarked that it was an honor to be proud of even to be thought to be the father of a President . . . of these United States, 'But,' he said, 'I was only fifteen years old when Abe was born.' 'Then,' said Redman, 'you could not have been, being at that time only fourteen years old when he was begotten.' 'Now,' said Uncle Abe, 'not too fast, for I passed into puberty at fourteen and could have been his father at that age as easily as at any time from that until the present moment. Now to set the matter forever at rest, I will say I never put my hand on her naked flesh, or any part of her body save her hands, and never in my life had carnal intercourse with her. I think all this grew out of his name being the same as mine, but I can account for that name; his grandfather was named Abraham Lincoln." . . .

Charles Friend's letter continued: "You asked me a question, was he, Thomas Lincoln castrated? I heard a cousin of my father, Judge Jonathan Friend Cessna, say that his father, William Cessna, said that Thomas Lincoln could not have been Abe's father, for one of Thomas' testicles was not larger than a pea or perhaps both of them were no larger than peas." (Hertz, 1938.) Such was gossip's source of the myth of the birth of the hero.

Public Fascination for Myths of Illegitimacy

The myth of Lincoln's illegitimate birth will probably never die. It pleases the jealousy of man's frustrated egocentric desire to be somehow first in public importance by making supreme heroes like Moses, Buddha, Christ, and Lincoln have some kind of unusual quality of birth. It crops out in most unexpected ways with allegations of illegitimacy assumed to be true and spread by gossip without reservation of doubt. The pictorial magazine *Look* published (December 1953) the private diary of Harold Ickes, Secretary of the Interior in President Franklin Delano Rossevelt's cabinet. Ickes said, under the caption, "Lincoln Legitimacy:"

"While Speaker [Henry T.] Rainey and I were at the White House the President brought up a very interesting matter. He had been told that the greatest private collection of Lincolniana in the country was in the possession of an estate in New York, which was anxious to sell it.
    "The President and the Speaker discussed the possibility of the purchase by the Government of this collection; and it was agreed that the purchase should be made if the material could be bought at a reasonable price. . . . The Speaker said that some of the material had only recently been examined. He said that letters in the collection proved conclusively that Lincoln was illegitimate and he asked the President whether, in the event of a purchase by the Government, these facts should be suppressed or destroyed. The President said that they should not be, that Lincoln's parents were married before

Lincoln himself was born, and I made the remark that, even if he were born before the marriage of his parents, Lincoln was Lincoln just the same, and I thought it would be a great mistake to destroy documentary evidence, the destruction of which would be greatly deplored in times to come."

In the light of ample disproof of this old gossip the comments were unjustifiably speculative and the reckless publication of them by Ickes unfortunate. It was repeated in Ickes' diary, to be read by many impressionable young people who will take no more trouble than these men did to get their information straight and their impressions right on the parents of Lincoln.

Question of Tom Lincoln's Fertility

It seems quite certain that some of Tom Lincoln's household and neighbors in Kentucky and Indiana doubted his fertility and the paternity of his children during Abraham's boyhood. The doubt seems to have been based on the gossip of Dennis Hanks, who lived in Tom Lincoln's home many years, and of other men in Kentucky and Indiana, who observed that he had a small scrotum and assumed it to mean either undescended testicles or atrophy of the testicles following mumps. These observations must be given due consideration.

Ainsworth-Davis (1950), a medical authority on the genital diseases of human males, says that unilateral orchitis following mumps after 25 years of age is very rare, and bilateral orchitis is extremely rare. Sterility and atrophy of the testis follows, but sexual virility may be retained since the cells that produce the sex hormones remain viable, although the cells that produce the sperm are destroyed or rendered infertile.

The question of incomplete scrotal descent of the testes must also be considered. When a testis fails to pass through the external muscular ring of the abdomen it does not develop and does not become spertamogenic, because the normal temperature of the body is excessive for the germ cells, although not for the endocrine cells. When it passes through the external ring far enough to be covered only by skin, but does not descend into the scrotum, it is generally exposed to low enough external temperature to develop and become fertile. In such cases the scrotum remains undeveloped and is visibly smaller than normal. Many a family has a father with unilateral or bilateral testes that never completely descended into the scrotum (Ainsworth-Davis, 1950).

If Tom Lincoln had undescended testicles and ever doubted his own fertility, his wife's conceptions either convinced him of being a complete man or else sexually deficient, depending on his faith in her fidelity.

The evidence indicates that Tom Lincoln had an observable scrotal deficiency as the result of the failure of the testicles to descend completely but that he was fertile. This inference is supported by Herndon's admission of inability to find any neighbor in Indiana who knew if Tom ever had the mumps. It seems that sterility by disease can be disregarded as improbable.

Significance of Family Resemblance

With the exception of his coarse black hair, Abraham is said to have thought that he had more of his mother's physical and mental qualities than his father's. His unusual facial lines and muscles, as shown by comparable photographs, were definitely a Hanks characteristic and genetically maternal in origin. However, comparable portraits of Abraham Lincoln and his second cousin, David Lincoln, published by Tarbell (1924), also show a striking resemblance of the eyes, nose, mouth, and ego-attitudinal expression. It is remarkable that such unusual features were similar in both the Lincoln and Hanks families.

Strong evidence that Tom Lincoln was the father of Abraham exists in the likeness of a certain unusual hereditary trait in both men and in Tom's brother Mordecai. Abraham became an unusually clever story teller and humorist like his father and uncle. Although this is not a very uncommon trait and a son may have learned from watching the father how to tell jokes and amusing stories effectively, its development to an unusual degree, like any other art, requires more inheritance of such abilities than is found in most people. This kind of evidence, however, may not have been given much consideration by Lincoln.

Sarah, Lincoln's sister, who had a short thick body, and Abraham, with long thin body, were markedly different constitutional types. But such differences are not unusual in families. Sarah had more of her father's type of body, whereas Abraham had strongly his mother's. Based on physical similarities and differences between parents and children it would be as logical to say that Sarah could not have been Nancy's daughter as to say that Abraham could not have been Tom's son. Both children had very similar traits of personality found in both parents—talkativeness, kindness, good humored sociability, independence, honesty, dutifulness, and love of freedom and justice.

What Young Lincoln Was Told about His Parents

Whether or not Abraham Lincoln was the natural son of Tom Lincoln has now no historical significance. However, in an analytical biography of the development of mental attitude and personality and philosophy of human relations we must consider what he said that is relevant to it and the alternative possibilities of meaning.

There are many significant records indicating the biases of conditioning effects of young Lincoln's family's sexual ways on the development of his thinking in childhood on the moralities and immoralities of human nature and sexual relations. They must be given due consideration if we will understand his attitude. We have traced back to the earliest memories of his childhood his vigorous demands to be informed by his people so that he could understand the implied meanings of their double talk, and his uncompromising irritability as a child, and later as a man, over being confused by indefinite meanings. In counteracting contrast we find that he constantly practiced, as child and adult, the utmost accuracy, simplicity, and directness of self-expression in speaking and writing.

Young Abe's demands for explanations of the secret meanings of the double talk of his people naturally tended to develop the force and drive of restless urge to get the truths of sexual relations of his elders and the births in his family, after he learned of the illegitimacy of his mother, Dennis, and other cousins. Naturally the boy wanted to know about the sexual relations of his own parents in order to know the truth of his origin.

Young Abe probably saw in the intimacy of life in the one room cabin and in swimming in the creek that his father had a small scrotum. He probably learned also from his imaginative, 10 years older, "base born" cousin Dennis, that it was believed this meant his father had small testicles and could not produce children. No doubt he learned early in childhood that his mother and Dennis and other cousins in the family did not have fathers who were married to their mothers. He also might as a child have become influenced by the cunning talk of Dennis, who would naturally have liked to have him think he was "base born" like himself, to half believe this for some time.

Insofar as the boy questioned his father's fertility he then would naturally think that his mother had sexual relations with some other man, with her husband's approval, in order to have children. Since he felt constantly grateful to his mother for his birth, and they loved each other, he would be inclined to feel that he was a wanted child by both parents. If such had been the case, it is conceivable from what followed that an unusual boy might have become sufficiently inspired to regard his mother as a "heroic" woman and want to redeem her honor by making himself a thoroughly worth while, respectable man who would some day, somehow, vindicate his birth by making a contribution to the moral improvement of human relations.

Perhaps the most impressive statement from Lincoln, giving an unintentional indication that he might at times have been doubtful of the legitimacy of his own birth, was made in a speech at Columbus, Ohio, February 13, 1861, when on the way to Washington to accept the presidency. He compared his position as the leader of a nation facing secession with that of President Washington, as the "Father of his country."

> "I cannot but know what you all know, that, without a name [reputation], perhaps without a reason why I should have a name, there has fallen upon me a task such as did not rest upon even the Father of his country, and so feeling I cannot but turn back and look for the support without which it will be impossible for me to perform that great task. I turn, then, and look to the American people and to that God who has never forsaken them."

In interpreting the unconscious, involitional determination of this statement, which like all conscious volitional thinking is unconsciously determined by past as well as present environmental conditions, we must remember that he intended to express in humility his feelings about his lowly origin in contrast to Washington's aristocratic ancestry. However, the foregoing considerations do not enable us to feel that we understand how a youth of Lincoln's strength of character and independence of mind could have developed under continuous submission to illiterate, impulsive Tom Lincoln's unjust authority if he seriously doubted that he was his son.

In the letter that Dennis wrote to Abe in 1858 about his aging father longing to see him before he dies, he appealed to him as his "only child that is his flush [sic] and blood" to grant him this wish. Herein is definite indication from Dennis that he really believed Abraham was the real son of Thomas Lincoln and that Thomas Lincoln also believed this. It seems improbable that Dennis would have so sentimentally expressed his appeal to his old friend and relative had either he or Abe or Tom believed that Abe was an extramarital son of Nancy. This evidence discredits the interpretation by Herndon of the statement he claimed to have been made to him by Dennis, that Tom Lincoln was sterile and Abraham Lincoln could not have been his real son.

Lincoln's Faith in His Father

Proof for a child of its paternity can only be established by physical and personal resemblances between himself and his father and his faith in the loyalty and devotion of his mother to him.

The strongest indications that Abraham was the son of Thomas Lincoln are: (1) the probability that Tom Lincoln had fertile though undescended testes; (2) the physical likeness shown in photographs of Abraham for a Lincoln relative as well as for a Hanks relative; (3) the similarity of some hereditary personal characteristics in father and son; (4) Lincoln's own statements about his father; (5) his respect for his real mother and her devotion to her husband and his continued obedience and loyalty to the inconsiderate authority of his father after his second marriage; (6) Nancy named her first son Abraham after her husband's father and named her second son Thomas after her husband; and (7) Mr. and Mrs. Lincoln named their fourth son Thomas ("Taddie") after his father Thomas.

We have fairly evaluated the first three points and will now consider the remainder.

The most convincing evidence that Abraham Lincoln believed himself to be the son of Thomas Lincoln appears in the statements about his ancestry that he made in private letters to Lincoln relatives, many years before he thought that he might become a candidate for the presidency, and in the letter to his stepbrother with a special message to his dying father, and in autobiographical letters after his candidacy became possible.

To David Lincoln (3, 24, 1848):

"Your very worthy representative, Gov. McDowell has given me your name and address, and, as my father was born in Rockingham, from whence his father, Abraham Lincoln, emigrated to Kentucky, about the year 1782, I have concluded to address you to ascertain whether we are not of the same family. I shall be much obliged, if you will write me, telling me, whether you in any way know anything of my grandfather, what relation you are to him, and so on. Also, if you know, where your family came from, when they settled in Virginia, tracing them back as far as your knowledge extends."

To Solomon Lincoln (3, 24, 1848):

"Yours of the 21st. is received. I shall not be able to answer your interrogatories very fully; I will, however, do the best I can. I have mentioned that my grandfather's name was Abraham. He had, as I think I have heard, four brothers, Isaac, Jacob, Thomas and John. He had three sons, Mordecai, Josiah, and Thomas, the last, my father. My uncle Mordecai, had three sons, Abraham, James and Mordecai. Uncle Josiah had several daughters, and an only son Thomas. My father has an only child, myself, of course.

"This is all I know certainly on the subject of names; it is however my father's understanding that Abraham, Mordecai and Thomas are old family names of ours. The reason I did not mention Thomas as a family name in my other letter is because it is so very common a name, as to prove little, if anything, in the way of identification."

To Jesse Lincoln (4, 1, 1854):

"On yesterday I had the pleasure of receiving your letter of the 16th of March. From what you say there can be no doubt that you and I are of the same family. The history of your family, as you give it, is precisely what I have always heard, and partly know, of my own. As you have supposed, I am the grandson of your uncle Abraham; and the story of his death by the Indians, and of Uncle Mordecai, then fourteen years old, killing one of the Indians, is the legend more strongly than all others imprinted upon my mind and memory. I am the son of grandfather's youngest son, Thomas. I have often heard my father speak of his Uncle Isaac residing at Watauga (I think), near where the then States of Virginia, North Carolina, and Tennessee join,— you seem now to be some hundred miles or so west of that. I often saw Uncle Mordecai, and Uncle Josiah but once in my life; but I never resided near either of them. Uncle Mordecai died in 1831 or 2, in Hancock County, Illinois, where he had then recently removed from Kentucky, and where his children had also removed, and still reside, as I understand. Whether Uncle Josiah is dead or living, I cannot tell, not having heard from him for more than twenty years. When I last heard of him he was living on Big Blue River, in Indiana (Harrison Co., I think), and where he had resided ever since before the beginning of my recollection. My father (Thomas) died the 17th of January, 1854, in Coles County, Illinois, where he had resided twenty years. I am his only child. I have resided here, and hereabouts, twenty-three years. I am forty-five years of age, and have a wife and three children, the oldest eleven years. My wife was born and raised at Lexington, Kentucky; and my connection with her has sometimes taken me there, where I have heard the older people of her relations speak of your uncle Thomas and his family. He is dead long ago, and his descendants have gone to some part of Missouri, as I recollect what I was told. When I was at Washington in 1848, I got up a correspondance with David Lincoln, residing in Sparta, Rockingham County, Virginia, who, like yourself, was a first cousin of my father; but I forget, if he informed me, which of my grandfather's brothers was his father. With Col. Crozier, of whom you speak, I formed quite an intimate acquaintance, for a short one, while at Washington; and when you meet him again I will thank you to present him my respects. Your present governor, Andrew Johnson, was also at Washington while I was; and he told me of there being people of the name of Lincoln in Carter County, I think. I can no longer claim to be a young man myself, but I infer that, as you are of the same generation as my father, you are some older. I shall be very glad to hear from you again. Very truly your relative,"

"My Father's Child"

Lincoln, when president, liked to make brief informal remarks to troops passing through Washington to impress them with the importance of winning the war. On one occasion during the campaign of 1864 he said to the 166th Ohio regiment:

"It is not merely for today, but for all time to come, that we should perpetuate for our children's children that great and free government which we have enjoyed all our lives. I beg you to remember this, not merely for my sake, but for yours. I happen temporarily, to occupy the White House. I am a living witness that any one of your children may look to come here as my father's child has. It is in order that each of you may have, through this free government . . . equal privileges in the race of life, with all its desirable human aspirations. It is for this the struggle should be maintained, that we may not lose our birthright."

To Fell (12, 20, 1859) he wrote:

"My paternal grandfather, Abraham Lincoln, emigrated from Rockingham County, Virginia, to Kentucky, about 1781. . . . My father, at the death of his father, was but six years of age."

To Scripps (6, 1860):

"Abraham was born Feb. 12, 1809, then in Hardin, now in the more recently formed county of Larue, Kentucky. His father, Thomas, & grandfather Abraham, were born in Rockingham county Virginia."

Lincoln's frequent references in private and public letters, to Thomas Lincoln as "my father" and Abraham Lincoln as "my grandfather" are not unquestionable evidence that he believed himself to be Tom Lincoln's real son, for he addressed his stepmother as "mother," and signed his letters to her "affectionately your son;" hence other indications of the nature of his belief must also be given consideration.

It is conceivable that a sensitive boy, or man, would claim himself to be the son of his mother's husband, in order to avoid social defamation even though he secretely believed him to be sterile and himself the illegitimate son of another man. However, if this were so it is not likely that he would have repeatedly searched the history of his paternal ancestry and given repeatedly, under appropriate circumstances, consistent accounts of the origin of his father, grandfather, uncles, and cousins in order to trace connections between himself and distant paternal relatives. It is more natural that a man as fundamentally honest as Abraham Lincoln would not have pretended in private letters to be related to his father's distant cousins when there was no necessity for seeking such connections. It is also probable that, had he been doubtful of his paternity, he would not have lied in public letters to gain a political nomination or election. Lincoln said "an honest man is the noblest work of God," and this was the moral standard he applied rigorously to himself throughout life.

It seems almost inconceivable that an honest man who expressed so carefully, as Lincoln did, what he really knew and what he was doubtful about in his father's family and relatives, and repeatedly identified himself as the grandson of Abraham Lincoln and the son of Thomas Lincoln, in many letters to inquiring relatives and spontaneous public talks, would have any doubt about the truth of his positive statements. Whoever persists in doubting the truth of Lincoln's faith in his father and mother consistently questions the legitimacy of his own paternity and that of every child of every woman, for only by faith in the fidelity of the mother to her husband is the fatherhood of the child established in the family.

When we compare the indicative evidence of Lincoln's attitude toward his mother's family and his father's, we find that he was proud of his Lincoln connections, and reticent about his Hanks connections for obvious moral objections to the promiscuity of his mother's relatives. Nevertheless, he believed in the honesty of his mother and, as he liked to say, her word was "the truth and the law to me." Only one letter written by Lincoln to a member of the Hanks family about their relatives has been found, but this cannot be taken as proof of lack of interest in his mother's people for other letters may have been lost or destroyed.

Four letters, two public and two private, are known in which he referred to his mother or her family, and they all show no little reticence. In the autobiographical letter to Fell (1859) he said: "My mother, who died in my tenth year, was of a family by the name of Hanks, some of whom now reside in Adams and others in Macon County, Illinois." In his Scripps letter (1860) he said: "He [father[married Nancy Hanks—mother of the present subject—in the year 1806. She was also born in Virginia; and relatives of hers of the name of Hanks, and of other names, now reside in Coles, in Macon and in Adams Counties, Illinois, and also in Iowa."

In his letter to Sam Haycraft (5, 28, 1860) he said: "My father was Thomas Lincoln and Mrs. Sally Johnston was his second wife. You are mistaken about my mother—her maiden name was Nancy Hanks."

In the following letter, written August 24, 1860 to his mother's cousin, John Hanks, in reply to an inquiry from him, Lincoln showed definite fear of public prejudice for his mother's family's reputation being aroused against him during the campaign. Since boyhood Lincoln had always regarded John, who was four years older, with affection and respect. They had split rails together in Indiana and Illinois and John had presented some rails at the State Republican Convention as Lincoln's work. Lincoln had won the nomination as the "rail splitter" candidate for President when this letter was written.

> "Yours of the 23rd. is received. My recollection is that I never lived in the same neighborhood with Charles Hanks till I came to Macon county, Illinos [sic], after I was twenty-one years of age. As I understand, he and I were born in different counties of Kentucky, and never saw each other in that State; that while I was a very small boy my father removed to Indiana, and your father with his family remained in Kentucky for many years. At length you, a young man grown, came to our neighborhood, and were at our house, off and on, a great deal for three, four or five years; and during the time, your father, with his whole family, except William, Charles, and William Miller, who had married one of your sisters, came to the same neighborhood in Indiana, and remained a year or two, and then went to Illinois."

The letter recalled other contacts with the Hanks family in Illinois and then closed:

> "This is, as I remember it. Dont let this letter be made public by any means."

Significance of Young Lincoln's Acceptance of Paternal Authority

The most convincing indicative evidence that Abraham Lincoln believed that he was the son of Thomas Lincoln exists in obedient submission to his authority until he became of legal age, even though at times his commands were unreasonably impulsive, ill tempered, and painfully unjust. Despite his father's rough, inconsiderate attitude in killing his pet pig, and indifference to his mother's funeral rites, and many blunt attempts to discourage his efforts at extending his education and make him help with the work, Abe continued to live at home with him and his stepmother in Indiana and then moved with them to Illinois and helped them build a new cabin there, and later provided legal means of insuring their permanent security. It is improbable that a vigorous, healthy, highly independent minded, fearless, self-reliant youth like Abe Lincoln, who was far better educated and more intelligent than Tom Lincoln, and a good enough woodsman, farmer, carpenter, and boatman to have easily earned a living in a world teeming with exciting adventures and rich rewards for young braves, could have continued to live at home after his New Orleans experience in obedience to the authority of a man whom he believed was not really his father.

We have seen how deeply Lincoln was impressed in childhood by his mother's strength of character, candor and truthfulness, loyalty to her husband and his family, and, above all, her moral teachings. We will see, again and again, how he applied "her word as his law" to the social problems of his time. These convictions were often expressed with more candor and courage than any man of his time, despite intensely bitter public criticism. Biographical analysis must trace the origins of such important convictions back to the particular conditioning experiences of childhood.

Lincoln held masterfully as a lawyer, political debater with Douglas, and in the Cooper Institute address, and as president, that all laws should be obeyed until repealed, but judicial interpretations of their meanings, even by the Supreme Court of the United States, are open to question and political refutation by the people. The reaction pattern of dutiful submission to law and authoritative judgment was established in childhood, but the habit of questioning the interpretations and meanings and applications of law was also then established.

Perhaps the best illustration of Lincoln's strong moral attitude toward his father exists in his acceptance speech when nominated in 1858 by the Illinois republicans as their candidate for the United States Senate. Although strongly advised by his confidential friends against it, he said: "A house divided against itself cannot stand. I believe this nation cannot endure permanently half slave and half free."

He saw the people of the nation as one great family that needed to abide by the rules of good family life. We can be reasonably confident that no sensible man would have so conspicuously and forcefully presented this moral precept had he doubted his father's fertility and his mother's fidelity to him.

Lincoln's application of conviction that a house divided against itself cannot stand indicated definitely that he had easily repressed in childhood the naturally affectionate rivalry of a healthy boy with his father in claiming his mother's attentions, under belief in his mother's goodness and the truth of her word. He learned early that unity and fidelity were essential to happy family life, and he applied it with remarkable constancy as well in the house of his father's second marriage and later in his own marriage.

We can be reasonably certain in the light of modern psychopathology and attitude analysis that, if Nancy Hanks Lincoln were promiscuous before and after marriage, and her children were incidentally fathered by men other than her husband, she, having far superior energy, intelligence and literacy, would not have remained an obedient, respectful, dutiful, and loving wife to him. A young, vigorous, spirited woman, who had a sterile, lazy husband, would probably not have stopped being promiscuous after she had three children. She would inevitably have grown dissatisfied, irritable, contemptuous, and hated living with him. He would have grown jealous, suspicious, mean, and hateful toward her and the children, as he became more and more conscious of his inferiority to other men and sensed their scorn and ridicule of him.

If Abraham Lincoln had believed as a young boy and later in adolescence, that he was the son of some man other than his legal father, it would have had an insidious, profoundly demoralizing effect on the development of his personality. He probably would, as is generally the case with a wantonly promiscuous mother, have retained his immoral childhood erotic interest and therewith grown up in moral indifference. The stigma of bastard inferiority would have been contemptuously thrown up to him by children of legitimate superiority and he would have grown bitterly resentful and socially nihilistic. He would have felt himself to be irreparably inferior to other boys and cynical, if not hateful, of law and morals. His attitude toward his mother would have grown heedless if not disobedient and disrespectful. Toward his domineering, lazy, weak father, he would have grown challenging, rebellious, and disdainful. He would have developed under the vigorous erotism and temptations of adolescence into an unmoral boy, indulging himself freely in irresponsible, promiscuous sexual relations, in the tradition of his mother's relatives.

But he was always in childhood conscientious, truthful and obedient, and developed into a highly conscientious, dutiful, moral, and sexually self-controlled boy and man. He remained respectful and devoted to his father and new mother, and to his sister and stepsisters and stepbrother, and later a constant husband and affectionate father. His confession to Herndon, after his father's death, about the illegitimate birth of his mother only shows that he was still deeply impressed by it.

It seems, therefore, most logical from indicative evidence that we believe that Abraham Lincoln believed Thomas Lincoln was his real father.

Chapter VI

YOUTH

Tom Lincoln needed a wife badly to keep house for his family and help with the farm. Fourteen months after the death of Nancy he returned to Kentucky to persuade an old childhood friend, Mrs. Sally (also Sarah) Bush Johnston, now a widow with a son and two daughters about the ages of his children, to marry him. Sally Bush had once refused him, but now he would try again. With simple, straightforward business he made his proposal as soon as he found her. By the house he said, as retold by her neighbor Samuel Haycraft: "Well Miss Johnston, I have no wife and you have no husband. I came a purpose to marry you. I knowed you from a gal and you knowed me from a boy. I have no time to lose; and if you are willin' let it be done straight off." To this she replied after she had recovered her aplomb: "Tommy, I know you well, and have no objection to marrying you; but I cannot do it straight off, as I owe some debts that must first be paid." The debt was said by relatives to have been two dollars and fifty cents and Tom at once offered to pay it (Lamon, 1872).

Sally Bush came of a better educated family than Tom Lincoln's. She was an energetic, self-reliant, resourceful, thrifty, intelligent, honest, courageous, generous woman, and she knew Tom Lincoln to be a good, kindly, honest, straightforward and respectable, if easy-going man. Upon urging by her friends she yielded and married him the next day, December 2, 1819. They loaded her household furniture, bedding, cooking utensils and clothing into a wagon and, with her three children, John, Elizabeth, and Matilda, departed at once for the Indiana home.

Resolute Stepmother

Here she found that her new husband's representations of his property and possessions had been "too glowing," if not fancifully untrue. The meanness and poverty-stricken condition of the place appalled her, but her pride and Christian sense of duty and the pathetic needs of his children decided her to make the best of it. She firmly refused to sell her furniture upon her husband's request to raise money, and made him put a floor, door, and window into the cabin and improve the living conditions of the place. Later he built a new cabin of half-hewn timbers for her.

Dennis described it to Herndon:

> "In the fall and winter of 1819-20 we commenced to cut the trees, clear out the brush and underwoods and forest for our new grand old log cabin. . . . It was one story, eighteen by twenty feet, one passage [door], one window, no glass in it. The lights were made from the leaf coming off

from the hog's fat. This was good and mellow light and lasted well. The house was sufficiently high to make a kind of bedroom overhead, a loft. This was approached by a kind of ladder made by boring holes in the logs forming one side of the house, and thus peg over peg we climbed aloft, the pegs creaking and screeching as we went. Here were the beds; the floor of the loft was clapboards, and the beds lay on this. Here I and Abe slept."

With superior intelligence and resolute character Sally was able to work out a harmonious relationship with her husband. Apparently she had much of the character of Tom's mother for he willingly accepted her wishes and judgment. They became active members of the Pigeon Creek Baptist Church and Tom served on several of its committees.

With remarkable persistence, energy and resourcefulness, Sarah (Sally) succeeded in inducing Tom to improve himself and the family's livelihood, but the greatest reward for her genius came through her inspiring encouragement of young Abraham.

Abe and His New "Mother"

"She proved a good and kind mother to Abraham," he wrote in his Scripps letter. She found him still dressed, although nearly 11 years old, in a long, one piece, linsey shirt such as he had always worn as a child. She put him in pants and dressed him like other boys of his age. He responded with complete appreciation, love, and devotion for his new "mother." She made me "feel like a human being," he said, and often referred to her as his "saintly mother" in a tone much like his reference to his real mother as his "angel mother." No longer would paternal indifference and social ridicule blight his world. The two sets of children lived together harmoniously, and his new mother loved, encouraged, and rewarded him as her own son. She found him at first shy and cautious but easily alert, inquisitive, and intelligently talkative with a hearty-laughing sense of humor, regardless of an extremely lanky, leggy, awkward body and homely face with large ears and nose and uncut, unkempt hair.

Mrs. Lincoln, when 75, was interviewed by Herndon in 1865 (Hertz, 1938) on her relations with the Lincoln children. Her description of Abe as a boy, though 40 years retrospective, was understanding and largely dependable:

"When I landed in Indiana, the country was wild and desolate. Abe was a good boy; he didn't like physical labor, was diligent for knowledge, wished to know, and if pains and labor would get it, he was sure to get it. He was the best boy I ever saw. He read all the books he could lay his hands on. . . . I think newspapers were in Indiana as early as 1824. . . . Abe was a constant reader of them. . . . Abe . . . had no particular religion, didn't think of that question at that time, if he ever did. He never talked about it."

On his reading habits she said:

"He read diligently, studied in the day time, didn't after night much, went to bed early, got up early, and then read, ate his breakfast, got to work in the field with the men. . . . When he came to a passage that struck him, he would write it down on boards if he had no paper and keep it there till he did get paper, then he would rewrite it, look at it, repeat it. He had a copybook, a kind of scrap book, in which he put down all things and then preserved them. He ciphered on boards when he had no paper or no slate, and when the board would get too black, he would shave it off with a drawing knife and go on again."

About young Lincoln's compulsion to understand she said (italics inserted for characterization):

"Abe, when old folks were at our house, was a silent and attentive observer, never speaking or asking til they were gone, and *then he must understand everything, even to the smallest thing, minutely and exactly; he would then repeat it over to himself again and again, sometimes in one form and then in another, and when it was fixed in his mind to suit him, he became easy and he never lost that fact or his understanding of it.* Sometimes he seemed perturbed to give expression to his ideas and got mad, almost, at one who couldn't explain plainly what he wanted to convey.

"He would hear sermons, . . . come home, take the children out, get on a stump or log, and almost repeat it word for word, . . . His father made him quit sometimes, as the men quit their work. Mr. Lincoln (Tom) could read a little and could scarcely write his name. . . . I induced my husband to permit Abe to read and study at home. At first he was not easily reconciled to it, but finally he was willing to encourage him to a certain extent. . . . I can say what scarcely one woman, a mother, can say in a thousand and it is this: Abe never gave me a cross word or look and never refused in fact, or even in appearance, to do anything I requested him. I never gave him a cross word in all my life. He was kind to everybody and to everything and always accomodated others if he could, would do so willingly if he could. His mind and mine, what little I had, seemed to run together, more in the same channel. Abe could easily learn and long remember, and when he did learn anything he learned it well and thoroughly.

"He was fond of fun, sports, wit and jokes . . . he was always in good health, never sick, was very careful of his person, . . . cared nothing for clothes, so that they were clean and neat, further cut no figure with him, . . . he was more fleshy in Indiana than ever in Illinois. . . . He never drank whiskey or other strong drink, was temperate in all things, too much so, I thought sometimes. He *never told me a lie in his life, never evaded, never quarreled, never dodged nor turned a corner to avoid any chastisement or other responsibility.* He never swore or used profane language in my presence nor in others' that I now remember of. . . . He listened to the aged, argued with his equals, but played with the children. He *loved animals generally and treated them kindly; he loved children well, very well. . . . Abe didn't care much for crowds . . . was not very fond of girls . . . he sometimes attended church* . . . he was dutiful to me always. . . . I had a son John who was raised with Abe. Both were good boys, but I must say, both now being dead, that Abe was the best boy I ever saw."

The above sketch of Abe Lincoln's youth by his aged "mother," gives a consistent understanding of their attitudes toward each other. It also indicates how Abe displaced her own son John in her affections. This difference in her transference encouraged Abe to develop a consistent, self-reliant, constructive mind, whereas John became a shiftless, discontented neer-do-well, later dependent on Abe (see Chapter XXI).

Adolescent Growth

In his 11th year, not long after the injury of his brain, Abe grew from a long, thin, skinny boy to a tall, lean, lanky youth. In this period, he tired easily according to his neighbor, David Turnham: "He seemed to change in appearance and action. Although quick-witted and ready with an answer, he began to exhibit deep thoughtfulness, and was so often lost in studied reflection we could not help noticing the strange turn in his actions. He disclosed rare timidity and sensitiveness, especially in the presence of men and women, and although cheerful enough in the presence of the boys, he did not appear to seek our company as earnestly as before." (Herndon & Weik, 1889). This condition was probably a phase of physical recovery and neural readjustment in the beginning of adolescence.

Abe was a kindly, sympathetic, honest boy and made friends easily when he desired. He bore no prejudices and shirked no challenge of his rights, courage, or manliness, and never let himself be enticed into meanness by other boys. Although endlessly ridiculed about his extremely long arms and legs, awkward movements, and big ears, he continued to answer such joking with good natured wit and laughter and retain his self-confidence and respectability.

Self-Education

Young Lincoln, age 14 to 16 (1824-26) made a book by cutting wrapping paper into sheets and sewing them together. He entitled it "Abraham Lincoln, His Book." In it he copied from an arithmetic and other books such ideas as he wanted particularly to remember and use. He wrote in it:

> Abraham Lincoln,
> His hand and pen,
> He will be good
> But God knows when.

His question "What do you observe?" and careful notations give evidence of unusual determination to analyze things to the smallest detail and get his memory and understanding exactly right. Whenever he solved a problem in mathematics by addition or multiplication he verified the answer by subtraction or division, and vice versa. He checked each procedure by applying the opposite procedure—a principle now recognized as indispensable in modern science.

Later this early established, deeply habitual, careful analytical thinking became his strongest and most useful characteristic as a lawyer and president.

The records are not consistent but it seems that he attended school in Indiana, when a teacher was available, in short periods in the winter months for several years, mostly at 10, 14, and 17 years of age. The last school was four miles from home, and as he walked along the wilderness road he often

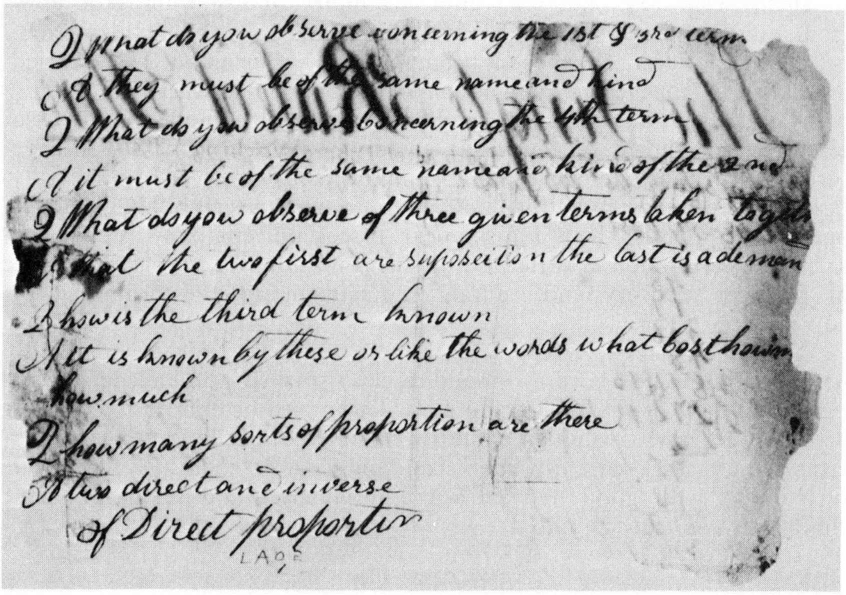
Q what do you observe concerning the 1st & 3rd term
A They must be of the same name and kind
Q What do you observe concerning the 4th term
A it must be of the same name and kind of the 2nd
Q What do you observe of three given terms taken toget[her]
A that the two first are supposition the last is a deman[d]
Q how is the third term known
A it is known by these or like the words what cost how[many]
how much
Q how many sorts of proportion are there
A two direct and inverse
Of Direct proportion

PLATE 4. Page from Young Lincoln's "Sum Book." "What do you observe?" From the original manuscript in the McLellan Lincoln Collection in Brown University Library.

recited aloud what he had learned. Abe's determination to educate himself reminds us of his grandmother Lucy Hanks.

He read over and over Bunyan's *Pilgrim's Progress,* Aesop's *Fables, Robinson Crusoe,* Franklin's *Autobiography,* and the *Bible.* His cousin Sophie Hanks, who lived in their house, told her descendants that when he learned from his teacher that grammars were written to teach people how to talk properly he walked for miles in the community in search of one that he could borrow. He then studied it so well that he knew more grammar than his

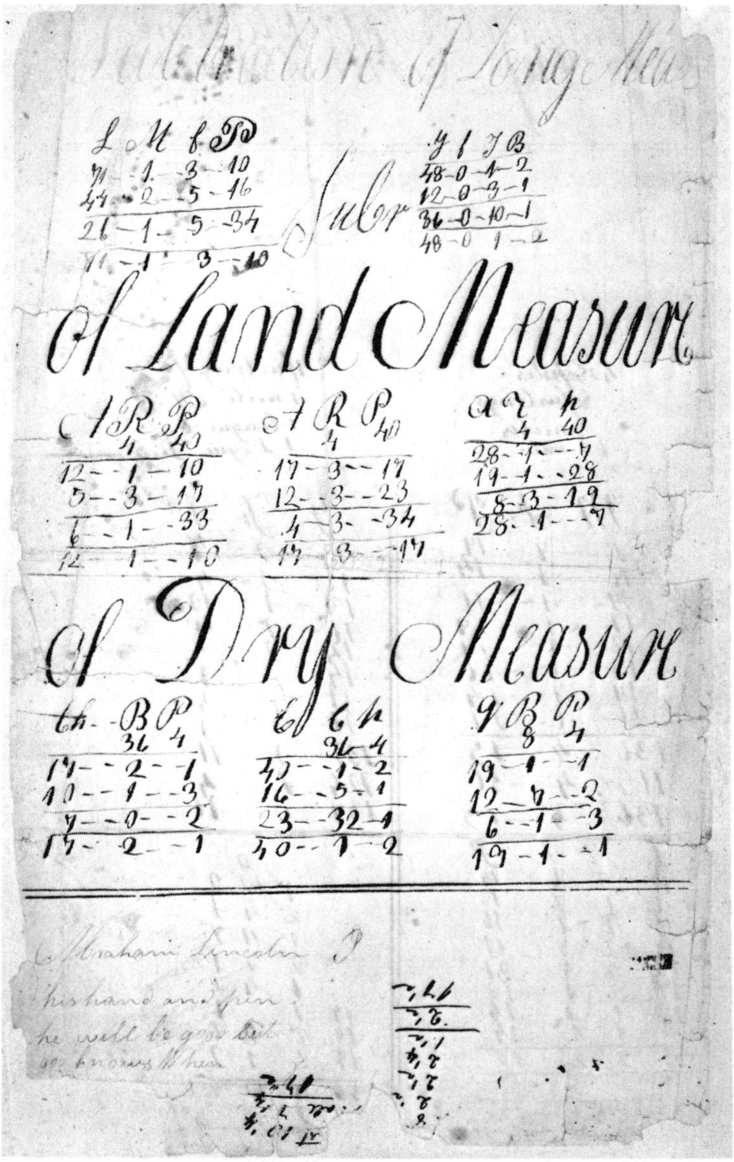

PLATE 5. Page from Young Lincoln's "Sum Book." "Land Measure and Dry Measure." From the Herndon-Weik Collection, Library of Congress.

teacher. He borrowed Pike's *Arithmetic* and copied many of its lessons in his scrap book. He also borrowed *Sinbad the Sailor* and the *Kentucky Preceptor* and memorized various poems for reciting in school. Weems' *Life of Washington* impressed him greatly by giving him the heroic, personal example of a great leader of the people. This book became soiled by rain and he paid for it several times over its real worth by working in the fields for "Old Blue Nose" Crawford, at 25 cents a day. He also managed to buy a copy of Barclay's *Dictionary.*

Dennis Hanks, who lived with the Lincolns for 12 years, and at 21 married Sarah's daughter Elizabeth Johnston, age 15, gave an intimate account of Abe's relations with his father: "Abe was a constant and I might say stubborn reader, his father having sometimes to slash him for neglecting his work by reading. Mr. Lincoln, Abe's father, often said: 'I had to pull the old sow up to the trough,' when speaking of Abe's reading and how he got to it then; and now he had to pull her away." (Hertz, 1938.)

Abe's brother-in-law and schoolmate, Aaron Grigsby, described him (Hertz, 1938) many years later as being the best pupil in school and a leader of the boys. Nat Grigsby, Aaron's brother, said they had spelling matches frequently and Abe was the best speller and was always ahead in his classes. "Crawford tried to learn us manners. He would ask the scholars to retire from the schoolroom, come in, and then some scholar would go around and introduce him to all the scholars. . . . Essays and poetry were not taught in the school . . . Abe took it up of his own accord."

Abe liked words and was the best at using them in the school. Since his side usually won in spelling matches he was sometimes eliminated in order to equalize the contests. On one occasion the word "defied" was misspelled by both sides and the teacher decided to try it around the second time. It finally came to pretty little Kate Robie whose charms pleased Abe. She began cautiously *"d-e-f"* and then was lost for what to guess next. Quickly she glanced at Abe for help who was grinning at her with encouragement from the back of the room. Slowly he put his finger up to his eye and taking the hint she finished *"i-e-d"* with a triumphant exclamation (Lamon, 1872).

Adolescent boys and girls must have heroes to worship in order to make sympathetic self-identifications with them and reflexly imitate their social attitudes, developing thereby consistency of mind. The idealized, exemplary meaning of Washington and his heroic feats for Lincoln, as a boy and later as a man, were often shown in his speeches. We quote here from one made as president-elect before the New Jersey Senate, February 21, 1861, in order to show what Washington meant to Abraham Lincoln in adolescence.

"Away back in my childhood, the earliest days of my being able to read, I got hold of a small book—Weems's *Life of Washington.* I remember all the accounts there given of battle fields and struggles for the liberties of the country, and none fixed themselves upon my imagination so deeply as the struggle here at Trenton, New Jersey." (Young Lincoln's impressions upon reading, at about 12, of Washington's crossing of the Delaware River with his army to attack Trenton, were no doubt conditioned by his experience as a boy of eight upon crossing the Ohio River in a small flatboat with his parents to conquer the wilderness of Indiana.) *"I recollect thinking then,"* he said, *"boy even though I was, that there must have been something more than common that those men struggled for"* (italics inserted).

John Hanks, age 20, lived for four years (1822-26) with the Lincolns. He described to Herndon (Hertz, 1938) how Lincoln read all the books he could get or lay hands on; he was a constant and voracious reader.

> "I never could get him in company with women; he was not timid in this particular but he did not seek such company. He was always full of stories . . . he would gather hickory bark, bring it home, and keep a light by it and read by it, when no lamp was to be had. . . . Abraham was a good, hearty eater [as many of his neighbors have testified]. . . . His own mother and step-mother were good cooks for their day and time. In the summer he wore tan linen pants and flax shirt and in the winter he wore linsey-woolsey, that is, during the time I was there.
>
> "When Abe and I returned to the house from work, he would go to the cupboard, snatch a piece of corn bread, take down a book, sit down in a chair, cock his legs up as high as his head, and read. He an I worked barefooted, grubbed it, ploughed, mowed and cradled together, plowed corn, gathered it, and shucked corn. Abraham read constantly when he had an opportunity."

His favorite books in his youth were the *Bible* and Aesop's *Fables*, largely for his interest in lessons on morality and equalitarian justice for the improvement of human relations. These two books, through teaching in adolescence the wisdom of understanding both the good and evil sides of human nature, by fact and fantasy, allegory and analogy, guided his way of thinking as well as his kind of thinking, probably, through endless reiteration, more than any other literary influence until he read Blackstone and Shakespeare in his mid-twenties. The most striking quality of young Lincoln's self-education was the eagerness and thoroughness with which he cultivated reasonable knowledge that gave him a well balanced, common-sense understanding of human nature and the ways of people with each other in everyday life.

Humorist and Orator

He liked to work for Mrs. Crawford. She was not only interested in him but owned more books than most of the neighbors. In her house, she said, he often "ciphered with a coal or with red keel that he got from the branches [creeks]; he smoothed and planed boards and wrote on them."

The few books that he could borrow were fortunately good ones and, reading them over and over, often at night in winter while lying on the floor by the light of a hickory bark flare, or while on his way to work, he memorized their best passages.

Abe liked to tell people about a new thing that he had learned, particularly when he thought it was something useful or wonderful. His passion for making stump speeches to anyone who would listen, grown-up or child, as well as for reciting aloud as he walked the trails to school or to work, gave amusement to the neighborhood. He was so clever and eloquent as a speaker by 16, that workmen would leave their jobs for the pleasure of listening to him. His stepsister, Matilda Johnston, recalled:

> "When father and mother would go to church, Abe would take down the *Bible*, read a verse, give out a hymn and we would sing." "He preached and we would do the crying and sometimes he would join in." "One day my brother, John, caught a land terrapin, brought it to the place where Abe was preaching, threw it against the tree and crushed its shell. It suffered much—quivered all over. Abe then preached against cruelty to animals, contending that an ant's life was as sweet to it as ours to us."

Girl-Shy Sublimation

When we consider the intimacy and temptations of Lincoln's adolescence while living in a one-room cabin with two stepsisters and several girl cousins, at least one of whom was illegitimate, we can best understand his shyness and modesty as being morally self- and home-defensive. He would generally leave the house early in the morning with his lunch and axe and walk several miles into the forest to where he was splitting rails. His "mother" strictly forbade her daughters, who were past puberty and extremely fond of Abe, to go with him. One morning Matilda, the younger, sneaked away from the cabin and followed him on the trail. She managed to creep up behind him and, with a scream, leaped on his back. Caught by surprise he fell and the axe cut her leg. He tore strips off his shirt and bound up the wound to stop the bleeding. Then he asked her, "What will you tell Mother?" She replied, "I'll tell her the truth. I cut my leg on the axe." "That won't be enough of the truth," Abe insisted, "you must tell her how it happened and trust her to understand it and do what is right." He was the soul of honor with his stepmother and stepsisters. He must keep the house from dividing against itself lest it fall.

Dressed in home-made deerskin pants that were much too tight and short for him, he would go to the dances but was too shy of physical contact with girls to be induced to learn the art. Eventually he would start telling droll stories to the boys and in uproarious laughter they would gather around him much to the distress of the neglected girls. His behavior in adolescence against the sexual temptations that surrounded him in a wilderness environment indicates a most unusually vigorous self-discipline in striking contrast to the freedom of his relatives. He was always a boy's boy and became later a man's man.

Lincoln grew up in an atmosphere of robust, pioneer vulgarity that was neither profane, indecent, nor immoral, but frankly unrestrained in enjoying the naturally humorous frustrations and incongruities of life. Many of the young people were sexually free, but respected each other in marriage. Dennis Hanks married Elizabeth Johnston, Abe's older step-sister, soon after her arrival in the family and John Hall later married her sister Matilda. Both couples fared well. Abe regarded sexual promiscuity as immoral and sublimated his repressions through hard study and the cultivation of an insatiable ambition to become a leader of his people. Like his father, he had an unusually good sense of humor and could elaborate scenes from everyday life for all they were worth. His wit was ready, keen and logical in making up elaborate stories out of homely observations. Talking in hill-billy vernacular, with slow, easy drawl and persuasive appeal, with a penchant for ending his tales with some witty but moral and practical philosophical Aesopian surprise, made him a delightful entertainer. In adolescence, and later as a man, he was morally obsessed to master his emotivations in consistent keeping with his inspiration of destiny to be a man of justice. No virtuous young knight ever sought the Holy Grail with higher principles or greater perseverence.

He told stories and jokes intentionally to make people laugh and thereby get himself to laugh, for then he was happiest as well as most influential. His productions, while apt and amusing, were in youth often grossly vulgar but never profane or vile. This effective technique continued unchanged as he grew into manhood. It became his best defense against the daily insidious tendency to yield to irrepressible, gloomy preoccupations over the futility of life.

Athletic Prowess and Mental Leadership

Abe's great height and unusual strength and determination in youth encouraged him to outdo the feats of physical skill that he saw others perform. In village gatherings he excelled in the tests of strength, courage, endurance, and will power. No one could equal him in using an axe. He could drive it deeper into a log and split more rails than anyone and he was generally the best wrestler in the crowd. He was proud of the weights he could lift and liked to stand with his feet flat and bend backwards until his hands touched the ground.

His egoistic attitude was always ready to defend the rights of weaker persons and of animals who were being mistreated. We have found evidence of this characteristic as early as six years of age, when he tried to save the life of his pet. As a boy in school and young man in the community, Lincoln was a natural mixer and leader of his age group, largely from confidence in his superior intelligence, size, and strength. As he grew older he tended to play the part of leader in more important groups, although his attitude was characterized by cautious, unaffected humility.

Cousin Dennis (Hertz, 1938) described Abe as "a tricky man."

> "Sometimes when he went to a log-house raising, corn shucking, and suchlike things, he would say to himself and sometimes to others, 'I don't want these fellows to work any more,' and instantly he would commence his pranks, tricks, jokes, stories, and sure enough all would stop, gather around Abe, and listen, sometimes crying and sometimes bursting their sides with laughter. He sometimes would mount a stump, chair, or box and make speeches . . . he never failed here. . . . He was . . . a kind of forward boy and sometimes too forward *when he got stubborn; his nature went an entire revolution.* . . . He was ambitious and determined, and when he attempted to excel man or boy his whole soul and his energies were bent on doing it, and he generally almost always accomplished his ends."

Postadolescent Poetry

At 15 Abe felt the urge to read and write poetry, although it was not taught in school and probably no one, unless it was his stepmother or Mrs. Crawford, read it. As Dennis told it: "At this early age he was more humorous than in after life, full of fun, wit, humor, and if he ever got a new story, new book, new fact or idea, he never forgot it." When 16 "he wrote a humorous rhyme on his friend Josiah Crawford that made all the neighbors, Crawford included, burst their sides with laughter."

Sarah (Abe's sister) married Aaron Grigsby when she was 19. She had grown up into a shy, sweet, kindly, understanding, truthful young woman. She was stocky and heavy muscled, more like her father than her mother and brother. But, according to Mrs. Elizabeth Crawford, for whom she often worked, she resembled Abe in disposition. Abe was 17 when in commemoration of the wedding he composed a poem to the meter of a folk song. We give four stanzas, as recalled by Mrs. Crawford (Hertz, 1938), since they show how his playful mood was colored by certain adolescent ideals which later, as we will see, dominated his own matrimonial interests.

Stanza 1

When Adam was created
He dwelt in Eden's shade,
As Moses has recorded,
And there sweet Eve was made.

Stanza 6

This woman was not taken
From Adam's feet we see
So he must not abuse her
The meaning seems to be.

Stanza 7
This woman was not taken
From Adam's head we know—
To show she must not rule him
Tis evidently so.

Stanza 9
Sweet Eve was taken near his heart
And so it seems quite clear,
Adam must always love her,
and she must hold him dear.

First Satire

From 30 to 45 years of age, Lincoln the politician passed through a phase of satirically ridiculing opponents. This disposition was preceded by a similar phase in youth. By his late teens, he had written many amusing satires and chronicles, most of them unprintable, on a variety of subjects such as weddings, fights, "Crawford's Nose," "Sister Gordon's Innocence," and the "Chronicles of Reuben."

Abe and his sister had been devoted to each other but she, too, was ill fated and died in childbirth in the first year of marriage. He was deeply distressed and blamed her husband for neglecting to provide medical care. This is the first definite evidence of his resentment for the death of a person he loved. In retaliation, the Grigsbys ignored him when they invited guests to a big double wedding in the family. Nettled by this cut Abe wrote the satirical "Chronicles of Reuben," and dropped the paper on the road near the house. The finder promptly gave it to the Grigsbys, as he anticipated, and his infuriated brother-in-law challenged him to fight. Abe refused because of being too big for his opponent but asked his stepbrother, John Johnston, to fight for him so that honor could be assuaged on both sides.

Although it is not entirely certain that Lincoln originated the "Chronicles," Mrs. Crawford's account of how he used them is, however, important. They show the biblical and Aesopian influence on his self-educated literary style at this time and are reproduced here as recited years later by Mrs. Crawford to Herndon (Hertz, 1938). Though probably not entirely accurate in wording, the fable gives invaluable insight into the development of Lincoln's personality and progress in self-education at 18.

"Now there was a man in those days whose name was Reuben, and the same was very great in substance in horses and cattle and swine, and a very great household. It came to pass that when the sons of Reuben grew up, that they were desirous of taking unto themselves wives, and being too well known as to honor, in their own country, they took to themselves a journey into a far country; and procured to themselves wives. And it came to pass that when they were about to make the return home, that they sent a messenger before them to bear the tidings to their parents; so, they inquired of the messengers, when their sons and wives would come. So, they made a great feast and called all their kinsmen and neighbors in, and made great preparations; so, when the time drew near, they sent out two men to meet the grooms and their wives with a treat to welcome them and to accompany them; so, when they came near to the house of Reuben, their father, the messengers came on before them and gave a shout, and the whole multitude ran out with shouts of joy, and music playing on all kinds of instruments of music, some playing harps, and some on viols, and some blowing on ram's horns, some casting dust and ashes toward Heaven; and amongst the rest Josiah blowing his bugle, making sound so great that it made the neighboring hills and valleys echo with the resounding acclamation; so when they played and harped, sounded, until the grooms and brides approached the gate, the father, Reuben, met them and welcomed them into his house, and the wedding dinner being now ready, they were all invited to sit down to dinner. Placing the bridegrooms and their wives at each end of the table, waiters were then appointed to carve and wait on the guests; so when they had all eaten, and were full and merry, they went out and sang and played till evening, and when they made an end of feasting and rejoicing, the multitude dispersed, each to his own home; the family took seats with their waiters to converse awhile, at which time preparations were being made in an upper chamber for the brides to be first conveyed by the waiters to their beds; this being done, took the two brides upstairs to their beds, placing one in a bed at the right hand of the stairs and the other on the left. The waiters came down, and Nancy, the mother, inquired of the waiters, which of the brides was placed on the right hand and they told her. So, she gave directions to the waiters of the bridegrooms, and they took the bridegrooms and placed them in the wrong beds, and came down stairs; but the mother being fearful that there might be a mistake, inquired again of the waiters and learning the fact, took the light and sprang upstairs, and running to one of the beds exclaimed: Reuben! You are in bed with Charles' wife! The young men, both being alarmed, sprang out of bed and ran with such violence against each other, that they came very near knocking each other down, which gave evidence to those below that the mistake was certain. They all came down and had a conversation about who had made the mistake, but it could not be decided."

Abe was working for the Crawfords at the time he presented the amusing chronicles, as a description of what had actually happened at the Grigsby wedding. The two brothers were put to bed by cunning deception with each other's wife, and Abe was suspected later of having been the politic genius that originated the idea and put some of the guests up to it.

Adolescent Sexuality

The chronicles included a doggerel which, though incomplete and not clearly connected, satirically portrays a homosexual relationship between two young men, Billy and Natty, and why Betsy rejected one as a suitor.

"I will tell you a joke . . . it is neither a joke nor a story, for Reuben and Charles had married two girls, but Billy had married a boy."

"The girls he had tried on every side
But none could he get to agree;
All was in vain, he went home again
And since that, he is married to Natty.

So Billy and Natty agreed very well;
And mama's well pleased at the match.
The egg it is laid but Natty's afraid,
The shell is so soft that it never will hatch.
But Betsy, she said: 'You cursed baldhead,
My suitor you never can be;
Besides, your low crotch proclaims you a botch
And that never can answer for me.''

We must consider this 18-year-old boy's fantasy of homosexual solution of heterosexual frustration, in relation to his own moral heterosexual repression and his great diffidence and confusion later in three efforts at heterosexual courtship when a man. They indicate that he was late in developing the natural transference of affection and interests because of severe self-repression of heterosexual motivations when they naturally tended to develop.

Young Lincoln, his personal history shows, did not develop as a personality in the free heterosexual pattern of his people. He was too girl shy and sensitive to learn to dance, preferred songs of cynical, frustrated love, and never had a deep emotional transference on a pretty girl in his youth.

Handy Man

Abe liked to work for Mrs. Crawford at doing odd jobs in the house and on the farm, and confided many of his thoughts and problems to her. He was very popular with the women of the village because of his willing, kindly attitude, genial sense of humor, and inexhaustible fund of stories and jokes. He had no inferiority complex about menial labor and did anything they desired from washing dishes and tending babies to cleaning house and working in the garden. He was not only an excellent woodsman but a fair carpenter and mended broken furniture ingeniously. He said humorously, in excuse of laziness, that his father taught him the carpenter's trade but never taught him to like to work with him.

Abe often sang when at work in a tune carried badly in a rasping voice that was off key but with a true sense of time and harmony. Mrs. Crawford memorized some of his songs of which the following seemed to be his favorite.

John Anderson's Lamentation

O Sinners! poor Sinners! take warning by me;
The fruits of transgressing, behold now and see;
My soul is tormented, my body confined;
My friends and dear children left weeping behind.

Much intoxication, my ruin has been;
And my dear companions have barbarously slain,
In yonder cold graveyard her body doth lie,
Whilst I am condemned, and shortly must die.

Remember John Anderson's death and reform
Before Death overtakes you and vengeance comes on.
My grief's overwhelming, in God I must trust;
I am justly condemned, my sentence is just.

I am waiting the summons, in eternity to be hurled;
Whilst my poor little orphans are cast on the world.
I hope my kind neighbors their guardians will be;
And Heaven, kind Heaven, protect them and me.

This satirical, morally meaning ballad, sung by Abe for his pleasure proved later to have been indicative of his sympathetic understanding of intemperance. It was also characteristic of the style of chant that he liked to hear many years later when president.

First Flatboat Trip to New Orleans

Abe, like his father, preferred to loaf and talk, and worked more from necessity than ambition. Standard pay then was 25 cents a day. At 18 he went with Dennis to Louisville where they worked on the canal then under construction around the falls of the Ohio River. Here he received his first pay in silver dollars, a proud experience. He also worked on a ferry that crossed the Ohio at Troy, and worked for John Romaine who described him as "awful lazy; was always reading and thinking; I used to get mad at him. . . . He would laugh and talk and tell stories but didn't ever work but did dearly love his pay. He worked a few days only at a time. His breeches and socks didn't meet by twelve inches. His shin bones were sharp, blue and narrow."

At 19 (1828) Abe and young Allen Gentry took a flatboat loaded with produce for Mr. Gentry down the Ohio and Mississippi Rivers to New Orleans. As Lincoln described it in the third person: "He was a hired hand merely; and he and a son of the owner, without other assistance, made the trip. The nature of part of the cargo-load as it was called—made it necessary for them to linger and trade along the Sugar coast—and one night they were attacked by seven negroes with intent to kill and rob them. They were hurt some in the melee, but succeeded in driving the negroes from the boat, and then 'cut cable' 'weighed anchor' and left." Young Lincoln could lift more than two men and throw most men in a wrestling match. Armed with a club he was a terrible adversary for a gang of marauders.

The trip to New Orleans was his first contact with a great city. Here he saw many foreign people dressed in strange, rich costumes, heard strange languages and gazed with wonder and admiration at the great ships and docks laden with produce from all parts of the world. He saw the brutally cynical slave auction, and the mental and emotional impact of this sordid worldly experience on this 19-year-old, raw, backwoods youth made a lasting confirmation of his biblical comprehension of man's need of better moral relations. Out of it came, we find, three decisive impressions—a stronger realization and abhorrence of the injustice and evils of slavery, the inspiration to prove that all men are created to have equal legal rights to freedom, and intuition of the inevitable development of a serious conflict in the Union between the advocates of slavery and freedom.

Common-Sense Preparation for Manhood

The parts of books that young Lincoln memorized were particularly consistent in bearing on rules of equal rights, on human aspirations, freedom, heroism, fortitude, and justice, and on the sadness of life's inevitable frustration in death. These he recited ambitiously over and over to himself aloud, when walking on the trails and roads, when at work or at home, always with consistent attitude. In the perseverance of such practical self-taught pursuit of knowledge he was most unusual, considering the uninspiring indifference to education of the people around him. It indicates that he was possessed of a constant subconscious drive towards becoming a leader of people through teaching them how the ways of equitable righteousness can be made to dominate over the evils of selfishness. Early in youth he saw how egocentric and altruistic cravings work more or less in endless conflict in all persons, and that as one dominated the other the characters of men changed. Herein young Lincoln reasoned in freedom with unprejudiced common sense. With conviction that his destiny would follow Patriarch Abraham in teaching his people a better way of treating each other, he gathered knowledge of practical ethics as avariciously as other men sought gold.

With learning from books he continued to carry along the usual beliefs and superstitions of pioneers in predestination and the revelation of its course in unusual signs and dreams. Lincoln's parents were Baptists but he did not become a "member" of any particular "church" or religious sect, and did not believe in the divinity of Christ. He seemed to think in youth as he did in maturity, that a universal, supernatural, lawful Intelligence exists, called God, which reveals determinations and intents to man's conscience by occult signs. He read the *Bible* so studiously that he knew the places and times in its different chapters that dreams and other mysterious signs gave people premonitions and warnings of God's will. He liked the New Testament better than the Old, and was most impressed by the Sermon on the Mount and Christ's golden rule of living for mankind. He saw man as the sublime creation of God and believed that Divine revelations to chosen people would be given at present time as well as to the ancient prophets.

The grand straightforward directness and simplicity of his manner of self-expression in speaking and writing was first biblical and Aesopian, to become a few years later more Shakespearean. As he budded into manhood he still liked to act the shouting, hell fighting, Baptist preacher for little groups of friends, and so vividly could he talk in biblical style that many of the simple, eager people would weep and love it. Even he would at times become tearful with his own portrayals of the prophets.

Although he was generally of happy disposition, at times he was sad. From our knowledge to be presented later of his melancholic depressions as a man, we may surmise that play preaching was a healthy expression of affections which had become, since boyhood, continuously involved in memories of the tragic death of his mother and her inspiration of his feeling of destiny. We must not, however, regard young Lincoln, although a natural introspectionist, as a constant introvert, as some biographers have assumed. He was a personality of variable dominant introvert versus extrovert affections. Although often a moody, contemplative introvert, he was at times more of an extrovert. He was always an entertaining, humorous story teller, characteristically with an ingenious, poetical flair for using dramatic metaphor and symbolism for greater clarity and impressiveness of illustration. He had learned that amusing, vulgar, witty stories best hold the interest of people, and thereby constitute the best means of illustrating a point and making a moral conviction.

It is quite probable that in adolescence Abe entertained imaginations of some day trying to become president. This is indicated by Mrs. Crawford's story. One day when he was teasing some girls, Sarah (his sister) exclaimed: "Abe, you ought to be ashamed of yourself. What do you expect will become of you?" "Be President of the United States," he promptly responded. Although this was a playful reply, when connected with his conviction of predestination to become a moral leader of his people, it is indicative of the constant purpose in his self-culture.

Embryonic Lawyer

Abe built a flat-bottom row boat in 1827 to take passengers out to steamboats in the Ohio River as they passed off shore from Anderson's Creek, when the water was too low to make a landing. In this lazy, haphazard way he earned a little money and on one occasion was given a dollar for his services. Abe had no license to transport passengers and aroused the ire of the licensed ferryman, John Dill, who lived across the river in Kentucky. According to law Kentucky owned the Ohio River as far as the low water level on the Indiana side, and Dill decided he would compel young Lincoln to respect his rights.

One day he beckoned Abe to come over to the Kentucky side, ostensibly to get some freight. When he landed, Dill and his brother seized him and threatened to throw him into the river unless he promised to quit taking business from them. They quickly learned that Abe was unimpressed by their threats of force but he was interested in their legal claims. He persuaded them to submit the question to Squire Sam Pate who lived nearby. According to Barton (1925) the Squire decided to hold a formal trial and Dill entered complaint and swore out a warrant which was immediately served on the defendant. The case of the Commonwealth of Kentucky against Abraham Lincoln was then called and both parties announced themselves ready for trial. Dill complained that the defendant had transported passengers from the Indiana shore to steamers in the Ohio River without license and that the act violated his rights.

Lincoln admitted the facts as alleged but denied having violated the law or having infringed on the rights of Dill's authority even though he had exclusive permission to transport passengers across the Ohio River for pay. He claimed that the law did not forbid others from transporting passengers to the middle of the stream. He said he thought he had not violated the law for he had not "set persons across the river," but had only rowed them out to steamboats in midstream. He held further with good natured common sense that since the ferryman could not always be on the Indiana side and steamboats could not stay in one position in midstream it seemed that passengers on the Indiana side should have the right to hire a boat to take them out to a steamer when it approached. Squire Pate acquitted the defendant and the Dill brothers went their way much disgruntled.

Then followed naturally a fortunate sequel for Abe Lincoln. Ever congenial and interested in getting information, he sat on the porch with the Squire and questioned him about legal statutes and their administration. Many well-meaning people, he learned, got into trouble through ignorance of the law and means should be provided for giving them proper information. Before Abe left he was invited to attend trials in the squire's court and read his law books. Here he obtained a copy of the *"Revised Statutes of Indiana."* On the title page it stated: "The Revised Laws of Indiana, adopted and enacted by the General Assembly at their eighth session. To which are prefixed the Declaration of Independence, the Constitution of the United States, and sundry other documents connected with the Political History of the Territory and State of Indiana. Arranged and published by authority of the General Assembly. Corydon. Printed by Carpenter and Douglas, 1824." (Tarbell, 1924.)

It proved a most impressive book for young Lincoln as he studied it thoroughly in his own way. From it he got a realistic conception of the long series of parliamentary steps that had been taken in order to found the nation and establish the Northwest Territory and the state of Indiana. In it he found a statement that prohibited the spread of slavery into the Territory. Article No. 6 read: "There shall be neither slavery nor involuntary servitude in the said Territory otherwise than in the punishment of crimes, whereof the party shall have been duly convicted; provided always that any person escaping into the same, from whom labor or service is lawfully claimed in any one of the original States, such fugitive may be lawfully reclaimed, and conveyed to the person claiming his or her labor or service, as aforesaid."

So carefully and thoroughly had he studied his subject that the clarity of his discussions of its laws won the admiration and respect of the lawyers of Booneville and Rockport, Ind., where he liked to attend court. Judge John Pilcher of Rockport was moved to invite him to make free use of his law library.

Booneville, Warwick County, Ind., was 15 miles from Gentryville, and Abe, at 19 and 20, walked the road many times to attend court there. He was most impressed by the skill of Mr. Breckenridge as he carried on the prosecution of a murder trial. Upon listening to his speech he felt himself grow convinced that he wanted to become a lawyer, but thought that great profession was out of reach because of insufficient education. Although he was dressed in buckskin breeches much too short and tight and his shaggy head was covered with a coonskin cap, he congratulated Mr. Breckenridge upon his speech with complete self-reliance in the dignity of what he had to say. Thirty-three years later, when Mr. Breckenridge called at the White House, President Lincoln recalled the trial and commented: "It was the best speech that I, up to that time, ever heard. If I could, as I then thought, make as good a speech as that, my soul would be satisfied."

First Published Essay

In 1829, Abe Lincoln wrote an article on national politics, as told by William Wood, long after, to Herndon. Abe and his father built Wood's house and furniture, and he knew them and Abe's mother well. "The article was the result of self-education based on one year of schooling. In it Abe stated that the American government was the best form of government in the world for an intelligent people; that it ought to be kept sacred and preserved forever; that general education should be carried all over the country; that the Constitution should be sacred, the Union perpetuated, and the laws revered, respected and enforced." This fine conception of lawful order under the constitution, although formed in youth, was so sound that it remained fixed and uncompromised for the rest of his life.

Abe used to borrow newspapers, including a temperance paper, Mr. Wood said.

> "One day he wrote a piece on temperance and brought it to my house, I read it carefully over and over, and the piece excelled for sound sense anything that my papers contained. I gave the article to Aaron Farmer, a Baptist preacher; he read it, it struck him, and he sent it to a temperance paper in Ohio . . . they published it. . . . I saw the printed piece and read it with pleasure over and over again." "The political article I showed to John Pilcher, an attorney of Posey County, Indiana, who was traveling on the circuit . . . and stopped at my house over night; he read it carefully and asked me where I got it. I told him that one of my neighbor's boys wrote it. . . . Pilcher . . . was struck with the article and said, 'The world can't beat it.' He begged for it. I gave it to him and it was published. . . . Abe was always a man though a boy."
>
> "I never knew him to swear," Wood continued, "he would say to his playfellows and other boys: 'Swear off your boyish ways and be more like men.'"

What We Learn from Young Lincoln's Intuitive Method of Self-Education

Young Lincoln sought and cultivated truth of knowledge at pedestrian pace and each step gained was logically correlated with a growing fund of well balanced common-sense concepts of right versus wrong in human relations that were to be lived by and never forgotten.

Judging from the consistency of his attitude and ways of thinking in boyhood and later in manhood, we may say that he possessed at birth a brain with extraordinary potentialities for high integrative organization (in modern psychological terms an unusually high I.Q.). However it was severely injured in boyhood it compensated sufficiently to carry on mentation at a remarkably high level despite visual decoordination and abnormal nervous instability.

The boy obtained from both of his mothers consistent encouragement and conviction to believe that self-reliance must be based on self-education and common-sense understanding of reality. Out of his transcendance in his stepmother's affections over her real son, and out of his moral compulsion to preserve the sanctity of his parents' house from dividing against itself came reinforcements of inspiration and belief in his destiny in virtuous service of law. By postadolescence he had grown so adept in applying Biblical and Aesopian morals to human interactions that he held the faith of contestants in his judgment of equal rights to retributive justice. Loyal to his mothers, he was dutifully submissive to paternal possessive authority but developed, after painfully unforgetable experiences, challenging resentment of injustice that became one of his most vigorous characteristics as a man.

As a keen analytical student of human nature Lincoln developed as a boy and later as a man extraordinary ability for discriminating logical essentials of reality in argument from the fiction of wishful assumptions. He was born with a genius for understanding implications of egocentric interests of social attitudes and motives of himself and other people, and for serving welfare with patient good will by resolving conflicts into compromises.

Abraham Lincoln had, in youth, to work endlessly to overcome the effects of a definitely conditioned, permanent, nostalgic emotional neurosis, that combined with a definite organic neurosis and produced a continuously melancholic self-doubtful outlook on life as each form of neurosis tended to reinforce the other in a vicious circle when excited by moral kinds of social frustration. He developed intuitively his own system of counterbalancing mental defenses and self-controls of this vicious circle by reducing its social excitations through the intentional culture of a common-sense philosophy of life, working always for the right, with genial, kindly good humor and inexhaustible patience and perserverence. By constantly making doubly sure that his thinking was right and not wrong, that what he upheld was really true and good, he avoided most causes of anxiety and depression of an overly sensitive nervous system.

We will observe in the following years that he learned his self-taught boyhood lessons in common-sense analytical thinking so thoroughly and retained them so tenaciously, as he did his social attitudes, habits of speech and dress, that little need to change them was ever necessary as a lawyer, legislator, politician, statesman, and president. Always diffident and cautious in approach with kindly, honest, and realistic considerations of every side of an issue, he eventually arrived at impartial, self-respectful convictions that he was treating other people as he wished to be treated. This constantly self-controlling, self-righting culture of moral rightwayness gave him the clear, directly expressive mind that made him so impressive as a man.

Chapter VII

EARLY MANHOOD

In the fall of 1829 Tom Lincoln decided unexpectedly (he was completing a new cabin of neatly hewn logs) that he was tired of living in the forest on Pigeon Creek where his cattle so often died of the "milk sick." He sold his 80-acre farm for $125 in cash after buying it for $160 and improving it for 14 years. Attracted by the news from John Hanks, who had moved to Illinois, that prairie land was more fertile and easier to farm than forest land, and cattle were healthier, Tom Lincoln, Dennis Hanks, and Squire Hall decided to move there. They built three covered wagons entirely of wood except for the iron rims of the wheels and, by selling much of their household furnishings, raised enough money to buy two yoke teams of young steers for each wagon. On March 1, 1830, they loaded into these rickety-rackety prairie schooners all their possessions, with the women and children sitting on top of the bedding, and started (Abe's father and Abe, his stepmother and her two daughters and their husbands and children—13 in all) for the land of promise. The five men walked and drove the oxen and hunted game on the way. They are said to have traveled northward to Jasper in Dubois County and then turned westward through Petersburg and crossed the Wabash at Vincennes. Abe, now 21 by three weeks, was his own boss, and no longer required by conscience to believe himself legally and morally bound to serve his father. However, he helped loyally with the moving and carried a pack of pins, needles, buttons, suspenders, and other notions for peddling on the way.

In the migration through Illinois a small pet dog was left by oversight across a flooded icy stream. The heavy ox-drawn wagon could not be turned back to recover it so they decided to move on. The dog ran along the bank barking in great distress but would not plunge into the water. Lincoln, who told the story, is quoted as saying: "I could not endure the idea of abandoning even a dog. Pulling off shoes and socks I waded across the stream and triumphantly returned with the shivering animal under my arm. His frantic leaps of joy and other evidence of a dog's gratitude amply repaid me for all the exposure I had undergone" (Herndon, 1889).

They finally arrived at John Hanks' place in Macon County. As Lincoln described it to Scripps: "His father and family settled a new place on the North side of the Sangamon River, at the junction of the timber-land and prairie, about ten miles Westerly from Decatur. Here they built a log-cabin, into which they removed, and made sufficient rails to fence ten acres of ground, fenced and broke the ground, and raised a crop of sow[n] corn upon it the same year. . . . The sons-in-law, were temporarily settled in other places in the county. In the autumn all hands were greatly afflicted with augue and fever, to which they had not been used, and by which they were greatly discouraged—so much so that they determined on leaving the county." They remained, however, through the succeeding winter of the very celebrated "deep snow season of Illinois." In the spring of 1831 Tom Lincoln moved his family from Macon to Coles County where conditions seemed to be healthier.

First Public Speech

One day early in 1830 Abe Lincoln went with John Hanks to nearby Decatur "to trade." They joined a crowd that had gathered around a man by the name of Posy who was making a speech. John didn't like some of Posy's statements and declared Abe could do better. Eager for a contest in anything the crowd yelled at the young stranger for a speech. Mounting a stump he delivered an argument for dredging rivers to improve transportation. His timely choice of subject, clarity of discussion, and magnetic manner of delivery made such a popular hit that he felt encouraged to believe he had a real ability for public speaking. Heretofore he had merely played at the game.

"During that winter," Lincoln continued in his description to Scripps. "A. together with his stepmother's son, John D. Johnston, and John Hanks, yet residing in Macon county, hired themselves to one Denton Offutt, to take a flat boat from Beardstown Illinois to New-Orleans; and for that purpose, were to join him—Offutt—at Springfield, Ill., so soon as the snow should go off. When it did go off which was about the 1st. of March 1831—the county was so flooded, as to make traveling by land impracticable; to obviate which difficulty the[y] purchased a large canoe and came down the Sangamon river in it. This is the time and manner of A's first entrance into Sangamon County."

Frozen Feet

Abe's canoe overturned in the Sangamon River and his feet were so badly frozen that he had to be taken to the home of Sheriff Warnick nearby until he recovered. He lived here for two weeks in a wealth of house furnishings and friendly administrations for his comfort that must have exceeded his fondest imagination. The sheriff's pretty daughter Polly was already engaged to marry Joe Stevens so Abe could only look upon her with admiration and gratitude, but years later Joe bragged that he won Polly from Abe Lincoln.

We are told by Warnick (Barton, 1925) that Abe spent most of the time in reading law books while lying on the floor resting his head against the back of a chair that he had turned upside down and padded with a cushion. This peculiar posture of lying on his back to read had become characteristic of Lincoln as a young man and we will see how he used it almost daily throughout his life. It has been regarded by most biographers as merely an eccentric habit carried over from boyhood, but it seems now that it was the best position that he could take in order to bring his upturned left eye into focus with the normal right and relieve the strain that would otherwise have produced severe headache, nausea, and gloomy discouragement.

Lincoln's feet never fully recovered a normal circulation and thereafter caused him no little discomfort. In repayment for Sheriff Warnick's board and room he split rails.

Lincoln Meets Offutt

Lincoln continued to Scripps:

"They found Offutt at Springfield, but learned from him that he had failed in getting a boat at Beardstown. This led to their hiring themselves to him at $12 per month, each; and gettin the timber out of the trees and building a boat at Old Sangamon Town on the Sangamon river, seven miles N.W. of Springfield, which boat they took to New-Orleans, substantially upon the old contract. It was in connection with this boat that occurred the ludicrous incident of sewing up the hogs eyes. Offutt bought thirty odd large fat live hogs, but found difficulty in driving them from where [he] purchased them to the boat, and thereupon conceived the whim that he could sew up their eyes and drive them where he pleased. No sooner thought of then decided, he put his hands, including A. at the job, which they completed—all but the driving. In their blind condition they could not be driven out of the lot or field they were in. This expedient failing, they were tied and hauled on carts to the boat. It was near the Sangamon River, within what is now Menard county."

Abe had been greatly disappointed when Offutt's plan was about to fail and it was he who proposed that they build the boat. The three men patched up an old shanty on the Sangamon River to live in, and then felled trees and cut logs on federal land and delivered them to a mill where Offutt had them sawed into boards of proper dimensions. In four weeks the boat, 80 feet long and 18 feet wide, with flat bottom sloped upward at each end, was launched and loaded with barrels of salt pork and corn and the live hogs. Unfortunately the spring freshet subsided faster than expected and the boat got stuck on top of the mill dam at New Salem. Pole as three strong men might, they couldn't budge it. A crowd of villagers gathered to shout advice and enjoy the excitement but all efforts proved futile, and unloading the boat seemed the only solution. The accounts of what happened are confusing but it seems that Abe hit upon an ingenious idea. He moved most of the cargo to the upstream end, raising the bow until they could pole the boat half over the top of the dam. Then they moved the cargo forward until the boat tilted downward. Next he bored a hole in the bottom to let out the bilge water and then corked the hole so that the boat would float and carry the rest of the cargo. After these operations they poled the boat off the dam—much to the hilarious delight of their audience. Such ingenuity in thinking his way out of a seemingly hopeless impasse by shifting forces where he had leverage, like a skillful wrestler, made him later a great lawyer and war president.

The three boatmen and Offutt floated down the Sangamon into the Illinois River and then the Mississippi. At St. Louis John Hanks had to return home but the others went on and reached New Orleans without mishap early in May. Here they stayed until Offutt sold his cargo for a handsome profit and all then returned by steamboat to St. Louis.

In New Orleans Lincoln had ample time to explore again the ways of the people and elaborate the impressions of his first visit. The sordid slave market with its brutal chain gangs, abuse of women and cruel separation of parents from children depressed him. Abe greatly admired the go-getter, optimistic audacity of his boss and Offutt liked Abe's genial good humor, cautious judgment, and self-reliance. In his letter to Scripps Lincoln wrote of their friendship with evident pride: "During this boat enterprise acquaintance with Offutt, who was previously an entire stranger, he conceived a liking for A. and believing he could turn him to account, he contracted with him to act as a clerk for him, on his return from New-Orleans, in charge of a store and Mill at New-Salem, then in Sangamon, now in Menard County."

New Salem

Offutt went to St. Louis to purchase a stock of goods for the New Salem enterprise and Abe Lincoln returned to Coles County. After a month spent in helping his father build a new cabin he decided to go to New Salem and wait for his boss.

Many biographers who have followed the decisive steps in Abraham Lincoln's career like to present them as a sequence of fortunate chances, i.e., if he had taken some other route of travel and not met certain people and gone to New Salem, he might not have been elected to the legislature and studied law, etc. This is a trivial and superficial comprehension of human nature. Actually, young Lincoln, as conditioned since boyhood by the most impressive influence in his life—the love and pride of both of his mothers in the ethical way of living—was, at 21, deeply hopeful of studying law and administering it with justice. No other way of self-expression could give him real happiness. He believed himself to have insufficient education ever to become a lawyer yet no other means of improving the ways of mankind could satisfy him. He could not become a Christian minister, since he believed neither in the divinity of Christ nor God as a personal being, although he did believe in God as a universal, impersonal, creative Intelligence. He might have become a great physician for he was inventive at repairing appliances and, like his mother, he was deeply sympathetic and ingenious at persuasion and helpful to people in distress. He could do farm work, wood work, run flatboats, and handle other simple odd jobs. He thought of becoming a blacksmith, a trade that his ancestors up to his father knew well. But the outlook of such ways of making a living for his intellectual capacity was dull and gloomy.

His nervous emotional instability since the injury of his brain in boy-hood influenced him, in order to maintain control of himself, to function cautiously, conservatively, honestly, truthfully, and safely lest he get in-volved in self-commitments and responsibilities that he could not fulfill or prove right. His obsession of predestination to serve mankind in the improvement of equalitarian justice, his aesthetic love for the use of words, and his intelligent wit and humor, set him to leave home and go among people wherever he might earn a living and accumulate knowledge in his heartfelt direction and unhappily reject anything else. We will see how quickly and intensely he seized upon each opportunity that fitted in with his great desire. Although at first he took almost any job that was offered, and would have done so in any place where he lived, he readily kept changing toward the greater opportunity, in the direction of his real love, the study of law for the improvement of human relations.

A long, lean, lanky, easy-going, smiling, awkward young stranger, wearing tight, home made pants shrunken far above his shoe tops, with all his worldly possessions tied up in a bandanna handkerchief, walked on a summer day into the straggling village of some 20 log cabins and 100 souls, on the bank of the Sangamon. He quickly made new friends and found employment until Offutt arrived with the merchandise. He worked as a farm hand and did odd jobs about the village, including the moving of flat boats, and helping Mentor Graham as an election clerk. Balloting was done by oral declaration. Every man, proud of his affiliations and his oppositions, expressed them before a partisan crowd of neighbors, by stating whom he wanted to vote for all down the list from the highest to the lowest office. The clerks recorded his vote in writing and placed the ballot in a box in his presence to be counted at the close of the polls. Lincoln's name with Graham's on the voting record shows that he served in this capacity three times a year for several years.

Offutt and Lincoln believed from their successful flatboat enterprise that the Sangamon River could be made navigable for small steamboats and New Salem had a big future as the inland shipping center of a rich farming community. Offutt, overconfident borrower and promotor, bought a lot for $10 in the village near the river and obtained a license to sell merchandise in September of 1831. With the help of Lincoln he put up a log store house and soon after rented the Rutledge mill and built a wharf nearby, all on loans and mortgages.

Abe Lincoln Wrestles Jack Armstrong

The famous wrestling match, which has been described in many ways, proved a good test of Lincoln's character and sportsmanship. In a small frontier town, physical strength and courage are more impressive than knowledge and intelligence in the minds of most of the inhabitants. A newcomer soon gets rated, by appearances, on such potentialities. If he seems to be unusually powerful he is pushed forward with no little mischievous delight to meet "the champ." Offutt, insatiable promotor of everything, soon had everybody agog by offering to bet $10 that Abe Lincoln was "the best man" in town and could throw Jack Armstrong. In nearby Clary's Grove a band of good natured young rowdies ruled the neighborhood under the leadership of this hero. A match was arranged and all the neighborhood turned out to see it. During the contest, one account says, the gang tricked Abe when he threw Jack, and tied him down. Much to their surprise, instead of getting frightened or enraged at their hilarious impositions he joked and laughed with them so heartily that they gave up trying to humiliate him and became converted with admiration for his wit and self-control. Armstrong and his wife, Hannah, and Lincoln became thereafter warm and loyal friends and Abe often stayed at Jack's house. (See later Lincoln's defense of their son against the charge of murder.)

Better Self Education

Mentor Graham, unusually capable village schoolmaster and a man of earnest character, liked to teach children and promote the interest of adults in self-education. Lincoln immediately took advantage of his friendship to improve his knowledge of history and mathematics. He borrowed Kirkham's *Grammar,* and with the help of Graham mastered its principles. He also read books on astronomy and chemistry. Managing the business of Offutt's mill and store greatly increased Lincoln's confidence in his ability to serve people, but in another way he found himself superior to anyone in the community. James Rutledge and Mentor Graham had organized a literary and debating society in New Salem, then remarkable for the number of its publicly interested people. Upon discovering Lincoln's unusually keen interest in study for mental improvement they invited him to become a member.

Robert Rutledge, then a boy of 14, was present and later described Abe's first debate: "As he rose to speak, his tall form towered above the little assembly. Both hands were thrust down deep in the pockets of his pantaloons. A perceptible smile at once lit up the faces of the audience, for all anticipated the relation of some humorous story. But he opened up the discussion in splendid style to the infinite astonishment of his friends. As he warmed with his subject, his hands would forsake his pockets and would enforce his ideas by awkward gestures; but would very soon seek their easy resting place. He pursued the question with reason and argument so pithy and forcible that all were amazed. The president [James Rutledge], at his fireside after the meeting, remarked—that he was already a fine speaker, that all he lacked was culture to enable him to reach the high destiny which he knew was in store for him. From that time Mr. Rutledge took a deeper interest in him." (Hertz, 1938.)

In this period Abe wrote numerous short essays on various subjects of common interest with the same natural simplicity, directness, and coherence that characterized his impromptu arguments in debate. And it was this consistency in self-taught expression in both media, in an age when people waxed grandiloquent in flowery interpolations, that made him unusually clear and convincing. It must be said to the historical credit of his New Salem friends that they first discovered and fostered the talent of Abraham Lincoln.

Jack Kelso, an eccentric, literary minded neighbor, who would rather go fishing than attend to business, introduced Abe to Shakespeare, Byron, Burns, and other poets; and Justice of the Peace Bowling Green, with whom he lived for some time, loaned his books on law. In these years, Tom Paine's *Age of Reason* and Volney's *Ruins* were much read and discussed in the community and awakened Lincoln's interest in natural philosophy.

His method of study, as in boyhood, was to write out, memorize, and recite aloud whole passages and pages that seemed important to him. He was rarely without a book under his arm wherever he went, and the neighbors enjoyed hearing Abe, on foot or horseback, reading or reciting aloud as he passed along. His interest in dramatic poetry, particularly Shakespeare, was most absorbing. He loved its masterful human insight and economy of words, its allegory, rhythm, and plots. He recited to his friends from *King Lear, Richard III, Henry VIII, Hamlet,* and *Macbeth.* The latter was his favorite. He cared little for the comedies.

Offutt's Bust

Offutt borrowed more money from his neighbors and started more enterprises than he could manage successfully. The people along the Sangamon were eager to prove their river navigable, and when Lincoln piloted the Talisman, a small river steamboat, from Beardstown below its mouth up to New Salem and Springfield he became the hero of the hour. But the steamer moved only four miles a day and got stuck badly on the New Salem dam. Abe earned $40 for his skill and refused to believe that sand bars and shoals had sealed the doom of New Salem as an inland shipping center.

Offutt's enterprises failed in less than a year and he had to sell out to irate creditors and get out of town. Lincoln was the only person who regretted his leaving. Himself, shy and cautious, he most admired self-confident, optimistic men with audacity to undertake building for the future. After his extremely narrow education and experience with unimaginative backwoods people he had been stimulated by Offutt to a greater vision of the possible development of the state and of his own powers as a man. Offutt's presuming manners anathematized himself in New Salem without reflection on Lincoln, who somehow always did the kindly, likable thing and never betrayed a trust or a friend.

First Step in Politics

Offutt's bust put Lincoln out of steady work, and for want of something better he did odd jobs and split rails again. He now took the first bold step of his political career. Encouraged by his admiration of Offutt's optimistic aggressiveness, and inspired by James Rutledge, Mentor Graham and other New Salem friends, who knew of his desire to study law and admired his ability as a debater, he decided to try his hand at politics. Within a year after moving into the community, on March, 1832, Abe Lincoln announced his candidacy for the state legislature by distributing, as customary, a small, printed handbill in which he stated his political principles.

Although his father was a Democrat, and most of the New Salem people were Democrats, he announced himself, in the customary manner in the *Sangamo Journal,* as a Whig candidate, for the more conservative policies of this party were more nearly like his own beliefs. He advocated the establishment of national banks, a high protective tariff, improvements of transportation in the state through building canals, good roads, and railroads, but, more particularly, in making rivers like the Sangamon navigable as fundamental to its development, and, curiously, a law against usury. Lincoln's sentence structure and coherence and reasoning should be compared with later addresses to observe the improvements he achieved as a lawyer and president. His inclination, that became so important later, to give philosophical reasons for his actions is apparent here.

> *"To the People of Sangamo County"* March 9, 1832 "Fellow-Citizens: Having become a candidate for the honorable office of one of your representatives in the next General Assembly of this state, in accordance with an established custom, and the principles of true republicanism, it becomes my duty to make known to you—the people whom I propose to represent—my sentiments with regard to local affairs.
>
> "Time and experience have verified to a demonstration, the public utility of internal improvements. That the poorest and most thinly populated countries would be greatly benefited by the opening of good roads, and in the clearing of navigable streams within their limits, is what no person will deny. But yet it is folly to undertake works of this or any other kind, without first knowing that we are able to finish them—as half finished work generally proves to be labor lost. There cannot justly be any objection to having railroads and canals, any more than to other good things, provided they cost nothing. The only objection is to paying for them; and the objection to paying arises from the want of ability to pay."

After discussing the superior advantages of railroads over rivers for transportation, he commented.

> ". . . however high our imaginations may be heated at thoughts of it—there is always a heart appalling shock accompanying the account of its cost, which forces us to shrink from our pleasing anticipations. The probable cost of this contemplated rail road [from the Illinois River to Springfield] is

estimated at $290,000:—the bare statement of which, in my opinion, is sufficient to justify the belief, that the improvement of Sangamo river is an object much better suited to our infant resources."

"Respecting this view, I think I may say, without the fear of being contradicted, that its navigation may be rendered completely practicable, as high as the mouth of the South Fork, or probably higher, to vessels of from 25 to 30 tons burthen, for at least one half of all common years, and to vessels of much greater burthen a part of that time. From my peculiar circumstances, it is probable that for the last twelve months I have given as particular attention to the stage of water in this river, as any other person in the country."

He then described, from his experiences with flatboats in the preceding year, how the river would have to be cleared of driftwood and many of its channels in its "zig zag course" straightened by cutting wide ditches across "the necks" of peninsulas.

"The whole river in a short time would wash its way through, thereby curtailing the distance, and increasing the velocity of the current very considerably . . . and being nearly straight, the timber which might float in at the head, would be apt to go clear through. . . ."

". . . Finally, I believe the improvement of the Sangamo river, to be vastly important and highly desirable to the people of this county; and if elected, any measure in the legislature having this for its object, which may appear judicious, will meet my approbation, and shall receive my support."

Then he proposed the passage of a law against usury.

"It appears that the practise of loaning money at exorbitant rates of interest, has already been opened as a field for discussion; so I suppose I may enter upon it without claiming the honor, or risking the danger, which may await its first explorer. It seems as though we are never to have an end to this baneful and corroding system, acting almost as prejudicial to the general interest of the community as a direct tax of several thousand dollars annually laid on each county, for the benefit of a few individuals only, unless there be a law made setting a limit to the rates of usury. A law for this purpose, I am of opinion, may be made, without materially injuring any class of people. In cases of extreme necessity there could always be means found to cheat the law, while in all other cases it would have its intended effect. I would not favor the passage of a law upon this subject, which might be very easily evaded. Let it be such that the labor and difficulty of evading it, could only be justified in cases of the greatest necessity."

His reasons for declaring in favor of supporting state education are based on his personal experience and his love of the morally equitable way of living.

"Upon the subject of education, not presuming to dictate any plan or system respecting it, I can only say that I view it as the most important subject which we as a people can be engaged in. That every man may receive at least, a moderate education, and thereby be able to read the histories of his own and other countries, by which he may duly appreciate the value of our free institutions, appears to be an object of vital importance, even on this account alone, to say nothing of the advantages and satisfaction to be derived from being able to read the scriptures and other works, both of a religious and moral nature, for themselves. For my part, I desire to see the time when education, and by its means, morality, sobriety, enterprise and industry, shall become more general than at present, and should be gratified to have it in my power to contribute something to the advancement of any measure which might have a tendency to accelerate the happy period."

His comment on the necessity of altering existing estray and road laws shows that, although progressive on improving means of transportation and education, he was conservative about changing established laws.

"Considering the great probability that the framers of those laws were wiser than myself, I should prefer [not?] meddling with them, unless they were first attacked by others, in which case I should feel it both a privilege and a duty to take that stand, which in my view, might tend most to the advancement of justice."

Lincoln's closing remarks reveal the potentialities of a rudimentary social-political attitude in an inexperienced, modest young man that will develop eventually into one of the greatest teachers of the meaning of government ever achieved by a citizen of a democracy.

"But, fellow citizens, I shall conclude. Considering the great degree of modesty which should always attend youth, it is probable I have already been more presuming than becomes me. However, upon the subjects of which I have treated, I have spoken as I thought. I may be wrong in regard to any or all of them; but *holding it a sound maxim, that it is better to be only sometimes right, than at all times wrong, so soon as I discover my opinions to be erroneous, I shall be ready to renounce them.*" (Italics inserted.)

Adoption of Shakespearean Heroic Style

Lincoln's final statement of this political appeal expresses the common sense, sincerity, humility, and modesty of his young political ambition with graceful submission to the *will of the people,* but it also shows, for the first time, the influence of memorizing and reciting Shakespeare on his literary style. Free to express himself here without argument, he swings with almost perfect rhythm into the heroic verse so effectively used by Shakespeare. I have rearranged, after the manner of Paul Hunter, the last few lines of his handbill to demonstrate his natural adoption of the poet's heroic meter. The quotation is given without change of wording.

"Every man is said to have his peculiar ambition.
Whether this be true or not,
I can say for one
That I have no other so great
As that of being truly esteemed of my fellow men
By rendering myself worthy of their esteem.
How far I shall succeed in gratifying this ambition

Is yet to be developed.
I am young and unknown to many of you.
I was born and have ever remained
In the most humble walks of life.
I have no wealthy or popular relations
To recommend me.
My case is thrown exclusively upon
The independent voters of this country;
And if elected, they will have conferred
A favor upon me, for which I shall be
Unremitting in my labors to compensate.
But if the good people in their wisdom
Shall see fit to keep me in their background,
I have been too familiar with disappointments
To be very much chagrined.
Your friend and fellow citizen,"

A. Lincoln.

Here is obvious the influence of Hamlet's soliloquy, "To be or not to be—that is the question," on an earnest, natural young man who, feeling life to be a sacred trust, regards his ambition to serve people with religious self-respect.

Indian War

In the spring of 1832, Black Hawk, a Sioux Chief, tried to lead his people back to their ancient tribal lands across the Mississippi River into Illinois. War followed and the governor of the state called for volunteers for 30 days. Many young men of Sangamon County enlisted as a company. Among them were Abraham Lincoln and the Armstrong boys. They were a tough, rowdy, wild, undisciplined, un-uniformed gang who loved to test each other's metal with ribald, practical joking. Private Lincoln "to his own surprise was elected captain" and found that all kinds of men liked him as a leader. Captain Lincoln's company was unmounted and formed part of General Whiteside's brigade. His ability to adapt himself to embarassing situations is shown by an occasion when drilling his company. As it marched toward a gate, he said that he found himself unable to remember the proper command for "getting the company through endwise. So as we came near the gate I shouted, 'the company is dismissed for two minutes when it will fall in again on the other side of the gate.' "

When old Chief Shabbona, a friendly Indian, wandered into camp he was surrounded by infuriated soldiers set upon lynching him. Lincoln confronted the shouting mob with such vigorous appeals for justice that it yielded to him. Dangerous emergencies that threatened rights and justice instantly aroused him to act in defense of the victim. His company never fought with the Indians but arrived after a battle in time to bury the dead. Lincoln, as previously reported, once said that he had no enjoyment of colors in sunsets and flowers like other people: but his account of the scene describes the colors of the sky vividly.

> "I remember just how those men looked as we rode up the little hill where their camp was. The red light of the morning sun was streaming upon them as they lay with their heads towards us on the ground. And every man had a round, red spot on the top of his head, about as big as a dollar where the redskins had taken his scalp. It was frightful, but it was grotesque, and the red sunlight seemed to paint everything all over." (Herndon, 1889.)

When his company disbanded at the end of the 30 days he enlisted twice as a private in other companies until the end of the war. In his Scripps letter he commented retrospectively on his experiences:

> "He has not since had any success in life which gave him so much satisfaction. He went the campaign, served near three months, met the ordinary hardships of such an expedition, but was in no battle. He now owns in Iowa, the land upon which his own warrants for this service, were located."

Speaks For Himself

Lincoln returned to New Salem 10 days before the election and, as he said, "encouraged by his great popularity among his immediate neighbors" resumed his candidacy for the legislature, although he had little time to present himself. He was only 23 and educationally unprepared for legislative duties, but faith in his ability to learn by the application of common sense what would be best to do was sufficient ground, he felt, to take the step. While making his first speech some ruffian attacked one of his friends. He leaped from the stand and clearing a row of benches in his stride grabbed the assailant and, lifting him at arms's length above his head, threw him to the ground. Then without further delay he returned to the stand and resumed his speech unruffled in temper.

In Lincoln's words to Scripps: he "was beaten—his own precinct, however, casting its votes 277 for and 7, against him. And this too while he was an avowed Clay man, and the precinct the autumn afterwards, giving a majority of 115 to Genl. Jackson over Mr. Clay. This was the only time A was ever beaten on a direct vote of the people."

Odd Jobber, Merchant

During the following two years, 1833 and 1834, Lincoln continued to live a poor man's easy-going but decent, try-and-try-again existence in New Salem. He served as town clerk and split rails until he bought with William F. Berry a failing merchandising emporium from the Herndon brothers (cousins of his future law partner). He gave his note to Herndon in payment and then gave additional notes for stocks of two other stores that had failed.

Lincoln became postmaster of the village on May 7, 1833 and moved the office into his store. The business outlook seemed hopeful except for one thing. On March 6, 1833, the Commissioners' Court of Sangamon County "ordered that William F. Berry, in the name of Berry and Lincoln, have license to keep a tavern in New Salem to continue twelve months from this date, and that they pay one dollar in addition to six dollars heretofore paid as per treasury receipt. And that they be allowed the following rates, viz: French brandy per pint 25," and so on, including peach and apple brandy, Holland gin, domestic gin, wine, beer, rum and whiskey; besides rates for lodging and food.

The license was taken out by Berry, who seems to have signed the bond for both men since Lincoln's name is not in his handwriting. According to New Salem tradition, Lincoln disapproved of Berry's action, and, as Berry was their best customer, Lincoln sold out his partnership to him after several months' trial. It was customary for general stores to sell without a license whiskey and beer in bulk, not to be consumed on the premises. A license was necessary to sell alcoholic drinks for consumption on the premises and Lincoln seems to have objected to this. He portrayed his experience as a merchant for Scripps as follows:

> "He was now without means and out of business, but was anxious to remain with his friends who had treated him with so much generosity, especially as he had nothing elsewhere to go to. He studied what he should do—thought of learning the black-smith trade—thought of trying to study law—rather thought he could not succeed in that without a better education. Before long, strangely enough, a man offered to sell and did sell, to A. and another [William F. Berry] as poor as himself, an old stock of goods, upon credit. They opened as merchants; and he says that was *the* store. Of course they did nothing but get deeper and deeper in debt. He was appointed Postmaster at New Salem—the office being too insignificant, to make his politics an objection. The store winked out."

To effect his business transactions not a cent of money was required, the buyer giving the seller his note and the latter assigning it to someone else in trade. (Herndon & Angle, 1942.)

Abe Lincoln as the village storekeeper has been vividly described by many people as a long, gaunt, shambling, kindly spoken, melancholy, leisurely fellow. He would sit on a box in front of the store with a dejected, sad, abstracted look on his face. An old friend, Abner Yates Ellis (Herndon, 1889), said Abe Lincoln, as a salesman, was "most unfit." He liked more to talk than sell goods, often letting people help themselves while he carried on about law or politics or told some entertaining vulgar story with a surprisingly amusing, witty, moral or practical philosophical ending. He had the reputation of disliking "to wait on the ladies" and preferring to wait on men and boys. At times he slept on the store counter when the village tavern of four rooms was crowded. In summer he wore flax and tow linen pantaloons, much too short in the legs, held up by one suspender, a calico shirt and coarse tan brogans, blue yarn socks and unbanded straw hat. On one occasion, according to Ellis, while he and Lincoln boarded at the Rutledge tavern, a lady and her son and three stylishly dressed daughters were guests for several weeks but Lincoln never sat at the same table with them.

As a society man Abe was "singularly deficient" while living in New Salem but he bore himself with a gentleman's gallantry. He never gossiped about ladies or circulated village scandal. Once a Major Hill, in violent temper, accused him of making defamatory remarks about his wife. Lincoln denied the charge and insisted that he had a high regard for Mrs. Hill. The only thing that he knew to her discredit was the fact that she was Major Hill's wife.

New Salem was called "a fast place" because of its wild, hard drinking, sporting young men, but Lincoln was always popular with everyone, although he never drank intoxicating liquor or used tobacco. He was keenly interested in tests of skill and strength and ready to accept any challenge, competing with high courage and wise caution, for the joy of it.

Lincoln's stories, and the poems and songs that he loved to recite or sing, constituted an important part of his daily mental activities, and the biographer must keep apace with these expressions of feeling, as with his changes in style of speech and writing, to catch each phase of his development of egoistic attitude. In the New Salem period, as "a mimic he was unexcelled," Ellis (Herndon, 1889) said, "and with his characteristic gestures, he built up a reputation for story-telling—although fully as many of his narratives were borrowed as original—which followed him through life. . . . his laugh was striking. Such awkward gestures belonged to no other man. They attracted universal attention, from the old sedate down to the schoolboy. Then in a few moments he was calm and thoughtful as a judge on the bench, and as ready to give advice on the most important matters; fun and gravity grew on him alike."

He liked to sing, though his voice was off key, ballads and doggerels to little groups of friends who gathered in his store in the evenings. The one most often repeated, Ellis said, was "How St. Patrick Came to be Born on the 17th of March." Where Lincoln acquired it is unknown. It gives valuable psychoanalytic indication on how, as a sociable young man, he was at this time solving his inferiority complex over his mother's birth. It is of sufficient importance to quote fully (Herndon, 1889).

> The first factional fight in old Ireland, they say,
> Was all on account of Saint Patrick's birthday,
> It was somewhere about midnight without any doubt,
> And certain it is, it made a great rout.

> On the eighth day of March, as some people say,
> Saint Patrick at midnight, he first saw the day;
> While others assert 'twas the ninth he was born—
> 'Twas all a mistake—between midnight and morn.

> Some blamed the baby, some blamed the clock.
> Some blamed the doctor, some the crowing cock.
> With all these close questions sure no one could know,
> Whether the babe was too fast or the clock was too slow.

Some fought for the eighth, for the ninth some would die;
He who wouldn't see right would have a black eye.
At length these two factions so positive grew,
They each had a birthday, and Pat he had two.

Till Father Mulcahay who showed them their sins,
He said none could have two birthdays but as twins.
'Now Boys, don't be fighting for the eight or the nine
Don't quarrel so always, now why not combine.

Combine eight with nine. It is the mark;
Let that be the birthday. Amen! said the clerk.
So all got blind drunk, which completed their bliss,
And they've kept up the practise from that day to this.''

Vocal self-expression with joy, as in other arts, is emotivated by constructive love. Lincoln's shyness with women was based more likely on the feelings of social inferiority over the illegitimate birth of his mother and other members of her family rather than crude manners, great poverty, and ill-fitting clothes. He was at this time obtaining through the friendship and idealism of Ann Rutledge, the lovely daughter of James Rutledge, encouragement for believing in himself. He relieved his feeling of social inferiority over his mother's birth by humorous reflections on the confusions over St. Patrick's birth.

Natural Humanitarianism

Lincoln had an unfailing sense of the needs of people and a spontaneous urge to help out wherever he could. Robert Rutledge has told the story of Ab Trout, a boy in bare feet in winter who was chopping a pile of wood when Abe passed by. Seeing the boy's condition Abe stopped to question him and upon learning that he would get a dollar to buy a pair of shoes when he finished the job, Abe sent him into the house to warm his feet and finished it for him.

Two neighbors became involved in a law suit but decided they would get more satisfaction by fighting it out with their fists. One chose Abe Lincoln as his second and the other chose John Brewer, a cocky little man, to serve for him. Brewer's man won the fight and in his excitement Brewer challenged: "Well Abe, my man has whipped yours and I can whip you." Abe laughingly agreed to fight on condition that John would mark off the size of his body on Abe and count every blow struck outside of the area a foul.

One day when riding to Springfield, a man named Chandler whom Lincoln scarcely knew overtook him, riding a jaded horse for all it could go. Lincoln asked about his hurry and upon learning that he was racing to beat a wealthy, avaricious land owner to Springfield to file a claim, Lincoln loaned him his horse and rode the jaded animal into town while Chandler hurried on to win the title.

How Lincoln Used Wit

Lincoln seemed to be perpetually set in an attitude ready to take homely little episodes from everyday life and by the witty addition of a few words convert them into humorous illustrations of the admirable or disgraceful qualities of a greater situation. He delighted in amusing his Illinois friends with Hoosier tales. He would join hilariously in a good laugh over his own stories, and none could retell an old chestnut with more prolific and vivid embellishments than Abe Lincoln.

An illustration of his characteristic method is taken from Ellis (Herndon, 1889). Abe was chosen to umpire a cock fight in which each man paid a quarter to enter his bird. The contestants formed a ring and at a given signal from the umpire all fowls were tossed into the center simultaneously, owner of the surviving bird in the fight that followed to take all. Bap McNabb had boasted proudly of the fighting qualities of his rooster and a crowd of excited fans gathered around to bet on their favorites. At the signal, in flew the birds and a great battle started with all of them in it except McNabb's rooster which turned tail and ran. Bap, in chagrin at the jeering, took the bird home and tossed it into the yard. Promptly it flew onto a wood pile and flapping its wings lustily gave a mighty crow. At this Bap exclaimed in disgust: "Yes, you little cuss, you're great on dress parade, but not worth a d--n in a fight." President Lincoln is said to have applied this story later to the war policy of General George B. McClellan.

The following "lizard story," as he liked to call it, was one of his favorites. It is probably a fair sample of his style at that time. It was retold as nearly verbatim as possible by J. Rowan Herndon (Herndon, 1889), who heard Lincoln tell it.

"The meeting house was in the woods and quite a distance from any other house. It was only used once a month. The preacher—an old line Baptist—was dressed in coarse linen pantaloons, and shirt of the same material. The pants, manufactured after the old fashion, with baggy legs and a flap in front, were made to attach to his frame without the aid of suspenders. A single button held his shirt in position, and that was at the collar. He rose up in the pulpit and in a loud voice announced his text thus: 'I am the Christ, whom I shall represent today.' About this time a little blue lizard ran up underneath his baggy pantaloons. The old preacher, not wishing to interrupt the steady flow of his sermon, slapped away on his legs, expecting to arrest the intruder; but his efforts were unavailing, and the little fellow kept ascending higher and higher. Continuing the sermon, the preacher slyly loosened the central button which graced the waist-band of his pantaloons and with a kick off came that easy-fitting garment. But meanwhile Mr. Lizard had passed the equatorial line of waist-band and was calmly exploring that part of the preacher's anatomy which lay underneath the back of his shirt. Things were now growing interesting, but the sermon was still grinding on. The next movement on the preacher's part was for the collar button, and with one sweep of his arm off came the tow linen shirt. The congregation sat for an instant as if dazed; at length one old lady in the rear of the room rose up and glancing at the excited object in the pulpit, shouted at the top of her voice: 'If you represent Christ then I'm done with the Bible.' "

Reading Law

Abraham Lincoln said of his education as a man (Scripps letter, 1860): "He was never in a college or Academy as a student; and never inside a college or academy building till since he had a law-license. What he has in the way of education he has picked up. After he was twenty-three, and had separated from his father, he studied English Grammar—imperfectly of course, but so as to speak and write as well as he now does." Lincoln's reference to his father indicates endless paternal opposition. He read Squire Bowling Green's law books studiously and often attended his court. Sometimes he contributed advice to disputants on the advantages of compromising their difficulties.

When he pleaded a bastardy case for a young unmarried mother in the Squire's court, he argued that the man's character was like a piece of cloth which, though soiled, could again be made clean by washing and hanging in the sun to dry. But the character of the girl, who was probably less to blame than the man, was like a broken and shattered vase, which could never be restored and made whole again. This estimation of the man's action, as not being held against him permanently, whereas the woman's would be regarded as guilty and remain damaging to her reputation for life unless he restored her honor by marriage, indicates how Lincoln continued to feel about the illegitimate pregnancy of his grandmother and the premarital conception of his own mother.

Lincoln's darkening cloud as a merchant obtained a silver lining by a chance of good furtune. As he described it to A. J. Conant, an artist who painted his portrait in 1860:

> "One day a man who was migrating to the West drove up in front of my store with a wagon which contained his family and household plunder. He asked me if I would buy an old barrel for which he had no room in his wagon and which contained nothing of special value. I did not want it, but to oblige him I bought it, and paid half a dollar for it. Without further ex-amination I put it away in the store and forgot all about it. Some time after, in overhauling things, I came upon the barrel and emptying it on the floor to see what it contained, I found at the bottom of the rubbish a complete edition of Blackstone's Commentaries. I began to read those famous works, and I had plenty of time, for during the long summer days, when the farmers were busy with their crops, my customers were few and far between. The more I read the more intensely interested I became. Never in my whole life was my mind so thoroughly absorbed. I read until I devoured them." (Whipple, 1908.)

Abe Lincoln read aloud from Blackstone, lying on the store counter with his head propped up by a bolt of jeans cloth; sometimes he would stretch out on the floor with a chair turned upside down to rest against, or in summer he would lie on the ground in front of the store under a tree and move around with its shade, evidently preferring this position (Barton, 1925). So earnestly did he study the *Commentaries* that within a few weeks he had memorized many of its fundamental rules, and these he would recite to whomever would listen. "Municipal law is a rule of civil conduct prescribed by the supreme power in a state, commanding what is right and prohibiting what is wrong." Herein, "we the people" as the founders of the Constitution, and no longer a king "by divine right," constitute the final authority of government.

> "The primary and principle object of the law are rights and wrongs. Rights are divided into rights of persons and rights of things. The rights of persons include the rights of personal security or the legal enjoyment of life, limbs, body, health and reputation; personal liberty; and the right to acquire property. Wrongs are simply violations of rights and are divided into private wrongs and public wrongs."

Abe explained to his neighbors how the absolute rights of individuals are preserved through the writ of habeas corpus. He liked to discuss the relative merits of democracy, aristocracy, monarchy, and slavery, in relation to principles of ethics. He studied the history and purpose of common law, the Magna Charta, trial by jury, the Petition of Rights, the Bill of Rights, and the development of jurisprudence as a system of defense against injustice and oppression.

"Honest Abe"

Berry failed within a few months and Lincoln, in fairness to his creditors, assumed responsibility for the notes they had given in establishing the store. With his meager earning capacity nearly 15 years must pass before he finished paying this debt. He became known as "Honest Abe," a reputation that proved later to be of the utmost value as a lawyer and politician. Since he might have avoided these obligations by declaring himself bankrupt, he gained enormously in self-respect as well as respectability among the people by this conscientious application of retributive justice to himself.

> "That debt was the greatest obstacle I have ever met in my life," he said; "I had no way of speculating and I could not earn enough money except by labor, and to earn even by labor eleven hundred dollars besides my living seemed the work of a lifetime. There was, however, but one way, I went to the creditors and told them that if they would let me alone I would give them all I could earn over my living, as fast as I could earn it."

Surveyor

The frontier country was being settled rapidly and surveyors were in great demand. John Calhoun, county surveyor, had found Lincoln a reliable assistant and appointed him as a deputy. With Mentor Graham's assistance Abe mastered within a year Gibson's *Theory and Practice of*

Surveying and Flint's *Treatise on Geometry, Trigonometry and Rectangular Surveying,* sufficiently to continue this work until he left New Salem. His records were written neatly and carefully, and have since proven accurate. They include surveyed maps of the towns of Huron and Albany in 1836. Lincoln commented in his Scripps letter about himself as a surveyor:

> "The Surveyor of Sangamo, offered to depute to A that portion of his work which was within his part of the county. He accepted, procured a compass and chain, studied Flint, and Gibson a little, and went at it. This procured bread, and kept soul and body together."

Abe Lincoln's ingenuity was demonstrated one day. When surveying near Mrs. Hornbuckle's home where he stopped at noon for dinner, she had no meal ready but willingly set about at once to prepare one, explaining that her clock had stopped and she had no way of knowing the time. Abe said he could remedy that. He set his compass on the floor and then with an awl scratched a line due north and south in a board near the door jamb. "When the jamb's shadow strikes this line," he said, "it will be high noon."

Postmaster

Lincoln moved the post office to Hill's store after Berry failed. His salary was proportional to the annual postal business and amounted to about $30 a year. He proved a likable postmaster in his pleasure at being accommodating. He believed thoroughly in the honesty and good will of the people and would sort the mail and leave the office unlocked so that the villagers could come and get their letters and newspapers while he was off splitting rails or helping to build a house or barn or surveying land. When about to pass the house of a neighbor who had unclaimed mail, he would carry it under his hat and make a free delivery. His office had other compensations. It made him acquainted with almost every settler in the country around, much to his future political advantage, and gave him ample opportunity for indulging freely in one of his greatest pleasures, reading newspapers.

His lax habits as postmaster were not entirely satisfactory and several complaints were filed against him. But he continued to hold the office until it was removed from New Salem. He favored one George Spears with delivering a paper on credit, only to find when the account was finally paid his friend demanded a receipt. Lincoln replied (7, 1, 1834), no little offended: "At your request I send you a receipt for the postage on your paper. I am some what surprised at your request. I will however comply with it. The law requires News paper postage to be paid in advance and now that I have waited a full year you choose to wound my feelings by insinuating that unless you get a receipt I will probably make you pay it again."

Although a bookkeeper of the government's accounts and finances Abe was not inclined to appreciate the importance of being exact in detail and punctual in opening the office. He trusted everyone, and kept the government's funds in an old blue sock in an unlocked drawer. Postal rates for letters varied with the number of pages and the distance traversed. A single sheet cost six cents for 30 miles and 25 cents for over 400. Two sheets cost twice as much and three sheets three times as much.

It was more than a year after the New Salem post office had been discontinued and Lincoln had moved to Springfield that he was finally called upon by the government to close his account. William Carpenter, the Springfield postmaster, made the following record. "For cash rec'd of A. Lincoln late P.M. New Salem $248.83." This sum was the correct receipt of the office for a year and the commission for it was between $25 and $30.

Sued for Debt

Lincoln, as a surveyor, postmaster, and odd jobber, earned enough to make small payments on his debts but this was insufficient to meet the notes when presented as due. One Peter Van Bergen bought up Lincoln's note to Radford for $379.82, dated October 19, 1833. He alone of Lincoln's creditors brought suit, in April, 1834, even though part payments had reduced it to $204.82. Judgment was rendered against Lincoln, and his worldly possessions, horse, saddle, bridle, and surveying instruments, by which he earned money to live and pay his debts, were taken from him according to law and sold at auction.

Why Van Bergen hated Lincoln so ruthlessly that he would destroy his means of earning a living is unknown. "Uncle Jimmy" Short of Sand Ridge bought the property and generously gave it back to Abe. With tears in his eyes the young man thanked his friend and in time paid the debt in full. Barton (1925) tells us that years later, when President Lincoln heard that old "Uncle Jimmy" was "penniless" in California, he appointed him as an Indian agent.

These were anxious days for Abe Lincoln. Though barely able to pay for board and room, with his notes a millstone around his neck, he humorously referred to them as "the national debt."

Chapter VIII
ANN RUTLEDGE: ROMANCE, TRAGEDY, INSPIRATION

It is of little historical importance whether Abraham Lincoln loved Ann Rutledge, but it is of the utmost importance, in an analytic study of the development of his mind, personality, self-education, understanding of human nature, and philosophy of living, to evaluate the evidence indicating the nature of their personal relations.

I will present first an account that seems most naturally true, based on the most reliable indicative evidence and on a psychological estimation of the sacred meaning of instinctive mating love for a virtuous, woman-shy, morally idealistic, conscientious young man like Lincoln. Then consideration will be given to the opinions of Herndon, the Randalls, and other biographers *for* and *against* the probability of Abraham Lincoln and Ann Rutledge having loved each other.

Information on the personal relations between them naturally falls into several categories—indefinite old memories of neighbor eye-witnesses, indicative implications in letters and other documents, reliably known conditions existing at the time that naturally tended to the development of interests in each other, consistency of testimony on Lincoln's nervous depression after Ann's death, and the consistency thereafter of Lincoln's continuation of sad meditations on the frustration of love by death, coupled with his neurotic conflicts each time he tried to love and marry. A man's unwillingness or inability to free himself from the effects of continuation of mood long after the death of a beloved person is impressive evidence of the depth of his feeling for that person.

We must bear in mind that most of the memories of the survivors of the Rutledge family and of neighbors closely associated with Abraham Lincoln and Ann Rutledge at the time of their attentions to each other (1833-35) were related 30 years after the event (1865) to Lincoln's law partner, W. H. Herndon, upon personal questioning to gather evidence and testimony with the intention of writing his biography, and not merely to tell the story of a romance as alleged by some biographers. By that time most of the informants were elderly except Mrs. Sarah Rutledge Saunders, Ann's youngest sister, and John Hill and Robert Rutledge, who were then middle-aged active business men. John Hill's unsolicited account, published in 1862, indicates that neighborhood gossip about Abe's interest in Ann had continued in circulation after he left New Salem.

Robert Rutledge was five years younger than Ann and at 12 to 17 years of age was an intelligent boy interested in his sister's beaux, particularly John McNamar and Abe Lincoln. He recorded his memories of observations in letters to Herndon with conscientious care and honesty after properly checking details with other members of his family. He has given the most direct and simple, objectively realistic descriptions of

Lincoln's physical constitution, dress, habits, manners, social attitudes, studies and characterizing interactions with his neighbors during his New Salem years of any contemporary. History is indebted to Robert for his faithful description of facts without embellishment of impressions and interpretations. Practically all of his testimony has been accepted as reliable and regarded as indispensable by most biographers—except his account of Lincoln's engagement to his sister Ann, which has been questioned by some. In October 1866, he wrote to Herndon in response to a list of questions:

> "Believing that any authentic statements connected with the early life and history of the beloved Abraham Lincoln should belong to the great American people, I submit the following replies to the interrogatories contained in your recent letter. I trust largely to your courtesy as a gentleman, to your honesty and integrity as a historian, and to your skill in writing for the public, to enlarge wherever my statements seem obscure, and to condense and remove whatever seems superfluous. Above all, I trust to your honor and your sense of right and consistency, to exclude from print anything which in your judgment may injuriously affect the surviving actors in the great drama which you propose to re-enact once more.
>
> "Many of my statements are made from memory with the aid of association of events; and should you discover that the date, location, and circumstances of the events here named should be contradictory to those named from other sources, I beg of you to consider well the testimony in each case, and make up your history from those statements which may appear to you best fitted to remove all doubt as to their correctness."

Some recent biographers have, not without prejudice of purpose, disposed of the testimony of Robert Rutledge and other members of his family on the relations of Abe and Ann as wishful reminiscences written after the death of President Lincoln to connect the Rutledge name intimately with his name. Such sweeping judgment is logical and valid only where testimony can be shown to have been fabricated for such purpose. The Rutledges neither initiated nor tried to propagate information to establish such impressions. Evidence given independently by neighbors, who would certainly have resented and denounced any ambitious faking of particular intimacy with Lincoln, shows that this was not the case. The Rutledges were modest, honest, respectable people who had the confidence and esteem of their neighbors. The evidence will show, in many ways, that Lincoln was more closely and sympathetically associated with the Rutledge family than with any other family thereafter, including his wife's relatives.

In the following presentation, passages will be quoted from Robert's letters as they present information on special subjects, since they constitute the most reliable material that has been collected on persons, conditions, and events of significant importance in the relations of Abraham

Lincoln and Ann Rutledge. (For a complete presentation of these letters see Hertz, 1938.)

After Lincoln's defeat for the legislature in 1832 and the failure of his store in 1833, which left him "penniless," in debt and often without work, it is quite certain that he was happy in New Salem since he continued to enjoy the use of books and sympathetic encouragement in self-education of kindly people—opportunities such as he had never known elsewhere. However, this is probably not enough to account for a capable, unattached, ambitious, strong young man, eager to study law, freely choosing to continue living in a dying village after he had made new friends in the Black Hawk War among prominent men including lawyer John Stuart, of thriving Springfield less than a day's walk away. New Salem had another attraction—the warm exchange of interests with a sweet, lovely, gracious, intelligent, understanding young woman, Ann Rutledge. Although engaged to another man, she was naturally sympathetically interested and fascinated by Lincoln's ability as a speaker in their community meetings and by his enthusiastic displays of progress in the study of law. This sympathetic intercourse was naturally conditioned to become inspirational to him as it was consistent with that between him and his mother. It must have had a vigorously constructive effect on his mind as such influences have for any shy, diffident, ambitious, morally idealistic young man. It would be absurd to assume that Abe's attitude toward Ann was not naturally inclined to grow, under encouraging circumstances, into the first and possibly the deepest instinctive mating-love-fixation of his life.

The Rutledge Family

Ann's father, James Rutledge, was a son of Edward Rutledge, an eminent South Carolina lawyer educated in England, a signer of the Declaration of Independence, member of the Continental Congress, officer of the Army of the Revolution, and governor of South Carolina. His father's brother John Rutledge, also an eminent lawyer and governor of South Carolina, was a member of the Federal Constitutional Convention. He played an important role in drafting the Constitution of the United States.

James was born in South Carolina in 1781. Three of his children including David and Ann were born in Kentucky, and the last six were born in Illinois. He, with his cousin, Reverend John Cameron, laid out the town of New Salem in the summer of 1829 and bought land, built houses, a tavern, store, a saw and grist mill, and a dam on the Sangamon River. When the river proved to be insufficiently navigable for shipping farm products in boats, the future of New Salem was doomed. Rutledge, once a relatively wealthy gentleman pioneer, lost his store, mill, farm and tavern and died in December 1835, a poor man.

Ann Rutledge

Ann, who was born in Kentucky, January 7, 1813, was the third of nine children. As described by Herndon, and other people who knew her, she was about five feet two inches tall, slender, affectionate, sympathetic, attractive, gracious and understanding, with reddish tinted, light auburn hair, red lips and blue eyes. She had a pleasing voice, was intelligent, self-reliant, sensible and practical, and managed her father's tavern after she was 20. Her fiancé, John McNamar, wrote to G. U. Miles (May 5, 1866):

> "Miss Ann was a gentle Amiable Maiden without any of the airs of your city Belles but winsome and comly withal a blond in complection with golden hair, cherry red lips & a bonny Blue Eye."

As Robert described Ann to Herndon in 1866:

> "My sister was esteemed the brightest mind of the family, was studious, devoted to her duties of whatever character, and possessed a remarkably amiable and lovable disposition."

We can be reasonably certain that Ann in her relations with her family and neighbors was practical, friendly, and understanding. She was sixteen and a favorite pupil of Mentor Graham, the village teacher, when her father founded New Salem in 1829. Robert has told about her beaux:

> "William Berry [the son of a local minister] first courted Ann and was rejected; afterward Samuel Hill; and then John McNamar."

John (NcNeil) McNamar

John McNamar came to New Salem in 1830 and boarded in the home of Reverend John Cameron. He gave his name as John McNeil and soon became interested with Sam Hill in establishing a general merchandizing store. Apparently he had superior ability as a merchant and sufficient cash to buy stock, for several competitors (including Offutt, Rutledge, and the Herndons) soon closed their stores. Ann was then seventeen and according to Robert:

> "A friendship grew up between McNeil and Ann which ripened apace and resulted in an engagement to marry. McNeil's real name was McNamar. It seems that his father had failed in business, and his son, a very young man, had determined to make a fortune, pay off his father's debts, and restore him to his former social and financial standing. With this in view he left his home clandestinely, and in order to avoid pursuit by his parents changed his name. His conduct was strictly high toned, honest, and moral, and his object, whatever any may think of the deception which he practised in changing his name, entirely praiseworthy.
>
> "He prospered in business and, pending his engagement with Ann, he revealed his true name, returned to Ohio [New York] to relieve his parents from their embarrassments, and to bring the family with him to Illinois. On

his return to Ohio, several years having elapsed, he found his father in declining health or dead, and perhaps the circumstances of the family prevented his immediate return to New Salem. At all events he was absent two or three years."

McNamar had suddenly sold his share in the store to his partner Sam Hill in the fall of 1832 when he decided to go home. He then owned three farms and a fortune estimated at $12,000. Lincoln, as seems sufficiently indicated, probably thought as other New Salem people did, that Ann Rutledge and John McNamar intended to get married upon his return to New Salem. McNamar did not return until late in 1835, several months after Ann's death. During the three years of his absence it seems, according to Barton (1927) he had not written to her about himself and had not answered her letters. According to Robert's memory Ann was sadly disappointed over her fiancé's neglectful attitude and grew perplexed about what to do about her self-commitment to him.

Robert knew McNamar for many years after the death of his sister and his expression of respect for his character and intentions inspires confidence in what he had to say about the relations of Lincoln and Ann as well as McNamar and Ann. Herndon knew McNamar and interviewed him personally in 1866 on his relations with Ann Rutledge. He was influenced by McNamar's recollections in forming his account of the engagement of McNamar and Ann, and why it lapsed after his absence and negligence leading to the engagement of Lincoln and Ann. Barton (1925, 1927) had personal interviews many years later with Ann's sister and McNamar's second wife. He found that McNamar was regarded as being honest, practical and thrifty but mercenary and, as his second wife expressed it "utterly without sentiment."

"Old Plain Abe"

When Lincoln settled in New Salem in August of 1831, as a clerk in Offutt's store, he boarded with Rowan Herndon. He was very poor and often had meals and spent nights as a guest in the homes of other friends including Jimmy Short, Jack Armstrong, and Squire Bowling Green. Neighbors found his gossip, comments, political ideas and humorous tales relieved the monotony of their lives. He had learned the value of entertaining conversation in his own wilderness home as a boy, and knew what lonely settlers liked to talk about. He seems not to have considered that out of politeness he should offer to pay money for meals and lodgings. The early settlers had little money to exchange but, proud of their hospitality, they graciously accepted repayment in equality of service. Lincoln's way of compensation lay in skillfully repairing broken tools and furniture, doing chores, tending babies and amusing children or helping around the farm. Married women urged their husbands to bring Abe home for, unlike most men, he was not too proud to lend a willing hand in the kitchen.

Abe learned in 1831, from Squire Green, how to write contracts, wills, deeds, mortgages and other minor legal papers. One of his friends was John McNeil (McNamar), who boarded with the Camerons. "Mack," as Abe called him, was then the best merchant and business man in town. Without wasteful habits, he saved money and shrewdly bought defunct farms at bargain prices. According to Barton (1925), he first purchased a farm in November 1831 under the name of John McNeil. Worried about the risk of holding property under an assumed name he later confided in his friend Abe that his real name was McNamar. He was advised to correct the use of his name on legal documents, and the village people soon learned of the misrepresentation. He bought the Cameron farm in December 1831 and, a few months later, the adjoining farm of James Rutledge, who was forced to sell when New Salem failed to develop as expected. According to Barton, Ann Rutledge learned in this way the real name of her betrothed. According to her brother's statement he had previously confided his true identity to her upon their engagement. The latter seems probably correct, for she continued to have faith in his promise, which, as shown later, he had honorably intended to keep.

After Lincoln took over the defunct Herndon store with Berry, he became a regular boarder in the home of Reverend John Cameron, practising Presbyterian minister and unsuccessful real estate operator, the father of one son and eleven daughters. Some of the girls were about his age but to them he was just "old plain Abe," amusing but awkward, unromantic and girl-shy, without attraction as a possible husband.

Lincoln Finds Himself

In sad contrast to John McNamar, handsome, well born, and educated young easterner who, in two years, had become the most successful business man in the community, Lincoln was in late 1833 an inexperienced, good natured, comtemplative, impractical failure as a merchant. He and Berry had bought with promissory notes the old stock of three closed stores, and when their store "winked out" he had accumulated a burden of debt that he had no prospect of paying off entirely in many years.

According to the statement of Robert Rutledge: after Berry failed

"Lincoln came to Rutledge [his father] and made him a tender to pay half the note. This Rutledge utterly refused to accept from Mr. L., alleging that he had taken Berry's note for the debt and, if he could not make it out of him, he would not accept it at all."

By committing himself to pay Berry's debt as well as his own, when he might have declared bankruptcy or left the community, Lincoln had proven to his friends that he was a man of honorable word, good will, generosity, sympathetic understanding and philosophical comprehension of the profound importance of living by kindness, service, honesty, truth, and justice. He had shown that he was a man who held self-respect and social respectability and social cooperation above material necessity.

The regard of the Rutledge family and of the people of New Salem for Abe Lincoln grew enthusiastic as he became an excellent surveyor and earned enough to make payments on his debts. In the summer of 1834 they urged him to try again for the state legislature.

Lincoln has told Scripps of the meaning, as a turning point in his life, of his election to the legislature and the encouragement of his friends to study law:

> "The election of 1834 came and he was then elected to the legislature by the highest vote cast for any candidate. Major John T. Stuart, then in full practice of the law, was also elected. During the canvass, in a private conversation he encouraged A. to study law. After the election he borrowed books of Stuart, took them home with him, and went at it in good earnest. He studied with nobody. He still mixed in the surveying to pay board and clothing bills. When the Legislature met, the law books were dropped, but were taken up again at the end of the session."

Lincoln's Ideal Woman

In a letter (1, [3?], 1842) to his close friend Joshua Speed, Lincoln persuaded him to overcome his self-doubt of love and marry Miss Fanny Henning. The reasons Lincoln gave indicate the qualities he admired and loved most in a woman and why he would instinctively want to court such a woman.

> "Not because you thought she desired it, and you had given her reason to expect it, not for her wealth, for you knew she had none, not because you reasoned yourself into it, but because you found yourself unable to *reason* yourself *out of it.* Did you partly form the purpose, of courting her the first time you ever saw her? What had reason to do with it, at that early stage? There was nothing *at that time* for reason to work upon. Whether she was moral, amiable, sensible, or even of good character, you did not, nor could you then know; except perhaps you might infer the last from the company you found her in. All you then did or could know of her, was her *personal appearance and deportment;* and these, if they impress at all, impress the *heart* and not the head."

In his earnest sincerity Lincoln spoke from his own experience of having fallen in love the first time he saw a certain girl and was unable to reason himself out of it. From his characterization of her as moral, amiable, sensible, and of a *"personal appearance and deportment"* that "impress the *heart"* she could have been none other than Ann Rutledge.

Records of the Rutledge tavern show that Lincoln boarded there in 1833-34 when Ann was in charge. We can be reasonably certain that he became sympathetically attentive to lovely Ann in her unhappiness when he saw, as postmaster, that she was not receiving letters from McNamar. A keen observer of human nature, he understood her increasing disappointment as one and then two years passed. Naturally, he became convinced that McNamar had grown indifferent in his engagement to her.

By mid-1834 Lincoln was no longer a total failure. As a surveyor and postmaster working and saving to pay his debts he had become one of the most liked and trusted young men in the community, although still one of the poorest. There can be little doubt that Ann, who was taking care of Abe's room and board, was observing with admiration the zeal of his studies, and her lively sympathetic interest in his progress gave him real satisfaction and heartfelt encouragement.

Lincoln's feelings for Ann Rutledge naturally passed, as indicated by the memories of neighbors collected by Herndon, into three phases of development—shy admiration and sympathetic attraction, hopeful love and conditional engagement, followed by bitter anguish and sacred resolution.

During the first year in New Salem Lincoln had frequently seen Ann responding happily to the attentions of his handsome, successful friend "Mack," and instinctively felt the inferiorities of his face, education, and family. In his highly moral conscientiousness, he regarded an engagement between man and woman as inviolate as marriage. No matter how much he admired the loveliest, most attractive and understanding young woman that he had ever the good fortune of talking with almost daily as a friend, he had to think of her as promised to another man. Even when, in December 1831, he had learned confidentially that McNeil's real name was McNamar, his attitude remained unchanged. In 1833 Ann respected her engagement to John McNamar, and even though Lincoln instinctively loved her, he had little hope of getting her. However, by 1834 he saw that she had become deeply disappointed by McNamar's silent indifference to her feelings.

The tavern failed in the fall of 1834, and the Rutledge family moved in with the Camerons on the farm that had been sold to McNamar. Hereafter Ann and her mother worked for various neighbors. That winter Lincoln was earning three dollars a day when attending the legislature in Vandalia. With his additional jobs as postmaster, deputy surveyor, and legal recorder, he was able to make sufficient payments on his debts to think of the possibility of getting married after being admitted to the bar. His diffident courtship of Ann probably grew hopeful and serious in 1834.

Herndon has told us from descriptions by neighbor witnesses of Lincoln's attentions to Ann. He escorted her to a quilting bee and, though men were supposed not to stay in the sewing room with the women, he braved the custom to sit near her and admire her skill. Such indifference to custom was certainly characteristic of Lincoln. His enchantment embarrassed her, and the mistakes she made in stitching a quilt were displayed for many years after as evidence of her affectionate responses to him.

Abe, now 24, and Ann, 21, were naturally congenial in their physical and mental constitutions, in education, in their veneration of the historical traditions of the founding the nation's independence and government, in respect for truth and honesty, for morality, for ambition, and for equalitarian legal rights with freedom in social relations. There can be little doubt of their affections' responding instinctively, warmly, to each other's sympathetic attentions. The courtship has been described as idealistic and sweet. He liked to recite to her favorite selections from Shakespeare, Blackstone, Clay, and other famous men that he had memorized in his studies, and she delighted him with songs.

Robert told Herndon in several letters in 1866 about Lincoln's attentions to Ann.

> "Mr. Lincoln courted Ann and engaged to marry her, on the completion of the study of law. In this I am corroborated by James Mc. Rutledge, a cousin about her age, and who was in her confidence. He says in a letter to me just received: 'Ann told me once in coming from a camp meeting on Rock Creek, that engagements made too far ahead sometimes failed, that one had failed (meaning her engagement with McNamar), and gave me to understand that as soon as certain studies were completed she and Lincoln would be married.' "

In another letter Robert told of McNamar's long absence and how

> "Mr. Lincoln paid his addresses to Ann, continued his visits and attentions regularly, and those resulted in an engagement to marry, conditional to an honorable release from the contract with McNamar. There is no kind of doubt as to the existence of this engagement. David urged Ann to consummate it, but she refused until such time as she could see McNamar, inform him of the change in her feelings, and seek an honorable release."

Since no evidence has ever been found of correspondence between Abe and Ann, many biographers have questioned the reality of their engagement. Since no evidence of correspondence exists between Ann and McNamar either, we cannot accept the lack of letters as being decisively significant of no engagement. Neither have letters been found by Lincoln to Mary Todd or Mary Todd to Lincoln before their marriage, but no one holds that none were written and therefore they could not have been engaged. The fairest assumption seems to be that probably Lincoln and Ann did correspond during the two months when he was away attending the Illinois State Legislature in Vandalia, but that the letters of both have been displaced and lost or destroyed. The Rutledge family moved from New Salem under impoverishing circumstances in this period, and either disposal is quite possible. Only one letter to Ann, written by her brother David as a postscript in a letter to his father, July 27, 1835, is known to exist. It was loaned to W. B. Barton by Ann's sister, Mrs. Sarah Rutledge Saunders, who had treasured it since childhood. It says:

> "Valued sister . . . . I am glad to hear that you have a notion of coming to school, and I earnestly recommend to you that you spare no time from im-

proving your education and mind. Remember that time is worth more than all gold therefore throw away none of your golden moments."

Ann's interest in improving her education has been interpreted by some biographers as indicating that probably she was not in love with Lincoln. It seems more likely to indicate that Lincoln, in the eagerness of his studies, had influenced her to want to improve her education and she had told her family that she was planning to attend the women's seminary in Jacksonville where David was in college. It would certainly have been most natural for these two highly conscientious, idealistic and capable young people in their affectionate influences on each other to have planned on improving their education as far as possible before marriage.

Ann became ill, probably of typhoid, in late July of 1835, while living with her family and the Camerons in the house on Sand Ridge that was then owned by McNamar. Lincoln was living seven miles away in New Salem and, according to Ann's older brother John (Herndon, 1889), he was permitted to visit her until her worsening condition led the physician to forbid it.

John said in a letter to Herndon, November 25, 1886:

> "I have heard mother say that Ann would frequently sing for Lincoln's benefit. She had a clear ringing voice. Early in her illness he called, and she sang a hymn for which he always expressed a great preference. It begins: 'Vain man, thy fond pursuits forbear.' You will find it in one of the standard hymn-books. It was likewise the last thing she ever sang." (Herndon, 1889.)

Barton undertook, long after Herndon, his own review of New Salem records and traditions, to throw better light on the relations of Ann Rutledge and Abraham Lincoln. In 1921, he personally interviewed Mrs. Sarah, "Aunt Sallie," Rutledge Saunders, then living in Lampoc, California. Although Mrs. Saunders was then ninety-two, he found her "a woman of clear mind, strong character and abiding faith." Sarah, the youngest of the Rutledge family, was born in the Rutledge tavern in 1829. She was only six when Ann died, but lived with her mother and brother Robert for so many years thereafter that her information from conversations in the family on the relations of Ann, John McNamar, and Abe Lincoln was definite enough to convince Barton that Ann first loved McNamar and then Lincoln.

In 1922, Mrs. Saunders dictated in a letter written by her son, James Rutledge Saunders, to Mr. George P. Hambrecht of Madison, Wisconsin, concerning Ann's illness:

> "Finally my brother David, who was attending school at Jacksonville, Ill., and Lincoln were sent for. I can see them as they each came, and when Lincoln went into the sick room where Sister Ann lay, the others retired. A few minutes later Lincoln came from the room with bowed head and seemed to me, at the time, to be crying. Soon after this Ann died, and was followed by my father."

Sarah's memories, given in 1921 and 1922, are so independently consistent with those of her brother that no biographer can fairly dismiss them as ambitious fabrications to identify the family name with that of Lincoln. Sarah's impressions, at six years of age, of Ann's fatal illness, of the family sending for her brother and Lincoln when death was impending, and of Lincoln's grief, certainly seems to mean that Ann and Lincoln were believed by the family to be in love with each other.

Sarah's letter is consistent with the other family accounts indicating that Ann asked repeatedly to see Abe during her illness but, as her condition grew worse, her physician advised that his visits be postponed until a more favorable time. When her condition grew alarming, word was sent to him. He was permitted to remain alone in the room with her, but nothing of what they said to each other was ever revealed by him. Lincoln had to endure the bitter anguish every person must know when the one he loves is dying. Ann passed away on August 25, 1835 and was buried in the little Concord Cemetary.

It is entirely consistent with the characters and the severely conscientious morality of Abe and Ann, his shyness and her sense of continuing obligation to McNamar until she had honorably ended their engagement, for us to infer that Lincoln and Ann Rutledge never realized the full extent of their love for each other. It may have been that after she became ill she felt she would not wait for McNamar to return, although her people were dependent on her decision and his good will for a house to live in. Perhaps not until then had she been able completely to commit herself to Abe. Such fatefully involved destiny of love seems most consistent with Lincoln's attitude later about the futility of love ending in death. On this we have abundant indicative evidence, to be given later in this chapter.

Some biographers, because of the lack of positive statements by witnesses that Lincoln attended the funeral, have inferred that he was not really in love with Ann, but was only her confidential friend and legal adviser. Barton (1925), a Baptist minister interested in this question, has explained that services were not usually held by the western settlers at the time of burial. It was customary to wait until several burials had accumulated and then hold one funeral service for all of them. This custom reduced travel and loss of time from work. If the funeral was held later, after the harvest, Lincoln might possibly have been in Vandalia and unable to attend.

Melancholy and Despair

Robert Rutledge wrote: "The effect upon Mr. Lincoln's mind was terrible; he became plunged into dispair, and many of his friends feared that reason would desert her throne. His extraordinary emotions were regarded as strong evidence of existence of the tenderest relations between himself and the deceased." Robert was then seventeen and his statements of personal observation, as a sensible young man, although given 30 years later, are impressive. His high-minded style of writing was characteristic of his time.

Old neighbors of New Salem told Herndon that for several days after the death of Ann, Lincoln was overcome by melancholy and despair. We give the gist of his report of their accounts for their indicative values. Unable to control his thoughts, unable to eat, sleep, work or rest, he wandered through the woods and fields, alone and disconsolate. He is reported to have been found by his friends lying by Ann's grave with one arm thrown over it in abject futility of spirit. In alarm they took him to the home of Bowling and Nancy Green where previously he had lived. He sat at the hearth in silence, his eyes staring and seeing no one. His usually smiling face had grown "terrible." It was useless to talk to him. Fearing that he might be suicidal, his friends deprived him of his pocket knife and razor. One night when a storm was raging he went to the door and looked out into the dark turmoil. Finally he exclaimed, "I can't bear to think of her out there alone. The rain and the storm shan't beat on her grave."

Lincoln's neighbors seem to have been impressed by this revelation of his feelings. John Hill wrote (6, 6, 1865): "Miss Rutledge died within a few days of September 1, 1835, *certain*. Lincoln bore up under it very well until some days afterwards a heavy rain fell which unnerved him." Hill's report of his parents' memory of gossip that Lincoln was nervously distressed by a severe change of weather has been discredited by Randall (1945) as an absurd fabrication, entirely out of character with Lincoln's dignity and good common sense. Such reaction to weather by Lincoln is certainly consistent with his statement several years later to Speed on the depressing effect of gloomy weather on himself (See Chapter XIII). Hill's recollection is also indicative of the reliability of some other reports of gossip about Lincoln's feelings for Ann Rutledge (see later in this chapter).

A letter of neighboring John Jones to Herndon about Lincoln's behavior expresses belief that he loved Ann Rutledge. Jones wrote (10, 29, 1866):

> "Having seen the statements made by R. B. Rutledge in reference to the early life of Abraham Lincoln and having known Mr. Lincoln and been an eye-witness to the events he narrated, from my boyhood, I take pleasure in saying that they are literally true.
>
> "As to the relation existing between Mr. Lincoln and Ann Rutledge, I have every reason to believe that it was of the tenderest character, as I know of my own knowledge that he made regular visits to her. During her last illness he visited her sick chamber and on his return stopped at my house. It was very evident that he was much distressed, and I was not surprised when it was rumored subsequently that his reason was in danger. It was generally understood that Mr. Lincoln and Ann Rutledge were engaged to be married. She was a very amiable and lovable woman and it was deemed a very suitable match—one in which the partners were in every way worthy of each other."

Mrs. Bennett Abell, in whose home Lincoln is said to have lived at the time of Ann's death, commented reminiscently in a letter to Herndon in 1867, on her neighbors' views of Lincoln's grief. "The community said he was crazy but he was not crazy but he was very desponding for a long time."

James (Uncle Jimmy) Short, a warm friend of Lincoln and the Rutledges, stated in 1865 that Mrs. Rutledge (Ann's mother) kept house for him until he married. [During this period Ann managed the tavern for her family and boarded Lincoln. Later the Rutledges lived about half a mile from the Shorts at Sand Ridge.]

> "Mr. Lincoln came over to see me & them every day or two. I did not know of any engagement or tender passages between Mr. L and Miss R at the time. But after her death . . . he seemed to be so much affected and grieved so hardly that I then supposed there must have been . . . something of the kind."

Several other of Lincoln's old friends testified that they inferred from his uncontrollable grief that he "must have been" in love with Ann. The most positive testimony from neighbors to Herndon was given by schoolmaster Mentor Graham, Lincoln's old advisory teacher, and probable confidential friend as Lincoln was characteristically inclined to be so dependent. According to Herndon's memo of April 2, 1866, Mentor Graham said: "Lincoln and she were engaged. Lincoln told me so—she intimated to me the same." Graham also described Lincoln's "momentary derangement," probably meaning temporary derangement, and his feeling to commit suicide after "the death of one he dearly and sincerely love[d]." Randall (1945) discredited these memories of Graham because of errors he made in stating the years and age of Lincoln when he had known him as a child in Kentucky.

McNamar wrote to G. U. Miles in 1899: "Bowling Green feared that Lincoln's grief might injure his mind and took him into his home for a week or two to cheer him up. . . . Mrs. Green thought Ann loved McNamar as much as Lincoln, though the former had been absent so long." Mrs. William Rutledge, an aunt, said she thought that Ann liked McNamar better than Lincoln and would have married the former. W. G. Greene, an intimate New Salem friend, stated he believed that Abe and Ann were engaged and that his friends feared he might commit suicide after her death. Other neighbors, Caleb Carman, J. R. Herndon, L. M. Greene, Henry Hohhiner, and Jason Duncan expressed similar views. It seems that these largely consistent retrospective opinions by Lincoln's neighbors were founded both on his behavior after the death of Ann Rutledge and the frequency of observation of their happy associations together for more than a year previous.

McNamar was not informed of Ann's death and returned with his mother a few months after in the expectation of marrying her. He found, he said to Herndon in 1866, Lincoln "desolate and sorely distressed," as if in love with Ann, but he was sure that she had remained true to her promise to him and he, not Lincoln, would have married her. When Herndon asked McNamar to show him where Ann was buried, McNamar was unable to point out her grave or that of his mother, both being unmarked in the same neglected cemetary.

When Dr. Shastid published his father's description of Lincoln's eyes and melancholic mood, as cited in a previous chapter, he was probably informed by his father, who had lived in New Salem when Lincoln lived there, as well as by other sources, about the courtship of Ann Rutledge. "Lincoln loved Ann Rutledge with all his great heart," Dr. Shastid said, but he did not think his melancholy began at her death but was produced by the mental strain of his "crossed" eye condition since both were "known to have existed long before meeting her." (Shastid, 1929.)

Since Dr. Shastid wished to establish, as historically important, Lincoln's hyperphoria as a cause of repetitive melancholy, he certainly would have discredited the belief of his father and other New Salem people that Lincoln loved Ann if he had known any valid reason for doing so.

Biographers accept that Lincoln became despondent over the death of Ann and after some time recovered self-control, but have insisted this does not mean that he was in love with her. Lincoln's advice to his friend Speed (2, 3, 1842) answers this skepticism. Speed had confided that he was not sure of the truth of his love for Miss Henning because he was unable to free himself of melancholy anticipation of her poor health ending in early death. Lincoln counseled with assurance from his own experience:

> "You well know that I do not feel my own sorrows much more keenly than I do yours, when I know them. . . . I hope your melancholly bodings as to her early death are not well founded. . . . Why Speed, if you did not love her, although you might not wish her death, you would be most calmly resigned to it."

The vivid reports of Lincoln's dramatic actions and distraught words after the death of Ann are not inconsistent with his mood and behavior as a boy under relative circumstances. As he has told us (in Chapter III), after his father slaughtered his pet pig he scraped from the ground the traces of its blood and hair and burned them, and thereafter he felt nausea when the meat was served. His emotional reactions over the death of Ann naturally tended to repeat his reactions over the death of his mother when she was buried in the forest near his home. He had probably visited her grave alone more than once with similar thought and mood. Later, as a man, when he returned to his mother's grave he left it unmarked, but expressed his melancholy sentiment in a poem (see Chapter XV).

Recovery of Self-Control

Lincoln's constantly nostalgic fixation of love since boyhood, on memories of his dead mother, indicates how he was conditioned to adjust himself to the loss of Ann. Her death from a wasting fever in late August was remarkably similar to his mother's death in October 16 years before. These two women had awakened in him the greatest depth of love that a man can know. Ann's affectionate nature, loyal character, and idealistic mind reinforced the same inspiring effect upon him that the ideals of his heroic mother had in his boyhood. He retained with devotion memories of his mother but said little about her to anyone, except the brief confidence on one unusually conducive occasion to Herndon after the death of his father (see Chapter XXI). Hence it is consistent to conclude that in his silence about Ann he held in the same way his memories of her as sacred. If he had talked about them, even confidentially, as is usually advised in psychotherapy when emotionally frustrated, unsublimated memories cause neuroses, he would have reduced their impressive effects on his mind. Without cherishing the memories of Ann as an inspiring influence on his mind Lincoln would have regressed into gloomy apathy. To restore hopeful integrity for himself and make life again worth living he must think out a philosophy of common sense that would keep alive in constant resolution Ann's ideals of living, consistently with those of his mother. In this intuitive sublimation of the depressing feeling of the futility of love ending in death, Lincoln was consistent with the almost universal religious culture of memorial rites dedicated to the dead and belief in the continuation of being of the spirit in peace when devoutly remembered in the ideals, prayers, and rituals of the living. His counsel to Speed (2, 3, 1842) reflects this philosophy:

"The death scenes of those we love, are surely painful enough; but we are prepared to, and expect to see. They happen to all, and all know they must happen. Painful as they are, they are not an unlooked-for-sorrow. Should she, [Fanny] as you fear, be destined to an early grave, it is indeed, a great consolation to know that she is so well prepared to meet it."

Lincoln's gloomy state of mind did not entirely incapacitate him. As in most cases of depression upon the death of a beloved person, he found relief in work, although in a miserably dejected way. Herndon (1889) has given Lincoln's friends' accounts of how they kept him busy helping with the harvest, how he walked alone on country lanes and recited and read aloud to himself. They regarded uneasily his tired, worried eyes and sad face, apprehensive of his growing ill from despair. Eventually he was able to maintain sufficient consistency of mind to resume surveying and the study of law. In December he attended the legislature in Vandalia, but he looked "a changed man."

The behavior of President Lincoln many years later (in 1862) upon the death of his son Willie was certainly characteristic of his desperate efforts to live out his miserable thoughts and master hopeless melancholy. We know more definitely about his nervous reactions then, and give them here to show how extremely difficult it was for him to accept the death of a person he loved.

F. B. Carpenter (1877), who lived in the White House in 1864 for six months while painting President Lincoln reading the Proclamation of Emancipation to his cabinet, has given an intimate description from what he learned from members of the household, of Lincoln's distress after Willie's death. "After the funeral, the President resumed his official duties, but mechanically, and with terrible weight at heart. The following Thursday he gave way to his feelings and shut himself from all society. The second Thursday it was the same; he would see no one, and seemed a prey to the deepest melancholy. . . . The setting apart of Thursday for the indulgence of his grief had gone on for several weeks, and Mrs. Lincoln began to be seriously alarmed for the health of her husband." Carpenter further relates that through her influence the President accepted a visit from the Reverend Francis Vinton of Trinity Church, New York. Reverend Vinton appealed to him to become reconciled over the death of Willie by thinking of him, as taught in the *Bible,* as being alive in spirit called by Divine Will. The President was thought to have accepted this advice as he ceased his weekly regression into mourning. Thereafter he rarely spoke, unless necessary, about the death of Willie.

Lincoln seems to have recovered, at least superficially, within a few months after Ann's death, from his first serious experience with melancholic depression upon frustration of mating love. We may say, summarily, from the best available accounts, that it was produced, following such predisposition after injury of his brain, in a mother revering, girl shy, love diffident, sexually virtuous, highly moral young man, by the irreplaceable loss of his idealized love mate. Once real love has been awakened, living becomes extremely difficult upon its unexpected frustration, producing for some time nervous depression, and, in extreme cases, suicidal melancholia or schizophrenia. Lincoln, we find, thereafter grew "hypochondriacal," that is, miserably depressed and self-doubtful every time he tried to make himself love another woman and commit himself to marry her. He had an increasing tendency to lapse into a state of gloomy abstraction when alone, and dreaded loneliness more than anything. Insomnia and at times nightmares distressed him. The latter, as psychoanalysis has shown, are caused by conditional associations of excitements during the day of previously repressed idea-emotion complexes involved generally with feelings about death.

In 1836 Lincoln confided to one of his close friends, R. L. Wilson, as retold by Herndon (1889), that although he appeared to enjoy life rapturously he was the victim of a terrible melancholy. He sought company and indulged in hilarity without restraint or stint of time; but when by himself he was so overcome by mental depression that he never dared to carry a knife in his pocket. This report seems an exaggeration until we see later his behavior over breaking his engagement to Mary Todd.

He wisely cultivated friendly contacts and a humorous attitude to prevent "melancholy." He liked to exchange stories and would laugh inordinately at his own stories, even when told several times in a day. His

stories were generally characteristic in that they made the frustrated
vanity of eccentric egotism ridiculous, and ended with a moral implication
of wisdom in self-restraint. Eventually he became a person of increasing
inner reserve and solitude, inclined to indulge in philosophical meditation
on the tragic futility of love ending in death.

"Oh! why should the spirit of mortal be proud?" became Lincoln's
favorite poem. Herndon had often heard him quote the lines, and said in
his lecture of November 1866, on Lincoln's love for Ann Rutledge, that
he got the poem from Jason Duncan in 1833 when living in New Salem.
Later, in his biography (1889), Herndon said that Lincoln obtained the
poem from Duncan in 1842 after he gave a eulogy at the funeral of his
friend Bowling Green. While Herndon's dates are not consistent, his
statement of Lincoln's love of reciting the poem was correct. He intimated
in his lecture and book that it reflected Lincoln's feelings about Ann
Rutledge. That the poem was Lincoln's favorite and that it was associated
with Ann has been rejected by some biographers as another unfounded
inference.

Carpenter (1877) has given a most intimate account of Lincoln's
feelings for these lines. One evening when he was alone with the
President in his study he read some favorite passages from Shakespeare.
"Relapsing into a sadder strain," Carpenter has told us, "he laid the
book aside, and leaning back in his chair, said, 'There is a poem that has
been a great favorite with me for years, to which my attention was first
called when a young man, by a friend, and which I afterward saw and cut
from a newspaper, and carried in my pocket, till by frequent reading I had
it by heart. I would give a great deal,' he added, 'to know who wrote it,
but I never could ascertain.' Then, half closing his eyes, he repeated the
poem."

> Oh! why should the spirit of mortal be proud?
> Like a swift-fleeting meteor, a fast-flying cloud
> A flash of the lightening, a break of the wave
> He passeth from life to his rest in the grave.
>
> The leaves of the oak and the willows shall fade,
> Be scattered around, and together be laid;
> And the young and the old, and the low and the high
> Shall moulder to dust, and together shall lie.
>
> The infant a mother attended and loved;
> The mother that infant's affection who proved;
> The husband, that mother and infant who blest,—
> Each, all, are away to their dwellings of rest.
>
> [The maid on whose cheek, on whose brow, in whose eye,
> Shone beauty and pleasure,—her triumphs are by;
> And the memory of those who loved her and praised,
> Are alike from the minds of the living erased.]

The hand of the king that the sceptre hath borne,
The brow of the priest that the mitre hath worn,
The eye of the sage, and the heart of the brave,
Are hidden and lost in the depths of the grave.

The peasant, whose lot was to sow and to reap,
The herdsman, who climbed with his goats up the steep,
The begger, who wandered in search of his bread,
Have faded away like the grass that we tread.

[The saint, who enjoyed the communion of Heaven,
The sinner, who dared to remain unforgiven,
The wise and the foolish, the guilty and just,
Have quietly mingled their bones in the dust.]

So the multitude goes—like the flower or the weed
That withers away to let others succeed;
So the multitude comes—even those we behold,
To repeat every tale that has often been told.

For we are the same our fathers have been;
We see the same sights our fathers have seen;
We drink the same stream, we view the same sun,
And run the same course our fathers have run.

The thoughts we are thinking, our fathers would think;
From the death we are shrinking, our fathers would shrink;
To the life we are clinging, they also would cling;—
But it speeds from us all like a bird on the wing.

They loved—but the story we cannot unfold;
They scorned—but the heart of the haughty is cold;
They grieved—but no wail from their slumber will come;
They joyed—but the tongue of their gladness is dumb.

They died—ay, they died;—we things that are now,
That walk on the turf that lies over their brow,
And make in their dwellings a transient abode,
Meet the things that they met on their pilgrimage road.

Yea! hope and despondency, pleasure and pain,
Are mingled together in sunshine and rain;
And the smile and the tear, the song and the dirge,
Still follow each other, like surge upon surge.

'T is the wink of an eye—'t is the draught of a breath—
From the blossom of health to the paleness of death,
From the gilded saloon to the bier and the shroud:—
Oh! why should the spirit of mortal be proud?

"The two verses in brackets," Carpenter said, "were not repeated by Mr. Lincoln but belong to the original poem." We can be quite certain that Lincoln knew them, and call attention to the fitness of the lines on the maid to Ann Rutledge and the lines on the saint and sinner to himself in his controversial position as President.

Lincoln liked to recite the poem to sympathetic friends and he was credited in some news reports as having written it. When asked if this was so he replied, Carpenter tells us: "I have heard that before . . . but there is no truth in it. The poem was first shown to me by a young man named 'Jason Duncan' many years ago."

Jason Duncan was one of many signers of a petition to the County Commissioners' Court for the County of Sangamon, written in New Salem by Abraham Lincoln, February 9, 1833, to consider the care of Benjamin Elmore who was insane. It seems that Lincoln became acquainted with this poem while living in New Salem when he and Duncan exchanged sentiments on the tragic ending of love. The poem was written by William Knox, a young Scotsman, contemporary with Sir Walter Scott.

President Lincoln also recited to Carpenter the lines of Oliver Wendell Holmes:

> The mossy marbles rest
> On the lips that he has pressed
> In their bloom;
> And the names he loved to hear
> Have been carved for many a year
> On the tomb.

"For pure pathos," Lincoln said, "in my judgment, there is nothing finer . . . in the English language." His love for memories of the dead was felt, as a boy, young man, and president, to be eternal.

Definite indication that Lincoln continued to cherish tender memories of his first mating love, lost in the time of its realization, exists in the reflective advice of the verses he wrote in the album of Rosa Haggard 23 years later (1858). Rosa was the daughter of an old friend in whose hotel he spent the night after making a speech. She was then blooming into young womanhood and her natural desire for love seems to have reminded him of Ann Rutledge.

> "You are young, and I am older;
>   You are hopeful, I am not—
> Enjoy life, ere it grow colder
>   Pluck the roses ere they rot.
>
> Teach your beau to heed the lay—
>   That sunshine soon is lost in shade—
> That now's as good as any day—
>   To take thee, Rosa, ere she fade."

The lines "You are hopeful, I am not . . . Teach your beau . . . That sunshine soon is lost in shade . . . To take thee, Rosa, ere she fade" are indeed, after 16 years of marriage, tragically reminiscent of what he felt might have been had Ann taught him, shy beau, to take her before it was too late.

Lincoln's Way in Love

People who fail to complete their instinctively idealized love often marry a substitute who becomes more or less practically satisfactory or hopelessly disappointing. After failure in love has led to displacement of affection toward a substitute, the ego becomes disposed to restore its feeling of superiority by ridiculing the love mistakes and failures of others. All the world admires successful, graceful, heroic lovers and weeps at their tragedies, but it laughs at bunglers and scorns cowards.

Lincoln was conscientiously real in his expression of feelings and never beguiling, affected or pretending, but he was always a shy, neurotic lover, ever sensitive lest he might bungle and be rejected and made ridiculous as a suitor. He had in youth expressed such apprehension in a poem upon his sister's marriage. He had also written satires on ambitious and unnatural affections of love. Later, feelings of egoistic inferiority distressed him when rejected in his courtships of Mary Owens and Mary Todd.

When a person reasons himself into an engagement to marry for economic and other social advantage, without sufficient instinctive attractions for the personality of the mate to excite love, imagination, and admiration, the union feels endlessly more or less strange and misfit. Conversely, marriage that feels unnatural is fundamentally deficient in the important qualities of sacred and romantic love. Lincoln had such difficulties with himself during three later attempts at courtship. He idealized love so highly, as will be shown later in confidential letters to two friends, that when he promised to marry and tried to induce himself to love Mary Owens, he found that he could not maintain repression of involitional reaction to avoid marriage and stay free. His letters to her (see next chapter) show his respect for his promise of engagement. She, and not he, must break it.

No emotions caused Lincoln so much self-doubt, perplexity, anxiety, and humiliation as his conflict over feelings of being in love or not in love during his later courtships. We cannot understand the development of his personality and his sublime expressions of philosophy of human relations without bearing this fact constantly in mind. As will be seen in the next chapters, in no other emotional interest did he become so confused himself and so mysterious, so badly misunderstood and characterologically misjudged by many people and yet, in no other emotion of other people was he more tenderly understanding and wisely considerate.

Lincoln has been morally condemned as a shallow lover by some biographers who, like Masters (1931), have judged him by prejudices of conventional notions and abstract moral standards of mating behavior regardless of vast differences in the physical constitution and cultural conditioning of people.

Love in the family, of the father and mother for each child, and the love of each child for its parents and siblings, differs in each person. Lincoln's love for his mother, his pig, and his sister and stepmother had important though different values in his life. His love for Ann Rutledge, I think the evidence now shows convincingly, was his first, real, mating love. His love for his wife, a few years later, as will be seen, became devotedly paternalistic.

Many biographers of Lincoln have spoken of love without discriminating that instinctive mating love is naturally an involitional selection which, as he said to Speed, "you cannot reason yourself out of." It is not like cultivated love, to be intentionally developed and volitionally transferred according to opportunity. Lincoln's love was not that kind. It was above all characteristically natural. When later he tried to cultivate love for Mary Owens he felt unnatural and hypochondriacal. We have correlated sufficient evidence in his own words that shows his love for Ann Rutledge was an instinctive mating urge, involuntarily awakened in his "heart" by her particular qualities of "personal appearance and deportment." Even though he was too honorable and conscientious to seek her love while he felt she was bound to McNamar, he could not keep from feeling attracted to her.

In order to understand the profound inspiration of love, followed by depression and confusion over its tragic frustration, that Lincoln had experienced at the ages of six, nine, and twenty-seven, and was to experience again, we must apply modern psychobiological information on the far greater force of instinctive mating love behavior over the superficialities of intentional culture of affected love.

Love is the natural, genetically determined feeling of autonomic nervous emotional drive toward mating and reproduction as completion of being. It is inborn-predetermined, and after birth it is experience-conditioned throughout life by what it seeks to acquire as feeling most fit to fulfill its instinctive needs. Such definitive determination reduces all other conditioning experiences to lesser substitutional values, if it does not avoid them as unfit. When a person is successful in the realization of his love-objective, it produces a highly integrated, energetic, pleasurably inspired, ego-progressive circular psychophysiological (mind-body) state of being. When he loses hope of this realization, it tends to produce an energy-depressing, ego-regressive, mentally uninspired circular psychophysiological state.

All of the involitional emotional drives of the personality—its loves, fears, hates, and sorrows—are specifically conditioned by particular experiences, and the past plays endlessly active, more or less unconsciously, subconsciously, and consciously determinative, allied, and antagonistic parts, in present conscious volitional behavior. Such determination becomes particularly evident in perplexing unavoidable situations that involve the necessity of making difficult discriminations and decisions of *what to do in order to be* versus *what not to do in order not to be.* When such trials are complicated by limitations of time, danger of failure, and interests that extend from the past into the future, such as unrequited love for someone who is unforgettable, its frustration may have extremely serious pathological effects on the mind. We will see evidence later, in many letters and public statements, that Abraham Lincoln was motivated constantly by nostalgic love of the past that projected itself into maintaining the present and future welfare of his fellow man. He never really hated any man although he detested lying, cheating, injustice, and selfish ambition. He was carefully consistent in the organization of his mind in that what he would love to acquire and construct was thoughtfully reinforced by what he would hate and fear and avoid. This salutary balance of common sense was maintained further by distrusting the insidiously destructive imaginative influence of jealousy on his mind. He consistently renounced jealousy and its serpentine ways and bitter objectives in every instance but one, as will be seen in his advice to Herndon on this and his counsels to himself in later chapters.

Indicative Sequels

Lincoln persisted from 1833 to 1836 in trying to arouse public interest in building roads and making the Sangamon River navigable. It proved a young man's impractical dream, but it indicates the strength of his interest in trying to save New Salem and its owners from financial disaster.

Upon recovering from his depression after the death of Ann, Lincoln is reported by Herndon (1889) to have written a "book" [paper] on "infidelity" in the winter of 1835-36. Herndon based his account on statements in conversations and letters by John Hill in 1865. John said that he was told by his father, Sam Hill, in whose store Lincoln clerked and kept the post office, that Lincoln showed him "the book." Sam Hill urged him to burn it and not expose himself to public resentment. It seems, according to the account, that Lincoln took his friend's advice.

John Hill affirmed his story by describing his early childhood impressions about his father who, he thought, was not a religious man, acting in defense of religion, and on hearing the incident "alluded to hundreds of times by different old settlers."

Herndon thought that probably Lincoln had argued, as he "often" heard him do later with his lawyer friends, that the Bible was unnatural and false in many claims and violated reason, that Jesus was not the son of God any more than any other man, that the Bible did not contain the full record of all divine revelations of God to man. We know that later Lincoln expressed belief that man today receives revelations from God through his conscience, and that he himself relied on the dictates of his conscience when he had to make a difficult decision between right and wrong for the public welfare. Herndon, who knew Lincoln's philosophical views better than any other man, has told us that he when a lawyer, "firmly believed in an overruling, impersonal Intelligence, Providence,

Maker, or God and his contact with man through the Soul." (See Chapter LXII.

The tradition of Lincoln's infidelism was not fabricated by John Hill, as recently charged by discrediting biographers. It was consistent with the defense Lincoln had to make 10 years later, when John was a boy, against charges of infidelism by his political opponents. He issued a handbill "To the Voters of the Seventh Congressional District," dated July 3, 1846, against "a charge having gotten into circulation in some of the neighborhoods of this District, in substance that I am an open scoffer at Christianity." Again, in a letter of August 11, 1846, to Allen Ford, he defended himself against "the whispering charge of infidelity" by Peter Cartwright, a rival candidate for election in the District, for Congress. (See Chapter XVI.)

It is certain that Lincoln's spirit was miserably shocked and depressed by the death of Ann Rutledge until he found a natural sublimation as legislator and lawyer in renewed dedication to work for equality of freedom and legal rights in human relations, which he knew was her idealism as well as his own and which he held to be based on the equalitarian rule of Christ. A strong indication that he had become so awakened exists in a declaration of his political philosophy, less than a year after the death of Ann (June 13, 1836), upon request of the editor of the *Sangamo Journal:*

> "In your paper of last Saturday, I see a communication over the signature of 'Many Voters,' in which the candidates who are announced in the Journal, are called upon to 'show their hands.' Agreed. Here's mine!
>
> "I go for all sharing the privileges of the government, who assist in bearing its burthens. Consequently I go for admitting all whites to the right of suffrage, who pay taxes or bear arms, (by no means excluding females)."
>
> "If elected, I shall consider the whole people of Sangamon my constituents, as well those that oppose, as those that support me."

Here was an unprecedented, idealistic declaration in favor of woman's suffrage, unique and bold in Illinois politics. Lincoln's belief that women should have equal political rights with men was certainly based on belief in their ability to exercise it intelligently. This realization could hardly have had other origin than his confidence in the intelligence, strength of character, and political acumen of a young woman who, in managing a tavern for her father, needed such impressive public influence. Inspired thinking has its source in hopeful virtuous love and, conversely, evidence of it is the strongest indication of such love.

We have some indication of the sources of Lincoln's inspirations in his expressions of grateful appreciation of old friendships. In 1861, President-elect Lincoln, a few days before leaving for Washington, went to Charleston, Ill., to see his aging "mother," Sally. Here, old neighbors from Coles County and some who had once lived in New Salem are said to have gathered to bid him farewell and wish him a successful administration. Among them was Isaac Cogdale (named Cogsdale by Herndon) who had an intimate conversation with Lincoln. Always interested in learning about the lives of old friends, Lincoln asked him about the Rutledges and other old families of New Salem. During the conversation Cogdale said he asked:

> "Abe, is it true that you fell in love with and courted Ann Rutledge?" To this question he said Lincoln replied: " 'It is true—true indeed I did. I have loved the name of Rutledge to this day. I have kept my mind on their movements ever since.' Of Ann he spoke with some feeling; 'I loved the woman dearly and sacredly; she was natural, and quite intellectual, though not highly educated. I did honestly and truly love the girl, and I think often—often of her now.' "

The record of this conversation was reported by Herndon (1889) from his collection of statements and testimony. It seems to have been written as a memorandum of what he was told by Cogdale some time after Lincoln's death. It purports to quote Cogdale's conversation with Lincoln. The style of the speech is Herndon's but it has the nostalgic, philosophical quality that Lincoln loved to indulge in when talking reminiscently with old friends. Sweetly proud of his ability to recall affectionately details of past times, as his letters show abundantly, he was always interested in talking over the course through life of his relatives and old neighbors. Even as president he invited some to visit with him for this pleasure.

Professor Randall (1945) says, "the record" [of Cogdale's conversation with Lincoln] seems "artificial and made to order" and presents Lincoln "in an unlikely role." I reply that it is improbable that Herndon invented this account although the wording of the quotation is in his idiom and no doubt inexact. Its meaning, however, is so consistent with Lincoln's personality and characteristic continuation of affectionate memories for old friends that we cannot pass off this interest in Ann Rutledge and her family as "unlikely."

Professor Randall has inferred with no little "psychoanalytic intuition" (to apply to his own reasoning the phrase that he has applied several times to Herndon's reasoning) that Cogdale's report is "uncharacteristic," on the assumption that Lincoln's friends addressed him as "Lincoln" or "Mr. Lincoln" and not as "Abe." This is probably true after he became President, but improbable for the friends of his New Salem and Springfield years when he was so humbly and intimately congenial and jovial with people, and addressed them by their informal names even as his friends called each other by nicknames or abbreviated first names. That Lincoln's friends continued to address him personally as "Abe" after he became an eminent lawyer and candidate for the United States Senate against Douglas, has been recorded by Carl Schurz (1892) in the description of his first meeting with him on a train during the debates. (See Chapter XXXII.) This record is consistent with that of people everywhere, in conversation, referring to him as "Old Abe," or "Good Old Abe," or "Honest Abe;" and Lincoln said repeatedly, when president, that the name "Honest Old Abe" won the confidence of the people and elected him.

Some biographers have inferred, since Lincoln is not known to have spoken of his interest in Ann Rutledge to any of his intimate friends except Cogdal, that she was only a dear friend. The following excerpt from a letter, now in the Library of Congress, written by Joshua Speed, November 30, 1866, to Herndon indicates that Speed, who knew Lincoln's affections more confidentially before he married than any other person, regarded this silence much the way Herndon did.

> "In the winter of [18] 40 or 41 he was very unhappy about his engagement to his wife. Not being entirely satisfied that his *heart* was going with his hand—How much he suffered then on that account none know so much as myself—He disclosed his whole heart to me . . . If I had not been married and happy he would not have married . . . I thank you for your last lecture on Lincoln's love for Ann Rutledge—It is all new to me—but so true to my appreciation of Lincoln's character that independent of my knowledge of you I would almost swear to it—Lincoln wrote a letter (a long one which he read to me) to Dr. Drake of Cincinnati descriptive of his case—Its date would be in Dec 40 or early January 41—I think he must have informed Dr. D of his early love for Miss Rutledge—as there was a part of the letter he would not read."

Speed's letter is presented more fully later as additional evidence of Lincoln's inability to love Mary Todd. His vigorous statement that Herndon's account of Lincoln's love for Ann Rutledge was so true of his own appreciation of Lincoln's character indicates that he had sensed intuitively that Lincoln was in love with a girl of the past.

It is known that in 1833 Lincoln was attentive for a short time to Mary Owens, who was then visiting her married sister, Mrs. Bennett Abell, in New Salem, and to other young women in the community, but such friendly interests reveal neither positive nor negative indication of his instinctive feelings then or later toward Ann Rutledge. At that time Ann was engaged to McNamar, as Lincoln knew.

The meaning of Lincoln's attentions to Mary Owens at this time will become more evident in his letters to her and to Mrs. Orville Browning, given in full in the next chapter. Here it should be mentioned that he said in his letter to Mrs. Browning written in 1838, when living in Springfield, that "in the autumn of 1836" he accepted, without having seen Mary since 1833, a conditional proposal from Mrs. Abell "a great friend" in whose home, near New Salem, he was then living, that he marry her sister. "I of course accepted the proposal for you know I could not have done otherwise had I really been averse to it, but privately, between you and me, I was confoundedly well pleased with the prospect. I had seen the said sister some three years before, thought her intelligent and agreeable and saw no objection to plodding through life hand and hand with her." This ironical comment was made in connection with even more satirical descriptions of the disappointing changes he found in Mary's physical appearance when he tried to keep his promise and make himself love her.

Professor J. G. Randall (1945) and his wife, Ruth Painter Randall (1957) have given a far-fetched psychoanalytic interpretation of the meaning of Lincoln's mood, when he wrote the Browning letter, as indicative evidence that he had considered Mary Owens as a desirable matrimonial partner in 1833 and therefore could not then have been in love with Ann Rutledge. Lincoln's comments to Mrs. Browning on his feelings about Mary Owens must be correlated with his letters to Mary in Chapter IX. They show that he was never able to feel more than a friendly interest in her and, try as he did, was never able to love her. Mrs. Abell's statement to Herndon many years later (1896), that Mary told her that Lincoln said he would rather have her "than any woman living," is certainly indicative of fixation of love on the memory of one who was dead. It seems more probable that Lincoln felt he might as well marry Mary Owens for he had no hope of ever loving again. His letters to her, and later his letters to Speed about his conflict of feelings for Mary Todd, reveal the hopelessness of his feelings about love and marriage to any woman, after Ann's death.

Herndon versus Other Biographers on Lincoln's Relations with Ann Rutledge

The endless controversy among Lincoln's biographers over whether or not he and Ann Rutledge loved each other and were engaged to marry has turned more around Herndon's account of such a romance, his evidence, inferences, and interpretations, than the previous evidence of Lincoln's own interests, behavior, letters and statements, revealing his personal experiences and understanding of "love." Because of the interest of American people in Herndon's account and the controversial opinions of his most recent important critics, they are reviewed here in relation to each other and to my interpretation of what happened.

Herndon was not the first to write about the love of Abraham Lincoln for Ann Rutledge. He seems to have learned, after the death of President Lincoln, of their interest in each other when his attention was called to an article "A Romance of Reality," published by John Hill in the *Menard Axis* of Petersburg, Ill. (near New Salem) on February 15, 1862. Hill based his story on reminiscences, often repeated, by his father and mother and old neighbors. His father courted Ann for some time in competition with McNamar when they owned the store where, later, Lincoln kept the post office at the time he courted Ann. Sam Hill was married in 1835 and his wife remembered Ann with admiration and envy. The article gave a realistic description of Lincoln in New Salem as "an awkward youth— dry goods clerk—soldier—keeper of a stallion—grocery keeper—bankrupt liquor merchant—day laborer, infidel, writer, surveyor, hog drover and legislator," who was love-sick over an attractive young lady and upon her tragic death became depressed and suicidal. Ann's name was not mentioned in the article but she was readily identified by New Salem people.

Later Hill corrected his statement that Lincoln owned a stallion to that of being interested in the services of a stallion owned by a friend. President Lincoln seems, from lack of record, to have ignored this article if it was brought to his attention.

Previously, in 1860, Hill published in the *Missouri Republican,* an article in opposition to Lincoln's candidacy, entitled "Opposing Principles of Henry Clay and Abraham Lincoln." In it he argued with a politician's generalization and several stretched misstatements of records of the Illinois State Legislature and of Congress, that Lincoln was an "abolitionist."

Among Lincoln's files a letter was found written by him to John Hill (8, 1860) which was not completed and which he seems to have decided not to send. With painstaking point by point comparison of Hill's statements with the facts in the records, Lincoln showed exactly wherein Hill was in error and admonished him for having stated "what is almost certainly false, and certainly what you do not know to be true." Lincoln admitted:

> "It is true, that he [referring to himself] drew up, and sought to get before the House of Representatives . . . a bill for the abolition of slavery in the District of Columbia, upon the conditions that the abolition should be gradual, and only upon a vote of the majority of the people of the District, and with compensation to unwilling owners, and also embracing a fugitive slave clause, and an exception in favor of Officers of the Government, while in the District on the public business; all of which appears in the same volume of the Congressional Globe, at pages 212-244."

Evidently, Hill intentionally ignored these important qualifications of Lincoln's opposition to slavery in making his sweeping charges and thereby exposed himself to question of sincerity and reliability.

The editors of Collected Works (Vol. 4) have stated: "Lincoln's resentment of Hill's lack of respect for the truth is all the more interesting in view of the fact that Hill became the prime source of the Ann Rutledge story, the tradition of Lincoln's infidelity, and a number of other spurious or dubious traditions concerning Lincoln's New Salem years." . . . "It was this article ["A Romance of Reality"] which led Herndon to elaborate on the Ann Rutledge episode when he began collecting material for his biography of Lincoln in 1866, and Hill rather than Herndon deserves recognition for primary irresponsibility in first publishing stories which have been perpetuated in popular belief."

This sweeping application of editorial judgment condemns by association as "irresponsible" the independent investigations of Herndon on the memories of people who knew Lincoln and Ann Rutledge. It is obviously meant to destroy faith in his evidence as well as his accounts by attributing their origin to Hill's story. Logic does not justify the assumption that he who has once made a mistake can never be right, and he who has lied or misrepresented facts will never tell the truth. As will be shown by Lincoln's own letters, John Hill was not the only source of the tradition of Lincoln's "infidelity." The prime source was Lincoln's own discussions of infidelism and biblical mythology.

Herndon saw, in Hill's story, an explanation of his own observations over many years of Lincoln's habitually melancholy outlook on life, his sad pleasure in meditation over memories and poetry on love frustrated by death, his compensatory culture of humor, his self-doubtful confusion about his feelings when engaged to Mary Todd, and his paternalistic attitude toward her after their marriage. When he obtained verifying evidence of the romance through questioning Ann's family, neighbors, and McNamar, he inferred that Lincoln had continued to cherish his memories and love of Ann, since after recovering from bitter anguish he had been characteristically silent about her.

Herndon's father was a cattle buyer, and friend of Ann's father, James Rutledge. Young Herndon was 15 in 1833 when he first met Ann. With his father he had stopped at the Rutledge tavern and become acquainted with the family and other people of the village. He said (1889) that he knew Miss Rutledge as well as her father and other members of her family, and was personally acquainted with every one of the score or more witnesses whom he interviewed after the death of Lincoln: "From my own knowledge and the information thus obtained I repeat, that the memory of Ann Rutledge was the saddest chapter in Mr. Lincoln's life." . . . "Ann . . . was a beautiful girl, and by her winning ways attracted people to her so firmly that she soon became the most popular young lady in the village." His collection of personal observations, neighbors' testimony and indicative evidence has been regarded by many biographers, including Lamon, Arnold, Hertz, Beveridge, and Angle, as honestly sought and mostly correctly recorded, although fanciful and extravagant in his interpretations of some of its meanings.

Herndon's method of questioning witnesses was that of a lawyer, and naturally suggestive of recall of memories fitting his purpose and objective. He chose what seemed to him to be the best of the evidence on the almost supernatural development of the character of the man he loved and venerated as a law partner and helped to make president. He wanted the American people to know the realities of Lincoln's greatness in overcoming unusual personal difficulties in working out his profoundly practical philosophical understanding of human nature. His information on the relations of Lincoln and Ann Rutledge, obtained through numerous personal interviews and letters of inquiry, 30 years after the event, was, as we would expect, not fully definite in detail and not entirely consistent in the minds of old neighbors, under the influence of gossip, time, the terrific emotional bias of the Civil War, and the assassination. However, it contains so much natural consistency with the characteristics of development then and later of Lincoln's philosophical attitude toward life and death that it would be sheer prejudice to deny all as does Thomas (1952) as "a legend for which no shred of contemporary evidence has been found."

Quotations of statements in interviews with people were generally written out by Herndon in his own idiom but this does not, as such, discredit the truth of their essential meanings. Neither is his understanding of the natural development of affection in four years, between shy, supersensitive, idealistic "penniless," Abraham Lincoln with lovely, sensitive, idealistic, morally obligated Ann Rutledge to be passed off as imaginary and fantastic. We must interpret his use of words by his own meanings and not by the meanings in use today. For instance, he characterized Lincoln's state of mind on different occasions as being "crazy" and "crazy as a loon"—when a boy after being kicked in the head by a horse, when a man after the death of Ann Rutledge, and after the breaking of his engagement with Mary Todd. "Crazy" was obviously meant in a loose popular sense, as Mrs. Abell gave it (see previous quotation).

The biographer must also differentiate what Herndon said in his letters about his collections of evidence in the sixties, when he was in the prime of life but neurotically shocked by Lincoln's death, from what he said later in his letters as an harassed old man still trying to get Weik, Nicolay, and other biographers not to hide the real Lincoln from the American people. He based his intuitive inferences of Lincoln's feelings toward Ann on 18 years of closely personal observation of his partner's nostalgic moodiness and positive indicative evidence from eye witnesses of their affectionate relations, whereas when he said that Lincoln seemed to think of himself as being an illegitimate child, that Lincoln's father was probably sterile, and that Tom Lincoln and Nancy Hanks were probably not legally married, he based his inferences on negative indications from lack of positive evidence to the contrary. Although Herndon was proven later, by the discovery of positive evidence, to have been in error in these inferences, the biographer cannot logically conclude that he erred in all of his evidence and inferences.

Herndon regarded himself as being "somewhat of a psychologist," and "mind reader." Actually he was more interested in psychology, philosophy and sociology than law, and wisely cultivated the ability to read "hidden" as well as obvious motives of people in their attitudes, faces, manners and statements. The keenness of his observation is evident since he was the only person of record who knew Lincoln, including his physicians, who suggested that his chronic melancholy might have an "organic" as well as an "occult" basis.

Herndon lived in the same room with Joshua Speed and Lincoln during Lincoln's first courtship of Mary Todd. Later, as his law partner, he observed repeatedly the pleasing and disappointing effects on his mind of his harmonious and frustrating relations with his wife, far more intimately than any other person. Lincoln's letters to Herndon when in Congress (see Chapter XVII) reveal the intimacy of their confidential relationship.

Although nine years younger than Lincoln, Herndon was his respected law partner for 16 years. He was not a dabbler in introspective psychology as some of his critics have portrayed him, but a searching student of the best books then published on the introspective study of the mind. Neither was he Lincoln's partner "to do his legal chores," as one biographer has put it. As a lawyer, he developed an unusually comprehensive philosophical, legal, and political discrimination, and not only tried cases with Lincoln as well as alone, but was far better read in psychology, philosophy, history and sociology than most of his contemporaries. As an astute political adviser he did more than any other person to foster Lincoln's interest in becoming president. Lincoln chose Herndon to represent his views in the decisive series of conferences with Eastern Republican leaders that won their support for his candidacy. After Lincoln was elected president, he asked Herndon to keep the office and name sign going so that they could resume the practice of law together upon the completion of his time in office. Herndon was a guest at the White House and President Lincoln sought his advice on several appointments.

In November of 1866, about 18 months after the death of President Lincoln, when Mrs. Lincoln and the American people were still in a state of shock and mourning, Herndon committed an impulsive, tactless, and unnecessary violation of public sentiment in his lecture in Springfield entitled "Abraham Lincoln, Miss Ann Rutledge, Pioneering and the Poem." Consistent with the literary culture of that time, he gave an elaborately detailed sentimental description of New Salem, its people and environs when Lincoln lived there, in contrast with the last remaining, empty, decaying log house standing in 1866. In this fateful setting he twice portrayed Lincoln's courtship of Miss Rutledge, in general accordance with the memories of their old friends, colored with his own imagination of the cause of Ann's illness and how Lincoln probably felt when called to her bedside, his despondency upon her death and the sad continuation of his love for her for the rest of his life, as symbolically expressed in his love of reciting the poem "Oh! why should the spirit of mortal be proud."

> "I do not *think,*" he said, "wishing to arrogate to myself—that any living man or woman so well understands, the many delicate wheels and hidden springs of the story of Lincoln, Miss Rutledge, the Poem, and its relation to the two, in time and place, as I do." . . . With earnestness and sincerity he said: "You know my Religion, my Philosophy, namely; that the highest thoughts and acts of the human soul in its religious sphere, are to think, love, obey and worship God, by thinking freely, by loving, teaching, doing good to and elevating mankind. My first duty is to God, then to mankind, and then to the individual man and woman. I wish to perform my duty honestly and truthfully. I do not wish to awaken or injure the dead, nor to wound or injure the feelings of any living man or woman."

Herndon described Ann as a beautiful, gifted, intelligent, lovely girl of 19, who had three good and influential young men [Hill, McNamar, and Lincoln] of the village fall in love with her "simultaneously," meaning obviously at the same time. One man, he said, she quickly rejected [Hill] but became involved, through unavoidable circumstances in loving the other man [McNamar] and Lincoln and engaged to both men "at one and the same time."

> "No earthly blame can be attached to the girl and none to the men in their fidelity and honor to her. It all so happened or was decided by fate." . . .
> "The young girl saw her condition. Her word of promise was out to two men at the same time, both of whom she loved, dearly loved. The consciousness of this, and the conflict of duties, love's promises, and womanly engagements, made her think, grow sad, become restless and nervous. She suffered, pined, ate not and slept not. Time and struggle, as supposed and believed by many, caused her to have a raging fever, of which she died on the 26th day of August, A.D. 1835."

The inference that Miss Rutledge died of "brain fever" brought on by intense emotional conflict and a perplexed state of mind was rejected by her brother Robert:

> "I think you are in error as to the cause of Ann's sickness; you will pardon my frankness, as I wish to assist you in developing the truth, the whole truth, and nothing but the truth. I have no doubt but Ann had fully determined to break off the engagement with McNamar, but presume she had never notified him of the fact, as he did not return until after her death."

This inference has been ridiculed by some recent biographers as being more evidence of Herndon's unreliable "psychoanalyzing" propensities. It is, however, common knowledge in medical practice that such deep emotional conflicts of love and conscience as Ann probably had become involved in may cause extremely serious complications in infectious fevers, such as typhoid or pneumonia.

> Herndon asserted that "Abraham Lincoln loved Miss Ann Rutledge with all his soul, mind and strength. She loved him as dearly, tenderly and affectionately. They seemed made in heaven for each other though opposite in many things . . . It is said and thought that the young lady was conditionally promised to Mr. Lincoln, to be consummated upon a release from her first engagement with Mr. — [McNamar]."

The testimony of family and friends, that Lincoln was called in to see Ann sometime before she died and that he became visably greatly distressed is accepted by most biographers as well established. As Herndon said:

> "The meeting was quite as much as either could bear, and more than Lincoln, with all his coolness and philosophy could endure. The voice, the face, the features of her, the love, sympathy and interview fastened themselves on his heart and soul forever. Heaven only knows what was said by the two. God only knows what was thought."

Then Herndon went on to describe Lincoln's despondent behavior after the burial of Ann and his final sadly meditative adjustment and love of the Poem.

> "Mr. Lincoln has stated that his heart, sad and broken, was buried there."
> "He said in addition, to the same friend, 'I cannot endure the thought that
> the sleet and storm, frost and snow of heaven should beat on her grave.' "

His lecture was not too shocking but he added an inference that dis-
paraged Lincoln's love for his wife and deeply offended Mrs. Lincoln and
her friends. He said:

> "He *never* addressed another woman in my opinion, 'yours affec-
> tionately,' and generally and characteristically abstained from the use of the
> word 'love.' The word cannot be found more than half a dozen times, if that
> often, in all his letters and speeches, since that time. I have seen some of his
> letters to other ladies, but he never says 'love.' He never ended his letters with
> 'yours affectionately' but signed his name, 'your friend, A. Lincoln.' "

The extant letters written by Lincoln to women with whom we would
expect him to have expressed tender affections indicating love, if not the
use of the word "love," show that Herndon was largely correct. In his
letters to Mary Owens, during their engagement, he began with "Friend
Mary" and ended with "Your friend, Lincoln." The first letter of known
existence from Lincoln to his wife (4, 16, 1848) was written while he was
attending Congress in Washington and she was staying with her people in
Kentucky. He began with "Dear Mary" and ended with "most affectionately, A. Lincoln." It contains several expressions of tender affection for
her and the children, but not the word "love." The letters written a few
weeks later (5, 24, 1848) and (6, 12, 1848) begin with "My dear wife" and
end "affectionately, A. Lincoln." Another letter (8, 2, 1848) begins with
"My dear wife" and ends with "Kiss and love the dear rascals, affectionately, A. Lincoln." This is the only letter to his wife in which we find the
word "love." The first letters of Lincoln, when President, to Mrs. Lincoln
begin with "My dear wife" and end "affectionately, A. Lincoln." The
letters of 1863 and later begin "Mrs. A. Lincoln" and are very pointed,
brief, and signed without expression of affection "A. Lincoln." In none of
President Lincoln's telegrams to Mrs. Lincoln do we find expression of
love for her. We assume that the collection of letters and telegrams of
Mr. Lincoln to his wife is a characteristic representation of his expressions
of feelings for her, although probably he wrote many others which she did
not save.

In letters to his friend Joshua Speed in persuading him to marry Miss
Fanny Henning, Lincoln used the word "love" several times. In a letter to
his friend Mr. Orville Browning (6, 24, 1846) he sent "our love to Mrs.
Browning and yourself." Lincoln chose his words habitually with measured care to say what he felt in his personal as well as in legal and
political communications. The few instances in which he used the word
"love" after the death of Ann Rutledge to express his feelings largely
support Herndon's inference. Unfortunately we know little of how he
used the word before this time.

Mrs. Lincoln and her son Robert deeply resented the unhappy implication of Herndon's statements. Mrs. Lincoln, as will become evident later (see Chapters XIII, XXI and LXI), was a well-educated, intelligent, proud and ambitious, graciously sweet and jealously bitter, ill-tempered, extremely sensitive, narcissistic and at times remorseful person. This mental attitude was naturally augmented by the extreme shock and unconsolable bereavement that followed upon seeing the assassination of her husband. She seems to have felt disgraced, probably not so much by Herndon's assertions that her husband had loved another woman before he knew her, but by the implication, in his assertion that he had continued to retain such sad reminiscences of love of Ann Rutledge, that he did not love his wife. Then, still in a very unhappy, remorseful state of mind, she became greatly agitated and, as said, called Herndon's story "a myth" and him "a liar." We know, as shown later, that she was unable to convince herself before and after Lincoln's death that she was the only living woman that he, as her husband, ever loved. Robert Lincoln, to relieve his mother's unhappiness, persuaded Nicolay and Hay to disregard the biographical value of Herndon's evidence on his father's first love as well as his interpretation of its meaning, by giving it only passing notice in their 10 volume biography as the sad ending of a brief affection.

Biographical analysis must differentiate Herndon's evidence from his interpretations of its meanings. It must consider the evidence as circumstantial and naturally indicative, and not as positive "proof." It must differentiate the indications first of Lincoln's love for Ann, and second of her love for him, and third their conditional engagement. Biographical judgment based entirely on documentary evidence, without regard for testimony of contemporaries, as indefinite and contradictory as it may be, becomes forced, dry and unnatural. Conversely, interpretation elaborated by making negative assumptions based on lack of positive evidence in permanent records becomes fanciful and unreliable. When a biographer quotes chosen parts of a testimony that support his own opinion and ignores the contrary, as done by some for Lincoln, often when in the same sentence, he is being prejudiced and unreliable. The biographer must not assume, when a close neighbor, after 30 years, has stated that he has no memory or only vague and questionable memory of Lincoln's courtship of Ann, that it is disproving evidence, for actually it means nothing. Only positive statements of observations, for or against, are to be considered. We would expect that most old neighbors remembered the relations of Abe and Ann only casually with passing years, and became interested in recalling details after Lincoln became President. It is the common experience of most people that neighbors, and even members of a family, rarely have true, positive knowledge of each other's idealized love interests, and far less so after 30 years. People normally keep such thoughts to themselves lest they become embarrassing.

Direct or straight testimony only is permissible in law, and indirect quotation of what one person may say that another has said about a sub-

ject in question is not. The biographer, however, must give due consideration to quotations of sayings when they come from honest, reliable,
unprejudiced persons living close to the situation. When similar testimony
is repeated independently by several witnesses, as Herndon obtained it,
and is consistent with the indicative evidence of the behavior of that
person under similar conditions many years before and afterwards, it
becomes relatively impressive, if not entirely convincing.

The Herndon-Weik (1889) account of the interest of Abe Lincoln in
Ann Rutledge has been repeated by many biographers without adequate
discrimination of positive and negative statements of witnesses and
Herndon's interpretations of their meanings. He was not entirely convinced of the truth of many of his inferences, as his letters show, and
invited critical review of the testimony in each case. Within recent years
this material and additional collections have been reappraised more carefully by several professional biographers.

Sandburg (1932) has given sympathetic consideration of Herndon's
information on the intimacy of relations of Lincoln and Ann Rutledge,
apparently without deciding whether or not he thought they were engaged.

Angle (1942) republished "Herndon's Life of Lincoln" and reviewed
his evidence and argument on the relations of Lincoln and Ann Rutledge.
On the basis of what he called "competent medical opinion" that it is
next to impossible, psychologically, for an emotional attachment to endure for anything like a lifetime unless it is stimulated by frequent
personal contacts, Angle concluded that if Lincoln loved Ann Rutledge
his affection must have faded out within a few years after her death. I
reply, as a physician and psychiatrist, who has specialized for over 50
years in the analytical study of this particular subject, that this medical
opinion and Angle's conclusion are erroneous, generalized assumptions.

The scientific analysis of permanently fixed memories of experiences
that have conditioned love, jealousy, shame, fear, sorrow, or hate, and
produced obsessive feelings and compulsions, beliefs, delusions, or hallucinations, moral convictions or religious sentiments has shown that one
intense experience in childhood after three years of age, or later, can make
sufficient impression in the associative neurons of the brain to continue
vividly in the mind throughout life, even into old age. Most people do
not forget their first idealized mating love experience and although its
influence may fade with passing years, many of its details are not extinguished. Every adult mind retains specific, emotionally conditioned
memories of childhood, youth and maturity that are never forgotten,
although based on only one experience. Every mind has memories of long
past impressions that persist involuntarily in influencing his acquisitive
and/or avoidance choice of thinking throughout life. Even though the
particular conditioning experience with a certain person, pet, or beautiful
or terrifying object occurred many years past, any similar later experience,
in a similar state of mind, becomes conditionally reflexly associated with
it, and recall of either memory is sufficient to revive, in detail, the

feelings and memories of the other experience. This is particularly true in a mind like Lincoln's with supermemory, when love has been repeatedly frustrated by death as a fateful interference and memories are repeated almost daily as reliving of experience. Many of Lincoln's own letters and poems, like his recitations of favorite poetry, after 1835, reveal his nostalgic pleasure in reviving sad memories of beloved persons who were dead. He liked to think of them as "dear ones" who had passed on, and "ere long" he would join them.

Thomas (1952), after admitting that "in the face of affirmative reminiscences, Lincoln students can scarcely declare with certainty that no such romance took place," has asserted that "most of them regard it as improbable, and utterly reject its supposed enduring influence upon Lincoln." Such supposition of improbability is based on a cool, academically abstract understanding of human nature. It does not realize that, in a nostalgic attitude, characteristically silent meditative self-containment of memories of love for a person after his death can be cherished as feeling too sacred in its sweet sad influence to discuss with anyone.

J. G. Randall (1945), after a meticulous review of the Ann Rutledge evidence, credited Herndon with having "loved the truth and eagerly sought it" but discredited him with being unable to resist giving it "his inevitable psychoanalysis" and dramatic elaborations. Randall has concluded that "two elements on which there is agreement are Ann's engagement to McNamar and Lincoln's grief at her death." Whether Lincoln was in love with Ann, or grieved her untimely death because of her loveliness as a dear friend, whether his temperament was subject to gloom and deeply sensitive to the tragedy of death, whether there was an engagement between them, whether Ann loved him or was just friendly and still intended to marry McNamar, are, Randall has said, "unanswerable questions." "As to a romantic attachment," he has advised, "it has not been *dis*proved. It is more correct to characterize it as *un*proved."

Professor Randall charged Herndon repeatedly, twice in the introduction of his book, "Lincoln the President," and four times in the chapter on Ann Rutledge, with forming "psychoanalytic" inferences on the meaning of his evidence. Here is, indeed, evidence of prejudice of Randall's own forethought. He must have known that psychoanalysis was originated after Herndon's time by Sigmund Freud. However, he seems not to have understood that psychoanalysis is a special psychological method of inducing a person to recall and release specific involitional determinations, by repressed unconscious idea-emotional complexes of past experiences, of present volitional thinking. Through the sympathetic induction of a relaxed egoistic attitude and free association and expression of thoughts and feelings in connection with specific nervous symptons or obsessive thinking, delusions, hallucinations, alcoholism, drug addiction, dreams, impractical habits, attitudes or prejudices, and other undesirable behavior, the mind becomes able to relieve itself of socially impressed hyperconscientious fear of itself and thereby naturally readjusts itself toward regaining a more normally self-determining, self-balanced common-sense attitude and working capacity. When a person candidly confides to a sympathetically understanding friend, as Lincoln did to Mrs. Browning after Mary Owens refused him, and as he did to Speed and Dr. Henry after Mary Todd jilted his trust and love, he relieves himself from frustrated, involuntarily persistent anxiety. He is naturally, intuitively using a social method of regaining self-control and peace of mind common to all humanity through the ages and developed by psychoanalysis as a science.

Lincoln's biographer must certainly give due consideration to the characteristic consistency of the natural interest shown by Lincoln and Ann in each other, almost daily for two years, after McNamar's long silent absence, their relations during Ann's fatal illness, Ann's desire and the family's desire for his presence, his despondency and behavior after her death, and above all his confidential advice on the meaning of "love" to Speed. Furthermore, he must correlate these well-established points of evidence with Lincoln's continuation, for the rest of his life, of sadly meditating on his memories of love frustrated by fate, as shown in his repeated pleasure in reciting to friends his favorite poem, "Oh! why should the spirit of mortal be proud," learned in his New Salem days. His advice written 23 years after the death of Ann, in the little poem to Rosa Haggard, to teach her beau to take her before it becomes too late, is certainly reminiscent of his own shyness and sad regrets.

Lincoln's Sources of Inspiration

Most biographers agree that Lincoln was always an unusually inspired man. Any person's inspiration to work creatively in a particular field begins in the child's love for a parent as stimulated by the parent's love for the child's special abilities. It grows upon earning encouraging admiration in that direction from other supremely esteemed persons. We know from Lincoln's declarations of purpose as a candidate for the legislature that his inspiration to work in law and politics, to extend human welfare through maintaining equal legal rights for all people under constitutional government, had become intensely reinforced while living in New Salem. The admiration of James Rutledge, Bowling Green, Mentor Graham and Ann Rutledge for young Lincoln as a debater, led him to study law. Biographers have varied greatly in estimating the extent of inspiration his love with Ann Rutledge might have had later on his course of thinking.

We must recognize, if we will understand the deeper motivations of consistent development of Lincoln's personality and philosophy of life, that he felt life and love to be sacred gifts of God. He held his memories and feelings about his mother and Ann Rutledge, and later his son William, as being too deep and tender to himself to speak of with other people. Ann, a granddaughter of a signer of the Declaration of

Independence and a grandniece of a founder of the U.S. Constitution, was a self-respecting, unaffected, amiable, idealistic, attractive, intelligent, sympathetic person who, in virtue and modesty, pride of family and love of truth, honor, freedom and human welfare, had all of the qualities that Lincoln admired and loved in a woman. Her moral idealism was consistent in character with his mother's, and, instinctively, he consciously and subconsciously associated these impressive influences into one sublime, practically idealized inspiration that gave him the force of consistent mental integrity in his ambitious pursuit of greatness.

No idealistic young man with Abraham Lincoln's sensitive nature, intensely virtuous independence of mind, democratic traditions, profoundly moral attitude and political ambition could have done other, in his love for Ann Rutledge, then worship with her at the same altar of democracy. It seems quite natural that her virtuous idealism stimulated in Lincoln more intense appreciation and reverence for the Constitution than he had previously felt, and that he became more resolutely determined for the rest of his life to preserve and defend it against any violation, although it was still being held in many states, by important people, to be of doubtful value as an experimental foundation of federal rights over states' rights in national government. Such highly patriotic determination, as we will see later, dominated his mind as a state legislator, public lecturer, congressman, lawyer, and President so persistently and forcefully against all opposition and criticism, that it must have had an unusually deep, persistent, experience-conditioned motivation in the ideals of persons he loved.

Reflections of this influence on Lincoln are expressed in his first public lecture in January, 1838, on "The Perpetuation of our Political Institutions" two and a half years after the death of Ann Rutledge (see Chapter X).

In silent reminiscences on his loves he retained the wellspring of his expressions of thought on history and patriotism, friendship, law and order, slavery and freedom, government and union, and life and death, that have become immortal. He dedicated himself to carry on the ideals and traditions of his beloved, lest they died in vain. In due time he would say that by honoring the heroic patriotism of the free men who founded the nation and of those who saved the nation, government by the people, for the people will not perish.

Chapter IX

LEGISLATOR, LAW STUDENT,
NEUROTIC COURTSHIP

Lincoln had borrowed $200 from his friend Coleman Smoot in order to attend the legislature at Vandalia, then the state capital, when it convened in the winter of 1834-35. Unable to purchase a suit of clothes that would fit his unusually long arms and legs he had one made by a tailor. Unused to such regalia he felt at first somewhat ill at ease until he got it thoroughly wrinkled and baggy. During his first term in the Illinois General Assembly, from 1834 to 1836, Lincoln played his little part cautiously as a Whig under the leadership of Major John Todd Stuart, listened wisely in council and made many friends but avoided self-commitments as he learned the game of inside political manipulation under parliamentary rules of order.

His maiden effort was the introduction of a bill on December 9, 1834, to limit the jurisdiction of justices of the peace so as not to entertain "any civil case whatever—unless it be in the precinct in which the defende[nt] resides or [sic]—or in which the contract on which suit is brought was made and entered into, or made payable—any thing in former laws to the contrary notwithstanding." This act was probably advised by his friend Bowling Green as a means of preventing the wealthy from taking cases outside of local situations to favorable judges, thereby forcing the poor to yield for lack of means of defense. It was much revised and amended in committee and passed by the house but was tabled by the senate. Such restrictions have since been generally adopted in most states.

Two days later he introduced an amendment to the house rules making it "not in order to offer amendments to any bill after its third reading," and on December 15th he introduced a bill authorizing Samuel Musick to build a toll bridge. His activities were numerous but restricted to minor interests of law, such as the disposal of stray horses and cattle; the building of state roads, bridges, and canals; disposal of revenues from the sale of public lands; relief of insolvent debtors; and reports of his committee

In the campaign for his second term he said in the *Sangamo Journal:*

"If elected, I shall consider the whole people of Sangamon my constituents, as well those who oppose, as those that support me.

"While acting as their representative, I shall be governed by their will, on all subjects upon which I have the means of knowing what their will is; and upon all others, I shall do what my own judgment teaches me will best advance their interests."

As a freshman legislator, Lincoln believed, as did Thomas Jefferson and the fathers of the Constitution, that democratic government must be founded on the will of free people through the election of officers to serve as their representatives. We will see later how firmly he applied this principle to administrative situations against the sophistry of demagogic politicians seeking unilateral privileges.

Lincoln served four consecutive terms (1834-42) in the General Assembly and his interest and influence grew progressively until he became leader of the Whig minority. He learned what influential people thought of the increasing implications of the extension of slavery in the territories and its limitation by federal and state law under the Constitution, the value of state banks, a national bank, federal tariffs, public education, federal and state aid in constructing railroads and public buildings, taxation and expenditure of state funds, sale of federal lands, temperance, and causes of panic. As a Whig, and even more so characterologically, he opposed the political philosophy of President Andrew Jackson "to the victors belong the spoils," as the culture of party favoritism and official incompetence at the expense of the people.

Resolute Law Student

Practically all of his law and other reading, like his stories and jokes, dealt in some manner with the egoistic emotivations of mankind under sympathetic or antipathic adjustments arising necessarily out of cooperative and competitive human relations and the necessity of legal regulation and proper authoritative interpretation of such relations. His invaluable habit of writing out and rereading gems of literary expression and of legal knowledge and judgment until he had memorized them, and his reading and reciting aloud to himself or to anyone who would listen, helped him greatly in cultivating the ability to think clearly and speak with familiarity and conviction in debate before a critical public. This habit was a natural continuation of copying and reciting in the "blab" schools of childhood.

He had long learned the value of practising the audible vocalization of his thought as the best means of preparing himself for a speech. He thereby not only grew used to the sound of his own voice, so that it no longer split his attention from the main line of thought that he wanted to express, but he learned how to project best his erratically rasping voice from a weakened vocal chord so that people liked to listen to him. He probably also learned in this particular way to take advantage of human nature, in its natural tendency to wish sympathetically to help those who work willingly to overcome a disability.

In the village store, over the counter, around the stove, Postmaster Lincoln liked to stir up his idle friends into common-sense discussions of the philosophy of law and government. Who are the best law makers and what is the best form of government? What are the advantages and disad-

vantages of slavery? What should the people of Illinois do about it? Can
it exist without violating the free will and Christian intelligence of master
as well as slave?

No man ever developed himself as a lawyer more naturally. Law became his absorbing interest and rarely gave way to anything else. As he
said, he "went at it in good earnest." When alone in the store or at home,
when walking or riding along the road, he read and reread books of law
with bulldog tenacity until he felt that he had mastered each one. Years
later (1858), when asked by young Reavis for advice on the best method of
studying law, he wrote:

> "If you are resolutely determined to make a lawyer of yourself, the thing
> is more than half done already. It is a small matter whether you read *with*
> anybody or not. I did not read with anyone. Get the books, and read and
> study them until you understand them in their principal features; and that is
> the main thing. It is of no consequence to be in a large town while you are
> reading. I read in New Salem, which never had three hundred people living
> in it. The *books* and your *capacity* for understanding them are just the same
> in all places. . . .
>
> "Always bear in mind that your own resolution to succeed is more im-
> portant than any other thing."

Lincoln's manner when he came to the office to borrow law books
upon invitation, has been described by H. E. Dummer, Stuart's law partner from 1833 to 1837.

> "Sometimes he walked, but generally rode. He was the most uncouth
> looking young man I ever saw. He seemed to have little to say; seemed to feel
> timid, with a tinge of sadness visible in his countenance, but when he did talk
> all this disappeared for the time and he demonstrated that he was both strong
> and acute. He surprised us more and more at every visit."

Although ambitious, Lincoln cultivated humility, and carefully avoided
the development of vain, egotistical pretensions and affectations to hide
his feelings of social inferiority, as do most people under more highly
sophisticated and civilized education. He remained shy and cautious, and
became able with maturing experience to understand and measure the interests of greatest value in interpersonal and general social situations. He
learned with increasing confidence in himself to separate more clearly and
accurately than most people the relativity of essentials from verbiage, fact
from fancy, truth from lie, reality from wishful artifice, sincerity from
affectation, honesty from deception, right from wrong, love from hate,
good from evil, justice from injustice, domination from submission, impartiality from prejudice, innocence from guilt, and freedom from
coercion.

The simple, natural, primitive attitudinal organization of Lincoln's
personality, as he became a man of serious responsibilities, exposed his
emotivating-autonomic visceral organs to react excessively in professional
conflicts and other social stresses, although he succeeded in maintaining

a smiling facial appearance and courteous manner. He worked with such complete mental concentration that he was inclined to develop repeatedly eye strain, headaches, constipation, and gloomy visual outlook from nervous fatigue.

His best self-protection against this almost daily tendency was the earnest, hopeful culture of sweetness and light with peace of mind and a resolute determination to make life worth living for himself by helping others. Characteristically calm, deliberate, thoughtful, considerate, unashamed, slow and easy-going, he was inclined to ignore the attempts of others to provoke him to anger and indignation if not too unjust and insulting. He avoided bearing malice and making derogatory remarks about people, but he liked to satirize and exaggerate the personal pretensions of political opponents with humorous analogies and caricatures, even as he was often treated.

During the campaign of 1836 his opponent for election ridiculed him in a speech as a young upstart. When he finished Lincoln replied:

> "The gentleman commenced his speech by saying that this young man would have to be taken down, and he was sorry the task devolved upon him. I am not so young in years as I am in the tricks and trade of a politician; but live long or die young; I would rather die now than, like the gentleman, change my politics, and simultaneous with the change, receive an office worth three thousand dollars a year, and then have to erect a lightening-rod over my house to protect a guilty conscience from an offended God."

Possession of lightning rods, as a new invention adapted for protection at some expense, aroused no little envy in the minds of many people and Lincoln cleverly tied his opponent's hypocrisy to it with witty implications that delighted his audience.

Spartan Respectability

The early settlers were, above all things, a highly independent, self-respecting and respectful people, whatever their lack of education, wealth or social standing. This seriously cultivated tradition led them naturally, with pride and courage, to express prompt resentment against designed attempts at belittlement of character. During the election campaign of 1836 Colonel Robert Allen tried to destroy the confidence of New Salem people in Lincoln through spreading malicious insinuations against his character. When Lincoln heard of this he immediately wrote the following letter to Allen.

New Salem, June 21, 1836

> "Dear Col.
> "I am told that during my absence last week, you passed through this place, and stated publicly, that you were in possession of a fact or facts, which, if known to the public, would entirely destroy the prospects of N. W. Edwards and myself at the ensuing election; but that, through favour to us, you should forbear to divulge them.

"No one has needed favours more than I, and generally, few have been less unwilling to accept them; but in this case, favour to me, would be injustice to the public, and therefore I must beg your pardon for declining it. That I once had the confidence of the people of Sangamon, is sufficiently evident, and if I have since done any thing, either by design or misadventure, which if known, would subject me to a forfeiture of that confidence, he that knows of that thing, and conceals it, is a traitor to his country's interest.

"I find myself wholly unable to form any conjecture of what fact or facts, real or supposed, you spoke; but my opinion of your veracity, will not permit me, for a moment, to doubt, that you at least believed what you said.

"I am flattered with the personal regard you manifested for me, but I do hope that, on more mature reflection, you will view the public interest as a paramount consideration, and, therefore, determine to let the worst come.

"I here assure you, that the candid statement of facts, on your part, however low it may sink me, shall never break the tie of personal friendship between us.

"I wish an answer to this, and you are at liberty to publish both, if you choose.

Verry Respectfully,

A. Lincoln"

This letter was characteristic of Lincoln's profound faith that respect for honest, frank challenge of poisonous, serpentine attempts at defamation of character, would prevail in the minds of most people over the pleasure in half-believing such lies. We marvel at the cleverness with which he took advantage of Allen's attack and levered him into a hopelessly self-destructive political position. Later Lincoln repeatedly used such methods in self-defense, particularly when president, against disloyal cabinet officers. The letter to Allen seems to have been the earliest political occasion in which such courageous philosophical wisdom was applied.

Whig Leader

Lincoln's natural ability for leadership, even as a young man, showed to advantage wherever he went. His free imagination, easy flow of speech, convivial disposition, and keen sense of the importance of dignity and respectability and equalitarian justice, combined with his unusual powers for presenting his views consistently and persuasively, and his ever ready humorous appeal as the situation required, enabled him to lead many people willingly to change their minds and adopt compromising views. He studied endlessly how best to express himself so as to convince others. Although he liked to talk and to write letters, we find that he intentionally cultivated economy and precision in the use of words so as to make his meaning clear for everyone. His usage of simile and metaphor, allegory, satire, wit and humor, to win approval or demolish opposition in favor of some principle or idea, by setting its critical points in estimable or ridiculous connections with customary standards of acceptance or rejection as good or evil, were usually adequate for winning arguments. He liked to illustrate a point by telling a story in his unique, arresting, raspy drawl, so that it ended in a laugh-provoking surprise. This method was now becoming perfected as his most effective instrument of persuasion. His good humored willingness to be helpful to others and his cautiousness about offending the self-respect of people when opposed to them won him many friends wherever he went, although he loved to argue on the basic principles involved in any human issue, particularly politics, government, law, and religion.

Major John Todd Stuart, Springfield lawyer, the son of a Kentucky college professor, with all of the advantages in education that had been denied to Lincoln, had attained enviable professional and social standing in the state. As the leader of the Whig minority in the legislature Stuart exercised important influence in the development of state legislation and politics. He had known Lincoln in the Black Hawk War and shared confidences and political influence with him in the campaign of 1834. Impressed by his ability as a speaker and politician he encouraged Abe to study law and invited him to share his room when attending the legislature in Vandalia. Here Lincoln met many important people—lawyers, politicians, office seekers, farmers, educators, business men—as they came to influence the passage or defeat of some measure, moved generally more according to personal or community interests than state and public welfare.

Stuart and Lincoln worked as a team. Many bills were written out by Abe to be introduced by other members, indicating no little dependence on his legible penmanship. Stuart aspired for election to Congress and as he built up political affiliations in this direction Lincoln took over leadership of the Whigs on the floor of the General Assembly. Politics mixed with legislation at every turn and he became adept at perfecting log-rolling schemes and compromises. He learned to yield individual interests in favor of party organization. Personal influence and popular appeal rather than merit were often more important in getting laws passed. The party system was superceding rugged individualism and a man no longer bucked it by announcing his candidacy for office without obtaining the nod of the party's leaders. This cultivation of personal transferences among men for political influence intrigued Lincoln and we find him from now on developing its artistry with fascination and supreme self-confidence in his estimation of the character, wiles, motives, vanities, humors, and wishes of men.

Admission to the Bar

It was September 1836 before Abraham Lincoln mastered sufficient confidence in his knowledge of law to ask for an examination for admission to the bar. He found the Board a convivial group of lawyers who gladly passed him upon proper certification of his moral character after asking a few perfunctory questions. As customary he then invited his

PLATE   6a. Mary Owens. Courtesy of Lincoln National Life Foundation.

PLATE 6b. Sarah Rickard. Courtesy of Lincoln National Life Foundation.

PLATE 7a. Lincoln's Law Partner, John T. Stuart. Courtesy of the Illinois State Historical Library.
PLATE 7b. Lincoln's Law Partner, Stephen T. Logan. Courtesy of the Illinois State Historical Library.

PLATE 7c. Lincoln's Law Partner, William H. Herndon. Courtesy of the Illinois State Historical Library.

examiners to dinner. He was enrolled and licensed to practise law in the state of Illinois on September 9th and two days later participated in his first case, a minor damage suit tried in a Springfield court. He substituted for Stuart who could not attend the trial and a few months later he accepted an offer of partnership with him.

On March 1, 1837 the name of Abraham Lincoln was formally enrolled by the State Supreme Court as an attorney and counsellor licensed to practise law in all the courts of the state of Illinois.

Neurotic Courtship of Mary Owens

With the decrease of melancholia which had followed the death of Ann Rutledge, Lincoln became obsessed with a dread of gloomy loneliness and thought of marriage as a means of preventing it. Seemingly confident of being able to live pleasantly with any considerate, attractive woman and probably convinced that he could never love another as he had Ann Rutledge, he decided to make the best of it for himself. Such reasoning is characteristic of people with Lincoln's type of neurosis-disposing love fixation and it rarely works out happily.

A young legislator, politician, and lawyer of much promise, though poor, he was regarded as a good catch, and Mrs. Abell proposed to Lincoln, when he was living in her house, that if he would promise to become her brother-in-law she would have her sister Mary Owens return to New Salem for another visit. Abe was one year older than Mary and, three years earlier when she visited her sister, he had paid her some attention but, as will be seen from his letters, he had not been seriously interested in her. Longing to be married as a means of relief from loneliness if not of realizing love, Lincoln gave his promise with characteristic sincerity and hopefulness and not jestingly as Thomas (1952) and Mrs. Randall (1953) would have us believe. No doubt Mrs. Abell talked over the promise seriously from every angle with her sister.

Mary S. Owens was the daughter of a prominent Kentucky banker and well educated for that time. Her photograph shows that she had good features though perhaps somewhat overly positive and masculine in character. Upon her arrival in the autumn of 1836 Abe was shocked to find her unlike his memory of her but felt himself bound in conscience by his promise. Try as he might, he could not induce himself to fall in love with her and could neither wish for the marriage nor tell her frankly of his dilemma. Three letters which Lincoln wrote to Mary in 1836 and 1837 and one to Mrs. Browning in 1838 show the serious nature of his mental and emotional conflict and its danger for him if he did not find a solution. Parts of the first letter are quoted here italicized by me to emphasize their neurotic qualities. Other letters will follow in due course.

"Vandalia, Decr. 13, 1836

"Mary

"I have been sick ever since my arrival here, or I should have written sooner. *It is but little difference, however, as I have verry little even yet to write.* And more, the longer I can avoid the moritfication of looking in the Post Office for your letter and not finding it, the better. You see I am mad about that *old letter* yet. I dont like verry well to risk you again. I'll try once more any how."

Lincoln then discussed briefly a speech by the Governor and the chances of getting the "seat of the Government moved to Springfield." He then closed the letter as follows:

"You recollect I mentioned in the outset of this letter that I had been unwell. That is the fact, though I believe I am about well now; but that, with other things I can not account for, have conspired and have gotten my spirits so low, that I feel that I would rather be any place in the world than here. I really can not endure the thought of staying here ten weeks. Write back as soon as you get this, and if possible say something that will please me, for really I have not [been] pleased since I left you. This letter is so dry and [stupid] that I am ashamed to send it, but with my pres[ent] feelings I can not do any better. Give my respects to M[r. and] Mrs. Abell and family. Your friend*

Lincoln"

Obviously Lincoln was moody over the inability of himself and Mary to get really in love with each other, although they had entered into an understanding for the purpose of marriage. He was pleased with himself as a young legislator and lawyer and naturally expected that any girl who was to become his wife would be overcome with enthusiasm and admiration for his abilities and future prospects. Instead he found that Mary Owens, with her superior education and self-reliant intelligence, measured him with a critical eye and often not without finding unpleasant faults in his manners. His ego reacted painfully with feelings of inferiority to her noncommittal reserve and though obliged to attend the legislature his emotivation disposed him to withdraw into a regressive, nostalgic attitude. He loathed the prospect of remaining in Vandalia for 10 weeks and had not been pleased since he left her but could not say that he longed to see her. He disliked risking his pride again but would "try once more any-how." This was not an unhappy state of unrequited love but inability to love.

We cannot understand Lincoln in his early maturity and his developing philosophy until we know how his hypochondriacal mind worked in reaction to frustration. A man in such a perplexed state about himself is highly sensitive to ridicule and tends to resent other reflections on his dignity. Lincoln did not get into physical fights, although he had proved himself brave enough to resent offense, and many Vandalia people who hated him for advocating the removal of the state capital probably tried to break his spirit. He reacted to Mary Owens' unintentional frustration of his pride by developing a compensatory *egoitis* that grew sarcastic and satirical in debate.

Abe Lincoln's First Clash with Steve Douglas

At this time (1836) another young man, Stephen A. Douglas, had been elected to the legislature as a Democrat from Morgan County. The people of Sangamon, as the largest county in the state with the largest representation in the House, were urging vigorously, though not unanimously, for the selection of Springfield, their largest town, as the site of the new state capital. Douglas, a member of the committee on petitions, filed for the supporters of Vandalia a petition to divide Sangamon County into two parts, with the idea of splitting the strength of its representation. Lincoln met this threat by proposing that part of Morgan County be included in the formation of the new county. Since this would reduce Douglas' representation in Morgan County he withdrew his move against Sangamon.

Lincoln's project made him immensely popular in Springfield but it eventually cost the state many times the true value of its real estate and buildings. He derived no economic benefit from the manipulation but was held responsible by the Democrats, including Douglas, for getting the state into debt beyond its actual carrying capacity. The panic of 1837, precipitated by President Jackson's obliteration of the Federal Bank in favor of State Banks and hard money, almost forced Illinois into bankruptcy and brought upon Lincoln intensely bitter political blame.

Lincoln was also attacked from another, personally sensitive direction, as a member of the committee responsible for the finances of the state. U. F. Linder (Democrat) offered a series of resolutions to examine the management of the State Bank located in Springfield. His move was planned to frighten Springfield stock holders into yielding on the state capital in order not to lose the bank, for the majority of an examining committee would be Democrats, unfriendly to maintaining it as an institution. Lincoln opposed Linder and sparred with him for several days until he had time to marshall evidence in favor of the Bank. On January 11, 1837, he made a prepared but unusually sarcastic speech against his opponent in the legislature, of which the first paragraph is quoted here.

"Lest I should fall," he said, "into the too common error, of being mistaken in regard to which side I design to be upon, I shall make it my first care to remove all doubt on that point, by declaring that I am opposed to the resolution under consideration, in toto. Before I proceed to the body of the subject, I will further remark, that it is not without a considerable degree of apprehension, that I venture to cross the track of the gentleman from Coles [Mr. Linder]. Indeed, I do not believe I could muster a sufficiency of courage to come in contact with that gentleman, were it not for the fact, that he, some days since, most graciously condescended to assure us that he would never be found wasting ammunition on *small game*. On the same fortunate occasion, he further gave us to understand, that he regarded *himself* as being decidedly the *superior* of our common friend from Randolph [Mr. Shields]; and feeling, as I really do, that I, to say the most of myself, am nothing more than the peer of our friend from Randolph, I shall regard the gentleman from Coles as decidedly my superior also, and consequently, in the course of what I shall have to say, whenever I shall have occasion to allude to that gentleman, I shall endeavor to adopt that kind of court language which I understand to be due to *decided superiority*. In one faculty, at least, there can be no dispute of the gentleman's superiority over me, and most other men; and that is, the faculty of entangling a subject, so that neither himself, or any other man, can find head or tail to it."

Lincoln used the pronoun *I* 16 times in the first paragraph of this prepared speech, in relation to feelings of personal inferiority. Although meant sarcastically, it obviously indicates the neurotic state of his mind. The speech was successful in that it obtained a fair investigation, and a clean record for the Bank and safeguarded the confidence of the people in its management and the specie it issued. His discussion of Linder's resolutions shows that he had by this time thoroughly digested the logical limitations of Federal and State constitutions on legislation. He upheld the judgments of the State Supreme Court on the constitutionality of the State Bank and the importance for commerce of public faith in its principles and management. Lincoln's philosophy of constitutional democratic government was becoming highly progressive, and moving far in advance of the economic theory and political practise of his time.

First Protest Against Extension of Slavery

As a leader of the Whig minority, Lincoln suddenly found himself confronted in the General Assembly by the passage of a deceptively devised scheme to promote the interests of slavery. On January 12, 1837 the Democratic majority had unexpectedly passed, under instigation by its southern dominated national organization, the following set of resolutions in both Houses before public alarm and opposition could be organized.

"That we highly disapprove of the formation of abolition societies and of the doctrines promulgated by them,

"That the right of property in slaves is sacred to the slaveholding States by the Federal Constitution, and that they cannot be deprived of that right without their consent,

"That the General Government cannot abolish slavery in the District of Columbia, against the consent of the citizens of said District, without a manifest breach of good faith,

"That the Governor be requested to transmit to the States of Virginia, Alabama, Mississippi, New York and Connecticut, a copy of the foregoing report and resolutions."

Lincoln was incensed at this outrageous betrayal by the State Legislature of the people who, in large majority, opposed the retention of slaves in the state or the District of Columbia or the territories. He openly circulated a petition on the second last day of the session, March 3, 1837, stating that the undersigned protested against the above resolutions. All of his political friends refused to sign it save one. It read:

"Resolutions upon the subject of domestic slavery having passed both branches of the General Assembly at its present session, the undersigned hereby protest against the passage of the same.

"They believe that the institution of slavery is founded on both injustice and bad policy; but that the promulgation of abolition doctrines tends rather to increase than to abate its evils.

"They believe that the Congress of the United States has no power, under the Constitution, to interfere with the institution of slavery in the different states.

"They believe that the Congress of the United States has the power, under the Constitution, to abolish slavery in the District of Columbia; but that that power ought not be exercised unless at the request of the people of said District.

"The difference between these opinions and those contained in the said resolutions, is their reason for entering this protest.

Dan Stone,
A. Lincoln,
Representatives from the County of Sangamon."

The Democrats and Abolitionists both condemned and ridiculed the resolutions and all the Whigs except one shunned them.

This bold, singular action reveals the consistency of Lincoln's courage and independence of mind and the great force in his personality of the conscientious compulsion to uphold equitable legal rights of all men as established under the Constitution. It also reveals the innate wisdom and well-balanced judgment in his inclination to arbitrate uncompromising conflicts and discourage radical abolitionism. We will see again that 10 years later Congressman Lincoln felt compelled to express himself vigorously against the injustice of authoritarian imposition on the people and on the constitutional rights of Congress on limiting slavery. It was shown previously that his intense hatred and opposition to authoritarian injustice was established in his mind in childhood unconsciously by the tyranny of his father and the equitable justice of his mother, and influenced later by the idealism of Ann Rutledge in upholding the founders of the Constitution. His attitude toward the slavery question and the Constitution continued unchanged for the rest of his life. In 1860, as a presidential candidate, he said in reference to this protest, "It was then the same that it is now."

Springfield State Capital

The first capital of Illinois had been located in Vandalia, in the southern half of the state where most of its people were settled along the Wabash, Ohio, and Mississippi Rivers. As Chicago grew and the center of population moved northward the demand for transferring the capital to a more central location increased. The old state house at Vandalia was in such dilapidated condition that a new one had to be built and Lincoln played a leading part in having the capital transferred in 1837 to Springfield, then in Sangamon County, nearer the physical center of the state. The people of Vandalia put up a bitter fight to retain their political and economic advantage. They tore down the old state house when the legislature was not in session and built a new one on the site without legal authorization, hoping thereby to coerce the government into accepting it and repaying the costs.

Lincoln, unimpressed by such methods, organized a movement against Vandalia and, with the approval of Sangamon County's representation, he engaged in numerous political alliances whereby he traded support with various sections that desired the capital by promising the building of local roads, canals and other improvements in return for supporting the selection of Springfield.

R. L. Wilson, one of Lincoln's supporters, has described his political sagacity.

> "In those darkest hours when our bill to all appearances was beyond resuscitation, and all our opponents were jubilant over our defeat and our friends could see no hope, Mr. Lincoln never for a moment despaired; but collecting his colleagues to his room for consultation, his practical common sense, his thorough knowledge of human nature, then made him an overmatch for his compeers and for any man that I have ever known."

Lincoln Meets Speed

New Salem was doomed as a community, and Springfield as the new state capital was destined to grow and prosper. Lincoln, as the man of the hour, was persuaded by Stuart, Ninian Edwards, and other friends to move there and engage in the practice of law. On April 15, 1837 he rode into the town on a borrowed horse, dressed in the dignified, long black coat and high hat of a legislator, with a shawl over his shoulders and all his personal belongings packed in a pair of saddle bags.

Lincoln was familiar with the town but had little ready money to carry on until he could earn a living in the practice of law. He stopped at the prosperous general store of Joshua Fry Speed to inquire how much it would cost to have a bedstead built and equipped long enough for himself. As Speed (1896) has told it: "When he learned that the price would be about seventeen dollars he said: 'It is probably cheap enough; but I want to say that cheap as it is, I have not the money to pay. But if you will credit me until Christmas, and my experiment here as a lawyer is a success, I will pay you then. If I fail in that I will probably never pay you at all.'

"The tone of his voice was so melancholy that I felt for him. I looked up at him and I thought then, as I think now, that I never saw so gloomy and melancholy a face in all my life." Speed suggested that he had a large room upstairs with a very large double bed in it which he was willing to share. The congeniality of these two men was so spontaneous that it could only have been established by the natural harmony of the similarities and contrasts in their constitutional dispositions. Lincoln asked how to get to the room and took his saddle bags upstairs without further ado. In a few minutes he returned and with a face beaming pleasure exclaimed, "Well, Speed, I am moved."

Since Speed became Lincoln's most intimately confidential friend, a brief sketch of his life is inserted here.*

William Butler, active in state politics and owner of the Butler House, had a heavy stake in getting the state capital transferred to Springfield. He graciously invited Lincoln to board with him and supported his candidacies and political policies. This made good business, for, as Whig leader, Lincoln attracted many guests. He grew warmly attached to the Butler family and never, it seems, felt obliged to pay for his meals although he continued this dependence for several years. He has been criticized for having been a "sponge" and "working a racket" but the modern view does not apply here, for the practice among the early settlers of trading helps for benefits was customary.

J. T. Stuart and A. Lincoln, Attorneys

On the day of Lincoln's arrival in Springfield the *Sangamo Journal,* a Whig newspaper, carried a professional card announcing, "J. T. Stuart and A. Lincoln, Attorneys and Counsellors at Law, will practise conjointly in the courts of the Judicial circuit. Office No. 4 Hoffman's Row upstairs. Springfield."

Judge Logan, whose partner Lincoln became a few years later, has given impressions of Abe's first speech in Springfield:

> "He was a very tall and gawky and rough looking fellow then; his pantaloons didn't meet his shoes by six inches. But after he began speaking I became very much interested in him. He made a very sensible speech." . . . His manner was "very much the same as his speeches in after life—that is the same peculiar characteristics were apparent then, though of course in after life he evinced more knowledge and experience. But he had then the same novelty and the same peculiarity in presenting his ideas. He had the same individuality that he kept through all his life." (Herndon, 1889.)

---

*Joshua Fry Speed was born November 14, 1814, near Louisville, Ky., the fifth of ten children. His parents were both descendants of Virginia's aristocracy and socially prominent in Kentucky. Joshua was considered well educated for his time and quit college in order to work in a wholesale store. In 1834 he established a general store in Springfield, Ill., then a booming town of 1,500 people in the center of the State, inhabited largely by Kentuckians. He took a lively interest in public and social affairs and assisted in editing a local newspaper, and became a popular member of the leading social set.

He sold his store in Springfield on January 1, 1841 and returned to Kentucky to attend to his mother's estate. Here he married Fanny Henning in 1842. They never had children but they lived happily in complete devotion to each other for over 30 years, until her death.

Speed became a leading man in the business and political circles of Kentucky, and during the war was a close friend and advisor to President Lincoln. He was a frequent guest at the White House and an important factor in holding Kentucky loyal to the Union. He died in 1882.

John Todd Stuart was more of a politician than lawyer. Not a careful student of law but clever at building up sympathetic transferences and prejudices for or against an idea in the minds of a jury, he depended upon witty generalizations rather than factual argument. Lincoln, although a better thinker, was similarly but more logically inclined and the two made an unbalanced team. Their practice consisted mostly of minor suits. Stuart had run for Congress in 1836 and, though defeated, was preparing for another attempt in 1838 in which Lincoln was to play an influential part.

Lincoln's "Hypo"

While handsome, debonair Stuart enjoyed numerous friendly connections in Springfield's aristocratic society, his slouchy young partner found life lonely and discouraging. He had become a social lion in New Salem only to find himself neglected in Springfield, where he had expected to be well received after working so effectively in making it the state capital. His letter at this time to Mary Owens best portrays his neurotic state of mind (characteristic statements italicised by me).

"Friend Mary   Springfield, May 7, 1837

"I have commenced two letters to send you before this, both of which displeased me before I got half done, and so I tore them up. The first I thought wasn't serious enough, and the second was on the other extreme. I shall send this, turn out as it may." (Such vacillation was characteristic of Lincoln until he knew what he wanted to say.)

"This thing of living in Springfield is rather a dull business after all, at least it is so to me. I am quite as lonesome here as [I] ever was anywhere in my life. I have been spoken to by but one woman since I've been here, and should not have been by her, if she could have avoided it. I've never been to church yet, and probably shall not be soon. I stay away because I am conscious I should not know how to behave myself."

"I am often thinking about what we said of your coming to live at Springfield. I am afraid you would not be satisfied. There is a great deal of flourishing about in carriages here, which it would be your doom to see without shareing in it. You would have to be poor without the means of hiding your poverty. Do you believe you could bear that patiently? *Whatever woman may cast her lot with mine, should any ever do so, it is my intention to do all in my power to make her happy and contented; and there is nothing I can imagine, that would make me more unhappy than to fail in the effort. I know I should be much happier with you than the way I am, provided I saw no signs of discontent in you."* (Obviously Lincoln and Mary Owens were still unable to fall in love with each other and he was fearful of marrying her under such conditions. His letter continued with a patent attempt at getting out of his promise although he considered himself bound by it.)

. . . . "What I have said I will most positively abide by, provided you wish it. My opinion is that you had better not do it. You have not been accustomed to hardship, and it may be more severe than you now imagine. I know you are capable of thinking correctly on any subject; and if you deliberate maturely upon this, before you decide, then I am willing to abide your decision.

"You must write me a good long letter after you get this. You have nothing else to do, and though it might not seem interesting to you, after you had written it, it would be a good deal of company to me in this 'busy wilderness.' Tell your sister I dont want to hear any more about selling out and moving. That gives me the *hypo* whenever I think of it.

Yours, etc.

Lincoln"

Lincoln had previously consulted his physician, Dr. Anson G. Henry, about his morbidly depressed nervous condition and was told that he had "hypochondria," then regarded as a special form of nervous malady characterized by miserable feelings of weakness under the chondrium (breast bone), particularly in the heart and stomach. It is a miserably depressing state of mind from conflicting, unreciprocal autonomic nervous activation of vital organ functioning and the inhibition of endocrine release of energic materials in the blood. It is generally augmented upon becoming morally or economically bound by a distressing obligation, in a loveless personal relationship from which no means of escape seems possible.

Lincoln wanted Mary to warm up enthusiastically about him and so break down his inhibitions but it was not in her nature to do so. In his hypochondriacal irritability he had become dependent upon Dr. Henry, a humanely wise general practitioner, though not medically well educated in the modern sense, who was serving as a state commissioner appointed by the State Legislature. Lincoln defended his doctor in June of 1837, when he was accused of incompetent spending of state funds to build the new state house.

In August of 1837, Dr. Henry, a Whig, and General James Adams, a Democrat, became rival candidates for election as probate judge. A few weeks previously Stuart and Lincoln had been engaged by Mrs. Mary Anderson, a widow, to bring suit against General Adams, who posed as a lawyer, for title to 10 acres of land that she claimed he had obtained from her husband by fraud. Upon thorough examination of the records and deeds, Lincoln found evidence that Adams had written the will dishonestly. As was then customary in politics, he with friends publicly circulated a report in the form of letters under the pseudonym "Sampson's Ghost" in the *Sangamo Journal,* that caricatured Adams' unfitness as a lawyer and justice.

Adams replied vigorously and a series of recriminating public personal charges and countercharges followed in which each claimed to have proven the other "a liar" and said so repeatedly. Adams charged that Lincoln and "a knot of lawyers and doctors" were trying to defame his character in order to defeat him in the coming election. Lincoln replied (10, 18, 1837) with bold ridicule in a long letter, characteristic excerpts of which only can be given here.

"Now, let it be remembered that when he [General Adams] first came to this country, he attempted to impose himself upon the community as a *lawyer,* and actually carried the attempt so far, as to induce a man who was under a charge of murder to intrust the defence of his life in his hands, and finally took his money and got him hanged . . . If he is not a lawyer, he *is* a liar, for he proclaimed himself a lawyer, and got a man hanged by depending on him. . . .

"General Adams' publications and out-door manoevring, taken in connection with the editorial articles of the [Illinois] Republican [Democratic paper], are not more foolish and contradictory than they are ludicrous and amusing. One week the Republican notifies the public that Gen. Adams is preparing an *instrument* that will tear, rend, split, rive, blow up, confound, overwhelm, annihilate, extinguish, exterminate, burst asunder, and grind to powder all his slanderers, and particularly Talbott and Lincoln—all of which is to be done *in due time.* . . . Again the Republican comes forth with a mere passing remark that 'public opinion has decided in favor of Gen. Adams,' [who won the election] and intimates that he will give himself no more trouble about the matter. . . . (I really believe the editor of the Ill. Republican is fool enough to think General Adams is an honest man.) Suddenly the Gen. appears to relent at the severity with which he is treating us and he exclaims. 'The condemnation of my enemies is the inevitable result of my own defense.' For your health's sake, dear Gen. do not permit your tenderness of heart to afflict you so much on our account. For some reason (perhaps because we are killed so quickly) we shall never be sensible of our suffering.

"Farewell, General, I will see you again at court, if not before—when and where we will settle the question whether you or the widow shall have the land."

General Adams died before the suit was tried and it was abated by the court.

Such violence of expression to serve a friend, needlessly making bitter enemies for himself, was at this time characteristic of his neurotic state of mind. His emotional dilemma continued unsolved, although he and Mary Owens repeatedly muddled it over. The self-doubtful man persisted in revealing that he really wished freedom and the woman knew it. Three months later he wrote (neurotic indications italicised by me):

"Friend Mary.   "Springfield, August 16, 1837

"You will, no doubt, think it rather strange, that I should write you a letter on the same day on which we part; and I can only account for it by supposing, that seeing you lately makes me think more of you than usual, while at our late meeting we had but few expressions of thoughts. You must know that I can not see you, or think of you, with entire indifference; and yet it may be, that you, are mistaken in regard to what my real feelings towards you are. If I knew you were not, I should not trouble you with this letter. Perhaps any other man would know enough without further information; but I consider it *my* peculiar right to plead ignorance, and your bounden duty to allow the plea. *I want in all cases to do right, and most particularly so, in all cases with women. I want, at this particular time, more than anything else, to do right with you, and if I knew it would be doing right, as I rather suspect it would, to let you alone, I would do it.* And for the purpose of making the matter as plain as possible, I now say, that you can now drop the subject, dismiss your thoughts (if you ever had any) from me forever, and leave this letter unanswered, without calling forth one accusing murmer from me. And I will even go further, and say, that if it will add any thing to your comfort, or peace of mind, to do so, it is my sincere wish that you should. Do not understand by this, that I wish to cut your acquaintance. I mean no such thing. What I do wish is, that our further acquaintance shall depend upon yourself. If such further acquaintance would contribute nothing to your happiness, I am sure it would not to mine. *If you feel yourself in any degree bound to me, I am now willing to release you, provided you wish it; while, on the other hand, I am willing, and even anxious to bind you faster, if I can be convinced that it will, in any considerable degree, add to your happiness. This, indeed, is the whole question with me. Nothing would make me more miserable than to believe you miserable—nothing more happy, than to know you were so.*

"In what I have now said, I think I cannot be misunderstood; and to make myself understood, is the only object of this letter.

"If it suits you best not to answer this—farewell—a long life and a merry one attend you. But if you conclude to write back, speak as plainly as I do. There can be neither harm nor danger, in saying, to me, any thing you think, just in the manner you think it.

My respects to your sister. Your friend
Lincoln"

This was Lincoln's last letter to Mary Owens. She doubtless realized that he did not love her and could not make up his mind to marry her, however he tried to persuade himself; and discouraged by his impotent, neurotic vacillation she firmly rejected him and disregarded his final letter.

Frustrated, Sarcastic Egotism

The letters to Mary Owens show clearly that Lincoln's decision to marry would be determined, not by his love of a woman, which he could not even anticipate, but by the forlorn hope that that woman would be miserable without him even though not really in love and happy with him. His egoistic self-respect was hurt by Mary Owens' rejection and he blamed her for causing his painful feeling of inferiority, in a manner typical of the rejected suitor. He must have an emotional cartharsis to release his repressions and restore his integrity. He chose to write a confidential letter to Mrs. O. H. Browning, a close friend whose husband was in the legislature with him (neurotic expressions italicized by the author).

"Springfield, April 1, 1838
"Dear Madam:
"Without appologising for being egotistical, I shall make the history of so much of my own life, as has elapsed since I saw you, the subject of this letter. And by the way I now discover, that, in order to give a full

and inteligible account of the things I have done and suffered *since* I saw you, I shall necessarily have to relate some that happened *before*.

"It was, then, in the autumn of 1836, that a married lady of my acquaintance, and who was a great friend of mine, being about to pay a visit to her father and other relatives residing in Kentucky, proposed to me, that on her return she would bring a sister of hers with her, upon condition that I would engage to become her brother-in-law with all convenient dispatch. I, of course, accepted the proposal; for you know I could not have done otherwise, had I really been averse to it; but privately between you and me, I was most confoundedly well pleased with the project. I had seen the said sister some three years before, thought her intelligent and agreeable, and saw no good objection to plodding through life hand in hand with her. Time passed on, the lady took her journey and in due time returned, sister in company sure enough. This stomached me a little; for it appeared to me, that her coming so readily showed that she was a trifle too willing; but on reflection it occurred to me, that she might have been prevailed on by her married sister to come, without any thing concerning me ever having been mentioned to her; and so I concluded that if no other objection presented itself, I would consent to wave this. All this occurred upon my *hearing* of her arrival in the neighborhood; for, be it remembered, I had not yet *seen* her, except about three years previous, as above mentioned.

"In a few days we had an interview, and, although I had seen her before, *she did not look as my immagination had pictured her.* [Author's italics.] I knew she was over-size, but now she appeared a fair match for Falstaff; I knew she was called an "old maid," and I felt no doubt of the truth of at least half of the appelation; but now, *when I beheld her, I could not for my life avoid thinking of my mother* [aging stepmother]; *and this, not from withered features, for her skin was too full of fat, to permit its contracting in to wrinkles; but from her want of teeth, weather-beaten appearance in general, and from a kind of notion that ran in my head, that nothing could have commenced at the size of infancy, and reached her present bulk in less than thirty five or forty years; and, in short, I was not at all pleased with her.* [Author's italics.] But what could I do? I had told her sister that I would take her for better or for worse; and *I made a point of honor and conscience in all things, to stick to my word, especially if others had been induced to act on it, which in this case, I doubted not they had, for I was now fairly convinced, that no other man on earth would have her, and hence the conclusion that they were bent on holding me to my bargain.* [Author's italics.] Well, thought I, I have said it, and, be the consequences what they may, it shall not be my fault if I fail to do it. At once I determined to consider her my wife; and this done, all my powers of discovery were put to the rack, in search of perfections in her, which might be fairly set-off against her defects. I tried to immagine she was handsome, which, but for her unfortunate corpulency, was actually true. *Exclusive of this, no woman that I have seen, has a finer face. I also tried to convince myself, that the mind was much more to be valued than the person; and in this, she was not inferior, as I could discover, to any with whom I had been acquainted.* [Author's italics.]

"Shortly after this, without attempting to come to any positive understanding with her, I set out for Vandalia, where and when you first saw me. During my stay there, I had letters from her, which did not change my opinion of either her intellect or intention; but on the contrary, confirmed it in both.

"*All this while, although I was fixed "firm as the surge repelling rock" in my resolution, I found I was continually repenting the rashness, which had led me to make it. Through life I have been in no bondage, either real or immaginary from the thraldom of which I so much desired to be free.* [Author's italics.]

"After my return home, I saw nothing to change my opinion of her in any particular. She was the same and so was I. I now spent my time planning how I might get along through life after my contemplated change of circumstances should have taken place; and *how I might procrastinate the evil day for a time, which I really dreaded as much—perhaps more, than an irishman does the halter.*

"*After all my suffering upon this deeply interesting subject, here I am, wholly unexpectedly, completely out of the "scrape"; and I now want to know, if you can guess how I got out of it. Out clear in every sense of the term; no violation of word, honor or conscience.* [Author's italics.] I don't believe you can guess, and so I may as well tell you at once. As the lawyers say, it was done in the manner following, towit. After I had delayed the matter as long as I thought I could in honor do, which, by the way, had brought me round into the last fall, I concluded I might as well bring it to a consumation without further delay; and so *I mustered my resolution, and made the proposal to her direct; but, shocking to relate, she answered, No.* [Author's italics.] At first I supposed she did it through an affectation of modesty, which I thought but ill-become her under the peculiar circumstances of her case; but on my renewal of the charge, I found she repeled it with greater firmness than before. *I tried it again and again, but with the same success, or rather with the same want of success. I finally was forced to give it up, at which I verry unexpectedly found myself mortified almost beyond endurance. I was mortified, it seemed to me, in a hundred different ways. My vanity was deeply wounded by the reflection, that I had so long been too stupid to discover her intentions, and at the same time never doubting that I understood them perfectly; and also, that she whom I had taught myself to believe no body else would have, had actually rejected me with all my fancied greatness; and to cap the whole, I then, for the first time, began to suspect that I was really a little in love with her. But let it all go. I'll try and out live it. Others have been made fools of by the girls; but this can never be with truth said of me. I most emphatically, in this instance, made a fool of myself, I have now come to the conclusion never again to think of marrying;* and for this reason; I can never be satisfied with any one who would be block-head enough to have me. [Author's italics.]

"When you receive this, write me a long yarn about something to amuse me. Give my respects to Mr. Browning.

Your sincere friend

Mrs. O. H. Browning   A. Lincoln"

This letter does not mention the name of Mary Owens, and Mrs. Browning never guessed whom it referred to until Lincoln told her.

A year of unhappy courtship and noncommittal talk about marriage convinced Mary of Abe's indifference toward her and she wisely rejected him. His wounded ego vainly compensated with imaginations about being "a little in love" with her and to get even he ridiculed her physical imperfections that had inhibited him. Although the letter to Mrs. Browning showed esthetic deficiency to his discredit, it proved an adequate idea-emotional cartharsis. Thereafter he found himself relieved at having escaped from a bondage that would probably have submerged him in a life of uninspired mediocrity.

Mary Owens was not a toothless old maid that no man would have, as Lincoln had vulgarly described her. This unchivalrous picture was probably exaggerated for amusement in the manner characteristic of his sarcastic state of mind toward her. She was a respectable, well-educated, resolute minded woman, one year younger than Lincoln. A few years later she married Jesse Vineyard and had two sons who eventually served in the Confederate army. When Herndon asked her, 28 years later, for an account of the courtship, she admitted that her sister was anxious for her to marry Lincoln but she found him "deficient in those links which make up the chain of a woman's happiness." To illustrate this statement she described how he ungallantly let her cross a muddy road without offering his hand and yet had proudly told her how, in pity for a hog mired in a mudhole, he had pulled it out although dressed in his best pants.

> "Not that I believed that it proceeded from a lack of goodness of heart," she continued, "but his training had been different from mine; hence there was not that congeniality which would otherwise have existed. . . . His heart and hand were at my disposal; and I suppose that my feelings were not sufficiently enlisted to have the matter consummated. . . . The last message I ever received from him was about a year after we parted. He said to Mrs. Abell, 'Tell your sister that I think she was a great fool because she did not stay here and marry me:' characteristic of the man."

Lincoln's dread of being made "a fool" by a girl was yet to be far more vividly realized and his neurotic disposition frustrated to the point of self-destructive melancholy.

Chapter X

PRACTICAL POLITICAL PHILOSOPHER
OF LAW AND ORDER

Congressman Stuart spent most of his time in Washington and Lincoln carried on the firm's work on the basis of equally dividing their law earnings. At first he kept a neat record of accounts, but soon tired of such unnecessary bookkeeping and merely divided the collected cash into two equal amounts and kept them in separate packages in a drawer. Litigation in this period of American history was simple, and settled more on a common-sense application of fact, human appeal, and equitable principles of fairness and justice than on finely-drawn legal interpretations and involved citations of judgments of parallel cases. As a trial lawyer on questions of violations of personal rights and obtaining just retribution or compromise Lincoln soon demonstrated extraordinary abilities.

Realistic Analyzer

His success was based more on his astute common-sense analytical observation of human motivation and equalitarian application of moral principles than his knowledge of law. His natural method of cross-examination of evidence, characteristic as a boy solving problems in mathematics, continued with refinement of experience as a lawyer and politician arguing an issue.

He habitually analyzed quantitatively as well as qualitatively the evidence of conditioning forces *for* and *against* a claim or proposition, and differentiated and systematically arranged it into a series of allied factors to be acquisitively asserted and opposing factors to be avoidantly negated. Thereby he arrived at well-balanced judgment, and maintained a most reliable self-assurance against cautious self-doubt, traces of which, fortunately, he was unable or uninclined to repress. 'Don't be too sure of the truth of any premises and don't be too satisfied with any conclusions, but depend on the reasoning of common sense and beware of the emotional bias of wishful thinking' seemed to be his self-counsels. Although naturally idealistic, he avoided binding his imagination to striving for perfection or committing himself to uphold a declaration of principle beyond the limits of common sense. He avoided being an extremist in anything lest he would find he had lost control of his obligation.

Lincoln's fascination for practical analysis of news, petitions, and editorial opinions in sectionally representative newspapers, kept him well informed on trends and changes in public sentiment for and against state and federal legislative action in which he had interest. Consensus of public sentiment, he believed, was the most powerful force in politics. He liked particularly to estimate the personal interests and political actions of officials and candidates relative to the strength of their public influences.

Mentally highly independent, Lincoln first opposed the party caucus, then increasing in importance in the East and being adopted by the Democratic party in Illinois, for its Jacksonian tendency to consider the party welfare and that of its members above that of the state and its people. However, he naturally became a close party organizer through keeping his confederates posted and lined up as a harmonious team of workers for whatever was planned, but he carefully avoided subordinating the welfare of the state and its people in favor of anyone. The practical experience gained as a minority leader in the legislature became enormously useful in organizing political actions.

> "The people," he said, "know their rights and they are never slow to assert them, when they are invaded. Let them call for an investigation, and I shall ever stand ready to respond to the call.
>
> "I believe it is universally understood and acknowledged, that all men will ever act correctly, unless they have a motive to do otherwise."

Lincoln was a keen analyst of apparent and hidden motives and characteristically questioned obvious explanations of policy until he saw through the personal advantages involved. It was his philosophy of democracy that the people's political interests, in their freedom to work for self-preservation, naturally differentiate into selfish desires for advantages to be gained directly at the expense of the public welfare, and patriotic desires to increase public welfare as an indirect means of increasing personal welfare. The greatest good for the greatest number is served best by keeping individual or class welfare subordinated to state and public welfare, and this, he held, must be achieved principally through educational and legal processes. His natural inclination would subordinate political power to efficiency in government and the welfare of the people, but his party experience forced him to accept that independence of mind must compromise with party organization as well as majority opinion. In his minority position, as Whig leader, he resented intensely the subordination of government service and welfare to the Jacksonian system of patronage.

An indication of his political philosophy at work is evident in his letter (12, 24, 1836) to his old friend John McNamar, who wanted a road routed to improve his property.

> "Dear Mack: . . . I have received the petition for the change of the state road, so as to make it run by Tilman Hornsecker's and Bowman's, and . . . unless you, who are opposed to the change, get up a remonstrance and send it on, I shall be forced to have a bill passed upon the petition. . . . If you feel any particular interest in this affair don't fail to bestir yourself."

Lincoln would serve the interests of his friend provided he showed them to be consistent with the best interests of the community by obtaining a majority approval. This philosophy, though not unerring, generally served better the will of the common people, and strengthened, when he served it, his own public influence. We have seen that, as a boy in Indiana and as a young man in New Salem serving as elected captain of volunteers, Lincoln was a natural organizer and leader of group interests. He won confidence by directing its sentiments toward improving the common welfare and disapproving special privileges. He applied these principles as strictly to himself as he did to other persons. When he bought cheap land as a speculation along a highway that had been authorized by the legislature, he did not violate legislative ethics by exerting influence to have its value increased through making further improvements.

Lincoln's astute, untiring interest in political organization is indicated in his letter to J. W. Fell (7, 23, 1838): "If we do our duty we shall succeed in the congressional election, but if we relax an *iota,* we shall be beaten." He supported a protective federal tariff, a United States bank, the state bank, the improvement of transportation, and the state's purchase of federal land to sell at a profit for reduction of the state debt. Such progressive, liberal views held the approval of most people including the wealthy, aristocratic families of the state. An important Springfield citizen, Ninian Edwards, the son of a former governor of the state, became an enthusiastic Lincoln supporter and offered to finance him in opening his own law office. After some consideration Lincoln declined, largely out of fear of the possibility of failure to make a living in his profession and getting deeper into debt, reminiscent of his experience as a merchant, even though he was becoming socially as well as politically popular in Springfield.

Cultivation of consistent, logical thinking, as the basis of clear, convincing speaking and writing, continued to be characteristic of Lincoln's self-education. However, he carelessly retained some of his early misspellings, like "verry," and hillbilly pronunciations and habits of speech, such as splitting infinitives and saying "myself" instead of "I." He grew more impressive as he learned to refrain from speaking unless he could think of something worthwhile to say, whether serious or amusing, although he loved to talk. He once commented on the ordeal of making impromptu speeches: "I believe I shall never be old enough to speak without embarrassment when I have nothing to say." He spoke, even in humor, persuasively to induce moral convictions and not merely to entertain. Practical ways of dealing with human nature, in its sympathies and antipathies of cooperative and competitive social relations, were the most interesting subjects for him. He generally began a story or discussion of a subject in argument or lecture with a statement that indicated his essential thought about it and then followed with an elaboration. He also liked to close with a clincher that expressed the whole idea as simply and clearly as possible with the least number of words. To achieve such effects he often spent hours, and even days, working an idea over and over until he thought he had succeeded in expressing it so that everyone would understand its meaning.

Principles of Jeffersonian Government

James Rutledge probably had more impressive influence than any other man on Abraham Lincoln when in his formative state of mind, by inviting him into New Salem's debating society and urging him to try for the legislature and study law. His father, Edward Rutledge, a governor of South Carolina and signer of the Declaration of Independence, was a close friend of Thomas Jefferson. His father's brother John Rutledge, also a governor of South Carolina, was one of the framers of the Constitution. Here were indeed intensely intimate, direct lines of personal connection with the men who created the most important documents in the history of the United States, authorizing the revolt of the 13 colonies from Great Britain and organizing their solidarity in a national democratic form of government. The nation was hardly 50 years old when Lincoln came under the stimulating influence of the close living ties of the Rutledge family with American history, and we can be quite certain that no subjects were more often discussed and reflected upon by him in New Salem, for their many implications in human relations. He probably memorized both documents, as he did Blackstone's principles, and became interested in the personal history of each of the signers, as his later discussions evince. He read Jefferson's philosophical arguments on the political involvements of the inalienable, God-given rights of man to self-government and became an ardent reader of Senators Daniel Webster and Henry Clay, leading interpreters of liberty in the United States government at this time.

The faith expressed in the Declaration of Independence had become Lincoln's "political religion;" and the author, Thomas Jefferson, whom he called "the most distinguished politician in our history," became his chief authoritarian reference on political philosophy. Like Jefferson he upheld human rights and human labor above property rights and economic values, and ever retained faith in the intelligence of a free people to govern themselves without being dominated by a self-appointed ruling class. Like Jefferson and his New Salem friends, he abhorred slavery and believed it to be too unjust and cruel to survive. Unlike Jefferson, he held consistently that states' rights should be subordinated to federal rights in order to maintain the government's solidarity under the Constitution.

Lincoln saw that the basic precept of the natural need of freedom and equal legal rights for each person, as asserted by the fathers of the

Revolution and the Constitution in opposition to the ancient claim of divine rights of kings to govern, was based on the social rule of Christ, to treat others as you wish to be treated. This profoundly influential moral conviction remained, throughout his career as a lawyer, politician, statesman and president, the guiding principle of all of his arguments and judgments on legal regulation of human relations.

Probably without planning to develop a consistent moral philosophy of law and order, Lincoln was becoming so set in mind. In applying the principle that all men are created to be free and enjoy equal legal rights, under the limitations of the Constitution, he logically deduced, as consequences, the necessity of cultivating equitable cooperative self-giving by each person, to counteract his natural egocentric propensity for social domination and "distinction" and getting more and more power and wealth for giving less and less. He arrived, through his habitual rigorous analytical studies of the motivation of himself and of other people, at an unequivocal monistic philosophical comprehension of the inevitable economies in the cooperative and competitive social interactions naturally inherent in the self-preservative and reproductive compulsions of life. As we review his speeches, letters and lectures in the order of production we find that intentional self-discipline of cool, logical, realistic reasoning, and repression of wishful personal bias develops increasingly, to give him eventually superiority over most lawyers, editors, judges, legislators, politicians, statesmen, and generals of his time in analytical discrimination of essentials from nonessentials and practical evaluation of allied and conflicting legal, moral and physical forces in a situation.

Philsophy of Perpetuation of Political Institutions

Lincoln's natural aptitude for public speaking soon expanded from political to popular lecturing. His choice of subject for the first lecture after leaving New Salem reflects the liveliness in his mind of memories of discussions with his friends on the ideals of the Revolution leading to his greater realization of the restless forces in human nature that must be regulated by constitutional law. His lecture, delivered before the Young Men's Lyceum in Springfield on January 27, 1838, contains the roots of consistent application of moral perception, that he was now inspired to repeat in different ways to different audiences and that eventually matured into the practical philosophy of democracy that led the people to elect him their president.

His earlier humility of expression was now expanding into an egoistic phase of cultivating, with sophomoric elan, the redundant and extravagent use of dramatic allegory, and vivid, though broad, analogy and metaphor, much after the popular style of the famous political orators of his time. Most biographers have regarded this lecture as historically unimportant and only mention some of its studied, flowery phrases to compare them with the magnificent simplicity of his later, more mature-minded expressions.

This address is psychologically important, however, as evidence on the development of his manner of expression as well as reflecting the influence of his personal experiences on his philosophy of law and order. With characteristic plan of presentation he gave, in the introductory and closing statements, his reasons why and how posterity must preserve the constitutional form of democratic government founded by its fathers. He began:

> "As a subject for the remarks of the evening, *the perpetuation of our political institutions,* is selected.
> "In the great journal of things happening under the sun, we, the American People, find our account running, under date of the nineteenth century of the Christian era. We find ourselves in the peaceful possession, of the fairest portion of the earth, as regards extent of territory, fertility of soil, and salubrity of climate. We find ourselves under the government of a system of political institutions, conducing more essentially to the ends of civil and religious liberty, than any of which the history of former times tells us. We, when mounting the stage of existence, found ourselves the legal inheritors of these fundamental blessings. We toiled not in the acquirement or establishment of them—they are a legacy bequeathed us, by a *once* hardy, brave, and patriotic, but *now* lamented and departed race of ancestors. Their's was the task (and nobly they performed it) to possess themselves, and through themselves, us, of this goodly land; and to uprear upon its hills and its valleys, a political edifice of liberty and equal rights; 'tis ours only, to transmit these, the former, unprofaned by the foot of an invader; the latter, undecayed by the lapse of time, and untorn by usurpation—to the latest generation that fate shall permit the world to know. This task of gratitude to our fathers, justice to ourselves, duty to posterity, and love for our species in general, all imperatively require us faithfully to perform.
> "How, then shall we perform it? At what point shall we expect the approach of danger? By what means shall we fortify against it? Shall we expect some transatlantic military giant, to step the Ocean and crush us at a blow? Never! All the armies of Europe, Asia and Africa combined, with all the treasure of the earth (our own excepted)—could not by force, take a drink from the Ohio, or make a track on the Blue Ridge, in a trial of a thousand years.
> "At what point then is the approach of danger to be expected? I answer, if it ever reaches us, it must spring up amongst us. . . . As a nation of freemen, we must live through all time, or die by suicide.
> "I hope I am over wary; but if I am not, there is, even now, something of ill-omen amongst us. I mean the increasing disregard for law which pervades this country; the growing disposition to substitute the wild and furious passions, in lieu of the sober judgments of Courts."

He followed with a broadly generalized sketch of "outrages committed by mobs" that "have pervaded the country, from New England to Louisiana, . . . not the creature of climate—neither are they confined to the slaveholding, or the non-slaveholding States. Alike, they spring up among the pleasure hunting masters of Southern slaves, and the order loving citizens of the land of steady habits."

The nation, it seems, was even then differentiated in his mind into two great cultural systems of contrasting ideals and similar faults. He recounted an epidemic of lynchings in Mississippi that had spread from an attack first on gamblers then to Negroes and to white citizens and even strangers on business in the state, "till, dead men were seen literally dangling from boughs of trees upon every road side; and in numbers almost sufficient, to rival the native Spanish moss of the country, as a drapery of the forest."

He then described the seizure and burning to death of a free mulatto in St. Louis by a mob after he had killed a respected citizen. He used these episodes of disregard of legal justice as a basis for discussing the future consequences of the mob spirit on the integrity of the government. In analytical sequence he first disposed of the immediate consequences of local mob action as minor, when the innocent are abused with the guilty, and then enlarged on its eventual major cultural effects.

"The perpetrators of such acts going unpunished, the lawless in spirit, are encouraged to become lawless in practice; and having been used to no restraint, but dread of punishment, they thus become, absolutely unrestrained. Having ever regarded Government as their deadliest bane, they make a jubilee of the suspension of its operations; and pray for nothing so much, as its total annihilation."

Lincoln's intuitive grasp of insidious processes of social moral degeneration was clear:

"Good men, men who love tranquility, who desire to abide by the laws, and enjoy their benefits, who would gladly spill their blood in the defence of their country; seeing their property destroyed, their families insulted, and their lives endangered; their persons injured; and seeing nothing in prospect that forbodes a change for the better; become tired of, and disgusted with, a Government that offers them no protection; and are not much averse to a change in which they imagine they have nothing to lose. . . . Whenever the vicious portion of population shall be permitted to gather in bands of hundreds and thousands, and burn churches, ravage and rob provision stores, throw printing presses into rivers, shoot editors . . . this government cannot last. . . . If the laws be continually despised and disregarded, if their [the American people's] rights . . . are held by no better tenure than the caprice of a mob, the alienation of their affections from the Government is the natural consequence; and to that, sooner or later, it must come."

The mob lynching of the abolitionist editor Elijah P. Lovejoy, in Alton, Illinois, two months before, had greatly incensed Lincoln and he used this cautiously politic method of indirectly arousing the law-abiding citizens of the state to realize the importance of supporting their government and making its officers execute the laws. He avoided making direct accusations which would have antagonized the proslavery element. Lincoln proposed a "simple" idealistic solution of this "internal danger" to the nation:

"Let every American, every lover of liberty, every well wisher to his posterity, swear by the blood of the Revolution, never to violate in the least particular, the laws of the country; and never to tolerate their violation by others. As the patriots of seventy-six did to the support of the Declaration of Independence, so to the support of the Constitution and Laws, let every American pledge his life, his property, and his sacred honor;—let every man remember that to violate the laws, is to trample on the blood of his father, and to tear the character of his own, and his children's liberty. Let reverence for the laws, be breathed by every American mother, to the lisping babe, that prattles on her lap—let it be taught in schools, in seminaries, and in colleges; let it be written in Primmers (sic), spelling books, and in Almanacs; let it be preached from the pulpit, proclaimed in legislative halls, and enforced in courts of justice. And, in short, let it become the *political religion* of the nation; and let the old and the young, the rich and the poor, the grave and the gay, of all sexes and tongues, and colors and conditions, sacrifice unceasingly upon its altars."

Obey Bad Laws Until Repealed

Bad laws, Lincoln held, should be obeyed by the people and just grievances against them should be expressed through urging legislative repeal and reform:

"There is no grievance that is a fit object of redress by mob law. In any case that arises, as for instance, the promulgation of abolitionism, one of two positions is necessarily true; that is, the thing is right within itself, and therefore deserves the protection of all law and all good citizens; or, it is wrong, and therefore proper to be prohibited by legal enactments; and in neither case, is the interposition of mob law, either necessary, justifiable, or excusable."

Lincoln's Thirst for Distinction—Would Emancipate Slaves

Lincoln saw the Constitution as a political institution that had been established as an experiment in self-government by the people and preserved successfully "for more than fifty years." He then showed how man's egocentric love of freedom, ruling, and superior distinction, that established it, could make it last "fifty times as long" or destroy it.

"Then all that sought celebrity and fame, and distinction, expected to find them in the success of that experiment. . . . Their ambition aspired to display before an admiring world, a practical demonstration of the truth of a proposition, which had hitherto been considered, at best no better, than problematical; namely the *capability of a people to govern themselves.* If they succeeded, they were to be immortalized; their names were to be transferred to the counties and cities, and rivers and mountains; and to be revered and sung, and toasted through all time. If they failed, they were to be called knaves and fools . . . then to sink and be forgotten. They succeeded . . . and thousands have won their deathless names in making it so. But the game is caught; and I believe it is true, that with the catching, end the pleasures of the chase. This field of glory is harvested . . . but . . . men of ambition and talents will spring up amongst us . . . and they will as naturally seek the gratification of their ruling passion, as others have so done before them . . . can that gratification be found in supporting and maintaining an edifice that has been erected by others? Most certainly it cannot. Many great and good men . . . would aspire to nothing beyond a seat in Congress, a gubernatorial or a presidential chair; *but such belong not to the family of the lion, or the tribe of the eagle.* What! think you these places would satisfy an Alexander, a Caesar, or a Napoleon? Never! Towering genius disdains a beaten path. . . . It *scorns* to tread in the footsteps of *any* predecessor. . . . It thirsts and burns for distinction; and, if possible, it will have it, whether at the expense of emancipating slaves, or enslaving freemen. Is it unreasonable then to expect, that some man possessed of the loftiest genius, coupled with ambition sufficient to push it to its utmost stretch, will at some time, spring up among us? And when such a one does, it will require the people to be united with each other, attached to the government and laws, and generally intelligent, to successfully frustrate his designs."

Lincoln had grown apprehensive lest the potentiality of man's passion to rule and gain distinction under the Jacksonian system of cultivating political power and party loyalty would dominate national patriotism. Then he was not worried about the possibility of abolitionism leading to secession and civil war. He foresaw that a political genius, morally unrestrained by the intent of the fathers of the Constitution and the precedent of two terms established by President Washington, might develop a system of propagating official distribution of economic patronage so as to keep repeating his election and maintaining his party in power. Lincoln's understanding analysis of the strength and weakness of the Constitution and of human nature proved true. Within a 100 years such egoistic realization of supreme political distinction was achieved by Franklin Delano Roosevelt. Through turning the prejudices of the poor against the rich, and by appointing judges and bureaucratic systems of demogogic officials, and by taxing wealth and spending revenues so as to cultivate the support of a voting majority and, worst of all, by exploiting the future of unborn generations in making them pay the consequences of an expanding national debt, he had himself elected President of the United States four times, even though in the last campaign for reelection he was obviously mentally and physically too deteriorated by progressive nervous disease to be able to complete the term.

"Distinction," as Lincoln said, "will be the paramount object" of a "lofty genius;" and "although he would as willingly, perhaps more so, acquire it by doing good as harm; yet, that opportunity being past, and nothing left to be done in the way of building up, he would set boldly to the rask of pulling down." Lincoln warned that the passions of egotism for gaining political power and superior distinction must be restricted by the common people, as lesser passioned egotists, uniting with each other and intelligently demanding equality of rights under constitutional law to retain freedom of speech and self-determination in order to enjoy self-respect. He applied indeed the wisdom of Ecclesiastes (1: 2), "Vanity of vanities, all in vanity."

Fading Memories, Dangerous Passions, Cold Reasoning

The naturally dangerous potentiality towards degeneration in our democracy is enhanced, Lincoln warned, by the fading influence of the ideals of the revolution:

. . . "By this influence, the jealousy, envy, and avarice, incident to our nature, and so common to a state of peace, prosperity, and conscious strength, were, for the time, in a great measure smothered and rendered inactive; while the deep rooted principles of *hate,* and the powerful motive of *revenge,* instead of being turned against each other, were directed exclusively against the British nation. And thus, from the force of circumstances, the basest principles of our nature, were either made to lie dormant, or to become the active agents in the advancement of the noblest of causes—that of establishing and and maintaining civil and religious liberty. . . .

"But this state of feeling *must fade, is fading, has faded,* with the circumstances that produced it. . . . [Not] that the scenes of the revolution *are now or ever will be* entirely forgotten; but that like everything else, they must fade upon the memory of the world, and grow more and more dim by the lapse of time. In history, we hope, they will be read of, and recounted, so long as the bible shall be read;—but even granting that they will, their influence *cannot be* what it heretofore has been. . . . At the close of that struggle, nearly every adult male had been a participator in some of its scenes. . . . a *living history* was to be found in every family. . . . a history . . . that could be read and understood alike by all, the wise and the ignorant, the learned and the unlearned. But *those* histories are gone. They *can* be read no more forever. . . .

"They *were* the pillars of the temple of liberty; and now, that they have crumbled away, that temple must fall, unless we, their descendants, supply their places with other pillars, hewn from the solid quarry of sober reason. Passion has helped us; but can do so no more. It will be future be our enemy. Reason, cold, calculating, unimpassioned reason, must furnish all the materials for our future support and defence. Let those be moulded into *general intelligence,* morality and, in particular, a *reverence for the constitution and laws;* and, that we improved to the last; that we remained free to the last; that we revered his [Washington's] name to the last; that during his long sleep, we permitted no hostile foot to pass over or desecrate his resting place; . . .

"Upon these reasons let the proud fabric of freedom rest, as the rock of its basis; and as truly as has been said of the only greater institution, *'the gates of hell shall not prevail against it.' "*

These closing comments reflect Lincoln's own experience with the fading memories of the "living history" he loved in the Rutledge family, as one which, with Washington, had fought the revolution and founded our constitutional government. His sentiment 'those histories are gone and can be read no more forever' is similar to that he loved in the lines of "Oh! why should the spirit of mortal be proud." He would carry on their ideals and thereby make living worthwhile.

Here Lincoln expressed the common sense by which he recovered will of mind and purpose to live, after dangerous despondancy upon frustration of love by the death of Ann Rutledge. By cultivating the self-reservations of cold reasoning and regarding his passions as the enemy of his intelligence, he became able to dedicate himself to preserve the Constitution and the Union with the families who fought to create it, and in this way he hoped to achieve political distinction within the precedents of Washington and, through such idealism of work, prevail against the potential hell of melancholy within himself.

He believed in fateful predestination and solved its involvements for himself with such common-sense aphorisms as: "It may be true, if it must, let it." "Let none falter, who thinks he is right, and we may succeed. But, if after all, we shall fail, be it so."

Abraham Lincoln, finding himself in boyhood to have the genius to lead people, believed he was destined to become a moral lawgiver somehow toward a more equitable way of life, as had Patriarch Abraham. He revealed in this speech his own passion to gain "distinction," as the paramount interest of living. Believing that he belonged to "the family of the lion or the tribe of the eagle" he aspired to achieve eventually supreme leadership, even as had Alexander, Caesar, and Napoleon, not however by international conquest and expansion which he hated, not by exploitation or enslavement which he detested, but toward increasing life, liberty and pursuit of happiness of all people, which he loved.

In this address Lincoln also revealed that he would emancipate the slaves if ever he had the legal power and official opportunity to do so. The foreboding significance of his remarks at 29 years of age have not heretofore been given due consideration by his biographers.

Self-Analysis and Self-Control

Lincoln felt moved to emphasize, in this lecture, that people should cultivate cool reason to control passion in their interpersonal interactions and in government, in order to safeguard against man's natural disposition to yield to passion and revert to gangs and mob rule. The lecture shows characteristically how Lincoln reasoned in accordance with his personal experiences when we correlate it with his letters to Mary Owens, the last written a few months previously, and the sequel letter to Mrs. Browning written a few weeks later. They show constant striving of egoistic attitude to develop a higher level of volitional integrity against subconscious involitional unhappy impulses of frustrated love.

In due time, after Mary Owens had not answered his last letter, Lincoln felt relieved of "the hypo" as her silence meant that she had liberated him from his promise. However, he sent the letter (see previous chapter) to Mrs. Browning in which he satirically described his engagment and Mary's physical inferiorities, to relieve his injured vanity. His self-analytical comments reveal the insight of genius on the minutiae of counterbalancing adjustments of his egoistic attitude.

> "My vanity," he said, "was deeply wounded by the reflection, that I had long been too stupid to discover her intentions, and at the same time never doubting that I understood them perfectly; and also that she . . . had actually rejected me with all my fancied greatness, and to cap the whole, I then, for the first time, began to suspect that I was really a little in love with her. . . . Others have been made fools of by girls; but this can never be with truth said of me. I . . . made a fool of myself—and have come to the conclusion never again to think of marrying."

Through such honest, astute self-analysis of egoistic instinctive tricky motivations to acquire the pleasures of being desired, socially superior, and admired, and avoid the displeasures of being rejected, inferior, and scorned, and frankly expressing them to a friend, Lincoln was developing keen understanding of the social needs of the vanities of his egotism relative to the egotism of other people. He learned how to relieve neurotic miseries attending discouraging frustration and rejection by obtaining sympathetic acceptance and encouragement.

Lincoln's powers of self-control of passion by cool reasoning were yet to be tried to the limit. He was yet to become jilted by a vain girl to please the vanity of a rival for her affections. As we follow him we will see how he passed through a series of stronger self-reorganizations of egoistic integrity after each painful experience, by holding, with resolute conviction, that he, and not another person, must be the moral judge of right and wrong for himself. He became more distant, reserved, idealistically practical and morally abstracted in his interpersonal relations as he repressed and controlled passion and achieved higher levels of intelligent reasoning. He needed, however, to express his feelings in writing or talking to a respected sympathetic person who he felt understood him. When he could not have this stabilizing help he would write out the *pros* and *cons* of his thoughts in notes to himself and thereby relieve his feelings.

Chapter XI

ABE LINCOLN VERSUS STEVE DOUGLAS

Herndon (1889) and Speed (1986) have pointed out that a most unusual interweaving of conflicting and paralleling personal and political interests and endeavors eventuated in the public careers of Abraham Lincoln and Stephen A. Douglas. History has no other episode the equal of it. They first met in Vandalia in 1834. Lincoln was then 25, a Whig member of the House of Representatives and Douglas was 21 and lobbying for the position of a state's attorney. In 1836 Douglas became a member of the House as a Democrat and the political policies and personal interests of the two men thereafter became intimately interactive and generally opposed to each other, while yet each respected the other's abilities as a legislator, lawyer, and politician.

After the capital of Illinois was transferred to Springfield through Lincoln's legislative manipulations despite Douglas' oppositions, Lincoln and Douglas with other young men became nightly habitues of Speed's store where they generally argued on the affairs of the state and nation. Abe and Steve usually presented antagonistic views, and the impromptu discussions eventually grew into several series of formal political debates, to be presented later in their chronological order.

Natural Rivals

In 1839 both men were admitted to practice in the Supreme Court of Illinois on the same day. In 1840 both courted Mary Todd, and in 1846 both represented Illinois in Congress at Washington, Douglas in the Senate and Lincoln in the House. From 1854 to 1856 Lincoln and Douglas vigorously disputed, in numerous speeches, each other's policies on the national issue of slavery. In 1858 they were rival candidates for the United States Senate and in 1860 they were rival candidates for the Presidency. Eventually Senator Douglas became a vigorous supporter of President Lincoln's effort to preserve the Union and died shortly after the South took Fort Sumter. It will become evident later how Douglas made Lincoln make himself a statesman out of a lawyer.

The fundamental political attitudes and mental qualities of these two young men, who would eventually influence the course of history, were remarkably dissimilar and naturally antagonistic, based largely on polar opposites of inherent physical constitution. Both, the antithesis of the other in every way, were destined, through conflicting, overlapping personal as well as legal interests and political ideals to clash intensely for the rest of their lives until the supreme issue of preserving the Union suddenly made them allies.

In 1838 Douglas was 25, short and thick, five feet four inches, with large head, bull neck, barrel chest, and full-sized body with grotesquely short, well-muscled arms and legs, deep, bass voice, strong, commanding, egoistic face and piercing blue eyes. He was highly extroverted, bold, aggressive, audacious and fiery, full of fun and mischief, eloquent and flamboyant of speech, earnest, self-confident, honest, sincere, ambitious, progressive, academically educated, a positive optimist, an able lawyer and business man, a strong party politician, an intolerantly domineering leader, clever with women and popular with men. He dressed well, read widely, ate heartily and drank whiskey robustly, told humorous stories lustily, orated dramatically, spent money freely, enjoyed being a social lion, and never considered differences in size a deterrent for a fist fight. Douglas was popularly known as the "Little Giant."

Lincoln at this time was 30, long and thin, six feet four inches, with average-sized head, high cheek bones, powerful jaw, thin, scrawny neck, narrow chest, sloping shoulders, grotesquely long arms and legs, high-pitched, squeaky voice, kindly smiling face and sad, enigmatical gray eyes. He was introverted, cautious, brave and resolute but peaceable, earnest, gentle, humble, patient and kind, honest, sincere, eternally ethical, ambitious, self-educated, simple, logical and direct in thought and speech, nervous, a fine trial lawyer and astute, calculating politician, a skeptical opponent, a poor business man, shy, slightly self-doubtful until self-assured, diffident with women, but a good mixer and extremely popular with men, a master of wit and humor and wise in applying the practical philosophy of common sense. He was slouchy and unvarying in dress, awkward in manner, generally indifferent in appetite, abstemious, inconsistently read, and socially unimportant except under conditions favorable to providing an audience for his endless fund of humorous humanitarian stories, told in slow, drawling, unenergetic but unique, highly interesting and appealing manner. Both men were physically and mentally brave, ambitious, democratic and tenacious, but Douglas was more of a plunging opportunist than Lincoln who was more conscientiously careful and logically consistent. He had become known as Herndon (1889) and Speed (1896) have said, as "Honest Abe" in New Salem for his fairness in judging horse racing and other competitive sports and the payment of debts incurred by his failure as a storekeeper.

> "I have often thought," Speed (1896) said reminiscently many years later, "of the characters of the two great rivals, Lincoln and Douglas. They seemed to have been pitted against each other from 1836 till Lincoln reached the Presidency. They were the respective leaders of their parties in their State. They were as opposite in character as they were unlike in persons. . . . Douglas in all elections was the moving spirit in the conduct and management of an election; he was not content without blind submission to himself.

He could not tolerate opposition to his will in his party organization. He held the reins and controlled the Democratic chariot. With a large state majority, with many able and ambitious men in it, he stepped in front in his youth and held it till his death.

"Mr. Lincoln, on the other hand, shrank from any controversy with his friends. Being in a minority in his State he was forced to the front because his friends thought he was the only man with whom they could win."

Discussions in Speed's Store

The large upstairs room in Speed's store was converted into a dormitory where Joshua Speed, Abraham Lincoln, Charles R. Hurst, and William Herndon* slept. Downstairs in the winter evenings a number of progressive young lawyers, business men, and politicians liked to gather and talk with Lincoln, even as others had in New Salem.

Herndon (1889) and Speed (1896) have given intimate descriptions of their convivial group and its various interests.

> Speed saw Lincoln as "a social man, though he did not seek company; it sought him. After he made his home with me, on every winter's night, by a big wood fire, no matter how inclement the weather, eight or ten choice spirits assembled without distinction of party [Whig or Democrat]. It was a sort of social club without organization. They came there because they were sure to find Lincoln. His habit was to engage in conversation upon any and all subjects except politics."

Lincoln, Douglas, and their friends, Herndon tells us, organized the Young Men's Lyceum for holding public meetings and taking turns at reading their literary compositions. These young men were remarkable for earnestness, progressive public spirit, and mental ability. The group included, besides Lincoln, Speed, Herndon, and Douglas, James Matheny, Noah Rickard, Evan Butler, Milton Hay, David Davis, Newton Francis, and others who eventually became prominent in the state. Douglas eventually became the Democratic leader of the United States Senate and three times candidate for his party's nomination for president, Lincoln became President of

---

*William H. Herndon, age 19, was attending college at Jacksonville when Editor Elijah P. Lovejoy of Alton was cruelly murdered and his press destroyed in the fall of 1837 by a proslavery mob because of his exposition of abolitionism. Thereafter the people of the state became divided into intensely opposed pro- and antislavery factions. The unjust violation of the rights of freedom aroused the faculty of eastern educated professors as well as the students, to unrestrained indignation. Young Herndon became so imbued with the spirit of abolitionism that his father, an advocate of slavery, compelled him to withdraw from college and return home. Unable to endure his father's tyranny, Herndon hired out as a store clerk to Joshua Speed, at the liberal salary of 700 dollars per annum.

the United States, and Davis a member of the United States Supreme Court.

Abe versus Steve

As Whig minority leader and member of the Committee on Finance in the legislature, Lincoln exerted strong influence and was said to have confided to his friends that he "aspired to become the Dewitt Clinton of Illinois." (Clinton was a contemporary political leader of New York who accelerated the development of his state through promoting progressive legal measures for building the Erie Canal, highways and railroads.)

Lincoln foresaw for Illinois a great political and economic future, based on the increasing western migration and its size and location in the center of the Union with fertile soil and great rivers and lakes on every side for transportation. He pushed constantly in the Legislature for funds to improve education, with the idea that the success of democratic government depends upon the intelligence of the people, hence every person capable of learning must have the opportunity of acquiring the fundamentals of literacy.

He argued in the Legislature for the purchase of public (Federal) lands in Illinois, estimated at 20 million acres. He proposed to buy all of it from the government at 25 cents an acre, for five million dollars, which sum the State would borrow. The land could then be sold for $1.25 an acre and the principal repaid together with interest at five per cent over a period of 30 years. This would provide means of paying the State's heavy debts for public works and farm land for many new people.

He would also change the customary practise of taxing land at a uniform rate per acre regardless of its actual worth, which "favored the few rich" and "worked a hardship on the many poor," to taxing land according to an assessed valuation relative to its actual economic value. This policy he urged upon the Whigs as a wise political move since there were only a few of the rich to oppose it.

Lincoln vigorously advocated the building of roads and held at first that canals and rivers were preferable for transportation to the then inefficient railroads, being less expensive and more service- able to the greater number. He held that the future of the state depended on the development of transportation and a system of banking, and after he succeeded in locating the state capitol in Springfield these became his chief legislative interests.

Friends praised Lincoln for being progressive, but Representative Stephen A. Douglas and other Democrats criticised him mercilessly during the panic of 1837 and 1838 for getting the State excessively into debt. Douglas in particular seemed to have had a penchant for attacking Lincoln and the Whigs, calling them "Federalists," "Tories," and "Aristocrats," "opposed to freedom, justice and progress." Lincoln replied sagely that Douglas only made loose, unwarranted assertions to catch votes and cheat men out of judging issues fairly. Douglas was naturally inclined to influence reason through arousing passion and intolerant prejudice whereas Lincoln tried to arrive at impartial judgments based on facts.

Lincoln's Dislike of Douglas

In 1838 Douglas, after only one term in the state legislature, became the Democratic candidate for Congress, with Lincoln's partner Stuart his Whig opponent. Douglas and Stuart were at first good friends and often traveled together and addressed the same audience, but before the campaign finished their arguments grew bitter and ended in a barroom fight. Lincoln's shrewd advice and astute political management enabled Stuart to win by a small margin. Douglas, thereafter, became set to even the score against Lincoln and eventually succeeded, as shown later, by humiliating him in competing for the affections of Mary Todd.

We obtain some information on Lincoln's attitude at this time toward Douglas from remarks in letters to Stuart and other political friends. To W. A. Minshall (December 7, 1837):

> "We have adopted it as part of our policy here, to never speak of Douglas at all. Isn't that the best mode of treating so small a matter?" To J. W. Fell (July 23, 1838): "I again repeat you may deny the charges made by Douglass against Stuart in relation to a government Bank."

In June 1838 Lincoln appealed to the editor of the *Chicago American* to investigate the legality of certain people who had voted for Douglas in the previous election, lest the same thing might be repeated. To Stuart on November 14, 1839 he wrote:

> ". . . Douglass has not been here since you left. A report is in circulation here now, that he has abandoned the idea of going to Washington; though the report does not come in verry authentic form, so far as I can learn. Though, by the way, speaking of authenticity, you know that if we heard Douglass say that he had abandoned the contest, it would not be verry authentic. . . ." On December 23, 1839, three days before his speech on the Sub-Treasury, he commented in a letter to Stuart: "The Democratic giant is here; but he is not now worth talking about."

First Lincoln-Douglas Debate

Whig Lincoln and Democrat Douglas, both ambitious and highly progressive young lawyers and budding statesman rarely failed to hold opposite views on the best way of solving the problems of the state and nation. Herndon has described an incident in Speed's store of December 1839 that was to become important in American history. Speed's (1896) account of this argument fully agrees with Herndon's.

> "One evening while the usual throng of loungers surrounded the inviting fireplace . . . the conversation turned on political matters. The disputants waxed warm and acrimonious. . . . I . . . seated myself on a keg and listened with eager interest to the battle. . . . Douglas, I recollect, was leading on the Democratic side. He had already learned the art of dodging in debate, but still he was subtle, fiery and impetuous. He charged the Whigs with every blunder and political crime he could imagine. . . . At last, with great vehemence, he sprang up and abruptly made a challenge to those who differed with him to discuss the whole matter publicly."

Then followed the first public Lincoln-Douglas debate. It was arranged to hold a series of meetings in the Presbyterian Church, in in which Douglas, Calhoun, Lamborn, and Thomas represented the Democrats, and Logan, Baker, Browning, and Lincoln the Whigs. One evening was given to each man and the debate required a week. The financial status of the state and nation was extremely depressed, and the subject chosen for discussion was how to relieve it and establish a sound economic system.

Lincoln spoke last (December 26, 1839) to a small audience. The people had tired of the series of eight lectures and became interested in Christmas festivities. He would discontinue the Federal Sub-Treasury in favor of reestablishing a national bank. His plan of discussion marks an important step in the development of his economic intelligence. It is characterized by a strictly Euclidian presentation of argument in the form of a series of logically related propositions supported by citations of relevant facts. It is evidence of a decisive change of attitude from the sophomoric lecturer on law and order of one year previous, to that of a seriously thoughtful, highly patriotic, young statesman. It should be mentioned here that he had become acquainted with Mary Todd, the attractive, coquettish young cousin of his law partner, a few months before this debate. She was then encouraging the attentions of Douglas, and judging from the near tragedy for Lincoln that followed within the year, the political rivalry of the two men was even then becoming involved with jealousy over the new girl from Kentucky.

Lincoln began:

> "It is peculiarly embarrassing to me to attempt a continuance of the discussion, on this evening, which has been conducted in the Hall on several preceding ones. It is so, because on each of those evenings, there was a much fuller attendance than now, without any reason for its being so, except the greater *interest* the community feel in the *Speakers* who addressed *them,* than they do in *him* who is to do so *now.* I am, indeed, apprehensive that the few who have

attended, have done so, more to spare me of mortification, than in the hope of being interested in any thing I may be able to say. This circumstance casts a damp upon my spirits, which I am sure I shall be unable to overcome during the evening. But enough of preface."

We are at once profoundly impressed by the frank, simple humility of Lincoln's confession of personal disappointment and embarrassment at the people's lack of interest in what he might have to say. He reached out for the sympathetic support of his friends and won their hearts. He did not approach his audience in the grand manner with a cocksure attitude that he, only a year past, aspired to cultivate in imitation of the great orators of the time. He was learning that naturalness of expression and clear, simple reasoning from facts, with humility of appeal for fair consideration and judgment, spiced with relentless disproof, incisive wit and kindly humor in criticising the opposing argument, would win the interest and support of earnest people, whereas bombastic showmanship and high sounding ambiguous phrases and designed accusations only aroused the approval of prejudiced minds.

"The subject heretofore, and now to be discussed, is the Sub-Treasury scheme of the present Administration, as a means of collecting, safe-keeping, transferring and disbursing the revenues of the Nation, as contrasted with a National Bank for the same purposes. Mr. Douglass has said that we (the Whigs), have not dared to meet them (the Locos), in argument on this question. I protest against this assertion. I assert that we have again and again, during this discussion, urged facts and arguments against the Sub-Treasury, which they have neither dared to deny nor attempted to answer. I now propose, in my humble way, to urge those arguments again; at the same time, begging the audience to mark well the positions I shall take, and the proof I shall offer to sustain them, and that they will not again permit Mr. Douglass or his friends, to escape the force of them, by a round and groundless assertion, that we 'dare not meet them in argument.'

"Of the Sub-Treasury then, as contrasted with the National Bank, for the above enumerated purposes, I lay down the following propositions, to wit:

"1st. It will injuriously affect the community by its operation on the circulating medium.

"2nd. It will be a more expensive fiscal agent.

"3d. It will be a less secure depository of the public money."

First Proposition

"To show the truth of the first proposition" he gave a short review of conditions under the National Bank (which had been discontinued by the Democrats). Between collecting and disbursing revenues, the Bank, as a depository, had been permitted to loan them out to individuals. Hence the large sums annually collected were kept constantly in circulation and not held idle as in the present operation of the Sub-Treasury. Lincoln maintained that "money is only valuable while in circulation . . . any device which will keep government revenues in constant circulation . . . is no inconsiderable advantage." (This view is much like the modern theory of national economics.)

"By the Sub-Treasury, the revenue is to be collected, and kept in iron boxes until the government wants it for disbursement; thus robbing the people of the use of it, while the government does not itself need it. . . . The natural effect . . . is to *reduce* the quantity of money in circulation." The revenue, Lincoln asserted from the record, was intended by President Van Buren to be collected in *specie*. Since there was only between 60 and 80 millions of specie in the United States and the government expended 40 millions in 1838, it will take more than half the specie in circulation from the total population of fifteen million souls. This throws more than half of all the specie into the hands of public office holders and public creditors, some quarter of a million in number, "leaving the other fourteen millions and three-quarters to get along as best they can, with less than one-half of the specie of the country. . . . By this means, every office-holder, and other public creditor, may, and most likely will, set up a shaver; and a most glorious harvest will the specie men have of it. . . . In all candor, let me ask, was such a system of benefiting the few at the expense of the many, ever before devised? And was the sacred name of Democracy, ever before made to endorse such an enormity against the rights of the people?"

Jacksonian Democratic justification of managing the government's economic system for the benefit of the political party in power, above serving the national and public welfare, distressed Lincoln, as it did most other conscientious citizens who held the spoils system in local, state and national government degenerative and unpatriotic. He demonstrated the relative values of property to the amount of money in circulation and the advantages to debtors and disadvantages to creditors of inflation and cheap money and the reverse effects of deflation and dear money. When economic distress is imposed upon one class, he pointed out, it eventually involves the other likewise through reduction of trade and work.

Lincoln then showed how decrease of money in circulation produced "a *peculiar* and *permanent* hardship upon the citizens of those States and Territories in which the public lands lie." Here the money "is swallowed up" by the Land Offices and, since the price of lands is fixed by law, the capacity of labor and produce, that would earn money to purchase land, decreases with reduction of money in circulation. His argument evidently stemmed from the experience of his own and other poor families in purchasing public lands in Indiana and Illinois.

He then defended the old national bank against the Democratic charge of being unable to prevent contractions and expansions in the currency, by pointing out that it had been able, for 40 years, to maintain a sound and uniform currency until the Government withdrew its funds from the bank.

Second Proposition

Lincoln then discussed the relative expense of the National Bank versus the Sub-Treasury as fiscal agents. He showed that the bank had paid $75,000 annually to the government out of earnings on its loans whereas the estimated cost of operation of the Sub-Treasury to the government was about $400,000 annually. This fund, he claimed, would produce public lands for 8,000 poor families.

Third Proposition

Lincoln argued from "the experience of the past" that the Sub-Treasury would be less secure than a national bank. He diverted here briefly with a philosophical discussion of how we know the present and future by the past. His reasoning gives us a precious glimpse into how carefully he studied his own mental processes in order to know what he thought he knew.

"I rely chiefly upon experience to establish it, let me ask, how is it that we know any thing—that any event will occur, that any combination of circumstances will produce a certain result—except by the analogies of past experiences? What has once happened, will invariably happen again, when the same circumstances which combined to produce it, shall again combine in the same way. We all feel that we know that a blast of wind would extinguish the flame of the candle that stands by me. How do we know it? We have never seen this flame thus extinguished. We know it, because we have seen through all our lives, that a blast of wind extinguishes the flame of a candle whenever it is thrown fully upon it. Again, we all feel to *know* that we have to die. How? We have never died yet. We know it, because we know, or at least we think we know, that of all the beings, just like ourselves, who have been coming into the world for six thousand years, not one is now living who was here two hundred years ago.

"I repeat then, that we know nothing of what will happen in future, but by the analogy of experience, and that the fair analogy of past experience fully proves that the Sub-Treasury would be a less safe depository of the public money than a National Bank." He pressed this point by showing, with citation of names and sums, that among the politically apointed Treasurers of the Mint, Custom-House officers, and Land officers not a year had passed "without numerous defalcations." In comparison, the services of the National Bank covered over five hundred million dollars in a period of forty years without the loss of "one dollar, nor one cent."

Lincoln was careful to point out that he did not mean to say that bank officers were more able and honest than public officers. By the best method of selection "there will be some unfaithful and dishonest in both classes. . . . The Saviour of the world chose twelve disciples, and even one of that small number, selected by superhuman wisdom, turned out a traitor and a devil. And, it may not be improper here to add, that Judas carried the bag—was the Sub-Treasurer of the Saviour and his disciples."

"The *interest* of the Sub Treasurer is *against his duty*—while the *interest* of the Bank is *on the side of its duty.* . . . And who that knows anything of human nature, doubts that, in many instances, interest will prevail over duty." Whereas a political appointee will often prefer "oppulent knavery" the Bank must perform faithful service in order to retain its charter.

In his discussion of the government's economic system Lincoln was earnestly intent upon working out an equitable means of providing a sound currency rather than merely arguing to support a political policy. Question of the constitutionality of a National Bank *versus* a Sub-Treasury was raised by the Democrats and he disposed of it logically with citing the approval of no less authorities than the framers of the Constitution, the first President, General Washington, and the judgment of the Supreme Court. A national bank was no less "necessary and proper" than a Sub-Treasury, for it was provided in the Constitution that Congress had the power to make all laws necessary "to lay and collect taxes, duties, imposts and excises;" and "pay the debts," hence to keep, transfer and disburse revenues. The exact method, he held, of performing this indispensable service for maintaining the integrity of the Union was not specified in the Constitution. Lincoln was becoming a deep and thorough research student of the history and motives of "the Patriarchs" who had contributed to the production of the Constitution. In debate he liked to cite such information, as the most authoritative of references, for its impressive effect. We will see later how enormously influential this ability became politically.

Following this reasonable demonstration of three major propositions Lincoln reviewed critically the statements made by his opponents, Lamborn and Douglas. The argument of the former was composed mostly of weak analogies which Lincoln humorously stretched into boomeranging absurdities. The latter's claims, however, were taken seriously and disproven point by point. Both opponents had admitted apologetically that "errors" had been made in the administration of the Sub-Treasury, but they were not, Lincoln replied, an acceptable 'excuse' for the weakness of the system.

"We admit that errors may have occurred under all administrations; but we insist that there is *no parallel* between them and those of the two last. If they can show that their errors are no greater in number and magnitude, than those of former times, we call off the dogs. But they can do no such thing."

The last 10 years, under Jackson and Van Buren, had cost more than the first 27, "including the heavy expenses of the late British war" (1812). The last year of J.Q. Adams' administration cost about 13 millions, or, "about one dollar to each soul," whereas the year of 1838 under Van Buren cost 40 millions or *"two dollars and fifty cents to each soul,"* although in time of peace. (Lincoln's position was made relative to the increase in population but not to the increase in the cost of labor hence depreciation of the dollar.)

The argument of Douglas, Lincoln claimed, presented a few true statements that proved nothing, and numerous ones that were untrue. He methodically reviewed and disproved each point and then summed up its ethical meaning with uncompromising denunciation. His manner indicates significantly that their personal rivalry was more than political.

Congress, Douglas had asserted, was under Whig domination and that party was as responsible as the Democrats for the expenditures of 1838. Lincoln cited statistics showing that both Houses then had Democratic majorities and they had approved of Van Buren's Sub-Treasury policy for that year.

> "Those who heard Mr. Douglass," he said, "recollect that he indulged himself in a contemptuous expression of pity for me. 'Now he's got me,' thought I. But when he went on to say that five millions of the expenditure of 1838, were payments of the French indemnities, *which I knew to be untrue;* that five millions had been for the Post-Office, *which I knew to be untrue;* that ten millions had been for the Maine boundary war, *which I not only knew to be untrue, but supremely ridiculous also;* and when I saw that he was stupid enough to hope, that I would permit such groundless and audacious assertions to go unexposed, I readily consented, that on the score of both veracity and sagacity, the audience should judge whether he or I were the more deserving of the world's contempt."

Lincoln's closing statement, reverberating with patriotic fervor, was indicative, as proved later, of the resolute, fatalistic attitude of working for the right that he would maintain throughout life against any political opposition or disaster.

> "Mr. Lamborn refers to the late elections in the States, and from their results, confidently predicts, that every State in the Union will vote for Mr. Van Buren at the next Presidential election. Address *that* argument to *cowards* and to *knaves;* with the *free* and the *brave* it will effect nothing. It *may* be true; if it *must,* let it. Many free countries have lost their liberty; and *ours may* lose hers; but if she shall, be it my proudest plume, not that I was the *last* to desert, but that I *never* deserted her. . . . The *probability* that we may fall in the struggle *ought not* to deter us from the support of a cause we believe to be just; it *shall not* deter me. If ever I feel the soul within me elevate and expand to those dimensions not wholly unworthy of its Almighty Architect, it is when I contemplate the cause of my country, deserted by all the world beside, and I standing up boldly and alone and hurling defiance at her victorious oppressors. Here, without contemplating consequences, before High Heaven, and in the face of

the world, I swear eternal fidelity to the just cause, as I deem it, of the land of my life, my liberty and my love. And who, that thinks with me, will not fearlessly adopt the oath that I take. Let none faulter, who thinks he is right, and we may succeed. But, if after all, we shall fail, be it so. We shall have the proud consolation of saying to our consciences . . . that the cause approved of our judgment, and adored of our hearts, . . . we NEVER faultered in defending."

Here indeed, we find in this young lawyer, just thirty, the expression, with keen analytical insight, of a philosophy of personal obligation to his country's welfare that will carry him to the highest development of spirit as he defends without faltering at any cost of pain or disaster, what he conscientiously believes is right.

Lincoln was pleased with this speech. To his partner Stuart he wrote (1, 20, 1840) with his usual touch of humor about himself:

"Well, I made a big speech, which is in progress of printing in pamphlet form. To enlighten you and the rest of the world, I shall send you a copy when it is finished."

Political Organizer

Lincoln's speech against the political exploitation of Treasury funds made people, who heard him, see the institution as an increasing threat to national integrity and patriotism. He had found political graft in government becoming more serious than indifference to mobs and, as a reformer who would establish sound government with sound currency, he won public support, particularly among the younger people. In order to reduce the heavy indebtedness of the state, for which he was largely responsible, he continued to urge the legislature to buy the Federal lands within its borders and sell them at a profit and to tax lands according to their values. Both proposals were unpopular with a land grabbing aristocracy.

As he grew in caliber above the level of contemporary state legislators, he built his political fences thoroughly. Although extremely lax and careless about most personal things, in contests involving pride of respectability of character and logical intelligence his ego was always spurred to the quick.

We get some idea of how carefully and thoroughly Lincoln planned political battles, from his management of the campaign of 1840. It shows how inherently characteristic it was for him to consider meticulously every contingency in advance of an anticipated conflict in order to win, or reduce the consequences of defeat. His advice to Madison Miller, Whig candidate for the state legislature, on how to organize his county, and the campaign circular to the Whig county committeemen of January 31, 1840, are so much alike in plan that Lincoln no doubt was the principal author of the latter although signed by several names with his. The following citations illustrate his practical philosophy.

> "Gentlemen:—In obedience to a resolution of the Whig State Convention, we have appointed you the Central Whig Committee of your county. The trust confided to you will be one of watchfulness and labor; but we do hope the glory of having contributed to the overthrow of the corrupt powers that now control our beloved country, will be a sufficient reward for the time and labor you will devote to it. . . .
>
> "Our intention is to organize the whole State, so that every Whig can be brought to the polls in the coming presidential contest. We cannot do this, however, without your co-operation; and as we do our own duty, so we shall expect you to do yours.
>
> "After due deliberation, the following is the plan of organization, and the duties required of each county committee.
>
> "1st. To divide their county into small districts, and to appoint in each a sub-committee, whose duty shall be to make a perfect list of all the voters in their respective districts, and to ascertain with certainty for whom they will vote. If they meet with men who are doubtful as to the man they will support, such voters should be designated in separate lines, with the name of the man they will probably support.
>
> "2nd. It will be the duty of said sub-committee to keep a CONSTANT WATCH ON THE DOUBTFUL VOTERS, and from time to time have them TALKED TO by those IN WHOM THEY HAVE THE MOST CONFIDENCE. . . .
>
> "3d. It will also be their duty to report to you, at least once a month, the progress they are making, and on election day see that every Whig is brought to the polls."

The circular was completed with seven other duties of similar nature, to elect "the gallant HARRISON at our head."

Having learned the value of political organization, Lincoln developed it into a regimental system for personally soliciting the pledge of each voter to support the party's candidates. Naturally in sympathy with the common people, he made it his business to keep himself informed on their needs and sentiments. His 1840 campaign was successful in his state. General W. H. Harrison was elected President and he was himself returned to the legislature. He never lost interest in the welfare of the common man and we will see later how tirelessly he cultivated the potentialities of this vast political garden.

Chapter XII

IMPORTANCE OF FRIENDSHIPS—
MORE NEUROTIC COURTSHIPS

Lincoln's toast at a public dinner in Springfield in July 1837 gave his value of cultivating friendly personal relations. "To all our friends,— they are too numerous to be named individually, while there is no one of them who is not too dear to be forgotten or neglected."

In a letter to Speed (2, 25, 1842) he said:

> "If we have no friends, we have no pleasures; and if we have them we are sure to lose them, and be doubly pained by the loss."

In 1839, two of his best friends, William Butler and Edward Baker, became involved in a bitter quarrel over the legislative division of Sangamon County. Butler seems to have been hot tempered and inclined to make unfair charges against his opponent. Three letters written by Lincoln within a week indicate how strongly he desired to bring about a peaceful reconciliation between them. With characteristic, kindly, paternal forthrightness, he urged Butler (1, 26, 1839):

> "Your letter of the 21st Inst. is just received. You were in an ill humor when you wrote that letter, and, no doubt, intended that I should be thrown into one also; which, however, I respectfully decline being done."

Lincoln had learned from experience that he must not allow himself to become ill humored and bear malice upon being meanly treated by anyone, no matter how unjust. This intelligent culture of self-control and equable fraternalism with forthright wisdom became the best means of keeping his unstable nervous system functioning in a comfortably equilibrating condition.

> "All you have said," he continued, "about our having been bought up by Taylor, Wright, Turley, enemies, etc., *I know you would not say, seriously, in your moments of reflection;* and therefore I do not think it worth while to attempt *seriously* to prove the contrary to you."
> In good natured appeal he added; "I only say now, that I am willing to pledge myself in black and white to cut my own throat from ear to ear, if, when I meet you, you shall *seriously* say, that you believe me capable of betraying my friends for any price."
> After answering each point in Butler's complaint he concluded with: "My respects to Mrs. Butler & Salome (his oldest daughter). Your friend in spite of your ill nature."

A few days later (2, 1, 1839) Lincoln wrote again (italics inserted):

"Your letter enclosing one to Mr. Baker, was received on yesterday evening [in which Butler apologized to Baker with the explanation that 'under a misapprehension' he had 'felt himself badly treated']. There is no necessity of any bad feeling between you. . . . Your first letter to him was written while you were in a state of high excitement, and therefore ought not to be considered as an emanation of deliberate malice. Unfortunately it reached Baker while he was writhing under a severe toothache, and therefore he at the time was incapable of exercising that patience and reflection which the case required. . . . *It is always magnanimous to recant whatever we may have said in passion;* and when you and Baker shall have done this, I, am sure there will be no difficulty left between you. I write this without Baker's knowledge; and *I do it because nothing would be more painful to me than to see a difficulty between two of my most particular friends.*"

Lincoln was unusually senstive about maintaining respectable friendly relations and felt endlessly the sympathetic need of them. This personal trait made him painfully reactive to humiliating disappointments, particularly when they violated his trust and self-respect. We will find hereafter, in his earnest comments on the value of cultivating friendly personal relations to increase the enjoyment of living, that it was the very foundation of his philosophy of democracy. However, as he advised Stuart (December 17, 1840), he was opposed to removing competent men from office "to make room for friends."

Virile Justice

Lincoln's sense of social justice was automatically quick to express itself when offended by someone's unfairness or lack of consideration for others.

Shy and cautious with women lest he might make some embarrassing mistake, he was bold and audacious with men, ready to meet any critical emergency. When he and other Whig members of the Legislature were prevented, by someone locking the door, from leaving a meeting to break up a quorum and avoid voting on a bill that was brought up in a surprise maneuver by the Democrats to insure its passage, he immediately led his group to escape by jumping from a window.

Lincoln's law office was above a meeting room where people gathered to hear speeches. A trapdoor opened into it and he liked to lie on the floor and peep through at the crowd. On one occasion his friend E.D. Baker was attacking some corruption of the Democrats when a powerful man in the audience took offense at his charges. Shouting "pull him down" he started for the platform. The situation grew rapidly desperate for Baker as he bravely stood his ground against overwhelming odds. Realizing that he might be mobbed, Lincoln quickly jerked away the trapdoor and lowered himself onto the platform. Grabbing a stone water pitcher by the handle he shouted: "Hold on, gentlemen. This is the land of free speech. Mr. Baker has a right to speak and ought to be heard. I am here to defend him and no man can take him from this stand if I can prevent it." Quiet was soon restored and Baker finished his speech.

Lincoln was once distressed by the screaming of a neighbor's wife from the blows of her worthless, drunken husband. No longer able to endure the outrage he felt himself compelled to warn the fellow that if it was repeated he would beat him until he promised to stop it. Within a few days the woman was heard screaming again, Lincoln enlisted two friends to help him intervene. They tied the ruffian to a tree and urged his wife to apply a lash to his back. Taken by surprise she hesitated until she comprehended that it was Lincoln's determination to teach her husband a lesson in justice. She then did her part so thoroughly that she was never attacked again.

Upholding fairness and justice with retributions, in the everyday life of a man shows the metal he is made of and what may be expected of him in greater emergencies. We will see that Lincoln sacrificed his own interests to be kind and just rather than take an unfair advantage, and he never avoided a fight for the right.

When Lincoln had insufficient funds for carrying on his campaign for reelection in 1838, Speed collected 200 dollars among friends and presented it to him for defraying personal expenses. After the election Honest Abe returned 199 dollars and 25 cents to be redistributed among the subscribers. He said that he had not needed the money, having traveled on his own horse and lived in the homes of friends, except for 75 cents that he used to buy a barrel of cider for some farm hands upon their request.

Conversion from Ideal to Natural Sexuality

Joshua Speed was a handsome young bachelor, a descendant of a slave-holding, aristocratic Kentucky family, socially well accepted, and famous among the ladies for transferring his affections easily from one to the next without undue pangs of conscience. An unusually amorous man, as his photograph shows, Speed's close friendship with Lincoln was a paradox of contrasts, for the latter, although born of "the poorest class of whites," was conscientiously ascetic. Both men were honest, trusted each other completely, and developed a lifelong friendship, the warmest each ever knew.

Speed, it seems, had no little suggestive influence in converting Lincoln from idealistic to natural heterosexuality. Lincoln was sexually normal in direction of development, although somewhat endocrinologically retarded and morally self-repressed. Lincoln's arrangement with village friends when living in New Salem, as described by Hill (Hertz, 1938), for watching Joe Watkins' stallion serve mares is indicative of a natural masculine interest. Herndon has also given an account of Speed's sharing his mistress with Lincoln.

The story, indicating the manner of Lincoln's conversion to practical heterosexualism, was told by Speed to Herndon as told to him by his mistress (Hertz, 1938.) Speed was keeping a pretty woman in Springfield and Lincoln eventually cautiously approached his friend with hints that he would like to have an introduction. Speed gave him a note to the girl. After some convivial exchanges he approached her and she accepted. After they had gone to bed he began to worry over the cost. "How much do you charge?" he asked. The girl replied, "Five dollars." After some thought he said dubiously, "I've only got three dollars." At this she encouraged him with, "Well, I'll trust you, Mr. Lincoln, for two dollars." After further consideration Lincoln commented: "I do not wish to go on credit. I'm poor and I don't know where my next dollar will come from and I cannot afford to cheat you." This honest self-revelation moved her to accept his offer. Later, after they had dressed, he handed her the money but she refused to take it, saying: "Mr. Linoln, you are the most conscientious man I ever saw." We can take her willing sacrifice as evidence of satisfaction with his charm and potency.

The little group of literary minded friends who met in Speed's store entertained each other with their essays, poems and other effusions. One of Lincoln's offerings contained the following stanza as recalled years later by James Matheny:

> "Whatever spiteful fools may say,
> Each jealous, ranting yelper,
> No woman ever went astray
> Without a man to help her."

Similar expressions of sentiment at other times have been cited in previous chapters, showing that since youth Lincoln believed that men should protect women and share with them the moral responsibilities of sexual relations.

Courtship of Sarah Rickard

During 1840 Lincoln seems to have courted the affections of Sarah Rickard. Having had no social consequence it was entirely forgotten by Herndon and other close friends, in the passing of 23 years between Lincoln's marriage and his death. Sarah was a younger sister of Mrs. William Butler with whom she had lived for some time when Lincoln boarded with the family. On November 30, 1886 Speed sent to Herndon the letters he had received from Lincoln written in 1841 and 1842, and asked him to use them "carefully so as not to wound the feelings of Mrs. Lincoln," who had been offended by Herndon's lecture on Lincoln and Ann Rutledge, delivered two weeks earlier. The letters contained references to Lincoln's unhappiness during his engagement

to Mary Todd and also some ambiguous references to "Sarah."
In sending these letters Speed said: "I have erased a name which I
do not wish published—If I have failed to do it anywhere strike it out
when you come to it—That is the name Sarah." This strange request
naturally raised the question: Did Speed want to avoid embarrassing
Sarah by connecting her name with Lincoln or with himself? Or did
he want to avoid offending Mrs. Lincoln by connecting Sarah's name
with her husband before their marriage?

Lincoln made three references to Sarah in these letters.

> June 19, 1841:
> "I have not seen Sarah since my long trip, and I am going out
> there as soon as I mail this letter." February 3, 1842: "I have seen
> Sarah but once. She seemed very cheerful, and so I said nothing to
> her about what we spoke of." March 27, 1842: "One thing I can tell
> you which I know you will be glad to hear; and that is that I have seen
> Sarah and scrutinized her feelings as well as I could, and am fully
> convinced she is far happier than she has been for the last fifteen months
> past."

Sarah had become Mrs. Barrett but Herndon knew her well enough,
as the sister of his wife's stepmother, to obtain an explanation of
Speed's request. Many years later Weik (1922) made his own personal
investigation with Mrs. Barrett, and since his report corroborated her
statement as given by Herndon we review them for additional information on Lincoln's neurotic attitude towards women.

In a written statement to Herndon, Mrs. Barrett said:

> "Mr. Lincoln did make a proposal of marriage to me in the summer
> or perhaps later, in the year of 1840. . . . My reason for declining
> his proposal was the wide difference in our ages. [She was then
> sixteen and he thirty-one.] . . . He seemed almost like an older brother,
> being, as it were, one of my sister's family."
>
> According to Weik (1922) Mrs. Barrett "related that Mr. Lincoln
> was an unusually interesting talker with many winning and even
> fascinating traits . . . his conduct could not have been more thought-
> ful and considerate. He was delicate and attentive to the point of
> gallantry; made her several beautiful presents; attended her at numerous
> social functions and escorted her to public entertainments. Among
> them she recalled 'The Babes in the Wood,' the first real theatrical
> performance, with regulation stage and curtain, ever given in Spring-
> field." She also recalled that Lincoln, in pressing his suit, urged that
> "because the Sarah of Bible times became the wife of Abraham,
> therefore she, Sarah Rickard, in view of the precedent, was fore-
> ordained to marry Abraham Lincoln."
>
> "Droll and curious," Weik continues, "though this argument was,
> the lady admitted that it was not without some weight in her own
> mind, but that it failed eventually to win her consent because of the
> objection of an elder sister who contended that she was too young to
> think seriously of matrimony. But even that probability was not the

real reason; for, in a letter . . . Sarah herself says: 'Mr. Lincoln became daily more attentive and I found I was beginning to like him; but you know his peculiar manner and general deportment would not be likely to fascinate a young lady entering the society world."

Mrs. Barrett's statement that Lincoln proposed marriage to her has been called by some modern biographers "fantastic," and the details in Herndon's and Weik's interviews "fictitious." Masters (1932) has interpreted the proposal as placing Lincoln "in no admirable light," for having been frivolously inconsiderate of a young woman's feelings. Sandburg (1932) reviewed the available evidence and rejected Mrs. Barrett's claim as an unfounded attempt to link her name with that of the great martyred President. He concluded that the references which Lincoln made about Sarah to Speed indicate that he had not been interested in Sarah for himself but that he had entertained her at Speed's request, who needed to relieve his conscience for having courted her affections and then neglected her before leaving Springfield.

A reconsideration of Sandburg's conclusion with the times, which he neglected, of Lincoln's and Speed's statements, makes a strong case against it. Speed sold his store on January 1, 1841, but did not leave Springfield until March 1841, and he returned to Springfield in September of 1841 and stayed until January 3, 1942—ample time to settle his love affairs himself. Lincoln's letter in which he timed Sarah's unhappiness as of 15 months past, was written in 1842, three months after Speed left Springfield. Mrs. Barrett placed the time of Lincoln's gifts, attentions and proposal in the summer or perhaps fall of 1840. Lincoln's timing of Sarah's unhappiness placed it in December of that year, which was the time of his engagement to Mary Todd.

Lincoln's remarks showing that he had been worried about Sarah's unhappiness were written when he was still unhappy over the breaking of his engagement with Mary Todd. The last remark was made in the same letter in which he expressed happiness at Speed's marriage and warned him of return of doubts of love, and spoke of his own continued unhappiness. It seems to me that Lincoln, in his highly conscientious attitude of 'always wanting to do right by women,' was continuing to be remorseful as well as self-doubtful over having proposed marriage to Sarah and then disappointing her to court and propose to Mary and then disappointing her also. Therefore Speed's request of Herndon not to publish Sarah's name, made in the same letter which urged him to be careful in using Lincoln's letters so as not to wound the feelings of Mrs. Lincoln, suggests strongly that he wanted to avoid causing the latter more unhappiness by bringing to light another early romance.

If Lincoln did propose to Sarah, as she said he did, we may infer that he tried to induce himself to believe that he loved her, even as he had tried before with Mary Owens. Marriage of substitution after the death of a beloved person is a common solution of loneliness. It seems probable that, in his lonely, woman-shy attitude, he had felt himself becoming increasingly encouraged and attracted to Sarah while boarding in the same house with her and seeing her grow into a lovely young woman of marriageable age. This interpretation gives a reasonable explanation of why, in his poverty and indebtedness, he had spent money on presents and entertainments for her in the summer and fall of 1840. He would not likely have done so much to make her happy if she had been courted and then neglected by Speed who was still living in Springfield.

The most impressive point in Sarah's statement of Lincoln's courtship is his revelation to her that he thought her marriage to him was "foreordained;" that he, like patriarch Abraham, would take a wife named Sarah. Such seemingly absurd superstition was characteristically consistent with other notions of predestination that he habitually entertained for himself, and his inclination when in doubt, and under emotional pressure to make a fateful decision, of looking for occult signs that pointed the way of his destiny. We will see later how he interpreted himself as having been "drawn by fate" to bring about the marriage of Joshua Speed and Fanny Henning.

> "I was always superstitious," he wrote (7, 21, 1842) to Speed, "and as part of my superstition, I believe God made me one of the instruments of bringing your Fanny and you together, which union, I have no doubt He had foreordained. Whatever he designs he will do for me yet."

Lincoln certainly would not, in his highly conscientious, neurotic state of mind, have made humorously joking or frivolous talk of marriage to a trusting, unsophisticated girl of sixteen. This proposal was no more "fantastic" than the manner of his engagements to Mary Owens and Mary Todd, as well as the manner of his marriage, as will be seen. All were neurotic but sincere trial attempts at finding love and getting married.

Mary Ann Todd

The most important woman, although not the most inspiring, in Abraham Lincoln's mature years was Mary Todd. We have seen from his own words that all of his great inspirations and ideals were clearly and firmly established before he knew her. She eventually became his wife although the courtship was at times extremely distressing to both. In order to understand the dangerous emotional conflict that Mary's ambitious, flirtatious, egoistic vanity produced in Lincoln's sensitive, neurotic personality and how he eventually solved it philosophically, and the directive effects of his commonsense adjustment on his great political career, we must know Mary.

Important recent biographies of Mary Lincoln have been written by Sandburg and Angle (1932) and Ruth Painter Randall (1953). They both maintain that Lincoln's marriage was on the whole a happy love match for himself and his wife, and negate the accounts of Herndon (1889) on their naturally incompatible constitutions and unhappiness. The most pointed correlations of evidence of these and other studies are included here with my own interpretations of their meanings.

The most revealing documentary evidence exists in the letters of Abraham Lincoln and Mary Todd, not to each other, for none have been found written previous to their marriage, but to their friends. Also the reminiscences of friends and relatives who knew them both before and after their marriage show definitely how their personalities were congenial and how they clashed.

Mary Ann Todd was 21 years old when she came to Springfield, in 1839, to live with her sister, Elizabeth, now Mrs. Ninian W. Edwards, who had married into the important, aristocratic, wealthy and politically powerful Edwards family. Nearby lived another sister, Frances, who had married Dr. William Wallace. The Todds of Kentucky, although not as influential as the Edwards family of Illinois, also enjoyed aristocratic culture. Mary, one of the charming, socially assured belles of this period, besought by many gallant beaus, lost no time in playing the prospective game with the unmarried eligibles wherever she went.

She had light brown hair with a bronze glint, a round head, a wide forehead, straight nose, sharply defined eyebrows, clear grey-blue eyes, long lashes, pink, dimpled cheeks, lovely complexion, and a pretty, round, animated, though not beautiful, face. Her figure, although short and chunky, was attractive with a well-developed bosom and perfectly molded arms, hands and feet. She dressed stylishly, designed her clothes, liked to wear flowers, and carried herself gracefully, with a proud, lively, engaging dignity. She spoke with quick, decisive animation, with sparkling, audacious wit and friendly aggressiveness.

She was an excellent horsewoman and dancer, well mannered, and widely read, spoke French fluently, was talkative, and had the habit of smiling pleasantly as she carried on with her chin up. She was constitutionally tough-minded, extroverted and inclined to be impatient as she intuitively estimated the true and false and right and wrong values in praises and criticisms of herself and other people. She was naturally disposed to dominate other people more than adapt herself to them. She had keen understanding of the motives and interests of people but little insight into her own egotism and less self-control of its tricky, tempestuous jealousies and resentments. Unfortunately she was overly ambitious, could not endure antagonism, and tended to grow bitterly sarcastic and infuriated in retaliation. She was highly narcissistic and flirted incorrigibly to win admiration.

Herndon lived with Lincoln and Speed during the first part of Lincoln's attentions to Mary and met her many times at parties and balls and occasionally danced with her. He also knew her later as the wife of his law partner, hence we accept his account of Lincoln's courtship and marriage, when supported by indicative evidence, as being highly important, although his interpretations of character and intent of Mrs. Lincoln seems, at times, to have been biased.

He described Mary Todd as being at this time "rather pleasant, polite, civil, rather graceful in her movements, intelligent, witty and sometimes bitter too; she was a polished girl, well educated, a good linguist, a fine conversationalist, shrewd, sharp, and a fine judge of human nature and of the appropriateness of conditions." The following story of Mary's prompt, sharp reply to Herndon's well intentioned but awkward compliment shows how readily her mind worked. He had finished a waltz with her and wanting to praise the gracefulness of her gliding movements compared them with "the ease of a serpent." She halted for a moment, drew back and her eyes flashed as she retorted: "Mr. Herndon, comparison to a serpent is rather severe irony, expecially to a newcomer." (Herndon, 1889).

Mary was remarkably like Stephen Douglas in short-thick body build and tough quick-minded, hyperkinetic, impulsive, aggressive, extroverted, ambitious, socially dominating constitutional type. It is most interesting that Lincoln, with his long-thin body, slow thinking tendermindedness, hypokinetic, cautious, adaptively extroverting-introverting constitution, political ambition and social indifference, should naturally be incompatible with a man extremely opposite to him in type, and yet fascinated by such a woman. It has often been observed that man, like other bisexual animals, tends in sexual selection to be attracted by opposite physical and personal qualities in a mate, although feeling compelled to hate them in a rival, as if nature would thereby restore constitutional balance through reproduction.

Mary's description of herself in a letter to her most intimate friend, Mercy Levering, shows that when pleased she had a good humored attitude and regarded her physical and mental constitution with satisfaction: "I still am the same ruddy *pineknot,* only not quite so great an exuberance of flesh, as it once was my lot to contend with, although quite a sufficiency." She had a warm, animated, passionate personality, overflowing with energy in seeking excitement and enjoyment of happy living. Unfortunately for Lincoln, who, as we have seen, dreaded nothing so much as being made a fool by a woman, Mary enjoyed nothing so much as flirting with men to win admiration and flattery through charming displays of cleverness and intelligence.

The characterizations of Mary by herself and her sisters and friends who knew her best are largely consistent with Herndon's estimations of her personality. Her disposition to swing to extremes of being sunny, cheerful, warmly affectionate and effusively kind in her sociable moods, when hoping to get what she wanted, and bitterly sarcastic and uncontrollably enraged when frustrated, appear repeatedly throughout her life. Through habitual repetition without self-restraint, Mary's culture of egoistic pride made her become eventually a jealous, sensitive, quick tempered, unjustly accusing woman and at times a bitterly sarcastic, laugh-ridiculing shrew. This propensity gradually developed, after her marriage, into a disposition to explode in hysterical fugues and rages, resulting in over-development of her facial muscles, with coarseness of expression. Hence her naturally vigorous, warmly affectionate personality must be regarded as having been psychopathologically inclined through social conditioning since early childhood, and in order to understand her fate as a woman we must understand her as a child.

Mary's Childhood

In human, as in lower animals, development of the ways the egoistic, consciously volitional, self-determining attitude of the personality will work is based on the inborn genetic constitution and prenatal nutritional influences, followed postnatally by environmental conditions of stress, nutrition, and social interactions. The latter are particularly impressive in the form of the sympathetic appeals and approvals it likes to acquire which enable it to see itself as being superior, good, beautiful, right, clean and desirable; contra to the inferior identifications of self as being ugly, evil, wrong, unclean and undesirable, as forced upon its mind by antagonistic suggestions, criticisms and disapprovals of members of its social group, family, school and community which it would like to avoid but cannot.

Mary was born in Lexington, Kentucky, on December 13, 1819, the fourth child of married cousins Robert Smith Todd and Elizabeth Parker Todd. The Todd and Parker antecedents were old, hardy, well disciplined, colonial American families that had produced generals and statesmen with distinguished records in the War for Independence. Her grandparents on both sides had moved into Kentucky shortly after the Daniel Boone migration and established themselves among the successful, prominent, aristocratic, slave-holding families of the state. Many of her immediate relatives were important in the professions and business, and few young American girls had the right to regard their ancestors and family connections with greater pride for their contributions to the founding of the nation.

Besides Elizabeth and Frances, Mary Ann had an older brother Levi and a younger sister Ann Maria; and then later by her step-mother, four half-brothers and five half-sisters of whom Emily [Helm] remained the most congenial with her. Mary's attitude toward her full sisters through childhood and womanhood has been expressed frankly in an intimate letter to a cousin, Elizabeth

Todd Grimsly (9, 29, 61), written six months after the inauguration of her husband as President. Because of the potential psychopathy of its insidiously vindictive jealousy it is quoted in part in Chapter LXI. It shows this sinister motivation began to develop early in childhood and continued its unhappy influence in womanhood before and after the death of her husband when it became progressively active under increasing distress of frustration.

Mary Ann was six years old when her mother died (age 31) in giving birth to a child, and Ann Maria was then probably about three, as a brother was born between them. Ann Maria was named after her father's young sister who, with Grandmother Parker, took care of his children and home after his wife died until he married again. The letter indicates that Mary and Ann became bitter rivals for the first place in the attentions of their father. Later Mary dropped "Ann" from her name except for legal signatures. As Mary was three years older than Ann and a pretty, bright, extroverted, aggressive, vivacious, jealously affectionate, cute, chubby, winsome and interesting child, she probably dominated Ann and became her indulgent father's spoiled darling.

Mary's father was a soldier in the War of 1812, interested in politics, served in the Kentucky legislature, and for 20 years held the office of president of the State Bank of Lexington. He was a sensitive, temperamental aristocrat who believed in strict discipline and honorable respectability. He was devoted to his family and after the death of his wife depended on his sister Ann Maria and Grandmother Parker, who lived nearby, to look after his home and children. The history of the family's daily life and Mary's later development of character indicates that she had the joy and inspiration of being her lonely, indulgent father's spoiled pet and, as her constitution disposed, she became egotistically set upon holding first place in his affections. Her cute, self-confident displays of ability, learning and intelligence seem to have succeeded generally in catching his admiring eye and complimentary word, for she became infatuated with winning recognitions of her social superiority over her sisters for its narcissistic satisfactions.

The pattern of this infatuation seems to have been retained as a woman, for later she liked being first in the affections of people she admired and was pleased when her husband, Abraham Lincoln, called her his "child wife." As will be seen later, he certainly had to become an indulgent fatherly husband to please her.

Unfortunately for little Mary, her father, continuing to be unhappy, decided to marry again despite her tragic disappointment and the bitter opposition of the Parker family. The new Mrs. Todd proved a woman of good will and high moral character who cared for his first wife's children conscientiously and in time produced nine (four sons and five daughters) of her own. But Mary remained intensely jealous of her stepmother and resisted her authority and disciplinary requirements with unrestrained outbursts of temper and blame for her unhappiness.She was encouraged and abetted in this paranoid twist of motivations of thwarted egotism by conniving, gossiping Grandmother Parker who sympathized with her and was hostile toward the new Mrs. Todd.

The analysis of origins of acquisitive and avoidance prejudices of motivations of the self-determinative egocentric attitude of the personality, in the early period of development of man (as in lower animals), has shown that the conditioning effects of reward, success and social approval and/or punishment, frustration and social disapproval continue throughout life. They remain unconsciously and consciously more or less active in the brain as excited or inhibited by the particular conformation of the egoistic attitude interacting with the particular conditioning stimuli of its social situation.

As the study of personality development in childhood and the attitude analysis of many normal and neurotic adults has shown, the ambitiously jealous egoistic attitude that would continue to give and get exchanges of love with another person, less for its reciprocally constructive value to each than for narcissistic reflections of superiority, remains parasitically and psychopathologically childish. It lacks the realistic cultivation of the heterosexually maturing, sociable qualities of considerate, judicial self-restraint with willing self-sacrifice and renunciation of primitively self-centered pleasures. When not reverberating with autistic imaginations about itself as being first, the narcissistic ego feels incomplete, depressed, restless, dissatisfied, irritated and unjustly annoyed. It cannot resist blaming the loved person, whose special attentive praises and justifications it needs, and the rival who defeats its ambitions, with plotting together to destroy its happiness. Conversely, it delights in getting intense feelings of being wanted, through jilting a person, who really loves it, into a jealous state of uncontrollable pain and mortification, by flirting with his detested rival.

Mary had these socially trying predispositions and never developed insight into the conditioned, subconscious emotivations of her childish egotism but, as usual, learned to discriminate skilfully the signs of sympathetic admiration and antipathic criticism of her arts and wishes. As she grew up she, like other constitutionally wilful, neurotic egotists, found happiness in cultivating other people intensely for first place in their affections, only to tire of them or become bitterly disappointed upon finding herself becoming secondary in importance. Pride in the distinction of being superior, with ardent affection for those who humored her and sarcastic intolerance of opponents, inclined her to live joyously with success, and tempestuously and tragically in defeat.

Mary's Schooling

The history of Mary's mental development shows that she was highly intelligent, industrious, precociously impulsive, learned easily in school and liked to improve her knowledge and abilities. At eight she was sent to a coeducational private school in Lexington conducted by Dr. John Ward, a strict Episcopalian minister. Here over 100 boys and girls of the "best families" were taught under a rigid moral system that imposed arduous physical and mental discipline to cultivate the dominance of mind and will power over discomfort, fatigue and sensuous pleasures.

School began early in the morning, and local pupils had to get up before dawn in winter in order to arrive on time. Much has been made of this discipline by some biographers, as if it had been a hardship imposed upon a sensitive child resulting in the production of a tempestuous disposition. This trivial explanation ignores the fact that Mary's brothers and sisters as well as other children in the school did the same thing. Millions of children have developed the best of rugged, independent characters by getting up long before dawn, doing chores on the farm and trudging miles in all weather to school with pride and joy of achievement, and this hardy, ambitious little girl measured up fully to her duties with the other children in her social group.

Mary was highly superstitious; and a faithful old slave, "Mammy Sally," seems to have been an important suggestive influence in this culture, as she ministered daily to the needs of the Todd children and disciplined waywardness with dark forebodings of evil consequences for wrong doing. Mary loved her mammy devotedly and never lost belief in signs, portents and dreams, or the weak pleasure of being softly flattered for her vanities. (Later, as mistress of the White House she again intimately cultivated the sympathies of a colored woman.)

Elizabeth Humphreys, a niece of the second Mrs. Todd, lived with the family and shared Mary's room and attended the Ward school with her. She described her as a bright, intelligent student who was industrious and practical, and knitted and sewed skilfully, but had a "sharp tongue."

From 14 to 18 Mary attended the select finishing school of Madam Mantelle, where she chose to learn to speak and write French, with the fine arts of letter writing, conversation and dancing, as became the social graces and proprieties and domestic niceties of Southern aristocratic culture. At 20 her education, refinement and intelligence exceeded that of most young women of her time. But her disposition, described by another cousin as being "very highly strung, nervous, impulsive, excitable, having an emotional temperament much like an April day, running all over with laughter at one moment, the next crying as if her heart would break," showed little improvement in self-renunciation.

Lincoln's Interest in Mary Todd

Abraham Lincoln met Mary Todd, the niece of his law partner, Congressman John Todd Stuart, late in 1839 when she was living in the grand home of her sister, Mrs. Ninian W. Edwards. Unhappy with her stepmother in Lexington she had come to Springfield to make a new circle of friends and catch a husband. An aristocratic thoroughbred, more vivacious, better educated, more imaginative and stronger minded than most of the young women, Mary soon became a popular leader of the younger social set in a growing border state capital seething with politics.

Lincoln had eventually been accepted by Springfield's "coterie," as they styled themselves, largely through his abilities as an orator, political leader and legislator, and as the law partner of one of its prominent members. We are interested particularly in the time that he courted Mary Todd and when they became engaged and separated. Since Lincoln courted Sarah Rickard in the summer of 1840 and according to her word, proposed to her in the fall of that year, and according to Mary's comments about her beaus in her letters to Mercy Levering which, as will be seen, mention Lincoln for the first time in December of 1840, it seems that his attentions had not been particularly impressive for her.

Apparently their friendship developed slowly under the skeptical consideration of the Ewards family. According to Herndon (1889), Mrs. Edwards, a clever matchmaker, thought Lincoln and Mary "had no congeniality—no feelings alike." She saw him as an honorable, rugged, capable, promising young man but too cold, indifferent, unsociable, and generally inclined to withdraw into abstract thinking. She found that he could not hold a lengthy conversation with a lady because of lack of sufficient education and training to make himself interesting. He "seemed ill constituted" she said, "by nature and education to please such a woman as my sister. Mary was quick, gay and in the social world somewhat brilliant. She loved show and power, and was the most ambitious woman I ever knew. She used to contend (when a girl and later in Springfield) that she was destined to marry a President."

We gather from Mrs. Edwards' estimation of Mr. Lincoln that he never was particularly interested in entertaining her and avoided answering her searching questions about his family. As a careless, easy-going individualist and an ardent philosopher of democracy and champion of the common people, he was distrustful of the lust for power of wealthy aristocrats and not at ease in an elaborate social environment of formally cultivated tastes and proprieties. However, he found that most wealthy people were interested in progressive government and regarded him respectfully as a man, despite his out of bounds manners.

Lincoln's love of good natured wit was well matched by Mary's sharp, quick thinking. She generally led the conversation and often interjected apt French expressions much to his amusement. Mary was religious and, as a conscientious student of the Bible, could quote important verses as well as Lincoln. She also had a true artistic sense for words, and recited favorite passages from Burns, Shakespeare and other poets with a relish for their rhythm and meaning.

Lincoln obviously was attracted physically as well as mentally by Mary Todd as she gracefully displayed her charms with an artful audacity that opened his eyes and challenged the staid womanly restraints of her time. The homely, long, slim, slow thinking, shy, cautious, self-educated, socially self-doubtful bachelor became naturally fascinated with the little, graceful, vivacious, bright-eyed, smiling, beautifully formed, quick witted, well educated, self-assured, wilful young lady; and, as he found her politically minded and able to express herself intelligently on current issues, she became more interesting to him than Sarah Rickard. According to the history given by Herndon (1889) he grew infatuated with Mary long before she felt similar affections for him.

Retaining strongly many of the cultural influences of his childhood, Lincoln seemed to like best the speech and manners of Kentuckians. Nearly all of the people who became his intimate friends, even in later years, were born in that state. Mary Todd's home in Lexington, not far from Hodgenville, and her personal friendship with Senator Henry Clay, then a leader in national government and Lincoln's ideal statesman, gave the pair many delightful interests in common. Lincoln, by nature a compromiser of conflict in law and government, could discuss practically with Mary the political effects of Clay's measures for keeping peace between the pro- and anti-slavery interests in Congress. Mary knew intimately the better side of slavery, and both held that abolitionism was unconstitutional and not a just solution of the great problem. Both were also Whigs and advocated Harrison for President.

Mary's Beaux

Mary is said to have commented once in a family discussion that she would marry not for wealth but for love, but would only consider a man who had an important future. She liked to boast that she was destined to be the wife of a President and would marry a man "who had the best prospects" (Hertz, 1948). These remarks have been interpreted by many biographers as expressing ambition to be the wife of a President of the United States. It was probably no more than the gay expression of desire of a young woman to marry a man with such impressive mental powers as her father had, when, as her hero, he was president of Lexington's State Bank. Among all of the eligible young men that she knew at this time two had such potentialities to an extraordinary degree. Both paid her attentions and she did not hesitate to play one against the other as rivals for her favors. Biographers generally agree that it has been well established that gossip said she "flirted outrageously" with Douglas and other beaux.

The first preserved letter by Mary Todd, written when visiting her uncle in Columbia, Missouri, to Mercy Levering on July 23, 1840, gives evidence of her unusually extroverted, romantic sociability, ideals for marriage and intimately confidential, intense affection for Mercy and a particular beau. She makes no reference to Lincoln, even though he had attended the Missouri State Whig Convention at Rocheport, a month previous (Barton, 1927) and, as her family stated, he had called on her. It seems that Mary was then not seriously interested in him. Since her letters constitute significant revelations of her personality as well as documents on this important question, the following excerpts (Sandburg and Angle, 1932) are presented at some length in order to include the contexts of the parts that are often quoted by biographers as evidence for their inferences. Brief discussions on the meanings of the parts and some inferences follow the quotations. (Italics Miss Todd's.)

Mary Todd, as will be seen, was infatuated with Mercy Levering, an attractive Baltimore girl of about her age who visited with relatives living near the Edwards home. They had become warm, confidential friends. Her letter starts:

> "Many thanks Dearest Merce for your kind letter, yet in spite of the pleasure of hearing from you, it brought many feelings of sorrow and regret, to know that you were as near as St. Louis, & [I] was debarred the happiness of seeing one I love so well. A few days before receiving yours, Elizabeth wrote to me & spoke of the possibility of seeing you again as you did not quit these western wilds until August. . . . In spite of the *agreeable visitation* I have already made, I had determined to forego all, once more to see you, and shorten my visit here. You will really credit me Dearest, when I tell you my time has been most delightfully spent. This portion of the state is certainly most beautiful, and in my wanderings I never encountered more kindness & hospitality. As my visit was particularly to my relations & [I] did not expect to remain for any length of time, I was not anxious to mingle with the strange crowd, and form new associations so soon to be severed, yet every lady almost that called extended an invitation to us to spend an evening with them, so I have necessarily seen more society than I had anticipated. . . . Were Missouri my home, with the exception of St. Louis, Boonville would certainly in my estimation have the preference. A life on the river to me has always had a charm, so much excitement, and this *you* have deemed necessary to my well being; every day experience impresses me more fully with the belief. I would such were not my nature, for mine I fancy is to be a quiet lot, and happy indeed I will be, if it is, only cast near those, I *so dearly love.*"

Some biographers have assumed that Mary's words, "mine I fancy is to be a quiet lot," indicates that she was then engaged to Lincoln. That this is not true seems evident in her fancies of how she would like to live in Missouri near Mercy, as expressed in the same letter.

> "My feelings & hopes are all so sanguine that in this dull world of reality tis best to dispell our delusive day dreams as soon as possible. Would it were in my power to follow your kind advice, my dear Merce and turn my thoughts from earthly vanities, to one higher than us all. Every day proves the fallacy of our enjoyments, & that we are living for pleasures that do not recompense us for the pursuit.—I wrote you a lengthy document, soon after reaching this place. As you did not mention having received it, I feared it had not reached you. The mail comes in today, and I am on the wing of expectation, hoping to hear from my dear sister Fanny. Dr. Wallace I hear has been sick, & Fanny I fear is unable to play the part of a devoted nurse at *this time,* to both child & husband."

"I am on the wing of expectation," has been excerpted from its context by some biographers as indicating hope for a letter from a particular beau, even though it definitely refers to a letter from her sister giving news about her husband who was ill and to whom Mary was devoted. Later she named a son after him.

> "Every week," the letter continues, "since I left Springfield, have had the felicity of receiving various numbers of their interesting papers. Old Soldiers, Journals & even the Hickory Club, has crossed my vision. This latter, rather astonished your friend, *there* I deemed myself forgotten.—When I mention *some letters* I have received since leaving S— you will be somewhat surprised, as I *must confess* they were entirely *unlooked for.* This is *between ourselves,* my dearest, but of this more anon. Every day I am convinced this is a stranger world we live in, the *past* as the future is to me a mystery."

Some biographers have assumed that all of these papers were sent to Mary by Lincoln since he was one of the editors of the biweekly campaign publication, *The Old Soldier,* advocating General Harrison for president. *The Hickory Club,* named after President "Old Hickory" Jackson, was the publication of the Democratic party, of which Douglas was state boss. It is not likely that Lincoln would have sent this paper to Mary. It seems more probable that various people were writing to Mary and sending copies of the local papers. The pointed expression of delight and astonishment upon receiving a copy of *The Hickory Club,* and letters that were entirely unlooked for from a man who she thought had forgotten her indicates that she was referring to Steve Douglas and was still affectionately interested in him and not Lincoln.

Mary's letter continues:

> "How much I wish you were near, ever have I found yours a congenial heart. In your presence I have almost *thought aloud,* and the thought

that paineth most is, that such may never be again, yet, I trust that a happier day will dawn, near you, I would be most happy to sojourn in our earthly pilgrimmage. To me it has ever appeared that those whose presence was the sunlight of my heart have departed—separated—far and wide, to meet when? In Boonville I met with two or three former schoolmates endeared to me by the ties of early memories, also several young gentlemen. . . . This, at all times I have deemed a hard lesson . . . to have so many beaux 'dancing attendance' on us at one time, and the little throng were hosts within themselves. Our Sucker friends would have opened their orbs, at such strange doings."

The preceding and following fancies of how she and Mercy might find husbands and live near each other in Boonville also show quite conclusively that she had not yet become seriously interested in any man.

"I there met with a young Cousin, by my mother's side, who has a few weeks since, wended his way westward, a young lawyer, and gives hopes of bright promise. Already the old lawyers, have extended a patronizing smile & I trust & feel that he may one day, ere long weave a bright chaplet of fame for his youthful brow.—Were you to see him, I almost fancy & hope that others in your eye would be forgotten. No other cousin save *him* would I deem worthy of your acceptance— and he has that Dear Merce which I have heard you say would be *indispensable,* good Morals & Religion and the most affectionate heart in the world, yet I much fear yours is a *gone case.* Though far separated, do not deem your confidence misplaced, tell me all—every thing, you know the deep interest I feel for you, time can never banish your remembrance, how desolate I shall feel on returning to Springfield without you, your kind and cheering presence has beguiled many a lonely hour of its length. . . . If you conclude to settle in Missouri, *I will do so too.* There is *one* being here, who cannot brook the mention of my return [to Springfield] an agreeable lawyer & grandson of *Patrick Henry—what an honor!* I shall never survive it—I wish you could see him, the most perfect original I ever met. My beaux have *always* been *hard bargains* at any rate. Uncle and others think, he surpasses his *noble ancestor* in *talents;* yet Merce I love him not, & my hand will never be given, where my heart is not. Be as unreserved as you find me. I forget myself writing to you. Pass my imperfections lightly by, and excuse so miserable a production from your most attached friend."

This intimate letter contains many indications that Mary Todd was not as yet affectionately interested in Lincoln in July of 1840, and certainly not engaged to him. It does indicate, however, that Mary liked Douglas and was hopeful of his attentions but still free to fantasy living near Mercy in Boonville, and still more inclined to love her than any man that she knew.

Herndon (1889) and Mrs. Randall (1953) agree that it was generally recognized by those who knew Mary Todd intimately that she liked to flirt in public with Douglas and other beaus. According to one accepted story, Mary mischievously challenged Douglas to bedeck himself with a wreath of roses that she had just made and how gallantly he did it to everyone's amusement as they walked gaily along the street. Emily Todd Helm, Mary's half sister, and Katherine Helm, a cousin, both described how Lincoln "forgot" a date to take Mary to a dance but she went nevertheless and carried on gaily with Douglas.

James C. Conkling, a warm friend of Mary Todd, had become engaged to Mercy Levering, and his letter to her of September 21, 1840 gives news about Mary of a nature that would almost certainly have mentioned Lincoln had he been high in her favor at the time. He wrote of seeing Miss Todd in the Journal office where they heard the Tippecanoe Singing Club (Harrison for President). He also told of how Miss Todd and he were standing partners in the marriage of friends and how remarkably well and attractive she looked. "She regrets your absence very much and feels quite lonesome. And now that Martha Jane has gone as well as yourself I do not doubt but she is quite solitary . . . she is the very creature of excitement you know and never enjoys herself more than in society and surrounded by a company of merry friends."

Mary's Loneliness

According to Mary's relatives (Herndon, 1889), she developed a state of nervousness over her infatuations, and the comment by Conklin, in his letter of October 24, 1840 to Mercy Levering, that "she did not appear as merry and joyous as usual" seems indicative of worry. Mary is said to have confided her troubles to Dr. Wallace, her brother-in-law, and he induced Douglas, who was famous as a lady killer, "to end his pursuit, which he did with great reluctance."

Mrs. Harriet Chapman, who lived with the Lincolns two years after their marriage, told Herndon that Mrs. Lincoln said confidentially to her that she "loved Douglas, and but for her promise to marry Lincoln, would have accepted him."

Mary Todd's letters and the accounts of her friends and relatives show that she liked having the attentions of many beaus, and carried on with Douglas, Webb, Lincoln and other men at the same time, with no little neurotic vacillation of interest. Her letter to Mercy of the week beginning December 13, 1840 is symptomatic of involved moodiness.

> "Many, many weary days have passed my ever dear Merce, since mine has been the pleasure of hearing from you. Some weeks since I received your kind, soul cheering epistle & had I been *then* told such a length of time would have intervened ere I had availed myself of an opportunity of replying to it, I would not have given credence to the tale, yet such has been the case & I feel I owe you many apologies & sincerely trust our

further correspondance may be more punctual. My time has been much occupied of late . . . *sewing,* necessary for winter comfort. . . . On my return from Missouri, my time passed most heavily. I feel quite made up in my present companion, a congenial spirit I assure you. I know you would be pleased with Matilda Edwards, a lovelier girl I never saw *Mr. Speed's* everchanging heart I suspect is about offering *its young* affections at her shrine, with some others. There is considerable acquisition in our society of *marriageable gentlemen,* unfortunately only 'birds of passage.' Mr. Webb, a widower of modest merit, last winter, is our *principal lion,* dances attendance very frequently. We expect a very gay winter, evening before last my sister gave a most agreeable party, upwards of a hundred graced the festive scene. I trust the period is not very distant when your presence will be among us to cheer us & moreover I trust *our homes* may be near, that as in times past, so may it *ever be,* that our hearts will acknowledge the same kindred ties."

Mary diverted from this bit of nostalgia with humorous references to Speed, Lincoln and Webb.

"Speed's 'grey suit' has gone the way of *all flesh,* an interesting suit of *Harrison blues* have replaced his *sober livery, Lincoln's lincoln green,* have gone to dust, Mr. Webb sports a mourning p[—?] by way of reminding us *damsels,* that we *'cannot come in.'* Of the new recruits I need not mention, some few are gifted & all in our humble estimation interesting."

The above terse remark on poor Lincoln's once black suit faded to "Lincoln green" and gone to dust is hardly consistent with the thoughts of a young woman if she were then happily engaged to him, or hopefully in love with him.

Her letter continues with comments on her married girl friends, much quoted by biographers as indicating that she was then contemplating marriage for herself.

"Harriet Campbell appears to be enjoying all the sweets of married life. *Mrs. Abell* came down two or three weeks since. . . . Her *silver tones,* the other evening were not quite so captain like as was the wont in former times. Why is it that married folks always become so serious? Miss Lamb, report says is to be married next week. *Mr Beauman* . . . looked *becomingly* happy at the prospect . . . I am pleased she is about perpetrating the *crime of matrimony,* like some of ones friends in *this place,* I think she will be much happier."

After some diversion about herself having become "quite a *politician,* rather an unladylike profession" in behalf of General Harrison, Mary indulges in another poetical, lonesome fantasy about living near Mercy.

"The icy hand of winter has set its seal upon the waters, the winds of Heaven visit the spot but roughly, the same stars shine down, yet not with the same liquid, mellow light as in the olden time. Some forms & memories that enhanced the place, have passed by, many weary miles are you dear Merce removed from us. The star of hope, must be a guiding *star*, and we must revel in the happy anticipations of a reunion, may the day be not far distant.—Once more, allow me my dear friend to wish you were with us."

After this romantic expression of affection Mary became more realistic.

"We have a pleasant jaunt in contemplation, to Jacksonville, next week there to spend a day or two. Mr. Hardin & Browning are our leaders the van brought up by Miss E, my humble self, Webb, Lincoln & two or three others whom you know not. We are watching the clouds most anxiously trusting it may snow, so we may have a sleigh ride.—Will it not be pleasant?"

Again the casual mention of Webb and Lincoln gives no indication of love for either man, and almost certainly means that no engagement to marry has yet been made with Lincoln. Again she reverts to an expression of infatuation for Mercy, this time more significant of the continuation of an adolescent samesex loving disposition.

"We cannot do much longer without you, *your mate* misses you too much from her nest, not to marvel at your delay. Do trust a friend and be more communicative in your next, feeling as you must do the great interest I take in you, would you deny me the consolation of being a sharer of your joys & sorrows, may the latter never be known to you."

Most psychiatrists of analytic experience would conclude from the personal history of two foregoing letters of Mary Todd that she was an ardent, affectionate extrovert who liked many beaus to excite for her happy feelings of narsissistic superiority. She was still intensely infatuated with Mercy, her "mate," and had not found a man who loved her whom she could really love. She certainly had not written as late as mid-December to her most intimate and confidential friend anything to indicate that she was, as yet, even in love with Lincoln, although we know that he had become attentive to her. Neither do her sentences, if we disregard those expressing love for Mercy, have the quality we would expect of an affectionate young woman who had found the true answer to her heart's desire and was eager to get married. Her gloomy note about the passing of "weary days" suggests continuation of disappointment over Douglas' not having fallen in love with her although she had indicated such anticipations for him.

Lincoln and Douglas, Rivals in Politics and Love

Douglas had organized the Democratic party of the state and most of the counties into an efficient political machine with a majority in both houses of the legislature. Though not yet 30, he had become its progressive leader, and was well on the way up as a statesman, when he became interested in Mary Todd. Whereas Lincoln was looked upon as a suitor by the Edwards family with some dislike for his lack of culture and poor earning capacity, Douglas, well educated and a political and social lion with a well established, lucrative law practice, held their admiration and encouragement. Douglas was probably sincere in his intentions to Mary although he had a reputation for promiscuity. He was a master of women whereas Lincoln was submissive to them.

Mary, it seems, was fascinated by the strength of character, education and intelligence, ready wit, and gay, jovial disposition of Douglas. Her father had been successful in law, politics, and business and, measuring the ways and needs of such careers by him, she probably saw a greater future in Douglas than in Lincoln. Indications for this inference exist in Mary's hints of affection for Douglas to Mercy Levering in 1840 and to Harriet Chapman (Lincoln's cousin) two years after her marriage, and her enigmatic reply on another occasion, to Mrs. Edwards' remark that she used to think Mr. Douglas would be her choice, "No, I liked him well enough, but that is all."

That both men were jealous of each other as political leaders and statesmen has been shown in previous chapters. Lincoln's humorous comments in letters to Stuart on the behavior of Douglas show continuation of this rivalry.

> December 23, 1839: "The Democratic giant is here, but he is not now worth talking about."
>
> March 1, 1840: "Yesterday Douglas, having chosen to consider himself insulted by something in the 'Journal,' undertook to cane Francis in the street. Francis caught him by the hair and jammed him back against a market-cart, where the matter ended by Francis being pulled away from him. The whole affair was so ludicrous that Francis and everybody else (Douglas excepted) have been laughing about it ever since."

Neurotic Engagement

Documentary evidence on the courtship and first engagement of Lincoln and Mary Todd is extremely limited but sufficiently definitive. There is an enormous collection of gossip by Herndon and other investigators from Mary's relatives and friends which has been largely reviewed and plausibly evaluated by many biographers but will not be discussed here. No letters written by Lincoln to Mary or Mary to Lincoln before their marriage have been found. Since he was often away from Springfield for protracted periods and both liked to write profusely, such letters would surely have been written if they were in love for any length of time before their engagement.

The events recorded in letters and documents indicate that the affectionate relations between them developed rapidly, if not unexpectedly and impulsively for both, late in December of 1840, possibly during the "jaunt" to Jacksonville. An engagement followed immediately and, after a short, stormy commitment Lincoln tried to break it, only to continue, followed by Mary's breaking it.

Herndon, who was still working for Speed at this time, published (1889) an account of what transpired from his memories and inquiries of Speed and her family made after 1865. Herndon's version became the basis of endless controversy largely because of assumptions that did not harmonize with the letters of Lincoln to Stuart and to Speed, of Speed to Herndon, of Conklin to Mercy Levering, and of Mary to Mercy. However, reconsideration of the parts of his material that date consistently with the indications in these letters, and discounting doubtful details of memories of various old members of the family, given two decades after, makes a fairly consistent picture.

It is quite clear by her last letter that Miss Todd was interested in three rival suitors at the same time, all lawyers like her father—Lincoln, Douglas, and the new widower, Webb—as prospects. Upon being much attended she was again looking forward to a gay winter, when Lincoln seems to have become spurred to propose marriage. Mary accepted his offer which, probably, as indicated by what followed, he had made with characteristic secret self-doubts of the reality of his love for her and of her constant loyalty, since she would not or, probably, could not quit flirting with other beaus. Lincoln soon regarded himself as being treated dishonorably in public and made to feel unendurably inferior in her eyes to his arch rival, Douglas, by the woman he would marry. As will become evident later, he was not jealous of Webb. Naturally needing to receive confirmation of his personal superiority through getting spontaneous signs of whole hearted devotion from his fiancée, he grew increasingly self-doubtful and despondant as he realized her impulses to continue flirting with Douglas were irrepressible.

We must bear in mind that Lincoln, as leader of the Whigs, had brought about the defeat of Douglas for Congress by his partner Stuart, and in turn, as a member of the finance committee of the House, he had been charged by Douglas with such extravagent expenditures of the State's money as to threaten the collapse of its financial credit. During their first public debate a year previous, he had been so insulted by Douglas that he came to detest his arrogance, opportunistic policies and promiscuity. When Mary, knowing all this, persisted in flirting with Douglas in a manner that humiliated Lincoln, he became unable to endure the injury of his self-respect. His most obsessive fear, that of being made ridiculous by the girl he would love, had become a miserable reality.

After a short, unhappy engagement, Lincoln wrote Mary a letter to break it, but before sending it he decided to ask his friend Speed for advice. Herndon has described how one evening (unfortunately undated) Lincoln came into the store and called for Speed. Together they walked back to the fireplace, where Lincoln drew a letter from his pocket and asked him to read it. Many years later (9, 17, 1866) Speed wrote to Herndon:

> "The letter was addressed to Mary Todd, and in it he made a plain statement of his feelings, telling her that he had thought the matter over calmly and with great deliberation, and now felt that he did not love her sufficiently to warrent her in marrying him. This letter he desired me to deliver. Upon my declining to do so he threatened to intrust it to some other person's hand. I reminded him that the moment he placed the letter in Miss Todd's hand, she would have the advantage over him. 'Words are forgotten,' I said, 'misunderstood, unnoticed in private conversation, but once put your words in writing and they stand a living and eternal monument against you.' Thereupon I threw the unfortunate letter in the fire. 'Now,' I continued, 'if you have the courage of manhood, go see Mary yourself; tell her, if you do not love her, the facts, and that you will not marry her. Be careful not to say too much, and then leave at your earliest opportunity.' Thus admonished, he buttoned his coat, and with a rather determined look started out to perform the serious duty for which I had just given him explicit directions."

Lincoln took his experienced friend's advice and went to see Mary. Herndon (1889) continues:

> "Speed did not go upstairs to bed with us,* but under pretense of wanting to read, remained in the store below. . . . Ten o'clock passed, and still the interview with Miss Todd had not ended. . . . after eleven he came stalking in. . . . 'Well, old fellow, did you do as I told you and as you promised?' were Speed's first words.
>
> " 'Yes I did,' responded Lincoln, thoughtfully, 'and when I told Mary I did not love her, she burst into tears and almost springing from her chair and wringing her hands as if in agony, said something about the deceiver being himself deceived. . . . it was too much for me. I found the tears trickling down my own cheeks. I caught her in my arms and kissed her.'
>
> " 'And that's how you broke the engagement,' sneered Speed. 'You not only acted the fool, but your conduct was tantamount to a renewal of the engagement, and in decency you cannot back down now.'
>
> " 'Well,' drawled Lincoln, 'if I am in again, so be it. It's done, and I shall abide by it.' " (Herndon, 1889)

---

*Although Herndon had married on March 26, 1840 he seems to have continued to sleep at times in Speed's store.

Chapter XIII

SELF-REVELATIONS OF TWO
NEUROTIC BACHELORS

It is necessary to correlate the verifiable evidence of Lincoln's ways in love and marriage with the frustrations of January 1841, in order to understand how his cerebral condition and melancholic disposition developed hypochondriacal anxiety upon the breakdown of his resolution 'to control passion by cold reason.'

Thereby we can better follow the further development of his personality, his egoistic ambitions and intense need of moral self-respect and pride in being respectable, his constant need of getting sympathetic reassurance from confidential friends to counteract his endless tendency to melancholic mental detachment under loneliness, his dread of humiliation by the irrepressible flirtatious vanities of the woman he would marry, his jealousy of her continuation of affectionate interest in Douglas, and his eventual paternalistic common-sense adjustment of the resistances of his continued nostalgic fixation of love on his mother and Ann Rutledge, so as to be able to love Mary Todd and marry her.

Then we can understand more consistently and realistically how the political moves of Douglas, many years later, as United States Senator, to legalize extension of slavery and thereby obtain the Democratic nomination for the presidency, aroused in Lincoln, who was ever envious of him, the intensely moral compulsion to defeat him and his project.

Herndon concluded, from his correlations of evidence and gossip, that Lincoln continued his attentions to Miss Todd and, although Mr. and Mrs. Edwards questioned the fitness of Lincoln for Mary on the grounds of his lack of culture and means, they planned to get married on the evening of January 1st, 1841, in the Edwards home. What really happened between Lincoln and Mary remains an unsolved question. Biographers differ enormously in their interpretations. Herndon, then a very close friend of Lincoln, told Lamon for his biography 25 years later and repeated it in his own biography (1889) and in his letters to Weik (Hertz, 1938), that on the wedding evening preparations had been completed and the guests had arrived and the nervously expectant bride was all dressed and ready for the ceremony but the groom never appeared. After waiting for more than an hour Mary grew hysterical, the guests withdrew, the house was darkened and a party of friends, led by Speed, made a search for Lincoln.

They found him, Herndon said, "by daybreak—restless, gloomy, miserable, desperate . . . an object of pity. His friends, Speed among the number, fearing a tragic determination, watched him closely in their rooms day and night." Twenty-five years later (January 6, 1866) Speed described Lincoln's condition to Herndon as recorded by him (Herndon, 1889), "knives and razors, and every instrument that could be used for self-destruction were removed from his reach" Herndon continued: "Mrs. Edwards did not hesitate to regard him as insane, and of course her sister Mary shared in this view. But the case was hardly so desperate. His condition began to improve after a few weeks."

Herndon's dramatic account of Lincoln's failure to appear for his wedding was published by Lamon in 1872 and aroused bitter dispute of its authenticity among Springfield's citizens. Weik personally interviewed the Edwards family and friends in 1883 and published an account of it in his own book on Lincoln (1922). He was unable to verify Herndon's tale further than, now aged, Mrs. Edwards' statement that preparations had been made for a wedding but Lincoln failed to carry out his part. Ruth Randall (1953) and other modern scholars, after considering available letters and other sources of gossip for possible clues on Lincoln's behavior in this affair, have judged Herndon's version as being no better than imaginary revamping of memories without substantial foundation. Not a single contemporary letter, or local newspaper or other publication has been found that contains any reference to preparations at this time for a wedding of Abraham Lincoln and Mary Todd in the home of the Edwards family, as would naturally have been reported for such an important social event.

However, Herndon's account is supported by Lincoln's comments to Speed (see next chapter) on his own dread of the ceremony of being married and "the fatal first of Jany." It is also supported by the reaction of Mrs. Mary Lincoln to it. Although she was greatly mortified by Lamon's and Herndon's publications of accounts of Lincoln's failure to appear for their wedding, there is no record of her correcting or disproving it.

"Hypo"

Positive documentary evidence showing that Lincoln suffered a nervous breakdown of a so-called hypochondriacal form of depressive anxiety, in January 1841, exists in a statement made by himself in a letter of the 20th of that month to his law partner, Congressman John Todd Stuart:

> "I wish now to speak of our Post-Office. You know I desired Dr. Henry to have that place when you left; I now desire it more than ever. I have, within the last few days, been making a most discreditable exhibition of myself in the way of hypochondriaism and thereby got an impression that Dr. Henry is necessary to my existence. Unless he gets that place he leaves Springfield. You therefore see how much I am interested in the matter.
>
> "We shall shortly foward you a petition in his favour signed by all or nearly all the Whig members of the Legislature, as well as other Whigs.

"This, together with what you know of Dr.'s position and merits I sincerely hope will secure him the appointment. My heart is verry much set upon it.

"Pardon me for not writing more; I have not sufficient composure to write a long letter."

Lincoln's previous letter to Stuart (12, 17, 1840) was purely political and impersonal, indicating, as his legislative record does, no lack of self-composure or good health at that time. However, this is inconclusive for he wrote a week or so later to Dr. Daniel Drake, dean of the medical college of Cincinnati, a friend of Dr. Anson Henry, and probably upon his advice. The letter has not been found but Lincoln read it to Speed, whose remarks about it in a letter to Herndon, although made many years later (11, 30, 1866), give reliable evidence on its nature:

"In the winter of 40 & 41 — he was very unhappy about his engagement to his wife — Not being entirely satisfied that his *heart* was going with his hand. — How much he suffered then on that account none know so much as myself. He disclosed his whole heart to me. . . . One thing is plainly discernable if I had not been married & happy — far more happy than I ever expected to be — he would not have married. . . .

"Lincoln wrote a letter (a long one which he read to me) to Dr. Drake of Cincinnati discriptive of his case. Its date would be December 40 or early January 41. I think he must have informed Dr. Drake of his early love of Miss Rutledge — as there was a part of the letter he would not read . . . I remember Dr. Drake's reply — which was that he would not undertake to prescribe for him without a personal interview."

Herndon was present when Lincoln sought Speed's advice the first time that he tried to break his engagement with Mary Todd and said many years later (1889) that he then thought Lincoln had grown so jealous and nervous over her flirtations with Douglas that he felt he could not marry her. We find, as we correlate pertinent evidence in letters, chronologically, that Lincoln did again want his freedom and contributed to making Mary break the engagement; and this emotional conflict, combined with another precipitating factor, produced a prolonged and serious breakdown of self-composure and working ability.

According to Beveridge (1928), Lincoln, as the Whig floor leader of the Illinois House of Representatives then in session, had been in constant attendance in December, having missed but five or six of the many roll calls during the five busy weeks preceding Friday, January 1, 1841. He was only present once on that day and twice on the next. On Monday, January 3, he was absent, notwithstanding that business was transacted of particular interest to him. On Tuesday he was again absent except at the opening of the House when he voted for the incorporation of Galensburg. On Wednesday he voted twice. On Thursday Lincoln answered one roll call in the forenoon but did not vote on two important questions immediately thereafter. He addressed the house briefly on the 8th and 9th. From January 13 until January 21 he attended the legislature only once.

The editors of *Collected Works* have suggested, after a thorough study of the documentary evidence, that Lincoln's absence from the legislature from January 13 to 19 was due to "illness of a psychopathic nature" brought on in all probability by whatever happened on the first of January. This view is based on a letter Lincoln wrote to Speed (3, 27, 1842) fifteen months after that date, in which he said:

> "Your last letter gave me more pleasure, than the total sum of all I have enjoyed since that fatal first of Jany. '41. Since then, it seems to me, I should have been entirely happy, but for the never-absent idea, that there is *one* still unhappy whom I have contributed to make so. That still kills my soul. I can not but reproach myself, for even wishing to be happy while she is otherwise."

Lincoln's remarks about "the fatal first of January '41" indicate that, in his miserably vacillating, self-doubtful, split-minded state over whether or not he really loved Mary Todd and whether to marry her or not to marry her, he had felt himself compelled to obtain release from his promise, in order to get relief from his dangerous emotional state of mind. Thereby he "contributed" the provocation that made her break their engagement, either on that day or a few days later.

Lincoln's emotional compulsion about Mary Todd was quite different from his compulsion to get out of his promise to marry Mary Owens. With Miss Owens he found himself disliking her physically and thinking that he was getting a woman so easily that no man would have her; and, however he tried to convince himself that he loved her for her face and intelligence, he continually 'repented the rashness which had led him to make the promise,' so the affair ended with his being happy in regaining freedom. With Miss Todd he found himself intensely attracted by her physical and mental charms and getting a woman that many men wanted, but he felt too jealously humiliated by her flirtatious vanities to marry her, only to find after he was free again that, instead of being happy, he was endlessly reproaching himself for having caused her the unhappiness of breaking their engagement and endlessly wishing to see her happy again. His attitudinal readjustment after getting free of Mary Owens was consistent and healthy, but after Mary Todd it continued to be inconsistent and neurotic.

The *Illinois State Register,* the authorized annals of the State Legislature, shows that in his brief address on the ninth he referred to himself humorously as being the "longest" of the "long nine" (a group of prominent Whig representatives) and added that "if any woman, old or young, ever thought there was any peculiar charm in this distinguished specimen of number 9, I have, as yet, been so unfortunate as not to have discovered it." (Loud applause.)

A physician would assume that Lincoln's humorous reference to himself at this time of his illness, implying that he was too "long" to be attractive to any woman, indicates that he had regained considerable self-composure after his engagement to Mary Todd had been broken. If *he* had broken the engagement, or failed to appear for his wedding on January 1st, as alleged by Herndon, this remark would have been an unnecessarily cruel expression of sardonic flippancy, exhibiting a despicably vindictive trait of character that Lincoln did not have.

It seems more indicated that Mary Todd ended the engagement before the eighth, if not on the first, and that, instead of being shocked and breaking down as she did the first time Lincoln tried to get out of his promise, she let him have it in no uncertain terms. The extroverted, tough-minded constitution of the little woman, with strength of character, hot temper and sharp tongue, seems to have devastated the composure of the introverted, tender-minded, self-doubtful, self-pitying, long thin lawyer in a way that let him understand that she was able to take care of herself. After a few days of thinking it over, he felt sufficiently reassured of this to see the humorous side of their quarrel. This view is consistent with his humorous references later on to their marriage as "the long and short of it." He would probably have continued his recovery after the ninth but for the cause of relapse of depression by another factor.

Lincoln's reference to the fatal first of January had certainly an additional meaning that has not been given heretofore, sufficient consideration by any of his biographers. Speed and Lincoln, in living together for four years, had developed an unusually strong and intimately confidential, mutually dependent sympathetic friendship, in which each influenced the courtship and marriage of the other, as shown definitely by their correspondence. (See Chapter XIV).

Speed sold his store on January 1, 1841, after having been influenced by his aging mother to do so and return to Kentucky and manage the family's estate. Lincoln tried repeatedly after the sale, and probably before, to persuade him to remain in Springfield. He seems to have been so greatly depressed by the sale and the imminence of losing his friend's intimate sympathetic encouragement in his miserably frustrating conflict of love and jealousy over Mary Todd that he completely lost self-composure on that fatal day and broke down into the vacillating state of hypochondriacal confusion that made her end the engagement. From this state of mind he was recovering by the ninth, only to relapse.

Lincoln's entire absence from the 13th to the 19th, and his letters to Stuart of the 20th (previously quoted) and the 23rd (see later), indicate the conditions of his relapse and how he regained sufficient self-composure to carry on his duties in the legislature. It seems that when Lincoln had regained sufficient composure to put on a brave face about his break with Mary Todd, Speed firmly expressed his intention of leaving Springfield permanently. It was then that Lincoln lost hope of dependence on his friend's intimate assurances and slumped into the dangerously self-pitying, miserably nostalgic, gloomy state of mind that totally incapacitated him until he found a solution.

Speed (1896) said of Lincoln's condition:

> "In the winter of 1841 a gloom came over him till his friends were
> alarmed for his life. Though a member of the legislature he rarely attended
> its sessions. In his deepest gloom, and when I told him he would die unless
> he rallied, he said, 'I am not afraid, and would be more than willing. But
> I have an irrepressible desire to live till I can be assured that the world is a
> little better for my having lived in it.' "

It was probably for these reasons that Speed continued to postpone
his departure from week to week until March, when he felt sure that his
friend had recovered sufficient self-control and will power to work.

Lincoln's pathetically appealing letter of January 20 to Stuart in which
he said, "I have an impression that Dr. Henry is necessary to my existence" and "my heart is verry much set" on his appointment as postmaster
of Springfield, shows how much he was habitually dependent on maintaining a mutually sympathetic transference with some friend who held
his respect and confidence for loyalty and wisdom. Thereby he could
talk out confidentially his perplexing self-doubts, self-accusations, and
moral and emotional conflicts so as to regain self-confidence and peace
of mind; very much in the way now found indispensable in modern
psychotherapy and religion.

On January 23 Lincoln appealed again to Stuart:

> "Yours of the 3rd. Inst. is recd. & I proceed to answer it as well as
> I can, tho' from the deplorable state of my mind at this time, I fear I shall
> give you but little satisfaction." He then discussed at considerable length,
> with all of his political astuteness, the implications for the future of the next
> congressional election and the part he was playing in it, and continued:
> "On the last evening there was a meeting of our friends at Butler's; and I
> submitted the question to them & found them unanamously in favour of
> having you announced as a candidate." . . . Although he had recovered
> sufficiently to fulfill his legislative obligations and attend to political affairs
> he added: "For not giving you a general summary of news, you *must* pardon
> me; it is not in my power to do so. I am now the most miserable man
> living. If what I feel were equally distributed to the whole human family,
> there would not be one cheerful face on the earth. Whether I shall ever be
> better I can not tell; I awfully forbode I shall not. To remain as I am is
> impossible; I must die or be better, it appears to me. . . . I fear I shall be
> unable to attend to any business here, and a change of scene might help me.
> If I could be myself, I would rather remain at home with Judge Logan. I can
> write no more. Your friend as ever—"

Dr. Anson Henry, as much politician as physician, recently beaten
in election for probate justice, did not get the post office, and he did not
leave Springfield. His treatment of Lincoln's illness is said to have consisted principally of rest, tonics, calomel, and listening sympathetically
to complaints and making intuitive suggestions. Although not well educated in medicine, Dr. Henry had such deep understanding of human
nature and its trials over unavoidable conflicting social obligations that

he remained Lincoln's chief sympathetic prop for the rest of his life, even through his presidency, when he often visited the White House.

Some nonmedical biographers have made medical diagnoses of Lincoln's illness. Sandburg and Angle (1932) have offered the plausible explanation that it was probably brought on by poor food, exposure to bad weather and overwork. Ruth Painter Randall (1953) has added the suggestion of "flu," and sensitiveness and discouragement over opposition by the Edwards family to Mary Todd's marriage to him because of his origin, poverty, and lack of culture. Such opinions do not account for the logic of his idea-emotional reactions to his social situations relative to his physical symptoms, as is necessary in modern medical practice.

My Diagnosis of Lincoln's Neurosis

We cannot believe that a man of Lincoln's age, experience, intelligence, and understanding of human nature, however sensitive he might have been about the moral inferiority of his mother's family, would have let the cool notions of Mary's proud relatives crush him. Neither would Mary, with her independence of mind, have listened to her sister if she really loved him.

Lincoln's work at that time was neither excessive nor frustrated. He was living comfortably in Springfield, made no complaint about the food, was attending the legislature, had been reelected, had helped impressively as the state leader of the Whigs in electing William Henry Harrison president of the United States, and was quite sure of his law partner's reelection to Congress.

Real hypochondriasis is a persistent functional malady of obscure origin in an apparently weak nervous system, characterized by endless self-pity, weakness of will power and endless self-conscious preoccupation over miserable feelings of weakness of heart, lungs, stomach, and intestines, causing fear of being unable to continue to live. This psychophysiological condition tends to continue for years and is very difficult to cure after it is once established. Because of the manner of onset of Lincoln's "hypo" over his engagement to Mary Owens and again over his engagement to Mary Todd, and the way he recovered each time, I think he did not have real hypochondriasis. He had repetitions of anxiety neurosis producing similar miserable feelings, but of temporary duration and quick recovery.

Lincoln had to fight constantly against the repetitive nervous tendency, when alone too long, to lapse into a lower egoistic state of gloomy, dull, regressive, nostalgic distraction. Observations, expressed in various ways, by himself to his friends and to Dr. Henry, and by his contemporaries in law, and when President by members of his Cabinet, on such lapsing of mental integrity and quick recovery, will, from now on, become increasingly impressive. This nervous pathology and its effects upon his mind was produced, it seems, by two sets of functionally interactive factors—an injury of his brain in childhood leaving him with an overly sensitive nervous system, diplopia, tendency to develop anxiety, headache, and gastric nausea, indigestion and constipation, upon egoistic humiliation, emotional conflicts and fatigue; and his repressed, idealized love fixation on the memories of two people, his mother and Ann Rutledge.

Lincoln's attacks of anxiety neurosis were characteristically attended by a regressive form of depression and were produced by particular kinds of moral frustration and humiliation of self-respect with feelings of egoistic disgrace and public dishonor. Then followed quickly recovery of self-respect upon making an understanding self-analysis of his attitude and situation. This unusually active sensitivity, instability and resiliency was probably augmented by the partial destruction of the left frontal lobe of his brain. In this lobe in a right-handed person is normally integrated the highest level of the self-conscious ego and its volitional control of emotional reactions, towards directing thought and action in space and time so as to acquire social admiration and approval of rightwayness and success and avoid disapproval of wrongwayness and failure. In compensation for the left frontal lobe deficiency a new system of higher egoistic integrations is developed in the right frontal lobe. Such crossing of reintegrations after left frontal injury are not as automatically stable as normal and need to be kept activated by acquiring the right kinds of repetitive social sympathetic encouragements. Lincoln needed to work more than a normal man so that he could see himself and think of himself as being morally honorable and personally desirable, and not see himself, and think of himself, as being disgraced or accused of dishonesty or rejected as undesirable, in order to enjoy self-respect. By cultivating an extremely conscientious attitude of wanting "in all cases to do right, particularly in all cases with women" and restless ambition to achieve superior political distinction, he was inclined to make his overly sensitive nervous system undergo stress, frequently to the limit of endurance.

In serving the equalitarian rights of mankind with moral conviction, he functioned comfortably as long as he was able to see his way clearly and justifiably through frustrations and oppositions to win goals that reflected credit upon himself. When he became involved in any kind of personal obligation, as with Mary Owens and Mary Todd, or as a lawyer in representing a case that developed involvements that he could not honestly support, he grew excessively worried and developed miserable anxiety until he found a way of correcting his obligations and honorably withdrawing from the situation. Naturally his chosen fields of work, as legislator, politician and lawyer, exposed him repeatedly to the limit of endurance as his ambitions forced him to take on ever greater commitments. He learned to protect himself against himself, through intentionally cultivating a kindly, tolerant, good-humored common-sense understanding of human nature and human relations. He loved particularly to debunk unfounded claims and pretensions, by judiciously applying a logical series of analytical questions and clever metaphors that exposed their absurdities. The people loved him for this healthy social service in reequilibrating their own egos, even as they did Will Rogers 100 years later.

It is quite probable that during the augmented phase of Lincoln's attack in January 1841, which lasted about a week, he was too agitated and unreasonable about himself to be able to work, but never irrational and delusional about his personal relations. He always knew why he was in a state of moral conflict and regret over the way he had contributed to breaking his engagement, and never lost insight nor tried to repress it by lying to himself and making himself believe anything but the precious truth. (See his advice later to Speed on this.) His "irrepressible desire," despite his deeply distressing feelings, was to recover a resolute, normally composed state of mind and make the world a little better for his having lived in it. The feebleness of will power as expressed in his letters to Stuart has been regarded as being characteristic of hypochondriasis in a broken nervous constitution, but real hypochondriasis would have almost certainly destined him to have a permanently weak, indecisive mind. However, Lincoln's remarkable resiliency and recoverability and power to work shows that he did not have a genetically weak or broken nervous constitution but a melancholic disposition as the result of an organic deficiency following an old cerebral injury in a constitutionally strong nervous system.

Contemporary Impressions of Lincoln's Illness

That Lincoln's "discreditable exhibition" of himself was the subject of common gossip in Springfield is indicated by several references in contemporary letters. The following comment, January 22, by Martin McKee to John J. Hardin—"We have been very much distressed, on Mr. Lincoln's account; hearing that he had two Cat fits and a Duck fit since we left"— shows how some people regarded him.

J. C. Conkling, contemporary lawyer and political opponent, wrote a letter of sarcastic gloating over Lincoln's distress and Speed's leaving, on January 24 to Mercy Levering:

> "Poor L! how are the mighty fallen! He was confined about a week, but though he now appears again he is reduced and emaciated in appearance and seems scarcely to possess strength enough to speak above a whisper. His case at present is truly deplorable but what prospects there may be for ultimate relief I cannot pretend to say. I doubt not but he can declare 'That loving is a painful thrill, And not to love more painful still' but would not like to intimate that he has experienced 'That surely 'tis the worst of pain, To love and not be loved again.'
> "And Joshua [Speed] too is about to leave. I do not know what dreadful blow may be inflicted upon the interests of our State by his departure. But having taken a very prominent part in the last political canvass I really fear that great convulsions and tumult will follow for want of his superintending care and protection."

Miss Levering's reply from Baltimore to Conkling of February 7, 1841 shows that she had also communicated with other people in Springfield about Lincoln's illness and it was her opinion as well as Conkling's that he had been jilted by Mary: "Yesterday I wrote a long letter to Bri- in answer to her particulars. . . . Poor A—I fear his is a blighted heart! perhaps if he was as persevering as Mr. W— [E. B. Webb] he might finally be successful."

It seems that Miss Levering believed Lincoln had timidly let himself be defeated by Webb. A letter written by Mary (to be presented in chronological order) indicates that for a time she was inclined to consider Webb as well as Lincoln and Douglas for a husband.

Lincoln's Resiliency

It is not surprising that Lincoln's intimate friends referred to his self-pitying anxiety as "cat fits." He was obviously inclined, when depressed, to exhibit his distress, with little restraint, to the whole human family.

On January 25, 1841, Lincoln addressed the legislature in support of a bill and amendment to provide payment for work on the State House. An opposing member had objected to completing the construction because of the high cost of unsatisfactory living accomodations in Springfield. Lincoln humorously chided him: "If the gentleman from Fulton thought he was paying too high for his bread and meat let him go home and invite his constituents to come over and set up a competition in this line of business."

Lincoln had, it seems, fairly recovered by the 25th, as his record in the legislature shows. On February 5 he declared himself, in a letter to Stuart, as being in favor of having their mutual friend, E.B. Webb, appointed a district attorney. "I really have my heart set upon Webb's appointment to the place," he said, but not a word about his own health.

On February 5 he also wrote a vigorous circular letter against subordinating the Judiciary to the political tricks of the Legislature. If the independence of the Judiciary is dominated "our rights of property and liberty of conscience can no longer be regarded as safe from the encroachments of unconstitutional legislation."

On February 26, in a clash of wits before the Legislature, Lincoln showed that he had regained his ability to think quickly with effective repartee. He had offered an amendment allowing the state to pay its debts for labor with a three million dollar issue of bonds. Mr. Kitchell (from Montgomery County), objecting to increasing the debts of the state, said Lincoln's policy reminded him of the story of a drunkard who fell insensible from indulging to excess and would not be aroused until they offered him more toddy. To this ridicule Lincoln replied immediately that the argument of the gentleman from Montgomery reminded him of an eccentric old bachelor who lived in the Hoosier State. He was famous for seeing *big bugaboos* in everything and lived on a farm with his brother. One day he went squirrel hunting and fired so many shots into the top of a tree near the house that his brother went out to ask what he was shooting at. "He replied a squirrel—and kept on firing. His brother believing there was some humbug about the matter examined his person, and saw on one of his eye lashes a *big louse* crawling about. It is so with the gentleman from Montgomery. He imagined he could see squirrels every day, when there were nothing but *lice*." The House was convulsed with laughter.

J.C. Conkling, in a letter of March 7 to Miss Levering, took delight in contrasting the differences in the reactions of Miss Todd and Lincoln to their broken engagement. He described well the superiority of integration of the egoistic attitude of the rejector and the miserable inferiority of the rejected:

> "The Legislature have dispersed. Whether any persons regret it I cannot pretend to say. Miss Todd and her cousin Miss Edwards seemed to form the grand centre of attraction. Swarms of strangers who had little else to engage their attention hovered around them, to catch a *passing smile*. By the way, I do not think they were received, with even ordinary attention, if they did not obtain a *broad grin* or an *obstreperous laugh*. And L, poor hapless simple swain who loved most true but was not loved again—I suppose he will now endeavor to drown his cares among the intricacies and perplexities of the law. No more will the merry peal of laughter ascend *high in the air,* to greet his listening and delighted ears. He used to remind me sometimes of the pictures . . . of old Father Jupiter, bending down from the clouds, to see what was going on below. As an agreeable smile of satisfaction graced the countenance of the old heathen god, as he perceived the incense rising up—so the face of L. was occasionally distorted into a grin as he succeeded in eliciting applause from some of the fair votaries by whom he was surrounded. But alas! I fear his shrine will now be deserted and that he will withdraw himself from the society of us inferior mortals."

Logan and Lincoln, Attorneys

Lincoln decided in April, 1841 that his health had improved sufficiently for him to remain in Springfield but he would end his partnership with Stuart and accept Logan's invitation to establish a new firm. The change from socially prominent, easy-going Congressman Stuart to hard, analytical, thorough-going Judge S.T. Logan proved of the utmost practical importance for Lincoln. Logan was then known as the greatest *nisi prius* lawyer in Illinois. Ten years older than Lincoln, small, thin, wiry of stature, large of head, weazened of face and weak of voice, lover of fact and intolerant of fancy, vast of memory, methodical in preparation, and endlessly logical in calculation, he was a remarkable teacher of young lawyers. Four became United States Senators, three state Governors and one President.

Logan and Lincoln belonged to the same political party and had served together in several law suits. As Logan's competitor Lincoln had won the last three trials. On oratory and pleading before judge and jury he was developing masterful skill, but in preparation of evidence for or against his client he was still poorly trained, slipshod, careless, haphazard and sentimental. Logan and Lincoln made a magnificent team that soon impressed the legal profession of the state. This choice of partner no doubt greatly impressed the practical Edwards family, for Logan's thorough-going way of doing business was their way.

Logan has given his estimation of Lincoln as a young lawyer: his "knowledge of law was very small when I took him in. I don't think he studied very much. I think he learned his law more in the study of cases. He would work hard and learn all there was in a case he had in hand. He got to be a pretty good lawyer though his general knowledge of law was never very formidable. . . . After a while he began to pick up a considerable ambition in law. He didn't have confidence enough at first.

"Both he and Baker were exceedingly useful to me in getting the good will of juries. Lincoln seemed to put himself at once on equality with everybody—never of course while they were outrageous, never while they were drunk or noisy. . . .

"Lincoln was growing all the time, from the time I first knew him. . . . before he left this country he got to be quite a formidable lawyer.

"But he had one peculiarity: he couldn't fight in a bad case.

"So far as his reading knowledge of law went he had a quite unusual grasp of the principles involved. When he was with me, I have seen him get a case and seem bewildered at first, but he would go at it and after a while he would master it. He was very tenacious in his grasp of a thing that he once got hold of." (Herndon, 1889)

Wins First Murder Trial

In a letter to Joshua Speed of June 19, 1841, Lincoln gave a humor-ously dramatic description of a murder trial that created "the highest state of excitement here for a week past that our community has ever witnessed." It was in regard to the sudden disappearance without trace of an epileptic man, the people's apprehension that he had been murdered by three brothers of low reputation, the excited search for the body and failure to find it, the prosecutor's charge of murder against the brothers, their trial, and how he with Logan and Baker, as lawyers for the defense, saved them from hanging through obtaining the testimony of "an old man from Warren called Doctor Gilmore," who said he saw and treated the victim the day after he was supposed to have been murdered.

"When the doctor's story was first made public," Lincoln commented, "it was amusing to scan and contemplate the countenances, and hear the remarks of those who had been actively engaged in search of the dead body. Some looked quizzical, some melancholy and some furiously angry. Porter, who had been very active, swore he always knew the man was dead . . . looked most awfully wo-begone; he seemed to be the '*wictim of hunrequited haffection'* as represented in the comic almanac we used to laugh over; and Hart the little drayman that hauled Molly [Mary Todd] home once, said it was too damned bad to have so much trouble and no hanging at all."

The case was dismissed on Dr. Gilmore's testimony. Three years later Lincoln published it as a mystery story. His joke about the "wictim of hunrequited haffections" that he and Speed used to laugh over and his incidental mention of "Molly" indicate that he had taken a philosophical view of his past experiences with her and was not interested in resuming affectionate relations.

The letter closes with "I stick to my promise to come to Louisville," which is evidence that Speed did not take Lincoln with him in March in order to relieve his melancholy, as Herndon (1889) reported. Lincoln largely managed his own recovery as he did his education, through carefully thinking and talking out his needs and motivations in relation to the opportunities and frustrations of his situations.

Mary Todd's Regrets

Mary Todd's letter of June 18, 1841 to Mercy Levering repeats her usual expressions of intimate affection for her:

"When I reflect my own dear Merce, that months of change have passed by since I last wrote you, and that your letters during that time have been far, very far more unfrequent than I could have desired, these circumstances would lead an *unknowing one* to imagine that time had wrought its changes upon us, and lessened the love which I feel has ever been ours towards each other. . . . I have been much alone of late and my thoughts have oft been with thee. . . . Were you aware of the delight given by hearing from you, dearest Merce, surely you would more frequently cheer my sad spirit.—The last two or three months have been of *interminable* length. After my gay companions of last winter departed, I was left much to the solitude of my own thoughts, and some *lingering regrets* over the past, which time can alone overshadow with its healing balm. Thus has my *spring time* been passed. . . . I have much to tell you, of all that is daily occurring around us, that I scarcely know where the narrative shall commence. . . . The June Court is in session. . . . We have an unusual number of agreeable visitors, some pleasant acquaintances of last winter, but in their midst the *winning widower* [E.B. Webb] *is not. Rumor* says he with some others will attend the Supreme Court next month. In your last, you appeared impressed with the prevalent idea that we were *dearer* to each other than friends. The idea was neither new nor strange, dear Merce, the knowing world, have coupled our names together for months past, merely through the folly & belief of another, who strangely imagined we were attached to each other. In your friendly & confiding ear allow me to whisper that my *heart can never be his.* I have deeply regretted that his constant visits, attentions &c should have given room for remarks, which were to me unpleasant. There being a slight difference of some eighteen or twenty summers in our years, would preclude all possibility of congeniality of feeling, without which I should never feel justifiable in resigning my happiness into the safe keeping of another, even should that other be, far too worthy for me, with his two sweet little objections" [children].

Mary's remark that her name had been connected with Webb through 'the folly and belief of another who strangely imagined we were attached to each other' is generally accepted as referring to Lincoln. It is interpreted as meaning that she "deeply regretted" having offended him by accepting Webb's constant visits. Lincoln may have given some such impression, but he and Webb were very good friends as lawyers and political affiliates. The manner of Lincoln's recommendation, only a few weeks after the first of January, of Webb for district attorney—"I really have my heart set on Webb's appointment to the place"—indicates that he had not been jealous of him, who was inferior in ability, as a rival for Mary's affections.

It seems more likely that Lincoln did not let himself break down in self-respect so far as to reveal his egoistic jealousy of Douglas, who had humiliated him in debate and politics and then in love by winning Mary's admiration of his great abilities and instinctive enjoyment of his gay attentions.

Mary continued significantly:

> "Mr. Speed, our former most constant guest has been in Kentucky some weeks past, will be here next month, on a visit *perhaps, . . .* He takes a friend's privilege, of occasionally favouring me with a letter, in his last he spoke of his great desire of once more inhabiting this region & of his possibility of returning.—*His* worthy friend, deems me unworthy of notice, as I have not met *him* in the gay world for months. With the usual comfort of misery, imagine that others were as seldom gladdened by his presence as my humble self, yet I would that the case were different, that he would once more resume his station in Society, that 'Richard should be himself again,' much, much happiness would it afford me."

Evidently Mary was regretting the way in which she had offended Lincoln's self-respect, after she decided that Webb was too old and Douglas no longer courted her. After brief mention of the doings of several mutual friends, she confided revealingly to Mercy on an "interesting genleman:

> "Mr. Trumbull, is Secretary of State in lieu of *Judge Douglass,* who has been rapidly promoted to office [as a judge of the State Supreme Court]. . . . I feel much disposed to lay in my *claims,* as he is talented & agreeable & sometimes *countenances* me."

Mary continued to prospect for the admiration of beaus but none could compare with Douglas in impressiveness as a politician and statesman, even though she seems to have given up hope of getting him for a husband.

Love Trials of Two Bachelors

The brotherly love of Lincoln and Speed for each other was mutually deep and dependent. It lasted, though weakened in time after their marriages through differences of opinion on slavery. Lincoln visited Speed's family on their Kentucky plantation, Farmington, from early August to mid-September of 1841. He formed delightful friendships with Joshua's mother and half sister, Mary, and his fiancée, Miss Fanny Henning.

During Lincoln's engagement to Mary Todd, and Speed's engagement to Fanny Henning, each man experienced a severe anxiety neurosis with miserable self-doubts and "horrible" feelings, the nature of which were described by Lincoln in his letters to Speed and Speed's letter (11, 30, 66) to Herndon. They contain the most intimate revelations of Lincoln's personality known, and must be read closely in order to understand how his vacillating neurotic disposition affected his thinking and how he continued to improve his common-sense self-analysis to better understand and control his conflicting involitional motivations.

Speed described their neurotic mutually sympathetic involvements. He said:

> "In the summer of 1841, I became engaged to my wife. He was here on a visit when I courted her—and strange to say something of the same feeling which I regarded as so foolish in him—took possession of me and kept me very unhappy from the time of my engagement until I married. This will explain the deep interest he manifested in his letters on my account."

Speed knew that Lincoln had been more deeply interested in Mary Todd than any other living woman, and would have loved, honored and married her had she respectfully honored his self-respect during their engagement. He still believed, even so, that Mary and Lincoln were well suited to each other and wanted to see them married. Upon Lincoln's visit to Louisville Speed learned that he was much improved in health but still unhappy over the way he had managed his affair with Mary. Taking upon himself the delicate task of acting as love's emissary Speed tactfully began to let each know that the other still regretted, under the crust of egotistical pride, having offended the other's self-respect.

Lincoln knew that Speed loved dark-eyed, sweetly sad Fanny Henning far more than any other of the dozens of women he had charmed, even though he was neurotically lacking conviction that he loved her enough to marry her. Lincoln, greatly admiring Fanny and believing that she was the right girl for his friend, applied sympathetic suggestion to reassure him of his love with all the skill of a professional psychotherapist. His letters to Joshua and to Mary Speed reveal true self-insight, as well as understanding other people's difficulties with conflicting emotional impulses, gained through analyzing himself and the practice of inducing moral and legal compromises.

Tender Regard for Adolescence

The Speeds were aristocratic slave holders living in a slave state and Lincoln saw here evidence of the beneficient relations that were maintained in better Southern families between masters and slaves. Soon after his return to Illinois he wrote a letter (9, 27, 1841) to Mary Speed in appreciation of the family's hospitality. It shows that he gave much time and thought to understanding persons of all ages as individuals, as well as the different ways of people in their group relations as free men and slaves. His interest in the interpersonal relations of families was unusually sympathetic and understanding.

"My Friend:
    Having resolved to write to some of your mother's family, and not having the express permission of any one of them [to] do so, I have had some little difficulty in determining on which to inflict the task of reading what I now feel must be a most dull and silly letter; but when I remembered you and I were something of cronies while I was at Farmington, and that, while there, I once was under the necessity of shutting you up in a room to prevent your committing an assault and battery upon me, I instantly decided you should be the devoted one. . . .

    "You remember there was some uneasiness about Joshua's health when we left. That little indisposition of his turned out to be nothing serious; and it was pretty nearly forgotten when we reached Springfield. We got on board the Steam Boat Lebanon, in the locks of the canal about 12 o'clock, M. of the day we left, and reached St. Louis the next monday at 8 P.M. Nothing of interest happened during the passage, except vexatious delays occasioned by the sand bars be thought interesting.

    "By the way, a fine example was presented on board the boat for contemplating the effect of *condition* upon human happiness. A gentleman had purchased twelve negroes in different parts of Kentucky and was taking them to a farm in the South. They were chained six and six together. A small iron clevis was around the left wrist of each, and this fastened to the main chain by a shorter one at convenient distance from, the others; so that the negroes were strung together precisely like so many fish on a trot-line. In this condition they were being separated forever from the scenes of their childhood, their friends, their fathers and mothers, and brothers and sisters, and many of them, from their wives and children, and going into perpetual slavery where the lash of the master is proverbially more ruthless and unrelenting than any other where; and yet amid all these distressing circumstances, as we would think them, they were the most cheerful and apparently happy creatures on board. One, whose offense for which he had been sold was an over-fondness for his wife, played the fiddle almost continually; and the others danced, sung, cracked jokes, and played various games with cards from day to day. How true it is that 'God tempers the wind to the shorn lamb,' or in other words, that He renders the worst of human conditions tolerable, while He permits the best, to be nothing better than tolerable. [In another letter written to Speed many years later, when slavery had become a furious political issue, Lincoln spoke of the distress that he had experienced over thinking about the fate of these slaves.]
    . . ."Do you remember my going to the city while I was in Kentucky, to have a tooth extracted, and making a failure of it? Well, that same old tooth got to paining me so much, that about a week since I had it torn out, bringing with it a bit of the jawbone; the consequence of which is that my mouth is so sore that I can neither talk, nor eat, I am literally 'subsisting

on savoury remembrances'—that is, being unable to eat, I am living upon the remembrance of the delicious dishes of peaches and cream we used to have at your house. . . .

"Tell your mother that I have not got her 'present' [Oxford Bible] with me; but I intend to read it regularly when I return home. I doubt not that it is really, as she says, the best cure for the 'Blues' could one but take it according to the truth."

His letter closed with a sympathetic comment on Miss Fanny Henning's tendency to melancholy as a "misfortune and not a fault," and the offering of his regards to each member of the family individually, from baby to mother, in a manner that fitted each one. This letter reveals the extraordinary tenderness of sympathetic understanding Lincoln had for the feelings of people, young, adult, and old.

Psychotherapeutic Advice to Speed

Speed had returned with Lincoln to Springfield in September 1841 to settle old business accounts and remained until January 3, 1842, when he started back to Louisville. Greatly concerned over the indecisive state of mind of his friend, whether or not to marry Fanny Henning, Lincoln wrote the following letter with obviously studied care, before Speed's departure. He gave it to him just before leaving, expressly with the idea that he would read it carefully when alone on the boat. It is perhaps one of the most considerately thought out psychologically analytical letters that Lincoln ever wrote. My discussion of significant parts is inserted in brackets. The italics are Lincoln's.

"My dear Speed: Feeling as you know I do, the deepest solicitude for the success of the enterprise you are engaged in, I adopt this as the last method I can invent to aid you, in case (which God forbid) you shall need any aid. I do not place what I am going to say on paper, because I can say it any better in that way than I could by word of mouth, but because, were I to say it orrally, before we part, most likely you would forget it at the verry time when it might do some good. As I think it reasonable that you will feel verry badly some time between this and the final consummation of your purpose, it is intended that you shall read this just at such a time.

"Why I say it is reasonable that you will feel verry badly yet, is, because of *three special causes,* added to the *general one* which I shall mention.

"The general cause is, that you are *naturally of a nervous temperament;* and this I say from what I have seen of you personally, and what you have told me concerning your mother at various times, and concerning your brother William at the time his wife died.

"The first special cause is, your *exposure to bad weather* on your journey, which my experience clearly proves to be verry severe on defective nerves." [This is the first definite evidence from Lincoln that excessive stress of weather aggravated his nervous instability and that he thought his own nervous system was somehow defective. See J. Hill's observation of the depressive effect of a rain storm on Lincoln in Chapter VIII, following the death of Ann Rutledge.]

"The second is, *the absence of all business and conversation of* friends, which might divert your mind, and give it occasional rest from that *intensity* of thought, which will some times wear the sweetest idea thread-bare and turn it into the bitterness of death." [Lincoln sought witty conversation with friends in order to keep his own melancholy thoughts from becoming too intense.]

"The third is, *the rapid and near approach of that crisis on which all your thoughts and feelings concentrate.*" [It was Lincoln's experience that, as the day of marriage approached, his self-doubtful thoughts and involitional aversions grew unbearably intense.]

"If from all these causes you shall escape and go through triumphantly, without another 'twinge of the soul,' I shall be most happily, but most egregiously deceived." [Herein Lincoln showed analytical sense of the recurrence of obsessive feelings and ideas.]

"If, on the contrary, you shall, as I expect you will at some time be agonized and distressed, let me, who have some reason to speak with judgment on such a subject, beseech you, to ascribe it to the causes I have mentioned; and not to some false and ruinous suggestion of the Devil." [Lincoln's determination to hold on the real causes of his emotional neurosis and not let himself adopt some self-excusing delusion preserved the clarity of his mind.]

" 'But' you will say 'do not your causes apply to everyone engaged in a like undertaking?'

"By no means. *The particular causes,* to a greater or lesser extent, perhaps do apply in all cases; but the *general one,* nervous debility, which is the key and conductor of all the particular ones, and without which *they* would be utterly harmless, though it *does* pertain to you, *does not* pertain to one in a thousand. It is out of this, that the painful difference between you and the mass of the world springs."

Lincoln's self-analysis of his own miserable experience with uncontrollable increases of nervous debility, because of undesirable repetition of horrible ideas and emotions, producing a vicious circle of excitations, led him to the sound conclusion that the physical constitution and environmental stimulation together determine the nature of a person's behavior. Speed's "nervous temperament" and love of freedom, and the binding conditions of his promise to marry Fanny, were, as Lincoln saw, the causes of his neurosis. Herein his theory of behavior has proven remarkably parallel with that of modern neurology and psychiatry. We will see furthermore in his psychotherapeutic discussions of his own and his friend's neurosis that he had worked out, over 100 years before the discoveries of modern psychopathology and psychoanalysis, its most important dynamic processes. The letter to Speed is continued:

"I know what the painful point with you is, at all times when you are unhappy. It is an apprehension that you do not love her as you should. What nonsense!—How came you to court her? Was it because you thought she desired it; and that you had given her reason to expect it? If it was for that, why did not the same reason make you court Ann Todd [Mary Todd's younger sister]; and at least twenty others of whom you can think, & to whom it would apply with greater force than to *her*? Did you court her for her wealth?

Why, you knew she had none. But you say you *reasoned* yourself *into* it. What do you mean by that? Was it not, that you found yourself unable to *reason* yourself *out of it?* Did you not think, and partly form the purpose, of courting her the first time you ever saw or heard of her? What had reason to do with it, at that early stage? There was nothing *at that time* for reason to work upon. Whether she was moral, aimiable, sensible, or even of good character, you did not, nor could not then know; except perhaps you might infer the last from the company you found her in. All you then did or could know of her, was her *personal appearance and deportment*; and these, if they impress at all, impress the *heart* and not the head.

"Say candidly, were not those heavenly *black eyes*, the whole basis of all your early *reasoning* on the subject?

"After you and I had once been at her residence, did you not go and take me all the way to Lexington and back, for no other purpose but to get to see her again, on our return, [in that] seeming to take a trip for that express object?

"What earthly consideration would you take to find her scouting and despising you, and giving herself up to another? But of this you have no apprehension; and therefore you cannot bring it home to your feelings.

"I shall be so anxious about you, that I want you to write me every mail."

Lincoln knew from experience that love begins instinctively upon first sight in reaction to the physical and personality characteristics of the prospective mate and we cannot reason ourselves out of it and do not reason ourselves into it. This sense was convincing enough for Speed but he had another cause of anxiety.

Anxiety Over Death Wish

Unfortunately we do not have Speed's reply, but Lincoln's next letter to him (2, 3, 1842) reveals further his deep concern over his friend's anxiety neurosis and his insight into the motivation of the particular obsessive thought that most harassed him in his engagement to Fanny Henning. He shows that it was the same kind of thought that had tortured himself when he was engaged to Mary Todd.

. . . "You well know that I do not feel my own sorrows much more keenly than I do yours, when I know of them; and yet I assure you I was not much hurt by what you wrote me of your excessively bad feeling at the time you wrote. Not that I am less capable of sympathising with you now than ever; not that I am less your friend than ever, but because I hope and believe, that your present anxiety and distress about *her* health and *her* life, must and will forever banish those horid doubts, which I know you sometimes felt, as to the truth of your affection for her. If they can be once and forever removed, (and I almost feel a presentiment that the Almighty has sent your present affliction expressly for that object) surely, nothing can come in their stead, to fill the immeasurable measure of misery. The death scenes of those we love, are surely painful enough; but these we are prepared to, and expect to see. They happen to all. . . . Painful as they are, they are not an unlooked-for-sorrow. Should she, as you fear, be destined to an early grave, it is indeed, a great consolation to know that she is so well prepared to meet it. Her religion, which you once disliked so much, I will venture you now prize most highly.

"But I hope your melancholy bodings as to her early death, are not well founded. I even hope, that ere this reaches you, she will have returned with improved and still improving health; and that you will have met her, and forgotten the sorrows of the past, in the enjoyment of the present.

. . . "It really appears to me that you yourself ought to rejoice, and not sorrow, at this indubitable evidence of your undying affection for her. Why Speed, if you did not love her, although you might not wish her death, you would most calmly be resigned to it. Perhaps this point is no longer a question with you, and my pertenacious dwelling upon it, is a rude intrusion upon your feelings. If so, you must pardon me. You know the Hell I have suffered on that point, and how tender I am upon it. You know I do not mean wrong.

"I have been quite clear of the hypo since you left,—even better than I was along in the fall." . . .

Speed's worry about the possibility of the premature death of Fanny because of her lack of robust health and inclination to be melancholy, Lincoln showed realistically, did not make him feel that he did not love her, since he loved her instinctively for her personal qualities and could not reason himself out of it. However, being a sensuous, nervous man, who enjoyed making amorous conquests of women, he was being harrassed by his egoistic will to be free. It became obsessive in contra-reaction to his moral ego in having bound itself to marry. When his moral ego became unable to repress his free ego's will, or reasonably accept and patiently assimilate it, "horrible thoughts" were produced of wishing Fanny's death as the way to freedom. Fear of her "early death" and belief that he did not really love her followed naturally. Such intensely conflicting emotivations, to be or not to be free, to marry or not to marry made him suffer miserably, with increasing incompetence for work, with indecision and self-doubt of his own mental integrity. As the time of marriage approached he questioned his sanity and even began to fear insanity, for lack of self-understanding.

Lincoln, an esthetically inclined student of human nature, who lived abstemiously and loved freedom and self-respect more than anything, had also been harassed by a self-liberating wish for the death of the woman he had promised to marry, greatly augmented by her promiscuous flirtations, but he realistically interpreted it as meaning that he was unable to feel that he loved her as he knew he should in order to be happy when bound to her.

Critical people, ignorant of the miserable psychodynamics of the ubiquitous, ego-liberating death wish, usually blame the person who has it for being morally weak and excessively selfish in character. The natural origin and function of the ego's wish or desire for the death of a particular person has been revealed by the attitude analysis of numerous cases of severe states of anxiety and obsessive thinking in men, women, and children, and of the use of taboos, religion, ritual, art, morals, and laws the world over, among civilized and primitive peoples as preventives and controls.

Its source exists involuntarily, automatically in the person's naturally inborn egoistic need of the pleasure of freedom of will to think, work and create in the reproductive direction in accordance with its strongest inherent biological aptitudes and abilities. Thereby it can attract a mate that it desires instinctively for particular physical and personal qualities essential to fulfil its own genetically determined biological destiny.

In order to keep from consciously thinking about the horrible death wish and its motive and objective, the moral ego must concentrate consciously upon doing the particular thing, as conditioned by the situation, that enables him to keep it repressed at subconscious or unconscious levels of mental integration. Thereby the mind becomes obsessed with a particular kind of covering phobia, habit, compulsion, belief, tic, organic tension, drug addiction etc., that must be repeated as long as the death wish repeats.

The symptoms of anxiety produced by a guilty conscience over involuntary death wishes include distressing fluctuations of rate and amplitude of cardiac contractions, ranging from slow, large, pounding beats to small, fast, weak racing with, at times, momentary pauses producing fear of imminent hear failure, suffocation and death. Weak blood pressure and difficulties with respiration generally attend extreme conditions of cardiac anxiety. Other complications often include gastrointenstinal distress with indigestion and diarrhea or constipation, loss of appetite, insomnia, feelings of dizziness with muscular weakness, and incapacity to carry on decisive work.

The wish for death of the obstructing person (mate, parent, child, sibling, business partner or rival, love rival, tyrant, ruler, or feeble dependent) is produced automatically by the egoistic organization of the self-righting reflex systems of the body, in the same way that it rights itself against gravity and works to remove or destroy other opposing forces and frustrating obstructions. The death wish is generally limited to particular ideas of getting out of a particular binding situation, through the death of the obstructing person. It may grow into extroverting actions and break its barriers by killing the obstructing person, or by introverting itself and committing self-destruction by alcoholism, drugs, accident, psychosis, or suicide.

The intensity of the death wish is relative to the degree of narcissism of the egoistic attitude and the intensity of its desires and ambitions to enjoy happiness through developing self-perfections reflected in social supremacies. Assimilation of the death wish depends upon inducing a conversion of the egoistic attitude to a more naturally tolerant, less intensely conscientious, self-sacrificing, socially cooperative, generously sharing altruistic attitude; or in legally and equitably breaking the bonds of the contract. Cure of the anxiety symptoms comes almost immediately with the disruption of the binding conditions, or through making a conversion of egoistic attitude to willing acceptance of the binding person's rights and needs, who then becomes changed in value from being an undesirable cause of the death wish to being a desirable promoter of the life wish.

Debt of Gratitude

Lincoln was a severe critic of himself, despite his neurotic disposition to pity himself at times, ever analyzing how he was successful and how he failed in carrying out his work of adjusting interpersonal relations in law and politics. His self-estimation of having been weak in character for not firmly keeping either resolution, to marry or not to marry, was morally severe. Naturally affectionate and grateful, he must continue so in order to enjoy living, but he must not become the dupe of another person's whim or will. That he carefully considered how to control such predispositions in his easy-going, careless nature is shown by the manner in which he protected his stepmother from the whims for moving of his father and her son.

Upon receiving a fee of several hundred dollars for winning a lawsuit, Lincoln bought from his parents, in October 1841, the 40 acres on which they lived in Coles County. Then, by indenture, he gave it back to them for their free use for the rest of their lives, and deeded the land to his stepbrother, John D. Johnston, provided he paid back to him, upon the death of both parents, the sum of 200 dollars. By this means Lincoln assured himself that his parents would always have a place to live, and his stepbrother, a neer-do-well, would continue to live with them and work to repay this expenditure.

Chapter XIV

TWO NEUROTIC MARRIAGES

Lincoln improved constantly in understanding the motivations of human nature through honest, fearless self-analysis of excitements of his nervousness and undesirable thoughts and feelings in reaction to particular conditions of binding or otherwise unavoidable situations. His letters to Speed show progressive reduction of "hypo" and improvement in health with improvement of ego-organization, through more consistent self-understanding. Only persons who analyze the emotional biases and antisocial compulsions of their egoistic attitudes in relation to the particular interpersonal interactions that excite them, and do not repress them from consciousness as morally guilty or socially weak, can change their attitudes and master and convert their forces naturally so as to work constructively and not destructively in the mind.

As a practical psychologist, Lincoln understood the psychotherapeutic value of consistently practising self-denial and renunciation of the unilateral interests of egotism, by cultivating the morally equitable give and take of altruism. He had successfully persuaded his dearest friend, Speed, that he really loved Fanny Henning and would be happier if he married her, which he did a few weeks after returning to Kentucky from his visit to Springfield.

On February 13, 1842, Lincoln wrote:

> "Yours of the 1st. Inst. came to hand three or four days ago. When this shall reach you, you will have been Fanny's husband several days. You know my desire to befriend you is everlasting—that I will never cease, while I know how to do anything.
>
> "But you will always hereafter, be on ground that I have never occupied, and consequently, if advice were needed, I might advise wrong.

Lincoln habitually reasoned carefully, as his counsels show, from his own experience and not wishful fantasy or theoretical conjecture. He continued:

> "I do fondly hope, however, that you will never again need any comfort from abroad. But should I be mistaken in this—should excessive pleasure still be accompanied with a painful counterpart at times, still let me urge you, as I have ever done, to remember in the depth and even the agony of despondency, that verry shortly you are to feel well again. I am now fully convinced, that you love her as ardently as you are capable of loving. Your ever being happy in her presence, and your intense anxiety about her health, if there were nothing else, would place this beyond all dispute in my mind. I incline to think it probable, that your nerves will fail you occasionally for a while; but once you get them fairly graded now, that trouble is over forever."

Herein Lincoln indicates his fears and hopes for his own future. We will see later how he solved his troublesome doubt of his love for Mary Todd by making a final resolution that settled it forever. The letter proceeds:

> "I think if I were you, in case my mind were not exactly right, I would avoid being *idle;* I would immediately engage in some business or go to make preparations for it, which would be the same thing.

It is remarkable that Lawyer Lincoln had advised from his own experience that occupation to divert attention relieves neurotic anxiety. Realization that light occupation is indispensable in modern psychiatric treatment did not develop until nearly a century later. He encourages Speed:

> "If you went through the ceremony *calmly,* or even with sufficient composure not to excite alarm in any present, you are safe, beyond question, and in two or three months, to say the most, will be the happiest of men.

Lincoln has described here his own miserable anxiety over going through the marriage ceremony and his dread of the alarm his nervousness might excite in those present, as if it had actually been his experience. This is consistent with the description by Herndon (1889) and Weik (1922), as told to them separately by Mrs. Edwards, of Lincoln's inability to appear for his marriage in her house to her sister Mary. We will see later how anxiety troubled him again when he married and how he reduced his dread of alarming witnesses as much as possible by having the ceremony quick, simple, and private. He concludes:

> "I hope with tolerable confidence, that this letter is a plaster for a place that is no longer sore. God grant it may be so. I would desire you to give my particular respects to Fanny, but perhaps you will not wish her to know you have received this, lest she desire to see it. Make her write me an answer to my last letter to her at any rate. I would set a great value upon another letter from her. Write me when you have leisure. Yours forever,
> "P.S. I have been quite a man since you left."

Speed's next letter to Lincoln seems to have said that his marriage had intensified rather than eased his anxiety and horrible thoughts, upon finding that he was unable to love his wife as ardently as he had hoped. Lincoln's advice of February 25th in answer to his friends worries shows how intimately he understood him and how he used the force of their mutual sympathetic transference with hypnotic specificity to induce him to feel happily contented with having married Fanny:

> "I opened the letter, with intense anxiety and trepidation—so much, that although it turned out better than expected, I have hardly yet, at the distance of ten hours, become calm.
> "I tell you, Speed, our *forbodings*, for which you and I are rather peculiar, are all the worst sort of nonsense. I fancied, from the time I received your letter of saturday, that the one of wednesday was never to come; and yet it *did* come, and what is more, it is perfectly clear, both

from its *tone* and *handwriting*, that you were much *happier*, or, if you think the term preferable, *less miserable*, when you wrote *it*, than when you wrote the last one before. You had so obviously improved, at the verry time I so much feared, you would have grown worse. You say that 'something indescribably horrible and alarming still haunts you.' You will not say *that* three months from now, I will venture. When your nerves once get steady now, the whole trouble will be over forever. Nor should you become impatient at their being verry slow, in becoming steady.

It is evident from the repetitions of Lincoln's counseling that Speed's "indescribably horrible thoughts" were still being caused by involitional desire to be free and fear of the wish that his wife would die:

"Again: you say you much fear that that Elysium of which you have dreamed so much, is never to be realized. Well, if it shall not, I dare swear, it will not be the fault of her who is now your wife. I now have no doubt that it is the peculiar misfortune of both you and me, to dream dreams of Elysium far exceeding all that any thing earthly can realize. Far short of your dreams as you may be, no woman could do more to realize them, than that same black eyed Fanny. It you could but contemplate her through my imagination, it would appear ridiculous to you, that any one should for a moment think of being unhappy with her. My old Father used to have a saying that 'if you make a bad bargain, *hug* it the tighter;' and it occurs to me, that if the bargain you have just closed can possibly be a bad one, it is certainly the most pleasant one for applying that maxim to, which my fancy can, by any effort, picture.

In his eagerness to cultivate his friend's loving contemplation of his wife, Lincoln adopted the suggestive part of a surrogate lover of Fanny. His realization that their dreams of attaining Elysium through marriage were too idealistic and impractical, and therefore unwise to live by, seems to have greatly relieved his intentions for himself as well as for Speed. His surprising application of his father's advice, who was still living, 'to hug a bad bargain all the tighter' certainly indicates that he was now prepared to become more tolerant of Mary Todd's irrepressible vanities. He concludes:

"I write another letter enclosing this, which you can show her [Fanny], if she desires it. I do this, because she would think strangely perhaps should you tell her that you receive no letters from me; or, telling her you do, should refuse to let her see them.

"I close this, entertaining the confident hope, that every successive letter I shall have from you, (which I pray may not be few, nor far between) may show you possessing a more steady hand, and cheerful heart, than the last preceding it."

Realizing that Speed must conceal the cause of his nervousness from Fanny, Lincoln enclosed the following letter. It shows extraordinary consideration of her feelings and contains a significant statement of his own great need of friendship:

"Yours of the 16th. Inst. announcing that Miss Fanny and you are 'no more twain, but one flesh' reached me this morning. I have no way of telling how much happiness I wish you both . . . . I feel som[e]what jealous of both of you now; you will be so exclusively concerned for one another, that I shall be forgotten entirely. . . .

"I regret to learn that you have resolved not to return to Illinois. Shall be verry lonesome without you. How miserably things seem to be arranged in this world. If we have no friends, we have no pleasure; and if we have them, we are sure to lose them, and be doubly pained by the loss. I did hope she and you would make your home here; but I own I have no right to insist. You owe obligations to her, ten thousand times more sacred than any you can owe to others; and, in that light let them be respected and observed." . . .

Lincoln's Continued Unhappiness over Mary Todd's Unhappiness

Speed had written that he was growing happier as he accepted his marriage to Fanny. In his letter to Speed of March 27, Lincoln expressed his great pleasure at this change of feeling and spoke of Mary Todd affectionately for the first time since the disruption of their plans to marry. The comments of this revealing letter are followed by my interpretations of psychodynamic meaning:

"Yours of the 10th. Inst. was received three or four days since. You know I am sincere, when I tell you, the pleasure its contents gave me was and is inexpressible. As to your farm matter, I have no sympathy with you. *I* have no farm, nor ever expect to have; and, consequently, have not studied the subject enough to be much interested with it. . . .

"But on that other subject, to me of the most intense interest, whether in joy or sorrow, I never had the power to withhold my sympathy from you. It can not be told, how it now thrills me with joy, to hear you say you are *'far happier than you ever expected to be.'* That much I know is enough. I know you too well to suppose your expectations were not, at least sometimes, extravagent; and if the reality exceeds them all, I say, enough dear Lord. I am not going beyond the truth, when I tell you, that the short space it took me to read your last letter, gave me more pleasure, than the total sum of all I have enjoyed since that fatal first of Jany. '41."

Most biographers hold that January 1st was the day either Lincoln or Mary Todd broke their engagement, or, according to Mrs. Edwards' account to Herndon, Lincoln failed to appear for his wedding. As previously noted, Speed sold his store on that day, with the purpose of returning to Kentucky, and it is now evident that both men were so intimately dependent on each other for sympathetic advice and encouragement about marriage that it produced an augmenting emotional shock for Lincoln, already bitterly harassed by his inability to decide with finality whether or not to marry, that started his nervous breakdown on that day.

"Since then, it seems to me," he continued, "I should have been entirely happy, but for the never-absent idea, that there is one still unhappy whom I have contributed to make so. That still kills my soul. I can not but reproach myself, for ever wishing to be happy while she is otherwise. She accompanied a large party on the Rail Road cars, to Jacksonville last Monday and on her return, spoke, so that I heard of it, of having enjoyed the trip exceedingly. God be praised for that.

Lincoln's self-reproach for enjoying his freedom while Mary Todd remained unhappy evidently continued from the time of breaking their engagement, and was to become naturally the basis for somehow making her happy again. It reminds us of how he once pleaded with Mary Owens. The letter said:

"You know with what sleepless vigilance I have watched you, ever since the commencement of your affair; and altho' I am now almost confident it is useless, I can not forbear once more to say that I think it is even possible for your spirits to flag down and leave you miserable. If they should, don't fail to remember that they can not long remain so."

The faith that he would always recover the happiness of will to work after a period of gloom, enabled Lincoln to carry on through each attack. He added:

"One thing I can tell you which I know you will be glad to hear; and that is, that I have seen Sarah, and scrutinized her feelings as well as I could, and am fully convinced, she is far happier now, than she has been in the last fifteen months past."

As told in a previous chapter Lincoln had courted Sarah Rickard in the summer of 1840 and proposed marriage to her and then quit her and courted Mary Todd. The context of the immediately preceding paragraphs about the transitory nature of depressions in relation to his conscientious regret of having made Mary unhappy seems to have reminded him also of Sarah as another courting for which he had some regret.

The letter then asked Speed and Fanny to read his speech on temperance and discussed several matters of business interest to Speed, and closed with a charming expression of tender affection for Fanny:

"The sweet violet you enclosed, came safely to hand, but it was so dry, and mashed so fla[t,] that it crumbled to dust at the first attempt to handle it. The juice that mashed out of it, stained a [place] on the letter, which I mean to preserve and ch[erish] for the sake of her who procured it to be se[nt.]"

The often repeated statement that Lincoln was unsympathetic, cold, and too abstractly withdrawn and calculating to form close personal friendships is obviously not only untrue, but the direct opposite of his real nature.

Temperance Address

Lincoln's speech on temperance of February 22, 1842, before the Springfield Washington Temperance Society in the Second Presbyterian Church, as published in the *Sangamo Journal*, has been long ignored as of little importance by most biographers. This is one of his most important statements giving evidence on the development of his philosophy of human relations. He regarded this paper highly as an expression of his understanding of human nature. The following excerpts are selected particularly in this regard, without noting many of the picturesque metaphors that he still liked, under appropriate circumstances, to shower upon his audience. In order to appreciate the soundness of his common-sense analysis of the causes and treatment of intemperance, we must compare it with the modern medical concepts of the physiology, psychopathology, and psychotherapy of alcoholism as a disease.

Each person has a limited, genetically determined and habitually acquired degree of metabolic capacity to assimilate alcoholic drinks without becoming so intoxicated as to lose control of his mental and bodily functions. This metabolic capacity differs also for each person according to his physical and mental state at a particular time. Whereas some people are able to consume relatively large quantities of alcohol, others are so allergic as to become intoxicated by one drink. Whereas most persons have the will power to limit the intake to feeling pleasant without having more desire, others crave it more intensely as they drink more. While most persons do not like to relieve emotional frustrations, conflicts or elations with alcohol, those who crave it tend to drink more in such mental states. Alcoholic craving is frustrating and confusing to mental integrity, and its indulgence tends to become progressive toward establishing physical deterioration and mental helplessness.

Frustrated, introverted, self-pitying jealousy is the most pernicious cause of self-destructive alcoholism or other drug addiction, as a slow, insidious form of suicide. Jealousy of a loved person involves a form of hate that is aroused when one thinks that person loves another more. Jealousy then either extroverts and works to punish the loved person and/or the rival, or it introverts and works self-destructively to punish those he loves who are dependent upon him for constructive support.

The treatment of this dangerously diseased, self-pitying egoistic state the nature of his antisocial depravity, and give him kindly persuasive supporting suggestion but never moral advice. The latter implies superior social egoistic self-satisfaction and is instinctively offensive to inferior social egoistic weakness. With these points in mind we can better appreciate the deep realism of Lincoln's analysis of the insidious depressive causes of intemperance and its sympathetic treatment; and see how it was a logical application, although he was an abstainer, of his method of treating his own melancholic neurosis.

of mind rests in cultivating a mutually sympathetic transference with
some person for whom he has the deepest respect and confidence for
mental integrity and wisdom of understanding, in order to recall freely
and analyze confidentially how his self-pity and frustrated love, hate,
and jealousy work subconsciously as well as consciously. The recon-
structive influence of this friend depends upon his ability to be sympathetically understanding of the alcoholic person's debility, whatever

It is clear that he spoke earnestly from the depths of his own personal experience. He had recently recovered from an attack of melancholic regression in which he had allowed his offended feelings to
introvert to the degree of self-pity, that is, "retreat within himself,"
until they had to be relieved by making a mutual sympathetic transference with a respected, trusted friend. He had learned from his own
miserable experience, as have many other wise men, that the friendly
influence of confidential sympathetic persuasion is an effective means
of treating mental depression and loneliness from any cause, including
alcoholism or any other illness:

> "Although the Temperance cause has been in progress for near twenty
> years, it is apparent to all, that it is, *just now*, being crowned with a
> degree of success, hitherto unparalled. . . .
>
> "For this new and splendid success, we heartily rejoice. That that suc-
> cess is so much greater *now* than *heretofore*, is doubtless owing to
> rational causes; and if we would have it to continue, we shall do well to
> enquire what those causes are. The warfare heretofore waged against the
> demon of Intemperance, has, some how or other, been erroneous. Either
> the champions engaged, or the tactics they adopted, have not been the
> most proper. These champions for the most part, have been Preachers,
> Lawyers, and hired agents. Between these and the mass of mankind, there
> is a want of *approachability,* if the term be admissible, partially at
> least, fatal to their success. They are supposed to have no sympathy of
> feeling or interest, with those very persons whom it is their object to con-
> vince and persuade. . . .
>
> . . . "But when one, who has long been known as a victim of intem-
> perance, bursts the fetters that have bound him, and appears before his
> neighbors 'clothed and in his right mind,' a redeemed specimen of long
> lost humanity, and stands up with tears of joy trembling in eyes, to tell
> of the miseries *once* endured, and now to be endured no more forever;
> of his once naked and starving children, now clad and fed comfortably;
> or a wife long weighed down with woe, . . . now restored to health,
> happiness, and renewed affection; and how easily it is all done, once it
> is resolved to be done; however simple his language, there is a logic, and
> an eloquence in it, that few, with human feelings, can resist. . . . his
> sincerity [cannot] in any way be doubted; or his sympathy for those he
> would persuade to imitate his example, be denied.
>
> "In my judgment, it is to the battles of this new class of champions
> that our late success is greatly, perhaps chiefly, owing. But, had the old
> champions themselves, been of the most wise selecting, was their *system*
> of tactics, the most judicious? It seems to me, it was not. Too much

denunciation against dram sellers and dram drinkers was indulged in. This, I think, was both impolitic and unjust. It was *impolitic*, because, it is not much in the nature of man to be driven to anything; still less to be driven about that which is exclusively his own business; and least of all, where such driving is to be submitted to, at the expense of pecuniary interest, or burning appetite. When the dram-seller and drinker, were incessantly told, not in the accents of entreaty and persuasion, diffidently addressed by erring man to erring brother; but in thundering tones of anathema and denunciation, . . . it is not wonderful that they were slow, very slow, to acknowledge the truth of such denunciations, and to join the ranks of their denouncers, in a hue and cry against themselves.

. . . "When the conduct of men is designed to be influenced, *persuasion,* kind, unassuming persuasion, should ever be adopted. It is an old maxim, that a 'drop of honey catches more flies than a gallon of gall.' So with men. If you would win a man to your cause, *first* convince him that you are his sincere friend. Therein is a drop of honey that catches his heart, which, say what he will, is the great high road to his reason, and which, when once gained, you will find but little trouble in convincing his judgment of the justice of your cause, if indeed that cause really be a just one. On the contrary, assume to dictate to his judgment, or to command his action, or to mark him as one to be shunned and despised, and he will retreat within himself, close all avenues to his head and heart; and tho' your cause be naked truth itself, . . . you shall no more be able to pierce him, than to penetrate the hard shell of a tortoise with a rye straw.

"Such is man, and so *must* he be understood by those who would lead him, even to his own interest.

. . . "Denunciations against dram-sellers and dram drinkers, are *unjust* as well as impolitic. . . . The use of intoxicating drinks . . . is just as old as the world itself. . . . Physicians prescribed it in this, that, and the other disease. Government provided for it for its soldiers and sailors; and to have a rolling or raising, a husking or a hoe-down, any where without it, was *positively insufferable.*

"So too, it was everywhere a respectable article . . . like any other of the real necessaries of life."

Herein was justification of licence to sell Berry's whiskey in his store in New Salem, nearly ten years past. Universal public opinion not only tolerated, but recognized and adopted its use. He continued:

. . . "many were greatly injured by it but none seemed to think the injury arose from the *use* of a *bad thing,* but from the abuse of a *very good thing.* The victims to it were pitied and compassionated, just as now are the heirs of consumptions, and other hereditary diseases. Their failing was treated as a *misfortune,* and not a *crime* or even as a *disgrace.* . . .

"Another error, as it seems to me, into which the old reformers fell, was, the position that all habitual drunkards were utterly incorrigible, and therefore, must be turned adrift, and damned without remedy, in order that the grace of temperance might abound to the temperate *then,* and to all mankind some hundred years *thereafter.* There is in this something so repugnant to humanity, so uncharitable, so cold-blooded and feelingless, that it never did, nor ever can enlist the enthusiasm of a popular cause. We could not love the man who taught it—we could not hear him with patience. The heart could not throw open its portals to it. The generous man could not adopt it. It could not mix with his blood. It looked so fiendishly selfish, so like throwing fathers and brothers overboard, to lighten the boat for our security—that the noble minded shrank from the manifest meaness of the thing."

Lincoln's sage reflection that we can not love the man who teaches moral superiority—'the heart can not throw open its portals to him'—has the wisdom of political philosophy as well as modern psychotherapy. He saw that self-preservative economic interests dominate affection in most human relation:

. . . "Few can be induced to labor exclusively for posterity; and none will do it enthusiastically. Posterity has done nothing for us; and theorize on it as we may, practically we shall do very little for it, unless we are made to think, we are, at the same time, doing something for ourselves. What ignorance of human nature does it exhibit, to ask or expect a whole community to rise up and labor for the *temporal* happiness of *others* after *themselves* shall be consigned to the dust, a majority of which community take no pains whatever to secure their own eternal welfare, at a no greater distant day? Great distance, in either time or space, has wonderful power to lull and render quiescent the human mind. . . .

"Still, in addition to this, there is something so ludicrous in *promises* of good, or *threats* of evil, a great way off, as to render the whole subject with which they are connected, easily turned into ridicule. . . .

"By the Washingtonians, this system of consigning the habitual drunkard to hopeless ruin, is repudiated. *They* go for present as well as future good. *They* teach *hope* to all—*despair* to none. As applying to *their* cause, *they* deny the doctrine of unpardonable sin. As in Christianity it is taught, so in this *they* teach, that

'While the lamp holds out to burn,
The vilest sinner may return.'

"To these *new champions,* and this new system of tactics, our late success is mainly owing; and to *them* we must chiefly look for the final consummation. . . .

"But if it be true, as I have insisted, those who have suffered by intemperance *personally,* and have reformed, are the most powerful and efficient instruments to push the reformation to ultimate success, it does not follow, that those who have not suffered, have no part left them to perform. Whether or not the world would be vastly benefited by a total and final banishment from it of all intoxicating drinks, seems to me not *now* to be an open question. . . .

"In my judgment, such of us as have never fallen victims, have been spared more from the absence of appetite, than from any mental or moral superiority over those who have."

Here was foresight of the therapeutic service of the organization of sympathetic fellowship against intemperance, as we now have in Alcoholics Anonymous. He also preceded the modern physiochemical theory of the allergic origin of alcoholic craving, by which those who have it become drunk on one drink, or crave to drink until they become drunk, whereas more fortunate people have an avoidance satiety for alcohol, like other food.

Lincoln realized that "public sentiment," for or against a way of life, is the most powerful force in personal relations. It was his experience that the influence of "fashions" rests in sympathetic suggestion and imitation as the social determinant of egoistic acquisitive preference or avoidance prejudice, as held now in modern psychology, sociology, and anthropology.

> "What is the influence of fashion," he said, "but the influence that *other* people's actions have [on our own?] actions, the strong inclination each of us feels to do as we see all our neighbors do?—Nor is the influence of fashion confined to any particular thing or class of things. It is just as strong on one subject as another."

In his concept of fashions in social attitudes and thinking, Lincoln made a true application of his dependence on particular kinds of sympathetic suggestion from particular friends to do what would be thought right by other persons.

He concluded his address with a characteristically optimistic profession of faith in the goodness of the future of mankind, which should be considered in relation to his endless repetitive need to rise above his nervous tendency to lapse into a gloomy view of life for himself:

> [In the] "temperance revolution . . . we shall find a stronger bondage broken; a viler slavery, manumitted; a greater tyrant deposed. . . . By *it,* none wounded in feeling, none injured in interest. Even the dram-maker, and the dram seller, will have glided into other occupations *so* gradually, as never to have felt the shock of change; and will stand ready to join all others in the universal song of gladness.
>
> "And what a noble ally this, to the cause of political freedom. With such aid, its march cannot fail to be on and on, till every son of earth shall drink in rich fruition, the sorrow quenching draughts of perfect liberty. Happy day, when, all appetites controled, all passions subdued, all matters subjected, *mind,* all conquering *mind,* shall live and move the monarch of the world. Glorious Consummation! Hail fall of Fury! Reign of Reason, all hail!
>
> "And when the victory shall be complete—when there shall be neither a slave nor a drunkard on the earth—how proud the title of that *Land,* which may truly claim to be the birth-place and the cradle of both those revolutions, . . . How nobly distinguished that People, who shall have planted, and nurtured to maturity, both the political and moral freedom of their species.
>
> "This is the one hundred and tenth anniversary of the birth-day of Washington. We are met to celebrate this day. Washington is the mightiest name on earth—*long since* mightiest in the cause of civil liberty; *still* mightiest in moral reformation. On that name, an eulogy is expected. It cannot be. To add brightness to the sun, or glory to the name of Washington, is alike impossible. Let none attempt it. In solemn awe pronounce the name, and in its naked deathless splendor, leave it shining on."

Lincoln, at the age of 33 was organizing with authoritative confidence his sense of the basic values for life, liberty, and the pursuit of happiness in democracy, of the healthy mindedness and intelligent reasoning of each person. He could not resist the opportunity of arousing the enthusiasm of his audience with eloquent phrases hailing the glorious triumph of reason over uncontrolled passion.

Opposed Prohibition

In a later speech for temperance and against prohibition Lincoln said:

"Teach all men temperance and moderation but let Man have his freedom and his conscience! The cause of temperance can be but injured by prohibition, which is but a form of harsh intolerance—intemperance! It goes beyond the bounds of law and reason, when it attempts to seek a firm control of man's appetites by legislation, and make a crime of things that are not crimes. Such prohibition strikes a traitor's blow against the very principles of freedom whereon our law and government are founded. I have always been found on the side of the weaker classes, laboring to protect them from the stronger. Never can I give consent to such oppressive, lawless laws. Until my tongue is silenced by cold death I will fight forever for rights of man, for tolerance and freedom of all people."

Must Regain Self-Confidence to Keep Resolves

Lincoln's communication to Speed of April 13, 1842, was devoted entirely to the business of lawsuits and collecting accounts for him. It contains no reference to his friend's neurosis nor to his own, nor to Miss Todd, but expresses love for Fanny and hope for their visit to Springfield in the coming summer. It would seem that both men were now functioning well enough; but his letter of July 4, 1842, shows that he had again become troubled with recurring self-doubt and self-accusation about Mary Todd, after Speed had advised him to renew his courting of her or give her up entirely:

. . . "As to my having been displeased with your advice, surely you know better than that. I know you do; and therefore I will not labour to convince you. True, that subject is painfull to me; but it is not your silence, or the silence of all the world that can make me forget it. I acknowledge the correctness of your advice too; but before I resolve to do the one thing or the other, I must regain my confidence in my own ability to keep my resolves when they are made. In that ability, you know, I once prided myself as the only, or at least the chief, gem of my character; that gem I lost—how, and when, you too well know. I have not yet regained it; and until I do, I can not trust myself in any matter of much importance. I believe now that, had you understood my case at the time, as well as I understood yours afterwards, by the aid you would have given me, I should have sailed through clear; but that does not now afford me sufficient confidence, to begin that, or the like of that, again."

Lincoln's understanding of his involitionally vacillating state of mind had the clarity of astute self-analysis of common sense. His realization that he had not recovered sufficient egoistic integrity to dare to trust himself to come to a decision "in any matter of much importance," as well as of deciding whether he really did or did not want to marry Mary, indicates freedom of mind from the influence of sentiment against him by her family. With typical neurotic retrospection he was now inclined to believe that he would have "sailed through clear" of anxiety and self-doubts about his love and future happiness and married her, had Speed understood him as well as he had understood Speed and persuaded him to do it, even as he had persuaded Speed to marry Fanny. The letter continues:

> "You make a kind of acknowledgment of your obligations to me for your present happiness. I am much pleased with that. . . . The truth is, I am not sure there was any merit, with me, in the part I took in your difficulty; I was drawn to it by fate; if I would, I could not have done less than I did. I always was superstitious; and as part of my superstition, I believe God made me one of the instruments of bringing your Fanny and you together, which union, I have no doubt He had fore-ordained. Whatever he designs, he will do for *me* yet. 'Stand *still* and see the salvation of the Lord' is my text just now. If, as you say, you have told Fanny *all*, I should have no objection to her seeing this letter, but for its reference to our friend here. Let her seeing it, depend upon whether she has ever known anything of my affair; and if she has not, do not let her.
>
> "I do not think I can come to Kentucky this season. I am so poor, and make so little headway in the world, that I drop back in a month of idleness, as much as I gain in a year's rowing. I should like to visit you again. I should like to see that 'Sis' of yours, that was absent when I was there; tho' I suppose she would run away again, if she were to hear I was coming."

In saying that he would "stand still until he saw the salvation of the Lord," Lincoln expressed the essence of common sense. He believed in submitting to the conscientious, self-righting, socially equilibrating dictations of the inner voice of the subconscious mind, as it works out just solutions of the *pros* and *cons* of perplexing situations relative to the vital needs and motivations of itself in interaction with other people.

Reconciliation Through a Scapegoat

Abraham Lincoln and Mary Todd were brought together socially in the summer of 1842 through the connivance of mutual friends—Joshua Speed, Mr. and Mrs. Simeon Francis, owners of the *Sangamo Journal*, and Dr. Henry. Thereafter they met often in the Francis home without the knowledge of her sister's family.

It was the fashion of the time to write for newspapers anonymous or pseudonymous articles, critically ridiculing the policies of political opponents. James Shields, Auditor-General of Illinois, as the principal object of derision of Abraham Lincoln and Mary Todd, became their mutual scapegoat. Lincoln publicly ridiculed him in the "Rebecca" letter of August 27, 1842 for his administrative economies, and Miss Todd's contri-

PLATE   8. Mary Todd. Courtesy of the Lincoln National Life Foundation.

bution, published about two weeks later, was so bitterly sarcastic as to increase his feeling that he had been intentionally insulted. The excitement of writing the letters contributed to the revival of emotional rapport between Lincoln and Mary and led him to forget his jealousy of her flirtation with Douglas, and her to forgive him for the previous failure of their plan to marry.

Shields, a popular member of Springfield's "coterie" and an important Democratic officer, was a close friend of Douglas, now a judge of the Supreme Court of the State and boss of the Democratic party. At one time Shields and Mary were good friends, but it seems that she had become vindictively inclined for some reason to ridicule him about marriage.

PLATE 9. Joshua Speed and His Wife, Fanny Henning Speed. Courtesy of the Illinois State Historical Library.

Lincoln's "Rebecca" Letter

Lincoln's Rebecca letter is interesting in that it shows the remarkable intimacy of his observation of the egoistic attitudes and mannerisms of people. Later, when President, he derived pleasurable relaxation from reading to his Cabinet satirically picturesque articles from the press. We have seen that he used this ridiculing way in adolescence, as a protest against the selfish and unkind interests of some of his neighbors. He regarded himself humorously, with his big ears, divergent eyes, curious nose, scrawny neck, long arms and legs and flat feet, as one of the ugliest of men; and his satirical style reflected a good natured self-defense. His wit, though sharp, was tempered by considerately measured, kindly, good natured wisdom, which debunked the egotistical pretensions of political opponents by placing them in such relatively exaggerated, grotesquely awkward positions as to be amusing to themselves as well as others and yet give them opportunity to readjust in better proportioned, more acceptable ways. It is interesting that Lincoln chose to impersonate the character of a redoubtable pioneer wife to make his argument. It reflects much of his own social culture.

"Lost Townships, Aug. 27, 1842.

"Dear Mr. Printer:

"I see you printed that long letter I sent you a spell ago—I'm quite encouraged by it, and can't keep from writing again. I think the printing of my letters will be a good thing all round, . . . it will give me the benefit of being known by the world, and give the world the advantage of knowing what's going on in the Lost Townships, and give your paper respectability besides. So here come another. Yesterday afternoon I hurried through cleaning up the dinner dishes, and stepped over to neighbor S— to see if his wife Peggy was as well as might be expected, and hear what they called the baby. Well, when I got there, and just turned round the corner of his log cabin, there he was setting on the door-step reading a newspaper.

" 'How are you, Jeff,' say I,—he sorter started when he heard me, for he hadn't seen me before. 'Why,' says he, 'I'm mad as the devil, aunt Becca.'

" 'What about,' says I, 'aint its hair the right color? None of that nonsense, Jeff—there ain't an honester woman in the Lost Township than—'

" 'Than who?' says he, 'what the mischief are you about?'

"I began to see I was running the wrong trail, and so says I, 'O nothing, I guess I was mistaken a little, that's all. But what is it you're mad about?'

" 'Why,' says he, 'I've been tugging ever since harvest getting out wheat and hauling it to the river, to raise State Bank paper enough to pay my tax this year, and a little school debt I owe; and now just as I've got it, here I open this infernal Extra Registra, expecting to find it full of 'glorious democratic victories,' and 'High Comb'd Cocks,' when, lo and behold, I find a set of fellows calling themselves *officers of State,* have forbidden the tax collectors and shool commissioners to receive State paper at all; and so here it is, dead on my hands. I don't now believe all the plunder I've got will fetch ready cash enough to pay my taxes and that school debt.'

The Illinois State Bank, a Whig establishment, had failed in the depression of 1841-42 and its currency was declared, by Auditor General James Shields, to be acceptable in payment of taxes only at a discount. This official act was legal and probably in the best interest of the state but it caused severe hardship for many citizens. Lincoln, as a leader of the Whigs, had been blamed by Douglas and Shields for the State's economic policy as extravagent and the cause of the failure of the bank. In reaction he opposed the financial policies of Shields and Douglas, and used the letter to present his self-defense to the people. The letter continued:

"I was a good deal thunderstruck myself; for that was the first I had heard of the proclamation, and my old man was pretty much in the same fix with Jeff. We both stood a moment, staring at one another without knowing what to say. At last says I, 'Mr. S— let me look at that paper.' He handed it to me, when I read the proclamation over.

" 'There now,' says he, 'did you ever see such a piece of impudence and imposition as that?' I saw Jeff was in a good tune for saying some ill-natured things, and so I tho't I would just argue a little on the contrary side, and make him rant a spell if I could.

" 'Why,' says I, looking as dignified and thoughtful as I could, 'it seems pretty tough to be sure, to have to raise silver when there's none to be raised; but then you see *'there will be danger of loss'* if it ain't done.'

" 'Loss, damnation!' says he, 'I defy Daniel Webster, I defy King Solomon, I defy the world,—I defy—I defy—yes, I defy even you, aunt Becca, to show how the people can lose anything by paying their taxes in State paper.' 'Well,' says I, 'you see what the *officers of State* say about it, and they are a desarning set of men.' 'But,' says I, 'I guess you're mistaken about what the proclamation says; it don't say *the people* will lose any thing by the paper money being taken for taxes. It only says *'there will be danger of loss,'* and though it is tolerable plain that the people can't lose by paying their taxes in something they can get easier than silver, instead of having to pay in silver; and though it is just as plain, that the State can't lose by taking State Bank paper, however low it may be, while she owes the Bank more than the whole revenue, and can pay that paper over on her debt, dollar for dollar; still *there is danger of loss* to the *'officers of State,'* and you know, Jeff, we can't get along without *officers of State.'*

" 'Damn officers of State' says he, 'that's what you Whigs are always hurraing for.' 'Now don't swear so Jeff,' says I, 'you know I belong to the meetin, and swearin hurts my feelins.' 'Beg pardon, aunt Becca,' says he, 'but I do say its enough to make Dr. Goddard swear, to have tax to pay in silver, for nothing only that Ford [democratic governor] may get his two thousand a year, and Shields his twenty-four hundred a year, and Carpenter [democratic state treasurer] his sixteen hundred a year, and all without 'danger of loss' by taking it in State paper.' 'Yes, yes, its plain enough now what these *officers of State* mean by 'danger of loss.' Wash [clerk in Shield's office] I s'pose, actually lost fifteen hundred dollars out of the three thousand that two of these 'officers of State' let him steal from the Treasury, by being compelled to take it in State paper. Wonder if we don't have a proclamation before long, commanding us to make up the loss to Wash in silver.' "

The letter continued with a droll, grotesque argument by Jeff to convince Aunt Becca that Shields was a Whig and not a Democrat and therefore "a fool as well as a liar." Jeff's description of Shields as a lady's man expresses Lincoln's ability for satirical repartee without insolence.

"I tell you, Aunt Becca, there's no mistake about his being a whig—why his very looks shows it—every thing about him shows it—if I was deaf and blind I could tell him by the smell. I seed him when I was down in Springfield last winter. They had a sort of gatherin there one night, among the grandees, they called a fair. All the galls about town was there, and all the handsome widows, and married women, finikin about, trying to look like galls, tied as tight in the middle, and puffed out at both ends like bundles of fodder that hadn't been stacked yet, but wanted stackin pretty bad. . . . They wouldn't let no democrats in, for fear they'd disgust the ladies, or scare the little galls, or dirty the floor. I looked in at the window, and there was this same fellow Shields floatin about on the air, without heft or earthly substance, just like a lock of cat-fur where cats had been fightin.

"He was paying his money to this one and that one, and tother one, and sufferin great loss because it wasn't silver instead of State paper; and the sweet distress he seemed to be in,—his very features, in the exstatic agony of his soul, spoke audibly and distinctly—'Dear girls, *it is distressing,* but I cannot marry you all. Too well I know how much you suffer; but do, *do* remember, it is not my fault that I am *so* handsome and *so* interesting."

The letter closed with an artful appeal to voters to change their officers of state. His portrayal of the character of Aunt Becca as a Whig and Jeff as a Democrat is so natural and vivid, and their expressions of outraged reasoning so sensible and pertinent, that he proved himself a master of satirical humor. His paternally kind but audacious and incisive way of looking at the prides and prejudices of people was the essence of his wisdom.

Mary Todd's "Rebecca" Letter

About two weeks after Lincoln's Rebecca letter appeared, Mary Todd published a letter anonymously in the same paper. Having heard that Shields was fighting mad over Lincoln's Rebecca letter she assumed the same character and sarcastically ridiculed his threatening attitude into that of being too cowardly to fight:

"I was so skart that I tho't I should quill-wheel right where I was." After commenting on herself as a modest, blushing, toothless widow, and Shields as a handsome gentleman of high social position, she proposed to become his wife as the best way of ending their grudge. "I'm not over sixty, and am just four feet three in my bare feet, and not much more around the girth . . . and . . . isn't marrying better than fightin' though it does sometimes run into it. . . . I never fights with anything but broomsticks or hot water. . . . I will give him his choice, however, in one thing, and that is, whether, when we fights, I shall wear breeches or he petticoats, for I presume that change is sufficient to place us in an equality." (Herndon, 1889.)

This letter was followed by the publication of a doggerel by Miss Todd that further ridiculed Shields as a marriageable gentleman.

Duel with Shields

Shields, an honorable lawyer, and an important member of Springfield's best society, a hot tempered Irishman, handsome, witty, clever, entertaining, popular with men and women and a brave man, as proven later by his splendid Mexican and Civil War records, felt himself to have been needlessly and bitterly insulted. He demanded of Editor Francis the name of the author of the letters, and Lincoln permitted his name to be given on condition that Miss Todd's name would be kept secret. As her valiant protector he made himself subject to blame for the offense. According to the code of chivalry then prevailing in the West, the people expected Shields to demand an apologetic retraction in the *Journal* or challenge the author to a duel.

He wrote to Lincoln and published the letter, saying:

"I have become the subject of slander, vituperation and personal abuse, which were I capable of submitting to, I would prove myself worthy of the

> whole of it. . . . I take the liberty of requiring a full, positive and absolute retraction of all offensive allusions by you in these communications in relation to my private character and standing as a man. . . . This may prevent consequences which no one will regret more than myself."

Lincoln replied evasively to Shields that his demand for retraction of certain articles in the *Journal* contained "so much assumption of facts and so much menace as to consequences" that he could not submit to answer them. Whereupon Shields followed with a specific public request to know if Lincoln wrote any or all of the Rebecca articles. This information Lincoln said he would give if Shields would retract his former threatening letter.

The public had become so thoroughly aroused that an honorable duel became unavoidable. Shields felt himself obliged to challenge Lincoln, and both men appointed seconds. Lincoln, as the challenged party, exercised his right to choose the weapons, conditions, time and place for the duel. He elected to fight with "cavalry broad swords of the largest size" identical in construction, across a line "marked by a plank" over which "neither was to pass his foot upon the forfeit of his life." These specifications gave him, with his long, powerful arms, a ridiculous advantage over Shields, a much smaller man. Lincoln detested dueling as the proper means of getting honorable satisfaction, and chose this burlesque way with the express purpose, as he said, of protecting himself and his adversary from being killed.

Lincoln also wrote to his second the following apologetic explanation to be given to Mr. Shield's second:

> "I did write the 'Lost Township' letter . . . but had no participation, in any form, in any other article alluding to you. I wrote that, wholly for political effect. I had no intention of injuring your personal or private character or standing as a man or a gentleman; and I did not then think, and do not now think that that article, could produce or has produced that effect against you, and had I anticipated such an effect I would have forborne to write it. And I will add that your conduct toward me, so far as I knew, had always been gentlemanly; and that I had no personal pique against you, and no cause for any."

Upon the intervention of friends of both parties, Shields finally accepted Lincoln's explanation and the affair ended peaceably between them but not without involving their seconds in recriminations with embarrassing reflections upon Lincoln. For the rest of his life he reacted with obvious chagrin to any reference to this "duel." He had been forced into this undignified position by Miss Todd's aggressive interference in his political conflict with Shields and he, no doubt, realized, in his keen appreciation of human nature, that her vigorous propensity for sarcastic resentment was an irrepressible misfortune of personality for which she would always need protection more than correction.

We will see that hereafter Lincoln's witty criticisms of opponents grew less satirical and more considerate of their self-respect.

Again to Marry or Not to Marry

The editors of the *Sangamo Journal,* Lincoln, Mary Todd, and their Whig friends had a hilarious time over the way Lincoln's Rebecca letter had aroused public approval and the indignation of Shields and other Democratic officials. We can easily imagine their amusement as they read Aunt Becca's and Jeff's humorous dialogue at Shield's expense, and no doubt the pleasure of its emotional momentum made it easier for Lincoln and Mary to become more affectionately interested in each other. Shields had been used intuitively by each as a scapegoat for ridicule to relieve the offended prides that each had held against the other.

Lincoln's willingness to assume responsibility for his letter, and fight a duel with Shields without disclosing Mary's name, and the paternal manner in which he protected her rashness, aroused her affection as he had not before. He had developed greatly as a chivalrous gentleman and she had found in him the counterpart of a kindly enduring father who could understand and forgive her impulsive behavior.

In the next letter to Speed, of October 5, 1842, Lincoln humorously described his "duel" with Shields and its secondary implications for his friends. Then he said:

> "I began this letter not for what I have been writing but to say something on that subject which you know to be of such infinite solicitude to me. The immense suffering you endured from the first days of September till the middle of February [period of Speed's engagement] you never tried to conceal from me, and I well understood. You have now been the husband of a lovely woman nearly eight months. That you are happier now than you were the day you married her I well know; for without, you would not be living. But I have your word for it too; and the returning elasticity of spirits which is manifested in your letters. But I want to ask a closer question— 'Are you now, in *feeling,* as well as *judgement,* glad you are married as you are?' From any body but me, this would be an impudent question not to be tolerated; but I know you will pardon it in me. Please answer as I feel impatient to know."

Speed's reply seems to have been so reassuring that Lincoln finally succeeded in persuading himself to ask Mary Todd again to marry him. As Speed wrote to Herndon after Lincoln's death (previously quoted with context): "One thing is plainly discernable; if I had not been married and happy—far more happy than I expected to be—he would not have married."

Lincoln's ability to make up his mind to marry came, finally, after a long period of doubt of his love and doubt of his ability to keep his resolution. We have indications of how he reasoned himself into this resolute state of mind by the way he had previously tried to do it with Mary Owens. To her he had written (5, 7, 1837): "Whatever woman may cast her lot with mine . . . it is my intention to do all in my power to make her happy and contented; and there is nothing I can imagine, that would make me more unhappy than to fail in the effort. I know I should be much happier with you than the way I am, provided I saw no signs of discontent in you."

Only after Lincoln had convinced himself that Mary Todd had been regretfully unhappy over having offended him by her vain flirtations and was again happy over his renewal of affection for her, and he had his most intimate friend's reassuring answer to his specific question, was he able to make a final decision to marry and relieve his "haunted soul." His actions were entirely consistent with his former statement of feeling of obligation to Mary Owens; "I want in all cases to do right, and particularly so, in all cases with women."

Having intuitively persuaded Speed into wanting to marry Fanny, Lincoln had intuitively persuaded him to persuade himself into wanting to marry Mary. The mutual needs of Lincoln and Speed for giving each other such intimate suggestions in order to develop such attitudinal conversions toward their women was the natural result of their unusually strong, intimate, sympathetic dependence on each other. As each encouraged the other to feel as much tender regard for his woman as he did for his friend, gradual transference of affections by each from the other was naturally and effectively facilitated. It is not unusual for intimate friends of the same sex to encourage each other in the transference of affections to friends of the opposite sex, leading eventually to marriage.

Lincoln had advised Speed, in encouraging him to marry: "Your nerves will fail you occasionally for a while; but once you get them fairly graded now that trouble is over forever;" and now he hopefully applied this suggestion to himself.

It is certain from Lincoln's own words to Speed in July that he was at this time unable to make up his mind either to court Mary Todd again with the idea of marrying her, or to give her up entirely. Certainly he was not engaged to her.

Lincoln's Lost Townships Rebecca letter was published on the 27th of August, and Shield's resentment had been placated by mid-September.

On October 5, Lincoln was, obviously, still doubtful of his judgment about the wisdom of marrying Mary. His "closer question" of Speed is almost conclusive evidence that he had not decided to ask her again to marry him until sometime after he had received Speed's specifically reassuring answer that he was happier than he had expected to be.

Mrs. Lincoln's statements in letters to friends, written after the death of her husband, are utterly contradictory of what her husband had said in his letters to Speed. To Dr. J. G. Holland she wrote (12, 4, 1865):

"The foolish and uncalled for rencontre, with Gen. Shields . . . occurred about six months before our marriage, when, Mr. Lincoln thought, he had some right, to assume to be my champion, even on frivolous occasions. . . . My beloved husband, had so entirely devoted himself to me, for two years before my marriage, that I doubtless trespassed, many times & oft, upon his great tenderness & amiability of character."

Hurried Wedding

Lincoln's most respected relative, John Hanks, seems to have been the only member of his family that he invited to attend his wedding. To him Lincoln is said by Hanks' granddaughter to have written late in October; "I am to be married on the 4th of next month to Miss Todd. I hope you will come over. Be sure to be on deck by early candle light." (Weik, 1922.) The authenticity of this letter has been questioned by Weik and Barton. However, its style is much like that of a letter he wrote to John Hanks 18 years later on the occasion of his visit to his stepmother.

The plan to marry was kept secret in Springfield until the morning of November 4th, when a license was obtained and Lincoln called on Reverend Charles Dresser. "I want to get hitched tonight," he said. He then called on his friend, lawyer James H. Matheny, and asked him to serve as best man. Miss Todd as abruptly requested Miss Julia Jayne to serve as her bridesmaid, and notified the Edwards family of her intentions only a few hours before the ceremony. Incredibly astonished, Mr. and Mrs. Edwards first tried to persuade Mary to reconsider her decision and then yielded to her resolution and invited her to hold the ceremony in their home as more appropriate evidence of family pride and loyalty.

While dressing for the wedding in his room at Butler's house, Sonny Speed Butler, seeing Lincoln so handsomely attired, asked him where he was going. "To hell I suppose," was his worried reply, as retold by Salome Butler (Herndon, 1889).

According to Matheny, Lincoln was "as pale and trembling as if being driven to slaughter" until the spell of his anxious ordeal was suddenly broken by the ludicrous outburst of Thomas C. Brown, a judge of the Supreme Court and a blunt speaking, hard of hearing, old pioneer. The service was Episcopalian, and as the minister, in canonical robes, handed Lincoln the ring and asked him to repeat after him, "With this ring I thee endow with all my goods and chattels, lands and tenements" Judge Brown, who had never seen such an elaborate marriage ceremony, whispered (overheard by all), "God Almighty! Lincoln, the statute fixes all that." (Herndon, 1889.)

Abraham Lincoln, age 33, and Mary Todd, age 24, were married in the evening of November 4, 1842. Therewith began a new way of life and a new phase in the development of his philosophy of human relations.

On the inside of the wedding ring was engraved "From Abraham to Mary—Love is Eternal." By making this complete self-commitment Lincoln had finally recovered confidence in his ability to keep his "resolves when they are made," and regain his "lost gem of character." He had firmly repressed beyond self-doubt all impulses to the contrary and arrived at a rational philosophical conviction that dominated his rebellious passions. He had finally made up his mind to bind himself and his wife together for life under the idealistic moral proposition that "love is eternal." It was a truly characteristic statement of the enduring nature of his idealization of love. Its inspiration was consistent in the inclusion of Mary with his lifelong continuation of love for the memories of his mother and Ann Rutledge, and for his living stepmother.

Lincoln had naturally a very sympathetic, love-cherishing constitution. He had to live with persons whom he could love; otherwise he would feel miserably gloomy and frustrated. This is evident in his affectionate dependence on his friends Joshua Speed and Dr. Anson Henry, to counteract his melancholic disposition. His problem had been how to induce himself and have himself induced to believe that he loved Mary Todd, in a way that he could feel happy in giving up his freedom in binding himself to her for life.

Each decade produces a crop of sentimental poems, papers, and novels eulogizing the marriage of Abraham Lincoln and Mary Todd as the ideal consummation of a great spontaneous love. The record of Lincoln's own statements does not warrent such romantic fabrications, no matter how pleasing the mental pap may be for some people.

Lincoln's resolution to marry was not formed with the easy, natural compelling urge characteristic of instinctive love between a man and a woman. It was formed in the vacillating "superstitious" way of a neurotic personality who is split-minded over conflicting emotions to love or not to love, to be free or not to be free, to marry or not to marry. Subconscious feelings urged him to remain free and avoid the legal bondage of marriage, and natural sexual motivations and conscious admirations and affections urged marriage to the woman who was personally and physically most attractive to him, and who was unhappy without him and would always need his paternal protection. She had deeply injured his self-respect and happiness by vain flirtations with the man he most disliked and he had deeply injured her happiness and self-respect by yielding to jealousy and quitting her, and now he had finally relieved his doubtful conscience by declaring that their love was to be "eternal," come what may.

Five days after his marriage Lincoln wrote to a friend: "Nothing new here except my marrying which to me is a matter of profound wonder."

Two months after his marriage (1, 18, 1843) he wrote a business letter to Speed and included the comment: "Mary is very well and continues her old sentiments of friendship for you. How the married life goes with us I will tell you when I see you here, which I hope will be verry soon."

On May 18, 1843 he concluded another business letter to Speed in happier vein: "We are not keeping house but boarding at the Globe tavern, which is very well kept now by a widow lady of the name of Beck. Our room (the same Dr. Wallace occupied here) and boarding only costs four dollars a week . . . I reckon it will scarcely be in our power to visit Kentucky this year. Besides poverty, and the necessity of attending to business, those 'coming events' I suspect would be somewhat in the way. I most heartily wish you and your Fanny would not fail to come. Just let us know the time a week in advance and we will have a room provided for you at our house and all be merry together for a while."

He closed a letter of July 26, 1843 with the happy greeting: "Your Fanny can not be more anxious to see my Molly than the latter is to see her; nor as much so as I am. Don't fail to come. We are but two, as yet."

Chapter XV

NOSTALGIC POET

Lincoln's feelings in reaction to his marriage behaved very much as he had predicted they would for his friend Speed. He foresaw that "miserable thoughts" would recur but they would let up and grow weaker in time. He got along happily enough, with improvement in conversion of attitude, as his habitual love of personal independence yielded to the new love of being bound to care for the needs, interests, and feelings of his wife and their son. However, congenial exchanges of sympathetic affections did not run a continuously undisturbed course for the Lincolns in the following years. As will become evident, Mrs. Lincoln's energetic, aggressive, amorous but meddling and vindictive disposition to have her way to enjoy her vanities or have a tempest about it did not let him have peace at home.

His mind continued upon insufficient environmental stimulation, as a permanent effect of his cerebral injury, to lapse into melancholic distraction. To relieve the unpleasantness of this disposition he continued to indulge in the repetition of the same old nostalgic reminiscences and poetical sublimations that he had always loved. He would counteract this unhealthy mental cycle when too insidious by wisely exercising his self-saving sense of humor and good natured wit, in exchanging comments, stories, poems, and letters with friends of kindred spirit in the practise of law and politics. His correspondence, wirtten carefully by hand, became voluminous and remarkable for considerate expression of essential details. He constantly needed to think conscientiously that he was doing right and being truthful and honest and just, in everything he did in interaction with other people, in order to keep a healthy sense of self-righting self-respect and avoid being haunted by depressing regrets.

Many comments and aphorisms of President Lincoln on the rights and obligations of freedom in democracy, expressed in state papers and proclamations, in the Gettysburg and other public addresses, and in letters to bereaved relatives of men killed in battle, have become enshrined in the minds of freedom-loving peoples the world over, not only for their philosophical recognition of the part each person must want to play in preserving democratic government but for their poetical beauty of expression.

We can only understand Lincoln's extraordinary development of this talent and the nostalgic hue of his thoughts, in the light of his love for reading, memorizing, and writing such poetry in relation to his meditations on memories of people he loved who were dead. He was a fervent reader of poems contemplative of the destinies and fates of life, particularly by Shakespeare, Scott, Goldsmith, Burns, Gray, Holmes, Bryant, and the *Bible*. He memorized and repeated frequently so many favorite lines that their influences are apparent in both his prose and verse. He wrote numerous doggerels in youth and later, but his best productions came a year or more after a visit to his boyhood home in 1844. Later, except for the little verses to Rosa and Linnie Haggard, he neglected this form of expression in favor of the more practical prose of letters, lectures, and speeches, although he continued his love of reading and reciting poetry even through the trying years of the war.

The following cantos were presented to the Library of Congress by Mrs. Charles Isham, Lincoln's granddaughter by Mr. and Mrs. Robert Lincoln. In a letter to his friend Andrew Johnston, a lawyer of Quincy, Ill. (4, 18, 1846), Lincoln spoke of how he came to write them:

> "In the fall of 1844, thinking I might aid some to carry the State of Indiana for Mr. Clay, I went to the neighborhood in that State in which I was raised, where my mother and only sister were buried and from which I had been absent fifteen years. That part of the country is, within itself, as unpoetical as any spot on the earth; but still, seeing it and its objects and inhabitants aroused feelings in me which were certainly poetry; though whether my expression of those feelings is poetry is quite another question. When I got to writing, the change of subjects divided the thing into four little divisions or cantos, the first only of which I send you now and may send the others hereafter."

The poem is now generally divided into three cantos, of related subjects: "My Child-Hood Home I See Again," "The Mad Man," and "The Bear Hunt." The first two are reminiscent in rhyme, rhythm, and sentiment of Goldsmith's "Deserted Village" and Gray's "Elegy, Written in a Country Church Yard," both of which he probably had memorized. The first two cantos really constitute the expression of the same mood and are composed of 24 stanzas though separated under two headings.

"My Child-Hood Home I See Again" reveals his deep attachment to memories of his old home, mother and friends, and his love of dwelling on thoughts of the past. The fading away in the distance of space and time of the memories of persons and places and events in everyday life intrigued his imagination as he continued to have compensatory feelings of destiny in contributing some improvement to the welfare of mankind, which he felt was yet to be revealed to him, and which in doing would preserve his name against the inevitable dimming of fate. The stanzas were written at different times as his mood moved him.

> "Feeling a little poetic this evening," he wrote to Andrew Johnston (2, 24, 1846), "I have concluded to redeem my promise this evening by sending you the piece you expressed the wish to have. You find it enclosed. I wish I could think of something else to say; but I believe I can not. By the way, how would you like a piece of poetry of my own making? I have a piece that is almost done, but I find a deal of trouble to finish it."

The first 10 stanzas with minor changes were enclosed in this letter to Johnston, and the remainder were sent on later as completed.

My childhood-home I see again,
    And gladden with the view;
And still as mem'ries crowd my brain,
    There's sadness in it too.

O memory! thou mid-way world
    'Twixt Earth and Paradise;
Where things decayed, and loved ones lost
    In dreamy shadows rise.

And freed from all that's gross or vile,
    Seem hallowed, pure, and bright,
Like scenes in some enchanted isle,
    All bathed in liquid light.

As distant mountains please the eye,
    When twilight chases day—
As bugle-tones, that, passing by,
    In distance die away—

As leaving some grand water-fall
    We ling'ring list its roar,
So memory will hallow all
    We've known, but know no more.

Now twenty years have passed away,
    Since here I bid farewell
To woods, and fields, and scenes of play
    And school-mates loved so well.

Where many were, how few remain
    Of old familiar things!
But seeing these to mind again
    The lost and absent brings.

The friends I left that parting day—
    How changed, as time has sped!
Young childhood grown, strong manhood grey,
    And half of all are dead.

I hear the lone survivors tell
    How nought from death could save,
Till every sound appears a knell
    And every spot a grave.

I range the field with pensive tread,
    I pace the hollow rooms;
And feel (companion of the dead)
    I'm living in the tombs.

The Mad Man

In the same mood and meter Lincoln continued reminiscently about
a boyhood schoolmate who lost his mind. This canto is generally re-

ferred to as "The Mad Man." It expressed his feelings about the fate of Matthew Gentry. Lincoln said of him:

> "He was a rather bright lad, and the son of *the* rich man in our very poor neighborhood. At the age of nineteen he unaccountably became furiously mad, from which condition he gradually settled down into harmlessly insanity. When . . . I visited my old home in the fall of 1844 I found him still lingering in this wretched condition. In my poetizing mood I could not forget the impression his case made upon me."

We should see Lincoln's vivid impression of his friend's illness in relation to his interest in his own dreadful experiences with melancholia.

> But here's an object more of dread,
>   Than ought the grave contains—
> A human form with reason fled,
>   While wretched life remains.
>
> Poor Matthew! Once of genius bright,
>   A fortune-favored child—
> Now locked for aye, in mental night
>   A haggard mad-man wild.
>
> Poor Matthew! I have ne'er forgot
>   When first, with maddned will,
> Yourself you maimed, your father fought,
>   And mother strove to kill;
>
> And terror spread, and neighbours ran,
>   Your dang'rous strength to bind;
> And soon a howling crazy man,
>   Your limbs were fast confined—
>
> How then you writhed and shrieked aloud,
>   Your bones and sinnews bared;
> An fiendish on the gaping crowd,
>   With burning eye-balls glared.
>
> And begged, and swore, and wept, and prayed,
>   With maniac laughter joined—
> How fearful are the signs displayed,
>   By pangs that kill the mind.
>
> And when at length, tho' drear and long,
>   Time soothed your fiercer woes—
> How plaintively your mournful song,
>   Upon the still night rose.
>
> I've heard it oft, as if I dreamed,
>   Far-distant, sweet, and lone;
> The funeral dirge it ever seemed
>   Of reason dead and gone.

To drink it's strains I've stole away,
        All silently and still,
Ere yet the rising god of day
        Had streaked the Eastern hill.

Air held his breath; the trees all still
        Seemed sorr'wing angels round;
Their swelling tears in dew-drops fell
        Upon the list'ning ground.

But this is past, and naught remains
        That raised you o'er the brute.
Your mad'ning shrieks and soothing strains
        Are like forever mute.

Now fare thee well; more thou the cause
        Than subject now of woe.
All mental pangs, by time's kind laws,
        Hast lost the power to know.

O death! Thou awe-inspiring prince,
        That keepst the world in fear,
Why dost thou tear more blest ones hence
        And leave him ling'ring here?

And now away to seek some scene
        Less painful than the last—
With less of horror mingled in
        The present and the past.

The very spot where grew the bread
        That formed my bones, I see.
How strange, old field, on thee to tread,
        And feel I'm part thee!

The third last stanza does not appear in the original manuscript but was added later.

In the sixth stanza he said, "Now twenty years have passed away." This would have taken his thoughts back to 1824, or age 15, possibly the time his friend lost his mind. Lincoln showed in this tragic poem such remarkably intelligent understanding of the mind splitting process of conflicting passions, which is the basis of precocious dementia, now called schizophrenia, as to do credit to any psychiatrist. He could naturally have been a great physician and healer of the split minded person as well as becoming the master statesman who understood best the psychopathology of the split minded political state of the Union. These cantos express his endless love of philosophical contemplation of how Nature produces and destroys life and mind.

The Bear Hunt

"The Bear Hunt," which Lincoln called a "doggerel," in humorous vein, is in striking contrast to the sadness of thought on his childhood home and the tragic loss of mind of his schoolmate. He commented to Johnston (2, 25, 1847): "To say the least, I am not at all displeased with your proposal to publish the poetry. I consent that it be done, together with the third canto, which I now send you." His boyhood enjoyment of hunting a pig-killing bear is recalled in vivid detail. The lines are suggestive of the stag hunt in Scott's "Lady of the Lake."

> A wild-bear chace, didst never see?
>   Then hast thou lived in vain.
> Thy richest bump of glorious glee
>   Lies desert in thy brain.
>
> When first my father settled here,
>   'Twas then the frontier line;
> The panther's scream filled night with fear
>   And bear preyed on the swine.
>
> But wo for Bruin's short lived fun,
>   When rose the squealing cry;
> Now man and horse, with dog and gun,
>   For vengence, at him fly.
>
> A sound of danger strikes his ear;
>   He gives the breeze a snuff;
> Away he bounds with little fear,
>   And seeks the tangled *rough*.
>
> On press his foes, and reach the ground,
>   Where's left his half munched meal;
> The dogs, in circles, scent around,
>   And find his fresh made trail.
>
> With instant cry, away they dash,
>   And men as fast pursue;
> O'er logs they leap, through water splash,
>   And shout the brisk halloo.
>
> Now to elude the eager pack,
>   Bear shuns the open ground;
> Th[r]ough matted vines, he shapes his track
>   And runs it, round and round.
>
> The tall fleet cur, with deep-mouthed voice,
>   Now speeds him, as the wind;
> While half-grown pup, and short-legged fice,
>   Are yelping far behind.
>
> And fresh recruits are dropping in
>   To join the merry *corps*:
> With yelp and yell,—a mingled din—
>   The woods are in a roar.

And round, and round the chace now goes,
    The world's alive with fun;
Nick Carter's horse, his rider throws,
    And more, Hill drops his gun.

Now sorely pressed, bear glances back,
    And lolls his tired tongue;
When as, to force him from his track,
    An ambush on him sprung.

Across the glade he sweeps for flight,
    And fully is in view.
The dogs, new-fired, by the sight,
    Their cry, and speed, renew.

The foremost ones, now reach his rear,
    He turns, they dash away;
And circling now, the wrathful bear,
    They have him full at bay.

At top of speed, the horse-men come,
    All screaming in a row.
"Whoop! Take him Tiger, Seize him Drum.'
    Bang,—bang—the rifles go.

And furious now, the dogs he tears,
    And crushes in his ire.
Wheels right and left, and upward rears,
    With eyes of burning fire.

But leaden death is at his Heart,
    Vain all the strength he plies.
And, spouting blood from every part,
    He reels, and sinks, and dies.

And now a dinsome clamor rose,
    'Bout who should have his skin;
Who first draws blood, each hunter knows,
    This prize must always win.

But who did this and how to trace
    What's true from what's a lie,
Like lawyers, in a murder case
    They stoutly *argufy*.

Aforesaid fice, of blustering mood,
    Behind, and quite forgot,
Just now emerging from the wood,
    Arrives upon the spot.

With grinning teeth, and up-turned hair—
    Brim full of spunk and wrath,
He growls, and seizes on dead bear,
    And shakes for life and death.

> And swells as if his skin would tear,
>   And growls and shakes again;
> And swears, as plain as dog can swear,
>   That he has won the skin.
>
> Conceited whelp! we laugh at thee—
>   Nor mind, that not a few
> Of pompous, two-legged dogs there be,
>   Conceited quite as you.

"Angel Mother"

It is quite certain that Lincoln visited the ruins of his childhood home on the occasion of his return to southern Indiana in 1844, as he wrote of how he felt as if "living in the tomb" upon seeing it in decay. Happy memories of childhood and sad memories of loved ones lost, he said, crowded his brain.

Under the influence of this visit, he is said to have written the lines expressing his profound love and gratitude for his real mother (presented in Chapter IV). No doubt he went alone to the graves of his mother and sister which were on a knoll in the forest with the graves of other relatives, less than a quarter of a mile from the cabin. He certainly would not have desired anyone to accompany him in this sacred moment. There is no definite record of this visit in anything he said later to neighbors where he stayed, and no evidence that he did anything to mark his mother's grave so that it would not be lost in oblivion, although, in his deepest melancholy, three years previous, he had expressed regret lest he would not recover and his name would be forgotten because he had not made a lasting contribution to human welfare.

Lincoln reasoned (2, 22, 1842) that the strongest argument in favor of belief "in the existence of an over-ruling Providence mainly depends on the universal *sense* of mankind." It was his sense that all life is a natural extension of being of its Maker, and death, as its dissolution, is the return of its elements to its Maker. As it was his characteristic inclination to say least about those he loved most, we can understand why he was not inclined to mark the grave of his mother. He preferred to express, in a few simple lines, his heartfelt sentiment and leave her to rest alone with her Maker forever, in the forest where she had lived and loved. Herein Lincoln's sentiment about his mother was reverent and sublime, and his love of his memories of her was a sacred love, beautifully expressed by the thought:

> "God bless her soul, God bless her memory,
>   Nancy, my angel mother."

Lincoln was earnestly and sincerely determined to be a natural man. He was not impressed by marking graves permanently in order to preserve memories of the dead.

Sadness, Sweetness, and Light

"Lincoln once told me," Herndon said, "of a song a young lady had sung in his hearing at a time when he was laboring under some dejection of spirits. The lines struck his fancy, and although he did not know the singer— having heard her from the sidewalk as he passed her house—he sent her a request to write the lines out for him. Within a day or two he came into the office carrying in his hand a delicately perfumed envelope which bore the address, 'Mr. Lincoln—Present,' in an unmistakable female hand. In it, written on gilt-edged paper were the lines of the song. . . . Something about it charmed Lincoln, and he read it and reread it with increasing relish. . . . In going over some old papers and letters turned over to me by Mr. Lincoln, I ran across the manuscript . . . The envelope, still retaining a faint reminder of the perfumed scent given it thirty years before, bore the laconic endorsement, 'Poem—I like this' in the handwriting of Mr. Lincoln." Unfortunately no name accompanied the poem so the lady's name was never discovered. The author was Charles Mackey, an English war correspondent for a London newspaper during the Revolution. It was set to music as a chant and rendered in public by the Hutchinson singers." (Herndon, 1889.)

"Tell me, ye winged winds
That round my pathway roar,
Do ye not know some spot
Where mortals weep no more?
Some lone and pleasant vale
Some valley in the West,
Where, free from toil and pain,
The weary soul may rest?
The loud wind dwindled to a whisper low,
And signed for pity as it answered, No.

"Tell me, thou mighty deep,
Whose billows round me play,
Knows't thou some favorite spot,
Some island far away,
Where weary man may find
The bliss for which he sighs;
Where sorrow never lives
And friendship never dies?
The loud waves rolling in perpetual flow
Stopped for a while and sighed to answer, No.

"And thou, serenest moon,
That with such holy face
Dost look upon the earth
Asleep in Night's embrace—
Tell me, in all thy round
Hast thou not seen some spot
Where miserable man
Might find a happier lot?
Behind a cloud the moon withdrew in woe,
And a voice sweet but sad responded, No.

"Tell me, my secret soul
Oh, tell me, Hope and Faith,
Is there no resting-place
From sorrow, sin and death?
Is there no happy spot
Where mortals may be blessed,
Where grief may find a balm
And weariness a rest?
Faith, Hope and Love, best boon to mortals given,
Waved their bright wings and whispered, Yes, in Heaven."

Religion is the art, and philosophy the science, of soothing the lonely human soul, wandering blindly hopefully through life seeking the meaning of it all, without ever obtaining a satisfactory answer. Lincoln, like other naturally meditative people with profound mother attachment, was inclined to become sadly but fondly engrossed in yearning for life after death, not for the sake of personal immortality but to relieve the hope of meeting again those he loved who had passed on.

Favorite Poems

It is fitting to recall here that Lincoln is said never to have read a book through completely. However, he memorized favorite passages from many that interested him. As previously quoted in Chapter VIII, he loved the "Last Leaf," by Oliver Wendell Holmes, but the whole poem that he recited most often when in a meditative mood, to himself and to close friends, when a lawyer and president, was the ode "Immortality." He had learned it in New Salem where he courted Ann Rutledge and his love of reciting it can hardly mean anything else than continuation of love of meditation on memories of Ann after her tragic death. It began:

Oh! why should the spirit of mortal be proud?
Like a swift-fleeting meteor, a fast-flying cloud
A flash of the lightening, a break of the wave
He passeth from life to rest in his grave.

Herndon often heard him recite the lines of the ode, and Mrs. Lois E. Hillis (Weik, 1922) gave a reminiscent account of Lawyer Lincoln's recital to a group of friends who had gathered one evening in a hotel to hear a concert. Ward Lamon (1872) has described scenes in which the President asked him to chant the lines. Carpenter (1866) has also told of President Lincoln's meditative moods and recitations on several occasions of the poem, except the lines:

The maid on whose cheek, on whose brow, in whose eye,
Shone beauty and pleasure, her triumphs are bye;
And the memory of those who loved her and praised,
Are alike from the minds of the living erased.

Similar quality of nostalgic love is expressed in the meditative stanzas Lincoln wrote to Miss Rosa Haggard in her album in 1858, also quoted in full in Chapter VIII. We repeat the first stanza for comparison of its thought with that of the ode.

> You are young, and I am older;
> You are hopeful, I am not—
> Enjoy life ere it grow colder
> Pluck the roses ere they rot.

The same evening he wrote for Rosa's younger sister Linnie:

> A sweet plaintive song did I hear,
> And fancied that she was the singer—
> May emotions as pure, as that song set astir
> Be the worst that the future shall bring her.

Chapter XVI

CONGRESSIONAL CANDIDATE

Lincoln's appeal for the sympathetic redemption of alcoholic addicts before the Washington Temperance Society greatly pleased most of its 700 members, some of whom were trying to reform. However, his charge that ministers often did more harm than good for lack of "approachability" offended some influential religious people who created a political sentiment against him, that contributed to the defeat of his first attempt to win the Whig nomination for Congress in 1843.

Lincoln Persuades Whigs to Adopt Convention System

President W. H. Harrison's untimely death, one month after his inauguration, had dealt a severe blow to the popularity of Whig policies through the failure of his successor, President John Tyler, to fulfill the party's promises. The next congressional election gave the Democrats a large majority in Illinois, and Lincoln, with S. T. Logan and A. T. Bledsoe as assistant committeemen, restated their party's principles in a campaign circular (3, 4, 1843). It was intensely American and nationalistic.

They demanded a protective tariff on foreign importations designed to encourage the growth of home industries, and the employment of more people in factories and less in agriculture. The advantages thus gained for the young nation would include greater material independence, with better balance in production and consumption of necessary commodities leading to higher prices for the farmer and better wages for labor. A larger part of the national income would be paid by the wealthy, through duties on imports which, they assumed, would eventually consist mostly of luxuries.

They were opposed to paying government debts by loans, as a pernicious system that must insidiously increase and "soon fail and leave us destitute." They opposed a system of direct taxation because "the land must be literally covered with assessors and collectors" . . . from whom "none can escape however strictly any citizen may exclude from his premises all foreign luxuries."

They again urged the adoption of a National Bank to stabilize the currency, and upheld Clay's Land Bill by which states would share with the Federal government in the sale of public lands within their boundaries, and advocated the convention system for the nomination of candidates. The arguments for these steps are evidence of Lincoln's ability to adopt new political principles and methods in keeping with the pressure of eastern social and economic conditions.

283

To keep the Whig party alive they urged that a candidate run for Congress in every district, "regardless of the chances of success."

> "We are aware," they said, "that it is sometimes a temporary gratifica-tion, when a friend cannot succeed, to be able to choose between opponents; but we believe that gratification is the seed time which never fails to be fol-lowed by a most abundant harvest of bitterness. By this policy we entangle ourselves. . . . no one portion of our friends, can ever be certain as to what course another portion may adopt; and by this want of mutual and perfect understanding, our political identity is partially frittered away and lost. And again, those elected by our aid, ever become our bitterest prosecutors" [persecutors].

After citing names of men elected by such aid who had thereafter "denounced us as the designing enemies of human liberty itself," they reasoned sophistically; "If it be the will of Heaven that such men shall politically live, be it so, but never, never again permit them to draw a particle of their sustenance from us."

Though independent minded, Lincoln became a convert to the con-vention system as a necessity "of the very first importance:"

> "Whether the system is right in itself, we do not stop to enquire; con-tenting ourselves with trying to show, that while our opponents use it, it is madness in us not to defend ourselves with it. Experience has shown that we cannot successfully defend ourselves without it." . . . Because aspirants for nomination who are not nominated rebel and become candidates "on their own hook" and factions fight furiously with one another, . . . "of all the Whigs in the State, who ran against regular nominees, a single *one only* was elected. . . . and the spoils [were] chucklingly borne off by the common enemy." He would tactfully not censor Whigs who opposed the convention system but "the disastrous results" without it were "forever after to be avoided."

These statements of the elemental needs for party organization and party loyalty in a system of self-government by a free, highly individ-ualistic, provincial people were followed by a philosophical comment that is now historically important for having become the prelude to a statement made 17 years later that contributed enormously to Lin-coln's nomination and election to the presidency:

> "That 'union is strength' is a truth that has been known, illustrated and declared, in various ways and forms in all ages of the world. That great fab-ulist and philosopher, Aesop, illustrated it by his fable of the bundle of sticks, and he whose wisdom surpasses that of all philosophers, has declared that 'a house divided against itself cannot stand.' It is to induce our friends to act upon this important, and universally acknowledged truth, that we urge the adoption of the Convention System."

The modern politician who would cite Aesop as an authority to illustrate a principle in human relations would be subjected to endless caricature and ridicule. But the less sophisticated, more simple and direct manner of thinking of the elementary pioneer mind liked metaphorical appeals to its intelligence so long as they were sensible and natural. Lincoln, in his self-education on human relations, ever searching for its fundamentals, had found in boyhood, in the teachings of Aesop and of Christ, moral truths that reinforced each other and carried, with sweetness and light, a conviction that would lead to the liberation of mankind through teaching individuals how to serve as free thinking units in a grand national union.

In application of this principle the committee said:

> "we know there will be incidents temporarily painful; but, after all, we believe those incidents will be fewer and less intense, with, than without, the system. If two friends aspire to the same office, it is certain both cannot succeed. Would it not, then, be much less painful to have the question decided by mutual friends some time before, than to snarl and quarrel till the day of election, and then both be beaten by the common enemy? . . . we do not understand the resolution as intended to recommend the application of the Convention System to the nomination of candidates for the small offices no way connected with politics; though we must say, we do not perceive that such an application of it would be wrong.

In the convention system, Lincoln foresaw that habitual party loyalty would become largely subjected to the gangsterism of boss dictators in the selection of candidates and policies. National welfare, becoming subordinated to party welfare and ruthless boss power, must be protected by the independence of mind and the legal exercise of personal rights by revolutionary minorities. He was to remain a loyal Whig until some 15 years later when he would feel forced to revolt against its outmoded conservatism and become a leader in its reorganization as the Republican party, with the express policy of restricting slavery and preserving the Union.

Cautious Candidate

Lincoln's confidential letter to Richard S. Thomas (2, 14, 1843) reveals the cautious manner of pushing himself forward.

> "Now if you should hear any one say that Lincoln don't want to go to Congress, I wish you as a personal friend of mine, would tell him you have reason to believe he is mistaken. The truth is, I would like to go very much. Still, circumstances may happen which may prevent my being a candidate.
> "If there are any who be my friends in such an enterprise, what I now want is that they shall not throw me away just yet."

E. D. Baker won the delegation's support and Lincoln commented with genial good humor to Speed (3, 24, 1843):

> "We had a meeting of the Whigs of the county here on last monday to appoint delegates to a district convention, and Baker beat me & got the delegation instructed to go for him. The meeting, in spite of my attempt to decline it, appointed me one of the delegates; so that in getting Baker the nomination,

I shall be 'fixed' a good deal like a fellow who is made groomsman to the man what has cut him out, and is marrying his own dear 'gal'."

Religious Prejudice in Politics

In a more serious letter to M. S. Morris (3, 26, 1843) after the Whig meeting Lincoln explained his defeat by Baker:

> "It is truly gratifying to me to learn that while the people of Sangamon have cast me off, my old friends of Menard who have known me longest and best of any, still retain there confidence in me. It would astonish . . . the older citizens . . . who twelve years ago knew me as a strange, friendless, uneducated, penniless boy, working on a flat boat—at ten dollars per month to learn that I have been put down here as the candidate of pride, wealth, and arristocratic family distinction. . . . There was too the strangest combination of church influence against me. Baker is a Campbellite, and therefore as I suppose, with few exceptions, got all that church. My wife has some relatives in the Presbyterian and some in the Episcopal Churches, and therefore, wherever it would tell, I was set down as either one or the other, whilst it was every where contended that no ch[r]istian ought to go for me, because I belonged to no church, was suspected of being a deist, and had talked about fighting a duel. With all these things Baker, of course had nothing to do. Nor do I complain of them. . . ."

Menard County had offered to instruct its delegation for him and he continued:

> "You say you shall instruct your delegates to go for me unless. I object. I certainly shall not object. That would be too pleasant a compliment for me to tread in the dust. And besides if any thing should happen (which however is not probable) by which Baker should be thrown out of the fight, I would be at liberty to accept the nomination if I could get it. I do however feel myself bound not to hinder him in any way from getting the nomination. I should despise myself were I to attempt it."

Lincoln made a public speech in support of Baker, but John J. Harden obtained the nomination and was elected to Congress in 1843. Loyal to party principles, Lincoln and Baker supported him and obtained enough votes in Sangamon County to win by a strong majority.

Clay's Influence on Lincoln

Henry Clay, United States Senator from Kentucky, enjoyed an enviable national reputation as the "Great Pacificator" between the contending northern, antislavery, manufacturing and southern pro-slavery, cotton growing factions in Congress. Lincoln had been greatly impressed since boyhood by his eloquent oratory and impartial reasoning in support of the Missouri Compromise, a protective tariff, a National Bank, the government disposal of public lands, support of the building of railroads and other national internal improvements, opposition to

President Jackson and his spoils system, and the organization of the Whig party out of conservative democratic and other discontented political factions.

When Clay gained the Whig nomination as a presidential candidate in 1844, Lincoln supported him with numerous speeches in Illinois and his old home county in southern Indiana. Unfortunately no published account of what he said has been found.

Lincoln and Herndon, Attorneys at Law

Logan and Lincoln, although partners, were rivals in 1843 for the Whig congressional nomination. Logan, as senior, thought he was entitled to Lincoln's support but the latter, as leader of the Whigs and a legislator of eight years' experience, believed himself to be the logical nominee. Herndon, who was then a law student in the firm, maintained later (1889) that the private contest led to acrimonious arguments and Lincoln decided to end their partnership. However, the firm was not actually dissolved until a year later (1844) when Logan decided to take his son David for a partner.

That the relations of Lincoln and Logan continued to be friendly thereafter is evident in the following letter written by Lincoln (3, 19, 1855) to one of Logan's old partners, H. E. Dummer:

> "Logan is willing to take the vacant seat on the Supreme Bench; but he is very anxious not to be beaten, if he is put on the track as a candidate. Our friends here, and everywhere, so far as I have heard, are for him; but it behooves us to be wide awake. . . . I am quite anxious for Logan's election, first, because he will make the best Judge, & second because it would hurt his feelings to be beaten worse than it would almost any one else."

Logan's scrupulously critical, industrious methods had often been too authoritative, exacting and annoying for Lincoln's easy-going attitude. Until he came of age he had endured with toleration his father's authoritative dictations, but never again did he submit his intelligence obediently to any man without questioning the right or best way of doing things. To everyone's astonishment he invited his young friend, Billie Herndon, to become his partner, in December 1844.

"I confess I was surprised," Herndon said, "when he invited me to become his partner. I was young in the practise and painfully aware of my want of ability and experience, but when he remarked in his earnest, honest way, 'Billy, I can trust you, if you can trust me,' I felt relieved and accepted his generous proposal—we never had any personal controversy or disagreement." Herndon always addressed his partner as "Mr. Lincoln," who called him "Billy."

"Billy" Herndon

William Henry Herndon was born in Kentucky in 1818. His family moved to Illinois in 1821 and settled in Springfield where his father established a store and bought cattle. Young Herndon clerked in this store for several years when not attending school. He first attended a private tuition school and then the city high school for three years and finally Illinois College for one year. While in college he became radically opposed to slavery and his father refused to support him for being "a damned abolitionist pup." His father, once a slave holder, and intolerant and tyrannical in attitude on the subject, aroused in his son an irrepressible compulsion to demand freedom for all men.

When Lincoln lived in New Salem he knew "Billy" Herndon as a boy and, later, in Springfield, they lived in the same room with Speed while he clerked for Speed. He married Miss Mary Maxey on March 26, 1840, and had several children by her. She died in 1860 and he married Miss Annie Miles in 1861.

Herndon had a naturally argumentative, legalistic mind, and through the encouragement of Lincoln became interested in the study of law. In 1842 he accepted a position as clerk in the firm of Logan and Lincoln and was admitted to the bar in 1844.

Herndon was five feet nine inches tall, of medium weight, handsome, energentic, impulsive, aggressive, and a hot abolitionist. Although he never achieved fame as a lawyer, he was an unusually progressive student, for his time, of law, psychology, sociology, politics, and philosophy, and read widely American and European publications in these fields. He carried on a voluminous correspondence and exchanged ideas with many political and social leaders and reformers. He frequently showed Lincoln this correspondence and such publications as might interest him. It was this vigorous, enthusiastic interest in legal and social progress toward establishing freedom and justice and better ways of living for mankind, with uncompromising hatred of tyranny, that attracted Lincoln and Herndon to each other. Herndon had a far more widely informed, restless and aggressive mind than Lincoln, and it was through his numerous communications with the progressives of the East that Lincoln came to realize that slavery was becoming a national problem of the first importance, although legal under the Constitution.

Lincoln was cool, slow thinking, affable, conservative, cautiously progressive, forethoughtful, and abstemious; whereas Herndon was warm, friendly, impulsive, excitable, quick thinking, hot headed, radically progressive, and inclined to drink too much. Although men largely of opposite constitutional type, they were highly cooperative in division of labor and generally understood and tolerated each other's points of view. Their firm continued active until Lincoln became President, and remained undissolved though inactive until his death. Herndon continued thereafter to occupy the old office with other partners.

Herndon admired Lincoln for his endless fatherly patience, kindness, tolerance, honesty and goodness, and unusual ability at effecting compromises in legal and political conflicts. He saw the grasp and clarity of Lincoln's thinking on the constitutional solution of the slavery problem

and great potentiality for political leadership. It was his natural, in-
cessant drive to push his partner forward politically; and Lincoln,
himself ambitious, was appreciative of this sympathetic encouragement.
Many years before anyone, including Lincoln himself, became interested,
Herndon began the subtle culture of his partner's potentialities for the
presidency. He did this by keeping Lincoln well informed on Eastern
sociopolitical inclinations and pressures of the time and by promoting
political influences in the state that led him to present himself as candidate
for Congress and the Senate and finally for President.

After Lincoln's death, Herndon continued with equal foresight, zeal
and devotion, at great cost of time and money and professional work,
to collect first hand evidence for a biography of Lincoln from people
who knew him personally at any time in his life or had important business
or other personal transactions with him. All biographers of Lincoln
are forever indebted to Herndon for carrying on this great work. In
Chapter VIII other characteristics of Herndon have been presented in
connection with his account of Lincoln's courting of Ann Rutledge.

He said of himself: "I am a social creature, generous, love my fellow
man, am progressive, somewhat radical, liberal in religion, a democrat
and freetrader, a contented, happy man who believes in the universal
progress of all things, especially in the force and onward march of the
Eternal Right and in the *oneness* of the Universe" (Hertz, 1938).
Herndon's philosophical views were similar to Lincoln's. He died in
1891, after his biography of Lincoln, written in collaboration with Weik,
had been published.

Basis of Consistency in Whig and Abolitionist Views

The Democratic administration under President James K. Polk was
in favor of the annexation of Texas after its successful secession from
Mexico. This involved the political question of extension of slavery. To
Williamson Durley, Lincoln wrote (10, 3, 1845):

> "Until I . . . saw you I was not aware of your being what is generally
> called an abolitionist, or, as you call yourself, a Liberty-man; . . . I was
> glad to hear you say that you intend to attempt to bring about, at the next
> election in Putnam [county], a union of the whigs proper, and such of
> the liberty men, as are whigs in principle on all questions only that of
> slavery. So far as I can perceive, by such union, neither party need yield any
> thing, on *the* point in difference between them. If the whig abolitionists
> of New York had voted with us last fall, Mr. Clay would now be president,
> whig principles in the ascendent, and Texas not annexed; whereas by
> division, all that either had at stake in the contest, was lost. . . . As I
> always understood, Liberty-men deprecated the annexation of Texas
> extremely; and, this being so, why they should refuse to so cast their votes
> as to prevent it, even to me, seemed wonderful. What was their process of
> reasoning, I can only judge from what a single one of them told me. It was
> this: 'We are not to do *evil* that *good* may come.' This general, prop-

osition is doubtless correct; but did it apply? If by your votes you could have prevented the *extension,* &c. of slavery, would it not have been *good* and not *evil* so to have used your votes, even though it involved the casting of them for a slaveholder? . . .

" . . . I perhaps ought to say that individually I never was much interested in the Texas question. I never could see much good to come of annexation; inasmuch, as they were already a free republican people on our own model; on the other hand, I never could very clearly see how the annexation would augment the evil of slavery. . . . I hold it to be a paramount duty of us in the free states, due to the Union of the states, and perhaps to liberty itself (paradox though it may seem) to let the slavery of the other states alone; while, on the other hand, I hold it to be equally clear, that we should never knowingly lend ourselves directly or indirectly, to prevent that slavery from dying a natural death—to find new places to live in, when it can no longer exist in the old."

Ten years later, Lincoln advanced the fusion of Whig and Abolitionist principles into a Republican party organization, and caused the splitting of the Democratic party into rival factions over the question of how to support slavery in the slave states but prevent its spread in the territories.

"For the Sake of Peace"

J. J. Hardin, E. D. Baker, and Lincoln, as leaders of the Whig party in their congressional district, had made a gentlemen's agreement that each one would contest for only one term in Congress and then withdraw in order not to interfere with the next man's race. Hardin had served in 1844 and 1845, and, as the election of 1846 approached, Lincoln grew worried over his inclination to contend for renomination. His confidential letters reveal intimately the character of his philosophy of political interpersonal relations during this period.

He confided to H. E. Dummer (11, 18, 1845):

"Before Baker left, he said to me, in accordance with what had long been an understanding between him and me, that the track for the next congressional race was clear to me, so far as he was concerned; and that he would say publicly in any manner, and at any time I might desire. I said, in reply, that as to the manner and time, I would consider a while, and write him. . . .

"I now wish to say to you that if it be consistent with your feelings, you would set a few stakes for me. I do not certainly know, but I strongly suspect, that Genl. Hardin wishes to run again. I know of no argument to give me a preference over him, unless it be 'Turn about is fair play.' "

To Robert Boal (1, 7, 1846):

"Since I saw you last fall, . . . All has happened as I then told you I expected it would—Baker's declining, Hardin's taking the track, and so on.

"If Hardin and I stood precisely equal—that is if *neither* of us had been to congress, or if *both* had—it would only accord with what I have always done, for the sake of peace, to give way to him; and I expect I should do it.

That I *can* voluntarily postpone my pretentions, when they are no more than equal to those to which they are postponed, you have yourself seen. But to yield to Hardin under present circumstances, seems to me as nothing else than yielding to one who would gladly sacrifice me altogether. This I would rather not submit to. That Hardin is talented, energetic, usually generous and magnanimous, I have, before this, affirmed to you, and do not now deny. You know that my only argument is that 'turn about is fair play.' This he, practically at least, denies.

"If it would not be taxing you too much, I wish you would write me, telling the aspect of things in your county, or rather your district; and also send the names of some of your whig neighbours, to whom I might, with propriety write. Unless I can get some one to do this, Hardin with his old franking list, will have the advantage of me. My reliance for a fair shake (and I want nothing more) in your county is chiefly on you, . . ."

As Hardin's pressure for the nomination increased, Lincoln wrote numerous letters to editors of newspapers in his district. They show his remarkable capacity to estimate realistically the strength of public opinion in various sections *for* and *against* him.

To B. F. James he wrote (1, 14, 1846):

"Hardin is a man of desperate energy and perserverance; and one that never backs out; and, I fear, to think otherwise, is to be deceived in the character of our adversary.

"I would rejoice to be spared the labour of a contest; but 'being in' I shall go it thoroughly, and to the bottom. As to my being able to make a break in the lower counties, I tell you that I can *possibly* get Cass, but do not think I will. Morgan & Scott are beyond my reach. Menard is safe to me. Mason—neck and neck. Logan is mine. To make the matter sure, your entire Senatorial District must be secured.

Lincoln wisely tended to overestimate the strength of his adversaries, thereby keeping himself stimulated to do his best until the contest was finished.

Hardin proposed special conditions for a poll of the Whigs to be held on the same day in each precinct throughout the district for selecting a candidate. He also proposed that each candidate restrict his personal electioneering to the county in which he resided. If adopted, this would have given him certain advantages over Lincoln since he was better known, being then the representative of the district in Congress.

Lincoln replied (1, 19, 1846):

"I do not wish to join in your proposal for a new plan for the election of a whig candidate for congress, because 1st. I am entirely satisfied with the old system [the convention system for which Lincoln had worked] under which you and Baker were successively nominated and elected to Congress; and because the whigs of the District are well acquainted with that system, and, so far as I know or believe, are universally satisfied with it." He followed with three additional fair reasons and ended his differences of policy with a characteristic appeal for reconciliation. "I have always been in the habit of acceeding to almost any proposal that a friend would make, and I am truly sorry that I cannot do this."

Frustrated by Lincoln's influence, Hardin made a public charge in the *Morgan Journal* that he used the argument for rotation in office "improperly" by claiming that each candidate should support the other, thereby preventing other men in the party from contending for the office. Lincoln denied the charge in a personal reply (2, 7, 1846):

"I never expressed, nor meant to express, that by such an arrangement, any one of us should be, in the least restricted in the right to support any person he might choose, in the District, but only that he should not *himself,* be a candidate out of his turn. . . .

"In this, the true sense of my proposition, I deny that there is any thing censurable in it—any thing but a mutual concession, for harmony's sake."

This letter, which cannot be entirely reproduced here, shows how meticulously Lincoln differentiated justifiable and erroneous and unfair particulars from generalizations, in the claims of contending parties. He seems finally to have persuaded Hardin to "think *better* and think *differently* in the matter" for he withdrew from the race and Lincoln was nominated by the Whigs.

Defense Against Charges of Infidelism

Reverend Peter Cartwright, a famed Methodist circuit rider, was the Democratic candidate opposed to Lincoln for election. Cartwright unethically started a whispering campaign against Lincoln, charging him with being an "infidel" and therefore unfit to serve in Congress.

Lincoln defended himself with the following statement in the form of a handbill to the voters of the district (7, 31, 1846).

"Fellow Citizens:

"A charge having got into circulation in some of the neighborhoods . . . that I am an open scoffer at Christianity, I have by the advice of some friends concluded to notice the subject in this form. That I am not a member of any Christian Church, is true; but I have never denied the truth of the Scriptures; and I have never spoken with intentional disrespect of religion in general, or of any denomination of Christians in particular. It is true that in early life I was inclined to believe in what I understand is called the 'Doctrine of Necessity'—that is, that the human mind is impelled to action, or held in rest by some power, over which the mind itself has no control; and I have sometimes (with one, two or three, but never publicly) tried to maintain this opinion in argument. The habit of arguing thus however, I have, entirely left off for more than five years. And I add here, I have always understood this same opinion to be held by several of the Christian denominations. The foregoing, is the whole truth, briefly stated, in relation to myself, upon this subject.

"I do not think I could myself, be brought to support a man for office, whom I knew to be an open enemy of, and scoffer at, religion. Leaving the higher matter of ethical consequences, between him and his Maker, I still do not think any man has the right thus to insult the feelings, and injure the morals, of the community in which he may live. If, then, I was guilty of such conduct, I should blame no man who would condemn me for it; but I so blame those, whoever they may be, who falsely put such a charge in circulation against me."

Cartwright started his sly defamation of Lincoln's reputation too late in the campaign for him to defend himself in some of the counties. These were lost to the minister, but he won in the others by a handsome majority. Upon being informed that a Mr. Woodward, personally unknown to him, had magnified the slander in an obnoxious way, Lincoln's moral indignation was aroused. He wrote a letter to A. N. Ford (8, 11, 1846), editor of the *Illinois Gazette* with a request that he publish it with his handbill:

"... If Mr. Woodward has given such assurance of my character as your correspondant asserts, I can still suppose him to be a worthy man; he may have believed what he said; but there is, even in that charitable view of his case, one lesson in morals which he might, not without profit, learn of even me—and that is, never to add the weight of his character against his fellow man, without *knowing* it to be true. I believe it is an established maxim in morals that he who makes an assertion without knowing whether it is true or false, is guilty of falsehood; and the accidental truth of the assertion, does not justify or excuse him. This maxim ought to be particularly held in view, when we contemplate an attack upon the reputation of our neighbor." ...

We will see later how Lincoln defended himself against the charge by Douglas of violating this maxim.

"Being elected to Congress," he wrote to Speed (10, 22, 1846), "though I am very grateful to our friends, for having done it, has not pleased me as much as I expected."

Cautious Progressive

Lincoln's conservative but cautiously progressive nature becomes increasingly evident in the development of his political philosophy. As a lawyer and congressman he habitually took carefully considered progressive positions on questions that involved the future welfare of state and nation. In the summer of 1847, as one of a committee, he favored the continuation of a railroad from Springfield to Alton for local development and the formation of a link with other railroads connecting the eastern cities with the Mississippi. He urged the people to support the eastern capitalists through the purchase of stock. "The whole of this great route will ultimately get into the hands of one company, and ... those who are really interested in prosecuting to completion this grand scheme of improvement, will soon overcome the difficulty arising from conflicting ownership and interests."

Preparation for Congress

Lincoln leased his "dwelling house and lot on which it now stands" in October of 1847 for one year for $90 in quarter yearly payments, with the right to store his furniture in "the North-up-stairs room, during the term" . . . and "to return the premises at the end of the year in as good repair as he [C. Ludlum] may receive them ordinary decay only excepted."

The most important interest Lincoln seems then to have had in Congress was the protective tariff. Little attention has been given to this by most biographers though it shows how he was educating himself in the principles of economics. After his election and before taking office he wrote at different times on scraps of paper his reasons *for* and *against* a protective tariff that he might present at some opportune time before Congress, then Democratic and opposed to it. His introductory outline shows his systematic Euclidian procedure.

"Whether the protective policy shall be finally abandoned, is now the question.

"Discussion and experience already had; and question now in greater dispute than ever.

"Has there not been some great error in the mode of discussion?

"Propose a single issue of fact, namely—'From 1816 to the present, have protected articles [co]st us more, of labour, during the *higher* than during the *lower* duties upon them?'

"Introduce the evidence.

"Analyze this issue, and try to show that it embraces the *true* and the whole question of the protective policy.

"Intended as a test of *experience.*

"The *period* seclected [sic] is fair; because it is a period of peace—a period sufficiently long to furnish a fair average under all other causes operating on prices—a period in which modifications of higher and lower duties have occurred.

"*Protected* articles, only are embraced. Show that *these only* belong to the question.

"The *labour* price only is embraced. Show this to be correct."

These notes, though elementary and insufficient, give some idea of his political reasoning on labor and internal improvements. He would have the producer, distributor, and consumer share in the cost of a protective tariff, through some increase in price for the consumer with reduction of profits for the producer and distributor.

As an example of useless labor he mentioned transportation of articles to distant consumers instead of manufacturing them at the place of consumption. Useless labor and idleness were merely burdens on useful labor and should be driven out of existence. He discussed useless production and developed the progressive effects for labor of maintaining on a national scale a circular interaction system of agricultural

needs for manufactured goods and manufacturers' needs for food and
other products of agriculture.

After giving a series of elementary illustrations he dwelt on the fallacy
of "buying cheapest" and "selling dearest" "because, with both these,
we might have scarcely any thing to sell—or, which is the same thing, to
buy with."

> "We must look not merely to buying cheap, nor yet to buying cheap *and*
> selling dear; but also to having constant employment, so that we may have the
> largest possible amount of something to sell. This matter of employment can
> only be secured by an ample, steady, and certain market, to sell the products
> of labour in."

He showed how such a national, internal system would develop best
under a protective tariff, through eliminating the need of importing foreign
products.

> "In the early days of the world, the Almighty said to the first of our race
> 'In the sweat of thy face shalt thou eat bread;' and since then, if we expect the
> *light* and *air* of heaven, no good thing has been or can be enjoyed by us, with-
> out first having cost labour. And inasmuch [as] most good things are produced
> by labour, it follows that [all] such things of right belong to those whose
> labour has produced them. But it has so happened in all ages of the world,
> that *some* have laboured, and *others* have, without labour, enjoyed a large
> proportion of the fruits. This is wrong, and should not continue. To [secure]
> to each labourer the whole product of his labour, or as nearly as possible, is a
> most worthy object of any good government."

Lincoln obviously wished to develop a national policy that would
reduce idleness, parasitic wealth, and useless labor to a minimum and
cultivate useful labor so that its products would increase the welfare of
the nation and the common man.

The notes on labor close with the following tentative estimation of
their value:

> "Believing that these propositions and the [conclusions] I draw from them
> cannot be successfully controverted, I, for the present, assume their correct-
> ness, and proceed to try to show, that the abandonment of the protective
> policy by the American Government, must result both in the increase of both
> useless labor, and idleness; and so, in pro[por]tion, must produce want and
> ruin among our people."

Herein is evidence for understanding Lincoln's tentative, never too
positive, method of reasoning. It is essentially the method of science,
and not vacillating and indecisive as often charged later. He reduced
problems or questions of issue to their fundamental assumptions or
propositions, and then drew from them what seemed to be the most
practical conclusions which he held to be the proper basis of action
until proven impractical. This method kept his mind free from establishing compelling convictions and enabled him to take up each day's

problems as and when presented. We will see later how this method clashed with the fixed idea systems of reasoning of prominent men of his time.

Chapter XVII

NATIONAL POLITICAL ORIENTATION

Lincoln, in his brief career in Congress, made no contribution to legislation that became historically important. Though limited to one term, it gave him, however, more practical understanding of the "back stage" party machinations of the nation's government, and the great sociopolitical problems and prejudices confronting it under conflicting interpretations of the intent and purpose of the Constitution. The legislative experience, information, beliefs, opinions, and friends gained became influential in the development of his own interpretation of the Constitution and political philosophy. The principles he advocated in addresses before the House and in letters and speeches in these years were morally and economically so soundly equitable that they became the foundation of his later thinking. That he never had to revise any of them except one to meet changing conditions will appear as we correlate the documentary evidence.

The Lincolns arrived in Washington on December 2, 1847, after a tiresome journey from Springfield by stage coach and noisy, smoky trains of puffing and chugging little engines and bouncing coaches. They visited on the way with Mrs. Lincoln's family in Lexington, Ky., where he again saw the better side of master and slave relations.

Lincoln spent less than two years in Washington, accompanied for about six months by his wife and two boys. The family lived in Brown's Hotel, and later, when alone, he moved to Mrs. Sprigg's boarding house. Here he ate at a large table with other guests. Dressed in a long, black coat, plain and dignified if not well pressed, his unpretentious, affable manner invited approach and soon he was on genial terms with everyone, regardless of official rank, nationality, or social class.

Dr. Samuel Bussey, a young physician who sat near Lincoln at Mrs. Sprigg's table, has given a precious bit of description for history of his way of telling a story. "I soon learned," he said, "to know and admire him for his simple and unostentatious manners, kind-heartedness, and amusing jokes, annecdotes and witticisms. When about to tell an annecdote during a meal he would lay down his knife and fork and place his elbows on the table, rest his face between his hands and begin with the words 'that reminds me' . . . Everybody prepared for the explosion sure to follow."

This little sketch of Lincoln's way in conversation, like many others of similar quality, indicates that he had a "single track" mind, generally giving his entire attention at the moment to whatever he was doing.

Washington in 1847

Washington was, at this time, a sprawling, malaria, rat and flea in-
fested city of 40,000 people, with some 8,000 free Negroes and 2,000
slaves. Its mixed extremes of architecture ranged from brick or stone
government buildings, churches, hotels, stores and homes, to squalid,
run down, unpainted, ramshackle frame houses scattered among
them. The White House looked much as it does today, but the Capitol
had an old wooden dome, and the wings now occupied by the Senate
and House were not then built. Numerous saloons and brothels com-
peted with the churches for the interest of the people. Only a few streets
were paved; and open sewage disposal on most of them, with pigs and
fowl roaming in search of food among the refuse, gave much of the city
a squalid, malodorous character.

Social Washington was dominated by the aristocratic families of
Virginia and Maryland, many of whom were slave holders and maintained homes in the city for entertaining and cultivating political influence. Most of these families were well educated and treated their
slaves with affectionate kindness and due regard for the importance of
self-respect in servitude, which won loyal devotion in return. Although
the slave owners generally held ardent church affiliations, they avoided
admitting to themselves that personal freedom and equality of legal
rights were Christian doctrines which apply logically to all people regardless of race or color. The city was an important center for the slave
trade, and Negroes chained together in gangs, trudging dumbly to the
slave market, were a common sight in the streets.

Northern abolitionists criticised bitterly the immorality of such self-
contradictory ethics, and succeeded in producing a guilty sensitivity of
conscience in many intelligent slaveholders. The sociopolitical pro- and
antislavery mixup of Washington was even then working itself into a
clash of intolerant, bitter criticisms and recriminations. At this time all
of the battles of the Mexican War had been fought but a treaty of peace
for defining boundaries and indemnities had yet to be established.

"To Distinguish Myself"

Stephen A. Douglas, who had served two successful terms in the
House, began his impressive career in the Senate in March 1847, as an
advocate of liberal Democratic policies. He married Martha Martin of
North Carolina, in April 1847. She was a beautiful, well educated daughter of a wealthy, aristocratic, slaveholding family. Senator Douglas then
dominated his state politically and was enjoying national importance and
high popularity in Washington society. The Douglases moved in social
and political circles where Lincoln, who could only hope to play a short,
minor part as a representative, and his wife were not entertained.

A few days after Congress convened Lincoln described in a letter to
Herndon (12, 13, 1847) how he took his position in that august body,

ambitiously but tempered with a genial sense of humor. "As you are all so anxious for me to distinguish myself, I have concluded to do so, before long." Although a member of the committee on post office and post roads, he decided to seize the bull by the horns and attack the untruthfulness of President Polk's charge in his message to Congress that Mexico had invaded "the territory of the United States and caused the war."

The Whig minority was accusing the Democratic administration of having perfidiously intervened in the struggle of the settlers from the United States living in Texas, for independence from Mexico, by admitting the young republic into the nation in 1845. During his campaign for election to Congress, Lincoln had taken a lukewarm position on the Mexican War and made no effort to arouse patriotic fervor except on one occasion when, at a rally, he urged young men to enlist in the defense of their country.

When Lincoln began his term in Congress the Mexican army had been hopelessly defeated several months previous by General Zachary Taylor at Buena Vista, deep in Mexico; and President Polk was now determined to make himself an angel of righteousness in the eyes of patriotically aroused American people by demanding that the defeated nation pay an enormous indemnity as well as surrender a large part of the conquered territory. The injustice of his trumped up charges against Mexico, as an invader of "our own soil," aroused the young congressman to denounce them with a series of resolutions, based on an array of historical facts.

Lincoln had judiciously investigated the history of the issue and, as an ardent believer in the Jeffersonian philosophy of obtaining territory by purchase rather than conquest, boldly challenged the truth of the President's statement. The facts of the issue were in part indefinite. The Louisiana Purchase of 1803 purported to extend to the Rio Grande, but the United States had sold the territory between the Sabine River (which now forms the eastern boundary of Texas) and the Rio Grande (on its present southwestern boundary) to Spain in 1819. After Mexico revolted from Spain the people of this territory revolted successfully from Mexico in 1836 and formed the Republic of Texas. The Mexican commander, General Santa Anna, had been captured and compelled, under duress, to sign a document, not a treaty, promising, in order to obtain his release, that the Mexican army would not cross the Rio Grande again. This action was later repudiated by the Mexican government as dishonorable, although Texas had reciprocated by promising not to send her army within five leagues (about 20 miles) of the Rio Grande. By this commitment Texas had seemingly limited her claim of jurisdiction far short of that river.

President Polk had repeatedly asserted in his messages of state that Mexico had broken her agreement with Texas by sending an army across the Rio Grande. The whole issue turned on whether the southern boundary of Texas was the Rio Grande or the Nueces, nearly 200 miles farther north, or in the desert lying between the two rivers. The actual limit of occupancy by the Texan people, after their revolt from Mexico, was the Nueces, except for a few squatters; whereas Mexican families continued to live south of it as they had for many generations. Mexico, and not the United States, had thereby actually exercised jurisdiction over this area.

Lincoln's resolutions (12, 22, 1847), presented in the House in amendment of those presented by W. A. Richardson (Democrat) from Illinois in support of President Polk's war and peace policy, shocked the Whigs and Democrats as well as his constituents at home. They began:

> "Whereas the President of the United States, in his message of May 11th. 1846, has declared that 'the Mexican Government not only refused to receive him' (the envoy of the U. S.) 'or listen to his propositions, but, after a long continued series of menaces, have at last invaded *our territory* and shed the blood of our fellow *citizens* on *our own soil*' " . . .

This point of issue was reinforced by quotations from two later messages of the President which reiterated the charge that the Mexican government struck the first blow and shed the blood of our citizens on United States soil. Then followed the critical attack:

> "Resolved by the House of Representatives, that the President of the United States be respectfully requested to inform this House—
> "First: Whether the spot of soil on which the blood of our *citizens* was shed, as in his messages declared, was, or was not, within the territories of Spain, at least from the treaty of 1819 until the Mexican revolution.
> "Second: Whether that spot is, or is not, within the territory which was wrested from Spain, by the Mexican revolution.
> "Third: Whether that spot is, or is not, within a settlement of people, which settlement had existed ever since before the Texas revolution, until its inhabitants fled from the approach of the U. S. Army."

These "spot resolutions" were accompanied by others which reinforced the argument that the area in question belonged to Mexico and had been invaded by the United States army even though its commander, General Zachary Taylor, had advised the President against such action as unnecessary to the defense of Texas.

"Badly Scared"

Lincoln addressed the House on postal contracts (1, 5, 1848) and later commented to Herndon (1, 8, 1848) on his maiden attempt.

> "As to speech making, by way of getting the hang of the House, I made a little speech two or three days ago on a post office question of no general interest. I find speaking here and elsewhere about the same thing. I was about as badly scared, and no worse, as I am when I speak in court. I expect to make one in a week or two, in which I hope to succeed well enough to wish you to see it."

"Personally I Would Not Object"

Lincoln was bound by an agreement with other leaders of his party to limit himself to one term in Congress, but young Herndon, ever ambitious for his champion of democracy, took the liberty of courting affiliations to keep him in office. When informed of this Lincoln wrote (1, 8, 1848):

> "It is very pleasant to learn from you that there are some who desire that I should be reelected. I most heartily thank them for their kind partiality; and I can say, as Mr. Clay said of the annexation of Texas, that 'personally I would not object' to a reelection, although I thought at the time, and still think, it would be quite as well for me to return to the law at the end of a single term. I made the declaration that I would not be a candidate again, more from a wish to deal fairly with others, to keep peace among our friends, and to keep the district from going to the enemy, than for any cause personal to myself; so that, if it should so happen that nobody else wishes to be elected, I could not refuse the people the right of sending me again. But to enter myself as a competitor of others, or to authorize any one so to enter me, is what my word and honor forbid."

Denounces President Polk's Deception

On January 12th Lincoln repeated his attack on Polk's claims for justifying the war on Mexico with a speech before the House. The following excerpts give his reasons and explain his actions as a citizen during the war. (They are indicative of what he was later to ask of every citizen during the Civil War.)

> "When the war began, it was my opinion that all those who, because of knowing too *little,* or because of knowing too *much,* could not conscientiously approve the conduct of the President, in the beginning of it, should, nevertheless, as good citizens and patriots, remain silent on that point, at least till the war should be ended. . . . I adhered to it, and acted upon it, until since I took my seat here; and I think I should still adhere to it, were it not that the President and his friends will not allow it to be so."

President Polk claimed that the war had the overwhelming approval of Congress by citing the vote in favor of war supplies as a vote in favor of beginning the hostilities by the United States. Lincoln protested:

> "This open attempt to prove, by telling the *truth,* what he could not prove by telling the *whole truth*—demanding of all who will not submit to be misrepresented, in justice to themselves, to speak out."
>
> "Upon these [Richardson's] resolutions—I shall be *compelled* to vote; so that I can not be silent, if I would. Seeing this, I went about preparing myself to give the vote understandingly when it should come. . . ."
>
> "Upon these [Richardson's] resolutions—I shall be *compelled* to vote; so that I can not be silent, if I would. Seeing this, I went about preparing myself to give the vote understandingly when it should come."

[The President's basic claim] "that the soil was *ours* on which hostilities were commenced by Mexico . . . to my judgment . . . is the *very point*, upon which he should be justified, or condemned." "The whole of this—issue and evidence—is, from beginning to end, the sheerest deception.—it assumes as true, that *one* river or the *other* is necessarily the boundary; and cheats the superficial thinker entirely out of the idea, that *possibly* the boundary is somewhere *between* the two, and not actually at either. A further deception is, that it will let in *evidence* which a true issue would exclude."

Lincoln maintained correctly, as history has proven, that since the territory between the Nueces and Rio Grande rivers had been sold by the United States to Spain the administration had no right to reclaim it after the annexation of Texas, for that state and Mexico both claimed it. His elementary method of applying logic to debunk authoritative assumptions was characteristic.

"How, Mr. Chairman, the line, that once divided your land from mine, can *still* be the boundary between us, *after* I have sold my land to you, is, to me, beyond all comprehension. And how any man, with an honest purpose only, of proving the truth, could ever have *thought* of introducing such a fact to prove such an issue is equally incomprehensible."

The habit, established in boyhood, of reducing issues, major or minor, to their most simple logical terms in order to compare the values of conflicting claims, is further shown in a note that he inserted later in the text for the record:

"The outrage upon common *right*, of seizing as our own what we have once sold, merely because it *was* ours *before* we sold it, is only equalled by the outrage on common *sense* of any attempt to justify it."

Political philosophy based on the logic of common sense and not the sophistry of wishful assumption was becoming the strongest characteristic of our young statesman.

On the justice of the claim of Texas to the Rio Grande boundary he said:

"If I should claim your land, by word of mouth, that certainly would not make it mine; and if I were to claim it by a deed which I had made myself, and with which, you had nothing to do, the claim would be quite the same, in substance—or rather, in utter nothingness."

He reduced to absurdity Polk's argument that General Santa Anna's forced signature to an agreement with Texas, not to cross the Rio Grande, constituted a "treaty" with the Government of Mexico, and showed further that exercise of jurisdiction by both governments overlapped in this area. "The true rule for ascertaining the boundary between Texas and Mexico," is that of "exercising jurisdiction" and *"whatever* separated" the areas of jurisdiction of one from the other was "the true boundary between them."

Right to Revolution

Lincoln's remarks in this speech on a people's right to revolt were portentious.

> "The extent of our territory in that region depended, not on any *treaty-fixed* boundary (for no treaty had attempted it) but on revolution. Any people anywhere, being inclined and having the power, have the *right* to rise up, and shake off the existing government, and form a new one that suits them better. This is a most valuable,—a most sacred right—a right, which we hope and believe, is to liberate the world. Nor is this right confined to cases in which the whole people of an existing government, may choose to exercise it. Any portion of such people that *can, may* revolutionize, and make their *own,* of so much of the territory as they inhabit. More than this, a *majority* of any portion of such people may revolutionize, putting down a *minority,* intermingled with, or near about them, who may oppose their movement. Such minority, was precisely the case, of the tories of our revolution. It is a quality of revolutions not to go by *old* lines, or *old laws;* but to break up both and make new ones."

He argued that the might to revolt makes it right, but he denounced Polk's policy of might to conquer as wrong. It is interesting to compare Congressman Lincoln's views on the rights of a people to revolt against their government, in 1848, with his views in 1861, as President, that the government must crush rebellion and preserve the Union. He held, consistently in each case, that the right of the majority to form a government and prevent revolution or anarchy is as sacred and liberating as the right of the majority to revolt and form a new government, so long as whatever government is formed permits equitably the free expression of the minority. Later this philosophy of democratic relations tempered his efforts at preventing secession and determined him to restore the Southern States to their full part in the government immediately after the close of the war.

Lincoln's criticism of President Polk for deliberately attacking Mexico was as severe as any that he himself had later to endure during the Civil War. In closing his speech he said:

> "I more than suspect . . . that he [Polk] is deeply conscious of being in the wrong—that he feels the blood of this war, like the blood of Abel, is crying to Heaven against him. . . . He is a bewildered, confounded and miserably perplexed man. God grant he may be able to show, there is not something about his conscience, more painful than all his mental perplexity!"

The "spot resolutions" and this speech were bitterly denounced in the Democratic press of Illinois as unpatriotic and disloyal to the nation in time of war. He was nicknamed "Spot" Lincoln and likened to the loathsome disease, "spotted fever" then epidemic in the west. "Out Damned Spot" was blazed in headlines by the *Illinois Register* and the name stuck for many years with unhappy political and social consequences, and arose again in his campaign for the Senate and the Presidency a decade later.*

Stephens of Georgia

It has been said by some biographers that Lincoln was so intensely interested in distinguishing himself that he was generally indifferent to the efforts of his contemporaries. His comment on the speech of Alexander H. Stephens, Whig member of Congress, 1848-1859, from Georgia (before the House), shows this to be an erroneous prejudice. In a note to Herndon (2, 2, 1848) he expressed his profound admiration: "I just take up my pen to say, that Mr. Stephens of Georgia,† a little, slim, pale-faced, consumptive man, with a voice like Logan's has just concluded the very best speech, of an hour's length, I ever heard.

"My old, withered, dry eyes, are full of tears yet." . . .

Anti-Lincoln Sentiment

President Polk enjoyed great popularity for having forcefully established the Rio Grande as the new boundary of Texas. He ignored Representative Lincoln's argument and took steps to include in the United States the vast conquered territory extending to the Pacific and north to Oregon. Lincoln achieved nothing of personal political value by this attack on the Democratic administration but it may have had some influence on the election of Zachary Taylor the next year.

Herndon was unable to check the anti-Lincoln sentiment that swept their congressional district, and pleaded with him repeatedly to change his position and vote for the administration's war policy. He even outdid President Polk in arguing that the war was a just defense against invasion

*Despite Lincoln's denunciation of Polk's invasion of Mexico as being unconstitutional for not having the consent of Congress, a Sunday evening radio commentator, infamous for the intensity of his prejudices, wrongfully twisted the facts of history in January 1951, and asserted that Lincoln had justified Polk's actions. This precedent, he maintained, established such presidential authority above the constitutional powers of Congress that it justified President Truman in sending troops to Korea and Europe without the consent of Congress.

†Alexander Stephens, who became one of Lincoln's best friends in Congress, was a thin, 90 pound, wiry, fiery, black eyed, little man who also believed that the problems of slavery could be worked out peaceably through sensible measures of compromise. He, like many Southerners, foresaw the necessity of accepting the natural, eventual decline of slavery, through the moral need of all people in the United States to enjoy Christian freedom and legal equality. After Lincoln was elected President he exchanged letters with Stephens in 1860, but he did not see him again until the last days of the Civil War, when they met in a conference between Northern and Southern emissaries on finding a means of restoring peace. The personal friendship in Congress of Mr. Lincoln of Illinois and Mr. Stephens of Georgia is evidence that the views on slavery of the two opposed cultures were reconcilable among well tempered people. The Jefferson-Clay-Lincoln philosophy of its gradual decline and extinction was not entirely unacceptable to the intelligent people of the South.

(a lie still taught in American schools). Lincoln replied (2, 1, 1848) confidentially:

> "You fear that you and I disagree about the war. I regret this, not because of any fear we shall remain disagreed, after you shall have read this letter, but because, if you misunderstand, I fear other good friends will also. . . . the war was unnecessarily and unconstitutionally commenced by the President and I will stake my life that if you had been in my place you would have voted just as I did. Would you have voted for what you felt and knew to be a lie. I know you would not."

Most of the Whigs in Congress, including 31 from the slave states, had voted against the declaration of war on Mexico, but voted for measures supplying the necessities of war. Lincoln's discrimination of the differences between the injustice of starting the war and the necessity for survival of carrying it on to victory after it had begun was consistent with his affiliates' but unsatisfactory to a war enthusiastic public. In order to carry on hostilities patriotically the people had to believe it to be a morally justifiable, self-defensive act; hence it was easier to support President Polk than Congressman Lincoln. In Illinois they held indignant mass meetings and denounced him as "little better than a traitor to the country." Nevertheless Lincoln was proud of his speech and sent copies to his friends, including one to his law partner with the request: "After you get over your scare, read it over again, sentence by sentence, and tell me honestly what you think of it."

Herndon persisted in defending President Polk against Lincoln's speech. In answer (2, 15, 1848) Lincoln shows the respectful care and consideration but firmness with which he logically analyzed the points of his argument:

> "Your letter of the 29th. Jany, was received last night. Being exclusively a constitutional argument, I wish to submit some reflections upon it in the same spirit of kindness that I know actuates you. Let me first state what I understand to be your position. It is, that if it shall become *necessary, to repel invasion,* the President may, without violation of the Constitution, cross the line, and *invade* the territory of another country; and that whether such *necessity* exists in any given case, the President is to be the *sole* judge.
>
> "Before going further, consider well whether this is, or is not your position. If it is, it is a position that neither the President himself, nor any friend of his, so far as I know, has ever taken. Their only positions are first, that the soil was *ours* where hostilities commenced, and second, that whether it was rightfully ours or not, *Congress had annexed it,* and the President, for that reason was bound to defend it, both of which are as clearly proved to be false in fact, as you can prove that your house is mine. That soil was not ours; and Congress did not annex or attempt to annex it. But to return to your position. Allow the President to invade a neighboring nation, whenever *he* shall deem it necessary to repel an invasion, and you allow him to do so, *whenever he may choose to say*

he deems it necessary for such purpose—and you allow him to make war at pleasure. . . .

"The provision of the Constitution giving war-making power to Congress, was dictated, as I understand it, by the following reasons. Kings had always been involving and impoverishing their people in wars, pretending generally, if not always, that the good of the people was the object. This, our Convention understood to be the most oppressive of all Kingly oppressions; and they resolved to so frame the Constitution that *no one man* should hold the power of bringing this oppression upon us. But your view . . . places our President where kings have always stood."

For Old Acquaintance Sake

We get a warm, intimate feeling of how Congressman Lincoln loved to keep his friends for the sake of friendship from his letter to Josephus Hewett (2, 13, 1848), and also why he approved the electoral vote for president.

"Your voting representative from Mississippi, P. W. Tompkins, has just shown me a letter of yours to him. I am jealous because you did not write to me. Perhaps you have forgotten me. Dont you remember a long black fellow who rode on horseback with you from Tremont to Springfield nearly ten years ago, swimming your horses over the Mackinaw on that trip? Well, I am that same one fellow yet. I was once of your opinion, expressed in your letter, that presidential electors should be dispensed with; but a more thorough knowledge of the causes that first introduced them, has made me doubt. Those causes were briefly these. The convention that framed the constitution had this difficulty: the small states wished to so frame the new government as that they might be equal to the large ones regardless of the inequality of population; the large ones insisted on equality in proportion to population. They compromised it, by having the House of Representatives on *population,* and the Senate on *states* regardless of population; and the executive on both principles, by electors in each state, equal in numbers to her senators and representatives. Now, throw away the machinery of electors, and the compromise is broken up, and the whole yielded to the principle of the large states. There is one more thing. In the slave states, you have representatives, and consequently, electors, partly upon the basis of your black population, which would be swept away by the change you seem to think desirable. Have you ever reflected on these things?

"But to come to the main point, I wish you to know that I have made a speech in congress, and that I want you to be *enlightened* by reading it; to further which object, I send a copy of the speech by this mail.

"For old acquaintance sake, if for nothing else, be sure to write me on receiving this. I was very near forgetting to tell you that on my being introduced to Genl. Quitman, and telling him I was from Springfield, Illinois, he at once remarked 'Then you are acquainted with my valued friend Hewett of Natchez,' and on being assured I was, he said just such things about you as I like to hear said about my own valued friends."

"If I Were President"

Senator Clay continued to be Lincoln's ideal as an American statesman although defeated by Polk for the presidency in 1845. However,
when Clay tried to obtain the party's nomination again in 1848 Lincoln
decided to support General Taylor, the conqueror of Mexico. In a letter
to Jesse Lynch (4, 10, 1848) he gave the following reason for this change:
"Our only chance is with Taylor. I go for him, not because I think he
would make a better president than Clay, but because I think he would
make a better one than Polk, or Cass, or Buchanan, or any such creatures,
one of whom is sure to be elected if he is not."

A few weeks previous to this letter Lincoln had written out a brief
outline of some policies which he though Taylor ought to present to the
people. They are cast in the first person and express some of his own ideas
about what he would do if he were president, showing how naturally he
was thinking of himself in this office even at this time.

[March ?] 1848.

"The question of a national bank is at rest; were I President I should not
urge its reagitation upon Congress; but should Congress see fit to pass an
act to establish such an institution, I should not arrest it by the veto, unless
I should consider it subject to some Constitutional objection, from which
I believe the two former banks have been free.

"It appears to me that the national debt created by the war, renders a
modification of the existing tariff indispensable; and when it shall be
modified, I should be pleased to see it adjusted with a due reference to the
protection of our home industry. The particulars, it appears to me, must
and should be left to the untramelled discretion of Congress.

"As to the Mexican War I still think the defensive line policy is the best
to terminate it. In a final treaty of peace, we shall probably be under some
sort of necessity of taking some territory; but it is my desire that we shall not
acquire any extending so far South, as to enlarge and agrivate the distracting
question of slavery. Should I come into the presidency before these things
shall be settled, I should act in relation to them in accordance with the
views here expressed.

"Finally, were I president, I should desire the legislation of the country
to rest with Congress, uninfluenced by the executive in it's origin or progress,
and undisturbed by the veto unless in very special and clear cases."

As a congressman, Lincoln would keep the president in a subordinate
position to the legislative body. Later as Chief Executive, he largely
dominated Congress.

Common-Sense Replies to Critics

Lincoln was severely criticised, more or less reasonably, by many
eminent men, for his argument in Congress that the United States and
not Mexico began the war. His replies (2, 20, and 3, 22, 1848) to critical
letters by U. F. Linder show the painstaking care of his aggressive defense:

"In law it is good policy to never *plead* what you *need* not, lest you oblige yourself to *prove* what you *can* not.

"Towards the close of your [second] letter you ask . . . 'Would it not have been just as easy to have elected Genl. Taylor without opposing the war as by opposing it?' I answer, I suppose it would, if we could do *neither—* could be *silent* on the question; but the Locofocos [Democrats] here will not let the whigs be *silent.* Their very first act in congress was to present a preamble declaring that war existed by the act of Mexico, and the whigs were obliged to vote on it—and this policy is followed up by them; so that they are compelled to *speak* and their only option is whether they will, when they do speak, tell the *truth,* or tell a foul, villainous, and bloody falsehood. But, while on this point, I protest against your calling the condemnation of Polk 'opposing the war.' In thus assuming that all must be opposed to the war, even though they vote supplies, who do not not [sic] endorse Polk, with due deference I say I think you fall into one of the artfully set traps of Locofocoism. . . . "There are in this H. R. some more than forty members who support Genl. Taylor for the Presidency, every one of whom has voted that the war was 'unnecessarily and unconstitutionally commenced by the President' every one of whom has spoken to the same effect, who has spoken at all." . . .

Linder had asked: "Have we as a party, ever gained anything, by falling in company with abolitionists?" Lincoln's reply was much in the pattern that he used later in his speeches against Douglas and in his Cooper Union and other addresses and in the organization of the Whigs. It is clear evidence of the great energy of his institinctive genius that he would keep himself informed on the political bias of each member of Congress as well as the more influential people of his state in order, not to adjust his premises and policies submissively to theirs, but aggressively to see how he could persuade them to accept the truth and logic of his reasoning.

"Yes. We gained our only national victory by falling in company with them in the election of Genl. Harrison. Not that we fell into abolition doctrines; but that we took up a man whose position induced them to join us in his election. But this question is not so significant as a *question,* as it is a charge of abolitionism against those who have chosen to speak their minds against the President. . . . There are in this H. R. whigs from the slave states as follows: one from Louisiana, one from Mississippi, one from Florida, two from Alabama, four from Georgia, five from Tennessee, six from Kentucky, six from North Carolina, six from Virginia, four from Maryland, and one from Delaware, making thirty seven in all, and all slave-holders, every one of whom votes the commencement of the war 'unnecessary and unconstitutional' and so falls subject to your charge of abolitionism!

"'En passant' these are all *Taylor* men, except one in Tenn. two in Ky. one in N.C. and one in Va. Besides which we have one in Ills—two in Ia, three in Ohio, five in Penn. four in N.J. and one in Conn. While this is less than half the whigs of the H.R. it is three times as great as the strength of any other candidate." . . .

PLATE 10. Congressman Lincoln, 1846. Daguerreotype by N. H. Shepard. Courtesy of the Library of Congress.

PLATE 11. Practical Lawyer, May 7, 1858. Ambrotype by A. N. Byers. Courtesy of the Illinois State Historical Library.

Horace Greeley, editor of the New York *Tribune,* then the leading Whig newspaper of the nation, had stated in an editorial on the boundary of Texas that all Whigs and many Democrats held that it stopped at the Nueces River. Lincoln saw herein a mistake that he disliked to see go uncorrected and he urged Greeley (6, 27, 1848):

> "I know a large majority of such Whigs of the House of Representatives as have spoken on the question have not taken that position. Their position, and in my opinion the true position, is that the boundary of Texas extended just so far as American settlement taking part in her revolution extended; and that as a matter of fact those settlements did extend, at one or two points, beyond the Nueces, but not anywhere near the Rio Grande at any point. The 'stupendous desert' between the valleys of these two rivers, and not either river, has been insisted on by the Whigs as the true boundary. . . . By putting us in the position of insisting on the line of the Nueces, you put us in a position which, in my opinion, we cannot maintain and which therefore gives the Democrats an advantage over us."

Federal Versus States' Rights on Necessary Internal Improvements

When President, Lincoln was the most discerning, logical, and convincing interpreter for the people of the constitutional limitation of rights, in the internal relations of the Union with the free and slave states. The close student of the practical development of his political philosophy will find in his speech to the House (6, 20, 1848), as a member of a committee on internal improvements, reporting on the state of the Union, the earliest evidence of his study of this problem, then becoming one of the most important confronting the rapidly developing nation. The following abstractions are presented, with comments on their psychological and political insight.

> "Mr. Chairman:
> "I wish at all times in no way to practice any fraud upon the House or the committee, and I also desire to do nothing which may be very disagreeable to any of the members. I therefore state in advance that my object in taking the floor is to make a speech on the general subject of internal improvements; and if I am out of order in doing so, I will give the chair the opportunity of so deciding, and I will take my seat."

He was informed by the Chair that any question of order raised would be decided at that time. By taking this simple, honest, equable position Lincoln won the respectful attention of everyone who desired to improve the internal conditions of the Nation.

As usual he first defined the political issues involved in the question as sufficient reason for his argument. He quoted the official statement of resolution of the Democratic party in its platform, as accepted and approved by General Lewis Cass, its nominee for president. The democratic position was "that the constitution does not confer upon the general government the power to commence and carry on a general system of internal improvements."

" . . . The question of internal improvements," Lincoln said, "has become more intense—than at any former period. . . . [It] is verging to a final crisis; and the friends of the policy must now battle, and battle manfully, or surrender all."

President Polk, in his message to Congress, had taken the position that internal improvements might not be made by the general government —as Lincoln said:

"1.   Because they would overwhelm the Treasury.

"2.   Because, while their *burthens* would be general, their *benefits* would be *local* and *partial;* involving an obnoxious inequality—and

"3.   Because they would be unconstitutional.

"4.   Because the states may do enough by the levy and collection of tonnage duties—or if not

"5.   That the constitution may be amended."

Obviously, making internal improvements involved the question of limitations of Federal versus states' rights as defined by the Constitution. It was a thorny question; with the northern, more populous, progressive, manufacturing states favoring the increase of internal harbor, river and other improvements by the Federal government, and the southern agricultural states adhering to the old policy of holding national improvements to a minimum, since naturally the northern states would receive more benefits. The problem had to be solved lest the development of the nation be greatly retarded.

The objection that Federal internal improvements would tend to overwhelm the treasury through undue expansion, as each congressman tried to obtain appropriations for local developments, Lincoln agreed, was true. But he maintained the danger was no worse than that found in state legislatures as each member worked to get appropriations for his county:

"Go where we will, the difficulty is the same. Allow it to drive us from the halls of congress, and it will, just as easily, drive us from the state legislature. Let us, then grapple with it, and test its strength. Let us, judging the future by the past, ascertain whether there may not be, in the discretion of congress, a sufficient power to limit, and restrain this expansive tendency, within reasonable and proper bounds."

He then demonstrated how Congress had recently expended less than two million where two hundred million had been requested. He admitted that the "burthen of improvements would be general while their benefits would be local and partial, involving an obnoxious inequality." However "no government patronage can be so exclusively *general* as not to leave some peculiar *local* advantage" and "nothing is so *local,* as not to be of some general advantage." He presented the Navy as the most general in its benefits to the nation attended by local benefits to the great harbor cities, with little extending to the towns of the interior states. Improving navigation on the Mississippi River and its tributaries would directly benefit 13 states. The Illinois-Michigan canal provided means of transportation whereby sugar produced in southern states could be delivered in New York cheaper than by ocean route.

"The result is, that the New Orleans merchant sold his ʼsugar a little *dearer;* and the people of Buffalo sweetened their coffee a little *cheaper;* than before—a benefit resulting *from* the canal, not to Illinois where the canal *is,* but to Louisiana and New-York where it is *not.* In other transactions Illinois will, of course, have her share, and perhaps the larger share too in the benefits of the canal; but the instance of the sugar clearly shows that the *benefits* of an improvement are by no means confined to the particular locality of the improvement itself.

"The just conclusion from all this is, that if the nation refuses to make improvements, of the more general kind, because their benefits may be somewhat local, a state may, for the same reason, refuse to make an improvement of a local kind, because it's benefits may be somewhat general. A state may well say to the nation ʻIf you will do nothing for me, I will do nothing for you.ʺ Thus it is seen, that if this argument of ʻinequalityʼ is sufficient anywhere,—it is sufficient everywhere; and puts an end to improvements altogether. I hope and believe, that if both the nation and the states would in good faith, in their respective spheres, do what they could in the way of improvements, what of inequality might be produced in one place, might be compensated in another, and the sum of the whole might not be very unequal.

. . . "Inequality is certainly not to be embraced for it's own sake; but is every good thing to be discarded, which may be inseparably connected with some degree of it? If so, we must discard all government. This capitol is built at the public expense, for the public benefit but does anyone doubt that it is of some peculiar local advantage to the property holders, and business people of Washington? Shall we remove it for this reason? and if so, where shall we set it down, and be free of the difficulty?"

If we bear in mind that the citizens of the individual states were then so jealous of their constitutional and physical autonomies within the Union that often they placed state above the national welfare, we see that Congressman Lincoln's argument was directed at the practical formation of a more perfect Union. He anticipated the necessity of a dominant national legislative policy as it operates today.

Lincoln made a humorous allusion to President Polk for his reactionary policy.

"There are few stronger cases in this world, of ʻburthen to the man, and benefit to the fewʼ—of ʻinequalityʼ—than the presidency itself is by some thought to be. An honest laborer digs coal at about seventy cents a day, while the president digs abstractions at about seventy dollars a day. The *coal* is clearly worth more than the *abstractions,* and yet what a monstrous inequality in the prices! Does the president, for this reason, propose to abolish the presidency? He *does* not and, and he *ought* not. The true rule, in determining to embrace or reject any thing, is not whether it have *any* evil in it; but whether it have more of evil, than of good. There are few things *wholly* evil or *wholly* good. Almost every thing, especially of governmental policy, is an inseparable compound of the two; so that our best judgment of the preponderance between them is continually demanded."

Lincoln then modestly presented an interpretation of the meaning of the Constitution relative to powers conferred upon Congress to make internal improvements.

"On the . . . constitutional question, I have not much to say. Being the man I am, and speaking when I do, I feel, that in any attempt at an original constitutional argument, I should not be and ought not to be, listened to patiently. The ablest, and the best of men, have gone over the whole ground long ago. I shall attempt but little more than a brief notice of what some of them have said."

President Polk had claimed, in his message, that President Jefferson in 1806 had recommended the need of an amendment to the Constitution for the purpose of applying the surplus in the Federal Treasury, "to the great purposes of public education, roads, rivers, canals, and such other objects of public improvements as it may be thought proper to add to the constitutional enumeration of the federal powers."

Lincoln held that a reconsideration of Jefferson's opinion in relation to the question of national *expediency* discredited Polk's interpretation of it. To support his argument he cited the opinion of Chancellor Kent, given in his *Commentaries on American Law,* as being superior in argument to any opposing opinions.

"He [Kent] was one of the ablest and most learned lawyers of his age, or any age. . . . His attitude was most favorable to correct conclusions. He wrote coolly, and in retirement. He was struggling to rear a durable [an enduring] monument to his fame; and he well knew that *truth* and thoroughly sound reasoning were the only sure foundations."

In idealizing Kent, Lincoln expressed his own strict self-disciplines for earning enduring fame. Kent favored the interpretation that, since the Constitution conferred upon Congress the power to levy taxes and regulate commerce, it also gave the power to make internal improvements for that purpose.

Lincoln pointed out that duties levied on tonnage coming into a harbor then in use, as the basis for determining improvements, were inadequate, since they provided no means for building new harbors or other means of interstate transportation. Because the Constitution failed to confer definitely this power upon Congress, the Democratic party, dominated by the southern states, held that if any general improvements became desirable an amendment passed by the States was necessary for this purpose. To this key argument Lincoln pointed out the inconsistency of states authorizing Congress to do what they believed it should not do.

"I have already said that no one, who is satisfied of the expediency of making improvements, needs to be much uneasy in his conscience about its constitutionality. . . . As a general rule, I think, we would much better let it [the Constitution] alone. No slight occasion should tempt us to touch it. Better, rather, habituate ourselves to think of it as unalterable. It can scarcely be made better than it is. New provisions, would introduce new difficulties, and thus create, and increase appetite for still further changes. No sir, let it stand as it is."

The thorny question of deciding what improvements should be made each year had to be answered, for some localities would be favored more than others. Lincoln suggested the method, now adopted by the social and economic sciences, of collecting statistics on the quantity and kind of needs of different districts, as the best means of working out a practical basis for the distribution of Federal funds:

"What is made unequal in one place may be equalized in another, extravagence avoided, and the whole country put on that career of prosperity, which shall correspond with it's extent of territory, it's natural resources, and the intelligence and enterprise of it's people."

Lincoln's speech on constitutional powers granted to Congress for making internal improvements shows important developments in his political interest and in his manner of expression. He had become a keen analyst of the meaning and content of the Constitution and a progressive advocate of its practical application. Politically, he had seized upon the critical issue of Federal versus states' rights in the construction of a more perfect Union and for a greater prosperity, and he boldly proposed how to carry it out:

. . . "Determine that the thing can and shall be done, and then we shall find the way. The tendency to undue expansion is unquestionably the chief difficulty. How to do *something,* and still not do *too much,* is the desideratum. . . . I would not borrow money. I am against an overwhelming, crushing system. Suppose, that at each session, Congress shall first determine *how much* money can, for that year, be spared for improvements; then apportion that sum to the most *important* objects. So far all is easy; but how shall we determine which *are* the most important? On this question comes the collision of interests. *I* shall be slow to acknowledge, that *your* harbor, or *your* river is more important than *mine*—and *vice versa.* To clear this difficulty let us have the same statistical information. . . . In that information, we shall have a stern, unbending basis of *facts*—a basis in no wise subject to whim, caprice, or local interest. The pre-limited amount of means, will save us from doing *too much* and the statistics will save us doing, what we do, in *wrong places."*

Lincoln was not the originator of the use of statistics in government but he urged its practical application. He had abandoned, in his constructive advice to Congress, the redundant metaphorical style of oratory of a few years previous for more mature minded, simple direct, logical, positive reasoning from demonstrable facts, as truth, reinforced by aversion for the loose, unfounded assumptions of President Polk. His wisely considerate style of argument was consistent with the beneficient paternal change of attitude that he was undergoing since he had married and become the good, proud father of two sons.

On Whig Nomination of "Old Rough"

Lincoln's description to Herndon (6, 12, 1848) of the nomination by the Whigs of General Zachary Taylor for president gives a vivid picture of how he enjoyed the performance and foresaw the results:

> "On my return from Philadelphia, where I had been attending the nomination of "Old Rough"—I found your letter in a mass of others, accumulated since my absence. By many, and often, it had been said they would not abide the nomination of Taylor, but since the deed has been done, they are fast falling in, and in my opinion we shall have a most overwhelming, glorious, triumph. One unmistakable sign is, that all the odds and ends are with us—Barnburners, Native Americans, Tyler men, disappointed office seeking locofocos, and the Lord knows what. This is important, if in nothing else, in showing which way the wind blows. . . . Taylor's nomination takes the locofocos on the blind side. It turns the war thunder against them. The war is now to them, the gallows of Haman, which they built for us, and on which they are doomed to be hanged themselves."

The Democratic Aministration was propagandizing the victory over Mexico and the enormous territory acquired, to win popular support for the coming presidential election (1848). Lincoln insisted, however, that restoration of truth and justice in public opinion and the nomination of General Taylor by the Whigs would turn the tide against continuation of the Democratic party in power. He regarded his party's position on the Mexican question as historically, constitutionally and ethically right, and continued to maintain and defend its principles with vigorous argument. We will see later how his moral attitude carried on in a similar way against the arguments of Douglas on extension of slavery in the territories.

Lincoln's Fatherly Advice to Herndon

Herndon persisted in justifying the war and giving gloomy forebodings of Whig defeat at home for having condemned it. Older men in the party, he complained, ignored the opinions of younger men. Lincoln's patient treatment of his young partner's temperamental prejudices, although repeatedly annoyed by them, is well illustrated in his advice of June 22, 1848:

> "You must not wait to be brought forward by the older men. For instance do you suppose that I should ever have got into notice if I had waited to be hunted up and pushed forward by older men. You young

men get together and form a Rough & Ready Club [named after "Old Rough and Ready Taylor"], and have regular meetings and speeches. Take in every body that you can get . . . gather up all the shrewd wild boys about town, whether just of age, or a little under age. . . . Let every one play the part he can play best—some speak, some sing and all hollow. Your meetings will be of evenings; the older men, and the women will go to hear you; so that it will not only contribute to the election of 'Old Zach' but will be an interesting pastime, and improving to the intellectual faculties of all engaged. Don't fail to do this.

"You ask me to send you all the speeches made about 'Old Zac' the war &c. &c. Now this makes me a little impatient. I have regularly sent you the Congressional Globe and Appendix, and you can not have examined them, or you would have discovered that they contain every speech made by every man, in both Houses of Congress, on every subject, during this session. Can I send any more? . . .

"You ask how Congress came to declare that war existed by the act of Mexico. Is it possible you dont understand that yet? You have at least twenty speeches in your possession that fully explain it. I will, however, try it once more." Lincoln then reviewed the history of the war and the Whig vote in Congress and added: "Even my little speech, shows how this was; and if you will go to the Library you may get the Journals of 1845-6, in which you can find the whole for yourself."

It has been said that Lincoln was not an extensive reader, but it is obvious now that he was a most patient, indefatigable and thorough-going investigator of legal records, authoritative opinions and other published reports on any subject that seemed important to him.

In his reply, Herndon seems to have repeated his complaints about the resistances of old men toward his efforts to win recognition. His resentful attitude of injured egoistic narcissism stemmed probably from the endless injustice and condemnation towards him in youth of his intolerant, violent tempered father, and more recently from unpleasant aversions by older contemporaries for his impatient disposition to argue from inadequately founded premises. Unlike Lincoln, who had decisively mastered his father intellectually and economically and obligated himself to protect his welfare, Herndon seemed to be unable to overcome such mental incumbence to the development of a healthy egoistic, altruistic attitude as a lawyer.

This now worried Lincoln and his sympathetically understanding fatherly advice (7, 10, 1848) to his young partner reveals the very essence of heartfelt interest in his mental integrity and that of humanity in general. Lincoln's deep understanding of the social involvements of each person's naturally inherent, self-loving, more or less envious egoistic rivalry with every other person is evident in the wisdom of his persuasive reasoning to induce conversion in Herndon's attitude:

"Your letter," he began, "covering the newspaper slips, was received last night. The subject of that letter is exceedingly painful to me; and I can not but think there is some mistake in your impression of the motives of old men. I suppose I am one of the old men."

By first kindly telling Herndon that his complaint of the motives of old men in opposition to his efforts to gain recognition was "exceedingly painful" to himself, being one of them, and that he must be mistaken in this, Lincoln expressed such sincere sympathetic interest in his egoistic involvements as to make him feel more important to his older partner than he had before realized. Herndon loved Lincoln sincerely but jealously, and this sympathetic bond naturally induced him to become more receptive to further suggestions. Lincoln followed this wise lead with consummate skill:

"I declare on my veracity, which I think is good with you, that nothing could afford me more satisfaction than to learn that you and others of my young friends at home, were doing battle in the contest, and endearing themselves to the people, and taking a stand far above any I have ever been able to reach, in their admiration. I cannot conceive that older men feel differently. Of course I can not demonstrate what I say; but I was young once, and I am sure I was never ungenerously thrust back. I hardly know what to say. The way for a young man to rise, is to improve himself every way he can, never suspecting that any body wishes to hinder him. Allow me to assure you, that suspicion and jealousy never did help any man in any situation. There may at times be ungenerous attempts to keep a man down; and they will succeed too, if he allows his mind to be diverted from its true channel to brood over the attempted injury. Cast about and see if this feeling has not injured every person you have ever known to fall into it."

By so firmly declaring that nothing could give him more satisfaction than to see Herndon and other young men win greater endearment and admiration of people in the contest for superiority than he could win, Lincoln expressed a healthy degree of renunciation of his own inborn egoistic self-interest in establishing his name in history, with conversion into an altruistic attitude interested in helping other persons to realize such ambitions. Analysis of the psychobiology of organization of development of man's egoistic attitude shows how deeply true and practical Lincoln's insight into its self-constructive and self-destructive processes had become.

The natural economies in the use of energy in the bodily organization of mind make the inborn egoistic attitude of each person desire to get firstness and mostness in the quickest and easiest way in its social interactions with other persons. In proportion to the qualities and quantities of social approval and economic security that it acquires, it enjoys greater integrity and self-respect. It is born to be always interdependently interactive with every other person, as more or less of a sympathetic energy-giving and -receiving ally when working in cooperative directions, and a jealous, energy-witholding rival in competitive directions. These psychobiodynamic reequilibrating versus disequilibrating personal involvements become conditioned by the interactions of family, age, sex, race, nationality, clan, community, occupation, or other social situations, as they tend to aid and decrease, or oppose and increase work to live. Primal egoistic love of self and drive to win social acceptability, and if possible superiority, tends to work more normally and healthfully, and less distressfully, for each person in an attitude that takes and gives with due consideration of the needs and rights, wishes, abilities, and work of other persons, as well as its own. Love the creative good will of other persons as that of thyself, and treat each as you wish to be treated, is man's most constructive moral philosophy. It disposes to the greater productivity and enjoyment of development of the mind of each person with greater progressive development of social organization. This was Lincoln's intuitive insight and strict rule of self-discipline and social discipline, to reduce stress of his overly sensitive nervous system and increase self-respect.

His philosophy did not mean that each person should give according to his abilities to each according to his needs as the best way of cultivating individual with community welfare. This political policy cultivates, as everyone knows, parasitic lazyness in dullards and weaklings and enslaves the more able by not giving them personal returns commensurate with harder work and the development of superior abilities.

Herndon, in his injured, narcissistic, resentful, impulsive, overly ambitious egoistic attitude, was disposed to let himself brood grievously over past frustrations, rejections and ridicules, rather than think about ways of working to make new conquests and win new approvals, as steps to increase self-respect. Lincoln saw both the individual and the social side of causes of mental deterioration in falling into the habit of yielding to the insidious growth of associations of painful and wishful ideas of suspicious jealousy, and reminded him of its fatal malignancy for mental integrity and social acceptability. He saw that it would inevitably turn people against him and establish an almost incurable, progressive vicious circle of interactions:

> "Now, in what I have said, I am sure you will suspect nothing but sincere friendship. I would save you from a fatal error. You have been a laborious, studious young man. You are far better informed on almost all subjects than I have ever been. You can not fail in any laudable object, unless you allow your mind to be improperly directed. I have some advantage of you in the world's experience, merely by being older; and it is this that induces me to advise.
>
> "You still seem to be a little mistaken about the Congressional Globe and Appendix. They contain *all* of the speeches that are published in any way. My speech and Clayton's speech, which you say you got in pamphlet form, are both, word for word, in the Appendix. I repeat again all are there. Your friend, as ever."

Lincoln had real cause to worry about his partner's social attitude, and wisely took the course of saving the young man's egoistic pride from developing a resentful disposition into a paranoid attitude, by cultivating, with fatherly kindness, patience, tolerance and encouragement, such sympathetic transference between them as would make him feel respect for himself and turn his thinking in constructive directions in order to increase his self-respect by winning Lincoln's increasing respect. It is not surprising that Herndon became therefore a most devoted and ardent disciple of Lincoln's moral political philosophy.

The following day Lincoln received a letter from Herndon, in answer to his previous letter, that seems to have expressed a more optimistic change of attitude, for he promptly replied in the following joyous vein (7, 11, 1848):

> "Yours of the 3rd. is this moment received; and I hardly need say, it gives me unalloyed pleasure. I now almost regret writing the serious, long faced letter, I wrote yesterday; but let the past as nothing be. Go it while you're young.
>
> "I write this in the confusion of the H. R. and with several other things to attend to. I will send you about eight different speeches this evening; and as to kissing a pretty girl, I know one very pretty one, but I guess she wont let me kiss her. Yours forever."

The interplay of their remarks indicates that their personal relations were unusually intimate and friendly as well as closely professional. Herndon seems, in his happier mood, to have suggested to Lincoln that he should kiss a pretty girl, as if he knew that Mrs. Lincoln was expected to return soon to Washington. Lincoln's reply was not meant in frivolity, as some of his biographers have assumed. His previous letters to Mrs. Lincoln (given in full in Chapter XXI) show that the remark expressed disappointment.

In Defense of Whig Principles

The nomination by the Whigs of General Zachary Taylor, hero of the Mexican war, as their candidate for President of the United States, proved so popular that it worried the leaders of the Democrats. Some made speeches in Congress contemptuously charging the Whigs with being a party without principles, and Taylor a man unfit for the presidency, because of inadequate schooling in constitutional law. Lincoln rose to the defense of his party and its candidate in a speech (7, 27, 1848) that proved him to have become a master of satire, before this critical, sophisticated audience.

> "Mr. Speaker:
> "Our democratic friends seem to be in great distress because they think our candidate for the Presidency dont suit *us*. Most of them can not find out that Gen: Taylor has any principles at all; some, however, have

discovered that he has *one,* but that that one is entirely wrong. This one principle, is his position on the veto power."

Lincoln then cited the attacks of several congressmen on General Taylor's position on this power and showed with quotations from him and Jefferson that they had similar ideas about it. From Jefferson:

> "A just respect for the wisdom of the legislature, would naturally decide the ballance in favor of their opinion: it is chiefly for cases, where they are clearly misled by error, ambition, or interest, that the constitution has placed a check in the negative of the President." From Taylor: "The power given by the veto, is a high conservative power; but in my opinion, never be exercised except in cases of clear violation of the constitution, or manifest haste, and want of consideration by congress."

Lincoln differentiated the principles of executive and legislative office as practiced by the Whigs from those of the Democrats by showing how the Whig president would honor legislation passed by the congressional majority as the indirect expression of the majority of the people whereas the Democratic president imposed executive policies upon the legislature and the people. The Democrats, Lincoln said, claimed that

> "the President is as much the representative of the people as Congress. . . . He is elected by them—but can he, in the nature [of] things, know the wants of the people, as well as three hundred other men, coming from all of the various localities of the nation? . . . I understand your idea, that if a Presidential candidate avow his opinion upon a given question, or rather, upon all questions, and the people, with full knowledge of this, elect him, they thereby distinctly approve all those opinions. This, though plausable, is a most pernicious deception. By means of it, measures are adopted or rejected, contrary to the wishes of the whole of one party, and often nearly half of the other." . . .

In relation to the probable positions of General Taylor and General Cass (the Democratic candidate for president) on the Wilmot Proviso,* Lincoln said:

> "I am a Northern man, or rather, a Western free state man, with a constituency I believe to be, and with personal feelings I know to be, against the extension of slavery. As such, and with what information I have, I hope and *believe,* Gen: Taylor, if elected, would not veto the Proviso. *But* I do not *know* it. Yet, if I knew he would, I would still vote for him. I should do so, because, in my judgment, his election alone, can defeat Gen: Cass; and because, *should* slavery thereby go

---

*The Wilmot Proviso was an amendment, introduced in 1846 by Representative Wilmot, to a bill providing money for purchasing territory from Mexico. It stipulated that 'neither slavery nor involuntary servitude shall ever exist in any part of said territory." Lincoln voted for it and it was passed by the House but defeated in the Senate. The dispute over the principles of the Wilmot Proviso eventually grew into the bitter feud between the anti- and proslavery factions in Congress.

to the territory we now have, just so much will certainly happen by the election of Cass; and, in addition, a course of policy, leading to new wars, new acquisitions of territory and still further extensions of slavery." . . .

Lincoln believed, like many prominent public men, that radical pro-slavery Democrats wished to extend slavery into Mexico, the Caribbean and South American countries as well as in the Territories.

Relativity of Democratic vs. Whig Principles

"You democrats, and your candidate, in the main are in favor of laying down, in advance, a platform—a set of party positions, as a unit; and then of enforcing the people, by every sort of appliance, to rectify them, however unpalatable some of them may be. We, and our candidate, are in favor of making Presidential elections, and the legislation of the country, distinct matters; so that the people can elect whom they please, and afterwards, legislate just as they please, without any hindrance, save only so much as may guard against infractions of the constitution, undue haste, and want of consideration." . . .

Satirical Characterization of Democratic Policy

Lincoln, the robust, western state legislator, once heedless and bludgeoning in satirical characterization, had grown, as a Congressman, wiser and more subtle in the art of restrained ridicule. He continued:

"The other day, one of the gentlemen from Georgia (Mr. Iverson), an eloquent man, and a man of learning, so far as I could judge, not being learned, myself, came down upon us astonishingly. He spoke in what the Baltimore American calls the 'scathing and withering style.' At the end of his second severe flash, I was struck blind, and found myself feeling with my fingers for an assurance of my continued physical existence. A little of the bone was left, and I gradually revived. He eulogized Mr. Clay in high and beautiful tones, and then declared that we had deserted all our principles, and had turned Henry Clay out, like an old horse to root. This is terribly severe. It can not be answered by argument. At least, I can not so answer it. I merely wish to ask the gentleman if the Whigs are the only party he can think of, who some times turn old horses out to root. Is not a certain Martin Van Buren, an old horse which your party have turned out to root? and is he not rooting a little to your discomfort now? But in nominating Mr. Clay, we deserted our principles, you say. Ah! in what? Tell us, ye men of principles, what principles we violated. We say you did violate principles in discarding Van Buren, and we can tell you now. You violated the primary, the cardinal, the one great living principle of all Democratic representative government—the principle, that the representative is bound to carry out the known will of his constituents. A large majority of the Baltimore convention of 1844, were, by their constituents, instructed to procure Van Buren's nomination if they could. In violation, in utter, glaring contempt of this, you rejected him—rejected him . . . for *avail-*

ability—that same 'General availability' which you charge upon us, and daily chew over here, as something especially odious and unprincipled." . . .

"But the gentleman from Georgia further says we have deserted all our principles, and taken shelter under Gen: Taylor's military coattail; and he seems to think it exceedingly degrading. Well, as his faith is, so be it unto him. But can he remember no other military coat-tail under which a certain other party have been sheltering for near a quarter of a century? Has he no acquaintance with the ample military coat tail of Gen: Jackson? Does he not know that his own party have run the five last Presidential races under that coat-tail? and are now running the sixth, under the same cover? Yes sir, that coat tail was used not only for Gen: Jackson himself; but has been clung to, with the gripe of death, by every democratic candidate since. You have never ventured, and dare not now venture, from under it. Your campaign papers have constantly been 'Old Hickories' with rude likenesses of the old general upon them; hickory poles, and hickory brooms, your never-ending emblems;" . . .

"Like a horde of hungry ticks you have stuck to the tail of the Hermitage lion to the end of his life; and you are still sticking to it, and drawing a loathsome sustenance from it, after he is dead. A fellow once advertised that he had made a discovery by which he could make a new man out of an old one, and have enough of the stuff left to make a little yellow dog. Just such a discovery has Gen: Jackson's popularity been to you. You not only twice made President of him out of it, but you have had enough stuff left, to make Presidents of several comparatively small men since; and it is your chief reliance now to make still another.

"Mr. Speaker, old horses, and military coat-tails, or tails of any sort, are not figures of speech, such as I would be the first to introduce into discussions here; but as the gentleman from Georgia has thought fit to introduce them, he, and you, are welcome to all you have made, or can make, by them. If you have any more old horses, trot them out; and more tails, just cock them, and come at us.

"I repeat, I would not introduce this mode of discussion here; but I wish gentlemen on the other side to understand, that the use of degrading figures is a game at which they may not find themselves able to take all the winnings. (We give it up.) Aye, you give it up, and well you may; but for a very different reason from that which you would have us understand. The point—the power to hurt—of all figures, consists in the *truthfulness* of their application, and, understanding this, you may well give it up. They are weapons which hit you but miss us."

Devastating Portrait of General Cass

General Taylor, as the conqueror of Mexico, was a real hero of the people, tried and proven true. In fear that he would be elected President, the Democrats had nominated General Cass. Even though Cass was a military figure of comparatively small reputation, Democratic propagandists outdid themselves in lavishing hollow praises upon him. Lincoln's satirical portrait of Cass before Congress brought him down to true size and probably contributed to his defeat. He continued:

"In my hurry I was very near closing on the subject of military tails before I was done with it. There is one entire article of the sort I have not discussed yet; I mean the military tail you democrats are now engaged in dovetailing onto the great Michigander. Yes sir, all his biographers (and they are legion) have him in hand, tying him to a military tail, like so many mischievous boys tying a dog to a bladder of beans. True, the material they have is very limited; but they drive it, might and main. He *in*vaded Canada without resistance, and he *out*vaded it without pursuit. As he did both under orders, I suppose there was, to him, neither credit nor discredit in them; but they constitute a large part of the tail. He was not at Hull's surrender* but he was close by; he was a volunteer aid to Gen: Harrison on the day of the battle of the Thames." . . .

"By the way, Mr. Speaker, did you know I am a military hero? Yes sir; in the days of the Black Hawk war, I fought, bled, and came away. Speaking of Gen: Cass' career, reminds me of my own. I was not at Stillman's defeat,† but I was about as near it, as Cass was at Hull's surrender, and like him, I saw the place very soon afterwards. It is quite certain I did not break my sword for I had none to break; but I bent a musket pretty badly on one occasion. If Cass broke his sword, the idea is, he broke it in desperation; I bent the musket by accident. If Gen: Cass went in advance of me in picking huckleberries, I guess I surpassed him in charges upon the wild onions. If he saw any live, fighting indians, it was more than I did; but I had a good many bloody struggles with the mousquetoes; and, although I never fainted from loss of blood, I can truly say I was often very hungry. Mr. Speaker, if I should ever conclude to doff whatever our democratic friends may suppose there is of a black cocade federalism about me, and thereupon, they shall take me up as their candidate for the Presidency, I protest they shall not make fun of me, as they have of Gen: Cass, by attempting to write me into a military hero."

Speeches in Eastern States

Congressman Lincoln made a number of speeches in eastern states advocating the election of General Taylor. The following comments by the press show how he was received. All are taken from the *Collected Works*.

The *Delaware State Journal* (6, 13, 1848): "The first speaker introduced to the assembled multitude [in Wilmington, Delaware—a slave state] was the 'Lone Star of Illinois,' Hon. Mr. Lincoln. He was received with three hearty cheers, and delivered an eloquent and patriotic speech on some of the principles of the Whig party and the standard-bearers they had selected to carry out their measures. He referred to the history of James K. Polk's administration—the abuse of power which characterized it—the high-handed and despotic exercise of the veto power, and the utter

---

*General William Hull surrendered Detroit to the British in 1812 and was court martialed and sentenced to be shot, largely on Col. Lewis Cass's testimony, which later proved to have been false, against his commanding officer *(Collected Works)*.

†Major Isiah Stillman, with three companies of volunteers, attacked a band of Black Hawk Indians and was defeated. Lincoln's company arrived after the fight and helped bury the dead.

disregard of the will of the people, in refusing to give assent to measures which their representatives passed for the good and prosperity of the country." . . .

The Boston *Daily Advertiser* (9, 14, 1848): "Mr. Lincoln has a very tall and thin figure, with an intellectual face, showing a searching mind, and a cool judgment. He spoke in a clear and cool, and very eloquent manner, for an hour and a half, carrying the audience with him in his able arguments and brilliant illustrations—only interrupted by warm and frequent applause. He began by expressing a real feeling of modesty in addressing an audience 'this side of the mountains,' a part of the country where in the opinion of the people of his section, everybody was supposed to be instructed and wise." . . .

Lincoln's ideas on the principles of republican government appealed to the Whigs, Abolitionists and Free Soilers. His modest, simple, logical, factual style of speaking won the respect of intelligent people who preferred to reason cooly from information rather than excited emotional prejudice.

The Boston *Atlas* (9, 16, 1848): "for sound reasoning, cogent argument and keen satire, we have seldom heard equalled." . . .

The Lowell *Daily Journal* commented (9, 18, 1848): "It would be doing injustice to his speech to endeavor to give a sketch of it. It was replete with good sense, sound reasoning and irresistible argument, spoken with that perfect command of manner and matter which so eminently distinguishes the Western orators." . . .

From the *Bristol County Democrat* (9, 29, 1848), politically unsympathetic, we have this gem: "The address as well as the speaker was such as to give unlimited satisfaction to the disheartened Taylorites. Such a treat it is indeed seldom their good luck to get, and they were in ecstacies. . . . It was reviving to hear a man speak as if he believed what he was saying, and had a grain or two of feeling mixed up with it." This paper's comments on Lincoln's speech, which he probably read, estimated the political situation on slavery with remarkable premonition of what was to follow in the next decade. "The aboliton of slavery in the territory of the United States can never be accomplished unless the North is united. But the North cannot be united until old party lines are broken down. But these lines cannot be broken down unless every man is willing to sacrifice his attachment to minor questions and make opposition to slavery the leading idea."

Whoever would accomplish this political reorganization would become one of the central figures in the national situation. We will see how he accomplished this within ten years.

Numerous personal discussions with eastern leaders on moral, economic and politic affairs taught Lincoln that prevention of the spread of slavery in the territories, leading eventually to its abolition in the slave states, was one of the most intensely active national interests. Here was the critical issue upon which he immediately seized with all of his natural compulsion to fight for the rights of freedom.

Resolutions for Abolition of Slavery in District of Columbia

Zachary Taylor had been elected President when the second session of the Thirtieth Congress opened and by this Whig good fortune Lincoln's political prestige was greatly increased. The constitutional restriction of slavery to the original states had again been violated, as in the case of Louisiana, by the admission of Texas where slavery had been legally established during its brief period as a Republic.

Representatives of the Northern states strove to abolish the sale of slaves in the District of Columbia, while those from the Southern slave states demanded its retention as a sacred Constitutional right. Lincoln, like Jefferson and Clay, tried to bring about a compromise (1, 10, 1849) that he thought would appease both sides and soften any attempts at too radical legislation.

He would direct the Committee of the District to bring in a bill limiting the retention of slaves in the District to those already living there or that might be brought in by Government officials from the slave states for their personal use. Children born of slave mothers would be educated, trained and freed after a certain age, producing a gradual decline in the number of slaves. *If any owner would willingly free a slave already in the District, he would be paid by the United States Treasury his fair value as determined by a special board.* His plan would also provide the municipal authorities of Washington and Georgetown with powers for apprehending and returning all fugitive slaves as property of their owners. He would call upon all white male citizens living in the District for one year or more to vote for or against the project.

His resolutions came to nothing, though he had obtained the approval of fifteen prominent citizens and declared his intention to introduce a bill himself. The plan for returning fugitive slaves aroused the bitter personal denunciations of many Northern commentators, including the eminent Wendell Phillips who called Lincoln "the slave hound from Illinois."

His basic antislavery principles were justly considerate under the Constitution of the rights of all parties concerned, slave holders and abolitionists, the Federal Government, the interests of the free states and slave states, and the future livelihood of the freed men. Combined with his attack on President Polk for starting a war on Mexico on unjust grounds, they brought him into extreme disfavor in his state and made him nationally ridiculous, in the North as well as the South. During this term, however, without his particular influence, trading in slaves in the District of Columbia was prohibited by Congress, and the rabble-rousing slave traders led a furious attack on the act as an infringement of their Constitutional rights, indicative of the conflict that would probably, within a few years, reach irreconcilable, warring proportions should efforts at compromise break down.

End of Congressional Career

Lincoln's career as a congressman ended in March, 1849. As he had previously agreed with his Whig friends, he was not a candidate for reelection. When he wrote an autobiographical sketch for Scripps ten years later, he briefly reviewed his criticism of Polk's war on Mexico and stoutly repeated his charges of injustice:

> "Mr. Lincoln thought the act of sending an armed force among the Mexicans was *unecesssary,* inasmuch as Mexico was in no way molesting, or menacing the United States or the people thereof; and that it was *unconstitutional,* because the power of levying war is vested in Congress, and not in the President. He thought the principal motive for the act was to divert public attention from the surrender of 'Fifty-four, forty, or fight' to Great Britain, on the Oregon boundary question."

Many biographers have looked upon Lincoln's congressional service as having been of little consequence for the nation or himself. Some have even estimated his career of two short sessions in Congress as having been "weak." We have found, however, in the study of his resolutions and speeches, though legislatively ineffective, evidence of a highly active, independent, morally courageous ethical mind that dared to challenge the rights of President Polk to start war on Mexico. In the face of bitter criticism, as being unpatriotic, he upheld the powers of Congress alone to declare war as conferred upon it by the Constitution. Representative Lincoln proved a vigorous defender of the Constitution and one of the best informed and keenest analytical students of its history in Congress.

Some historians think he blundered in presenting resolutions advocating the abolition of slavery in the District of Columbia, but herein we see again that he tried to put into practice his political philosophy that by equitably reducing slavery in the District it must become more disposed eventually to die out in all of the states.

If Abraham Lincoln's constituency had been such as to give him a long career in Congress he probably would have become one of the foremost legislators of his time. Perhaps we might then never have had a secession of the slave states and a war, for, as a master of compromise, he would have fought for their constitutional rights as well as their limitations.

Chapter XVIII

DISAPPOINTED POLITICIAN

The election of President Zachary Taylor in 1848 somewhat restored the lost prestige of Congressman "Spot" Lincoln in Washington and Illinois, but his influence in obtaining political appointments for his constituents soon waned. His letters at this time show how he allowed himself, through indecision, to become involved unwisely in the meshes of duplicity of rival politicians. However he tried earnestly and conscientiously to treat each man fairly, he suffered no little humiliation and anxiety over the blame of disappointed friends.

For 11 years, from the spring of 1849 until his election as President in November 1860, Lincoln practised law and lived in Springfield. This period divides naturally into three phases of dominant interest; failure in trying to build up political influence, resulting in transference of major interest to the practice of law, followed by revival of political interest in the national solution of the conflict over slavery in opposition to the policies of Stephen A. Douglas. Lincoln's letters in this and the following chapter reveal the attitude, principles, and methods by which he rose to prominence in his profession in the middle west, leading to his political rejuvenescence when the people needed a leader.

On Political Appointments

Lincoln's attitude and reasoning over President Taylor's appointments throws much light on his own subtle way of playing personal politics and the policy he would adopt later, when President, toward office seekers and government appointments.

He favored, as was then general practice, the appointment of capable Whigs who had worked for Taylor's election, to replace the partisan Democrats in office, although he admitted openly that he could not say they had been inefficient. In this he was not inclined to adopt the Democratic party's Jacksonian wholesale philosophy "to the victor belongs the spoils," for this placed party interest above national welfare and led to overloading the administration with lazy, inefficient yesmen. A young party's strength depends on placing in office capable, earnest men willing to work for its success with that of the nation. Even though it involved the discharge of some capable, experienced, ranking officials and reduced for a time the efficiency of government Lincoln stoutly urged such action. His recommendations, his letters show, were conscientiously studied for efficiency as well as practical politics and abhorrence of graft.

"No member of the cabinet knows so well as yourself," he wrote to W. B. Preston, Secretary of the Navy (4, 20, 1849), "the great anxiety I felt for Gen: Taylor's election, and consequently none could so well appreciate my anxiety for the success of his administration. . . . It is seen here that the government advertising, or a great part of it, is given to the Democratic papers. This gives offence to the Whig papers; and, if persisted in, will leave the administration without any newspaper support whatever. . . . I suppose Gen: Taylor, because both of his declarations, and his inclinations, will not go the doctrine of removals very strongly; and hence the greater reason, when an office or a job is not already in democratic hands, that it should be given to a Whig."

Importance of Being Consistent in All Things

Lincoln, however, was not radically partisan, as his letter to Secretary Preston (6, 24, 1849) shows, on the retention of democrats in office:

"I understand my personal friend and fellow Illinoisian, A. F. Patrick, has been removed from a clerkship in your Department, on some charge implicating his capacity or business habits as a clerk. In such an implication I suspect injustice has been done him, not by you, but by those on whose information you acted. If this be so you can ascertain it; and I shall be much obliged if you will wipe the injurious stigma from him. This is one thing; another is that if not inconsistent, I much wish he could have some temporary employment till about the meeting of Congress. When I say 'if not inconsistent' I mean that I wish you to be consistent in all things; and that if obliging Mr. Patrick, democrat as he is, in the matter of temporary employment, would at all interfere with your consistencey, I wish you not to do it."

Consistently Reverses His Reversal of Recommendations

Lincoln's great need of friends and his inclination to be sympathetically attentive to their wishes, often deferring to them at his own expense, has previously been demonstrated by a number of incidents. The following episode shows that he would not only reverse his recommendations to please a friend but upon finding that his confidence was being violated he would not hesitate to again reverse his reversal. He had recommended, to Secretary Ewing, W. Davis for the position of *Receiver* and T. R. King for *Register* in the General Land Office. A week later (4, 13, 1849) for "a personal reason, of no consequence," he wrote, "I now wish to transpose those recommendations; so that Davis may stand for *Register* and King for *Receiver.*"

This reversal of recommendations was done to please his old friend William Butler who also desired a position in the Land Office but seems not to have been regarded as fit for it by Lincoln. Butler was scheming to get the position of *Receiver,* but, not wishing to compete with his friend Davis he had his enemy King nominated for it so that he could discredit him. Lincoln's faith in Butler prevented him from seeing through the situation until King was publicly denounced as a disreputable person and a public tirade was turned upon himself for making the recommendation that threatened to break down his influence in Washington. Charges were forwarded by Butler or his friends to Secretary Ewing stating that King had been indicted three years previously "for keeping a gaming house."

Upon learning that his own reputation for reliability in recommending men of good character for office had been jeopardized Lincoln appealed to his friend P. H. Thompson, a merchant of Pekin, Illinois and a friend of King's, to sustain him. In his letter he enclosed a statement (4, 25, 1849) written on a scrap of paper that affirmed King's good character and asked him to copy it in his own handwriting and "get everybody (not three or four but three or four hundred) to sign it and then send it to me. "Also," he asked, "have six, eight or ten of the best known whig friends there, to write me individual letters, stating the truth in this matter, as they understand it."

Nowhere do we find better evidence of Lincoln's self-respectful character and strength of self-control than in the patience he exercised in this embarrassing situation.

> To Secretary Ewing he wrote the next day (4, 26, 1849) "to request that, if in this, or any other case, charges shall be sent against persons I have recommended, you will suspend action, and notify me. I will take pains to avoid imposing any unworthy man on the Department. Mr. King resides in the Land District, but sixty miles from me; and I recommended him to you, on the recommendation of his neighbors to me. I know him personally, and think him a good man; still my acquaintance with him is not intimate enough to warrent me in totally disregarding a charge against him. Accordingly I am making particular enquiry in the matter, and the Department shall know the result. I am not the less anxious in this matter because of knowing the principal object of the fault finders, to be to stab me."

Two weeks later (5, 10, 1849), after he had completed his investigation of King's reputation, Lincoln wrote Secretary Ewing a candid explanation of the whole affair.

> "I regret troubling you so often in relation to the Land Offices here; but I hope you will perceive the necessity of it, and excuse me. On the 7th. April I wrote you recommending Turner R. King for Register and Walter Davis for Receiver. Subsequently I wrote you that, for a private reason, I had concluded to transpose them. That private reason was the request of an old personal firend, who himself desired to be Receiver, but whom I felt my duty to refuse a recommendation. He said if I would transpose King & Davis, he would be satisfied; I thought it a whim, but anxious to oblige him, I consented. Immediately he commenced an assault upon King's character, intending as I suppose, to defeat his appointment, and thereby secure another chance for himself. The double offence of bad faith to me, and slander upon a good man, is so totally outrageous, that

I now ask to have King and Davis placed as I originally recommended—that is, King for Register and Davis for Receiver. . . .

."In writing to you a third time in relation to these offices, I stated that I supposed charges had been forwarded to you against King, and that I would enquire into the truth of them. I now send you herewith what I suppose will be an ample defense against any such charges. I ask attention to all the papers, but particularly to the letter of Dr. David Mark & the paper with the long list of names. *There is no mistake about King's being a good man.* . . . it would, in my opinion, be injustice, and withall, a blunder, not to appoint him."

Herndon saw (Hertz, 1938) Lincoln as a keen judge of juries and an accurate interpreter of public sentiment and the trends of the great moral and political movements of his time but a poor judge of the character and motives of individual persons. This idea has been generally adopted by biographers, but an analytical review of his personal letters shows that, quite to the contrary, Lincoln was an unusually careful and discriminating student of the ideas, beliefs, temperaments, motives, prejudices, and attitudes of individual people as well as of groups and organizations.

Muddles Appointment For Commissioner of General Land Office

As the end of Lincoln's term in Congress approached, he considered making an application for the position of Commissioner of the General Land Office but hesitated until too late because Mrs. Lincoln objected and he had promised to recommend a friend for the position. In a letter to Joshua Speed (2, 20, 1849) he gave the following reasons.

"I am flattered to learn that Mr. Crittenden [U. S. Senator from Kentucky] has any recollection of me which is not unfavorable; and for the manifestation of your kindness towards me, I sincerely thank you. Still there is nothing about me which would authorize me to think of a first class office; and a second class one would not compensate me for being snarled at by others who want it for themselves. I believe that, so far as the whigs in congress, are concerned, I could have the Genl. Land office almost by common consent; but then Sweet, and Col: Morison, and Browning, and Cyrus Edwards all want it. And what is worse, while I think I could easily take it myself, I fear I shall have trouble to get it for any other man in Illinois."

The office had charge of the vast Government lands in the States and Territories and carried extensive political influence. When Lincoln's term in Congress expired a Commissioner had not yet been appointed. Among the applicants from Illinois, Cyrus Edwards seemed to have built up the most impressive influence except for one man, Justin Butterfield of Chicago, who had the nod of Thomas Ewing, Secretary of the Interior, which included the administration of all Federal lands. However, competitors from Indiana and Ohio seemed to have worked up stronger political pressure on President Taylor than either of these men for the appointment.

The following abstracts from Lincoln's letters on this situation reveal how conscientiously he played the complex game of personal politics and eventually became involved in bitter recriminations, thereafter painful to him. He was eventually persuaded by Whig friends, who wanted the Commissioner of General Land office to go to Illinois, to apply for the appointment. He could not, however, conscientiously take this step without some change of agreements since he had recommended two of his friends for the position and promised to support the one selected between them upon their private arrangement. His reasons for this delicately ethical change of mind reveal again his unconsciously involved neurotic inclination to vacillate, under pressure of conflicting personal appeals, until his decision was made up by conditioned affections and external circumstances to pursue a course that felt to be honorably and legally consistent.

To Col. W. B. Warren he wrote (4, 7, 1849):

> "In answer to your note concerning the General Land Office, I have to say that, if the office can be secured to Illinois by my consent to accept it, and not otherwise, I give that consent. Some months since I gave my word to secure the appointment to that office of Mr. Cyrus Edwards, if in my power, in case of a vacancy; and more recently I stipulated with Col. Baker that if Mr. Edwards and Col. J. L. D. Morrison could arrange with each other for one of them to withdraw, we would jointly recommend the other. In relation to these pledges, I must not only be chaste but above suspicion. If the office shall be tendered to me I must be permitted to say "give it to Mr. Edwards, or, if so agreed by them, to Col. Morrison, and I decline it; if not, I accept.' With this understanding, you are at liberty to procure me the offer of the appointment if you can; and I shall feel complimented by your effort, and still more by it's success."

It seems that Lincoln's friends had informed him that they had been successful in getting Morrison to withdraw in order that he might conscientiously apply for the office for himself for he recommended (4, 10, 1849) Morrison to a sectional office in the Land Department. Although Edwards, as shown later, had not frankly acceded to the plan, Lincoln justified himself for his change of mind in order to defeat Justin Butterfield for the reasons expressed to W. B. Preston (5, 16, 1849).

> "It is a delicate matter to oppose the wishes of a friend; and consequently I address you on the subject I now do, with no little hesitation. Last night I received letters from different persons at Washington assuring me it was not improbable that Justin Butterfield, of Chicago, Ills, would be appointed Commissioner of the Genl. Land-Office. It was to avert this very thing, that I called on you at your rooms one sunday evening shortly after you were installed, and besought you that, so far as in your power, no man from Illinois should be appointed to any high office, without my being at least heard on the question. You were kind enough to say you thought my request a reasonable one. Mr. Butterfield is my friend, is well qualified, and, I suppose, would be faithful in the office. So far, good.

But now for the objections. In 1840 we fought a fierce and laborious battle in Illinois, many of us spending almost the entire year in the contest. The general victory came, and with it, the appointment of a set of drones, including the same Butterfield, who had never spent a dollar or lifted a finger in the fight. The place he got was that of District Attorney. . . . Again, winter and spring before the last, when you and I were almost sweating blood to have Genl. Taylor nominated, this same man was ridiculing the idea, and going for Mr. Clay; and when Genl. T. was nominated, if he went out of the city of Chicago to aid in his election, it is more than I ever heard, or believe. Yet, when the election is secured, by other men's labor, and even against his effort, why, he is the first man on hand for the best office that our state lays any claim to. Shall this thing be? Our Whigs will throw down their arms, and fight no more, if the fruit of their labor is thus disposed of. If there is one man in this state who desired B's appointment to any thing, I declare I have not heard of him. What influence operates for him, I cannot conceive. Your position makes it a matter of peculiar interest to you, that the administration shall be successful; and be assured, nothing can more endanger it, than making appointments through old-hawker foreign influences, which offend, rather than gratify, the people immediately interested in the offices."

Two days later (5, 18, 1849) Lincoln expressed even more vigorous dissatisfaction over Butterfield to Duff Green, a general political fixer about Washington and suggested a line of wire pulling. It shows decision to defeat Butterfield but hesitation on who to recommend instead.

"Can not you get the ear of Gen: Taylor? Ewing is for B; and therefore he must be avoided. Preston I think will favor you. Mr. Edwards has written me offering to decline, but I advised him not to do so. Some kind friends think I ought to be an applicant; but I am for Mr. Edwards. Try to defeat B; and in doing so use Mr. Edwards, J. L. D. Morrison, or myself, whichever you can to best advantage."

As the contest progressed Lincoln's anxiety increased and he wrote letters in the next few days to friends in Illinois, Ohio, and Indiana who might have some pull with the President on this appointment. To lawyer Joseph Gillespie:

"Butterfield will be Commissioner . . . unless prevented by strong and speedy efforts. Ewing is for him; and he is only not appointed yet because old Zach hangs fire. I have reliable information of this. Now, if you agree with me, that his appointment would *dissatisfy,* rather than gratify the whigs of this state; that it would slacken their energies in future contests, that his appointment in /41 is an old sore with them . . . that his appointment now would be a fatal blunder to the administration, and our political ruin here in Ills—write Mr. Crittenden to that effect. . . . You might write directly to Old Zach; you will be the judge of the propriety of that. Not a moment's time is to be lost."

In almost identical letters written on the same day (5, 29, 1849) to Congressmen E. Embree and R. W. Thompson of Indiana on this appointment he said:

"I am about to ask a favor of you—one which, I hope will not cost you much. I understand the General Land Office is about to be given to Illinois, and that Mr. Ewing desires Justin Butterfield, of Chicago, to be the man. I give you my word, the appointment of Mr. B. will be an egregious political blunder. . . . I wish you to write General Taylor at once, saying that either *I, or the man I recommend,* should in your opinion, be appointed to that office, if any one from Illinois shall be."

Lincoln finally made up his mind, when he found that Cyrus Edwards would certainly not get the appointment, to withdraw his support of him and present his own application. In the next two weeks, he wrote a number of letters to friends asking them frankly to write to the President and Secretary of the Interior recommending him for the office. He finally grew so intent upon getting the position that in June he made a long, tedious trip to Washington in a last effort to influence these men.

From Lincoln's memorandum (6, 15?, 1849) it seems that he had hoped to obtain an audience with the President in which he planned to say:

"Nothing in my papers questions Mr. B's competency and honesty, and, I presume nothing in his questions mine. Being equal so far, if it does not appear I am preferred by the Whigs of Illinois, I lay no claim to the office."

As to the only Whig representative from Illinois in Congress and a leader in the campaign for President Taylor's nomination and election, Lincoln felt that he was properly entitled to be heard on appointments involving the interests of his state. He continued:

"But if it does appear I am preferred, it will be argued that the whole Northwest, and not Illinois alone, should be heard. I answer I am as strongly recommended by Ohio and Indiana, as well as Illinois; and further, that when the many appointments were made for Ohio, as for the Northwest, Illinois was not consulted. When an Indianian was nominated for Governor of Minnesota and another appointed for Commissioner of Mexican claims, as for the Northwest, Illinois was not consulted. When a citizen of Iowa was appointed Second Assistant Postmaster General and another to a Land Office in Minnesota, Illinois was not consulted. Of none of these have I ever complained. In each of them, the State whose citizen was appointed was allowed to control, and I think rightly. I only ask that Illinois be not cut off with less deference."

Lincoln was informed that he would have been given the appointment but his personal application came after commitments had already been made to Butterfield, who was made commissioner. Before leaving Washington he obtained permission from Secretary Ewing to withdraw the papers on file recommending him for office. After reaching Springfield he opened the sealed packet, containing some forty letters, and found among them an harassing stab in the back by Cyrus Edwards.

Unhappy "Conflict of Feeling"

Lincoln wrote two letters to J. Gillespie on the same day (7, 13, 1849) expressing his unhappy embarrassment over the attitude of Cyrus Edwards whom he had regarded as a friend.

"Mr. Edwards is angry with me; and, in which, he is wronging me very much. He wrote a letter against me & in favour of Butterfield, which was filed in the Department. Ever since I discovered this, I have had a conflict of feeling, whether to write him or not; and, so far, I have remained silent. If he knew of your letters to me . . . and to the President . . . I suspect he would be angry with you too. Both those letters would help defend me with him; but I will not hazard your interest by letting him know of them. To avoid that, I write you a separate letter which I wish you would show him when it may be convenient.

"You will please accept my sincere thanks for your very flattering terms in which you speak of me in your letter to the President. I withdrew the papers on file in my behalf, by which means your letter is now in my possession."

In the letter to be shown to Edwards he said:

"Mr. Edwards is unquestionably offended with me, in connection with the matter of the General Land-Office. He wrote a letter against me, which was filed at the Department. The better part of one's life consists of his friendships; and, of these mine with Mr. Edwards was one of the most cherished. I have not been false to it. At a word, I could have had the office any time before the Department was committed to Mr. Butterfield— at least Mr. Ewing and the President say as much. That word I forbore to speak, partly for other reasons, but chiefly for Mr. Edwards' sake. Losing the office that he might gain it, I was always for; but to lose his *friendship* by the effort for him, would oppress me very much, were I not sustained by the utmost consciousness of rectitude. I first determined to be an applicant, unconditionally, on the 2nd of June; and I did so then upon being informed by a Telegraphic dispatch that the question was narrowed down to Mr. B and myself, and that the Cabinet had postponed the appointment three weeks for my benefit. Not doubting, that Mr. Edwards was wholly out of the question, I nevertheless would not then have been an applicant, had I supposed he would thereby be brought to suspect me of treachery to him. Two or three days afterwards a conversation with Levi Davis convinced me Mr. Edwards was dissatisfied; but I was then too far in to get out. His own letter, written on the 25th. of April, after I had fully informed him of all that had passed up to within a few days of that time, gave assurance I had that entire confidence from him, which I felt my uniform and strong friendship for him entitled me to. Among other things it says 'whatever course your judgment may dictate as proper to be pursued, shall never be excepted to by me.' I also had a letter from Washington, saying Chambers of the Republican had brought a rumor then that, Mr. E. had declined in my favor, which rumor I judged came from Mr. E. himself, as I had not then breathed of his letter, to any living creature.

"In saying I had never before the 2nd. of June determined to be an applicant, unconditionally, I mean to admit that before then, I had said substantially I would take the office rather than it should be lost to the state, or given to one in the state whom the whigs did not want; but I aver that in every instance in which I spoke of myself, I intended to keep, and now believe I did keep Mr. E. ahead of myself. . . .

"You may wish to know how Butterfield finally beat me. I can not tell you particulars now, but will, when I see you. In the mean time let it be understood I am not greatly dissatisfied."

Importance of the President's Appointments

Six weeks after Lincoln failed to obtain the appointment of Commissioner of General Land Office he wrote to his friend J. M. Clayton, Secretary of State (7, 28, 1849):

"It is with some hesitation I presume to address this letter—and yet I wish not only you, but the whole cabinet, and the President too, would consider the subject matter of it. My being among the People while you and they are not, will excuse the apparent presumption. It is understood that the President at first adopted, as a general rule, to throw the responsibility of the appointments upon their respective Departments; and that such rule is adhered to and practised upon. This course I at first thought proper; and, of course, I am not now complaining of it. Still I am disappointed with the effect of it on the public mind. It is fixing for the President the unjust and ruinous character of being a mere man of straw. This must be arrested, or it will damn us all inevitably. It is said Gen. Taylor and his officers held a council of war, at Palo Alto (I believe); and that he then fought the battle against the unanimous opinion of those officers. This fact (no matter whether rightfully or wrongfully) gives him more popularity than ten thousand submissions, however really wise and magnanimous those submissions may be."

"The appointments need be no better than they have been, but the public must be brought to understand, that they are the *President's* appointments. He must occasionally say, or seem to say, 'by the Eternal,' 'I take the responsibility.' Those phrases were the 'Samson's locks' of Gen. Jackson, and we dare not disregard the lessons of experience."

Later Lincoln, when President, held so strongly to this political philosophy that some members of his Cabinet and of Congress complained bitterly of loss of influence with their constituents and even ganged up to force him to yield such powers with, however, little success.

Declines Substitute Office

A short time after President Taylor's appointment of Butterfield, as Commissioner, Secretary of State Clayton notified Lincoln that he had been appointed Secretary of the Territory of Oregon. The position was unsolicited and Lincoln respectfully declined it and recommended (9, 16, 1849) his friend Simeon Francis, editor of the oldest Whig paper in the state, for the office.

"I know I have no right to claim the disposal of the office; but I do think, under all the circumstances, that he ought to receive the appointment."

Faithful but Unoptimistic Whig

Lincoln never held resentment against Ewing for his defeat, as a letter to his friend J. M. Lucas (11, 17, 1849) shows:

"I regret that the elections in the states have gone so badly; but I think there is some reason for hoping that this year has been the administration's 'darkest hour.' The appointments were its most difficult task; and this year it has necessarily been viewed in connection with them alone. These are pretty much through with, and next we can get on grounds of *measures*—policy—where we can unite & rally again. At least I hope so . . . Mr. Ewing is keeping faith with me [on appointments] in regard to my friends. By the way, I have a better opinion of Mr. Ewing than you, perhaps, suppose I have."

When Charles L. Wilson, Editor of the Chicago *Journal,* attacked Commissioner Butterfield as being an "autocrat" unfit for the office and involved Lincoln in the charge, Lincoln defended his rival in a letter to the editor (11, 21, 1849):

"When Mr. Butterfield was appointed commissioner of the land office, I expected him to be a faithful and able officer, and nothing has since come to my knowledge disappointing that expectation."

Dr. Henry "Is Number One With Me"

Lincoln's sympathetic attachment and dependence on Dr. Henry as his physician continued from the time of his first nervous breakdown for the rest of his life. The ardor of their friendship is evident in the following two letters.

To Secretary Clayton he wrote (11, 25, 1849):

"Allow me to introduce our friend, Dr. A. G. Henry of this place. I solicit for him your kindness and confidence; and this I do, not cerimoniously merely, but in all sincerety. You may perhaps remember his name, as that of the first person in whose behalf I made an appeal to you immediately after the inauguration of Genl. Taylor."

To Secretary Ewing (3, 22, 1850):

"I understand you have under consideration the question of appointing Dr. A. G. Henry to some Indian Agency. I wish now merely to say that of all those whom I have desired should receive appointments from this Administration, Dr. Henry was at first, has always been, and still is, No. One with me. I believe, nay, I *know,* he has done more disinterested labor in the Whig cause, than any other one, two, or three men in the state."

"My Feelings Were Wounded"

Lincoln's recommendation of Dr. A. G. Henry for an office in the Indian Agency disappointed G. W. Rives who supported another candidate. The following letter to Rives (12, 15, 1849) is remarkable for showing the extraordinary care with which he tried to keep his friends and how he suffered when he thought himself being unfairly used or blamed by anyone.

"From the beginning of our acquaintance I had felt the greatest kindness for you, and had supposed it was reciprocated on your part. Last summer, under circumstances which I mentioned to you, I was painfully constrained to withhold a recommendation which you desired; and shortly afterwards I learned, in such a way as to believe it, that you were indulging open abuse of me. Of course, my feelings were wounded. On receiving your last letter, the question occurred whether you were attempting to *use* me, at the same time you would *injure* me, or whether you might not have been misrepresented to me. If the former, I ought not to answer you; if the latter I ought, and so I have remained in suspense. I now enclose you a letter [presumeably of recommendation] which you may use if you think fit."

Declines Congressional Nomination

Lincoln's friends pressed him to become a candidate in the next congressional election but he declined in a letter to the *Illinois Journal* (6, 5, 1850).

"An article in the Tazewell Mirror in which my name is prominently used, makes me fear that my position, with reference to the next Congressional election in this District, is misunderstood, and that such misunderstanding may work injury to the cause of our friends. I therefore take occasion to say that I neither seek, expect, or desire a nomination for a seat in the next Congress, that I prefer my name should not be brought forward in that connection; and that I would now peremptorily forbid the use of it, could I feel entirely at liberty to do so. I will add, that in my opinion, the whigs of the district have several other men, any one of whom they *can* elect, and that too quite as *easily* as they could elect me."

Eulogy of President Taylor

Lincoln did not lose interest in Whig policies as a disappointed office seeker who could not overcome the opposition of a Whig clique against him as some biographers seem to infer. He was selected by his party in Illinois, upon President Zachary Taylor's untimely sudden death, to deliver the eulogy in Chicago (7, 25, 1850). Such unexpected prominence is sufficent evidence that he remained a respected leader in his party's councils. He gave a short biographical description of President's Taylor's life, and the choice of laudable characteristics he attributed to him reveals his own ideals of manhood, and indicates the attitude that he was constantly cultivating as a lawyer and statesman and would become characteristic as President. It was a balance of negatives in being above excitement and fear, hate and revenge, with positive unostentatious devotion to duty, working humbly and consistently without seeking applause. In it he said:

"Gen. Taylor's battles were not distinguished for brilliant military manoeuvers; but in all he seems rather to have conquered by the exercise of a sober and steady judgment, coupled with a dogged incapacity to understand that defeat was possible. His rarest military trait, was a combination of negatives—absence of *excitement* and absence of *fear*. He could not be *flurried,* and he could not be *scared.*

" . . . Terrible as he was to his country's enemies, no man was so little disposed to have difficulty with his friends. During the period of his life, *duelling* was a practise not quite uncommon among gentlemen in the peaceful avocations of life, and still more common, among the officers of the Army and Navy. Yet, so far as I can learn, a *duel* with Gen. Taylor, has never been talked of.

"He was alike averse to *sudden* and to *startling* quarrels; and he pursued no man with *revenge.* . . . As to Gen. Taylor's relations with his soldiers—all testify to the uniform kindness, and his constant care for, and hearty sympathy with, their every want and suffering; while none can be found to declare, that he was ever a tyrant anywhere, in any thing. . . .

"In Gen. Taylor's public relation to his country, what will strongly impress a close observer, was his unostentatious, self-sacrificing, long enduring devotion to his *duty*. He indulged in no recreations, he visited no public places, seeking applause; but quietly as the earth in its orbit, he was always at his post. . . .

"How well might the dying hero say at last, 'I have done my duty. I am ready to go.' . . . It is much for the young to know, that treading the hard path of duty, as he trod it, *will* be noticed, and *will* lead to high places. . . .

"The death of the late President may not be without its use, in reminding us, that *we,* too must die. Death, abstractly considered, is the same with the high as with the low; but practically, we are not so much aroused to the contemplation of our own mortal natures, by the fall of *many* undistinguished, as that of *one* great, and well known, name. By the latter, we are forced to muse, and ponder, sadly."

Lincoln's nostaligic preoccupation with the inevitability of life ending in death came strongly to the fore of his mind in closing his eulogy on President Taylor. He closed with quoting six appropriate stanzas from his favorite poem. "Oh, why should the spirit of mortal be proud." His eulogy of President Zachary Taylor might so fittingly have been delivered by another orator about himself 15 years later that it seems almost unconsciously premonitional of the eventual course of developments for himself. It illustrates how honest men, whose attitudes and minds are set upon establishing certain moral social orders for the people, will, in similar situations work in similar ways.

Eulogy of Henry Clay

Lincoln was being regarded with more respect by his party and was honored again with a request to deliver a eulogy in the Hall of Representatives of Springfield (7, 6, 1852), this time on Senator Henry Clay who died on June 29, 1852. Clay had been the most effective compromiser between the conflicting proslavery and antislavery members of Congress.

The limitations of space prohibit extensive quotations from his address other than to indicate the qualities in a man he had admired since his youth, and whose political philosophy, with that of Thomas Jefferson, had influenced most his development of practical views on democratic government. Again we find, in Lincoln's choice of descriptive characteristics, a reflection of the personal qualities that he desired most to cultivate for himself—passionate love of freedom and legal equality of all men, eloquence without use of hackneyed figures of speech, cool judgment and indominable will, doing everything with a view to its value for the whole nation and not for a section or a party of it.

He pointed out that the infant Henry Clay was born of obscure parents in the wilderness of Virginia in 1777, soon after

> "the oppressed colonies of Great Britain . . . declared their national independence. . . . Mr. Clay's education, to the end of his life, was comparatively limited. . . . [His] lack of a more perfect early education, however it may be regretted generally, teaches at least one profitable lesson; it teaches that in this country, one can scarcely be so poor, but that, if he *will,* he *can* acquire sufficient education to get through the world respectably."

Clay, like Lincoln, studied law and served in his twenties in his state (Kentucky) legislature before being elected to the House of Representatives. He had become prominent in the state as a legislator and an orator when Lincoln was born; and no doubt the boy's mind, in its formative years, was greatly impressed by his parents' expressions of admiration for the nobility of their senator's arguments to maintain freedom with equal rights and justice in government.

> "Throughout that long period" [1803-1852], Lincoln said, "he has been the most loved, and most implicitly followed by friends, and the most dreaded by opponents, of all living American politicians. In all the great questions which have agitated the country, and particularly in those great and fearful crises, the Missouri question—the Nullification question, and the slavery question, as connected with the newly acquired territory, involving and endangering the stability of the Union, his has been the leading and most conspicuous part. In 1824 he was first a candidate for the Presidency, and was defeated; and, although he was successively defeated for the same office in 1832, and in 1844, there has never been a moment since 1824 till after 1848, when a very large portion of the American people did not cling to him with an enthusiastic hope and purpose of still elevating

him to the Presidency. . . . It is probably true he owed his pre-eminence to no one quality, but to a fortunate combination of several. He was surprisingly eloquent; but many eloquent men fail utterly; and they are not, as a class, generally successful. His judgment was excellent, but many men of good judgment, live and die unnoticed. His will was indomitable; but this quality often secures to its owner nothing better than a character for useless obstinacy. These then were Mr. Clay's leading qualities. No one of them is very uncommon, but all taken together are rarely combined in a single individual; and this is probably the reason why such men as Henry Clay are so rare in the world.

"Mr. Clay's eloquence did not consist, as many fine specimens of eloquence does, of types and figures—of antithesis, and elegant arrangement of words and sentences; but rather of that deeply earnest and impassioned tone, and manner, which can proceed only from great sincerity and through a conviction, in the speaker of the justice and importance of his cause. This it is, that truly touches the chords of human sympathy; and those who heard Mr. Clay, never failed to be moved by it, or ever afterwards, forget the impression. All his efforts were merely for practical effect. He never spoke merely to be heard. He never delivered a Fourth of July Oration, or a eulogy on an occasion like this. As a politician or statesman, no one was so habitually careful to avoid all sectional ground. Whatever he did, he did for the whole country. In the construction of his measures he ever carefully surveyed every part of the field, and duly weighed every conflicting interest. Feeling, as he did, and as the truth surely is, that the world's best hope depended on the continued Union of these States; he was ever jealous of and watchful for, whatever might have the slightest tendency to separate them.

"Mr. Clay's predominant sentiment, from first to last, was a deep devotion to the cause of human liberty—a strong sympathy with the oppressed everywhere, and an ardent wish for their elevation. With him, this was a primary and all controlling passion. Subsidiary to this was the conduct of his whole life. He loved his country partly because it was his own country, but mostly because it was a free country; and he burned with a zeal for its advancement, prosperity and glory, because he saw in such the advancement, prosperity and glory, of human liberty, human right and human nature. He desired the prosperity of his countrymen partly because they were his countrymen, but chiefly to show the world that freemen could be prosperous."

When we express sincere admiration for certain qualities of another person's character we reveal what we wish to be. Conversely, expressions of contempt for another's character reveal what we would not be. Lincoln's admiring characterizations of Washington, Jefferson, Taylor, and Clay are consistently indicative of the altruistic attitude he was cultivating, to become with constant repetition impressed in the tissues of his brain and bone—"love of liberty and right, unselfishly, and for their own sakes." Hereby, we may add, the intelligent mind of good will obtains its deepest enjoyment of living.

Precepts of Jefferson and Clay

The informed people of the time saw in the vast southwestern territory acquired by the United States, from France through the Louisiana purchase and later from Mexico, the danger of dissolution of the Union over the question of expansion or restriction of slavery. It had now become the first national problem, and Lincoln was greatly preoccupied with searching for a just compromise within the precepts of the Constitution. When Missouri in 1819 had formed a state constitution without providing for the exclusion of slavery, and applied for admission to the Union, almost all of the non-slave-holding states rejected her. The bitter pro- and anti-slavery conflict that followed assumed a geographical division across the nation along the Ohio River to Missouri and westward. In reaction to this dangerous geographical political division of the nation Past-President Thomas Jefferson, father of the Constitution, made after his retirement the following statement, as quoted by Lincoln in continuing his eulogy on Clay:

> " 'I had for a long time ceased to read newspapers, or to pay any attention to public affairs, confident they were in good hands, and content to be a passenger on our bark to the shore from which I am not distant. But the momentous question, like a fire bell in the night, awakened, and filled me with terror. I considered it at once as the knell of the Union. It is hushed, indeed, for the moment. But this is a reprieve only, not a final sentence. A geographical line, co-inciding with a marked principle, moral and political, once conceived, and held up to the angry passions of men, will never be obliterated; and every irritation will mark it deeper and deeper. . . . a general emancipation, and *expatriation* could be effected; and, gradually, and with due sacrifices I think it might be. But as it is, we have the wolf by the ears and we can neither hold him, nor safely let him go. Justice is in one scale, and self-preservation in the other.' "

Jefferson's statement that the Union could be saved from division only through general emancipation gradually worked out, seems to have greatly impressed young Lincoln, a boy of 10 when it was made, for he held the same view throughout his life.

Clay's solution of the dangerous Missouri question, after the second rejection for admission to the Union as a slave state, was eulogized by Lincoln:

> "A sullen gloom hung over the nation. All felt that the rejection of Missouri, was equivalent to a dissolution of the Union: because those states which already had, what Missouri was rejected for refusing to relinquish, would go with Missouri. All deprecated and deplored this, but none saw how to avert it. . . . By some judicious modifications of his plan, coupled with laborious efforts with individual members, and his own over-mastering eloquence upon the floor, he [Mr. Clay] finally secured the admission of the State" [in 1821]. . . .

On the question of domestic slavery Lincoln said: [Mr. Clay] "was, on principle and feeling, opposed to slavery. The very earliest, and one of the latest public efforts of his life, separated by a period of more than fifty years, were both made in favor of gradual emancipation of the slaves in Kentucky. He did not perceive, that on a question of human right, the negroes were to be excepted from the human race. And yet Mr. Clay was the owner of slaves. Cast into life when slavery was already widely spread and deeply seated, he did not perceive, as I think no wise man has perceived, how it could be at *once* eradicated, without producing a greater evil, even to the cause of human liberty itself. His feeling and his judgment, therefore, ever led him to oppose both extremes of opinion on the subject."

We will see a few years later in his debates with Douglas, how strongly Lincoln held an attitude similar to that of Jefferson and Clay on the solution of slavery. He abhorred radicalism of any kind as a dangerous urge of emotional imbalance and excoriated it wherever it tended to force itself into the political situation.

"Those who would shiver into fragments the Union of these States; tear to tatters its now venerated constitution; and even burn the last copy of the Bible, rather than slavery should continue a single hour, together with all their halting sympathizers, have received, and are receiving their just execration; and the name, and opinions, and influence of Mr. Clay, are full, and, as I trust, effectually and enduringly, arrayed against them. But I would also, if I could, array his name, opinions, and influence against the opposite extreme—against a few; but an increasing number of men, who, for the sake of perpetuating slavery, are beginning to assail and ridicule the white-man's charter of freedom—the declaration that 'all men are created free and equal.' "

In closing his eulogy Lincoln expressed his own view on the solution of the slavery problem. It was entirely consistent with that of Jefferson and Clay:

"If as the friends of colonization hope, the present and coming generations of our countrymen shall by any means, succeed in freeing our land from the dangerous presence of slavery; and, at the same time in restoring a captive people to their long-lost fatherland; . . . and this too so gradually, that neither races nor individuals shall have suffered by the change, it will be a glorious consummation." . . .

A few years later, President Lincoln had to decide that it would be impractical to return freed slaves to Liberia.

Chapter XIX

PRACTICAL LAWYER

"Upon his return from Congress, he went to the practise of the law with greater earnestness than ever before," Lincoln wrote retrospectively for Scripps in 1860. We obtain better comprehension of how realistically and intelligently Lincoln constantly analyzed his personal efficiencies and deficiencies and successes and mistakes and how he continued cooly to discipline himself, from his own terse descriptions. In his Scripps letter he said:

> "He studied and nearly mastered the Six-books of Euclid, since he was a member of Congress. He regrets his want of education, and does what he can to supply the want."
>
> Lincoln explained his reasons for his study of Euclid: "In the course of my law reading I constantly came upon the word demonstrate—I thought at first I understood its meaning, but soon became satisfied that I did not. I consulted Webster's dictionary. That told of certain proof, 'proof beyond the probability of doubt:' but I could form no idea of what sort of proof that was. I consulted all the dictionaries and books of reference I could find, but with no better results. You might as well have defined blue to a blind man. At last I said: 'Lincoln, you can never make a lawyer if you do not understand what demonstrate means."

In choosing Euclid, as the best teacher of demonstration of mechanistic reasoning, Lincoln had the genius to see how he could apply geometrical principles of interaction to human behavior and the demonstration of logical determinants and sequelae in application of legal and political propositions.

> Herndon (1889) described how Lincoln, "as a member of Congress and otherwise immersed in politics seemed to lose interest in law," and how "political defeat . . . made a changed man of him. He was not soured —but made up for lost time in politics by studying law in earnest." On the circuit, he said, "we, usually, at the little county inns occupied the same bed. In most cases the beds were too short for him, and his feet would hang over the foot-board. . . . Placing a candle on a chair at the head of the bed, he would read and study for hours . . . till two o'clock in the morning. Meanwhile, I and others who occupied the same room would be . . . soundly asleep. On the circuit in this way he studied Euclid until he could with ease demonstrate all the propositions in the six books. How he could maintain his mental equilibrium or concentrate his thoughts on an abstract, while Davis, Logan, Swett, Edwards, and I so industriously filled the air with our interminable snoring was a problem that none of us could solve."

Lincoln seemed to labor under anxious doubt of his own understanding and application of what he had learned until he could describe it to some friend so that he could feel sure both understood it. This unusual trait, Herndon and other lawyers endured, generally with amusement and sometimes with admiration, and not infrequently with boredom, for once he seized upon a subject and a person there was no escape but to listen until he had finished.

Herndon should be credited with having had unusual psychological insight for a lawyer of his time. He was the first biographer who recognized in this particular characteristic of Lincoln the basis of development of his great mental powers. He discussed it with their contemporaries and traced its development back to his childhood through Mentor Graham, a friend of the Lincoln family in Kentucky. Abraham Lincoln's self-taught, systematic methods of study in New Salem greatly impressed Mentor Graham. "I have known him," he said, . . . to study for hours the best way . . . to express an idea." (We are reminded here of the story in Chapter IV that Lincoln told, of how as a child he felt he must understand what other people said so that he could repeat it intelligently to his playmates.)

Comments on these traits by Herndon show how consistently Lincoln continued to repeat his habits of mental training as a lawyer:

> "If he found anything worthy of his thoughts, he would write it down, commit it to memory, then analyze it—and tell it o'er and o'er to his . . . friends; and I can say . . . that he used to bore me terribly by his methods. . . . He would doubly explain things to me that needed no explanation. However, I stood it out of respect for the man; he was terribly afraid that I did not understand him when I understood even his thoughts at it. Lincoln despised 'glittering generalities' and even hated the men that used them. Mr. Lincoln was a very patient man generally, but if you wished to be cut off at the knee, just go at Lincoln with abstractions, . . . indefiniteness, mistiness of idea or expression. Here he flew up and became vexed and sometimes foolishly so; his mind was so organized that he could not help it. . . .he used to say to me 'Billy, don't shoot too high, shoot low down, and the common people will understand you; they are *the ones* which you wish to watch, at least they are the ones whom you ought to reach. The educated ones will understand you anyhow! . . . This Lincoln said to me many times when I was on the stump or at the bar, or writing letters for our newspapers." (1, 8, 1886, Hertz, 1938.)

Advice to Law Students

Between 1848 and 1856 Lincoln wrote letters and notes for lectures to law students. They give his practical comprehension of the philosophy and utility of law and his estimation of himself as a lawyer:

> "I am not an accomplished lawyer. I find quite as much material for a lecture in those points wherein I have failed, as those wherein I have been moderately successful. The leading rule for the lawyer, as for the man of every other calling, is diligence. Leave nothing to to-morrow which

can be done to-day. Never let your correspondance fall behind. Whatever piece of business you have in hand, before stopping, do all the labor pertaining to it which can then be done. When you bring a common-law suit, if you have the facts for doing so, write the declaration at once. If a law point be involved, examine the books, and note the authority you rely on upon the declaration itself, where you are sure to find it when wanted. The same of defenses and pleas. In business not likely to be litigated,—ordinary collection cases, foreclosures, partitions, and the like,—make all examinations of titles, and note them, and even draft orders and decrees in advance. This course has a triple advantage; it avoids omissions and neglect, saves your labor when once done, performs the labor out of court when you have leisure, rather than in court when you have not. Extemporaneous speaking should be practised and cultivated. It is the lawyer's avenue to the public. However able and faithful he may be in other respects, people are slow to bring him business if he cannot make a speech. And yet there is not a more fatal error to young lawyers than relying too much on speech-making. If any one, upon his rare power of speaking, shall claim an exemption from the drudgery of the law, his case is a failure in advance.

"Discourage litigaton. Persuade your neighbors to compromise whenever you can. Point out to them how the nominal winner is often a real loser—in fees, expenses, and waste of time. As a peace-maker the lawyer has a superior opportunity of being a good man. There will still be business enough.

"Never stir up litigation. A worse man can scarcely be found than one who does this. Who can be more nearly a fiend than he who habitually overhauls the register of deeds in search of defects in titles, whereon to stir up strife, and put money in his pocket? A moral tone ought to be infused into the profession which should drive such men out of it.

"The matter of fees is important, far beyond the mere question of bread and butter involved. Properly attended to, fuller justice is done to both lawyer and client. An exorbitant fee should never be claimed. As a general rule never take your whole fee in advance, nor any more than a small retainer. When fully paid beforehand, you are more than a common mortal if you can feel the same interest in the case, as if something was still in prospect for you, as well as for your client. And when you lack interest in the case the job will very likely lack skill and diligence in the performance. Settle the amount of fee and take a note in advance. Then you will feel that you are working for something, and you are sure to do your work faithfully and well. Never sell a fee note—at least not before the consideration service is performed. It leads to negligence and dishonesty—negligence by losing interest in the case, and dishonesty in refusing to refund when you have allowed the consideration to fail.

"There is a vague popular belief that lawyers are necessarily dishonest. I say vague, because when we consider to what extent confidence and honors are reposed in and conferred upon lawyers by the people, it appears improbable that their impression of dishonesty is very distinct and vivid. Yet the impression is common, almost universal. Let no young man choosing the law for a calling for a moment yield to the popular belief—resolve to be honest at all events; and if in your own judgment you cannot be an honest lawyer, resolve to be honest without being a lawyer. Choose some other occupation, rather than one in choosing of which you do, in advance, consent to be a knave."

Notes on the Philosophy of Improving Laws

"In law it is a good policy to never *plead* what you *need* not, lest you oblige yourself to *prove* what you *can* not. Reflect on this well before you proceed." (To U. F. Linder, 2, 20, 1848.)

Some time in 1858 Lincoln prepared notes for an argument on a case involving railroad legislation to be made before the Supreme Court of Illinois. They show again how methodically he developed his reasoning from carefully analyzed basic premises.

"*Legislation* and *ajudication* must follow, and conform to the progress of society.

"The progress of society now begins to produce cases of the transfer, for debts, of the entire property of Railroad corporations; and to enable transfereees to use, and enjoy, the transfered property, *legislation,* and ajudication, begins to be necessary.

"Shall this class of legislation, just now, now beginning with us, be *general* or *special?*

"Section Ten, of our constitution, requires that it should be general, if possible. (Read the section)

"Special legislation always trenches upon the judicial department; and, in so for, violates Section Two, of the constitution (Read it).

"Just reasoning—policy—is in favor of general legislation—else the legislature will be *loaded down* with the investigation of special cases—a work which the courts *ought* to perform, and can perform much more perfectly. How can the legislature rightly decide the facts in dispute between P. & B. [Page and Bacon] and S. C. & Co. [unknown].

"It is said that, under a general law, whenever a R. R. Co. gets tired of it's debts, it may transfer *fraudulently,* to get rid of them.

"So they may—so may individuals; and which—the *legislature* or the *courts* is best suited to try the question of fraud in either case?

"It is said, if a purchaser have acquired legal rights, let him not be robbed of them; but if he needs *legislation,* let him submit to just terms to obtain it.

"Let him, say we, have general law in advance (guarded in every possible way against fraud) so that when he acquires a legal right, he will have no occasion to wait for additional legislation—and if he has practiced fraud let the courts so decide."

Self-Reliance and Hard Study Makes a Good Lawyer

Lincoln's advice (11, 5, 1855) to I. Reavis, Illinois College student, upon receiving an application for permission to read law in his office, quoted in Chapter IX, shows how highly he valued self-reliance and constant application in the study of law.

The following advice to young W. H. Grigsby (8, 3, 1858) written during the climax of the debates with Douglas shows that he continued to hold the same views on methods of study, when highly successful as a lawyer, that he held as a student.

"Yours of the 14th. of July, desiring a situation in my law office was received several days ago. My partner, Mr. Herndon, controls our office in this respect, and I have known of his declining at least a dozen applications like yours within the last three months.

"If you wish to be a lawyer, attach no consequence to the *place* you are in, or the *person* you are with; but get books, sit down anywhere, and go to reading for yourself. That will make a lawyer of you quicker than any other way."

To J. T. Thornton, who had asked if he would instruct young J. H. Widmer in the study of law, Lincoln recommended (12, 2, 1858) the books of authorities on law that had most impressed him:

"I am absent altogether too much to be a suitable instructor for a law-student. When a man has reached the age that Mr. Widmer has, and has already been doing for himself, my judgment is, that he reads the books for himself without an instructor. That is precisely the way I came to the law. Let Mr. Widmer read Blackstone's Commentaries, Chitty's Pleadings— Greenleaf's Evidence, Story's Equity, and Story's Equity Pleadings, get a license, go to the practice, and still keep reading. That is my judgment of the cheapest, quickest, and best way for Mr. Widmer to make a lawyer of himself."

J. M. Brockman, a school teacher who asked, in 1860 after Lincoln's nomination, for advice on 'the best mode of obtaining a thorough knowledge of the law,' recieved the following answer (9, 25):

"The mode is very simple though laborious, and tedious. It is only to get the books, and read, and study them carefully. Begin with Blackstone's Commentaries and after reading it carefully through, say twice, take up Chitty's Pleadings, Greenleaf's Evidence, & Story's Equity &c. in succession. Work, work, work is the main thing."

When Colonel King was elected justice of the peace for Sangamon County he sought Lincoln's advice on how to conduct his court, and on what grounds to form his judgments. Lincoln is said by Herndon (Hertz, 1938)to have replied:

"There is no mystery in this matter, King; when you have a case between the neighbors before you, listen well to all the evidence, stripping yourself of all prejudice, if any you have, and throwing away if you can all technical law knowledge, hear the lawyers make their arguments as patiently as you can, and after the evidence and the lawyers' arguments are through, then stop one moment and ask yourself: What is justice in this case? and let that sense of justice be your decision. Law is nothing else but the best reason of wise men applied for ages to the transactions and business of mankind."

The Law Office

The law office of Lincoln and Herndon was located on the second floor at the end of a dark hall, in the back of a brick building on the west side of the public square, opposite the court house. It was a medium-sized room with two windows opening on a back lot. In later years it contained a long table and a short one placed across one end of it in the form of a letter T. Both were covered with green baize. In one corner was an old fashioned secretary with pigeon holes and a drawer, where the partners kept their law papers. A bookcase, containing some 200 volumes on law and miscellaneous subjects, a sofa and some chairs, completed the furnishings. Carelessness, or, rather, indifference to dust was its most striking characteristic. The paucity of books on law was made up by easy access to the state law library nearby.

The office of Lincoln and Herndon was never used as a headquarters for political organizations or meetings. Herndon said Mr. Lincoln rarely attended political gatherings until plans were organized, but was always ready to make a speech and reap any advantage that grew out of it.

One of the most vivid sketches of Lincoln, in his law office, has come from Gibson W. Harris (Weik, 1922).

"I was inducted into the office of Lincoln & Herndon as a student and clerk (1845). The office was in a room on the upper floor of a building which housed the post-office. Across the hall the Clerk of the United States District Court held forth. The furniture, somewhat dilapidated, consisted of one small desk and a table, a sofa . . . and chairs. The floor was never scrubbed. If cleaned at all it was done by the clerk or law student who occasionally ventured to sweep up the accumulated dirt. Over the desk a few shelves had been enclosed; there was the office bookcase holding a set of Blackstone, Kent's Commentaries, Chitty's Pleadings and a few other books. A fine law library was in the Capitol building across the street to which the attorneys of the place had access.

"And now as to Mr. Lincoln himself: The blue jeans in which he was clad the first time I saw him in 1840 had been discarded in favor of broadcloth shortly before his marriage. The day I entered his office in 1845 he had on a black suit—coat and trousers of cloth and a vest of satin; and the buckram stock about his neck was covered with black silk forcing him to carry his head more erect than would an ordinary tie. In summer he was accustomed to wear shoes known as the Wellington style; but in winter he wore boots. He had a great fondness for chess or checkers and also liked tenpins; but cared nothing for fishing or hunting.

"It would not be fair to speak of Mr. Lincoln as an idler save in his aversion to bodily labor. His brain was a singularly active one—seemed never to rest, never to tire; yet as a formal student he struck me as actually lazy. Days of leisure came frequently, and on such occasions he might sometimes be seen sitting in his chair with his feet on the office table reading the office copy of Byron or Burns. He would read an hour or two, then close the book and stretch himself at full length on the office lounge, his feet projecting over the end, his hand under his head, and his eyes closed, and in this attitude would digest the mental food he had just taken. He read but little at the office, and I have never imagined there was much burning of the midnight oil at his home. The truth is he never studied hard at any period of his life. He did not need to study hard. With him a single reading was sufficient to afford a clear insight into any ordinary subject."

It was generally Herndon's business to prepare briefs for cases that the two men would try together, for Lincoln disliked such work. When Lincoln wrote out the points of law for a case, his favorite position was to stretch both legs before him at full length on a chair with selected books on a table nearby or on his lap. No matter how deeply engrossed he became in his work, when a friend entered the room he would greet him pleasantly and often repeat some amusing story that was fresh in his mind.

"Lincoln had always on top of our desk a bundle of papers, into which he slipped anything he wanted to keep and afterwards refer to. It was a receptacle of general information. Some years ago [long after Lincoln's death], on removing the furniture from the office, I took down the bundle . . . Immediately, underneath the string was a slip bearing this endorsement in his hand: 'When you can't find it anywhere else, look in this.' " (Herndon, 1889.)

In their office, Lincoln and Herndon naturally repeated almost daily certain habitual adjustments to each other, some of which Herndon (Hertz, 1938) has sketched vividly:

"When he got to the office about 9 o'clock in the morning, the very first thing he did was to pick up some newspapers, if I had not hidden them, and read them aloud, much to my discomfort; he would spread himself out on the sofa, one leg on a chair and another on the table or stove. I have often said to him: 'Why, Lincoln, do you always read aloud?' and to which he said: 'When I read aloud, my two senses catch the idea. First, I see what I am reading and, secondly, I hear it read, and I can thus remember what I read the better.' Sometimes Lincoln would read something in the papers that would suggest to him an idea and he would say, 'That puts me in mind of a story that I heard down in Egypt in Illinois;' and then he would tell the story, and that story would suggest another, and so on. Nothing was done that morning. Declarations, briefs, pleas, and demurrers were flung to the winds. It was useless to attempt to read any more that morning."

Range of Practice

Like many of his contemporaries, Lincoln had for many years to take whatever cases he could get provided they had justifiable claims. These included partition suits, foreclosures, appeals from Justice Courts, actions in debt, trespass, replevin, suits over donor rights, damage suits and criminal prosecutions and defenses. Although most of his cases were civil suits he defended a woman accused of keeping a disorderly house, an adulterer, persons charged with gambling, larceny suits, perjury suits, indictments for the illegal sale of liquor, suits for slander (then much in fashion), assault cases, and two murder cases. He also served as prosecutor in a vicious case of rape (Angle, 1947).

Hundreds of pleadings in Lincoln's handwriting are still treasured in various court houses of the circuit. They were always neatly written and carefully drawn and usually signed A. Lincoln and the name of his associate. They show that besides conducting trials he often did the tedious work of writing out the preparation of a case for trial.

Eventually Lincoln and Herndon built up a large practice in Menard County. As the population increased, the eighth circuit was reduced from fourteen to eight counties and travel became less arduous.

Herndon has described their business arrangements (1, 27, 1888, Hertz, 1938):

> "While Mr. Lincoln and I were partners, we kept no books as to our partnership, though we did, for a while, as to others. Mr. Lincoln did most of the circuit court business while I stayed at the office. Sometimes I went on the circuit and, if I were with Lincoln around in the counties, all the money collected by us was instantly divided. If I . . . was at the office attending to our affairs at home, Lincoln would collect monies due us and our fees on the circuit and divide it, putting his half in his pocketbook and using it as he wanted to; he would wrap my half up in a roll, putting my name on a slip of paper and wrapping it, the slip, around the roll of money and then putting it in his pocketbook and when he came home he would come to the office and hand me my money; he did this always and at last it so excited my curiousity that I asked him . . . 'Why, Lincoln are you so particular in this matter?' and to which he instantly replied: 'Well, Billy, I do it for various reasons; first, unless I did as I do I might forget that I collected money or had money belonging to you; secondly I explain to you how and from whom I got it so you have not to dun the men who paid; thirdly, if I were to die you would have no evidence that I had your money and you could not prove that I had it. By marking the money it becomes yours and I have not in law or morality a right to use it. I make it a practice never to use any man's money without his consent first obtained.' "

Fees

Lincoln's fees for legal services were generally so small that his associates objected at times. Lincoln and Ward Lamon sometimes tried cases together. A young man, the brother of a feeble-minded young woman, employed them to protect his sister from an adventurer who wanted to marry her for her property which was worth about $10,000. He wanted to get a conservator appointed before the marriage and asked to know the fee in advance. Lincoln set the fee at $250, but advised him to wait until the case was settled for it might not take much time and would then cost less. The man, however, insisted on paying in full beforehand because he thought it would be a long and involved procedure. The case took less than an hour and was decided in the man's favor. He departed well satisfied, but when Lamon went to divide up Lincoln protested that the fee was too high, and made him return half of it or he would have none of it. Lamon, knowing Lincoln's attitude, agreed to the revision and made the refund.

Upon another occasion he wrote to G. P. Floyd (2, 21, 1856) upon receiving what he thought was an excessive fee:

> "I have just received yours of 16th, with check on Flagg & Savage for twenty-five dollars. You must think I am a high-priced man. You are too liberal with your money.
> "Fifteen dollars is enough for the job. I send you a receipt for fifteen dollars, and return to you a ten-dollar bill."

The biggest fee ($5,000) he ever charged was against the Illinois Central Railroad. Payment was refused and he had to bring suit for collection. His notes (6, 23, 1857) on the case give his reasons for the fee.

"Proof"

"Retainer.
"Brayman & Joy's letters, with proof of their signatures, and that they were the active agents of the Company.
That I did the service, arguing the case twice.
"Logan & Stuart.
What was the question. How decided—& on what point.
"The record—the final order—& the opinion. That *I,* and not Joy made the point & argument on which the case turned.
"Logan & Stuart.
"The Company own near two million acres; & their road runs through twentysix counties.
"That half a million, put at interest, would scarcely pay the tax.
"Are, or not the *amount* of *labor,* the *doubtfulness* and *difficulty* of the *question,* the *degree* of *success* in the *result;* and the *amount* of pecuniary interest *involved,* not merely in the particular case, but covered by the principle decided, and thereby *secured* to the client, all proper elements, by the custom of the profession to consider in determining what is a reasonable fee in this case.
"That $5000 is not an unreasonable fee in this case."

The jury found for Lincoln in the amount of $4,800, after deducting a retainer of $200 that had been paid to him by the railroad which he had forgotten.

As their office clerk, Gibson Harris described how, upon receiving the $4,800 fee, Lincoln said to Herndon; "Well, Billy, here is our fee, sit down and let me divide." Whereupon he counted out $2,400 and gave it to him with as much nonchalance as if it were a few cents.

Lincoln as a Lawyer

Herndon's notes (Hertz, 1938) give a frank description of his partner as a lawyer:

"Mr. Lincoln was purely and entirely a case lawyer, nothing more. He thought slowly and acted slowly; he must have his time to think, analyze the facts, and then wind them into a whole story. . . . I have seen him lose cases which anyone could have gained, just ones.

Even on the circuit, at *nisi prius,* if Mr. Lincoln had his time and thought that he was right, and could get the case swung to the jury, freed from technicalities, he was a good lawyer, but if he did not have his time, did not think that he was right, and could not get his case swung to the jury, freed from technicalities, then he was a very weak brother. In the circuit courts of the United States he was a good lawyer, because the practice of the courts was liberal, moved slowly, freed from technicalities, and gave Lincoln his own time to arrange his ideas and his plans for attack or defense. . . . But it was in the Supreme Court of the State of Illinois that he was truly a great lawyer, and nowhere else. The Supreme Court has its rules. . . . No man can be caught by surprise here and thrown out of court. . . . Except on special occasions, no oral evidence [is] admitted. The lawyers see each other's briefs, arguments, and the quoted law; they have ample time to hunt up the law and to argue the case, and in this court alone Lincoln was great truly and indeed. . . . In making his argument he referred to the history of law, a useless part as I then thought. . . . After the speech was through and Lincoln came into the law library . . . I said . . . 'why did you go so far back in the history of the law as applicable to this case?' and to which he instantly replied: 'I dare not trust this case on presumptions that this court knows all things. I argued the case on the presumption that the court did not know anything.' . . . Lincoln gained this very case by that very history which he was so careful to state fully. . . .

When a client came into our office and wanted advice, he listened to his story well, patiently, occasionally now and then breaking in as the story progressed by asking a question; the man would answer it, and then he wound proceed . . . after the man finished his story [Lincoln] would ask more questions . . . After the man was done telling his story fully and after Lincoln was done asking questions, he would generally think awhile before answering. When he answered, it was: 'You are in the right,' or: 'Your are in the wrong.' "

If Lincoln was not satisfied that the law was applicable to the case he would ask him to return later, and if he then thought he was not in the right he would advise him:

" 'You are in the wrong of the case and I would advise you to compromise, or if you cannot do that, do not bring a suit on the facts of your case because you are in the wrong and [will] surely get defeated and have to pay a big bill of costs.' . . . If the man was in a doubtful case Lincoln would say so, but say at the same time: 'if you must fight it out I will help you to do so the best I can.' "

"If you met with Mr. Lincoln on a case and you on one side and he on the other, you knew that you met a broad-minded and liberal gentleman, honest, fair, and that you would be defeated if you ought to be." . . .

"I was with Mr. Lincoln twenty-five years, and I can truthfully say I never knew him to do a wrong thing, a mean thing or any dirty little trick. He was always noble. I never knew so true a man—so incorrputed and incorruptible . . . he expressed his feelings in his thoughts and his great thoughts in his feelings . . . he was not speculative, but like Washington was severely practical . . . he never shaped his veracity, integrity or virtue to circumstances; he fashioned circumstances so far as he could to virtue and veracity."

Lincoln's brief statement (Hertz, 1938) to the Supreme Court of Illinois, upon his first appearance, illustrates this characteristic.

"This is the first case I have ever had in this court, and I have, therefore, examined it with great care. As the Court will perceive by looking at the abstract of the record, the only question in the case is one of authority. I have not been able to find any authority sustaining my side of the case, but I *have found* several cases directly in point on the other side. I will now give *these cases* to the Court, and then submit the case."

Manner in Court

Herndon said he was often asked:

"By what power, by what means, was it that Mr. Lincoln got such a firm hold on courts, juries, and lawyers?" He answered: "When Mr. Lincoln entered court he spoke to all persons in a polite way, calling them by some very familiar name, addressed the Court in his best and kindest manner. When Mr. Lincoln was addressing the Court on a law question only or on facts, he made the instantaneous impression on the Court that he was fair, honest, and would present the case fairly and honestly. The Court felt that there was no falsehood nor trick in his argument. The Court believed him to be a true gentleman, never suspecting that he would deceive or try to gain his point by an evasion or suppression of law or fact, but would meet each fairly and squarely. Mr. Lincoln did not glory in winning a case through a false argument, but rather had an ambition of gaining it on a substantial ground of justice. This seemed to be his pride. The jury, good common sense men of the country or the city, patiently listened to Mr. Lincoln's argument before them, and he was just as fair before them and to them as he was to the Court. Lincoln's statement of the case, both of law and of fact, was an argument, a plain, short condensed argument. This impression was stamped on the jury, nor did Lincoln ever seek to take advantage of it; he met all questions fairly and squarely, admitting what he could not deny and making the case plain to be seen by the jury. All rubbish and trash was away and from around the issues that now arose clear to the minds. If the case was a long, dry, tedious one and the jury got tired showed signs of weariness, or of sleepiness, Lincoln would tell one of his fine stories and arouse them up to a renewed attention, then he would take up the thread of his argument and proceed to the end of it."

Lincoln's manner of addressing a jury or audience has been realistically described by Herndon in a letter to T. H. Bartlett, sculptor (7, 19, 1887, Hertz, 1938).

"Mr. Lincoln was six feet four inches high in his sock feet; he was consumptive by build and . . . more or less stoop-shouldered. He was very tall, thin and gaunt. When he rose to speak to the jury or to crowds of people, he stood inclined forward, was awkward, angular, ungainly, odd, and, being a very sensitive man, I think that it added to his awkwardness. . . . Lincoln had . . . full and complete confidence in himself, self-thoughtful, self-helping, and self-supporting, relying on no man. Lincoln's voice was, when he first began speaking, shrill, squeaking, piping, unpleasant; his general look, his form, his pose, the color of his flesh, wrinkled and dry, his sensitiveness, and his momentary diffidence, everything seemed to be against him, but he soon recovered. . . . On rising to address the jury . . . he quite generally placed his hands behind him, the back part of his left hand resting in the palm of his right hand. As he proceeded and grew warmer, he moved his hands to the front of his person, generally interlocking his fingers and running one thumb around the other. Sometimes his hands, for a short while, would hang by his side. In still growing warmer, as he proceeded in his address, he used his hands—especially and generally his right hand—in his gestures; he used his head a great deal in speaking, throwing or jerking or moving it now here, now there in this position, now in that, in order to be more emphatic, to drive the idea home. Mr. Lincoln never beat the air, never sawed space with his hands [as reported by some biographers] never acted for stage effect; was cool, careful, earnest, sincere, truthful, fair, self-possessed, not insulting, not dictatorial; was pleasing, good-natured; had great strong naturalness of look, pose, and act; was clear in his ideas, simple in his words, strong, terse, and demonstrative; he spoke and acted to convince individuals and masses; he used in his gestures his right hand, sometimes shooting out that long bony fore finger of his to dot an idea or to express a thought, resting his thumb on his middle finger . . . he did not gesticulate much and *yet it is true* that every organ of his body was in motion and acted with ease, elegance, and grace, so it all looked *to me*.

"As Mr. Lincoln proceeded further along with his oration, if time, place, subject, and occasion admitted of it, he gently and gradually warmed up; his shrill, squeaking, piping voice became harmonious, melodious, musical, if you please, with face somewhat aglow; . . . and he rose up a splendid form, erect, straight, and dignified; he stood square on his feet with both legs up and down, toe even with toe—that is, he did not put one foot before another. . . . When Mr. Lincoln rose up to speak, he rose slowly, steadily, firmly; he never moved much about on the stand or platform when speaking, trusting no desk, table, railing; he ran his eyes slowly over the crowd, giving them time to be at ease and to completely recover himself, *as I suppose*. He frequently took hold with his left hand, his left thumb erect, of the left lapel of his coat, keeping his right hand free to gesture in order to drive home and clinch an idea. In his greatest inspiration he held both of his hands out above his head at an angle of about fifty degrees, hands open or clenched according to his feelings and ideas. If he was moved in some indignant and half-mad moment against slavery or wrong in any direction and seemed to want to tear it down, trample it beneath his feet, and to eternally crush it, then he would extend his arms out, at about the above degree, angle, with clenched big, bony, strong hands on them.

"If he was defending the right, if he was defending liberty, eulogizing the Declaration of Independence, then he extended out his arms, palms of his hands upward—as if appealing to some superior power for assistance and support; or that he might embrace the spirit of that which he so dearly loved. It was at such moments that he seemed inspired, fresh from the hands of his Creator. Lincoln's gray eyes would flash fire when speaking against slavery or spoke volumes of hope and love when speaking of liberty, justice and the progress of mankind. Such was the great man *to me,* and I think, I know, such he was to thousands, if not to millions of others."

"Harrassed" by Unjust Suit for Non-Payment of Collected Debt

A suit was filed in 1853 against Abraham Lincoln in Lexington, Kentucky by Oldham and Hemingway, partners of Robert S. Todd, deceased, (father of Mrs. Lincoln and Mrs. Edwards), alleging that Lincoln had collected $473.54 on an account owed to the firm and that he had not paid it. The suit came as a surprise to him. It seriously threatened his pride in reputation for honesty and moral integrity and he reacted with outraged indignation and harassed anxiety. His letters to his attorney, G. B. Kinkead, in Lexington, show how carefully he analyzed the situation in order to protect himself from unjust defamation of character.

"I am here [Danville, Illinois, 5, 27, 1853] attending court a hundred and thirty miles from home; and where a copy of your letter of this month, to Mr. [Ninian] Edwards, reached me from him, last evening. I find it difficult to suppress my indignation towards those who have got up this claim against me. I would really be glad to hear Mr. Hemingway explain how he was induced to *swear* he *believed* the claim to be just! I herewith inclose my answer. . . . You will perceive in my answer, that I ask the Petitioners to be ruled to file a bill of particulars, stating *names & residences* &c. I do this to enable me to absolutely disprove the claim. I can really prove by independent evidence, every material statement of my answer; and if they will name any living accessible man, as one of whom I have received their money, I will, *by that man* disprove the charge. I know it is for *them* to prove their claim, rather than for *me* to disprove it; but I am unwilling to trust the oath of any man, who either *made* or *prompted* the oath to the Petition."

In his answer to the Petition, Lincoln denied that he ever collected $472.54 or any sum whatever for the firm, or that any debt had ever been placed in his charge for collection or that he was ever employed as an attorney or in any other capacity by the Petitioners. He said he could only conceive a foundation for the charge to exist in the fact that after he had married Mary Todd her father, R. S. Todd, had visited Springfield in 1843.

During that visit Todd remarked "that there were two desperate or doubtful debts due Oldham Todd & Co"—*one* at, or near Beardstown, Illinois, . . . and the other at Shelbyville," and "that if any thing could be collected on said debts he desired Respondant to take and retain it as his own."

Of these debts Lincoln had collected fifty dollars from H. E. Dummer, attorney for one account, but denied that he acted as an attorney in the matter. He kept the money as Mr. Todd had requested and, in 1849 when in Lexington, he had given a statement of the whole matter to Mr. Todd's law partners. Again in 1852 he had given an account of it in "a sworn answer to a Bill filed for the adjustment of the estate of Robert S. Todd."

"Respondant cares but little for said fifty dollars," he said; "if it is his legal right he prefers retaining it; but he objects to repaying it *once* to the estate of said Robert S. Todd, and *again* to said firm."

Again he demanded that the Petitioners be required to file a Bill of particulars, stating the *names* and *residences* of the persons of whom they claim he had collected money belonging to them. As the time approached for the case to be tried in court Lincoln wrote to Kinkead (7, 6, 1853):

"I feel some anxiety about the suit which has been gotten up against me in your court; and I therefore hope you will pardon my requesting you to write me when your court sits . . . In the autumn of 1849 I was at Lexington several days, during which time I was almost constantly with L. O. Todd [attorney and son of R. S. Todd]; and if he shall, when the case comes on to be tried, *think* he *remembers* that I told him I had collected money for Oldham Todd & Co, the story would be plausible enough to require an answer. Such recollection would be an utter mistake; yet if something of the sort is not relied on, I can not conceive how Mr. Hemingway was induced to swear to the truth of the Bill. . . . I have said before, and now repeat, that if they will name the man or men of whom, they say, I collected money for them, I will *disprove* it. I hope you will write me at once."

The morally ugly little suit continued to worry Lincoln as the following letter to Kinkead shows. (9, 13, 1853):

"When, in your letter to me, of the 12th. of July, you gave the opinion that O. T. & Co. would abandon the suit, it was plain to my mind they intended no such thing, else they would have told you so plainly. The matter now takes me at great disadvantage, in this, that it will cost me more to leave the Circuit (which has just commenced) and attend to taking proof, than it would to give up the claim; and your letter does not mention the *time* of your next term.
"But the great difficulty of all is want of something definite, to take proof about. Without a bill of particulars stating the names of the persons of whom, O. T. & Co. claim that I have collected money for them, any proof I can possibly take will be wide of the mark."

Lincoln stated that he could prove by his former law partners, Stuart (1837-41) and by his present partner Herndon (since 1844) that

he individually or with any of them had not had any business with
O. T. & Co.

> "Also, by Ninian W. Edwards [Mrs. Lincoln's brother-in-law] of
> Springfield, Ills, that so far as he knows or believes the whole of the business
> of O. T. & Co in Illinois passed through his hands, and that so far as he
> knows or believes, none of it ever went into my hands—that the claims
> at Beardstown & Shelbyville both passed through his hands, and were,
> in the fall of 1843, given to me as desparate debts, by Mr. Todd, in manner
> as I have stated in my answer."

He could also show by court records that Ninian Edwards had
taken legal action on those claims and that judgments on both had
been passed and that the claims remained unpaid.

> "All this I can prove; but without a Bill of particulars, it seems to me,
> it will not meet the case."
> *"Can they not be ruled to give a Bill of particulars?*
> "This matter harrasses my feelings a good deal; and I shall be greatly
> obliged if you will write me immediately . . . whether I *can* or can
> *not* have a bill of particulars."

Lincoln's request was finally granted, much to his relief, as the following letter to Kinkead shows (9, 30, 1853):

> "Your letter . . . has just reached me through Mr. Edwards; and for
> which I thank you heartily. I now feel that the case is entirely manageable.
> I well know who Hawley and Edwards are. The 'Hawley' of that firm is
> Eliphalet B. Hawley; and the 'Edwards' is no other than Ninian W. Edwards,
> whom you know nearly as well as I do, & being the same who, on behalf of
> himself, and the rest of us here, has conducted all the business with you,
> in relation to Mr. Todd's estate."

Kinkead obtained favorable depositions from Hawley and Edwards
and the suit was dismissed. Lincoln saved his reputation as a lawyer
and man of honor from surrepititious charges.

Loyalty and Devotion, Intuition and Logic

Lincoln was guided by intuition and feeling as well as reasoning and
judgment in conducting a trial. He avoided taking part in the prosecution of criminals, probably for being too nervous, but twice he successfully defended men against charges of murder. His famous case
was that of William "Duff" Armstrong, the wild and wayward son of
Lincoln's old wild and wayward friend, Jack Armstrong, with whom
he had the wrestling match in New Salem and who had made Lincoln
captain of their company in the Black Hawk War many years before.
William was charged with murder. Woldman (1936) has given a history of
the case from which the following account is taken.

On the night of August 29, 1857, at a camp meeting, Duff Armstrong with his friend, Jim Norris, sided together in a quarrel with a man by the name of Metzker. In a fight that followed Metzker was killed. Jim Norris was accused by an eye witness, Charles Allen, of striking him on the head with a club, and Armstrong was accused of striking him on the head with a sling shot. Norris, in a separate trial, was convicted of murder on the testimony of Allen who claimed that he had seen the fight. Armstrong was still to be tried, and Lincoln, upon learning of it from the young man's desperately harassed old mother, was deeply moved to offer her his services.

Lincoln's conduct of the defense, his selection of a jury, the searching analysis of the testimony of the chief witnesses and the simple logic and sympathetic motivation of his pleas before the jury won the acquittal of his client. Today, lawyers still regard Lincoln's plan of defense as a masterpiece of criminal trial procedure.

He succeeded in getting a jury composed of men who averaged less than thirty years of age, in the belief that impulsive, hot blooded young men would be more understanding and tolerant of the accused than older men. The State's chief witness, Charles Allen, who had already testified in the trial of James Norris, again maintained that he had clearly seen the defendant, by the light of a bright moon, strike the victim on the head with a sling shot after he saw Norris hit him on the head with a club.

When Lincoln cross-examined Allen he led him to repeat this evidence and then followed with a series of searching questions on details, to which Allen replied that he had seen the assault in bright moonlight from a distance of about one hundred and fifty feet. Lincoln then introduced in evidence a current almanac showing that the moon could not have been shining brightly at the time of the murder for it was in an almost dark phase.

It was later alleged by some of the lawyers present, and repeated by some biographers, that the almanac introduced was one of the year previous and went unchallenged and the evidence on the state of the moon on the night in question was incorrect. This accusation implied that Lincoln was not really an honest man, but an actor who used honesty as a mask to conceal duplicity, trickery, and deception. The correlation of abundant evidence all through the development of his personality, from childhood throughout manhood, shows that Lincoln was more than an ordinarily honest man. He was obsessively honest and resentful of injustice toward himself or another person. Insecurity of self-respect by the doubt of himself or another person of his statement of fact excited a degree of nervousness and anxiety that was far more intense than normal.

E. J. Loomis, the Director of the Nautical Almanac of the United States Observatory, Washington, D. C., has stated that in Illinois, at 11 P.M., on the night of 29 August, 1857, the moon was very low in the southwestern sky, and its phase was about two days after the first quarter, about one hour of setting. The foreman of the jury of that trial, Mr. Milton Logan, stated that he examined the almanac and that it was of the year of the murder.

Lincoln maintained that at the distance claimed by Allen he could not have seen what happened, hence he had imagined it. Lincoln's questioning so completely destroyed Allen's testimony that it stood as an erroneous, if not largely prejudiced, fabrication. He also produced another witness who claimed that he and not Armstrong had made and owned the sling shot in question and that he had thrown it away where it was found. He then had this witness describe the inside structure of his sling shot, whereupon Lincoln boldly cut it open and proved its identity—it being constructed as described.

Lincoln's extemporaneous plea before the jury was unfortunately not recorded except by hearsay. The judge, prosecuting attorney and other lawyers who heard it said that he made one of the greatest speeches of his life. It was a hot day and the small court room was crowded. The prosecutor had finished an argument similar to the one that clinched the conviction of Norris. Lincoln removed his coat and tie and un-bottoned the throat of his shirt as he went along for an hour, carefully and methodically picking to pieces the testimony of Allen and other witnesses and building up the probability that Metzker died either from falling off his horse or from the blow by Norris. As he argued along with increasing earnestness of speech and awkwardness of gesture one suspender fell from his sloping shoulders but so deeply was his mind converged upon the jury and his argument that he seemed not to be conscious of it.

The earnestness of his appeal and faith in the righteousness of his own feelings and evidence was proven by the tears that trickled down his face as he told, in closing his speech, of his relations with the Armstrong family. How, years ago, when a stranger in New Salem, homeless and alone, without money or work, Jack and Hannah Armstrong had given him food and shelter in their humble cabin. He had rocked their baby, now this young man, in the home made cradle. Their home had been his home. He had often played with the baby and seen him grow up through childhood into manhood. He knew what kind of a boy he was and deep in his heart felt that he could not have committed murder. His good friend Jack Armstrong was gone and his son was now his grief-stricken widow's only support. Hopelessness and despair, loneliness, suffering and desolation were in store for this unfortunate woman if she lost her son. He was defending him without a fee. God, he said, had moved him to repay his debt of gratitude to his old benefactors by defending the boy and seeing that he had a fair trial. He prayed that he would not be unworthy of the task. Some of the jury wiped their eyes as Lincoln closed and sat down.

Judge Herriott instructed the jury on two points only, the question of reasonable doubt for the defendant and the possibility that the blow struck by Norris was alone the cause of the death of the victim, without referring to the evidence of the moon. At the dismissal of the trial Lincoln put his arm around the shoulder of the little, frail, old woman and helped her walk out of the courtroom. As they moved through the crowd he bent down to reassure her and was heard to say, "They'll clear him before dark, Hannah."

He was right. The jurors acquitted the defendant on the first ballot. Lincoln knew unerringly the quality and strength of the sympathetic bond of his argument and appeal. It is evidence of the certainty of his masterful intuition on the sympathies and antipathies of people, as individuals and in groups, toward one another over little and great issues.

Resents Injustice to Veteran's Widow

Herndon (1889) has given an unusual illustration of how easily Lincoln was aroused to resent an untruth or an act of injustice. When it involved taking an unfair advantage of a helpless person his indignation would grow intense and his denunciation of the offender before the court, merciless.

A pension agent by the name of Wright had collected from the government $400 for an old woman, the widow of a veteran of the revolutionary war, and retained half of the sum as his fee. She felt herself unjustly treated and appealed to Lincoln and Herndon for aid. Lincoln was at once aroused to sympathy for her almost helpless physical condition and to indignation at the tyranny of the pension agent. He immediately went to the agent's office and demanded the return of a fair portion of the money to his client but was refused. Suit was brought, and in preparing for it Lincoln declared that he was "going to skin Wright and get that money back." In his argument to the jury he portrayed in vivid details the hardships the soldiers of the revolution had endured. He described in sentimental colors the parting in old Virginia of the young husband from his wife and baby to go to war and the benefits the people of the nation were now deriving from such patriotism.

> "Time rolls by," he said in conclusion; "the heroes of '76 have passed away and are encamped on the other shore. The soldier has gone to rest and now crippled, blind and broken his widow comes to me, gentlemen of the jury, to right her wrongs. She was not always thus. She was once a beautiful young woman. Her step was elastic, her face was fair, and her voice sweet as any that rang in the mountains of old Virginia. But now she is poor and defenceless. Out here on the prairies of Illinois, many hundred miles away from the scenes of her childhood, she appeals to us who enjoy the privileges achieved for us by the patriots of the Revolution, for our sympathetic aid and manly protection. All I ask is, shall we befriend her?"

Half of the jury, Herndon tells us, were in tears, and the defendent squirming under the fire of Lincoln's appeal before he finished. A verdict was given in favor of the return of every cent to the plaintiff.

> "Lincoln was so much interested in the old lady," Herndon said, "that he became surety for costs, and paid her way home and her hotel bill while she was in Springfield. When the judgment was paid we remitted the proceeds to her and made no charge for the services. Lincoln's notes for the argument were unique. 'No contract.—Not professional services.—Unreasonable charge.—Money retained by Def' [Defendent] & not given Pl'ff [plaintiff]—Revolutionary War.—Describe Valley Forge privations.—Ice—Soldiers bleeding feet.—Pl'ff's husband.—Soldier leaving home. Skin Def't.—Close.' "

Lincoln's magnanimous urge to defend and cherish the helpless old woman in the Wright case, and defend the son of his old friend Hannah Armstrong, was motivated by deepest sympathy for their rights and needs, as was his devotion to the welfare of his mothers. They show consistently sympathetic interest in human welfare and how easily he was aroused to defend people against injustice and false accusation.

Lincoln's Most Important Trial

The Rock Island Railroad Company, extending its right of way westward from Chicago, built the first bridge across the Mississippi River and it soon became the center of litigation between the steamboat and the railroad interests. Boats and barges found it a hazard to navigation and an intrusion on their preestablished field of commerce in the vast western country. In 1856 the steamer *Effie Afton* crashed into one of the piers and burned to the hull, also burning a span of the bridge. Transportation in the west by railroad was still less efficient and important than by steamboat, so the latter carried greater prestige in popular opinion when the owners of the *Afton* brought suit for damages against the railroad company.

The Chamber of Commerce of St. Louis, Missouri, then center of traffic via the great rivers of the west, supported the steamboat interests, which would have the bridge removed, making the case a *cause celebre*. Lincoln defended the railroad company and the Chicago *Daily Democratic Press* published, from September 9th to 25th, 1857, an extensive daily report of the trial from which the following account (via *Collected Works*) of Lincoln's speech to the jury has been taken. It is one of the most complete records, although given in the third person, of an argument to a jury by Lincoln. It is an excellent example of his power for analytical examination of essential determinants in the evidence on both sides and foresight of the future part steamboat and railroad transportation would play in the development of the West. The reader will observe how Lincoln's previous river boat experience and Euclidian method of arguing from a series of demonstrable propositions gave him convincing advantages over the loose, slippery methods of his opponents.

"Mr. A. Lincoln addressed the jury: He said he did not purpose to assail any body, that he expected to grow earnest as he proceeded, but not ill-natured. There is some conflict of testimony in the case, but one quarter of such a number of witnesses, seldom agree, and even if all had been on one side some discrepancy might have been expected. We are to try to reconcile them, and to believe that they are not intentionally erroneous, as long as we can. He had no prejudice against steamboats or steamboatmen, nor any against St. Louis, for he supposed they went about as other people would do in their situation. St. Louis as a commercial place, may desire that this bridge should not stand, as it is adverse to her commerce, diverting a portion of it from the river; and it might be that she supposed that the additional cost of railroad transportation upon the productions of Iowa, would force them to go to St. Louis if this bridge was removed. The meetings in St. Louis were connected with this case, only as some witnesses were in it and thus had some prejudice [to] add color to their testimony.

"The last thing that would be pleasing to him would be, to have one of these great channels, extending almost from where it never freezes to where it never thaws, blocked up. But there is a travel from East to West, whose demands are not less important than that of the river. It is growing larger and larger, building up new countries with a rapidity never before seen in the history of the world. He alluded to the astonishing growth of Illinois, having grown within his memory to a population of a million and a half, to Iowa and the other young and rising communities of the Northwest.

"This current of travel has its rights, as well as that north and south. If the river had not the advantage in priority and legislation, we could enter into free competition with it and we would surpass it. This particular line has a great importance, and the statement of its business during a little less than a year shows this importance. It is in evidence since September 8, 1857, 12,586 freight cars and 74,179 passengers passed over this bridge. Navigation was closed four days short of four months last year, and during this time, while the river was of no use, this road and bridge were equally valuable. There is, too a considerable portion of time, when floating or thin ice makes the river useless, while the bridge is as useful as ever. This shows that this bridge must be treated with respect in this court and is not to be kicked about with contempt.

". . . Mr. Lincoln thought the proper mood of all of the parties in this affair is to 'live and let live,' and then we will find a cessation of this trouble about the bridge. What mood were the steamboat men in when this bridge was burned? Why there was a shouting, a ringing of bells and whistling on all of the boats as it fell. It was a jubilee, a greater celebration than follows an excited election.

"The first thing I will proceed to is the record of Mr. Gurney [bridge attendant] and the complaint of Judge Weed, that it did not extend back over all the time from the completion of the bridge. The principal part of the navigation after the bridge was burned passed through the span. When the bridge was repaired and the boats were a second time confined to the draw, it was provided that this record should be kept. That is the simple history of that book.

"From April 19, 1856 to May 6—17 days—there were 20 accidents, and all the time since then, there has been but 20 hits, including 7 accidents; so that the dangers of this place are tapering off, and, as the boatmen get cool, the accidents get less. We may soon expect, if this ratio is kept up, that there will be no accidents at all."

Lincoln then made an assumption on the motions, currents and floats that might have been challenged as being of unproven and therefore doubtful validity.

"Judge said, while admitting that the floats went straight through, there was a difference between a float and a boat, but I do not remember that he indulged us with an argument in support of this statement. Is it because there is a difference in size? Will not a small body and a large one, float the same way, under the same influence? True, a flat boat would float faster than an egg-shell, and the egg-shell might be blown away by the wind, but if under the *same influence* they would go the same way. Logs, floats, boards, various things, the witnesses say all show the same current. Then is not this test reliable? At all depths too, the direction of the current is the same. A series of these floats would make a line as long as a boat, and would show any influence upon any part, and all parts of the boat."

The lawyers for the plaintiff were content to produce merely witnesses who gave their ideas about the currents and the piers as so-called evidence, whereas Lincoln produced as witnesses the engineers who had tested the currents with various mechanical devices and calculated their forces and directions.

"I will now speak of the angular position of the piers. What is the amount of the angle? The course of the river is a curve and the pier is straight. If a line is produced from the upper end of the long pier straight with the pier to a distance of 350 feet, and a line is drawn from a point in the channel opposite this point to the head of the pier, Col. Mason [engineer of railroad construction and witness for the defense] says that they will form an angle of 20 degrees; but the angle if measured at the pier, is 7 degrees—that is, we would have to move the pier 7 degrees, and then it would be exactly straight with the current. Would that make the navigation better or worse? The witnesses of the plaintiffs seemed to think it was only necessary to say that the pier was angling to the current, and that settled the matter. Our more careful and accurate witnesses say, that though they have been accustomed to seeing the piers placed straight with the current, yet, they could see that here the current has been made straight by us, in having this slight angle—that the water now runs just right now—that it is straight and cannot be improved. They think that if the pier was changed the eddy would be divided, and the navigation [un]improved; and that as it is, the bridge is placed in the best manner possible.

I am not now going to discuss the question what is a material obstruction? We do not very greatly differ about the law. The cases produced here, are, I suppose, proper to be taken into consideration by the Court in instructing the jury. Some of them I think are not exactly in point, but I am willing to trust his honor, Judge McLean, and take his instructions as law."

After this neat compliment to the presiding Judge, Lincoln continued:

"What is *reasonable* skill and care? This is a thing of which the jury are to judge. I differ from them in saying that they are bound to exercise no more care than they took before the building of the bridge. If we are allowed by the Legislature to build a bridge, which will require them to do more than before, when a pilot comes along, it is unreasonable for him to dash on, heedless of this structure, which has been *legally put there.* The Afton came there on the 5th and lay at Rock Island until next morning. When the boat ties up, the pilot has a holiday, and would not any of these jurors have then gone around there, and got acquainted with the place? Parker [pilot of the Afton] has shown here that he did not understand the draw. I heard him say that the fall from the head to the foot of that pier was four feet! He needs information. He could have gone there that day and have seen that there was no such fall. He should have discarded passion, and the chances are that he would have had no disaster at all. He was bound to make himself acquainted with it.

"McCammon [assistant pilot on the Afton] says that 'the current and the swell coming from the long pier, drove her against the long pier.' Drove her towards the very pier from which the current came! It is an absurdity, an impossibility. The only reconciliation I can find for this contradiction, is in a current which White says strikes out from the long pier, and then like a ram's horn, turns back, and this might have acted somehow in this manner.

"It is agreed by all that the plaintiff's boat was destroyed; that it was destroyed upon the head of the short pier; that she moved from the channel where she was, with her bow above the head of the long pier, till she struck the short one, swung around under the bridge, and then was crowded under the bridge and destroyed.

"I shall try to prove that the average velocity of the current through the draw with the boat in it, should be five and a half miles an hour; that it is slowest at the head of the pier,—swiftest at the foot of the pier. Their lowest estimate, in evidence, is six miles an hour, their highest twelve miles. This was the testimony of men who had made no experiment—only conjecture. We have adopted the most exact means. The water runs swiftest in high water, and we have taken the point nine feet above low water. The water, when the Afton was lost, was seven feet above low water, or at least a foot lower than our time. Brayton [engineer in charge of construction of the bridge] and his assistants timed the instruments—the best known instruments for measuring currents. They timed them under various circumstances, and they found the current five miles an hour, and no more. They found that the water, at the upper end, ran slower than five miles; that below it was swifter than five miles, but that the average was five miles. Shall men, who have taken no care, who conjecture, some of whom speak of twenty miles an hour be believed, against those who have had such a faborable and well improved opportunity? They would not even *qualify* the result. Several men have given their opinions as to the distance of the Carson, and I suppose if *one* should go and *measure* that distance, you would believe him in preference to all of them.

"These measurements were made when the boat was not in the draw. It has been ascertained what is the area of the cross-section of the stream, and the area of the face of the piers, and the engineers say, that the piers being put there will increase the current proportionably as the space is decreased. So with the boat in the draw. The depth of the channel was 22 feet, the width 116 feet—multiply these and you have the square feet across the water of the draw, viz.: 2,552 feet. The Afton was 35 feet wide and drew five feet, making a fourteenth of the sum. Now one-fourteenth of five miles is five-fourteenths of one mile—about one-third of a mile—the increase of the current. We will call the current 5-1/2 miles an hour.

"The next thing I will try to prove is that the plaintiffs' boat had power to run six miles an hour in that current. It has been testified that she was a strong, swift boat, able to run eight miles an hour up stream in a current of four miles an hour, and fifteen miles down stream. Strike the average and you will find what is her average—about 11-1/2 miles. Take the 5-1/2, miles which is the speed of the current in the draw, and it leaves the power of the boat in that draw at six miles an hour, 528 feet per minute, and 8-4/5 feet to the second.

"Next I propose to show that there are no cross currents, I know their witnesses say that there are cross currents—that, as one witness says, there are three cross-currents and two eddies. So far as mere statement without experiment, and mingled with mistakes can go, they have proved. But can these men's testimony be compared with the nice, exact, thorough experiments of our witnesses. Can you believe that these floats go across the currents? It is inconceivable that they could not have discovered every possible current. How do boats find currents that floats cannot discover? We assume the position that those cross-currents are not there. My next proposition is that the Afton passed between the S. B. Carson and Iowa shore. That is undisputed.

Next I shall show that she struck first the short pier, then the long pier, then the short one again and there she stopped. [After citing testi-mony of eighteen witnesses on this point he continued:] Here is an endless variety of opinion. But ten of them say what pier she struck; three of them testify that she struck first the short, then the long, then the short pier for the last time. None of the rest substantially contradict this. I assume that these men have got the truth, because I believe it an established fact."

Lincoln stated carefully what he held to be true after acknowledging differences of opinion of expert witnesses. Most legal minds can not resist the temptation to become unilaterally dogmatic in argument under controversial conditions in order to feel more resolute. Lincoln had long learned that he must not disregard contradictory evidence until disproven, lest he be wrong and become nervous and worried over it. The onesided positive mind is disposed to become irritable, tense and angry upon being frustrated by controvertable facts that it has neglected or refused to consider, whereas Lincoln's understanding of human nature enabled him generally to avoid frustrations by giving fair consideration to both sides of an issue.

"My next proposition is that after she struck the short and long pier and before she got back to the short pier the boat got right with her bow out. So says the Pilot Parker—that 'he got her through until her starboard wheel passed the short pier.' This would make her head about even with the head of the long pier. He says her head was as high or higher than the head of the long pier. Other witnesses confirm this one. The final stroke was in the splash door, aft the wheel. Witnesses differ but the majority say she struck thus. . . .

"He [Mr. Lincoln] said the colored map of the plaintiffs, which was brought in during the advanced stages of the trial, showed itself that the cross currents alleged did not exist; that the current as represented would drive an ascending boat to the long pier, but not to the short pier as they urged. He explained from a model of a boat where the splash door is, just behind the wheel. The boat struck on the lower shoulder of the short pier, as she swung round, in the splash door, then as she went on round she struck the point or end of the pier, where she rested. Her engineers say the starboard wheel then was rushing around rapidly. Then the boat must have struck the upper point of the pier so far back as not to disturb the wheel. It is forty feet from the stern of the Afton to the splash door, and thus it appears that she had but forty feet to go to clear the pier.

"How was it that the Afton, with all her power, flanked over from the channel to the short pier without moving one inch ahead? Suppose she was in the middle of the draw, her wheel would have been 31 feet from the short pier. The reason she went over thus is, her starboard wheel was not working. I shall try to establish the fact that that wheel was not running, and, that after she struck, she went ahead strong on this same wheel. Upon the last point the witnesses agree—that the starboard wheel was running after she struck—and no witnesses say that it was running while she was out in the draw flanking over. Mr. Lincoln read from the testimony of various witnesses to prove that the starboard wheel was not working while she was out in the stream. . . . The fact is undisputed, that she did not move one inch ahead, while she was moving this 31 feet sideways. There is evidence proving that the current there is only five miles an hour, and the only explanation is that her power was not all used—that only one wheel was working. The pilot says he ordered the engineers to back her out. The engineers differ from him and say that they kept on going ahead. The bow so swung that the current pressed it over; the pilot pressed the stern over with the rudder, though not so fast but that the bow gained on it, and, only one wheel being in motion, the boat merely stood still so far as motion up and down is concerned, and thus she was thrown upon this pier.

"The Afton came into the draw after she had just passed the Carson, and, as the Carson no doubt kept the true course, the Afton going around her, got out of the proper way, got across the current, into the eddy which is west of a straight line drawn down from the long pier, was compelled to resort to these changes of wheels, which she did not do with sufficient adroitness to save her. Was it not her own fault that she entered wrong? so far, wrong that she never got right. Is the defence to blame for that? . . .

"The plaintiffs have to establish that the bridge is a material obstruction, and that they managed their boat with reasonable care and skill. As to the last point, high winds have nothing to do with it, for it was not a windy day. They must show 'due skill and care.' "

The jury disagreed, nine for the bridge and three against, and was discharged. Further litigation against the bridge was decided by the United State Supreme Court in 1862 in favor of the Rock Island Railroad Company and the public necessity of the bridge.

Chapter XX

CONTEMPORARY PORTRAITS

We cannot well understand the development of Lincoln's personality and his philosophy of personal interactions without considering the analytical portraits of his principle characteristics by his contemporaries. Wherein these agree and disagree, and offer particular impressions, our understanding of Lincoln's psychology is enriched.

Lamon (1871) and Herndon (1889), intimate contemporaries of Lincoln, each wrote a biography of him, and other members of the bar, also close associates, recorded their memories after his death in brief commentaries. These descriptions have thrown invaluable lights from different angles on Lincoln's personality and ways of working in everyday life as a lawyer, politician, and statesman. The most revealing portraits from these sources are given here. Since most were written retrospectively after the tragic death of Lincoln the President, who had won the Civil War, saved the Union, and emancipated the slaves, their impressions of him as a lawyer are colored by idealizing sentiments. However, when connected with Lincoln's own statements, records, letters, and accounts of unusual episodes, they present the social side of his personality, the sentiments, ideas, and methods that contributed to the development of his philosophy of law and government.

Personal Characteristics, Age Forty to Fifty

Herndon knew Lincoln more intimately and for a longer period than any other man and he did more than any other person towards cultivating and advancing his interest in becoming President. He was so greatly impressed by the practical strength of character and mind of Lincoln the lawyer that long before any other man, he saw in him the potential President, as the one man who could solve the slavery problem and save the Union. His analytical portrait of Lincoln's physique, personality and mind is indispensable, and we present it largely in his own words, lest its keen delineations be lost for the reader through interpretation by the author.

"In person and physique it can hardly be said that Mr. Lincoln was either dapper or handsome. Somewhat ill preportioned in figure, his movements seemed labored if not at times more or less awkward. He had a sad and rugged face which defied artistic skill to soften or idealize. It was capable of few expressions, but they were abundantly suggestive and unusual. When in repose his face was grave and thoughtful, pervaded by a look of dejection as painful as it was prominent. It brightened like a lighted lantern when animated. His dull eyes would sparkle with fun or express as kindly and tender a look as ever mounted a face when moved by some matter of human interest and sympathy. There was more difference between Lincoln grave and Lincoln animated in facial expression than almost any other man of his day.

"His forehead was narrow but high; his hair dark, coarse and rebellious. His cheek-bones were high, sharp and prominent, his jaws were long; nose large and a little awry toward the right eye; chin sharp and upcurved. His eyebrows cropped out like a huge rock on the brow of a hill; his face was sallow shrunk, and wrinkled, with here and there a hair on the surface and his cheeks leathery. His ears were large and ran out at almost right angles from his head, caused partly by heavy hats and partly by nature, his lower lip thick and undercurved while his chin reached for the lip upcurved; his neck slender and trim neatly balanced his head; there was a lone mole on the right cheek and an Adam's apple on his throat.

"His head was long and tall from the base of his brain and from the eyebrows. His head ran backwards, his forehead rising at a low angle like Clay's and unlike Webster's, which was almost perpendicular. The size of his hat measured at the hatter's block was seven and one eighth, his head, being from ear to ear six and one half inches and from the front to the back of the brain eight inches. Thus measured it was not below the medium size. The look of gloom and sadness, so often noted in the many descriptions of his countenance, was more or less accentuated by a peculiarity of one eye [left], the pupil of which had a tendency to turn or roll slightly toward the upper lid, whereas the other one maintained a normal position equidistant between the upper and lower lids.

"His legs and arms were very long and in undue proportion to the rest of his body. Sitting in a chair he was not taller than ordinary men; it was only when he stood up that he loomed above them."

"He was plain, unprepossessing, even commonplace, but when the gray eyes and every feature of that earnest and deeply thoughtful face were lighted up by . . . the fires of righteous zeal and determination, then it was that these apparently homely features beamed . . . as if his soul was fresh from the hands of Him who gave it being."

To biographer Lamon Herndon wrote (2, 25, 1870): "Mr. Lincoln was of a low physical organization, good digestion, slow circulation, slow functions, blood not hot, not impulsive, cold flesh, liver had no action, bowels slow, sometimes feverish, sometimes cold, had not a strong life but a tenacious one, . . . He took life easy, had no haste, no spontaneous emotion, no impulse, *was sympathetic and emotional in the presence of the object.* I know Lincoln better than I know myself. He was so good and so odd a man, how in the hell could I help study him! Mr. Lincoln's poverty, a curse of his origin, the origin and chasity of his near and dear relatives, his father's cold and inhuman treatment of him sometimes, the death of Ann Rutledge, his intense ambition, and society not energetically recognizing his greatness, etc., etc., intensified his melancholy."

Herndon repeatedly described Lincoln as "a peculiar, mysterious man" in numerous letters to various biographers in the course of twenty-five years. He had "a double consciousness, a double life. . . . This is the sole reason why L. so quickly passed from one state of consciousness to another and a different state. In one moment he was in a state of abstraction and then quickly he was in another state where he was a social talkative, and communicative fellow."

"He would to the observer's surprise, without warning, burst out in a loud laugh or quickly spring up and run downstairs as if the house were on fire, saying nothing. Sometimes it took a strong effort on his part to awake, arouse himself from one condition on purpose or with intent to live in another state of consciousness. To do this he would tell a story or read a chapter in such a book as Jack Downing, Nasby, Bill Nye, or Josh Billings [professional humorists]."

We are given a glimpse into Lincoln's own estimation of his mental processes in an account by Herndon (1, 1, 1886; Hertz, 1938) of a conversation between them.

"One day I somewhat earnestly complained to Lincoln that he was not quick and energetic enough in a particular case to accomplish our ends,—In a very good-natured way he replied: 'Billy, I am like a long strong jackknife doubled up in the handle. The extreme point of the blade has to move through a wider space before it is open than your little short woman's knife, which you hold in your hand, but when the jackknife is open, it cuts wider and *deeper* than your little thing. I am six feet four inches high and it takes me a good while to open and to act, so be patient with me. . . . These long convolutions of my poor brain take time, sometimes a long time, to open and gather force, but like a long, well-platted, heavy, and well-twisted ox lash, when swung around and around high in the air on a good whip stalk, well seasoned, by an expert ox-driver and popped and cracked and snapped at a lazy ox shirking duty, it cuts to the raw, brings blood, opens a gash that makes the lazy ox sting with pain, and so, when these long convolutions are opened and let off on something are they not a power and a force in action, as you say? You yourself have often complimented me on my force of expression and now in part you have the desired *why*.' "

Lincoln needed time, Herndon has told us, to think things through as a trial lawyer before acting, or else he would become confused, depressed and ineffective and lose his case. When President he characteristially protected himself, no matter what the emergency, from being rushed into making decisions.

"Mr. Lincoln's perceptions were slow, cold and exact," Herndon said (Weik, 1922). . . . "He saw all things through a perfect moral lens. There was no diffraction or refraction there; nor was he impulsive, fanciful, or imaginative. . . . He was pitiless and unrelenting in his search for the truth. His skill in the association of ideas was as marvelous as his memory was tenacious and unerring. His language indicated oddity of vision as well as expression. In his search for words he was sometimes hard pressed to give proper expression to his thoughts; first, because he was in no sense a master of the English language, and secondly, because in the vast store of words there were so few at his limited command that represented the exact shade of meaning that he intended to convey. . . .

. . . "Before he could form an idea of anything, before he expressed an opinion, he must know it in origin and history, in substance and quality, in magnitude and gravity. He must know his subject inside and outside, upside and downside.

"His reasoning through logic, comparison and analogy was unerring and deadly; his adversaries dreaded his originality of idea, condensation and force of expression, not less than they writhed under the convincing effect of singularly significant and apt stories. Woe be to the man who hugged to his bosom a secret error if Abraham Lincoln ever suspected or started in chase of it! Time and all the legerdemain of debate could hide it in no nook or angle of space in which he would not detect and expose it. . . . When his mind could not grasp premises from which to argue, he was weaker than a child, because he had none of the child's intuitions. . . . He was on the alert if a principle was involved or a man's rights at stake in a transaction; but he could see no harm in impropriety in wearing a sack-coat instead of a swallow tail at a dinner party, nor could he realize the offense of telling a coarse or questionable story if a preacher happened to be present.

"He did not care for the non substantial things of this world . . . nor did he manifest an intense interest in any individual man—the dollar, property, rank, order, manners, or similar things; neither did he have any avarice or other like vice in his nature. He distrusted somewhat all technical rules in law and the sciences, contending they were, as a general thing, mere forms founded on arbitrary ideas and not on reason, truth, and the right. . . . As a rule he took but slight interest in purely social affairs; was hardly ever present at a town meeting, and the few gatherings which he did attend almost invariably were political conventions. He seemed not to care who succeeded to the presidency of this or that society or railroad company; who made the most money; who was going to Philadelphia and what were the costs of such a trip; . . . No principle of justice, truth, or right being involved in these things, he could not be moved by them. It only remains to say that he was inflexibly steadfast in human transactions when it was necessary to be so and not otherwise. One moment he was as pliable and expansive as the gentle air; the next as firm and unerring as gravity itself.

"Mr. Lincoln's understanding, his conscience, yes, everything, yielded submissively to the despotism of his reason. His analytical power was profound. In his mental organization logic occupied the throne." [Lincoln's idealization of logical thinking as superior to emotional thinking has been cited in several previous chapters.] "His vision was clear, his pursuit of the truth intense and unremitting. His conscience ruled his heart; he was always just before he was generous. . . . he understood and comprehended his own capacity—what he did and why he did it— better, perhaps, than any other man of his day. He had a wider and deeper conception of his environments and limitations than men who made greater pretensions or had enjoyed the benefits of more thorough training."

"Mr. Lincoln's mind required much evidence to produce a conviction; it was an incredulous mind and naturally disposed to doubt. He often said 'I always was a fatalist' and quoted Shakespeare's 'There's a divinity that shapes our ends, roughhew them how we will.' "

"Lincoln kept aloof from men generally, few knew him; he would be cheerful and chatty, somewhat social and communicative, tell his stories, his jokes, laugh and smile, and yet you could see . . . that Lincoln's soul was not present, that it was in another sphere; . . . he was with you and he was not with you; he was familiar with you and yet he kept you at a distance. . . . Few [people] knew the man—[he] was reticent, secretive, incommunicable, in some . . . lines of his character. . . . I have seen and felt all this in Lincoln a thousand times."

"Mr. Lincoln was not at all times a popular man in Sangamon County . . . he was not understood by the mass of men; . . . When in one of his moods . . . he would stride along and not notice a friend on the street . . . nor reply to any good morning salutation. . . . All this was taken for *coldness, dignity and pride*, . . . and by some of his friends misjudged and disliked."

"Lincoln's individualism was great, so was his dignity, so was his reticence, abstractness and absent-mindedness . . . a peculiar man this Abraham was."

"Viewing his life as a whole the student of history will be sure to conclude that the elements which predominated in Mr. Lincoln's peculiar character were; first, *his great capacity and power of reason; second, his conscience and excellent understanding; third, an exalted idea of the sense of right and equity; fourth, his intense veneration of the true and good."* (Italics inserted.)

General Impressions

Lincoln was said by his intimate friends, in their exchanges of impressions about him, to have been an unusual and at times eccentric, diffident as well as self-reliant, highly independent and individualistic person. He had many peculiarities of speech, thought, manner, gesture, preference, dress, eating, appetite, and sleeping, that were accepted by the other lawyers as being a little odd and at times amusing. Although nearly six feet four inches in height, he usually weighed less than 180 pounds. He continued all his life to walk like an Indian, with slightly stooped shoulders and visibly bent knees, in an easy-going, almost loping swing that placed, as he stepped, the whole foot flat on the ground and so picked it up. His foot did not hit the ground by the heel first and leave by the toe last in stepping, as with most people who grow up walking on pavements. The natural continuation throughout life, under vastly improved urban and social conditions, of his primitive posture and style of walking and talking, as he had learned in childhood in the wilderness, shows how unconsciously his social attitude continued to evolve around love for the easy freedom of manners learned in boyhood.

Regardless of temperature, except in the extreme heat of summer, he wore a knee-long, double-breasted black coat. He covered his shoulders in winter with a shawl, or wound a muffler about his neck, and generally carried an enormous, shabby old umbrella. His clothes were probably unknowingly adopted for comfort to counterbalance low blood pressure and subnormal body temperature. In very hot weather he wore an old, sweat stained, long linen duster instead of a coat. Badly fitting shoes hurt his corns and bunions. When at home or in the office and later even in the White House he liked to remove his shoes regardless of whoever was present. As in his log cabin days, he would elevate his stocking covered feet on a chair, table or even a low mantle over a fireplace for relaxation.

His voice remained high pitched and more or less unpleasantly rasping and penetrating, and his pronunciation never lost its backwoods drawl, but his speech, generally deliberate and biblical in simplicity and Shakespearean in rhythm, was always direct, logical, practical, and interesting. Strangers soon learned to listen to him, for he was apt to express himself with an original, unique, witty or otherwise emotionally charged idea. He held it good business to speak thoughtfully, simply, logically, accurately and clearly. He rarely failed to hold the attention of his audience and never subjected it to an excess of words in expressing an idea, although he liked to talk.

One idea suggested another with most unusual freedom of associations, indicating little repression of motivation with regard for propriety, although he was naturally cautious about people's feelings. He talked in such kindly, simple, friendly, trustful manner that rarely did anyone care to interrupt him. His powers of conversation were remarkably developed, as usual with pioneering people, but unlike most of them he knew how to keep his ideas moving so as not to talk merely to be at it. His manner of speaking was always deliberate, dignified, and interpolated with homely, common-sense phrases. He liked to use picturesque allegory and metaphor in story telling, in legal arguments, debates, lectures, and speeches.

Unusually conscientious, kindly and patient about everything he did for people as a neighbor, lawyer and politician, he tended to worry when he thought he had offended someone unnecessarily or unfairly. This attitude inclined readily to make his overly sensitive nervous system develop visceral tensions with indigestion, constipation, severe headache and restless, dreamy sleep. He had, however, the good common sense to rely entirely on the inner voice of his conscience for guidance in times of trial and doubt, and never let any other person, judge, minister or whoever presumed, tell him what was right or wrong about anything. This inner voice of equilibrating proportions in human relations, he seems well to have believed, is, in man, the best means of knowing right from wrong and the way of sensing Divine will.

Lincoln generally assimilated the usual self-repressions of thought, impulse and emotion that everyone must make in the cooperative and competitive social adjustments of everyday life, for he consciously cultivated a generous, forgiving, unvindictive, good humored attitude toward opponents as well as friends. He seemed to assume with habitual caution and serene humility that the other fellow knew more about a special subject than he did, until he learned by a series of kindly but searching questions how to estimate his knowledge and character. Later photographs of Lincoln in groups of people, particularly with his generals or Cabinet, show in his serene, patient face, that he depended on intuitively, quietly sensing the acquisitive and avoidance interests and good and evil and loyal and tricky inclinations in other people's attitudes. In his interpersonal relations he used, like most wise men, his olfactory sense for "smelling out" the good attitudes and honorable intentions from the dirty tricks, cheats and "rats" in the flattery and honeyed proposals of everyday life. He was not, however, unduly suspicious or distrustful beyond such sensible evidence in the characters of people.

The High Hat

Abraham Lincoln began to wear a "stove-pipe" hat in the New Salem days and continued it throughout his career as a lawyer and President, except for a few trials with a soft hat which he did not like. The high hat on a man of six feet four inches increased his apparent height conspicuously, and after it had gone out of style in favor of lower, soft hats, it became an eccentric expression of social character. Lincoln, in his high hat, attracted immediate attention wherever he went and the public amusement it provided delighted him, but it was also the symptom of his unusual persistence of habit formation and how uncomfortable he became when he tried to adopt new styles of dress and manners.

Herndon (1889), who knew Lincoln all through the high hat period, has described one of its later variations.

> "This hat of Lincoln's—a silk plug—was an extraordinary receptacle. . . . In it he carried his bank book and the bulk of his letters. Whenever in his reading or researches he wanted to preserve an idea, he jotted it down on an envelope or stray piece of paper and placed it inside the lining. Afterwards when the memorandum was needed there was only one place to look for it."

Numerous comments have been written by people who felt they must express their reactions to Lincoln's high hat. They are of little interest, but his own remarks about it are invaluable for they reveal intimate traits of his personality.

> To C. R. Wells he commented in a latter (2, 20, 1849) explaining the loss of a letter: "To make it more secure than it would be in my hat, where I carry most all my packages, I put it in my trunk."
>
> T. R. S. Thomas (6, 27, 1850): "I am ashamed of not sooner answering your letter, herewith returned; and my only apologies are, first, that I have been very busy in the U. S. court; and second, that when I received the letter I put it in my old hat, and buying a new one the next day, the old one was set aside, and so, the letter lost sight of for a time."

Judge David Davis and his Round Table

Judge David Davis presided over the Eighth Circuit Court of Illinois from 1849 to 1862, largely during the latter half of the period that Lincoln practiced law in Springfield. The principal lawyers in his court included Edward D. Baker, later a United States senator from Oregon, Edward Hannegan and Daniel W. Voorhees, later senators from Indiana, Leonard Swett, Stephen T. Logan, John T. Stuart, U. F. Linder, Ward H. Lamon, Joseph Gillespie, Jesse B. Thomas, later judge of the Supreme Court, W. H. Herndon and Abraham Lincoln. Some of them (Davis, Swett, Lamon, Stuart, Herndon, Lincoln) formed a particular circle of intimate friends who liked to gather in the evenings after court and enjoy one another's company. This little group eventually became the first sponsors of Abraham Lincoln as a candidate for the nomination of the Republican party for President.

It was their custom to travel from one county seat to the next with Judge Davis while he held court for several days to a week in each place, twice a year. The circuit covered fourteen counties, and court work constituted the principal interest of the people of each county. Plaintiffs and politicians and those eager for social contacts then gathered in their respective communities to attend to business and enjoy the gossip and excitement of the court room.

Lincoln generally made the rounds of the circuit on horseback, or traveled with horse and buggy, over the dirt roads deep in snow in the winter, mud in the spring and dust in the summer. The little towns were many miles apart, and court was generally held in the largest available room if there was no court house. The inns were small, the meals poorly cooked, and often he had to share the short, hard, bumpy beds with Herndon or some other member of the bar.

Judge David Davis was a ponderous man with deep, booming voice, whose honor, wisdom and integrity commanded the respect of everyone. Herndon described him as being a man of veracity and integrity with quick, penetrating perceptions of human nature. He demanded strict obedience to legal procedure with rigid impartiality to all. Out of court he loved genial companionship, and gathered around himself, in the evenings at the inn, men he particularly liked. They were all men of strong character who had been well tried for honesty, honor, courage, generosity, integrity, friendship, and good will.

After supper in someone's room they held forth for merriment and expressions of mutual trust and admiration, common sense, and sympathetic rapport, using any passing subject as a medium of exchange. Lincoln's tolerant, kindly attitude, drawling speech and unique wit, and inexhaustible fund of stories, made him the favorite entertainer of the group. He characteristically designed his stories and comments so as to end in surprisingly apt wit that not only aroused laughter but had in it delightfully ingenious, practical wisdom and penetrating insight into human nature. When he was absent, the merry-go-round of commentaries lost so much of its interest that evenings dragged, and the disappointed group usually pressed him to explain why they had been neglected.

On one occasion Lincoln stayed away several evenings in succession. Knowing that he delighted in their company, the group grew uneasy lest he had become involved in some personal difficulty and insisted on knowing what might be the trouble. He replied that he had been going to the Academy to see a magic lantern show. Then he described in his entertaining way the interesting pictures of strange places and how the lantern worked, revealing, as naively as a school boy, what he had learned, although magic lantern shows were familiar experiences to most of his friends.

Lincoln was always an eager student of anything unusual. He was not merely an idle, casual observer of new inventions, but he habitually analyzed them for essential mechanisms until he understood how they worked. When his neighbor, for instance, put lightening rods on his house he became interested in lightening and electricity, and informed himself by reading an authoritative book on the subject.

Ludicrous incidents in everyday life that produced an unexpected, harmless deflation of his own or some other person's ego delighted Lincoln and he generally retold them several times during the day with hilarious pleasure each time. Herndon (1889) has given as typical of this quality the following story.

> Upon returning from the circuit Lincoln said, "Billy I heard a good story while I was up in the country. Judge Davis was complimenting the landloard on the excellence of his beef. 'I am surprised, he said, that you have such good beef. You must have to kill a whole critter when you want any.' 'Yes,' said the landloard, 'we never kill less than a whole critter.' "

Davis' Lincoln

David Davis, appointed Chief Justice of the United States Supreme court by President Lincoln, said of him as a lawyer in the United States Circuit, in a eulogy given at Indianapolis in May 1865:

> "In all the elements that constitute a lawyer he had few equals; he was great both at *nisi prius* [issue of fact] and before an appelate tribunal; he seized the strong points of a cause and presented them with clearness and great compactness. His mind was logical and direct, and he did not indulge in extraneous discussion. Generalities and platitudes had no charm for him. An unfailing vein of humor never deserted him, and he was always able to claim the attention of the court and jury when the cause was most interesting by the appropriateness of his anecdotes. His power of comparison was large, and he rarely failed in a legal discussion to use that mode of reasoning. The framework of his mental and moral being was honesty, and a wrong case was poorly defended by him. The ability which some lawyers possess of explaining any bad points of a cause by ingenious sophistry was denied him. In order to bring into full

activity his great powers it was necessary that he should be convinced of the right and justice of the matter which he advocated."

"This statement by Judge Davis," Herndon said, "is correct in the general, but it is not true in the particular, for these remarks were eulogistic, which would not admit of any limitations or modifications. Judge Davis said on his examination by me in '66 at Bloomington this [written as dictated]: 'Mr. Lincoln had no faculty or organizing power; hence a child could conduct the simple and technical rules, means and modes of getting at justice, better than Lincoln. The law has its own rules and a student could get them better than Lincoln. Sometimes Lincoln studied these, if he could not get the rubbish of a case removed, etc. He had no inventive or organizing ability, no administrative ability, etc.' "

The reader needs to correct the impressions given in these often quoted statements by remembering that Lincoln was an effective organizer of the Whig party, an effective leader in the state legislature and an effective organizer and leader of his Cabinet as President. He was mechanically ingenious and inventive and a keen student of devices of any kind. He made, as President, invaluable suggestions on guns and other mechanisms of the war as well as plans of strategy for battle and the government's reorganization of conquered territory. Lincoln's sense of the mechanics of interacting allied and conflicting social and mechanical forces of any kind proved to be far superior to that of most lawyers, politicians, statesmen, and generals and government officials in carrying on the war.

Man of Three Moods

To his circle of intimate friends Lincoln was known to be a man of three moods or attitudes towards life. When engaged in the business of counselling a client he became strict, matter of fact, and paid close attention to the problem involved without levity; when alone he tended to slump into serious, dark, melancholy preoccupation of thought; but when with jovial companions he became humorous, hilarious and even reckless of social proprieties in telling his tales and jokes.

He would be inclined to tell a good story a number of times in a day to different people and laugh as heartily over it each time as if it were entirely new. Having heard a good one, he seemed never to forget it. No matter how often he heard an old chestnut he would burst into laughter and his voice rang with contagious spontaneity. As a story teller Lincoln was ingenious and had few equals. He improvised as he went along, to paint his scenes and characters broadly in colors that he sensed would delight his audience. Generally his stories were told with obvious design to be entertaining but also to illustrate a moral or a particular human trait that he wanted to point out. He generally started with "that reminds me" and then began to spin a yarn related to the subject with such facility and novelty of interpolation that it seemed not to have been told that way before. Those who knew him well, however, suspected that one idea suggested another and he improvised a new story for later use as he was telling one for the immediate occasion.

A test of his ready wit, that has become famous, occurred one night when the members of "the Round Table" discussed confidentially among themselves the mean character of a certain contemporary lawyer (here referred to as Quirk) whose unethical methods had won the enmity of members of the bar. The round of commentaries finally included all those present except Lincoln, who, as it was well known, habitually refrained from making derogatory remarks about the character of anyone however disliked. This time Judge Davis mischievously cornered him by asking, "And what do you think of him, Lincoln?" They had all just previously been discussing the strange Asiatic belief in the transmigration of souls, that, when a human infant is born, the soul of some person who has died enters its body to begin life anew. Lincoln replied aptly without a moment's hesitation, "I reckon when Quirk was born no one died."

According to Judge Davis: "Mr. Lincoln was happy as he could be when on the circuit, and happy in no other place. This was his place of enjoyment. As a general rule when all the lawyers on a Sunday evening, would go to see their families and friends, Lincoln would refuse to go home." This comment, though probably somewhat exaggerated, indicates that Lincoln's friends knew that his married life was at times far from happy. Always devoted to his family, he enjoyed going home when his wife's better self made it pleasant.

Gillespie's Lincoln

J. Gillespie knew Lincoln well since 1832 in the Black Hawk War, and became one of his most trusted advisers in Springfield and in Washington. He was given an intimate sketch of his friend's personality in two letters to Herndon in 1866 (Hertz, 1938), selections from which are taken here for further description (author's italics). He saw Lincoln as being contemplative rather than speculative, and less given to abstraction than most thoughtful and investigative minds. He liked solid facts as a basis of thought and gave more importance to mathematical and physical science than metaphysical speculation. He was interested in astronomy and theories on the origin of the heavenly bodies. He was also interested in the origin and development of language, and once gave a lecture in Springfield on that subject and liked to comment on the instructive value for himself of these investigations.

> "His mind was made up of the traits which belong to mankind generally. He was a remarkably temperate man, eschewing every indulgence, not so much, as it seemed to me, from principle as from a want of appetites. I never heard him declaim against the use of tobacco or other stimulants although he never indulged in them. He was genial but not very sociable. He did not seek company, but when he was in it, he was the most entertaining person I ever knew."

Gillespie has described how Lincoln, though a Whig, was pressed into service by the Democrats of Rochester to entertain Mr. Martin Van Buren (then democratic candidate for president). The party proved so delightful that it lasted through most of the night and Lincoln was heartily praised by Van Buren for his entertaining stories.

"I am very sure that Mr. Lincoln was not aware of his own abilities or standing and that he never expected to attain a very marked distinction. . . . He said he had no capacity whatever for speculation and never attempted it. All the use . . . [he] had for wealth was to enable him to appear respectable. He never hoarded nor wasted but used money as he needed it and gave himself little or no concern about laying up."

Lincoln "was very sensitive where he thought he had failed to come up to expectations of his friends. . . . [When] he was pitted by the Whigs in 1840 to debate with Mr. Douglas, the Democratic champion . . . he did not come up to the requirements of the occasion. He was conscious of his failure and I never saw any man so much distressed. He begged to be permitted to try it again and was reluctantly indulged, and in the next effort he transcended our highest expectations. I never heard and never expect to hear such a triumphant vindication as he then gave of Whig measures on policy. (See Lincoln's first public debate with Douglas, Chapter XI.)

"He was never ashamed of the poverty and obscurity of his early life." This statement again contradicts attempts by Masters (1931) and other biographers to make him appear so. He talked so freely at times of his childhood to close friends (Speed, Herndon, Lamon, Swett and Gillespie) that he seemed, if anything, proud of his pioneer, log cabin days. "His most amusing stories consisted of incidents of his boyish days amongst his country playfellows. He had a marvelous relish for everything of that sort and the happiest faculty of turning his numerous reminiscences to good account in illustration in after life. No man could tell a story as well as he could. He never missed the nib of an anecdote. He always maintained stoutly that his best stories originated with country boys and in rural districts. He had great faith in the strong sense of country people and he gave them credit for greater intelligence than most men do. If he found an idea prevailing generally amongst them, he believed there was something in it, although it might not harmonize with science. He had great faith in the virtues of the *mad stone,* although he could give no reason for it and confessed that it looked like superstition," . . .

"Mr. Lincoln's love of justice and fair play was his predominating trait. I have often listened to him when I thought he would certainly state his case out of court. It was not in his nature to assume or attempt to bolster up a false position. He would abandon his case first." . . .

"Mr. Lincoln never, I think, studied history except in connection with politics; with the exception of the history of the Netherlands, and of the revolutions of 1640 and 1688 in England and of our revolutionary struggle, he regarded it as of trifling value as teaching by example. Indeed he thought that history as generally written was altogether too unreliable." . . . [Herndon recorded similar views of Lincoln of the unreliability of personal prejudices in history and biography.] . . . "I have heard him discourse upon the problem whether a ball discharged from a gun in a horizontal position would be longer in reaching the ground than one dropped at the instant of discharge from the muzzle of the gun, and he said it always appeared to him that they would reach the ground at the same time even before he had read the philosophical explanation."

Gillespie also observed that Lincoln had a "remarkably inquiring mind [that] roamed over the whole field of knowledge." "In religious matters, I think Mr. Lincoln cared but little for tenets or sects but had strong and pervading ideas of the infinite power, wisdom and goodness of Diety and of man's obligations to his Maker and to his fellow-beings." "He could not avoid believing in predestination although he considered it a very unprofitable field of speculation because it was hard to reconcile that belief with responsibility for one's acts." "He considered the means foreordained as well as the end and therefore he was extremely diligent in the use of the means."

Lincoln preferred to be philosophically practical, rather than entirely logical and consistent with indifferent acceptance of predetermined fate. He believed in improving the order of human relations with reason, self-determination and work. He was known for his unusual interest in dissecting mechanisms, as well as analyzing ideas and legal situations, into fundamentals.

According to Gillespie, he *"analyzed every proposition with startling clearness and only discussed those branches of his case upon which it hinged, leaving the others clear out of view. He was a marvel of fairness in debate both in the courts and the political arena and he never desired to obtain an unfair advantage."* His *"sense of right and wrong was extremely acute."*

Generally "undemonstrative," Lincoln "had to be studied to be understood." "He was by some considered cold-hearted or at least indifferent towards his friends. This was the result of his extreme fairness. He would rather disoblige a friend than to do an act of injustice to a political opponent. His strong sense of justice made him hate slavery intensely," and yet he seldom discussed it. He had "greater natural mental caliber than any man I ever knew. He was extremely just and fair-minded. He was gentle as a girl and yet as firm for the right as adamant. He was tender-hearted without much show of sensibility. His manners were kind without ostentation. He was unquestionably ambitious for official distinction but he only desired place to enable him to do good and serve his country." *He was "radical . . . so far as ENDS were concerned, while he was conservative as to the MEANS to be employed to bring about the ends. . . . He was an artful man and yet his art had all the appearance of simple-mindedness."*

The last characterizations of Lincoln by Gillespie are perhaps the most incisive made by any of his contemporaries. We have seen evidence of that as a trial lawyer and politician and will see it in his debates with Douglas, in the manner in which he, single handed, forced the schism of the Democratic party into Northern and Southern factions when it seemed impregnable, and in the manner in which when President he achieved the emancipation of the slaves, and the renomination of himself for President, and turned impending defeat into victory.

Gillespie commented that although Lincoln was rigidly logical in debate, he artfully clarified his arguments with illustrative humorous anecdotes and sentimental allegories. He used amusing stories for producing conviction of sentiment for or against an issue with remarkable skill and cultivated this method to make himself clearly understood by all classes. He diligently studied the law of a case and was extremely careful in preparing himself for it. After the task was finished he sought recreation (particularly in playing handball). Generally he appeared to be either extremely sad or extremely mirthful. As a humanitarian humorist he towered above all other men. No one vied with him in entertaining a crowd. He had an endless budget of anecdotes with which he illustrated any point that might arise.

> "His manner of telling a story was inimitable although there was no *acting* in it. He was not in the least degree histrionic. He never invented any of his stories but simply retailed them, but how he could gather up such a boundless supply and have them ever ready at command was the wonder of all his acquaintances." His humor never detracted from his dignity. "No man ever commanded greater respect from or inspired more confidence in an audience than Mr. Lincoln did."
>
> Lincoln was "economical without being parsimonious," "brave without being rash," and never refrained from expressing his views because they might be unpopular and yet he avoided giving needless offense. He never idolized particular men (other than Washington, Jefferson, Webster and Clay in his earlier years) but had unbounded faith in the honesty and good sense of the masses and in his own common sense. . . . He passed through every level of society and acted all through his career on such principles of common sense as every man would understand and approve. *"He had no superhuman qualities, such as might be called genius, but he had to an astonishing degree of what it takes to make a great common man."*
>
> *"Lincoln was before all things in favor of perfect equality and consequently disliked aristocracy in all its forms and loved our government and its founders almost to idolatry."*

Swett's Lincoln

Leonard Swett, a confidential friend who tried cases with Lincoln on the Eighth Circuit from 1849 to 1860, recorded for Herndon (Hertz, 1938) his ideas of him as a lawyer and President. We repeat his most important characterizations.

Lincoln was highly intuitive and liked to act on his impressions of the values of evidence as presented in a trial.

> "Where most lawyers would object he would say he 'reckoned' it would be fair to let this in, or that; and sometimes when his adversary could

not quite prove what Lincoln knew to be the truth, he 'reckoned' it would be fair to admit the truth to be so-and-so. When he did object to the Court, and when he heard his objections answered, he would often say, 'well I reckon I must be wrong.' Now, about the time he had practiced this three-fourths through the case, if his adversary didn't understand him, he would wake up in a few minutes learning that he had feared the Greeks too late and find himself beaten. He was wise as a serpent in the trial of a case, but I have had too many scars from his blows to certify that he was harmless as a dove. . . . By giving away six points and carrying the seventh he carried his case . . . he traded away everything which would give him the least aid in carrying that. Any man who took Lincoln for a simple minded man would soon wake up with his back in a ditch."

"He was extremely humane, yet, while these attributes were fully developed in his character . . . they never did control him contrary to his judgment. . . . Most men of such kindly feeling are controlled by this sentiment against their judgment, . . . It was never so with him. He would be just as kind and generous as his judgement would let him be—no more."

"If he told a good story that was refined and had a sharp point, he did not like it any the better because it was refined. If it was outrageously low and dirty, he never seemed to see that part of it. If it had the sharp ring of wit; nothing ever reached him but the wit. Almost any man that would tell a vulgar story has got in a degree a vulgar mind, but it was not so with him. With all his purity of character and exalted morality and sensibility, which no man can doubt, when hunting for wit he had no ability to discriminate between the vulgar and refined substances from which he extracted it. It was the wit he was after, the pure jewel, and he would pick it up out of the mud or dirt just as readily as he would from a parlor table."

"Lincoln's whole life was a calculation of the law of forces and ultimate results. The world was to him a question of cause and effect. He believed the results to which certain causes tended would surely follow. He did not believe that these results could be materially hastened or impeded."

Contemporary impressions of Lincoln's mind are consistent in recognizing this quality, which is essentially that of the scientific mind.

Lincoln's Philisophy of Wit

The philosophy of *wit* intrigued and baffled Lincoln and he frequently discussed it analytically with his friends. Gillespie has told us (Hertz, 1938) that Lincoln thought at first that it would be easy and simple to work out an explanation of its mental processes. The more he studied the question of what made a story or statement witty and excited laughter, the more he found that he could not explain one example by another further than the factors in common of *surprise* and *economy* with *originality* and *novelty* in association of ideas.

This theory, we may add here, was remarkably sound and not improved until Freud (1917) showed that wit produces reflex laughter through releasing the energy of repressed unconscious tensions bound up in idea-emotional complexes. These emotional forces have since been further shown by Kempf (1931, 1945) to be the product generally of the egotistical rivalry of each person with every other person for some kind of first placeness in the social world. The surprising downfall of the victim of the witty comment elevates the teller and the listener by so much. This gives the spontaneous enjoyment of excess of energy, expressed in laughing together in unexpected superiority.

Swett has said that Lincoln never told a smutty story to a woman but not infrequently his stories shocked the modesty of some of his male audience for he assumed that most men had a generously broad sense of humor. While he sometimes made jokes at the expense of some other person who tried his patience, he more frequently joked about himself, particularly his height, ears, awkwardness or dress, and then laughed heartily over it.

Lincoln had such an enormous fund of stories of such variety that he was reminded of one in almost every situation and one suggested another in an endless stream. Many of his friends thought that he was very original but he once remarked that he only originated two stories in his life, but told "tolably well other people's stories." This is probably misleading for he told many tales of what he had seen of his family and neighbors when a boy, with original shading, exaggeration, and fictitious elaboration to make them amusing.

Appreciating the educative value of humor and wit, Lincoln used it seriously for this purpose as well as for self-protection against his insidious tendency to gloominess. His remark, when President, to Senator Chauncey M. Depew, no less of a wit, has best expressed his philosophy.

> "They say I tell a great many stories; *I reckon I do, but I have found in the course of a long experience that common people, take them as they run, are more easily influenced and informed through the medium of a broad illustration than in any other way, and as to what the hypercritical think I don't care.*"

Lincoln's narrations in preparation for a delightful surprise although often vulgar were always entertaining, humorous and logical, leading to a witty conclusion that was so unerringly apt and practically just that, above all, his wit must be regarded as being philosophically moral.

A. K. McClure, a collector of Lincoln's stories from every period of his life, concluded that they showed he disliked vulgarity but loved the gem of humor that provoked laughter which he called "the joyous, universal evergreen of life."

Shastid, who had known Lincoln from the beginning of his career as a lawyer, attended a trial and told this story of it to his son (here somewhat abridged). Lincoln was a master of condensation, the soul of wit, and no one could trip an exaggerated statement of biased opinion more deftly. Once when defending a lawsuit for damages he refused to examine any of the witnesses except a famous surgeon whose statements were sure to establish the claim if not disproven. He only asked him, "Doctor, what fee are you being paid for your services as a witness in this case?" The eminent man declined to answer at first, but upon being told by the Judge that it was a proper question and must be answered he named a sum so large the everyone in the courtroom was astounded. When the time came for Lincoln to address the jury, he raised his long arm and pointed his long, bony finger at the jury and said: "Gentlemen of the Jury; big fee, big swear," and sat down. He won the case.

Shastid heard Lincoln conduct a number of trials and gave to history the following important characterological observation. (Author's italics.)

> *"Generally he was commonplace and uninteresting. But when he was defending a victim of injustice or oppression he would become transformed, inspired with holy determination, a veritable archangel of righteous advocacy. To speak well he must think that someone black or white had been abused."* (Shastid, 1929.)

Attorney and Pastor

Lincoln once served as attorney and pastor to a dying woman. He was a constant student of the Bible, and his copy showed much wear and stain of its pages from his fingers. He could recite Christ's Sermon on the Mount completely, and thought Paul's sermon on Mar's Hill the most able and eloquent expression of thought in history. He asked a friend (Iglehart) who told the story (Hertz, 1939), to go with him as a witness to the home of a woman who was dangerously ill and wanted to make a will.

> "We found the woman worse than we expected. She had only a few hours to live. When Lincoln had written the will and it was signed and witnessed, the woman said that she had great faith in Christ her saviour and was now really glad to die. Then she asked if he would read a few verses of the Bible to her.
>
> "Without picking up the book he recited from memory the 23rd Psalm, dwelling with deep pathos on the words 'Though I walk through the valley of the shadow of death, I will fear no evil, for thou art with me; thy rod and thy staff they comfort me.'
>
> "Then still without the book he continued from the first part of the 14th of John: 'In my father's house are many mansions. If it were not so I would have told you. I go to prepare a place for you. And if I go and prepare a place for you, I will come again, and receive you unto myself.' Then he gave other biblical quotations and recited several hymns, closing with the 'Rock of Ages, Cleft for me.' "

The woman died shortly afterwards and as they rode home Iglehart expressed surprise that Lincoln should have acted as pastor as well as attorney so perfectly, to which he replied, "God and eternity were very near to me today."

Altruism in Practice

Lincoln idealized Washington and liked, as a man, to present his belief of boyhood, that his hero was perfect. When his barrister friends in Judge Davis' Round Table questioned the wisdom of some of Washington's actions he protested: "It makes human nature better to believe that one human being is perfect; that human perfection is possible."

Lamon (1872) described how Lincoln, after proving an account for a client in a civil suit, learned during the trial from the evidence of the opposing lawyer, that he had been deceived by his client. He left the courtroom in disgust and went to his hotel. When the court called him to resume the case he sent word back: "Tell the Judge that I can't come; my hands are dirty and I came over to clean them."

Dr. Worral, a young physician, told the following story (Hertz, 1938). He had been in practice a few months when a woman came to his office with a fractured elbow. It was in a mean condition and he could not well reset the parts. Another physician talked the woman into bringing suit for damages and he was threatened with professional ruin. He employed Lincoln who won the case for him. When he asked for the bill Lincoln said:

> "You are a young man just starting out upon your career. I have easily earned a hundred dollars. I am only going to charge you twenty-five; and I will donate the other seventy-five to a worthy young man who has been the subject of malice."

This quality of Lincoln's generosity is further illustrated by the following story.

> When a friend came "to borrow a boiled shirt of him, he said, 'I have only two, the one I have just taken off and the one I have on. Which will you have?"

Stanton's Insult

Lincoln was not popular and well thought of in all barrister circles. Herndon (1889) has described the situation in which E. M. Stanton rudely offended him. M. Manny, an inventor, employed George Harding of Philadelphia and Lincoln in 1855 to go to Cincinnati, Ohio, and defend him, before Justice McLean, against the charge of infringement of a patent wherein Cyrus Hall McCormick (inventor of the reaper) was the plaintiff. Reverdy Johnson and W. H. Seward and other prominent attorneys had been employed by McCormick. The case was nationally famous and involved the future of the harvester manufacturing business. Lincoln realized the great opportunity and thoroughly informed himself on the history of the invention and the mechanistic principles involved, only to find that Harding knew more about it than he did. "When I came to compare notes with my associate," he told Gillespie,

"I found that he could lose all I knew and not miss it, and I insisted that he should take the lead." After reaching Cincinnati he first learned that Manny without consulting him had also engaged E. M. Stanton of Pittsburg as an attorney. Lincoln felt humiliated but acquiesced and derived satisfaction from the thought that he, as the original counsel, retained the privilege of addressing the jury. Since only two lawyers for each side could perform this function and by agreement Harding would speak first either Lincoln or Stanton would follow. Stanton proposed that Lincoln should address the jury, whereupon Lincoln politely said, "No, you speak." Stanton instead of deferring immediately grabbed the opportunity and replied "I will," and left the room. Lincoln felt that he had been treated discourteously and became gloomy and dejected as the case proceeded. He stayed through the trial but contributed little advice, and Stanton ignored him and ridiculed him to the other lawyers.

When Lincoln returned to Springfield he was still gloomy and mortified. He told Herndon that he had been ignored by Stanton and had overheard him remark to another lawyer, "Where did that long-armed creature come from and what can he expect to do in this case?"

Seven years later President Lincoln disregarded Stanton's insult and appointed him Secretary of War in his Cabinet. A few months preceding Lincoln's reelection for President Secretary Stanton schemed with other members of the Cabinet to bring about the defeat of their chief. Nevertheless, President Lincoln continued to retain him as Secretary because of his great capacity as a producer of war material.

Masters' Lincoln

The preceding selection of contemporary portraits of Abraham Lincoln the lawyer would be subject to the charge of bias towards establishing in the popular mind an idealistic and not realistic hero if it were not qualified by other records and interpretations and judgments of his actions by contemporaries who disliked Lincoln. Edgar Lee Masters, son of a lawyer who practised in the courts of Illinois with Lincoln, published (1931) an extensive correlation of such material. He has used it as a means of "examination of Lincoln's mind and nature," "just as an argument may be advanced in a court proceeding when all the evidence has been adduced." With the adoption of a lawyer's method of writing argumentative biography, Masters has gone the limit of reason in an embittered prosecution of Lincoln's record, abilities and reputation as a lawyer and man of honor. Masters judged Lincoln for what he read and did not read to inform himself on the great dissertations of his time on the social and political stresses of the nation. By such standards he then condemned Lincoln for what he did and did not do to solve the slavery problem and prevent the war.

Masters interpreted his arrays of evidence as showing that Lincoln was a "lazy man," "an undersexed man," "one of those manly men, whose mind made him seek masculine minds." Lincoln was "secretive," "cunning," "profoundly the actor," "he did not champion the poor and down trodden." "The stuff that has been written about Lincoln as the just, conscientious lawyer who would take no bad case is just unctious twaddle." "He was an honest lawyer just . . . as many of his contemporaries were."

"He disliked the work of the office." "He drafted few legal papers," "had no order, no method about law. He did not prepare his cases. He would go into court and lose a case that anyone should have won," "In a single year he was beaten in every case he had in the whole circuit." Masters has shown quite truly that Lincoln was for the most part a defendant's lawyer, taking advantage of the position that all men are innocent until proven guilty, a position that he also held in his debates with Douglas and later as President in defense of the Union. Masters said repeatedly that Lincoln was "a cold man," "he allowed no one to be familiar with him. There was no one besides Herndon whom he called by his first name . . . and no one called him Abe, not even Herndon."

"On the other hand," Masters said kindly, "there was his sense of humor, perhaps the only aesthetic gift that he had; and by this he drew people to him and held them."

Masters was utterly unable to appreciate the unusual sentiments of Lincoln's humor and the natural simplicity and poetical beauty of his heroic literary style in expressing his ideas and feelings on the causes of the conflict over slavery and the moral rights of mankind, that have become immortal in history.

Weik on Lincoln's Melancholic Disposition

"The most marked and prominent feature in Lincoln's organization," Weik (1922) gathered from interviews with Lincoln's contemporaries, "was his predisposition to melancholy or at least the appearance thereof as indicated by his facial expression when sitting alone and thus shut off from conversation with other people. It was a characteristic as peculiar as it was pronounced. Almost every man in Illinois I met, including not only Herndon, but John T. Stuart, Samuel L. Treat, James C. Conkling, James H. Matheny, David Davis, Leonard Swett, and Henry C. Whitney, reminded me of it. No one was able to determine what caused it. . . . Stuart told me and Herndon that Lincoln's liver failed to function properly. 'It did not secrete bile,' he said, 'and his bowels were equally inactive. It was this that made him look so sad and depressed. That was my notion and I remember I talked to him about it and advised him to resort to blue-mass pills which he did. This was before he went to Washington. When I came on to Congress in 1863, he told me that for a few months after his inauguration as President he continued the pill remedy, but he was finally forced to cease because it was losing its efficiency besides making him more or less irritable.'

"My inquiry on this subject," Weik continued, "among Lincoln's close friends convinced me that men who never saw him could scarcely realize this tendency to melancholy, not only as reflected in his facial expression, but as it affected his spirits and well being." -

Evidence of the tendency to melancholic distraction has been given as early as 1834 by Dr. Shastid. R. L. Wilson who was a member with Lincoln of the Illinois legislature in 1836 said:

> "Mr. Lincoln told me that although he appeared to enjoy life rapturously, still he was the victim of terribly melancholy. He sought company and indulged in fun and hilarity without restraint or stint as to time; but when by himself he told me that he was so overcome by mental depression he never dared carry a knife in his pocket; and as long as I was intimately acquainted with him previous to his commencement of the practice of law he never carried a pocket-knife."

Nervous Sleeper

Lincoln was generally a nervous sleeper. He had many disturbing dreams that sometimes reached the intensity of nightmares. He was introspectively interested in dreams as an occult medium of obtaining premonitary signs of right and wrong ways of doing in life, and could give many citations in discussing them, where, in the old and new testaments of the Bible, dreams are mentioned as warnings or revelations in times of trial and tribulation. The psychoanalysis of thousands of dreams by numerous investigators has shown that they are produced by the subconscious mind trying during sleep to reequilibrate itself with imbalancing forces in its environment through symbolically muddling over the helpful and opposing conditions of the previous day in conditioned association with earlier experiences.

Henry C. Whitney, a lawyer, who, with Judge Davis, sometimes shared a room with Lincoln, has desribed his behavior in a nightmare.

> "One morning, I was awakened early—before daylight—by my companion sitting up in bed, his figure dimly visible by the ghostly firelight, and talking the wildest and most incoherent nonsense all to himself. A stranger to Lincoln would have supposed he had suddenly gone insane. Of course I knew Lincoln and his idiosyncrasies, and felt no alarm, so I listened and laughed. After he had gone on in this way for, say, five minutes, while I was awake, and I knew not how long *before* I was awake, he sprang out of bed, hurriedly washed, and jumped into his clothes, put some wood on the fire, and then sat in front of it, moodily, dejectedly, in a most sombre and gloomy spell, till the breakfast bell rang, when he started, as if from sleep, and went with us to breakfast. Neither Davis nor I spoke to him; we knew his trait; it was not remarkable for Lincoln."

Such reactions to dreams show that although Lincoln assiduously cultivated composure he continued to be nervous and worried, with gloomy, self-repressive, regressive emotional reaction tendencies.

Chapter XXI

FAMILY MAN

The principal interest in the married life of Abraham and Mary Lincoln seems to have rested through the years in the love and care of their four boys and in similar political ideas and ambitions for the Whig, and later the Republican, party. Mrs. Lincoln, restlessly desirous of improving their social position and political influence, persisted in inciting her easy-going husband to strive more ambitiously. At times her critical nagging in the presence of friends annoyed him. He was out of place in refined and formal mixed social gatherings, but was magnificently at ease on any political occasion, so she seems to have believed that if she couuld teach him the necessary social proprieties his oratorical and political abilities would carry them to prominence, at least in state government. He detested the aristocratic social affectations of her family's set as they placed him at embarrassing disadvantages, but good naturedly he tried to please her and make the best of it. Mrs. Lincoln's estimation of her husband's abilities as a lawyer and politician seems to have been remarkably practical and as vigorously expressive. When she urged him to become a candidate for Congress, he liked it, and later when she objected to his acceptance of a minor political appointment that he was considering he acquiesced and refused it. She was obviously proud of her husband's abilities and addressed him always as "Mr. Lincoln" or "Father" and not by his Christian name, although he called her "Molly" and "Mary," except when he addressed her as "Mother."

Lincoln's interpretation of the meaning of the Constitution on State's rights and slavery, we have seen, was formed long before his marriage. As in most people, his egotistic social attitude was decisively integrated before physical maturity, and he developed thereafter principally in working out methods of self-projection as influenced by experiences as a lawyer, politician, statesman and, not least, husband and father.

Four Healthy Children

The Lincolns first lived in the Globe Tavern in Springfield, where the first child, Robert, was born. Late in 1843, about a year after their marriage, they bought for $1,500 a frame, one and a half story cottage, on the corner of Eighth and Jackson Streets.

Naturally, gossip said when Lincoln broke down from worry over inability to make up his mind to marry Mary Todd, that he had acquired a venereal disease which, he thought, rendered him unfit for marriage. Herndon's (Hertz, 1938) private notebook, in which he wrote that

Lincoln had confided to him that he feared he had contracted syphilis from a woman in Beardstown, became the source of such endless reports in biographies. The evidence shows now and for all time that this was not the case. His illness was the complicated product of a repetitively depressive *organic neurosis* following the injury of his brain in childhood, which interacted with a repetitive, depressive *emotional neurosis* through too idealistic fixation of love on the memories of his mother and Ann Rutledge. His resolution to renounce idealistic love and become a fatherly husband to a childishly temperamental wife, and a devoted father to their children, grew successful in certain ways with experience as a family man.

Four children were born of the marriage, Robert Todd on August 1, 1843, Edward Baker on March 10, 1846, William Wallace on December 1, 1850, and Thomas (Tad) on April 4, 1853. They were all fine healthy babies. Robert grew into a vigorous successful business man, Edward Baker died in his fourth year. William Wallace, named after Dr. William Wallace, family physician and brother-in-law of Mrs. Lincoln, became his father's favorite son largely through affinity of temperaments. Tad had some cleft of the palate, probably of genetic origin, involving slight impediment of speech, but as a child he compensated for this social inferiority through being highly alert, aggressive and ingenious.

The birth in due time of the first baby in good health was, in itself, positive evidence that both parents were free from venereal disease. Four healthy children in succession could not have been produced without a healthy father and mother. Hence Herndon's secret note that he suspected Lincoln had acquired syphilis before marriage must be regarded as unfounded.

Lincoln's record as a sire also shows that he was of average fertility, although his long limbs, low blood pressure and low autonomic pressure of energy indicate that he might have had, in addition to his nervous disability, a form of pituitary endocrinopathy that tends to reduce gonadal potency. Such nervous involvement of pituitary depression might have followed from his cerebral accident.

Constitutional Incompatibility

Constitutionally, Mary Todd was hyperkinetic. Her short, thick body build and intuitive, energetic, quick mental reaction-time, and her speech, varying impatiently in extremes of bitterly critical reaction-pattern when frustrated, to honeyed appeal when pleased, were quite the opposite of her husband's hypokinetic constitution and long, thin body build, drawling, contemplative speech, slow reaction-time and broadly elaborating, serenely patient and kindly mental reaction-pattern. Such fundamentally different constitutions naturally would have endless difficulty in harmonizing their interactions on family, political and other social problems sufficiently to understand sympathetically each other's likes and dislikes. He must wisely develop, since she could not, kindly patience and tolerance for differences in their opinions, taste and preferences, or else become irritated and provoked beyond endurance. Lincoln seems to have liked his pretty, vivacious little wife's prodding on political affairs and personal affiliations when she was not too strenuous and persistent, for it increased his discriminative comprehension of involved allied and conflicting personal interests and led generally to better understanding and more practical decisions on policies.

Lincoln sometimes remarked that he was one born of "the poorest class of whites." No doubt he had had anxious misgivings about his cultural fitness to marry a critically ambitious woman of the highest social class. The Edwards family was extremely undemocratic, aristocratic and snobbish, stylish in dress, and meticulous in speech. Could he learn to perform the proprieties of her social set without being ridiculously awkward and embarrassed, and still enjoy his old freedom of careless habits and backwoods manners? In his first public description of himself as a political candidate in New Salem he had referred to himself as being a man without influential family connections. Now he had them.

Naturalism Versus Conventionalism

Although the aristocratic conventionalism, manneristic affectations, ambitious social preferences, and prides and privilges, of family connections of Mrs. Lincoln contrasted and conflicted with the humble, crude, simple, straightforward naturalism and easy-going, provincial attitude of Mr. Lincoln, his growing character and impressiveness as a man and lawyer made up well for what he lacked in social refinements. His long hair, habitually disheveled by nervous fingers, his muddy facial skin, long, wrinkled, loose black coat and eternal stove pipe hat, and his careless personal habits were ever displeasing and irritating to his wife who was proper in speech and manners and neat and stylish in dress. She could love his many sterling qualities as a man, she probably reasoned to herself, if she could only teach him to observe the external niceties required of a gentleman. In this she was purblind. Lincoln, ever kind, sympathetic, patient, courteous, considerate, honest, just and good humored, was a natural gentleman, and the studied adoption of the superficial manners of social propriety would have made him feel painfully self-conscious and ridiculously shallow and misfit.

Mrs. Lincoln, proud of her French and flowery refinements of speech, tried persistently to induce her husband to give up his deeply ingrained backwoods' pronunciations. She believed that if he was to succeed as a lawyer and politician he must learn how to speak in the conventional manner in order to conduct himself with proper respect for the decorum of private social gatherings and state occasions. By nature, aggressive, alert, extroverted, ambitious, energetic, foreseeing, punctilious, intelligent but impatient, she conflicted with her husband, by nature shy, sensitive, introverted, deliberate, humble and easy-going, but as highly self-respecting and abmitious. Clashes of manners were inevitable and frequent, and eventually she developed the futile habit of nagging irritably at her husband to pay more attention to social proprieties.

Mrs. Lincoln grew sensitive about her height in contrast to her husband's and would become embarrassed by the little signs of amusement noticeable among people when they were seen together. She would not permit herself to be photographed with him. She rated him as coming from the "scrubs" and herself a well-bred, upper class patrician. Even on the night of her marriage she commented vexatiously on his "plebian" manners.

Lincoln's homely face developed spiritual refinement as his attitude grew more patient and humorously tolerant of his little wife's uncontrollable temper and sarcastic tongue lashing, while she grew more irritated at his drawling speech, uncouth pioneer enunciation, slouchy manners and careless habits. She easily lost her temper, and her face developed the muscular appearance characteristic of habitually weak self-discipline frequently broken by unrestrained outbrusts of rage.

Ever "Plain Old Abe"

Lincoln, generally patient, kind and considerate, learned to adapt himself more properly in some ways with social experience, but in his basic attitude he remained, fortunately for mankind, unchanged for life. It indicates how deeply, as a man, he felt that he must be natural in personal habits, though formed in boyhood. Never was his temperamental wife to accept or change this attitude. Patiently he endured and disregarded her annoyance and scolding. He had consistently cultivated serene humility, and as he grew in prominence he came to realize its value as most pleasing to the common people. Mrs. Lincoln liked men of distinguished, polished bearing and he tolerated this inclination with good humored joking. However, when she interfered with the habits that were expressive of his real inner self he would kindly but firmly refuse to listen. He liked to do what he could otherwise to make her and the children happy. It is quite certain that both people were in all things faithful to their marital promises and obligations, although they liked to tease each other occasionally about outside flirtations.

At home Lincoln seldom wore a coat, even though his wife objected to seeing him in shirt sleeves and suspenders. In the evening he liked to walk about the house in his blue woolen socks and read aloud to himself or anyone who would listen, even as he had in boyhood to the folks at home. Harriet Hanks Chapman, the daughter of Dennis Hanks, who lived with the Lincolns in 1846 while attending school in Springfield, has described his habit of reading for hours while lying on the floor with his back resting against a chair that he had turned upside down and cushioned with a pillow. We have shown in an earlier chapter how this seemingly eccentric habit relieved nervous strain produced by the left eye being turned upward slightly out of focus with the right eye. He liked to read poetry, and when some passage interested him in particular he would feel urged to read it aloud to the household. "The Burial of Sir John Moore" was one of his favorites. His voice was unpleasant and high pitched but enthralling with earnestness. His favorite resting and reading place was in the hall where he could be heard all over the house.

Mrs. Lincoln, always socially conscious and aspiring, was proud of having properly trained servants. She learned that she had to accept her husband's reading habits but she insisted that calls at the front door be answered by the maid. This social propriety Lincoln adopted so long as he didn't forget himself, which generally was his characteristic when completely entranced with what he was reading. In reaction to a knock or ring at the door he would then automatically get up and, still reading, open the door and invite whoever was there to come in, utterly oblivious of being in shirt sleeves and socks.

James Gourley (Hertz, 1938) knew Lincoln as early as 1834 in New Salem, and lived next door to him in Springfield for 19 years. He has given some preciously intimate glimpses of Lincoln's recreations. The two men often played handball together in New Salem and Springfield. He said Lincoln liked this game and played it up to the time of his presidential election. He would strip to the waist and play his best. He was also fond of wrestling and used side holds with great skill. "Lincoln used to come to our house," he said, "with slippers on, one suspender and an old pair of pants, for milk." He did not care much for trees and never planted fruit trees. He did plant a few rose bushes one year but they were neglected and died. He also once started a garden, worked it for a while, and then lost interest. He liked to curry his horse and milk his cow and attend to their feeding, and he sawed or cut wood for the house.

Persistent Tendency to Nervous Depression

After his marriage Lincoln seems not to have had another siege of "melancholy" severe enough to incapacitate him for more than a day or so at a time, except upon the death of his son Willie. However, frequently he had less depressive attacks attended by nausea, headache, insomnia, indigestion, and constipation, and we infer from his descriptions of himself that he never knew a day of freedom from the subconscious tendency to lapse into a state of detached gloominess unless he kept himself stimulated by work and conversation. This favorable change in his nervous motivations was probably largely due to having normal heterosexual functions and the dependence on him of his wife and children for fatherly protection and affection. Although unable to love his wife as ideally as he had loved Ann Rutledge, he was always devoted to her welfare and happiness, and seems not to have again desired freedom or been harassed by repressed wishes for her death.

In his boys he found a happy constant medium for his personal need for exchanges of affection, particularly with Willie who had the kind of meditative temperament and interests that established a deeper sympathetic rapport with him than with any other person.

Marital Fidelity

Herndon, who, when Lincoln's law partner, knew him more intimately than anyone, said that he "had a strong and terrible passion for women. He could hardly keep his hands off a woman, and yet, much to his credit he lived a pure and virtuous life. His idea was that a woman had as much right to violate the marriage vow as a man—no more and no less." (Hertz, 1938)

It is well known in psychiatry that any fairly well sexed adult who forces himself or herself from a natural heterosexual outlet, and is without profound interest in some exacting form of philosophical, scientific, religious, artistic, or other emotional sublimation, will suffer from a sexual neurosis that tends to summate with any other neurotic stress that he may have. Lincoln's wife was generally affectionate and physically attractive to him and at times he grew playful and amorous with her. But, as his verses of 1858 to Rosa Haggard, blooming into womanhood (see Chapter VIII) indicate, he probably never knew the inspiring personal effects of having sexual intercourse with a mate that he loved as deeply as he felt he needed. As he grew older he became increasingly self-controlled and reserved in attitude and more interested in the sublimations of demonstrative reasoning.

Mrs. Lincoln's Temperamental Annoyances

The accounts of the family life of the Lincolns, as given by servants and intimate friends of the family, and next door neighbors, generally agree in describing Mrs. Lincoln as being both an affectionate wife and mother and pleasing socially and at other times a bitter nagging scold who could work herself into uncontrollable rages. Sometimes she would even grow irrational in her accusations, and grieve and sulk until she became delusional. Disposed to be vain, jealous and sarcastic, she had difficulty in keeping friends or servants.

While her husband was away from home on a protracted trial, Mrs. Lincoln, without his knowledge, hired Gourley to convert the cottage into a two story house. When Lincoln returned he looked at it in astonishment and remarked to a passer-by: "Stranger, do you know where the Lincolns live? They used to live here." He protested to his wife for getting him into debt, but she continued to carry out plans and make extravagent purchases without consulting him. On another occasion she had Gourley buy a fine carriage for her and again her husband remonstrated without avail.

Once when Mr. Lincoln was away she had an idea that some men were coming to her house after the maid who, she said, was "a bad girl." Frightened and crying, she pleaded with Mr. Gourley: "Come, do come and stay with me all night. You can sleep in the bed with Bob and I. I don't want boys they go to sleep too soon and don't watch." Gourley called these ideas "hallucinations," leading some biographers to state incorrectly that Mrs. Lincoln was at times hallucinated.

The sexual wishfulfillment in such delusions is obvious. Naturally passionate, Mrs. Lincoln suffered no little from sexual neglect and her mentally absorbed husband's indifference to her need for petting. According to Gourley she said that she could love her husband better if he would stay at home at night as he ought to. Several times, Gourley claims, she asked him to kiss her, but the relationship seems never to have developed into further intimacy as he stated in his blunt fashion that he thought she was "a good woman" and "not a prostitute."

It is quite probable that Mrs. Lincoln's sexual repressions were excessive for her amorous constitution, making her progressively discontented, irritable, suspicious, and jealous of her husband's friendliness with other people. Although he was faithful to her she compensated with proud intolerance to conceal her feelings of inferiority as a neglected wife, a reaction that was consistent with her tendency later to become unreasonably jealous of President Lincoln's courteous attentions to women. This jealous disposition, as previously shown, began in childhood over her father's second marriage and extended throughout her girlhood and married life, and later dominated her mind in widowhood.

Love of Children

Mrs. Lincoln loved her children with obsessive intensity. She made clothes for them and herself with unusual artistry and skill and liked to display them on parade to church. When, in the early years of her marriage, she had callers or her husband's clients came to the house, she would dress up her boys and show them off, angling for flattery. She indulged their pranks and follies before people without discipline. Mr. Lincoln was known to remark, when the demonstration grew excessive:

> "These children may be something sometime, if they are not merely rare-ripe, or rotten-ripe, household plants. I have always noticed that a rare-ripe child quickly matures, but rots as quickly."

We get a clear impression of the nature of Lincoln's interest in his family, after three years of marriage, from the closing of a business letter to his old friend Speed (written in Springfield, 10, 22, 1846):

> "You, no doubt, assign the suspension of our correspondance to the true philosophical cause, though it must be confessed, by both of us, that this is rather a cold reason for allowing a friendship, such as ours, to die by degrees. I propose now, that, on the receipt of this, you shall be considered in my debt, and under obligation to pay soon, and that neither shall remain long in arrears hereafter. Are you agreed? . . .
>
> "We have another boy, born the 10th of March last. He is very much such a child as Bob was at his age—rather of a longer order. Bob is 'short and low,' and, I expect, always will be. He talks very plainly—almost as plainly as anybody. He is quite smart enough. I sometimes fear he is one of the little rare-ripe sort, that are smarter at about five than ever after. He has a great deal of that sort of mischief, that is the offspring of much animal spirits. Since I began this letter a messenger came to tell me, Bob was lost; but by the time I reached the house, his mother had found him, and had him whip[p]ed—and, by now, very likely he is run away again."

"Rare ripe" children who are "smarter at about five" years than later in mental development have generally been prematurely stimulated by overly indulgent parents giving too much attention and admiration for too little creative effort. Then the child develops a super-egotistical social attitude and wishful sense of unreality that conflicts with the more modest realism of extrafamilial playmates and soon finds itself critically rejected and frustrated.

As a father Lincoln was generally over indulgent and would let his boys crawl all over him and examine his watch or face or the papers on his desk without protest. Only when they ran too wild and imposed on other people would he gently discipline them. Mrs. Lincoln then generally sided with the children and undermined the impressiveness of his authority. According to Herndon, the father of six children himself, Lincoln's youngsters were a lot of undisciplined little "brats." Whenever their father brought them to the office they pried into everything and messed up the books and papers with ink, heedless of his protests and the trouble they made.

Lincoln liked on Sundays to take his boys on walks along the railroad track or roads into the country to show them the wonders of nature and enjoy their puppy pranks. At other times, with a shawl thrown over his shoulders and a basket on his arm he would stalk along to the market holding a son by the hand and, lost in contemplation, pay no attention to the youngster's eager comments and questions about things they passed.

Herndon (1889) has said that Lincoln did not care for children other than his own. We know that in New Salem he was fond of having them gather around him to listen to his stories and we may add here that in 1860, when in New York to speak at the Cooper Union, he stole away from his friends on Sunday morning and visited the House of Industry in the slums to watch the children do their religious exercises. Observing the unusual interest of the stranger, the superintendent asked if he would like to speak to the children. He said he would and they became so enthralled that twice, when he tried to end his talk, they shouted for him to continue.

Though life was at times tempestuous at home there were many tranquil, happy days when Lincoln enjoyed himself, often telling jokes to his family and servants for the fun of a good laugh. Neighbor Gourley said the Lincolns were generally happy "unless Mrs. Lincoln got the devil in her." The home was not always "dreary" as Herndon and some of the dissatisfied servants have reported, and Mrs. Lincoln was not always a "wild cat" in the house.

Mentally Preoccupied Eater

Some biographers have stated that Lincoln never used tobacco in any way, nor took an alcoholic drink in his life, and others have stated that at times in his early manhood he partook of the latter freely. Herndon, whose word is probably the most reliable on this, said that he did occasionally drink a glass of beer with his friends but he never took whiskey. It is known that on several occasions he treated himself with patent medicines that contained a large percent of alcohol, and in one period of depression whiskey was administered to him in liberal quantities by Dr. Henry. Lincoln said of himself:

> "I never drink much and am entitled to no credit therefore, because I hate the stuff. . . . It is unpleasant to me and always makes me feel flabby and undone."
>
> Herndon said that Lincoln "had a good appetite and a good digestion, ate mechanically, never asking why such a thing was not on the table . . . he filled up . . . never complained of bad food or praised the good. Lincoln was rather silent at the table, holding but little conversation there with anyone. I, on the circuit, have sat down with him a thousand times . . . at the table . . . he loved best . . . vegetable[s] . . . though his food was of a mixed kind. He loved a good, hot cup of coffee, and especially apples; he would wrap the forefinger . . . and . . . thumb around the equatorial part of the apple and commence eating it at the blossom end, never using a knife to cut or peel. . . ."
>
> "The door that entered our office was, the up half, of glass, with a curtain on the inside made of calico. When we did not wish anyone to see inside, we let down the curtain on the inside. Well, I say, many and many a time have I known Lincoln to come down to our office, sometimes his young son Bob, with him, with a small lot of cheese, crackers and 'bologna' sausages under his arm; he would not speak to me, for he was full of sadness, melancholy and I suppose of the devil; he would draw out the sofa, sit down on it, open his breakfast, and divide between Bob and himself. I would of course know that Lincoln was driven from home by

a club, knife or tongue,* and so I would lock the door behind me, taking the key with me. I would stay away an hour and then I would go into the office on one pretense or another, and if Lincoln did not speak, I did as before, go away. In the course of another hour I would go back and if Lincoln spoke, I knew it was all over, i.e., his fit of sadness."

His meals were very irregular and he partook mincingly of most foods when occupied with a legal case, showing how intensely he became interested in his problems. One night upon his return home late from business he had to chop wood and cook his own supper for none had been prepared for him. At times Mrs. Lincoln made conscientious efforts to regulate his meals but, when enraged over some disappointment, which was often, she would refuse to feed him. Inclined to grow fat, she set up such a stingy table that her husband gave up inviting friends to meals.

When Harriet Helm lived with the Lincolns in 1846 she observed that he was a "hearty eater and enjoyed a good meal of victuals as much as anyone I ever saw." Later he lost his appetite as worries over political debates and professional problems increased. He ate characteristicaliy anything put before him, without interest in it, as if preoccupied with thinking about something else. To reduce constipation he generally took blue mass pills. Eventually mercurial poisoning compelled him to give up this remedy. Paradoxically Lincoln said, of eating, "a large percent of professional men abuse their stomachs by imprudence in drinking and eating, and in that way health is injured and ruined and life shortened."

Social Life in Springfield

The Lincolns, largely through the influence of the important Edwards family, belonged from the beginning of their marriage, to the best social circle of Springfield. Later, as his eminence as a lawyer and politician became established, they carried on under their own prestige. An invitation in Lincoln's handwriting said: "Mr. & Mrs. Lincoln will be pleased to see you Thursday evening, Feb. 5 [1851] at 8 o'clock." Orville H. Browning's diary recorded under this date: "At night attended a large and pleasant party at Lincoln's." In a letter to her sister Emily Todd Helm (2, 16, 57, Sandburg and Angle, 1932), Mrs. Lincoln spoke of the many gay parties she attended with her husband and of one to which they invited 500 guests.

Mrs. Lincoln, stylishly dressed, entertained graciously when she gave a party. Although ready to be vexed by her husband's improprieties, she was obviously proud of his impressive abilities at self-expression. Despite his awkwardness and careless dress, he easily held

*Several times Mrs. Lincoln was said by next door neighbors to have chased her husband out of the house with a broom and once with a knife. As a tongue lasher she was pathologically bitter.

a large share of attention with humor and wit in any gathering. He, too, was proud of his plump, pretty, alert, intelligent little wife, as she easily carried on with vivacious conversation in any party.

Ward Lamon (1895) has told us of Mrs. Lincoln's enthusiastic appraisal of her husband in 1847. He had met her for the first time at an entertainment in the Lincoln home and had remarked that her husband was a great favorite in the eastern part of the state.

"Yes," she replied proudly, "he is a great favorite everywhere. He is to be President of the United States some day; if I had not thought so I never would have married him, for you can see he is not pretty. But look at him! Doesn't he look as if he would make a magnificent President?"

Gibson W. Harris (law clerk in Mr. Lincoln's office) wrote of the Lincolns:

"I was well acquainted with Mrs. Lincoln and was frequently at her house, being sent there now and then by her husband on errands from the office. On two occasions, I was her escort at a ball, instead of her husband who, because of absence from home, was unable to accompany her. I found her a good dancer; she was bright, witty, and accomplished, being able to speak French fluently. The sportive title or nickname she gave me was Mr. 'Mister,' but her husband invariably addressed me by my first name. She rarely visited the office. She was a member of the Presbyterian Church, but the statement that Mr. Lincoln attended divine service nearly every Sunday when in Springfield may have been true of later years, but to predicate it of the period I was in office, in the forties, would be more or less of an exaggeration. Mr. Lincoln showed great consideration to his wife. She was unusually timid and nervous especially during a storm. If the clouds gathered and the thunder rolled, he knew its effect on his wife and would at once hasten home to remain there with her till the skies cleared and the storm was safely over." (Weik, 1922)

Revealing Correspondence of the Lincolns

Mrs. Lincoln is said to have complained to friends that she could not endure the cold dampness of Washington in winter and its humidity and heat in summer. After three months she returned to her father's house in Lexington, Kentucky, with their two sons, Robert, age five, and Edward, two, and lived there during most of the time that her husband carried on his duties in Congress.The letters exchanged between them show their lives together were generally congenial and not always turbulent, and when separated for a time they grew sad and longed for each other's company. Both loved their children, and mutual interest in their welfare made strong bonds. The letter of April 16, 1848, to his wife, is one of Lincoln's most affectionate expressions of interest and desire for her, of record.

"Dear Mary:
"In this troublesome world, we are never quite satisfied. When you were here, I thought you hindered me some in attending to business;

but now, having nothing but business—no variety—it has grown exceedingly tasteless to me. I hate to sit down and direct documents, and I hate to stay in this old room by myself. You know I told you in last sunday's letter, I was going to make a little speech during the week; but the week has passed away without my getting a chance to do so; and now my interest in the subject has passed away too. Your second and third letters have been received since I wrote before. Dear Eddy thinks father is *'gone tapila'* [Capitol]. Has any further discovery been made as to the breaking into your grandmother's house? If I were she, I would not remain there alone. You mention that your Uncle John Parker is likely to be at Lexington. Don't forget to present him my very kindest regards.

"I went yesterday to hunt the little plaid stockings, as you wished, but found that McKnight has quit business, and Allen had not a single pair of the description you give, and only one plaid pair of any sort that I thought would fit 'Eddy's dear little feet.' I have a notion to make another trial to-morrow morning. If I could get them, I have an excellent chance of sending them. Mr. Warrick Tunstall, of St. Louis is here. He is to leave early this week, and to go by Lexington. He says he knows you, and will call to see you; and he voluntarily asked, if I had not some package to send to you.

"I wish you would enjoy yourself in every possible way; but is there no danger of wounding the feelings of your good father, by being so openly intimate with the Wickliffe family? [Bitter political enemies.]

"Mrs. Broome has not removed yet; but she thinks of doing so to-morrow. All the house—or rather, all with whom you were on decided good terms—send their love to you. The others say nothing.

"Very soon after you went away, I got what I think a very pretty set of shirt-bosom studs—modest little ones, jet, set in gold, only costing 50 cents a piece, or 1.50 for the whole.

"Suppose you do not prefix the 'Hon.' to the address on your letters to me any more. I like letters very much, but I would rather they should not have that upon them. It is not necessary, as I suppose you have thought, to have them to come free.

"And you are entirely free from head-ache? That is good—good—considering it is the first spring you have been free from it since we were acquainted. I am afraid you will get so well, and fat, and young, as to be wanting to marry again. Tell Louisa I want her to watch you a little for me. Get weighed, and write me how much you weigh.

"I did not get rid of the impression of that foolish dream about dear Bobby till I got your letter written the same day. What did he and Eddy think of the little letters father sent them? Dont let the blessed fellows forget father. . . .

Most affectionately, A. Lincoln"

The above letter shows that Lincoln had the usual difficulties in working of a professional man when living in close quarters with his family, as the endless demands of wife and children for attention "hindered" his studies. That his modesty and humility was real is evident in his objection to having letters addressed to him as "honorable" by his wife. In lonely times he missed her and the children and longed to have them return to Washington. He liked to shop at his wife's request and liked to tease her about getting fat and being flirtatious, and he doted on the pranks of his boys. In other letters he referred to his children as "dear codgers" and "dear rascals." His attitude toward them was extremely tender and affectionate and, if anything, too indulgent; entirely the reverse of his father's tyrannical attitude toward him (see Chapters III and IV). Although he had long dreaded marriage, he had become a good family man of the middle class American type.

The following letter from Mrs. Lincoln to her husband (Sandburg and Angle, 1932) retains much of her romantic style of expression and intelligently solicitous interest in her husband, children and father's family. Her pleasure in teasing her husband about her penchant for flirting, like his teasing her about liking to flirt, shows that both had learned to accept such interests as playful. She knew that her husband understood her vanities and impetuousness and tolerated her "little explosions" as being a relief for her tempestuous pressure of energy, although not infrequently of no little inconvenience to himself. (The italics are Mrs. Lincoln's.)

Lexington May - 48

"My Dear Husband-

"You will think indeed that *old age* has set *its seal,* upon my humble self, that in few or no letters, I can remember the day of the month, I must confess it as one of my peculiarities; I feel wearied & tired enough to know, that this is *Saturday night,* our babies are asleep, and as Aunt Maria B. is coming in for me tomorrow night, morning, I think the chances will be rather dull that I should answer your last letter tomorrow. I have just received a letter from Frances W. It related in an *especial* manner to *the box,* I had desired her to send, she thinks with you (as good persons generally agree) that it would cost more than it would come to, and it might be lost on the road. I rather expect she has examined the specified articles, and thinks as *Levi* says, they are *hard bargains.* But it takes so many changes to do children, particularly in summer, that I thought it might save me a few stitches. I think I will write her a few lines this evening, directing her not to send them. She says Willie is just recovering from another spell of sickness, Mary or none of them were well. Springfield she reports as dull as usual. Uncle S— was to leave there on yesterday for Ky. Our little Eddy, has recovered from his little spell of sickness. Dear boy, I must tell you a little story about him. Boby in his wanderings to day, came across in the yard a little kitten, *your hobby.* He says he asked a man for it, he brought it triumphantly to the house, so soon as Eddy spied it, his *tenderness* broke forth, he made them bring it *water* fed it with bread himself, with his *own dear hands.* He was a delighted little creature over it. In the midst of his happiness Ma came in, she you must know dislikes the whole cat race. I thought in a very unfeeling manner, she ordered the servant near, to throw it out, which of *course,* was done. Ed—screaming & protesting loudly against the proceeding, *she* never appeared to mind his screams, which were long & loud, I assure you. Tis unusual for her *now a days,* to do any thing quite so striking. She is very obliging & accomodating, but if she thought any of us, were on her hands again, I believe she would be *worse* than ever. In the next moment she appeared in a good humor, I know she did not intend to offend me. By the way, she has just sent me up a glass of ice cream, for which this warm evening, I am duly grateful. The country is so delightful I am going to spend two or three weeks out there, it will doubtless benefit the children. Grandma has received a letter from Uncle James Parker of Miss saying he & his family would be up by the twenty fifth of June, would remain here some little time & go on to Philadelphia to take their oldest daughter there to school. I believe it would be a good chance for me to pack up & accompany them. You know I am so fond of *sight-seeing,* & I did not get to New York or Boston, or travel the lake route. But perhaps, dear husband, like the irrisistible Col Mc, cannot do without his wife next winter, and must needs take her with him again. I expect you would cry aloud against it. How much, I wish instead of writing, we were together this evening, I feel very sad away from you. . . . It is growing late, these summer eves are short, I expect my long scrawls, for truly such they are, weary you greatly. If you come on, in July or August, *I* will take you to the Springs. *Patty Webb's,* school in S. closes the first of July. I expect *Mr. Webb* will come for her. I must go down about that time & carry on quite a flirtation, you know *we,* always had a *penchant* that way. I must bid you goodnight. Do not fear the children have forgotten you. I was only jesting. Even E— eyes brighten at the mention of your name. My love to all. Truly yours

M. L—

Lincoln was greatly occupied with advancing General Zachary Taylor for the Whig nomination for President when he wrote the following letter from the House of Representatives (6, 12, 1848). It reveals clearly the nature of his affectionate attitude toward his wife. Although at times she was difficult for him and their friends, he could become cutely playful with her and grow impatient to possess her.

"My dear wife:

"On my return from Philadelphia, yesterday, where, in my anxiety I had been led to attend the Whig convention I found your last letter. I was so tired and sleepy, having ridden all night, that I could not answer it till to-day; and now I have to do so in the H.R. The leading matter in your letter, is your wish to return to this side of the Mountains. Will you be a *good girl* in all things, if I consent? Then come along, and that as *soon* as possible. Having got the idea in my head, I shall be impatient to see you. You will not have money enough to bring you; but I presume your uncle will supply you, and I will refund him here. By the way you do not mention whether you have received the fifty dollars I sent you. I do not much fear but that you got it; because the want of it would have induced you [to] say something in relation to it. If your uncle is already at Lexington, you might induce him to start on earlier than the first of July; he could stay in Kentucky longer on his return, and so make up for lost time. Since I began this letter, the H.R. has passed a resolution for adjourning on the 17th. July, which probably will pass the Senate. I hope this letter will not be disagreeable to you; which, together with the circumstances under which I write, I hope you will excuse me for not writing a longer one. Come on just as soon as you can. I want to see you and our dear—*dear* boys very much. Every body here wants to see dear Bobby. Affectionately

A. Lincoln

It seems that Mrs. Lincoln resented having to promise to "be a good girl in all things" and gave plausible reasons for postponing her return to Washington, and then decided to abandon the plan entirely. The following is the last of the existing letters written by Mr. Lincoln to his wife during this period and it expresses affection, good humor, and patient resignation to her will.

Washington, July 2, 1848

"My dear wife:

"Your letter of last sunday came last night. On that day (sunday) I wrote the principle part of a letter to you, but did not finish it, or send it until tuesday, when I had provided a draft for $100 which I sent in it. It is now probable that on that day (tuesday) you started to Shelbyville; so that when the money reaches Lexington, you will not be there. Before leaving, did you make any provision about letters that might come to Lexington for you? Write me whether you got the draft, if you shall not have already done so, when this reaches you. Give my kindest regards to your uncle John, and all the family. Thinking of them reminds me that I saw your acquaintance, Newton, of Arkansas, at the Philadelphia Convention. We had but a single interview, and that was so brief, and in so great a multitude of strange faces, that I am quite sure I should not recognize him, if I were to meet him again. He was a sort of Trinity, three in one, having the right, in his own person, to cast the three votes for Arkansas. Two or three days ago I sent your uncle John, and a few of our other friends each a copy of the speech I mentioned in my last letter; but I did not send any to you, thinking you would be on the road here, before it would reach you. I send you one now. Last Wednesday, P. H. Hood & Co, dunned me for a little bill of $5.38 cents, and Walter Harper & Co another for $8.50 cents, for goods which they say you bought. I hesitated to pay them, because my recollection is that you told me when you went away, there was nothing left unpaid. Mention in your next letter whether they are right. [Mr. Lincoln was careful about getting into debt and making payment, whereas Mrs. Lincoln tended to be extravagent and careless.]

"Mrs. Richardson is still here; and what is more, has a baby—so Richardson says, and he ought to know. I believe Mary Hewett has left here and gone to Boston. I met her on the street about fifteen or twenty days ago, and she told me she was going soon. I have seen nothing of her since.

"The music in the Capitol grounds on saturdays, or, rather, the interest in it, is dwindling down to nothing. Yesterday evening the attendance was rather thin. Our two girls, whom you remember seeing first at Carusis, at the exhibition of the Ethiopian Seranaders, and whose peculiarities were the wearing of black fur bonnets, and never being seen in close company with other ladies, were at the music yesterday. One of them was attended by their brother, and the other had a member of Congress in tow. He went home with her; and if I were to guess, I would say, he went away a somewhat altered man—most likely in his pockets, and in some other particular. The fellow looked conscious of guilt, although I believe he was unconscious that every body around knew who it was that had caught him.

"I have had no letter from home, since I wrote you before, except for short business letters, which have no interest for you.

"By the way, you do not intend to do without a girl, because the one you had has left you? Get another as soon as you can to take charge of the dear codgers. Father expected to see you all sooner; but let it pass; stay as long as you please, and come when you please. Kiss and love the dear rascals. Affectionately

A. Lincoln

That Lincoln was disappointed over his wife's decision to delay returning to Washington indefinitely is shown in the letter he wrote a few days later (7, 11, 1848) to Herndon (quoted in full in Chapter XVII) in reply to his playful suggestion: "As to kissing a pretty girl, know one very pretty one but I guess she wont let me kiss her."

Ruth Painter Randall (1953) in her interesting book, "Mary Lincoln, Biography of a Marriage," has as the frontispiece presented a serenely contemplative profile photograph of President Lincoln facing a pleasing photograph of Mrs. Lincoln, taken at another time in the presidential period. Beneath are quotations from the preceding letters—although written twelve years before, in the congressional period.

"How they regarded each other," Randall said, "is revealed in their letters. He wrote her inquiring anxiously about her headaches, telling her to get a nurse to take care of the 'dear codgers,' and saying playfully: 'I am afraid you will get so well, and fat, and young, as to be wanting to marry again.' "

"She wrote him: 'How much, I wish instead of writing, we were together this evening, I feel very sad away from you.' "

Selecting photographs of one period and quotations from letters of another period in the married lives of the Lincolns, and placing them together so as to induce uncritical readers to feel and believe by association that they portray continuity of idyllic love for each other, may be permissible artistry in popular biography but it must be regarded as unrealistic and misleading in analytical biography.

Letters by Mr. Lincoln to Mrs. Lincoln after the congressional period grew shorter and less expressive of personal interest and affection for her until eventually, in the presidential period, they were almost barren of such thoughts. He continued throughout his married life to be constantly devoted to the welfare of his wife and children but his letters to her show that his attention became gradually, progressively transferred to professional and moral-philosophical and political interests. As will be seen later, the more he debated on the national implications of slavery and the more he grew involved in getting control of the Whig party in the state and the more the national public grew interested in his ideas and requested speeches from him, the less libido he had to give to his wife. And this kind of marital situation, every physician knows, must become increasingly trying and irritating to an energetic, ambitious, amorous woman who must repress her natural feelings and desires.

Lincoln's Father's Family

Mrs. Lincoln, Herndon said, was "terribly aristocratic" and remained coldly aloof to her husband's humble relatives. Although they lived in the state, only a day's journey away, during the first nine years of Lincoln's marriage none seem ever to have visited her house at Springfield except Dennis Hanks' daughter Harriet. When she lived with the Lincolns to attend school she took care of Bobby and helped with the housekeeping, but eventually she had to leave because of Mrs. Lincoln's temperamental berating. Despite his wife's rejection of his people, Lincoln maintained throughout his life the same protective interest in their welfare that he had before his marriage. We obtain, with deep sympathy for him, our most intimate understanding of his magnanimous attitude toward their problems from the letters he wrote to them from 1848 to 1852.

Besides buying his father's land and house and deeding all back to him guarded by legal stipulations that gave his stepmother a home as long as she lived, Lincoln had to provide frequently for them and his lazy stepbrother's family. He held his "mother" Sarah in profound gratitude and reverence and tried with patient devotion to make a respectable man out of his stepbrother. With all his law practice he frequently took time to send them letters of encouragement with advice and money.

John Johnston seems not to have been shy about asking for money. The weakness of his immoral, self-pitying reasoning shows, by contrast with the logical strength of Lincoln's firm moral self-discipline, the enormous difference in their egoistic attitudes and mental development. As two men who had grown up together in the same home since childhood, we must ask what differences in personal interactions in the family determined this. The following correspondence between them reveals the discouraging influence for John and the encouraging influence for Abe.

Johnston owed eighty dollars and, feeling dejected over not being able to pay his debt, tried to borrow money from his "brother." The pioneer backwoodsman's slurring vernacular of John's letters to Abe illustrate the way Lincoln probably learned to talk as a boy and had to correct in his self-education.

"I am dund and doged to death So I am most tired of living and I would Swop my Place in *Heaven* for that much money. I know you will think little of this for you never had the Tryal, but Abe, I would drother live on bread and wotter than to have men always dunning me. I could rayse a calf and Pig of my owen for Tom and Abe [his children] can now Doe nearly as much work in a crop as a man. I candadly would Drother never own a foot of land than not to pay my debts, nor lave any to my children. Indeed I would drother give possession now than to live here and have men watching me to see if I hadent something the law would take to sit a man wonst behind bares in this Country and no other way to make a Living only by his laber it will take a Life Time to get out and pay the Cash if he has a large family."

The careless, shiftless ways of John caused Abe, in his concern for the welfare of his "mother" Sarah, increasing worry and at times vexation. He answered one appeal for money with a proposition that should have aroused a neer-do-well's resolve to go to work.

Washington, Decr. 24th, 1848

'My dear father:

"Your letter of the 7th. was received night before last. I very cheerfully send you the twenty dollars, which sum you say is necessary to save your land from sale. It is singular that you should have forgotten a judgment against you; and it is more singular that the plaintiff should have let you forget it so long; particularly as I suppose you have always had property enough to satisfy a judgment of that amount. Before you pay it, it would be well to be sure you have not paid it; or, at least, that you can not prove you have paid it. Give my love to mother, and all the connections.

Affectionately your Son."

On the same page he began the following letter to his stepbrother. "Dear Johnston—

"Your request for eighty dollars, I do not think it best, to comply with now. At various times when I have helped you a little, you have said to me 'We can get along very well now' but in a very short time I find you in the same difficulty again. Now this can only happen by some defect in your *conduct*. What that defect is, I think I know. You are not *lazy,* and still you *are* an *idler.* I doubt whether since I saw you, you have done a good whole day's work, in any one day. You do not very much dislike to work; and still you do not work much, merely because it does not seem to you that you could get much for it.

"You are now in need of some ready money; and what I propose is, that you shall go to work, 'tooth and nails' for some body who will give you money [for] it. Let father and your boys take charge of things at home— prepare for a crop, and make the crop; and you go to work for the best money wages, or in discharge of any debt you owe, that you can get. And to secure you a fair reward for your labor, I now promise you, that for every dollar you will, between this and the first of next May, get for your own labor, either in money, or in your own indebtedness, I will then give you one other dollar. By this, if you hire yourself at ten dolla[rs] a month, from me you will get ten more, making twenty dollars a month for your work. In this, I do not mean you shall go off to St. Louis, or the lead mines, or the gold mines, in Calif[ornia], but I [mean for you to go at it for the best wages you] can get close to home [in] Coles county. Now if you will do this, you will soon be out of debt, and what is better, you will have a habit that will keep you from getting in debt again. If I should now clear you out, next year you will be just as deep in as ever. You say you would almost give your place in Heaven for $70 or $80. Then you value your place in Heaven very cheaply for I am sure you can with the offer I make you get the seventy or eighty dollars for four or five months work. You say if I will furnish you the money you will deed me the land, and if you dont pay the money back, you will deliver possession. Nonsense! If you can't now live *with* the land, how will you then live without it? You have always been [kind] to me, and I do not now mean to be unkind to you. On the contrary, if you will follow my advice, you will find it worth more than eight times eighty dollars to you.

Affectionately Your brother
A. LINCOLN

It seems that John's ambition was somewhat strengthened for a time as indicated by Lincoln's letter to him of February 23, 1850 from Springfield.

"Your letter about a mail contract was received yesterday. I have made out a bid for you at $120, guaranteed it myself, got our PM here to certify it and sent it on. . . . As you make no mention of it, I suppose you had not learned that we lost our little boy. He was sick fiftytwo days & died the morning of the first day of this month. It was not our *first,* but our second child. We miss him very much, Your Brother in haste."

John's desire to serve as a mail carrier came to naught despite his influential brother's enthusiastic efforts to get an appointment for him.

Attitudes of Abe and John for Mother's Welfare

No letter from Lincoln to his parents, since the preceding, seems to have been preserved until the one written on January 12, 1851 in regard to his father's illness. This was presented previously in Chapter V, on the development of his attitude towards his parents. His father died on January 17, 1851 and the next letter shows how Lincoln disposed of the property in order to protect his mother Sarah from the irresponsible schemes of her son John.

Lincoln and his wife Mary deeded (8, 12, 1851) their inherited interest in eighty acres of land, formerly owned by his father Thomas Lincoln, to John D. Johnston in consideration of the sum of one dollar, "subject to the right of dower of Sarah Lincoln." He seems to have thought that if John was given title to the farm he would take an interest in cultivating it and provide a home for his mother (now aged 63).

He was, however, soon disillusioned about this, as shown by his vigorously frank advice (11, 4, 1851).

"Dear Brother:

"When I came into Charleston day-before yesterday, I learned that you are anxious to sell the land where you live, and move to Missouri. I have been thinking of this ever since; and I can not but think such a notion is utterly foolish. What can you do in Missouri, better than here? Is the land any richer? Cany you there, any more than here, raise corn, & wheat & oats, without work? Will any body there, more than here, do your work for you? If you intend to go to work, there is no better place than right where you are; if you do not intend to go to work, you cannot get along anywhere. Squirming and crawling about from place to place can do no good. You have raised no crop this year, and what you really want is to sell the land, get the money and spend it—part with the land you have, and my life upon it, you will never after, own a spot big enough to bury you in. Half you will get for the land, you spend in moving to Missouri, and the other half you will eat and drink, and wear out, & no foot of land will be bought. Now I feel it is my duty to have no hand in such a piece of foolery. I feel that it is so even on your own account; and particularly on *Mother's* account. The Eastern forty acres I intend to keep for Mother while she lives—if you *will not cultivate it,* it will rent for enough to support her— at least it will rent for something. Her Dower in the other two forties, she can let you have, and no thanks to [me].

"Now do not misunderstand this letter. I do not write it in any unkindness. I write it in order, if possible, to get you to *face* the truth—which truth is, you are destitute because you have *idled* away all your time. Your thousand pretenses for not getting along better, are all non-sense—they deceive no body but yourself. *Go to work* is the only cure for your case.

"A word for Mother:

"Chapman [who married her grandaughter Harriet Hanks] tells me he wants you to go and live with him. If I were you I would try it for awhile. If you get tired of it (as I think you will not) you can return to your own home. Chapman feels very kindly to you; and I have no doubt he will make your situation very pleasant. Sincerly your son."

Johnston persisted in trying to sell his mother's land and seems to have succeeded in obtaining her consent to relinquish her rights to part of it. Lincoln was disgusted and determined to check him on the remainder (11, 9, 1851):

"When I wrote you before I had not received your letter. I still think as I did; but if the land can be sold so that I get three hundred dollars to put to interest for mother, I will not object if she does not. But before I will make a deed, the money must be had, or secured, beyond all doubt, at ten per cent.

"As to Abram (Johnston's 13 year old son) I do not want him *on my own account;* but I understand he wants to live with me so that he can go to school, and get a fair start in the world, which I very much wish him to have. When I reach home, if I can make it convenient to take him, I will take him, provided there is no mistake between us as to the object and terms of taking him."

The plan not to sell the land seems to have been finally established by Lincoln in his next letter (11, 25, 1851).

"Dear Brother
"Your letter of the 22nd. is just received. Your proposal about selling the East forty acres of land is all that I want or could claim for *myself,* but I am not satisfied with it on *Mother's* account. I want her to have her living, and I feel that it is my duty, to some extent, to see that she is not wronged. She had a right of Dower (that is, the use of one third for life) in the other two forties; but, it seems, she has already let you take that, hook and line. She now has the use of the whole of the East forty, as long as she lives; and if it be sold, of course, she is entitled to the interest on *all* the money it brings, as long as she lives; but you propose to sell it for three hundred dollars, take one hundred away with you, and leave her two hundred, at 8 per cent, making her the enormous sum of 16 dollars a year. Now, if you are satisfied with treating her that way, I am not. It is true, that you are to have that forty for two hundred dollars *at* mother's death; but you are not to have it *before.* I am confident that land can be made to produce for Mother, at least $30 a year, and I can not, to oblige any living person, consent that she shall be put on an allowance of sixteen dollars a year. Yours &c."

Lincoln's mother continued to live on the unsold part of the old homestead safeguarded by her grateful stepson, but her own son John, the self-pitying, scheming ne'er-do-well, could not rest contented. He married a second wife, Nancy Williams, age 16, and inveigled her parents into selling their farm and moving to Arkansas. Here he bought an old farm and for a short time made whiskey to sell at 50 cents a gallon. "I have bought me a Distillery & wont to commence makin Liqur in about 3 wekes" he wrote to his "brother" Abe.

John, the son of John Johnston by his first wife, when grown to manhood became a scheming, thieving rascal and finally landed in jail. Lincoln is said to have obtained his release on good behavior but his character seems to have improved very little, as indicated by a letter to him from Dennis Hanks, about his grandmother's farm. Written after Lincoln became President, it portrays the sequel of his efforts to provide his stepmother with a permanent home and also gives another vivid idea of the semiliterate mentations of Lincoln's boyhood associates, whose culture he first assimilated and then transcended.

"John and I want you to cum and take grand Mother and Keep her untill I see that your ant lived or NOT. It Looks Very strange to no that you have no more Simpany for your ant than you have that has waited on you a Many a time—Now John I have Bin to See old Abe and Now i Say to you that forty acres of Land was left for you grand Mother's support and if you Don't tend to it I will tend to it for you Shore. . . . Not one of them that She has cooked for and waited on is any a Count to her now So cum and take your grand Mother from here until your ant Lives or Dies I have packed shit and piss as long as I Entend to Do it is not a fitting place for your grand Mother I Entend to doo as I Say about it Shore take your Chies [choice] I want to here from you Mediaditly for I shall prosed in time." (Sandburg, 1950.)

The personalities of the two "brothers," Abraham Lincoln and John Johnston, contrast strikingly in their egoistic social attitudes, beyond differences in their inborn mental capacities.

John, born in 1816, was his mother's son by her first husband, and, as her last baby, no doubt enjoyed first place in her affections until some time after her second marriage in 1819. Abe, seven years older than John, was a sweet, lonely, neglected boy of ten when his father married Sarah Johnston. He soon won his new mother's heart through his forlorn, pathetic need for affection, eager, quick learning and willing devotion to her welfare, an attitude which never changed throughout his life. He thrived on the daily encouragement to educate himself that he received from his new "mother" despite opposition by his father to stop him when he had enough "larnin" to read and write. As a result he continued to develop a strong, considerate, self-confident egoistic integrity and remained ambitious throughout life and affectionately devoted to his stepmother and her family and his own family.

John, whose natural childhood rights and needs for first place in the affections of his real mother were frustrated, if not usurped by his stepbrother, developed the confused, self-doubtful, weakly integrated, indifferent traits of a child that always felt itself to be neglected in favor of its rival. As a man he continued in a weak, emotionally vacillating, self-pitying, scheming egoistic attitude that grew ever more socially frustrated, idle and unambitious, and more indifferent about the welfare of his mother and his own family.

It has been stated by some biographers that Lincoln was ashamed of his family because of the poverty of his youth and the unmoral connections in which he grew up. His endless care for their welfare and his letters to near and distant relatives and to the public about them show that he was proud of his father's connections and cautiously reticent about his mother's people. His letter to John Hanks (presented in Chapter V), written confidentially when he was a candidate for president, was wisely intended to safeguard his family's history of illegitimacy against exposure to the condemnations of bitterly vindictive political attacks. Although perhaps somewhat ashamed of his mother's illegitimate birth, he was too great a naturalist to be a moral prude about anyone's failures and deficiencies in life.

Lincoln loved his people, all of them, however good or bad, for he believed that no one was ever so bad as not to have some good in him. He always spoke simply and naturally of his humble birth, often referred to the log cabins of his childhood as "our home" and "our house," and the loft where he slept as "my little bedroom," and his people as "the dear ones." When President he invited John and Dennis Hanks to visit him in the White House and gave Dennis a silver watch.

In his tribute to his real mother Nancy and in conversations about his childhood he referred to her as his "angel mother," with profound devotion. He addressed his stepmother Sarah as "mother" and referred to her as his "saintly mother" and signed his letters to her "affectionately your son." He contributed to the support of his father and mother throughout his life. When in the vicinity of any relatives, though a busy lawyer sought after by clients and friends, he would leave the court room in time to walk to their homes, even though they lived several miles in the country. When president elect, one of his last acts before leaving Springfield for Washington was to travel by passenger and freight train to tell his mother Sarah goodbye, lest he might not see her again. Obviously, Lincoln was not a "cold man" as Masters (1931) said repeatedly.

Lincoln's profound love and respect for the honesty, good sense, passion for truth and freedom, patriotism and self-sacrifice of the common people was based mostly on the conditioning influences in the homes of his two mothers. He retained this elemental confidence throughout his political career and presented the organization of the family as the basic pattern of organization of the nation. This principle developed the comprehension of the people on the meaning of their own legal rights and relations under democratic government as members of one great political family, to be extended eventually to members of a world family of nations.